REBEL

SONG

Selected Writings
on
Peace, Life, & Spiritual Revolution

GEBRE MENFES KIDUS

authorHOUSE®

AuthorHouse™
1663 Liberty Drive
Bloomington, IN 47403
www.authorhouse.com
Phone: 1 (800) 839-8640

Published by AuthorHouse 09/26/2018

ISBN: 978-1-4969-5539-5 (sc)
ISBN: 978-1-4969-5540-1 (e)

To artists,

poets,

musicians,

writers,

peacemakers,

prophets,

revolutionaries,

healers,

and all people of faith.

And to my children – Noah, Zion, Adayah, and Hosanna – who are the greatest proof of God's unconditional love.

CONTENTS

(Poetry in *Italics* / short stories <u>underlined</u>)

INTRODUCTION

My beautiful wife has always supported my writing. She has been more than patient, perpetually encouraging my various creative endeavors and affirming my vocation of the pen. It's not easy living with someone who devotes countless hours to "artistic" work that generates little income and far too often deprives her of my availability and my time.

But if I did not write I would suffer emotionally and spiritually. If I did not write, my thoughts would have no release and my family would find me even more insufferable than I already am. As Franz Kafka said, *"A non-writing writer is a monster courting insanity."* (1) So I am deeply grateful for the tolerance and understanding shown to me by my wife and my children. Their love and acceptance encourages whatever is good in me and tames the demons with which I constantly wrestle. If everyone on earth could know such unconditional love for even a moment, then this world would surely begin to heal.

My wife is also my de facto editor. She kindly but forthrightly advises me to simplify, shorten, and temper my work. "Too many big words"... "Too long"... "Too redundant"..."Too provocative"... she will often say. And she's usually right. I talk too much. I preach too much. And my writing suffers from the arrogance of a man who always believes he has something important to say. But after many years of marriage, my wife still hasn't told me to shut up. Maybe she should. I'll let the reader decide.

The artist is inherently self-centered, and yet the artist is constantly striving to create something that transcends himself. At his worst the artist's words and work do nothing more than reveal his own narcissism. But at his best his creativity reaches out to touch the very edges of the universe.

My words are undoubtedly still mired in this terrestrial realm. Yet I take hope from the insight of Miguel de Cervantes, farcical though it may be: *"There is no book so bad that it does not have something good in it."* (2)

This book was written with my wife's sage advice in mind. So I hope that these offerings of poetry, prose, and polemics will be easy to read and easy to understand. And most of all, I hope that my words will usher the reader into a deeper commitment to peace, life, humanity, and love. The fire of my words is intended to purify, liberate, and heal, not to disparage and destroy. I pray that the reader will keep this in mind.

I must also emphasize that while the views and opinions in this book are deeply shaped by my Orthodox Christian faith, this book is by no means intended to be a dogmatic statement of the Orthodox Church. I am not a priest or a prophet, a teacher or a saint. I am just a simple child of God – as are we all (I truly believe) – offering up the convictions of my heart and soul with the hope that they will somehow contribute to peace, love, and healing in the world. I am a pilgrim: constantly seeking direction, constantly begging bread, and doing my best to share what I have been given with my fellow travelers on this trod through creation.

I can identify with Nikos Kazantzakis when he begins his interpretational biography of St. Francis of Assisi with the following words:

"I had taken up my quill to begin writing many times before now, but I always abandoned it quickly. Each time I was overcome with fear. Yes, may God forgive me, but the letters of the alphabet frighten me terribly. They are sly, shameless demons – and dangerous! You open the inkwell, release them; they run off – and how will you ever get control

of them again? They come to life, join, separate, ignore your commands, arrange themselves as they like on the paper – black, with tails and horns. You scream at them and implore them in vain, but they do as they please. Prancing, pairing up shamelessly before you, they deceitfully expose what you did not wish to reveal, and they refuse to give voice to what is struggling, deep within your bowels, to come forth and speak to mankind. As I was returning from Church this past Sunday, however, I felt emboldened. Had not God squeezed those demons into place whether they liked it or not, with the result that they wrote the Gospels? Well then, I said to myself, 'Courage, my soul! Have no fear of them! Take up your quill and write!' But I immediately grew fainthearted once again. The Gospels, to be sure, were written by the holy apostles. One had his angel, the other his lion, the other his ox, and that last his eagle. These dictated, and the apostles wrote. But I...?"(3)

Writing is indeed a dangerous and presumptuous endeavor. Will I one day look back on these words and regret something I said, or the way in which I said it? If not, then perhaps that will be a bad thing, because it will mean that I have not grown and matured as a man, as a writer, and as a Christian. In his journals, Thomas Merton lamented:

"I have always said too much, too soon. And then I've had to revise my opinions. My own work is to me extremely dissatisfying. It seems trivial. I hardly have the heart to continue with it – certainly not with the old stuff. But is the new any better?"(4)

The compositions herein simply reveal the condition of my heart and soul at this particular stage of my life. As far as my words reflect a consciousness that is wedded to peace, love, and life affirmation then I hope that my writing becomes more passionate rather than less. But as far as my words reflect spiritual pride, human intolerance, and the sin of self-righteousness then I pray that my writing will be increasingly tempered by divine mercy and true Christian grace.

I am not always responsible for that which resonates in my soul or flows through my mind. I am only responsible for what I permit to come forth, for what I allow to be unleashed. The heart guards the mind and tempers the spirit; and unless the heart is caressed by the Creator's hand then human intelligence and human pathos will produce all manner of lies, confusions, and horrors. Perhaps there are irresponsible words in this book. Perhaps there are soulful revelations that should have remained undisclosed. Perhaps there are unrestrained thoughts and feelings and opinions that made it past a heart that is still desperately in need of divine chastening. Only God knows. And only you, dear reader, can judge what speaks to you and what does not.

Albert Camus said: *"It seems to me that there is an ambition that ought to belong to all writers: to bear witness and shout aloud, every time it is possible, insofar as our talent allows, for those who are enslaved. The purpose of a writer is to keep civilization from destroying itself."*(5)

Well, I have no such grandiose notions about this book. But I can always hope. And it is my prayerful hope that the cry of these pages will uplift humanity and echo the divine truths by which humanity is ultimately sustained.

I suspect that some readers will find apparent contradictions in my philosophical views, or discrepancies in the words with which I express those views. And I make no apology for that. I have found peace in paradox. I am content to bathe in the antinomies of the Cross – the Cross that brings us both suffering and salvation simultaneously. So while I strive to be as logically consistent as possible, I dare not subvert the truth by crucifying truth with the rigid nails of my finite mortal rationale.

There are those who – in their desire to elevate consistency above all else – will disavow the sunset in order to affirm the sunrise, or who will deny the sunrise in order to affirm the sunset. But I choose to honor both sunset and sunrise as one inseparable cosmic mystery. And ultimately, I submit my fallible and finite words to the infinite Word of God who will judge everything that proceeds from the mouth, the pen, and the heart.

Ralph Waldo Emerson wrote:

"A foolish consistency is the hobgoblin of little minds, adored by little statesmen and philosophers and divines. With consistency a great soul has simply nothing to do. He may as well concern himself with his shadow on the wall. Speak what you think now in hard words, and tomorrow speak what tomorrow thinks in hard words again, though it contradict everything you said today. —'Ah, so you shall be sure to be misunderstood.' — Is it so bad, then, to be misunderstood? Socrates...and Jesus...and every pure and wise spirit that ever took flesh was misunderstood. To be great is to be misunderstood."(6)

But it is equally important to recall that Emerson also said, *"Let me never fall into the vulgar mistake of dreaming that I am being persecuted whenever I am contradicted."*(7) So I dare not pretend that my contradictions are proof of either greatness or victimhood. They are merely evidence of the weaknesses, fallibility, tensions, and struggles that swirl within this writer's soul – evidence of life and existence and all of their accompanying truth and turmoil. As Aldous

Huxley wrote: *"Consistency is contrary to nature, contrary to life. The only completely consistent people are dead."*(8)

Perhaps Kahlil Gibran's sentiment best expresses my own here: *"I have never agreed with my other self wholly. The truth of the matter seems to lie between us."*(9)

I must also confess that it is somewhat embarrassing to write about peace, justice, brotherhood, and truth – to pontificate about love, mercy, compassion, and grace – and yet do so little to actually help make these ideals a reality. As Kwame Nkrumah stated, *"Action without thought is blind; thought without action is empty."*(10) And to quote Huxley again:

"It is possible to make use of words as a substitute for effort, to live in a purely verbal universe and not in the given world of immediate experience. To change a vocabulary is easy; to change external circumstances or our own ingrained habits is hard and tiresome. The religious egoist who is not prepared to undertake a wholehearted imitation of Christ contents himself with the acquisition of a new vocabulary. But a new vocabulary is not the same thing as a new environment or a new character. The letter kills, or merely leaves inert; it is the spirit, it is the reality of underlying verbal signs, which gives new life."(11)

But the writer writes. Perhaps because that's the only way he can make any sense of the world, or the only way he knows how to make any difference in such a seemingly senseless world.

Dorothy Day – the radical pacifist, social revolutionary, and founder of *"The Catholic Worker Movement"* – wrote:

"Writing a book is hard because you are 'giving yourself away.' But if you love, you want to give yourself. You write as you are impelled to write, about man and his problems, his

relation to God and his fellow man. You write about yourself because in the long run all man's problems are the same. I have never felt so sure of myself that I did not feel the necessity of being backed up by great minds, searching the Scriptures and the writings of the saints for my authorities. The sustained effort of writing, of putting pen to paper so many hours a day when there are human beings around who need me – when there is sickness and hunger and sorrow – is a harrowingly painful job. I feel that I have done nothing well. But I have done what I could."(12)

I pray for the day when I too can say, "I have done what I could." As it stands I know that I have not done nearly enough, not nearly all that I could. My own words convict me. My own convictions haunt me. I am harshly judged by my own pen, and therefore I cry out: *"Lord have mercy on me, a sinner."*

There are various topics and themes included in this book: poetry, philosophy, social commentary, cultural criticism, essays, stories, personal reflections, and spiritual prose. The contents are not arranged in any particular order, so the book doesn't need to be read sequentially from beginning to end. There is much that I could have included but chose not to, and probably much that is included that would have been better left out. But the words contained herein were written with deep sincerity, fallible as they may be. I hope that God had something to do with them, and I hope that others will somehow benefit from them.

I must also issue this disclaimer:

Portions of this book contain profane language and disturbing material that is not suitable for children. So please be selective regarding which parts of this book you allow your children to read. (And I do encourage you to let your teenage children read most of the material contained herein. But please be responsible in exercising parental and adult censorship. I would never want to prioritize my own freedom of speech above protecting the welfare and innocence of youth.)

Ultimately, I echo the sentiments of Flannery O'Connor, who said:

"When a book leaves your hands, it belongs to God. He may use it to save a few souls or to try a few others; but I think that for the writer to worry is to take over God's business."(13)

So, this is just another *"Rebel Song."* It is in God's hands now. I pray that He will resurrect a divine melody out of any discordant notes.

May drops of ink
yield rivers of thought
that quicken the conscience
and open the heart.

+ GMK +

[A note about some of the terminology used in this book: Since this book is a compilation of writings I have composed over the years, some of the pronouns used are regrettably not gender neutral where perhaps they should have been, and some terms may not be politically correct according to the standards of the contemporary vernacular. I imagine that some of the adjective terminology contained herein might in time become anachronistic or even offensive. The linguistic standards of a culture are constantly changing, and there is simply no way to ensure that the vocabulary which is acceptable today will still be acceptable in the future. May the reader forgive me if I have unwittingly used socially offensive pronouns or adjectives throughout this book. I always wish to be culturally sensitive and as respectful as possible regarding language that addresses race, religion, and gender.]

Notes

1. Franz Kafka, *Letter to Max Brod, July 5, 1922*
2. Miguel de Cervantes, *Don Quixote*
3. Nikos Kazantzakis, *St. Francis*
4. Thomas Merton, *The Journals of Thomas Merton, Volume 7, 1967-1968*
5. Albert Camus, *Resistance, Rebellion, and Death*
6. Ralph Waldo Emerson, *Self-Reliance*
7. Ibid.
8. Aldous Huxley, *The Devils of Loudun*
9. Kahlil Gibran, *Sand and Foam*
10. Kwame Nkrumah, *Ghana: The Autobiography of Kwame Nkrumah*
11. Aldous Huxley, *The Devils of Loudun*
12. Robert Ellsberg (Editor), *Dorothy Day: Selected Writings*
13. Sally Fitzgerald (Editor), *The Habit of Being: The Letters of Flannery O'Connor*

Please note that the contents of this book have been revised, expanded, and updated since its original publication.

"Let the words of my mouth,
and the meditation of my heart,
be acceptable in thy sight,
O LORD, my strength, and my redeemer."
~ Psalm 19:14 ~

"Soon we'll find out who is the real revolutionary."
~ BOB MARLEY (BERHANE SELASSIE) ~

"Every act of rebellion expresses nostalgia for innocence and an appeal to the essence of being... Human rebellion ends in metaphysical revolt. It progresses from appearances to acts, from idealism to revolution... Rebellion cannot exist without a strange form of love... I rebel, therefore I exist."
~ ALBERT CAMUS ~

"You tell me that all the world is against me. And I tell you that I am against all the world."
~ ST. ATHANASIUS ~

"The more violence, the less revolution."
~ BARTHELEMY de LIGT ~

1. ~ COMPELLED BY MYSTERY ~

We are perpetually drawn to that which we fear and that which we do not understand. This is our human fascination. We are obsessed with love, with sex, and with God. Oh how badly we want to understand such matters! Oh how badly we want to tame and control such things! But, alas, we cannot. And thus we are ever intrigued.

This is why we compose books and poems and prayers and doctrines and songs and incessant works of art that cry out for answers, that cry out for understanding, and that cry out for some semblance of certainty – a certainty that will always elude our grasp in this mortal realm.

Oh how we both love and hate mystery! But by God, how empty life would be without it!

So, beware of those who presume to understand the incomprehensible nature of religion, love, and sex. Beware of those that claim to have conquered such mysteries by the dim light of human reason or the feckless might of carnal prowess. Such people are the most empty and dangerous among us.

There is beauty in mystery – fearful and perplexing though it may be. And beauty is truth. God calls us to bathe in it, not to understand it.

2. ~ REVOLUTIONARY ENDEAVORS ~

As revolutionaries we may overthrow governments, transform institutional structures, abolish social injustices, and reconstruct entire nations; but we will still have to stand before the Lord of creation and give an account of our individual and collective sins. And regardless of our temporal revolutionary achievements, unless we have experienced a revolution of our own spiritual condition, then all of our endeavors will wither in the pyretic winds of eternity.

3. ~ "OUR" LORD ~

Christ has redeemed all of creation. He has brought salvation to all mankind. He is the Bread of Life and the Light of the world. And yet we live, think, and act as if God is *for us* and *against them*. We raise our flags, sing our anthems, exalt our constitutions, and separate ourselves as islands of enlightened humanity amidst a dark sea of "terrorists," "savages," and "heathens." And we do so while invoking the name and blessing of Our Lord Jesus Christ. We call Him "Our Lord" as if this means that He is ours and not also theirs. But Christ is Our Lord – not ours alone, but ours as in Lord of all humanity and Lord of the entire universe. It is true that many refuse to acknowledge His Lordship, but is it not a greater sin to believe that Christ *loves us* and *hates them*? Is it not a worse blasphemy to live as though *our* lives are sacred and *theirs* are not? In the name of Our Incarnate God – who relinquished His own right to life – we claim the right to destroy the lives of others. In the name of Christ who humbled Himself to death on the Cross, we invoke *our* right to shoot, bomb, and abort *them*. But we will never be Christians, regardless of our professions or creeds, as long as we refuse to see Christ in all people – ally and enemy, born and unborn alike. Let us pray with Mother Teresa who said, *"Lord, break my heart so completely that the whole world falls in."*

4. ~ THROUGH the LOOKING GLASS ~

Some look through the kaleidoscope and see chaos and confusion. Others look through the kaleidoscope and see complexity, order, beauty and design. It is the same with the microscope and the telescope. It is not *what* we look at, but *how* we look at it that determines whether we will see truth or error, light or darkness, beauty or horror, heaven or hell.

5. ~ BLASPHEMIES and CURSES ~

When you bless bombs, you curse God. When you sanctify the sword, you blaspheme the Savior. When you condone violence, you curse the Prince of Peace. If you choose to support warfare, capital punishment, and abortion, then do so in your own name and not in the name of Our Lord. For when you honor killing, you dishonor Christ.

6. ~ THE MOST REVOLUTIONARY FORCE ~

Philanthropy is the charitable giving of one's resources, but love is the sacrificial giving of oneself. And love is the most revolutionary force in the world.

7. ~ PREVENTIONS and CURES ~

They say that abortion reduces poverty. They say that armies ensure peace. They say that prisons prevent crime. They say that politics facilitates progress. Well, decapitation also cures headaches.

8. ~ THE BULLET, THE BOMB, and THE BALLOT ~

As long as one seeks freedom through the bullet, the bomb, or the ballot, then they will never truly be free. This is because any freedom obtained by those means can just as easily be lost by those means. True freedom can never be compromised, stolen, damaged, or destroyed; because true freedom is ultimately spiritual, not material. True freedom comes from the knowledge of the Holy, and the spiritual soul can never be destroyed by material violence.

9. ~ SPIRITUAL LESSONS ~

Protestantism taught me the value of scripture.

Catholicism taught me the value of suffering.

Buddhism taught me the value of compassion.

Islam taught me the value of submission.

Hinduism taught me the value of reciprocity.

Judaism taught me the value of the Law.

Fundamentalism taught me the value of morality.

Liberalism taught me the value of tolerance.

Rastafari taught me the value of positivity.

And Orthodoxy teaches me to prayerfully struggle towards Christ – the Prince of Peace, the Lord of Life, the Friend of Sinners, and the Lover of Mankind – He from whom all divine values ultimately flow.

10. ~ FIRE in MY BONES, REVOLUTION in MY SOUL ~

I have cast my lot with the outcast and the insane, the dirty and the disinherited. I seek the company of the marginalized and maligned, the rejected and abused. I have no concern for the approval of the fashionable, the cool, the esteemed and the elite. My heart beats to a revolutionary drum, and my comrades are those who love social justice more than social acceptance.

My spirit is aligned with those who adore truth and rights above power, profit, or prestige. I seek the fellowship of those who suffer for Christ – those who are forsaken by family, friends, church, and state.

Give me the company of true rebels – those who exalt the values of peace and life, who carry the torch of true Christian love. Let me be blessed to abide with "fools for Christ," those whose words and actions light a fire to the status quo of inhumanity and evil.

Yes Lord, give me kinship with the person who stands alone on the street corner and calls all men to repentance. Give me fellowship with the radicals who endure heat and cold, insult and injury as they pray on the sidewalks of abortion clinics. Give me unity with those who refuse to lend voice, vote, and allegiance to a godless government and a blood-drenched flag.

I cannot help it. The Lord put fire in my bones and revolution in my soul. What have I to do with the pretty people, the popular people, the politicians and the profiteers? Give me the voices that cry in the wilderness. Give me those who are willing to lose their minds and their heads in order to preserve their souls and salvage the souls of others.

11. ~ A REFLECTION on EVIL ~

Evil thrives, but not because it is repugnant. Evil thrives because there is something about our fallen human nature that finds it seductive. We do not resist evil by pretending that we are above it, by pretending that we are repulsed by it. To do so is to pretend that we are as holy as God, which we certainly are not. We resist evil by acknowledging its attraction, and then recognizing that this attraction is utterly destructive to everything our souls were divinely created to experience. To presume that we are above evil is to render ourselves its prey. Better to stare evil in the face, to confess our desire for it, than to fool ourselves into believing that we do not love it on some base level. Satan fell because he thought he was holier than God. And now he seeks to replicate his insidious pride in our own human hearts. Let us acknowledge the brilliant and deadly light of Lucifer, and then flee headlong into the unfailing love of Christ.

12. ~ THE MYSTICAL PARADOX of CHRISTIAN DISCIPLESHIP ~

Why is it that some saints walked with lions and other saints were eaten by lions? I don't know. I just know that the saints were all saints because they had faith. Those that were eaten by beasts experienced the love of God just as surely as those that tamed the beasts. And this highlights the mystical paradox of Christian discipleship. We might be called to martyrdom or we might be called to a long and healthy and prosperous life. But wherever we find ourselves – in wealth or in poverty, in sickness or in health, in freedom or in prison, in joy or in despair – let us know that Christ is always in our midst. He is and always shall be!

13. ~ RADICAL EVIL, RADICAL PUNISHMENT, and RADICAL LOVE ~

Radically evil deeds deserve a radically commensurate punishment. But as Pumla Gobodo-Madikizela writes in her book, _A Human Being Died That Night_:

"The radically evil are unpunishable because no amount of punishment can balance what they have done. They are unforgivable because no yardstick exists by which we can measure what it means to forgive them, and there is no mental disposition we can adopt toward them that would correct the sense of injustice that their actions have injected into our world."

So whether it's the guillotine, the hangman's noose, or reciprocal endeavors of militaristic horror, radical evil will never be recompensed with radical punishment. The only answer, the only remedy, and the only truly effective response to radical evil is radical love.

14. ~ HUMBLE THYSELF and REJOICE ~

O man, humble thyself, for you were created on the sixth day, not the first. Yet rejoice, O man, for amongst all earthly and heavenly creatures you alone were created in the very image of God. (Cf. Genesis 1:26-31)

15. ~ TO BEAT SWORDS into PLOWSHARES and BULLETS into BREAD ~

I've grown tired of railing against Protestantism, railing against the Papacy, railing against homosexuality, railing against Islam, and railing against various heresies. In defending the Orthodox Christian Faith, God does not require me to crusade against all things heterodox. Rather, He requires me to love all men and to show them the same mercy that I seek from Him.

But I shall never grow tired of railing against the violent destruction of human beings created in the very image of God; for nothing is more unmerciful, unloving, and unchristian than refusing to confront and condemn the inhumane evils of warfare and abortion. Destroying life in the name of Christ is the greatest blasphemy I know, and I will perpetually condemn such blasphemy without apology.

I take up my cross to beat swords into plowshares and bullets into bread. In the name of Our Lord, I shall unceasingly proclaim peace amidst the idolatry of violence.

16. ~ MY REVOLUTION ~

If I can't help myself, then Lord help me to help someone else. If I can't find peace within, then Lord, use me to bring peace to my fellow man. And if I can't heal the world, then please Lord, heal my heart. Let me born again – again and again – daily arising from my sins. Let this be my revolution.

17. ~ A SIMPLE and AGE OLD CONCEPT ~

My rights end where your life begins. True individual freedom never infringes upon the freedom or lives of others. It's a simple and age old concept: *live and let live.*

18. ~ GIVING and RECEIVING ~

Politicians, economists, and sociologists view the problems of the world through the materialistic lenses of supply and demand, capital and labor, rich versus poor. And that's why their proposed solutions do nothing to truly alleviate the problem of human suffering. A materialistic worldview only produces materialistic solutions; and history demonstrates that these materialistic "solutions" often produce greater evils than the problems they attempted to redress.

The evil of human poverty will not be understood by philosophical dialectics or resolved by economic theories. And that's because the problem of poverty is fundamentally a problem of evil. It is a spiritual problem; and spiritual problems require spiritual solutions. And there is indeed an indelible spiritual law that can redeem the evil of homelessness and hunger, poverty and destitution: it's the universal principle of giving and receiving – to give without compulsion and to receive without shame; to give from the heart and to receive with gratitude; to offer without demands and to receive without obligation; to freely ask from one's need and to freely give from one's abundance.

You see, the fact is that Karl Marx simply plagiarized St. Luke the apostle. Marx stole a divine Christian principle and stripped it of its spiritual import. He used the example of authentic *spiritual community* to formulate his godless model of *materialistic communism*. In describing the first Christian community, St. Luke writes:

"They devoted themselves to the apostles' teaching and to fellowship, to the breaking of bread and to prayer. Everyone was filled with awe at the many wonders and signs performed by the

apostles. All the believers were together and had everything in common. They sold property and possessions to give to anyone who had need. Every day they continued to meet together in the temple courts. They broke bread in their homes and ate together with glad and sincere hearts, praising God and enjoying the favor of all the people. And the Lord added to their number daily those who were being saved." [Acts 2:42-47]

Karl Marx proclaimed, *"From each according to his ability and to each according to his needs."* And this principle is very similar to that which was actually practiced by the early Church. But Marx sought to formulate a materialistic philosophy that eliminated the spiritual component which was essential to the success of the first Christian community. Without devotion to God, without human fellowship, without corporate prayer and unconditional love, the needs of the human body and the human soul will never be adequately addressed.

So give freely. Receive freely. Forgive debts and demand nothing owed. Love God and love your neighbor. Ask when you have a need, and give before you are asked.

We are Christians, and the Gospel is the hope for the problem of poverty and the solution for human suffering. But instead of living according to the law of Christ, we live according to the philosophies of this world. We have been set free, but we continue to live like slaves. We cannot vote poverty away. We cannot work it away. We cannot horde it away. Such things may make us rich individuals, but they won't make for a wealthy world community. There are too many people that cannot work, that have nothing to save, that have no voice or vote, and that are completely dependent upon the mercy and kindness of their fellow man.

The only thing that will eradicate poverty is adherence to the divine law of freely giving and freely receiving. And this requires humility, faith, and love. It requires the humility to ask, to beg if need be. It requires the faith to give when we are afraid that we don't have enough of our own. And above all it requires love: loving our neighbors as ourselves.

19. ~ DO YOU SUPPOSE? ~

Do you suppose that diamonds and gold were divinely created only for the wealthy? Do you suppose that God blessed the fruit of the earth for the rich and not also for the poor? Do you suppose that fertile soil, abundant water, and aesthetic landscape are commodities that only the aristocracy can appreciate? Do you suppose that God intended for you to privately own what He has freely given to all? Do you suppose that God has anointed you to be the arbiter of who may drink from His rivers and feast from His land? You live as though the bounties of God's earth belong to you alone, and then you cry "foul" when the impoverished obtain their necessities by force. Wealth accrued at the expense of the poor is a greater violence than the poor man's struggle against such injustice. You fear the violence of the poor because you know that you rob them daily.

20. ~ THE PROFUNDITY of BEAUTY ~

The most profound beauty is that which has no pragmatic value or utilitarian import. It is simply beauty that requires no *"because."* It is the beauty that defies questions of "why," "what," or "how?" It is the beauty that renders logic impotent and superlatives superfluous. It is a sunset that splashes the horizon with a thousand shades of orange-red flames. It is a smile in the purity of a child's eyes. It is a melody that inexplicably milks our tears. It is the sweet aroma that evokes the mystical nectar of nostalgia. It's as simple as the twinkle of a single star and as complex as the expanse of a billion galaxies. The greatest beauty reveals, reflects, and radiates the divine. It says simply with its God, "I Am." Such beauty moves us by its mystery yet paralyzes us in its presence. There is no response to such sublimity other than to receive it and bathe in it, allowing its transcendence to transform its beholder. Perhaps this is why Dostoevsky said, *"Beauty will save the world."*

21. ~ THE PATHOLOGY of MANKIND ~

The earth is the womb of humanity. But we plunder, pillage, scar and abuse the very source of our life and nourishment. The pathology of mankind is evident: mother aborts child and humanity rapes its mother.

22. ~ THE COMPANY of PROPHETS ~

They may not be educated. They may not be creative. They may not be "socially conscious" in a socially acceptable way. They may lack tact. They may be devoid of cultural grace. They may be offensive, awkward, indelicate, and obtrusive. But give me those with passion. Give me those with heart. Give me those that care. Give me those that are not afraid to say, *"Thou shall,"* and *"Thou shalt not!"*

As sinful as I am, I nonetheless prefer the company of prophets to the company of politicians and poseurs, socialites and sycophants. I'd rather listen to the fool on the corner who curses Babylon than to "enlightened" intellectuals who do the whore's bidding.

23. ~ THEFT ~

The only purpose of unshared wealth is to provide temporal comfort on the road to eternal suffering. No one is more enslaved than individuals that shackle themselves to the chains of their own private riches. God gives to us so that we can give to others. To receive and not give is nothing other than theft.

24. ~ UNRAVELING MYSTERIES ~

Life is mystery. Love is mystery. God is mystery. Try too hard to unravel these mysteries and you will only unravel your soul.

25. ~ SPEAKING of PEACE ~

Speak of war,
They will call you "patriotic"

Speak of greed,
They will call you "ambitious"

Speak of lust,
They will say you are "passionate"

Speak of politics,
They will say you are "involved"

Speak of division,
They will call you "loyal"

Speak lies,
They will call you "pragmatic"

But when you speak of peace and love,
Nonviolence and truth,
They will call you "naïve," "foolish," "gullible" and "weak"

"Blessed are the peacemakers, for they shall be called the children of God."
[St. Matthew 5:9]

26. ~ INDIGO BLOOD ~

I carry a spear behind my ear
The battlefield is in my hands
The lines thirst,
And I must quench them
With the indigo blood of poetic truth

27. ~ PEOPLE of THE LIE ~

All human beings share an innate thirst for knowledge. But what separates us is that some people desire to know truth while others desire to know falsehood. Some strive towards good while others embrace evil. There will always be a spiritual and psychological conflict between people of the truth and people of the lie. And people of the lie are quite brilliant at disguising their lies as truth. Our world is in chaos because the masses exalt people of the lie and then ridicule, persecute, and murder people of the truth. They idolize politicians and curse the prophets. But no man can run away from himself. Those who perpetually embrace lies in this life will not escape those lies in the life to come. But there is hope for people of the lie, for as Our Lord said, *"The truth shall make you free."* [St. John 8:32]

28. ~ ROCK THE BOAT! ~

If our lives are devoid of controversy, then our lives are devoid of substance. The Cross is conflict. The horizontal clashes with the vertical – calling us to an agonizing, suffering, controversial truth. If our lives don't offend the world, then we aren't truly living. If our lives don't disrupt the status quo of apathy and evil, then we're merely existing. So pick up your instrument – whether pen or paint or sermon or song – and stir up some controversy today. Let the world be shaken by your witness to peace and life. Let the world be disturbed by your proclamations of justice and love. The path of salvation is a revolutionary road. So rock the damn boat before the boat rocks you to sleep!

29. ~ IT'S A BLESSING to BE at THE BOTTOM ~

It's a blessing to be at the bottom, because we can't look down on anyone and it's easier to stay grounded. What a tragedy to rise so high that you soar above humanity, to rise so high that you think you are God. Just look at the fate of Lucifer, who was cast into the depths of hell because he presumed to transcend his Creator. So we rejoice in our lowly lot in this life. For how can we be the salt of the earth if wealth, fame, power, and prestige have separated us from the majority of our human brethren?

30. ~ FUTILE SEARCHES / FAITHFUL ENDEAVORS ~

We search for justice. We search for truth. We search for love. We carry the flickering torch of Diogenes, waiting in futility for Godot. But when we decide to act justly ourselves, when we live truthful lives of unconditional love, then we illumine the darkness of our world with the inextinguishable Light of Christ. And then God becomes our experiential reality.

31. ~ THE WORDS of PEACE ~

Sometimes the words of peace are not peaceful words. Sometimes the words of peace echo the prophetic lament, *"They say 'peace,' 'peace' when there is no peace." [Jeremiah 6:14]* Sometimes the words of peace expose the insidious violence that masquerades as law and order. Sometimes the words of peace are angry, offensive, and disruptive. Sometimes the words of peace bring conviction rather than comfort. Sometimes the words of peace are provocative rather than palliative. But without the words of peace, the world would continue to systematically manufacture violence, destruction, and murder in unabated fashion. So I thank God for those who have the courage to speak words of peace in a violent and bloodthirsty world. They are the true revolutionaries - pointing us all to love, serve, follow, and obey the Prince of Peace, Our Lord Jesus Christ.

32. ~ BEWARE of CONDEMNING THE VOICES of TRUTH ~

It is not hateful, judgmental, or unchristian to condemn evil, rebuke injustice, and criticize corrupt powers. If such criticisms are wrong, then what are we to make of the prophets and saints who raised their voices against idolatry and gave their lives in the service of Truth? Upon Holy Baptism every Orthodox Christian becomes a prophet of the Church, empowered with the duty and grace to proclaim Christian truth and bring light to the darkness of this world. As St. Paul says, we must speak the truth in love. (Ephesians 4:15) But love is not always gentle, and love is not passive. True Christian love does not hesitate to rebuke injustice. True love does not turn a blind eye to evil. It is never apathetic towards suffering and oppression. As Bob Marley sang, *"Love would never leave us alone."* So beware, lest you condemn the voices of truth while defending the agencies of evil.

33. ~ AN UNACCEPTABLE ACCEPTABILITY ~

The Pharisees concerned themselves with what was "proper" and "acceptable" according to religious Law. But the prophets, saints, and martyrs prophesied against the perversion of truth that often masqueraded as religious custom. They refused to acknowledge the acceptability of idolatry and injustice. They refused to conform their thoughts and lives to that which was considered "proper" by a godless world. Their preaching and examples were not determined by a standard of what was merely "allowable;" instead, their lives were driven by a righteousness that finds its greatest expression in the holy folly of that irrational virtue called "unconditional love."

I am not a prophet, I am not a saint, and I don't presume to be a teacher. I am simply a struggling Orthodox Christian who refuses to call the destruction of those created in God's image "acceptable" or "proper." All killing is not equivalent. All killing is not necessarily *murder*. But while killing in self-defense or in defense of others may be technically "permissible" by legalistic interpretations of theology or the legalities of society, I shall never concede that any act of killing is "acceptable" or "proper." I cannot agree that it is ever acceptable or proper to destroy the very image of God, to stifle the divine breath that infuses every human being, and to presumptively appropriate the divine authority over life and death.

If affirming the unconditional sanctity of all human life makes me a heretic, then I shall revel in such a heresy. I am a servant of the Prince of Peace and a soldier in the army of His Church. I have no commands to kill, only commands to forgive, heal, serve, and love. And since I already fail to truly love my neighbors as myself, then the least I can do is dare not seek rationalizations to kill them.

34. ~ LIBERATION from HUMAN EXPECTATIONS ~

Do not live with the fear of disappointing other people. Don't enslave yourself to the anxiety of trying to live up to other people's expectations. No matter how hard we try, we will inevitably fail and disappoint even those we love the most. But God does not judge us by human expectations. His love is pure and unconditional, and we are never disappointments in His sight. Therefore, let us simply focus on loving others, serving others, and honoring God by honoring our neighbors. If we do this, then we will persevere and prevail – regardless of what anyone else thinks. Remember this truth and move forward in the peace, light, and love of Christ. Life is too short to do otherwise.

35. ~ THE MEDICINE of SUFFERING ~

Suffering is medicine for the soul. Redemption is born from suffering. And that's why the hope for our culture is not to be found in politics, education, or financial prosperity. Rather, our hope resides in the poor, the prisoners, and the unborn lives that possess unlimited promise for the future. Our willingness to endure suffering and to embrace the sufferers shall determine the redemptive blessings that God shines upon our society. God does not cause our suffering. He redeems our suffering. And He calls us to cooperate with Him in alleviating the pain and injustices that afflict our fellow man.

36. ~ ALL HE WANTED to DO WAS SING SONGS to JESUS ~

All he wanted to do was sing songs to Jesus. But the girls wanted him to sing songs to them. And as much as he loved Jesus in the morning, those girls would love him at night. So he sang to those pretty girls, and he made love to those pretty girls, and he went to heaven and hell with those pretty girls. But Jesus was always in his heart. And Jesus was always waiting on him when the sun came up.

37. ~ SOCIAL CAUSES and HUMAN LIVES ~

The devil is all too happy to have us embrace a righteous cause as long as we're willing to sacrifice innocent lives in pursuit of that cause. And that's the difference between politicians and revolutionaries: politicians prioritize "social issues" over the lives of individual people, but revolutionaries prioritize the sanctity of human lives above all other social causes. So beware of those who promote the "welfare of humanity" at the expense of innocent human beings – you know, those who tell us that the violence of war, capitalism, and legal abortion are necessary for the greater good of mankind.

38. ~ SOLIDARITY ~

I stand in solidarity
With the army of humanity
With the elderly, the unborn
And the homeless in poverty

I pray with the Buddhists
Under the Bodhi tree
I fight with the peaceful warriors
The true Jihadis

I struggle for theosis
In the Church of Orthodoxy
I chant JAH! Rastafari!
Burning Babylon without apology

I march toward Zion
But not politically
I fight injustice
Actively and prayerfully

I war against oppression
Militantly but nonviolently
I preach liberation
Freedom from mental slavery

I stand for truth and rights
One love, One aim, One destiny!
All men are brothers
And Satan is the enemy

The flesh is our prison
And sin is our captivity
But Christ has conquered
The Cross is our victory!

Death is defeated
And He is Risen...
Eternally!

39. ~ SELF-ENLIGHTENMENT ~

There can be so self-enlightenment apart from a desire to liberate the oppressed from suffering and bondage. We cannot have communion with God if we despise fellowship with our neighbors. It is useless to seek answers in the expanses of the universe while ignoring the questions in our brothers' cries.

40. ~ WHEN THEY CURSE YOUR CREATIVITY ~

It hurts when people curse your creativity. It hurts deeply when you labor to create something that you hope will glorify God and uplift humanity, only to have your work unfairly judged, condemned, and dismissed by those who have not even bothered to examine it. But do not despair. If your creative endeavors come from your heart, if they are motivated by a desire to make the world a better place, and if they seek above all to honor the God from whom all creativity flows, then know that your work will bear divine fruit. If you find that unknown enemies come out of the woodwork to attack your efforts, realize that whatever glorifies God also stirs up the wrath of demons. Ignore the hatred and continue to shine your light. Recognize that divine works will inevitably bring demonic opposition. And sometimes this opposition will try to masquerade itself as righteousness. But the *spirits* reveal themselves by their *spirit*; and although they may try, the hatred of demons cannot hide behind the façade of virtue. So continue to do JAH works; and if others don't receive your love, then shake the dust from your feet and move forward in positivity and peace. Continue to sow your creative seeds – for the glory of God, not for the praise of men – and your labor will never be in vain. Usually, those that curse our creativity are those who lack the courage and faith to create anything themselves. Rather than using their energies to uplift others, they exhaust themselves in efforts to tear us down. As Bob Marley (Berhane Selassie) sang:

"Many people will fight you down, when you see JAH light." [Exodus]

41. ~ SELECTIVE CONCERNS ~

People homeless and living on the streets? Not a big deal, because it's not happening to us.

Innocent civilians being murdered by American drones overseas? Not a big deal, because it's not happening to us.

People starving all over the world, and in our own country as well? Not a big deal, because it's not happening to us.

Unborn babies being butchered in the womb? Not a big deal, because it's not happening to us.

But Communism and Tsetse flies and Ebola and ISIS? Damn! We better take those things seriously, because those things could be coming for *us*!

42. ~ THE CHRISTIAN PACIFIST is NOT NAÏVE ~

We are not naïve; we understand that pacifism might get us killed. We are not naïve; we realize that the Cross means suffering and death. We are not naïve; we know that nonviolent struggle might not prevail in this temporal realm. But, as disciples of Christ, we have no other choice but to heed the divine commands and follow the holy example of the Prince of Peace.

There is nothing pragmatic, utilitarian, or expedient about the Cross. In the eyes of the world the Cross epitomizes weakness, defeat, futility, and superstition. But for us the Cross is salvation and strength. So we walk to His Cross, carrying our own crosses, by the power of the Cross. We march unarmed but eternally protected. We are lambs amongst wolves, and we will be vindicated by the Lion. We are followers of Christ, and therefore we have no right to walk in a different manner from Him. *"He who says he abides in Christ ought himself also to walk just as He walked." [I John 2:6]*

Make no mistake: following Christ can get you killed. But it will also gain you eternal life.

43. ~ CHRISTIAN COMPASSION and REVOLUTIONARY INJUSTICES ~

The term "social justice" has been misappropriated by the political left, and in reactionary manner it has been altogether discarded by the political right. But there is a Christian imperative to care about society and about justice. Society is comprised of our fellow man, our neighbors; and the Golden Rule compels us to seek the good for others that we desire for ourselves. However, it is not Christian to try to forcefully impose equality, fairness, and justice in society. Many "revolutionaries" started out as Christians, but they drifted away from the Church and became "wise in their own eyes." (Proverbs 3:7) Thus, their revolutionary endeavors inevitably resulted in creating greater injustices than the ones they were initially attempting to ameliorate. History demonstrates that mankind's attempts to establish an earthly Utopia have invariably ushered in conditions far more hellish than heavenly. The fact is, we cannot forcibly establish justice in the world; all we can do is strive to act justly ourselves. If we seek to violently impose justice, we will inevitably create only more injustice in the end; but if we seek to manifest mercy, compassion, and love, then we will shine the radiance of Christ and the world will be enlightened.

"Everyone thinks of changing the world, but no one thinks of changing himself." ~ Leo Tolstoy ~

44. ~ COLLECTIVE ACKNOWLEDGMENT ~

Let us collectively acknowledge – as we nestle into our soft beds tonight and arise to our warm breakfasts tomorrow – that we are in some measure responsible for the homelessness, hunger, and hopelessness that so many people around the world experience with each comfort and convenience we enjoy.

45. ~ WHAT I TRUST ~

I don't trust happiness and I don't trust pleasure. They are fickle, deceitful betrayers. But I do trust divine joy, that mystical *"peace that passes all understanding."* *[Philippians 4:7]* For when happiness fades into sorrow and pleasure turns into pain, the love of God endures – ever present, ever faithful, ever sure.

46. ~ ART and REVOLUTION ~

True artists have revolutionary vision, and true revolutionaries have artistic souls. Creativity and struggle are inextricably linked. Beauty, justice, freedom, and peace are born from a sacrificial concern for human dignity and a sacrificial love for human life. That's why Dr. Martin Luther King, Jr. was as much of an artist as Van Gogh, and why Van Gogh was as revolutionary as Dr. King. And it's why Dostoevsky could write: *"Beauty will save the world."*

47. ~ INSANITY ~

None of us are normal. Anyone who believes himself to be sane is crazy. We are all displaced from the Garden, the collective human Diaspora that wails because we long to go back home. Some people realize that they're sick and know that they're lost; therefore they have sense enough to cling to the Cross. All others are merely prisoners pretending to be free, perpetuating a corporate insanity in the name of reason.

48. ~ IN DEFENSE of THE INNOCENT ~

Christ stands with the innocent, the suffering, the helpless victims of violence and persecution. He stands in defense of them with His own Body and Blood. He stands in defense of them with eternal truth and divine reciprocity. He stands in defense of them with the promises of heaven and the company of His holy angels. He stands in defense of them with His words of life and His Spirit of comfort. He stands in defense of them with the prophecy of eternal justice and the certainty of His dreadful Judgment. He stands in defense of them with the wood of His victorious and life-giving Cross. Yes, Our Lord Jesus Christ is the surest defender of the defenseless, the greatest ally of the innocent and the oppressed. But He stands with them nonviolently and unarmed with weapons of mortal destruction. And His disciples must do the same.

49. ~ LIFE CONQUERS DEATH ~

Violence has the power to destroy nations, subjugate peoples, deface creation, abort the unborn, and inspire retaliatory acts of hate. But violence has no power to destroy the eternal ideals of peace, love, justice, and truth. Violence can exterminate the flesh but it cannot annihilate the soul. Life will forever conquer death. Christ is Risen! He is in our midst! He is and always shall be!

50. ~ AN UNTAMED WEAPON ~

Violence is a weapon that cannot be tamed. It is never wielded in moderation. When unleashed its horrors know no boundaries, limits, or restraints.

51. ~ KYRIE ELEISON ~

In my joy... Lord, have mercy.
In my pain... Lord, have mercy.
When I hope... Lord, have mercy.
When I despair... Lord, have mercy.
When I believe... Lord, have mercy.
When I doubt... Lord, have mercy.
When I laugh... Lord, have mercy.
When I cry... Lord, have mercy.
When I obey... Lord, have mercy.
When I sin... Lord, have mercy.
When I am afflicted... Lord, have mercy.
When I am comforted... Lord, have mercy.
When I suffer... Lord, have mercy.
When I am healed... Lord, have mercy.
While I live... Lord, have mercy.
When I die... Lord, have mercy.

For in this life nothing is constant, nothing is certain,
nothing is trustworthy except for Your unfailing mercy.

Teach me Lord to place my confidence in nothing else.
Spare me from the shackles of silver that purchased Judas's
judgment.
Take everything from me Lord, as you wish.
Snatch it all from my obstinate hands if need be.
But please Lord, let your mercy remain.

"Lord Jesus Christ, Son of God, have mercy on me a sinner."

+ Kyrie Eleison +

52. ~ FRIENDS ~

The encouraging words of our true friends heal the wounds inflicted by the spiteful words of our enemies. Even though many betray you, slander you, and fight you down, if you have but one true friend you are richly blessed. I can honestly say that in this regard, my cup runneth over. I am blessed beyond measure.

53. ~ IF PEACEMAKING IS WRONG, PERSUADE ME ~

If peacemaking is wrong, if nonviolence is the sin of cowardice, if forgiveness and love for our enemies is indeed a violation of the Christian gospel, then bring forth evidence from the entirety of the New Testament, submit clear confirmation from the Lives of the Saints, and let a tome of attestations from our holy Church fathers emerge.

Persuade me that Our Lord – in offering His own life on the Cross – was the epitome of cowardice and naïveté.

Persuade me that it is more honorable to kill than to forgive.

Persuade me that it is more Christian to hate than to love.

Persuade me that God actually turns His back on the innocent victims of unjust violence, and therefore our swords alone are their only hope of salvation.

Persuade me that in killing our enemies we will somehow save our enemies' souls.

Persuade me that might does in fact make right, and that the meek shall ultimately inherit hell.

Persuade me that Our Lord commanded us to turn the other cheek only so that we can reload our weapons.

Persuade me that Our Lord commanded us to bless those who persecute us only so that they might drop their guard and become easier targets for our bullets.

Persuade me that although the Christian no longer needs to slaughter bulls and goats to attain salvation, he nevertheless needs to slaughter his fellow man.

Persuade me of these things, and I will take up arms tomorrow.

But until then, I cannot take up arms, for my arms have taken up the Cross.

54. ~ REFORMATION, RENOVATION, and REVOLUTION ~

Spiritual maturation means leaving certain things behind. And spiritual maturation also means that some things will leave us behind. As the world inevitably progresses, the spiritually minded person will remain unmoved, rooted in timeless truths and unshaken by the capricious winds of demonic transformation.

"Progress," "growth," and "change" are often political euphemisms used to obfuscate immorality, injustice, and evil. For fear of being labeled "obscurantist," most people are afraid to oppose the proposed reforms of the day. The politician stands before the people and invokes the specious rhetoric of "progress and change." He cleverly points out the current problems, making the case that without his proposed reforms these problems will not be solved. And most people are afraid to oppose these "reforms" because they are terrified of appearing unenlightened and unprogressive.

But not all growth is good. Not all progress is positive. Cancerous tumors metastasize. Evil proliferates. The Tower of Babel was a wondrous achievement of human development, but it was ultimately a progress towards tragic self-destruction.

Political reformers are often right in diagnosing the problems, but they are almost always wrong in their proposed solutions. That's why the true revolutionary is not a politician. Politicians naïvely attempt to reform the disease. But the revolutionary understands that you can't reform a malignant tumor; you have to cut it out. Babylon cannot be renovated. Babylon must burn.

55. ~ IF IT'S TRULY GOOD, IT'S TRULY SHARED ~

Nothing truly good can be kept to oneself, for oneself. For everything good comes from God; and God offers Himself fully, wholly, and completely to all. The blessings He bestows upon His children are offered freely to the whole world. But many cling to the chains of evil and therefore cannot receive the abundant goodness of Our Lord. All things truly good are truly shared with all. God could not keep divine love to Himself. He died to share it with us.

56. ~ WAR and THE STATE ~

War is the health of the state. War is the wealth of the state. War is the need for the state. War is the cause of the state. Thus, the abolition of war is the abolition of the state; and men love the idol of the state more than they love their fellow man. And without the love of our fellow man as the supreme aspiration, we will never have peace; we will only have "states."

"You can only hide violence with lies, and you can only sustain lies with violence. Inevitably, anyone who proclaims violence as their method must take falsehood as their principle."
~ Alexander Solzhenitsyn ~

57. ~ WAR AGAINST OUR SOULS ~

Western culture pressures us to compete, to perform, to achieve. But these social pressures war against our souls, and they cause people to war against each other. How foolish are these worldly pursuits, for prince and pauper stand equally naked before God.

Stop racing ahead of your neighbor. Stop ascending on the back of your brother. Slow down and walk beside your fellow man. And if God blesses you with success, share the fruits thereof with unconditional generosity. Thereby you will achieve peace for yourself and peace with others.

58. ~ PRESUMPTUOUS TEACHERS ~

Anyone that thinks they cannot learn from another is a fool indeed. Beware of those who always presume to teach but never humble themselves to learn. Every person is created in the image of God, and therefore every human being has something of value to offer.

59. ~ GOD LOVES ME ANYWAY ~

God loves me anyway. That's the sum of it all. I cling to this truth above all else.

60. ~ WHY I EMBRACE NONVIOLENCE ~

I embrace nonviolence not because it *works*; I embrace nonviolence because it is *nonviolent*. Love does not love because it is loved in return. It loves because its true nature is unconditional. The principles of peace and love appear naïve, impractical, and idealistic to the worldly mind. But these values are rooted in an eternal God, and therefore they are infinitely enduring. We follow Christ not because He leads us to earthly success, but because He leads us to eternal salvation. Let the world be the world, and let us be Christians. We cannot embrace our fellow man if our hands are laden with guns. We cannot lead our enemies to Christ while aiming to shoot them down.

61. "JOHNNY ONE NOTE"?

I am frequently accused of being a "Johnny one note," of beating a single drum, of harping on a solitary issue to the exclusion of all others. But the cause of Life is not a single note. Life is a symphony composed of limitless chords; it is a tapestry woven with eternal colors; it is the mystery of existence that has its foundation and fulfillment in an infinite God. So if I bang the Pro-Life drum, it's because my heart beats to the rhythms of justice and my spirit is attuned to peace. I do not fight abortion to the exclusion of all other issues; I prioritize the right to Life because apart from Life there are no other issues.

62. ~ CLIMBING ~

Climb a ladder, and you might fall off. Climb a mountain, and you may never reach the top. But cling to the Cross, and you will ascend to heaven. Yet clinging to the Cross is the most difficult thing in life. Faith will indeed move mountains, but moving mountains sure ain't easy. It's hard enough just to climb them. But although we are weak, Our Lord can move heaven and earth. Our purpose is to struggle; God's purpose is to save. And unlike ladders, mountains, towers, and cliffs – the nearer we are to the foot of the Cross, the closer we are to heaven.

63. ~ YOUR ANGRY GOD UP IN THE SKY ~

Your angry god up in the sky
Is not the God who for us did die
So full of mercy, love and grace
That He gave His life for the human race

I serve no tyrant; I worship a King
I praise the One who removed death's sting
Transcending time and space and sin
Is the Lord of Eternity who lives within

64. ~ I REFUSE ~

I refuse to kill
for flag or "choice,"
to rob another
of their human voice.

I refuse to kill
for god or man,
to end a life
with my own hand.

I refuse to kill
for kings or laws;
I am a Christian
and life is my cause.

65. ~ CONFIDENCE ~

Have confidence in God and God will give you confidence in yourself. The sons and daughters of the King are princes and princesses, and they walk with assurance because of Him to whom they belong.

66. ~ TO BE TRUE AMBASSADORS of CHRIST ~

When we proselytize, preach, and evangelize without serving, listening to, and identifying with those we seek to reach, then we fail to be true ambassadors of Christ. The mindset of "the righteous" coming to save "the lost" has led to egregious evils committed in the precious name of Our Lord, conveying not Christ crucified but a crucifying Christianity. The hubristic triumphalism of "the saved" rescuing "the damned" is antithetical to the Orthodox Christian spirit. The mission fields of lost sheep do not need the polluted waters of a thousand disparate doctrines. They do not need modern day crusaders that come to conquer with Bibles for swords. Instead, what they need is for us to walk among them as brothers, to struggle beside them, to share in their suffering, and to offer them mercy as we ourselves cry out, *"Lord have mercy on us."*

67. ~ THE CONSISTENT LIFE ETHIC ~

I embrace the consistent Life ethic, which means I oppose any act or ideology that facilitates the deliberate destruction of human lives and undermines the sanctity of human life. I oppose abortion, war, and capital punishment because they intentionally destroy human beings created in the image of God. I oppose political, philosophical, and economic theories that elevate one group of people above another based on race, gender, creed, sexual orientation, or financial income. I believe that all human life – from conception to natural death – is sacred and worthy of dignity and respect. As long as people continue to demand their own rights at the expense of the rights of others, then our world will continue to be plagued by the evils of racism, war, poverty, and abortion. I stand for peace, love, and life – without apology. Who will stand with me?

68. ~ FREE ELECTION ~

The next time someone tells you that you have a duty to vote, remind them that Jesus was crucified by the consensus of a free election.

69. ~ BROKEN SWORDS ~

God honors broken swords, not bloody swords.

70. ~ MY THREE HEROES ~

Bob Marley (Berhane Selassie)... Muhammad Ali... Dr. Martin Luther King, Jr. ...

These are my heroes. A poet, a pugilist, and a preacher – three prophets of the 20th century. Their words and actions, their courage and grace, their struggle and conviction have influenced me more than anyone other than my own family and friends. These three souls showed me that with faith in God all things are possible.

As a little boy, long before I was a Christian, the words and example of Dr. King and Muhammad Ali helped me realize that evil is nothing more than cowardice, and that cowardice is conquered by reliance upon divine truth and divine exaltation. Later in my life, the music and message of Bob Marley showed me that God's children can conquer darkness, depression, injustice and oppression with imprecatory Psalms and rhythmic praise.

These three men were not saints. They stumbled and fell throughout their lives. They were tormented not only by systemic injustice, but also by their own sins and mistakes. As an Orthodox Christian, I honor and venerate the Saints and Fathers of the Church; but I personally identify with divine conviction accompanied by human passion and human failure.

Whenever I feel tempted to succumb to discouragement, defeat, or despair, I turn to the words Dr. Martin Luther King, Jr.; I look to the resilience of Muhammad Ali; and I listen to the music and message of Bob Marley. And then I depart from my worries. And with prayer in my heart and praises on my tongue, I rise up and fight these demons that assail my soul and attack our world. With sermon, song, and butterfly dance, I light fire to Babylon and chase vampires to their hellish graves.

Say what you will about these three men. There is plenty to criticize if criticism is your agenda. But if you choose to look for light and truth, goodness and grace, wisdom and beauty, then you will find an abundance of these things in their words, lives, and examples.

"Do not despair if you are condemned and persecuted for righteousness sake. When you testify for truth and justice, you are liable to scorn. Often you will be called an impractical idealist or a dangerous radical. But the end of life is not to be happy nor to achieve pleasure and avoid pain, but to do the will of God – come what may." ~ Dr. Martin Luther King, Jr. ~

"Old man river, don't cry for me;
I've got a running stream of love you see.
So no matter what they put us through...
We'll be forever praising JAH!"
~ Bob Marley (Berhane Selassie) ~

"If God is for me, who can be against me?!"
~ Muhammad Ali ~

71. ~ CREATIVITY ~

I believe that anyone who truly creates is acknowledging God in some way, whether they realize it or not. Human creativity is a reflection of the divine Creator, evidence of the fact that man has been created in the very image of God. There may be more hope for the creative atheist than for the professing Christian who closes his heart to all the beauty in the world and rejects the love of his fellow man.

"A Poet, a Painter, a Musician, an Architect: the man or woman who is not one of these is not a Christian." ~ William Blake ~

72. ~ SUICIDAL DEVIATION ~

Deviation from the norm is often revolutionary, but deviation from the truth is always suicidal.

73. ~ THINGS WE SHOULD NEVER OUTGROW ~

Don't ever outgrow Mr. Rogers, Big Bird, and Bert and Ernie. The lessons they taught us as children are timeless and universal:
1. We are all neighbors.
2. Everyone has something good to offer and something interesting to share.
3. Be courteous, be forgiving, and respect the God-given differences within humanity.
4. Never be afraid to create something positive.
5. When all else fails: join hands, dance, and sing a joyful song.

The world is in turmoil because people have outgrown the simple perspective of children. We forget that Our Lord told us to receive the Kingdom as a little child.

"Truly I tell you, anyone who will not receive the kingdom of God like a little child will never enter it." [St. Mark 10:15]

"When I think about heaven, it is a state in which we are so greatly loved that there is no fear and doubt and disillusionment and anxiety. It's where people truly look at you with the eyes of Jesus – the eyes of an advocate who sees you as good, valuable, and lovable." ~ Fred Rogers ~

74. ~ A FATALISTIC MINDSET ~

As Christians, let us not succumb to the fatalistic mindset that the only effective way to combat evil is with violence. We are all called to be warrior saints, and Our Lord has endowed us with spiritual weapons more powerful than weapons of the flesh. And even if we lose our lives, we shall gain our souls. We defend the innocent with our own bodies and blood, not by shedding the blood of others.

75. ~ FAÇADE of FOOLS ~

Spiritual revolutionaries are not those who are years ahead of their time, they are those who simply speak and act according to timeless truths. Prophecy is not novel innovation, but eternal revelation. "Progress and reform" that jettisons prophecy and truth is the façade of fools.

76. ~ THE PRODUCTION of OUR OWN POISON ~

There is perhaps no greater indication of the pathology of our society than the fact that we view a shorter work week as somehow being a threat to social progress and human productivity. And I guess that's because our cultural pathology also causes us to view progress and productivity as merely financial and material multiplication. Only an inherently sick society leads people to slowly commit physical, emotional, and spiritual suicide for the sake of paper dreams and temporal rewards. God gave us the earth, He gave us our souls, He gave us His Church, and He gave us one another. But we have traded paradise for blood, money, and for blood-money. Our sweat was meant to water the earth so that we could reap the blessings of beauty and abundance. But instead, we squander our sweat in the production of our own poison.

77. ~ SEEK PEACE and PURSUE IT ~

If we seek justifications for violence, we will find them. We can always manufacture rationalizations for sin and evil. In fact, one can even refashion the Prince of Peace into an idol that accommodates their violent ideologies. This is evidenced by the tragic fact that many people defend evils like war and abortion in the very name of Christ. We often find what we seek. We manifest the values we embrace. We reap what we sow. Let us therefore attune our hearts to love and our consciences to peace. Let us seek reasons to forsake the sword rather than searching for excuses to embrace it.

"Seek peace and pursue it." [Psalm 34:14; I Peter 3:11]

"Ask and it will be given to you; seek and you will find;
knock and the door will be opened to you."
[St. Matthew 7:7]

78. ~ OXYMORONS ~

Oxymorons:
"holy war;" "safe abortion;" "necessary evil;" "righteous kill"

79. ~ I FOLLOW THE TRUE SPIRITUAL REBELS ~

I follow the true spiritual rebels –

Those who lead revolutions
without firing a gun or striking a blow,

Those who transform society
without the coercion and corruption of politics,

Those who lay down their own lives
for a people and a cause
without ever destroying the lives of others.

I follow those who follow Christ –

The prophets, the saints,
the soldiers in the army of peace, love, and life.

The Gospel is my rebellion,
The Church is my army,
and theosis is the liberation I seek.

Don't hand me a gun and tell me
that my freedom depends
upon the death of my brother;

Rather, give me the Sacraments,
arm me with the Cross,
and show me how to love all men –
friends and enemies alike.

Redemption,
Restoration,
Reconciliation...

This is real revolution!

80. ~ A TIME for SILENCE ~

Sometimes we just need to remain silent. This is very difficult when lies and false accusations about us are being proliferated by those who are either mentally disturbed or demonically driven. Or maybe they just have some sort of personal grudge against us. But it gets to the point where answering every attack and responding to every false accusation saps one's energy and drains one's soul.

The truth will always prevail in the end, and our true friends and true brethren will not be swayed by the malicious opinions of those who falsely malign us. Sadly, not everyone who calls us "friend" and "brother" is truly a friend and a brother. Sometimes we have to remove ourselves from their negativity and spite, and simply allow their vitriolic torches to burn themselves out. Unfortunately, they may deceive a lot of people along the way, and they may even succeed in damaging our reputation and character. But when this happens, remember that Our Lord Himself was often falsely accused. (St. Matthew 11:19)

God knows our hearts; and when we are accused unjustly, unfairly, and untruthfully, the best response is to simply rest silently and peacefully in Our Lord's unconditional love. There is an old Turkish proverb: *"If you stop to throw stones at every dog that barks at you along the way, you will never reach your goal."*

81. ~ PREFERENCE and PRIORITY ~

God does not ask us to *prefer* the poor and the oppressed, for He shows no partiality among men. (Acts 10:34) But God does require us to *prioritize* those in need; for how can we minister to people's souls if by our apathetic indifference we allow their bodies to be crushed by the injustices of slavery, poverty, and abortion?

82. ~ THE HERESY of WAR ~

I believe war is heresy because it involves the deliberate destruction of human beings created in the very image of God. If we dare not desecrate icons made from wood and paint, then why would we think it Christian to destroy icons fashioned with the very breath of God?

I believe war is heretical because it is an abandonment of the hope and redemption of the Christian Gospel. Christ died on the Cross to conquer sin, death, and evil. Therefore, to call sin and evil "necessary," "justifiable," or "holy" is blasphemous in my opinion.

Christians are indeed called to be soldiers, defending the innocent and fighting for the Faith. But our warfare is spiritual not carnal; and we follow the command of Our Lord, who arms us only with the weapons of mercy, forgiveness, compassion, and love.

"Finally, be strong in the Lord and in his mighty power. Put on the full armor of God, so that you can take your stand against the devil's schemes. For our struggle is not against flesh and blood, but against the rulers, against the authorities, against the powers of this dark world and against the spiritual forces of evil in the heavenly realms. Therefore put on the full armor of God, so that when the day of evil comes, you may be able to stand your ground, and after you have done everything, to stand. Stand firm then, with the belt of truth buckled around your waist, with the breastplate of righteousness in place, and with your feet fitted with the readiness that comes from the gospel of peace. In addition to all this, take up the shield of faith, with which you can extinguish all the flaming arrows of the evil one. Take the helmet of salvation and the sword of the Spirit, which is the word of God. [Ephesians 6:10-17]

[I must emphasize that I am only speaking my own opinion on this matter. As far as I know, the Orthodox Church has not officially declared war to be a heresy. But the Church is very clear that all killing is sinful, even though the Church does make necessary distinctions between murder and defensive killing. But I maintain hope that one day my beloved Orthodox Church will indeed decry war as the heresy I personally believe it to be.]

83. ~ HOW CAN WE SHUN OUR BROTHER? ~

How can we shun our brother if we are truly aware of the poverty of our own souls? How can we say "no" to our neighbor in need when God has given so completely to us? How can we separate ourselves from any other God-honoring people unless we are full of self-righteousness and unholy pride?

84. ~ BABYLON'S SALE ~

First they sell you water. Then they sell you food. Then they sell you earth. Then they sell you air. Then they sell you knowledge. And once you have become accustomed to paying for the free gifts of God, Babylon can easily sell you war, abortion, destruction, and death.

85. ~ EMBRACE GOD / FLEE IDOLATRY ~

Embrace God by embracing truth. Embrace the truth by pursuing peace and living to love. Seek out and surround yourself with others who are doing the same. Flee from idolatrous man-made philosophies that rationalize division, discord, and death. And always look for God in the face of your fellow man.

86. ~ NO GLORY WITHOUT GHOSTS ~

There is no glory without ghosts, and no magic without madness. It is the haunted soul that finds its way to heaven. It is the mind driven mad by this world that finds peace in the next.

87. ~ DISTURBED BY INJUSTICE and EVIL? ~

Many people are disturbed by injustice and evil, they just aren't disturbed enough to do something about it.

88. ~ NAÏVE, IRRATIONAL, and INSANE ~

What could be more naïve, irrational, and insane than believing that war can establish peace or that abortion can bring liberation?

89. ~ RECIPROCITY ~

We are the image of God, knit together by the intricacies of Eternal energy. This terrestrial earth gives birth to us. We assimilate the earth, and inevitably the earth assimilates us. Then we return to the infinite realm. Reciprocity is an immutable universal law. What we do with the temporal will determine what we experience in eternity.

St. Paul declares, *"Be not deceived; God is not mocked: for whatsoever a man soweth, that shall he also reap." [Galatians 6:7]*

And King Solomon wrote:

"Remember your Creator until the silver cord is removed, and the golden flower is pressed together, and the pitcher is shattered at the well; then the dust returns to the earth as it was, and the spirit returns to the God who gave it." [Ecclesiastes 12:6-8]

90. ~ AT THE CENTER of ETERNITY ~

Wherever we may be – growing in our mother's womb or standing on the edge of the moon – we are at the center of eternity. And yet, although we are at the center of universe, God caresses the universe in His arms. If we fully understood this truth, then we would esteem our own lives with humility and reverence, and we would honor our fellow man the same. Just consider: we are the center of eternity, and yet eternity is at the center of God. We are creatures of finite dust bearing the indelible imprint of an uncreated and infinite God. And that's why regardless of how corrupted or fallen it may be, every human life is still worth celebrating.

91. ~ THE FIRE of MY SOUL ~

The fire of temptation, truth, love, and sin burns within my soul. If I let the fire rage, my soul will perhaps be damned. But if I extinguish the fire altogether, I will cease to have a soul.

92. ~ VIOLENCE AGAINST GOD ~

All humans are created in the image of God, and all people contain a divine spark. Therefore, violence against man is violence against God.

93. ~ THE CHRISTIAN IS A WARRIOR ~

The Christian is a warrior. He fights but he does not kill. He takes His orders from the Prince of Peace. He wages battle only with the spiritual weapons that have been issued him. He knows that the only way evil can prevail is if he allows evil to dictate the terms of engagement.

Violence perpetually crucifies, but peace eternally conquers. Killing is always a concession to evil, and the true followers of Christ refuse to concede to its demands or compromise with its insidious agenda.

94. ~ GIVE ME SUCH COMPANY ~

Give me the prophets
of pen and paint,
the everyday sinners
who might be saints.

Give me the rebels
who count the cost
and trade their bullets
for the nails of the Cross.

Give me the poets
who preach of love
with the souls of lions
and the hearts of doves.

Give me the warriors
whose weapons are truth,
who fight with innocence
and conquer fools.

Give me the mystics
who serve the poor,
who cry for the unborn
and weep for the world.

Give me the outcasts
with fire in their bones,
who the world has forsaken
but whose prayers save souls.

Give me such company
on this road of life,
to enlighten my heart
and open my eyes.

Yes Lord,
give me such company.

95. ~ A MEMORIAL DAY PRAYER ~

In the Name of the Father, the Son, and the Holy Spirit – One God – Amen

Dear Lord,

On this "Memorial Day," help us to remember the innocent unknown victims of warfare and violence.

Help us to remember the babies, the children, the mothers and fathers who wanted no part in the evils of war but nevertheless suffered from its cruelties.

Lord, give us the courage to reflect upon the horrors of burning flesh, the reality of severed limbs, the grotesque truth of mangled bodies and broken minds.

Lord, grant us the wisdom to see that war is not honorable, virtuous, or heroic, but rather sinful, shameful, and depraved.

Lord, help us to repent of the patriotism and prejudices that fan the flames of war and cause the blood of innocent children to be mercilessly shed.

Lord, make us understand that to kill in the name of country is idolatry, and that to kill in the name of Christ is blasphemy.

Lord, teach us that the Cross is mightier than the sword, and that love and forgiveness will eternally prevail over hatred and revenge.

Lord have mercy: on all those who have suffered and died from the evils of war.

Lord have mercy: on all fallen soldiers and all fallen civilians.

Lord have mercy: on those who prosecute wars and thereby manufacture hell on earth.

Lord have mercy: on those of us who hate war but refuse to love our fellow man enough to stop it.

Lord have mercy: on this fallen world and this fallen human race.

Forgive us Lord for beseeching your unfailing mercy while refusing to be merciful to the enemies and the innocent who suffer from our bombs, bullets, drones, and desecrations.

Forgive us Lord for acknowledging that war is hell and then celebrating war as if it were an act of heaven.

The earth runs red with innocent blood. But you see Lord, you see. And you hear the cries of those who suffer unjustly. You have commanded us to put away the sword, but we have refused. So we dare not complain when that same sword returns to sever our own stiffened necks.

"Put up again thy sword into its place: for all they that take the sword shall perish with the sword." [St. Matthew 26:52]

"Blessed are the peacemakers, for they shall be called the children of God." [St. Matthew 5:9]

In the Name of the Father, the Son, and the Holy Spirit – One God – Amen

96. ~ BLASPHEMOUS SUPERSTITION ~

Christ has trampled death, and yet too many Christians trample on His name by preparing for war. They proclaim the glorious truth that Christ is risen from the tomb while preparing to send men violently to their graves. I will say without apology that this is not faith; this is blasphemous superstition.

97. ~ DESIRING LIES MORE THAN TRUTH ~

It is easier to sell a lie than to give away the truth. That's why politicians are exalted and prophets are exterminated.

Every night she went to pray, to light a candle and ask for mercy. Gazing into the eyes of St. Mary she fell on her knees and begged for grace. A sinner she was, about to enter another evening of iniquity, willfully embarking on another mission of degradation and defilement. But she prayed anyway, as dusk descended with all of its lurid enticements and false hopes and inevitable horrors.

And every dawn, as the sun came up, she returned to pray again – ensconced in the earlier night's filth and stains and smells and trespasses, filled with the lusts and bruises and empty loves of many men – her purse heavier but her heart emptier. But still, she faithfully entered this sacred place, alone, to pray and confess. And she always wept for her sins, with tears melting her face like the wax of candles that burned before her. Clutching her rosary and crying from her heart, she knew she would repeat the same sordid cycle again after a few hours rest. She did not know why she did it – both why she continued to sin and why she continued to pray. But perhaps she could not help doing either.

I suppose like most of us – sinners that we all are.

Why do we do what we shouldn't do? And why do we not do what we know we should do? Why do we placate ourselves with the self-righteous assumption that our sins are somehow less egregious than the harlot's?

I don't have the answers to such questions. All I know is that Christ was merciful to those who fell at His feet and pleaded for mercy. All I know is that Christ forgave those who bowed before Him and begged forgiveness. And yes, He said "Go and sin no more." And yes, He tells us likewise to "Go and sin no more."

But who among us can truly say, "I have sinned no more"?

I know that I can't.

And I imagine that there are worse sinners than me whose faith far surpasses my own. And I trust that God will somehow welcome me too, in the company of hopeful reprobates that cast ourselves upon a Mercy that we can never hope to deserve.

And I am thankful for His Church, the Church that embraces prostitutes and drunkards and murderers and thieves – along with self-righteous fools like me. And I am thankful for the candles and incense and icons and sacraments that convey Christ to saints and sinners alike – unconditionally and always and ever-present, like the love of Our Lord Himself.

I pray for God to grant me the faith of a harlot who weeps day and night for her sins.

99. ~ CHRISTIANITY and SOCIAL AGENDAS ~

Christianity is not about social agendas; it's about loving God with all of our heart and loving our neighbor as ourselves. This is why I don't participate in the political process – because the Left and the Right both have their particular social policies, and yet with equal neglect they fail to adhere to the criteria of the Christian gospel.

Those on the Left often misappropriate Christ's message in order to justify their Socialist political ideologies. And those on the Right too often ignore the Christian imperative to pursue authentic social justice. A false dichotomy between the social and the sacred has crept into the contemporary Christian mindset. And we should reject this false dichotomy, for to accept it is to accept a perverse understanding of Our Lord and His meaning.

If we truly love our neighbor then we should not ignore their plight or their suffering. Rather than viewing human beings through the subjective mortal lens of political ideology, we should look at our fellow man with universal empathy and Christian compassion. We should endeavor to see all men truly liberated – both physically and spiritually.

100. ~ SPIRITUAL SIGHT ~

Those that only see sinners will never see Christ. Those that only see hell will never see heaven. Those that only see devils will never see the Divine. So change your perspective. Alter your focus. The love of God is everywhere you look, if you will simply look for it.

101. ~ WHY I CONDEMN VIOLENCE ~

I condemn violence – not because it is always unjust, not because it is always unnecessary, and not because it is always ineffective – but because it is always *unchristian*.

102. ~ CONDEMNING THE HOMELESS ~

Do not condemn your brother as lazy simply because he doesn't have a roof over his head and isn't getting paid. I can assure you that homelessness and poverty are hard work.

103. ~ THE CHOICE of FAITH ~

Call it "presuppositionalism." Call it "existentialism." Call it "superstition" even. But true faith is choosing to believe, even in the absence of any evidence, proof, feeling, or hope. To believe that God *is* and that He is *good*, even when all we experience is darkness and doubt: this is when faith is most real. The water becomes wine and the wine becomes Blood and the bread becomes Body and God becomes man and man becomes God. This is the truth of the mysteries of faith. A transcendent certainty, an unknowable knowledge, the choice to believe when we have no reason to believe. A god that is revealed through human proofs is not God at all. A syllogistic faith will not sustain us in the midst of depravity and horror. When nothing makes sense and it seems senseless to believe, this is when we must choose to cry out with the father of the demoniac boy: *"Lord I believe. Help thou my unbelief." [St. Mark 9:24]*

104. ~ SUNSET / SUNRISE ~

Last evening I paused
To watch the sun descend
In yellow orange peace
Slowly, taking its time
So I could breathe it in

Simple beauty, profound hope
Shaken by this morning's news
Of death, sorrow
And senseless loss

Random evil that precedes the dawn

I can only wish...
And pray...

That those who would pull the trigger
Would first pause to watch a sunset
Or a sunrise

"Lord have mercy"

105. ~ HEAR HIS WORD ~

If you will you truly seek God's will
and truly pray before you kill,
then you will clearly hear His word,
for clearly He says:
"Put away thy sword."

106. ~ TOO MUCH TO ASK? ~

To truly love, to truly serve – these are difficult things. But is it so hard to just simply be kind? To show kindness even to those we have not yet learned to love – is this too much to ask?

107. ~ ARE WE REALLY PRO-LIFE? ~

I often hear my Pro-Life comrades unequivocally declare that abortion is wrong from the moment of conception until the moment of birth. And I couldn't agree more. But there is one significant error in that statement that I believe reveals the reason why we have yet to see legalized abortion come to an end. You see, the abortion of human life is not only wrong from the moment of conception until the moment of birth, it is wrong from the moment of conception until the moment of natural death. In other words, just as it is wrong to violently abort an unborn human life because the mother doesn't want it, so it's also wrong to abort human lives in war because the "enemy" is unwanted by us.

Human life should never be violently aborted, at any stage of existence, for any reason. We Pro-Lifers are quick to condemn the euphemistic language behind the abortion movement: "It's only a 'fetus,' not a person;'" "It's a 'choice,' not a child;" "It's the 'product of conception,' not a human life;" etc. But we fail to be just as vigilant in condemning the demonic euphemisms behind war: "It's only 'collateral damage;'" "It's a 'necessary evil;'" "It's a 'just war;'" "It's not a war against humanity, it's a 'war on terror;'" etc.

Either we affirm the sanctity of human life or we don't. We cannot preach about the sanctity of life while defending, justifying, and supporting any action, ideology or endeavor that involves the premeditated, intentional, and violent destruction of human life. Period.

Abortion is never right – whether it be the violent negation of life in the womb or the violent negation of lives in war. So we need to seriously ask ourselves if we are really Pro-Life. We cannot expect

God to answer our "Pro-Life" prayers while we glorify the military, turn a blind eye to poverty, and condemn prisoners to death.

108. ~ PRISONERS of BABYLON / REVOLUTIONARIES of LOVE ~

I am aware that my opposition to politics is itself a political statement. I know that my refusal to vote does not entirely extricate me from the political system I oppose. The tentacles of Babylon are long, and we can never entirely free ourselves from their grasp. But there is a big difference between fighting the beast from within its belly and feeding the beast ourselves. Such are the paradoxes of the Christian pacifist. Our renunciation of the violence of politics, poverty, war, capital punishment, and abortion puts us in confrontational opposition to systems, powers, and people that perpetuate these evils. So we wage peace with spiritual militancy. We are simultaneously prisoners of Babylon and revolutionaries of love.

109. ~ WE ARE OUR BROTHER'S KEEPER ~

According to God, we are our brother's keeper. (Genesis 4:9-10) We have been commissioned by Christ to proclaim the Gospel throughout the world (St. Matthew 28:18-20; Acts 1:8), and we have a biblical mandate to love our neighbors as ourselves. (Leviticus 19:18; Galatians 5:14; St. Matthew 5:43-44)

In the tenth chapter of St. Luke's gospel, a lawyer asked Jesus what he must do to inherit eternal life. Christ engaged the lawyer in a discussion about the Law of God, and the lawyer demonstrated that he possessed an intellectual comprehension of the subject. The lawyer's understanding of the Law was superficial, however. Although he could sufficiently recite the *letter* of the Law, the lawyer did not understand the *heart* of the Law. He was confused and misguided about the identity of his neighbor. Therefore, Jesus preached the parable of the Good Samaritan, because He knew that mankind would perpetually stumble over the question of "Who is my neighbor?"

The point of the parable of the Good Samaritan is *personal responsibility*. Throughout the Bible, we see men attempting to exculpate themselves from the responsibility they have for their fellow man. Cain tried to evade personal responsibility for slaying his own brother, and King David sought to evade personal responsibility for Uriah's murder. Jonah fled from personal responsibility for Nineveh's darkness, and Pontius Pilate attempted to wash the responsibility for our Lord's death from his guilty hands.

In this parable of the Good Samaritan (St. Luke 10:25-37), we see the priest and the Levite attempting to avoid personal responsibility for the man who lay bloodied and beaten on the Jericho road. But Christ makes it abundantly clear that the priest and the Levite *were* responsible for this man's suffering. Unlike the Samaritan, who allowed the plight of his neighbor to become his immediate priority, the priest and the Levite passed by their neighbor unaffected and unmoved by his agony and suffering. The Samaritan, who was unlettered in the Law of God and theologically illiterate, nevertheless understood and obeyed the heart of divine Law; but those who had studied the Law of God all their lives refused to heed its essence at a critical moment.

When we deliberately pass by the helpless victims of our world, refusing to alter our lives on their behalf, then we are priests and Levites on the Jericho roads of life. When we fail to offer hope and compassion to those in need, then we are priests and Levites on the Jericho roads of society. When we fail to warn and admonish those who support and encourage the shedding of innocent blood, then we are priests and Levites on the Jericho roads of earth. We can curse our courts, criticize our politicians, and condemn evil rulers, but if we continue to pass by the innocent victims in our community without stopping to intervene, then God will hold *us* responsible for the continuation of bloodshed and suffering in the world.

"It is not the responsibility of knights errant to discover whether the afflicted, the enchained and the oppressed whom they encounter on the road are reduced to these circumstances and suffer this distress for their vices, or for their virtues: the knight's sole responsibility is to succor them as people in need, having eyes only for their sufferings, not for their misdeeds."

~ Miguel De Cervantes ~ *[Don Quixote]*

110. ~ THE SEAMLESS GARMENT ~

The "seamless garment" of social justice is woven with the fabric of Life. If we fail to preserve the fabric then we will never have a suitable garment.

111. ~ TWO VIEWS of WOMEN'S WORTH ~

Many people view women as animals that need to be sterilized and controlled with chemical pills, prophylactic potions, and the violent destruction of their unborn fruit. But I view women as human beings that are capable of exercising *self control*, not beasts that need to be tamed with *birth control*. I view women as human beings capable of creativity and virtue, not unrestrained savages whose reproduction must be violently curtailed. I view women as human beings that are strong enough, resourceful enough, and enlightened enough to give birth and nurture life even in the most difficult of circumstances.

So when people promote birth control and abortion, they disclose a fundamentally inhuman view of women. How sad it is that even in the 21st century women continue to be dehumanized and abused by chemical poisons and the violent invasion of their life-bearing wombs.

112. ~ THE WAY of CAIN or THE WAY of CHRIST? ~

The narrative of Cain and Abel demonstrates that man estranged from God is man at enmity with himself. But the narrative of the Gospel demonstrates that man reconciled to God is man compelled towards peace and love. Let us understand that the Cross has conquered the sin and curse of Cain. Those in Christ are no longer doomed to slay their fellow man, no longer cursed to wander through life bearing the bloodstained burdens of anguish and guilt. Let us lay down our weapons and pick up our cross. It is not the way of Cain that we are called to follow, but the way of Christ. Shall we enter Zion's gates defiled with the blood of our brother, or cleansed with the blood of Our Lord?

113. ~ "PROGRESS" ~

The most effective way to perpetuate evil is to call it "progress."

114. ~ THE POLITICS of "JESUS IS LORD" ~

"Jesus is Lord" is a radical political proclamation. In a world of Caesars and presidents and popes and kings that all vie for and demand human allegiance, the Christian confession of the Lordship of Christ is a subversive, seditious, and revolutionary statement. It is a profession and way of life that inevitably brings the disciples of Christ into conflict with the power of the State. In bowing to the Lordship of Jesus, the Christian rises up against political rulers and political systems that seek to usurp His Lordship. "Jesus is Lord" is not only our theology and our doxology, it is also our politics – and it is our *only* politics.

115. ~ THAT DAY ~

I'll never forget
that day
when you sent me away
with tears in your eyes
and a mind full of lies
that you made me believe.

As strangers locked me up
behind those walls
I cried for those
who abandoned me.
Crushed with guilt
for causing you sorrow...
asking God
to forgive me
for sins that were yours.

A troubled child
violently cast
into a strange, cruel reality
by those whose arms
were supposed to always
embrace and protect.

And yet as I lay
unjustly enclosed
in confinement and despair,
listening to cold, unfamiliar voices,
I never doubted
for a single moment...

that you loved me.

A wise Ethiopian Orthodox priest once explained to me that we are volitional pawns in a cosmic battle between God and the devil. Of course, God has already won the war, but He allows us to choose whether or not we will participate in the victory. The devil doesn't care about the righteousness of our particular "cause;" he is simply interested in fomenting division, discord, and hate – however he can. We may be absolutely right in our convictions and beliefs, and yet still be used as pawns of Satan to contribute to animosity and destruction. But God desires to use us as instruments of healing, reconciliation, and love.

Satan can work tremendous havoc through a doctrinally sound, theologically pure, and morally upright person who is arrogant and proud. Yet God can manifest His glory through a confused and ignorant sinner who possesses the gift of true humility.

As we enter this blessed season of Great Lent, I want to strive to be an instrument of God to facilitate peace, love, brotherhood, and understanding. This is a challenge for me because I am a prideful, impetuous, and arrogant human being. I am usually more concerned about being right than being loving. I too often prioritize beliefs above faith and truth above love. But faithless beliefs and unloving truths are the greatest of lies.

Satan can use a straight compass to disorient countless souls. And God can use a crooked stick to point people to eternal life. I've wasted too much time concerning myself with being an accurate compass. The reality is that I'm a broken vessel; and Our Lord came to redeem the sick and the suffering, the wandering and the weak.

The Saints and the Church Fathers tell us that humility causes the demons to tremble. Satan can take many noble virtues and pervert them in the incorporation of evil. But he can do nothing with humility. The Scriptures bear witness to this. (James 4:6; I Peter 3:8, 5:5; Psalm 138:6; Proverbs 3:34; Job 22:29)

Pray for me, that I will choose humility over "correctness." Pray for me, that I will choose to be an instrument of Christ rather than a pawn of the devil. Pray for me, that I will be a servant of the Holy Spirit rather than a servant of Satan. *"Lord have mercy."*

"Military service" is an oxymoron, a euphemistic term by which no Christian should be deceived. The New Testament word for service is "λειτουργία," (litoorg-eh-o) which means *"to minister; to do the work of worship."* This is the word from which "Liturgy" is derived.

Our Lord said, *"It is written, Thou shalt worship the Lord thy God, and Him only shalt thou serve." [St. Matthew 4:10]* And the apostle Paul writes, *"Therefore I urge you, brethren, by the mercies of God, to present your bodies a living and holy sacrifice, acceptable to God, which is your spiritual service of worship." [Romans 12:1]*

Nothing is more perverse than turning the proper definition of holy service to God and divine service to neighbor into a call to arms and a vocation of militancy, death, and destruction. The simple fact is that no Christian can serve Christ and neighbor while he is perpetually training to kill and destroy. Do not be deceived. Military service is not compatible with Christian service. *"No one can serve two masters. Either you will hate the one and love the other, or you will be devoted to the one and despise the other." [St. Matthew 6:24]*

(I realize that many people will disagree with me on this point, including many members of the Orthodox clergy. I do not presume to speak for the consensus of the Church on this issue. But I pray for the day when the Church will return to her nonviolent, pacifist roots and declare without ambiguity or equivocation that militarism is contrary to the Gospel. Until then, I will continue to speak my humble opinion on the matter and let others choose for themselves.

I cannot stop women from having abortions. I cannot stop people from taking up arms and going to war. I cannot stop murder and rape and child abuse. All I can do is preach the message of the Gospel, point to the perfect example of Our Savior, and urge us all to follow Him in every way possible. It is better to bear the splinters of the Cross than to bear the guilt of innocent blood.)

118. ~ SUFFERING and CREATIVITY ~

Suffering is the mother of creativity; and those who embrace suffering are those who are inspired, inventive, and visionary.

119. ~ PROPHETIC DISRUPTIONS ~

Prophets do not make good dinner guests, and they will certainly spoil a good cocktail party. So if you want to host your inane worldly entertainments without disruption, then be sure to keep the prophets away. But if you want to entertain the truth, then by all means welcome them openly.

120. ~ AN IRRECONCILABLE DIFFERENCE ~

Violence and nonviolence cannot be reconciled. They are as diametrically opposed as love and hate. The philosophy of violence is predicated upon a materialistic presupposition which leads to the godless principles of naked pragmatism and utilitarian expediency. Therefore the unjust means of bloodshed, torture, and evil are rationalized by the ends of temporal gains. But the philosophy of nonviolence is rooted in an eternal perspective. It eschews Machiavellian tactics and rejects the unchristian ideology of "by any means necessary." Nonviolence is the guiding principle in the revolution of peace and love – the only revolution that can truly and permanently eradicate systemic evil and social injustice.

That which is accomplished by violence can just as easily be undone by violence. But that which is accomplished by love will endure forever. For the Christian, violence is never an option. We strive to be "salt and light," working to positively transform our world with Christian love, seeking above all JAH's Kingdom which is to come. Our Lord has commanded us to put away the sword and take up our cross. Following the Prince of Peace – even unto death – is what separates His lambs from the world's wolves. Onward Christian soldiers!

121. ~ STRUGGLE ~

It is better to struggle and fall than to never struggle at all.

122. ~ EFFECTIVE OPPRESSION ~

The most effective way to further oppression is to convince people to oppress themselves in the name of "freedom," "liberty," and "choice."

123. ~ THE GREATEST NAME ~

For me, the greatest name for God in all of theology and in all of religion is the name "Emmanuel," which means: "God is with us." This beautiful name reveals the greatest of spiritual truths:

God so loved His creation that He became a man and dwelt amongst us. Infinite holiness walked amongst the vileness of sin. Eternal purity embraced mortal corruption.

There is no greater love, there is no greater truth, and there is no greater hope than this. The Almighty Creator – who is perfect righteousness and purest justice – remains our "Emmanuel." What a glorious reality, this Mystery of the Incarnation! In spite of our failures, our sins, our inadequacies, and our weaknesses, God is ever accessible to us. *God is with us!* What a liberating Truth!

124. ~ LIFE and LOVE ~

Every human being is the living, breathing, tangible proof of love. Life is the fruit of love. It is the blessed dividend of the love between two people expressed in sexual union. It is the realization of the love of a mother who embraced the nascent life within her, even though the circumstances of conception may have been painful. Life exists only because love was present somewhere, somehow. Life and love are symbiotic entities. Neither can exist apart from the other. Love is proven by life, and life is nothing without love.

125. ~ ENEMIES, SINNERS, and HERETICS ~

There are only enemies and sinners and heretics because we have been taught that there are enemies and sinners and heretics. Don't misunderstand: I certainly believe that enemies and sinners and heretics exist; they just don't exist outside of me.

126. ~ TRUE REBELLION ~

True rebellion knows nothing of half measures or compromise. True rebels are keenly focused upon justice, and therefore they refuse to embrace ideologies or tactics that are not rooted in just means and driven towards just ends. True rebels eschew the Machiavellian methods of political expediency, and they reject the feckless philosophy of incrementalism. The rebel sees his neighbor suffering – now, today – and therefore his primary concern is for the immediate amelioration of his brother's suffering. And yet, because the true rebel abhors all human suffering and death, he refuses to adopt suffering and death as legitimate means of opposing suffering and death.

127. ~ WHEN I BOWED ~

When I dropped
my mind arose
but my soul
remained unchanged.

With the microdot
I saw a lot
yet no further
than the windowpane.

But when I bowed
my heart awoke,
my spirit
was unchained.

Through water, Body,
Blood, and Word
my freedom
finally came.

128. ~ DON'T BLAME ME LORD ~

I'm not responsible for war,
I just build the bombs.
I'm not pro-abortion,
I just follow the laws.

So don't blame me for evil Lord,
I ain't killed no man.
I'm just a citizen of Babylon
with my head buried in the sand.

129. ~ CARRYING OUR CROSSES ~

Carrying our crosses is so hard indeed. It seems unbearable at times. It feels like it will kill us, and in fact it might. I love the Cross of Our Lord, but I hate the crosses that Our Lord calls me to bear. If I could choose a comfortable cross, I surely would. But there is no such thing. There is no easy road to heaven, no easy path to the Kingdom. It's a struggle, a struggle, a struggle... God help us. ~Amen~

130. ~ THE AGONY of BEAUTY ~

The experience of beauty in life is often accompanied by a profound angst. This is because we are intuitively aware that life's beauty is constantly threatened by the world's evil, ugliness, cruelty, and pain. Love, innocence, and purity rest precariously upon the precipice of corruption, possessing a tenuous and ephemeral existence that is too often negated by the merciless demon of time.

So, when the joys of life stir the depths of my being and flood my heart – the joy of gazing upon my children as they sleep peacefully in their beds at night; the joy of feeling their embraces of unconditional love; the joy of seeing my wife's radiant smile; the joy of seeing my little daughter's face light up as she gazes into my eyes – when I experience these joys I am simultaneously stricken with an ache in my soul. For I realize that I cannot contain the moment. I know it will pass.

My children will grow up in this callous world. They will not escape the clutches of life's cruelties. They will inevitably learn to harden their hearts to some degree, in order to shield themselves from the recurring pain that torments the innocence and naïveté of youth. And the joyous smile on my wife's face will always be replaced in time by expressions of fatigue and frustration, consequences of the daily battle she wages as a schoolteacher against the evils of apathy and ignorance.

Thus, as I relish the momentary reality of my wife's contentment, and as I gaze upon the joy of youthful innocence, I understand all too well that pain is somehow the ubiquitous companion of joy. I also know that peace prospers only as an agonizing struggle against those forces that incessantly seek to negate it. Any authentic consciousness of beauty is always accompanied by a subconscious awareness of forces that oppose it.

The reality is that there exist spiritual elements, principalities, and agencies of evil that hate children, despise innocence, abhor holiness, and wage perpetual war against everything in life that brings genuine joy and peace. Love is combated by lust; brotherhood and unity are opposed by political and racial division; objective righteousness is corrupted by the demand for subjective "rights;" and the glory of human life is assailed by euphemistic evils such as "national defense," "capital punishment," and "freedom of choice."

The nascence of the new millennium brings with it a void of love, a dearth of human kindness, and a lack of respect for life. Today, the notion of true love is often considered archaic, and the practice of unconditional peace is rejected as a quixotic absurdity. The concept of the brotherhood of man is mocked, and the ideal of the sanctity of human life is viewed as an annoying thorn in the side of scientific advancement.

Yet all of us are confronted with beauty; and this confrontation discloses a painful truth. To acknowledge beauty is to concede its antithesis. Life is the eye, the edge, and the epicenter of the storm. Try as we may to evade and ignore the agonies of our conscience, we cannot escape. The Creator has indelibly inscribed His immutable, universal laws upon our souls; and thus we are accountable. The audacity of humanism cannot save us, nor can any other philosophical fantasy that seeks to depose God from His eternal throne.

So, as I playfully wrestle with my children, basking in the glow of their gleeful shouts and vibrant laughter, I know that I must prepare to fight. And as I enjoy the radiant glow of my wife's glorious smile, I recognize that forces and ideologies of evil are out to eradicate her peace and our joy. We are all born into life and into war. Those who seek the victories of love, brotherhood, peace, and joy must understand that arrows of sorrow, heartache, and despair will come their way. And those who are content with lives of materialism, lust, power, or fame should know that the law of reciprocity is inescapable. It reverberates with eternal justice, and it echoes with imminent Judgment.

But I will accept each moment of joy in life as God's holy gift; and I will embrace the grief of soul that accompanies it. All pain is instructive for those who are willing to learn. And I will equip myself for battle. For it is up to us to work for the preservation of the beauty that we cherish, to prolong the innocence that we long to retain, to confront those forces that wage war against purity and peace, and to create a world more replete with joy and rarer with pain.

If we experience beauty in life and don't feel some accompanying agony in our souls, then we can be assured that we are only experiencing a façade, a mirage. And if we chase a mirage in the desert of life, then we will most certainly die of thirst.

"What earthly sweetness remaineth unmixed with grief? What glory standeth immutable on earth? All things are but shadows most feeble, deluding dreams: yet one moment only, and death shall supplant them all. But in the light of Thy countenance, O Christ, and in the sweetness of Thy beauty, give rest to him whom thou hast chosen, because Thou lovest mankind." ~ St. John of Damascus ~

"Beauty is unbearable, drives us to despair, offering us for a minute the glimpse of an eternity that we should like to stretch out over the whole of time." ~ Albert Camus ~

131. ~ CHRIST, COLOR, and CULTURE ~

I agree with a wise Ethiopian Priest who said, *"It matters not whether Christ is White or Black. What matters is that Christ is Lord."* However, a race of people that has not suffered the severe scars of slavery, colonialism, racism, and psychological warfare has no right to tell the Black man that he should ignore the significance of ethnicity and culture. If some Rastafarians see Christ as Black and proclaim Him as such, who am I to argue? What right do I have to dictate to anyone how they should perceive the color of Our Lord Jesus Christ? Let each man see Christ in the context of their own culture, and let them worship Him as such. Why should I as a White man be threatened by the image of a Black Christ? My icon corner is adorned with images of a Black Christ and a White Christ. But He is Christ all the same. Nothing in our Orthodox theology demands that one forsake their culture. We must forsake idolatry, yes. But forsake culture? No. The Rastaman is fighting to preserve African culture. And I support such efforts. My own ancestors wrought enough evil upon Africa. So if I can't help the Rastaman in his efforts to heal and preserve his culture, then I should at least stay the hell out of his way.

"We Negroes believe in the God of Ethiopia, the everlasting God. God the Father, God the Son, and God the Holy Ghost – the One God of all ages. That is the God in whom we believe. But we shall worship Him through the spectacles of Ethiopia." ~ Marcus Garvey ~

"To write a detailed and overall account of the Rastafarians and their beliefs in relationship to the Bible is a very difficult task. This is because there are many different concepts to be found among Rastafarians today. There are almost as many beliefs as there are Rastafarians. However, the concepts and philosophies that are based upon a more traditional foundation are to be found among the Rastafarians who have accepted the teachings of the Ethiopian Orthodox Church. Rastafarians should not be ridiculed or condemned. They must be brought gradually to Jesus Christ."
~ Archbishop Abuna Yesehaq ~ *[The Ethiopian Tewahedo Church]*

132. ~ IF OUR PEACE DISTURBS YOUR VIOLENCE ~

If our peace disturbs your violence, we do not apologize. If our love disrupts your hate, we will not repent. We resist your oppression and submit to Christ's liberation – incessantly, militantly, and without compromise. Crucify us if you must, but in doing so you will only fuel our divine revolution.

133. ~ ART and FAITH ~

Great art is the product of great faith. Great art inspires spiritual contemplation and internal reflection. It touches the moral component of man, stirring his heart and soul. It takes us beyond ourselves, elevating us to a transcendental consciousness. And above all, great art is always redemptive.

One need not be religious to produce profound works of art. But all great artists are ultimately people of faith. They must have the faith to view life as worthy of creatively reflecting, interpreting, and expressing. Whether they admit it or not, the creativity of their souls discloses a deep connection to the Creator of the Universe.

134. ~ VAMPIRES ~

They asked me, "Do you really believe in vampires?"

I answered:

"Yes. I know they exist. They walk among us every day. They disguise themselves as human, but in reality they are houses of demons ensconced in bodies of flesh. But their deeds reveal their true nature. And I observe their evil deeds and recognize them for what they are. So, beware of those that thirst for blood. Beware of those who love war and execution, abortion and euthanasia, and "scientific research" involving the destruction of human life. Beware of those who devise sophisticated weapons of mass destruction and invent modern methods of cruelty and torture. Beware of those who seek financial profit at the expense of the poor, the needy, and the weak. They may appear human, but they are in actuality *soulless vampires*."

But don't drive a stake through their hearts. Just make the sign of the Cross and pray. I've seen blood-thirsty vampires redeemed by the Blood of Christ, so there is hope even for them – just as there is hope for myself.

135. ~ RECEIVING THE ONE I REFUSED ~

I did not give to the panhandler, because I smelled alcohol on his breath. I did not speak to the prostitute, because I did not want my reputation damaged. I did not embrace the homosexual, because I did not want to condone his lifestyle. I did not help the beggar, because I did not want to enable his laziness. But I went to Church on Sunday to receive Him who I had refused all week long.

136. ~ MAN and ANT ~

Oh, the arrogance and foolishness of man! And yet, man cannot even match the accomplishment of a single ant. One man through greed, dishonesty, treachery, and the violation of his fellow human beings amasses a great fortune and erects materialistic monuments to his own glory; and yet the human society in which he lives is fraught with misery and suffering. How proud this one man is, thinking he has achieved something great because he has profited at the expense of his human brothers and sisters. The fool!

But the ant, with its microscopic brain and miniscule body, instinctively cooperates with his fellow ants to construct mountainous dwelling places that benefit the whole colony. And the ant instinctively assists his fellow ants in procuring great surpluses of food that can sustain the entire village. Anthropologists and archaeologists still marvel at how the Great Pyramids were built, but ants accomplish relative similar feats on a regular basis. Yet, I have never seen these tiny insects display arrogance. But there are plenty of fatuous human beings that act as if they were gods, while in reality they lack the sense of a simple ant!

137. ~ WE REFUSE TO BE QUIET ~

Wherever human beings are violently silenced, the true revolutionaries shall refuse to be quiet! We will decry injustice, inhumanity, killing, and evil – wherever it occurs – from the edges of the earth to the recesses of the womb. Until slaves are liberated, war is abolished, poverty is eradicated, and the unborn are free from the violence of abortion, then our voices will perpetually echo in the darkness of your conscience. We will speak the truth until you kill us also. But even then, divine truth shall haunt you. Silence us, perhaps. But you will never silence the Creator. His truth reverberates eternally.

138. ~ MY SUICIDE ~

One day I will write in detail about suicide, and how to overcome it, if indeed I am able to overcome it. But for now all I can write is the truth that we must all choose a suicidal path: some choosing the path of suicidal self-destruction and others choosing the suicidal path of the Cross. But either way, we all choose to die one way or another. And I confess that every day I waver between which death to choose. I want so badly to choose to die to myself, to be crucified with Christ, to let this world kill me so that I can live eternally. I want to choose the revolutionary suicide that leads to redemption and eternal life. But this earthly existence is so damn painful at times. And thus I am tempted to choose the reactionary suicide that will simply end the pain of the here and now. I am tempted to make the eternal gamble that whatever lies beyond will be easier than what I am forced to bear at the moment. But to choose that path would be to compromise everything I believe and know in my heart and soul. I may be losing, but I can't quit. I will continue to dwell in this mortal realm, fighting this battle until God decides when my time is up. If I do kill myself it will be fighting the injustices, evils, and lies of this world. That will be my suicide. And I will relish it. As Albert Camus wrote: *"It takes more courage to live than to shoot yourself."*

139. ~ HAUNTED ~

I think of you often
The child that I scarred
If indeed you survived
Or did you die?

I remember your mother
She was a "customer"
Who came to purchase the poison I sold
And one night I noticed
That her belly was swole

And for a moment
I turned away
Unable to keep my conscience at bay

But the laws of the block
And the loot from the rock
Were the choices I made
And thus the price you paid
An innocent babe

But don't blame your mother
Who was chemically enslaved

Blame me
Who with volitional evil
Scorned your life
And cursed your fate

Blame me
Who did not even know
Your mother's name

Forgive me, if you can
And know
That through eyes of my own children
You haunt me

140. ~ MAN HAS THE TRUTH ~

Man has been given the Truth. What he does with the Truth is what determines and defines his life. The gift of Truth is a divine endowment that man carries with him eternally. Truth cannot be stolen from him. It cannot be relinquished by him. It abides with him either as ally or enemy, depending on the condition of that person's soul. Man can neither extricate himself from the Truth nor jettison the Truth from himself. All he can do is adhere to it or ignore it, love it or despise it, live and die *for* it or live and die *against* it. But the Truth alone is the omnipresent companion of man, and man alone is responsible for how he responds to this divine gift. Will he worship the Truth in eternal heaven, or will he curse the Truth in eternal hell? What he does with the Truth now will determine what the Truth does to him forever.

"I am the Way, the Truth, and the Life.
No one comes to the Father except through me."
[St. John 14:6]

141. ~ ON POETIC and ARTISTIC EXPRESSION ~

There are two primary schools of thought regarding poetic and artistic expression. One is the Puritanical mindset, which views any artistic expression that is not overtly and explicitly Christian as demonic and evil. The other is the secular mindset, which views all artistic expressions as equally valid and morally equivalent. Both views are misguided in my opinion.

I believe the Psalms demonstrate perhaps the greatest example of poetic expression in all of history. The Psalms reveal the depth and height of emotional experience. The Psalms disclose sorrow and despair, torment and heartache; but they also reveal tremendous joy, abundant hope, and overflowing praise. But what makes the Psalms so profound is that they demonstrate the sublime beauty and poetic power that result from subjective emotions reaching out and embracing objective Truth.

Great art is ultimately transcendent. It takes us beyond ourselves. The Psalmists were able to go deep inside the recesses of their own hearts, expressing the darkness and pain that often resided therein. But they didn't remain in that darkness, brooding endlessly in self pity and hopelessness. Instead, they had the honesty to look deep within themselves – recognizing their mortality and sin –while having the courage to boldly reach out to the eternality and holiness of God.

Art begins with us, for we are the subjects who feel, experience, and struggle to interpret our lives. And artistic expression emanates from the human desire to interpret and convey the fears, the angst, and the hopes that resonate within our souls. But great artistic expression is never satisfied in the limited confines of self. By its nature, it takes us from the temporal and finite to the infinite and eternal. Real creativity always invokes an awareness of the Creator. Great art is unlimited, finding its ultimate expression in the creative articulation of transcendental truths. Great artists never remain in the realm of the subjective. Their burning creativity demands the acknowledgement of a mystical, objective reality far greater than themselves.

"He who works with his hands is a laborer.
He who works with his hands and his head is a craftsman.
He who works with his hands and his head and his heart is an artist."
~ St. Francis of Assisi ~

142. ~ MEANINGLESS RELIGION ~

Religion without mystery is religion without meaning.

143. ~ LOVE of COUNTRY? ~

If by "country" or "nation" one means the people who inhabit that land, then yes I love my country, for we have a divine command to love all people. But if by "country" or "nation" one means the values, ideologies, and politics of that land, then no, I do not love my country; for within me is a divine inclination to abhor and oppose the demonic idolatries of child sacrifice, materialism, warmongering, and capitalistic exploitation that are protected and promoted by this U.S. government.

"It is a virtue to restrain anger, to control desire, and to curb lust. For this is to flee from vice. For almost all things that are done unjustly and dishonestly arise from these affections. Also, if desire is restrained, no one will use violence by land or by sea. Nor will anyone lead an army to carry off and lay waste the property of others." ~ Lactantius ~

144. ~ CAUSES and RIGHTS ~

There is no cause that is greater than the life of an individual human being, and the rights of an individual human being are not greater than the cause of life and liberty for all.

145. ~ SIMPLE LOGIC ABOUT PEACE ~

"Nuclear war doesn't annihilate humans; people annihilate humans."

"Abortion doesn't murder babies; people murder babies."

"Guns don't kill people; people kill people."

Wait. What? I guess there's some semblance of logic to all that. But what seems far more logical to me is that if we abolished nuclear war, abortion, and guns, then we'd have a lot less killing and a lot more peace in the world.

But I will also say that I have no tolerance for the hypocrisy of those who want to disarm others without disarming themselves. Mr. USA President – whoever you are – don't tell the common man to put away his gun unless you first put away yours. Don't demand that other nations abolish their nuclear capacities unless your government first abolishes its own nuclear weapons. And don't you dare lecture the rest of the world about human rights as long as abortion is legal right here in America.

146. ~ A MORALLY GREAT NATION? ~

If America has produced any moral greatness it has usually been a response and reaction to its inherent immorality or a rebellion against its systemic injustices and evils. A morally great nation has no need for abolitionists, civil rights movements, anti-war protestors, and Pro-Life activists. A morally great nation has no need for revolutionary voices of social justice decrying its crimes against humanity. A morally great nation doesn't produce prophetic souls forged by the suffering and cruelty it inflicted upon them. America may be economically, militarily, and materialistically "great," but America is not and never has been a morally and spiritually great nation.

147. ~ CALLING and CONSCRIPTION ~

When the government calls the Christian, the Christian calls on God. We refuse to be conscripted by armies, for we have already been conscripted by Christ.

148. ~ EPISTEMOLOGICAL WONDER ~

To wonder why we wonder. All epistemological answers ultimately reside in this single question.

149. ~ DESTROYING EVIL ~

Whenever we presume to preserve the good by destroying evil, then we inevitably end up perpetuating evil in the name of the good. The fact is that we have no power to destroy evil; only God can do that. All we can do is destroy the evil human being, but the evil still remains. If it was possible to destroy evil with bullets and bombs, then we wouldn't need the Cross. If violence could conquer evil, then world peace would have sprouted from the ashes of mushroom clouds.

150. ~ CALLED TO FIGHT ~

The Christian has been called to fight, to fight to the death – to the death of ourselves so that Christ may live in us. (Galatians 2:20) The Christian has been called to war, to militancy – to wage battle against the spiritual forces of darkness that oppose Christ and His Church. (Ephesians 6:10-18) The Christian has been called to conquer – to conquer condemnation and sin through the love of Our Lord. (Romans 8:37)

So make no mistake: the Christian is most certainly called to warfare. But also make no mistake: the Christian is never called to kill.

151. ~ WHAT THEY ARE CALLED ~

A person who commits theft is called a "thief." A person who commits adultery is called an "adulterer." A person who lies is called a "liar." A person who sins is called a "sinner." But as long they wear a uniform and pledge allegiance to a flag, a person who kills is called a "soldier."

152. ~ A MUTUALLY SHARED DESTRUCTION ~

What is the one thing that is believed and embraced by the majority of Muslims and Jews, Catholics and Protestants, liberals and conservatives, atheists and (sadly) even most Orthodox Christians too? It is certainly not a shared belief in the same scriptures, the same religion, the same political ideology, or the same philosophy of human government. No. The one thing that most people believe in equally is the rationalization, permissibility, and necessity of "justifiable" violent "defense."

Now just consider that for a moment. The philosophy of the necessity of the sword is the one philosophy that most all men everywhere embrace to one degree or another. And of course, everyone believes that their own use of the sword is righteous and the other's use of the sword is evil. Everyone believes that their own use of the sword will bring peace and order, and that the other's use of the sword will bring evil and ruin.

The one ideology espoused by the majority of nations, religions, and individuals in the world is the very ideology that contributes to all the war, inhumanity, and unjust suffering that plagues our earth. The sword which is almost universally held by all is the sword by which we all universally suffer.

If the Christian cannot see the absurdity in all of this, if the Christian is not willing to follow the path of the Cross in opposition to the path of the sword, then who else will be a voice of reason amongst the madness? Who else will be an example of peace, love, light, and life in the midst of violence, hatred, darkness, and death?

153. ~ I SEE YOU ~

I see you
subtle light orb
deftly flashing
to distract me.

What are you?

You want me to wonder.
But I'm not interested.
You are of no concern to me.

I see through you
even more clearly
than I see through myself.

You are not the Light of Christ –
uncreated and unconditionally loving
infinite and eternally merciful.

No.

Your charms won't work here.
So cast your spells
upon someone else.
Because I cast you aside
with the sign of the Cross

I pay no attention
to your dark and feckless strobes.
The putrid lights of hell
will not deter me
from the pure Light of heaven.

154. ~ HEROISM ~

No heroic act of war can equal a heroic act of peace.

155. ~ PROCLAIMING PEACE and LIFE in A VIOLENT WORLD ~

I have reasoned about the issue of Christian nonviolence for many years now – forthrightly, lovingly, passionately, and (I believe) thoroughly. I'm sure that I have sometimes failed to be perfect in my logic and consistently Christian in my approach. But it has become quite evident to me that some people simply do not want to even consider the idea that militarism and violence may be wrong. Unless we agree to their insistent assertions that violence is sometimes necessary and permissible, then we are accused of being abrasive, confrontational, insulting, ignorant, and naïve.

I have also frequently referred people to numerous books, articles, and resources on the topic of Christian nonviolence. (I have listed some of these resources in the bibliography at the back of this book.) But most people who espouse a "Just War" philosophy don't want to take the time to consider another point of view. Many of them have been "educated" at universities and seminaries, and therefore believe that what they have been taught is impervious to scrutiny. They can't fathom the possibility that they achieved a Master's or Doctorate degree in theology while being taught something that is actually contrary to the Gospel. And how could uneducated folks like us possibly be right in our interpretation of the Gospel of peace? We are just ignorant pacifists who foolishly take Christ at His very word.

It took me many years to come to understand the Christian imperatives of peace and nonviolence. It didn't happen overnight. And it was certainly not easy for me to repent of the violent philosophies with which I had been thoroughly inundated for most of my life – philosophies that I had also been taught were quite acceptable with the Christian Faith. But I studied and read. I discussed and debated the issue with my Christian philosophy and theology professors, as well as with my Christian pastors and friends.

I steeped myself in the writings and philosophy of Gandhi, Dr. Martin Luther King, Tolstoy, Dorothy Day, and the Berrigan brothers. And most of all I prayed. And the years I spent praying and ministering on the sidewalks of abortion clinics proved to me that evil is not an abstract idea but a very concrete reality. More than anything else, the abortion issue forced me to understand the Gospel imperatives of nonviolence. For if violence is ever justifiable, then surely it is justifiable in defense of the weakest and most vulnerable members of the human race – unborn children. But I finally realized that there was One who was not only as innocent as an unborn child, but who was also as holy as almighty God. In fact, He *was* God and He *is* God. If ever any human life deserved a violent defense, it was the life of Our Lord Jesus Christ. But when His disciple sought to protect Him with the sword, Christ rebuked him with an unambiguous, unequivocal, and universal command: *"Put away thy sword! For all who live by the sword shall also die by the sword." [St. Matthew 26:52]*

But I didn't want to forsake the sword. Believe me. There is evil in this world that I wish I could rectify with my own mortal strength and authority. I wanted to be convinced that zealotry was permissible. I wanted to be convinced that God had called me to be a holy warrior in a righteous crusade to violently liberate the unborn, to exact vengeance on pedophiles, and to defend my family, my friends, and my Church by any means necessary. But I finally realized that as a Christian, Jesus Christ is my Lord, my Savior, my standard, and my authority. I cannot do other than what He commands and sanctions.

Proclaiming peace and nonviolence continues to cost me friends. It may even cost me my family. It may eventually cost me my own life. No matter how conciliatory and reasonable I try to be, some people just don't want to be told that killing is incompatible with the Gospel. If we speak this truth, then they will inevitably be offended and they will accuse us of being insulting, insensitive, self-righteous, etc. – just as those who support "abortion rights" will always be offended by the fact that we unapologetically state that abortion is murder. But that's the price and consequence of speaking peace and defending the sanctity of life. Violence permeates our culture so deeply that even many who profess to follow the Prince of Peace refuse to hear Him when He says, *"Put away thy sword, love your enemies, bless those that persecute you, and leave vengeance to God." [St. Matthew 26:52; St. Matthew 5:44; Romans 12:19]*

I am grateful for the many friends and brethren who have offered me encouragement and support as I try to promote peace, nonviolence, and respect for all human life. And I am also thankful for the many sincere, honest, and humble people who may disagree with me on the issue of pacifism but nevertheless desire to lean towards peace, with a willingness to learn more about Christian peacemaking.

I think all Christians will agree that peace is the divine standard. And through prayer, love, humility and faith we can work to eliminate those things within in our own hearts and within our world that cause violence, destruction, and human suffering. It is not easy to proclaim peace and life in a violent world. And it is even harder to live and act peaceably when we are surrounded by and confronted with so much injustice and evil.

As the Holy Spirit enlightened and empowered the Apostles 2,000 years ago, may also He enlighten and empower the children of God today.

"Lord have mercy."

+++

"The weapons we fight with are not the weapons of the world. On the contrary, they have divine power to demolish strongholds."
[II Corinthians 10:4]

156. ~ **HAPPINESS** ~

"I deserve to be happy!"

This mentality pervades our culture, and it leads to abortion, divorce, rape, war, and many other evils. And yet prior to the fall, Adam and Eve were happy in the Garden; so the pursuit of happiness is not necessarily wrong. The problem is not with the *pursuit* of happiness; the problem is with the *definition* of happiness. We confuse happiness with pleasure, comfort, and security rather than understanding happiness as nearness to God. God wants us to be happy in Him, and He has provided all we need to find that happiness. But too often we seek happiness in ourselves, in others, or in circumstances. And when we misplace the source of our happiness, we usually just make ourselves and those around us miserable.

"You make known to me the path of life; you will fill me with joy in your presence, with eternal pleasures at your right hand."
[Psalm 16:11]

"Delight yourself in the Lord, and He will give you the desires of your heart." [Psalm 37:4]

157. ~ IF I CAN DETER ONE PERSON ~

I can't save anyone from hell. I can't save anyone from sin. I can't save anyone from the pain and suffering of life. I am not Christ. He alone is the Savior. But if I can deter even one person from having an abortion, from joining the military, or from doing anything else that would cause them to shed the blood of another human being, then my life on earth will not be in vain. My heart breaks every time I see another young, naïve, desperate person enter the hellish gates of abortion clinics and military bases. What a shame to see the divine power of creative human potential wasted in the demonic pursuits of death and destruction.

158. ~ DO NOT MISTAKE OUR PACIFISM for WEAKNESS ~

Do not mistake our pacifism for weakness, for Christ is the epitome of strength. Do not mistake our pacifism for the tolerance of your evil, for Our Lord came to cast fire upon the earth. (St. Luke

12:49) Do not mistake our pacifism for cowardice, for the Cross of Christ was the bravest act in all eternity. Do not mistake our turning the other cheek for submission to your injustice; for when you violate us, you torment yourself. So we warn you: Do not mistake our pacifism; for although it is founded upon love, it will find satisfaction in divine vengeance. (Cf. Psalm 58:10) We condemn your violence against us, not only because we suffer, but because in violating us you persecute your own soul.

"If someone attempts to provoke you by physical violence, the admonition of the Lord is at hand. He says, 'To him who strikes you on the face, turn the other cheek also.' Let outrageousness be outworn by your patience. Whatever that blow may be, joined with pain and scorn, it will receive a heavier one from the Lord."
~Tertullian ~

159. ~ WEALTH and POVERTY ~

There is nothing Christian about stealing from the rich to give to the poor. Jesus Christ has nothing to do with Robin Hood. But it is equally unchristian to pretend that one man's wealth is not in some way related to another man's poverty. As St. Basil the Great said:
"The bread that you store up belongs to the hungry; the coat that lies in your chest belongs to the naked; the gold that you have hidden in the ground belongs to the poor."

160. ~ DOCTRINE and DISCRIMINATION ~

When we read Our Lord's words about who shall enter the kingdom and who shall be left out, they point to actions regarding how to treat one's fellow man rather than to specific doctrines or creeds. As Orthodox Christians, we uphold the Nicene Creed without apology; and we certainly defend sound doctrine. But we must understand that these doctrines always point us towards mercy, love, humility and forgiveness. Therefore, we dare not presume to have understood the infinite Mysteries of God, and we dare not discriminate against our neighbors based on our own finite reasoning. All doctrines that are truly divine point to true love for all humanity.

161. ~ NO SECURITY in THIS LIFE ~

I've come to realize that I will never have security in this life. And that's ok; because if this world ever becomes my comfortable abode then my soul will be in jeopardy.

Lord, grant me the strength to bear my crosses. In the midst of such pain, it's hard for me to understand that these trials are good for me. I just want a little relief, a little hope, a little assurance that it will all work out in the end.

But alas, my God has not promised me such things. He only tells me to follow Him, and that in doing so He will lead me to eternal life. So I cannot sell my soul for praise and approval, comfort and security. I'll live with my crosses the best I can, praying that they teach me to be more compassionate, more sensitive, more charitable, and more merciful to others who are suffering around me.

God bless all those who despise me, betray me, curse me, and neglect me. God just uses them to make me stronger. I'm still trodding through this vale of tears with my soul intact. And that alone proves the reality of Our Lord's love.

Forward through Babylon, and on to Zion!

162. ~ BLAMING BABYLON ~

I can't blame it all on Babylon. Babylon may be diseased, but if I feast on its pollution then I am responsible for the illnesses I incur.

163. ~ A FRAGILE THUNDER ~

Baby comes forth
With emergent cry
A fragile thunder
That shatters lies

Infant God
Gentle and meek
Eternal truth
That sages seek

164. ~ MYSTERY ~

The mystery of life and the mystery of death
The mystery of spirit and the mystery of flesh
The mystery of love and the mystery of hate
The mystery of youth and the mystery of age
The mystery of suffering and the mystery of sleep
The mystery of war and the mystery of peace
The mystery of pleasure and the mystery of pain
The mystery of doubt and the mystery of faith
The mystery of sorrow and the mystery of joy
The mystery of girl and the mystery of boy
The mystery of redemption, the mystery of the fall
The mystery of nothing and the mystery of it all
The mystery of fire and water and breath
But the greatest mystery is the mystery itself
Rejoice in it!

165. ~ GLORY and HONOR? ~

Whether I'm watching FOX News, CNN, ABC, or ESPN, it seems like I'm constantly seeing carefully choreographed stories about mothers and fathers in the military being reunited with their children after a tour of duty. Typically, the stories are set up where the parents surprise their children by their unexpected arrival at the child's school or at the halftime of some major sporting event. The segments are always accompanied by sentimental music that's meant to tug at the heartstrings. And honestly, only a completely callous individual would not be moved by seeing children reunited with their parents. But more often than not the parent usually redeploys for another tour of duty, and the poor children are once again left to live with the excruciating anxiety of wondering whether they will ever see their mothers and fathers again.

It seems that the only thing liberals and conservatives in this country agree upon is the insidious idea that it is somehow noble and glorious to abandon one's own children in order to go and kill people overseas. But I personally find such a notion repugnant. There is absolutely nothing honorable, decent, or heroic about abandoning one's family in order to violently shed the blood of one's fellow man. I guess such a sickening idea may be acceptable for those who don't pretend to follow the Prince of Peace, but it's by no means acceptable for the Christian. Shame on those who choose warfare and killing over raising their own children, especially while professing the glorious name of Our Savior!

166. ~ TWO MONKS ~

Once upon a time there were two monks who each lived alone in solitary caves, side by side, on a remote mountain far removed from the city. They spent their days and nights in prayer, and they subsisted on the little food that was occasionally brought to them by pilgrims from the nearest village. They rarely spoke to each other, for all their conversation was spent in talking with God. But they loved each other like brothers, and they each prayed for the other one's soul.

It had been many days since either one of them had eaten, because no pilgrims had come to visit them in quite a while. So they were very hungry and their faith was once again tested. But as they both emerged from their caves in the morning to thank God for another day, they noticed a hawk circling overhead. And both monks, each in their own silent prayer, asked God to bless the hawk and to bless all creatures great and small. For God created all living things, and therefore they prayed for all living things to continually be blessed by Him.

As they lifted their eyes and hearts to heaven, they observed the hawk beginning to circle lower and lower until it was almost close enough to touch. The monks noticed that it had something in its mouth, which it dropped at their feet and then glided back up into the great blue sky. They looked down and saw a large crust of bread on the ground.

One of the monks said to the other: "God has provided dear brother. Take and eat this crust of bread, because I know that you are hungry."

But the other monk said, "No my brother, you must take the crust of bread and eat it yourself, for I know that you are hungry and need it more than I do."

Then they began to argue over who should eat the crust of bread, each one insisting that the other one have it. Immediately they were both overcome with grief because they had started to quarrel.

"God has given us bread from heaven, and we have turned His blessing into a curse. I am sorry for arguing with you my dear brother."

"Indeed," said the other monk. "I too am ashamed. Please forgive me as well. I was more concerned about my own salvation than yours. I was willing to let you eat and thus benefit my own soul than to eat myself and allow your soul to be blessed."

"I too am guilty of feeling the same way my brother. I am ashamed."

They both looked down at the crust of bread, and then they looked up to see the hawk still circling high above.

"Let us return this blessing from whence it came," said the one monk to his brother.

"Yes, I agree. For we have allowed this blessing to be a source of sin for both of us. And look at the hawk who flies above us. It has lost its crust of bread, and perhaps it was taking it to feed its babies in the nest."

"You are right," said the other. "And the poor hawk has nothing to live for but food and water. But we are Christians, children of God, and even if we have nothing to eat or drink we nevertheless have the food of prayer to sustain us forever."

Suddenly they both began to weep over their sins and grieve out of pity for the hawk.

Then the two monks took the crust of bread, joined hands, and flew up to the sky and returned the bread to the hawk's beak. As soon as they put the bread into the hawk's mouth, the hawk transformed into a holy angel. The angel then flew with them back to their caves where they discovered multiple loaves of bread, cisterns of water, and gallons of wine waiting for them.

The two monks looked at each other with tears of joy streaming down their faces.

"Now we will have food and drink to share with the pilgrims who come to visit us!"

"Indeed!" said the other monk. "What a loving and merciful God we serve!"

167. ~ SEARCHING and SETTLING ~

It's better to be someone who is constantly struggling and searching than to be someone who comfortably settles for the wrong answers.

168. ~ AMERICAN VALUES ~

3 people are murdered at Ft. Hood, Texas, and it's an American tragedy. 100,000 Japanese civilians are murdered by an atomic bomb, and it's an American "victory." 3,000 innocent human lives are violently destroyed on 9/11, and it's an act of terror. 3,000 innocent human lives are violently destroyed in the womb every day, and it's an act of "choice." And America wonders why the rest of the world thinks we're full of hypocrisy when we lecture them about freedom, justice, and human rights.

169. ~ KILL THE WORLD ~

Kill the world in you, but don't you kill the world.

170. ~ TRUE PEACE and SYSTEMATIC ORDER ~

True peace is never achieved through violence or intimidation. Violence and intimidation may provide stability and order, but they can never provide peace. An orderly, stable society is not necessarily a peaceful and just society. Many wicked societies are well ordered in their evil. With systematic order, the slave trade thrived for centuries. With systematic order, the Nazis exterminated Jews. With systematic order, unborn babies are mercilessly butchered. And such evils are carried out under the protection of the sword of the state. We must never confuse the absence of tension with the presence of authentic peace. We must never confuse stability and order for truth and justice. True peace comes not from the sword, but from the Cross.

171. ~ TRULY SUFFER / FREELY GIVE ~

Some truly suffer and therefore they freely give. Others never freely give and therefore they truly suffer.

172. ~ WHAT GREAT ARTISTS TEACH US ~

When there is no difference between what we want to do and what we have to do, then we are truly happy. All great artists create because they *have* to and because they *want* to. For them there is no distinction, and therein lies their genius.

We can learn from this in the practice of our Christian Faith. Do we pray because we *have* to, or because we *want* to? Do we read the Scriptures because we *have* to, or because we *want* to? Do we worship because we *have* to, or because we *want* to? The reality is that we do *need* to do these things in order to be spiritually healthy. But if our Christian exercises are done only out of need and not from desire, then we are missing the fullness of the experience of God.

As a parent, there are certain things that I have to provide for my children: nurture, discipline, love, knowledge, and affection. But I never think of any of these things as duties or chores. I enjoy providing my children with all of these things; and in fact, doing so gives me the greatest pleasure. The Orthodox Christian Faith is the same. We come to God because of need, but we are drawn more by desire.

173. ~ PLANS and PREPARATIONS ~

Plan, prepare, and train for war and you will find war. Plan, prepare, and train for peace and you will find peace.

174. ~ DIVINE LIGHT ~

The Light which permeated the Garden of Eden...

The Light that radiated from Sinai's burning bush...

The Light which engulfed the summit of Mt. Tabor...

The Light that quenched Babylon's fiery furnace...

The Light which guided the Magi in the Palestine night...

The Light that Jonah felt in the belly of the whale...

The Light which blinded Saul on the Damascus road...

The Light that blazed from Elijah's fiery chariot...

The Light that obliterated Sodom and Gomorrah...

The Light that filled the heart and womb of the Virgin Mary...

The Light that infused the empty tomb...

The Light that descended on the Day of Pentecost...

The Light that illumines the righteous and scourges the heathen...

The Light that warms the faithful and burns the wicked...

The uncreated Light, which renders all other light as darkness...

This Light is the Light that is Christ Our Lord!

"Then spake Jesus again unto them, saying,
I am the light of the world:
he that followeth me shall not walk in darkness,
but shall have the light of life."
[St. John 8:12]

175. ~ THE FIRE of GRACE ~

The grace of God is like fire. We sinful human creatures are drawn by the offer of its warmth as we simultaneously fear its consuming power. Our souls crave divine grace, but the sinful flesh recoils against it. We don't deserve grace, a fact by which grace is defined.

It is a human instinct to choose the negative consequences of sin rather than accept divine grace. This is because most people are accustomed to sin and its consequential burdens, but they have little experience with unconditional forgiveness and divine mercy. And it is a human tendency to choose what is familiar over that with which we are unacquainted, even if what is familiar to us is also destructive to us.

Satan utilizes this dynamic against us, ushering us away from God's grace and back into a familiar pattern of sin and subsequent suffering. But the fire of divine grace will never consume us. It will only burn away sin, guilt, and shame, while bringing warmth to our souls. And although a person born into slavery is unfamiliar with freedom, would he not gladly forsake the familiarity of bondage for the uncharted experience of emancipation?

Therefore, let us throw ourselves into the fire of divine grace. Let us bathe in its warmth as we offer up our sin, guilt, and shame to its purifying incineration. God's grace will never consume us. It will only cleanse us.

Our Lord said, *"I have come to cast fire on the earth, and how I wish it were already kindled!"* [St. Luke 12:49] In commenting on this verse, *The Orthodox Study Bible* states:

"Fire references the proclamation of the gospel and the gift of the Holy spirit. The fire both enlivens the faithful and judges the faithless; it purifies virtue and destroys sin." [OSB p. 1393]

176. ~ HISTORY and TRUTH ~

Academics think that history judges the truth. Prophets know that the Truth judges history.

177. ~ GREAT HEARTS / BRILLIANT MINDS ~

I would much rather be surrounded by those who have average minds and great hearts than by heartless intellectuals. Consider the havoc in the world caused by men with brilliant minds and shallow souls!

178. ~ WHAT HAPPENED to MY CITY? (MOURNING the ATL) ~

What happened to my city, to my neighborhood, to my school and to the community where I grew up and spent so many joyous and tumultuous years? Does anyone remember Ray's Quick Mart, where I got caught stealing bubble gum as a kid? Or what about the Northside Pharmacy where you could get a Limeade and the best milkshake in town made by the curmudgeonly but lovable Herb? And then there was Oz Records where I purchased *Kiss Alive II* for $8.00 in 1978, when I was in the 5th grade.

Those wonderful places are long gone. Gone too is my beloved North Fulton High School where I played basketball, fell in love for the first time, and partied like there was no tomorrow. Gone too is Fulton County Stadium where I saw Hank Aaron, Pele, and Roger Staubach grace the sacred turf. And gone is the Omni Arena where I watched Dominique Wilkins, Dr. J, and Michael Jordan display their aerial prowess, and the venue where I once saw YES in concert.

It seems that the 1996 Olympics was the beginning of the ATL's demise. Did our beloved city really need the Olympics? Did we need to sell our soul and corrupt our identity for the almighty dollar? Were the jobs created and the revenue generated worth the loss of community, the loss of dignity, the loss of our essential uniqueness and collective individuality? Is it not better to struggle together than to "succeed" alone? Are we not all spiritually and culturally richer when we help each other than when we exploit one another in the pursuit of individual and material wealth?

What happened to the sanguine spirit of kindness, manners, and genuine friendship that we always had in Atlanta? We had a big city that resonated with small town southern charm. We were the city that was "too busy to hate." We produced Dr. Martin Luther King, Jr., who reflected our cooperative willingness to combat inhumanity and prejudice with love and tolerance. Dr. King, perhaps more than anyone, exhibited Atlanta's spirit of humble resilience and dignified strength. But we spat on Dr. King's grave by sacrificing the timeless values of humanity and decency for the financial expediency of the Olympics and the cheap lure of a proliferating sex industry.

Today our beautiful city is renowned not for its Southern hospitality, its Civil Rights history, or its iconic landmarks, but rather for its thriving adult entertainment culture. Sure, Atlanta was always content to have its Chesire Bridge Road and Clermont Lounge. Even our sleazy areas were unique and inherently reflective of the soul of our city. But now even our sleaziness has been co-opted, corrupted, and assimilated by the vultures of capitalism and the cold impersonality of international organized crime. Yes, we always had our own organized crime, but it was *our* organized crime. And we could reckon with it, because it was in our own backyard. But we no longer have our own backyard. We sold our backyard when we sacrificed our city to predatory political wolves and their false promises of a pot of gold at the end of the Olympic-ringed rainbow.

Atlanta was once a city where you could order sweet tea with Sole Meuniere. Now Atlanta is a city where you don't even know who your neighbor is from one day to the next, and where it now costs ten dollars for a couple of hot dogs and an order of onion rings at *The Varsity*.

I live in Jackson, Mississippi now. My parents sold our house in Atlanta a few years ago. The house is still there, in the same neighborhood. But it's not my home anymore. It is the abode of strangers. I no longer recognize it. And I no longer recognize my city. Atlanta will always be in my blood, it will always be my home. I guess some things will never change. I have close friends who are still holding down the fort, still living and maintaining the spirit of the Atlanta I know and love. God bless them.

I'm not sure if I left the city of Atlanta or if the city of Atlanta left me. But we have parted ways. I wish it well. I truly do. It was a great city once. Perhaps in some ways it still is. It's just so hard to tell now.

"I am reminded of a recent conversation I had with an acquaintance of mine, a native of the Midwest, who runs the Atlanta bureau of one of the nation's largest newspapers. He had been doing a story out in the Mississippi Delta, where time has stood still, and he had been touched by the patina of this older, inward South. The Delta had bewildered and intrigued him, for it has always both frightened and titillated the outsider.

'It's the other extreme from Atlanta,' he said. 'Southerners hate to be strangers to each other. That's why Atlanta is so traumatic for Southerners to visit. Southerners like to see you and say, 'Hi, how are you?' And the Yankees in Atlanta just don't respond to that. As for the native Atlantans, there's a city they remember that no longer really exists. But they still see it as if it were there – the gracious cotillions, the old Rich's department store, the old Peachtree Street, the Buckhead Boys.' He remembered what one old Atlantan had said to him: 'Maybe my city is only the way I remember it in my mind.'"

~ Willie Morris ~
[The South and Welcome to It: Does It Still Exist?]

179. ~ FIRES of LOVE / FLAMES of FEAR ~

Those who are secure in their own faith do not need to denigrate the faith of others. It is better to blaze the eternal fires of the Gospel than to ignite the ephemeral flames of hatred and fear.

180. ~ TELL THE TRUTH ~

Tell the truth. Always. Regardless of the consequences. Just don't tell the truth about *me!*

181. ~ REVOLUTION IS A PROCESS ~

Revolution is a process, *from* something *to* something. And the essence of true Christian faith is revolutionary, because it is a constant forward movement. To follow Christ is to move from violence to nonviolence, from the negative to the positive, from sin to righteousness, from death to life, from the ways of man to the ways of Our Lord, from the image of God to the likeness of God.

182. ~ CONSIDER THE CHILD CREATOR ~

Consider the Child Creator, working with Joseph the carpenter, fashioning wood as He once fashioned the universe, knowing that His blistered hands were but a mild foretaste of the agony He would ultimately endure. Consider the young omniscient Artisan, piercing wood with hammer and nails, knowing that spikes of sin would one day pierce His own holy flesh. Consider His mother Mary, removing her Child's splinters and binding His wounds while He knew she would soon anoint His crucified body with aloe and myrrh and tears. Consider the blessed grief and glory, the holy sorrow and joy, the profound mystery and hope of our salvation.

183. ~ WAR ~

A "just" war, a "necessary" war, a "defensive" war, a "legitimate" war, a "holy" war is still an evil, inhumane, and unchristian war.

184. ~ THE CICATRICES of OPPRESSION ~

The earth bears scars, and so does humanity. Wounds can be healed but the cicatrices run deep. The progeny of the oppressed must struggle to forgive and rise above the evils of history. And the progeny of the oppressors must never turn a blind eye to the scars that were inflicted by the crimes of the past. Instead, they must sacrificially reach out to lift the inheritors of such suffering to the same heights to which they themselves aspire.

Christ said, *"It is finished!"* Yet we nevertheless meditate upon His passion and venerate His Cross. We do not say, "That was in the past, get over it." Rather, we recognize that His historical suffering heals and saves us today. There is redemption to be found in the horrors of history, but only if we have the courage to gaze intently upon those horrors without rationalization or excuse.

I crucified my Lord. And I crucify my fellow man. I can't heal myself or my world until I acknowledge these truths and strive to live in reparative repentance.

185. ~ A PRESENT BLINDNESS ~

The problem is not that people forget the injustices of the past; the problem is that people are blind to the evils of the present. It's always easier to denounce the evils of history than to actually confront contemporary injustices.

186. ~ HOW TO GO TO HEAVEN ~

We cannot go to heaven unless we die. And yet we cannot go to heaven unless we live.

187. ~ LOST and FOUND ~

I looked for God in the sky, but I only saw blues.
I looked for God in Church, but I only saw sinners.
I looked for God in my heart, but all I saw was sorrow.
I looked for God everywhere, but I only found shadows.

But while I was searching for God,
God had already found me.

He looked at this child and saw His image.
He looked at this sinner and saw His handiwork.
He looked at me and saw something good.

I was lost in this world,
but I was never lost to God.

We may not always see Him,
but Our Lord always sees us.

And He looks upon us
with unfailing mercy and enduring love.

To cling to this truth is the true meaning of faith.

188. ~ OH HOW BRAVE ~

So you get paid
To put bullets in their brains
And their bodies in graves?

Oh how brave
Oh how brave

Their lives are wasted
But your medals are saved

Enjoy your parades

189. ~ PLEASE DON'T KILL on MY BEHALF ~

To all the soldiers in this world who risk their lives, health, and their sanity fighting for their various nations, ideologies, and causes: I can only beg you not to do so on my behalf.

I have never asked anyone to kill for me, and it offends me when soldiers claim that their violence and bloodshed is done for my benefit. I am a Christian, and the blood that Christ shed for me is enough for my salvation. So please don't presume to kill on my behalf. Please don't risk your life, your health, and your sanity because you think you are protecting my freedom.

My freedom is rooted in my faith in Christ, and such a freedom cannot be destroyed by bullets, bombs, prisons, or chains. Any ostensible faith that is predicated upon violent protection is certainly not a Christian faith. Christ has promised that the gates of hell shall not prevail against the Church (St. Matt 16:18), so His Church does not need to be defended at gunpoint. American soldiers may be killing for money, they may be killing for Obama, they may be killing for a constitution or a political philosophy, but they are not killing for me.

My heart breaks to see such beautiful human potential wasted in the foolish insanity of militaristic endeavors. That's why I join with all Orthodox Christians in praying for the peace of the armed forces, for the peace of *all* armed forces. And as I pray for peace I will persistently point out that peace will come when armed forces disarm and trust only in spiritual force.

But for those who are unrepentantly wedded to violence, I say to you forthrightly and unapologetically: don't dare think that you are engaging in this militaristic "service" on my account. If you really want to serve me, then save your life, preserve your health, and maintain your sanity by saying "no" to war and "yes" to peace."

190. ~ WOOD and STEEL ~

The wood of the Cross is stronger than the steel of the sword.

147

191. ~ THE SOLDIER'S OATH and THE CHRISTIAN'S CONSCIENCE ~

U.S. ARMED FORCES OATH OF ENLISTMENT:

"I, (name), do solemnly swear and affirm that I will support and defend the Constitution of the United States against all enemies, foreign and domestic; that I will bear true faith and allegiance to the same; and that I will obey the orders of the President of the United States and the orders of the officers appointed over me, according to regulations and the Uniform Code of Military Justice. So help me God."

Now I ask you, how can any true Christian take such an oath in good conscience? How can the follower of Christ pledge faith to a manmade constitution that might require him to compromise his fidelity to the commands of the Gospel? How can the citizen of heaven (Philippians 3:20) pledge allegiance to a secular government that requires him to defend its evils and injustices? How can a Christian swear to obey the orders of Barack Obama (or any president) and his godless minions? How can a Christian swear to place faith in any organization, institution, or document other than Christ, His word, and His Church?

Notice that there is no "conscience clause" in the soldier's oath. In taking the oath, the soldier willingly relinquishes his choice as to which orders he will obey. If the Commander in Chief gives an order, the soldier has pledged to obey it – even if that order violates his Christian conscience. If the President orders the National Guard to defend abortion clinics against Pro-Lifers engaged in nonviolent civil disobedience, the Christian soldier has taken a pledge to obey that order. He cannot say, "I am Pro-Life, so I won't obey this particular command." If the Commander in Chief issues drone strikes against a civilian population, the Christian soldier has pledged to carry out that order. If the U.S. government enters into war against a Christian country, the Christian soldier has taken an oath to violently side with this secular nation against his own Christian brethren.

Of course, the Christian soldier is always free to renege on his oath. He can always choose to disobey orders he deems to be unjust or unchristian, and he will have to suffer the consequences. But why would any Christian willingly take such a pledge to begin with, knowing that in doing so he is promising to obey a secular government that condones immorality and evil? Why would a Christian swear to defend a secular nation that protects the injustice of abortion?

To swear unconditional allegiance and obedience to anything other than Christ, His word, and His Church is a very dangerous thing. Our Lord was very clear that we cannot serve two masters: *"No one can serve two masters. Either you will hate the one and love the other, or you will be devoted to the one and despise the other."* [St. Matthew 6:24]

I for one shall never pledge obedience to any American president. I will never take an oath to defend a manmade constitution. And I will never swear allegiance to a government that defends the slaughter of innocents. I tremble at the thought of asking the "god of this world;" i.e. Satan (II Corinthians 4:4) for help. I serve One God alone – Father, Son, and Holy Spirit. ~ amen ~

192. ~ STUDY THE CHILDREN ~

Study the children, for they are our greatest teachers. Learn from their innocence, their purity, and their joy. Learn from their lack of prejudice, their honesty, and their exuberant play. Our Lord loves children, and He pointed to them as an example of how we should all receive the Kingdom of God:

"Verily I say unto you, Whosoever shall not receive the kingdom of God as a little child shall in no wise enter therein." [St. Luke 18:17]

193. ~ AUTHENTIC PACIFISM ~

Authentic pacifism is founded upon the twin pillars of courage and faith. Its courage is derived from faith in a God who will heal all wounds, resurrect all innocent victims, and avenge all injustice. Authentic pacifism is intrinsically spiritual and inherently theistic. It recognizes that it is braver to turn the other cheek than to swing in retaliation. It realizes that it is more courageous to use the spiritual weapons of nonviolent defense than to rely upon the carnal acts of might and force. Authentic pacifism demonstrates a genuine faith in a sovereign God and an eternal reward. It jettisons the security of temporal and material solutions in order to point humanity to the universal and infinite truths of Christ.

"Not by might, nor by power,
but by my Spirit,
sayeth the Lord of Hosts."
[Zechariah 4:6]

194. ~ OPPRESSION and DEMOCRACY ~

There is a fine line between oppression and democracy. The difference is only a matter of perspective. The oppressed view it as oppression; the oppressor calls it "democracy."

195. ~ BALANCE and HARMONY ~

Nature demonstrates that growth, beauty, and fruition are the result of balance. The earth revolves equally through night and day, its flora and sustenance emerging from the betrothal of sunshine and rain. And all life results from the union of male with female. It is therefore important to recognize the harmony of feeling and reason, emotion and logic. God has created us with both a head and a heart, and *"Those who worship Him must worship Him in spirit and in truth." [St. John 4:24]*

196. ~ READING and EDUCATION ~

If you want to be truly educated, then don't read the books they tell you to read. Instead, read books that speak to your soul, books that challenge your spirit, books that convict and burn while uplifting your mind and heart. Read books that are truly revolutionary, not the books that they tell you are revolutionary. Read history and poetry and parables and philosophy; but know that apart from divine prophecy, literature is worth no more than the paper upon which it is printed. This is why the Holy Scriptures are the greatest source of literary education and revolutionary fuel, and this is why the system fights so hard to keep the Scriptures out of the schools. So, in your pursuit of knowledge and wisdom, make this a rule of thumb: if they are trying to force you to read it, then read instead what they are trying to force you *not* to read.

197. ~ WHAT TO SEEK ~

If we seek to control our circumstances, then we will only find frustration and failure. But if we seek nearness to God in the midst of every circumstance, then we shall find peace even in our hardships and trials.

198. ~ CHRISTIANITY and SAFETY ~

I never understand why people keep trying to make Christianity "safe." What about the Cross is safe?

199. ~ GOD WITH US ~

*"The virgin will conceive and give birth to a son,
and they will call him Immanuel (which means 'God with us')."
[Isaiah 7:14; St. Matthew 1:23]*

*IMMANUEL – "God with us."
In the womb, God is with us.
In infancy, God is with us.
In childhood, God is with us.
In growth, God is with us.
In temptation, God is with us.
In doubt, God is with us.
In victory, God is with us.
In defeat, God is with us.
In sorrow, God is with us.
In joy, God is with us.
In darkness, God is with us.
In light, God is with us.
In despair, God is with us.
In hope, God is with us.
In suffering, God is with us.
In our struggles, God is with us.
On the Cross, God is with us.
In death, God is with us.
In the grave, God is with us.
In resurrection, God is with us.
In eternity, God is with us.*

*Indeed, God is with us!
Is there any greater truth?*

200. ~ POLITICIANS ~

Politicians will set your house on fire and then convince you that your greatest need is to let them sell you matches.

201. ~ CHAPELS of DEATH ~

Abortion clinics are chapels of death, houses of the unholy, idolatrous temples where children are sacrificed on the altars of comfort, convenience, materialism, and self. The shed blood of unborn innocents is the sacrament of demons, and the smoke produced from their incinerated bodies is the devil's incense. Those who burn babies ignite the flames of their own impending hell. Those who profit from abortion invite divine fire upon their own cowardly souls.

The brimstone is gathered and the lava boils. Lightning, earthquake, and thunder have given fair warning. The cup of Judgment is full to overflowing. The choirs of angelic unborn victims sing their imprecatory and intercessory prayers. The Lord hears the silent screams of those murdered in the womb, and He will soon ride upon the clouds with His scythe of justice.

So, Mr. Abortionist, don't fear me. It is not I who shall cut you down. It is not I who shall pay you the bitter harvest you are due. It is not my place to break your stiffened neck and send your soul to the devil you serve. But I worship the One who will. So I sheathe my sword and confront you only with prayer, love, and Gospel truth. Because as evil as you are, I only wish you the peace and love of Christ – the same peace and love that are the only hope for this sinner who now dares to rebuke you.

Repent while the hour is afforded you, and then perhaps you may find eternal peace in the reconciled company of those you have slain.

202. ~ NO ESCAPING GOD'S TRUTH ~

The stars of the heavens, the radiance of the sun, and the intricate rhythms of life all point to the Creator and to divine truth. God and truth are inseparable, irrefutable, and unassailable; yet truth is grasped at and groped for in the hallowed halls of Ivy League schools and ivory tower seminaries. It is discussed, debated, dissected, and discarded by educated fools who cynically query with Pontius Pilate, *"What is truth?" [St. John 18:37-38]*

Many people spend their entire lives in the futile attempt to evade the truth, because the recognition and embrace of truth will result in the radical alteration of one's own life. Confrontation and conformity with the truth requires a courage that can only come from the Creator. But the world is filled with individuals who are afraid to feel and afraid to think, because they are terrified of truth and of the God it serves.

People employ perverse reasoning, they sedate themselves with chemicals and potions, and they murder those who speak and live the truth. They deny the Creator and deify themselves. Human beings go to any and all lengths to escape the only thing that will free their confused minds and tormented souls. But there is no escaping God or His Truth; it will either heal us or torment us, according to how we respond to it.

> *"The truth does not change according to*
> *our ability to stomach it emotionally."*
> ~ Flannery O'Connor ~

> *"Do not rejoice in iniquity, but rejoice in the truth."*
> *[I Corinthians 13:6]*

203. ~ SNAKES SLITHER BENEATH THE FLOWERS ~

Snakes slither beneath the flowers. Behind the sunshine burns a fiery abyss. Life births you then breaks you. Love and hope and happiness are dangerous things. I do not trust them. And yet I seek them. I cling to them, no matter how often they crush me.

204. ~ DESTRUCTION IS WEAKNESS ~

How truly powerful is a weapon that destroys? Destruction is not a sign of power, but of weakness. True power is evident in acts of creation, life affirmation, and healing. Any fool can kill and destroy, but how many people can create and heal? Demonic minds conceive instruments of destruction, but righteous minds conceive creativity and life.

205. ~ UNCONDITIONAL LOVE ~

We usually show love only to those who have something to offer in return. But love is only authentic when it is unconditional. Love means giving even when we have been offended, disappointed, or hurt. True love gives freely without the manipulation of conditions imposed upon its recipients or expectations from its beneficiaries. True love is not coercive; it does not offer charity and kindness in order to gain the desired reciprocal results. We all struggle to practice unconditional love; but unconditional love is the only way to individual, familial, social, international, and spiritual peace.

"Our religion commands us to love even our enemies, and to pray for those who persecute us. For everyone loves those who love them. It is unique to Christians to love those who hate them." ~Tertullian ~

"He that has love is far from every sin." ~ St. Polycarp ~

206. ~ REBELLION ~

To rebel against God leads to detriment and destruction, but to rebel against idolatry leads to eternal life.

207. ~ MIND of THE CONQUEROR or THE MIND of CHRIST? ~

It is our Christian duty to actively work to change things for the better. But seeking to change the world by conquering the world is neither practical nor Christian. The mind of the conqueror is not the mind of Christ. History is littered with the detritus of human movements and social revolutions that committed unspeakable atrocities in the name of "progress and change." Salt seasons and light illumines; but violent force cuts down the wheat with the tares, leaving darkness and destruction in its wake.

208. ~ RACISM ~

Racism is often rooted in envy. People hate the beauty and strength they can't find within themselves. They don't recognize the image of God they inherently possess, and thus they are offended by the glory of God that radiates from their fellow man. So they create caricatures and stereotypes of other races in an attempt to obfuscate their own insecurities and weaknesses.

209. ~ IT'S NOT EASY to STAND for TRUTH ~

It is not easy to stand for truth. It is difficult enough to proclaim the ideals of truth – such as nonviolence, justice, and brotherhood – and it is even harder to live them. When you denounce evil, expose injustice, and promote peace, then you will be ridiculed, rejected, and assailed – even by some who may profess to be your brothers. But when you face such attacks, know that you are on the right path; for the road to heaven is paved with much resistance.

210. ~ WEEPING for SINS ~

I thought, "I will weep for the sins of the world when I have finished weeping over my own sins." But then I realized that my own sins are responsible for the sins of the world.

211. ~ BROKEN ~

It's better to have a broken heart than a broken soul.

212. ~ PEOPLE of VISION ~

People of vision carry a heavy burden. They have to maintain hope when others despair. They must focus on the positive amidst a sea of negativity. They have to keep the faith when their loved ones doubt. They must continue the struggle even when their comrades give up the fight. They have to see the good when everyone else sees only the bad. They must love even when they are met with hate. They must recognize the hand of God at work, even when their families and friends succumb to the voices of devils.

It is difficult to invest in the kingdom of heaven when those around you are slaves to the kingdoms of this world. And the effort to lead those you love from the darkness to the light is a thankless and arduous endeavor.

The true visionaries will suffer in this life. That is their fate. But their suffering is not in vain; it is eternally redemptive.

"Where there is no vision the people perish." [Proverbs 29:18]

213. ~ FREE ~

Oh how I'd love to be free
to preach like King
and dance like Ali.

Oh how I'd love to be free
to paint like Picasso
and write like Flannery.

Oh how I'd love to be free
to play like Santana
and sing like Marley.

And yet I know
that I'm already free,
because I don't have to be
anyone but me.

214. ~ LOSING IT ~

I might lose my possessions

I might lose my health

I might lose my family

I might lose my friends

I might lose my reputation

I might lose my mind

I might lose my life...

But by His grace
I won't lose my soul

215. ~ **PAPER HERO** ~

(The following is a true story. Some names and dates have been changed to protect the identity and privacy of the characters involved. Please be advised that this story contains some profanity.)

There was a book written about Friday night lights. It was a wonderful book. I've read it three times. They made it into a movie, and it was surprisingly good. I've seen the movie at least five times. A TV show followed, and it too was quite captivating for the first two seasons. *Friday Night Lights* is all about the passion, the mystery, the joys and crimes of that most American of traditions called high school football. In spite of the overt political agenda that somewhat detracted from it, H.G. Bissinger's book wonderfully captured the glory and pathos of a culture predicated upon the symbiotic hopes of teenage athletes and the adults who cheer them on, often to an unhealthy and idolatrous degree.

The story I am about to tell is not as ambitious as all that. It is simply a tale of something that occurred on a Friday night under the lights on a Florida high school football field in 1983. It is the story of something that happened to me.

I was 14 years old, and I was the quarterback for the Anneewakee Warriors. Or to be more precise, I was *a* quarterback for the Anneewakee Warriors. My best friend Tom was *the* quarterback, the leader of our team, tough as nails and with a rifle arm. I was his backup, the second string QB. But when I say I was the second string QB, please don't misunderstand. The only reason I found myself in that unenviable position was because other than Tom I was the only person on the team who actually knew how to throw a decent spiral.

I was 5'11" and weighed about 150 pounds – *with* helmet and pads on. This was my first time ever playing organized football, although I had dreamed of playing football from the time I could walk. But my mother wouldn't let me. Often overprotective in the wrong ways, she was worried about the risks of football while being heedless of the real dangers that were assaulting my childhood.

As a child, it broke my heart when I saw my friends headed to little league football practice after school, knowing that I couldn't participate with them. I would often follow along just to watch, dreaming of the moves and cuts and spins and speed that I could use against them – dreaming of how they would never catch me – if only my mother would give me the chance to don a helmet and put on pads.

When we played touch football during school recess I would score at will. I was the fastest person in my grade each of my elementary school years. And I would always convince my classmates to play tackle football before the teacher made us stop and go back to two hand touch. I relished the physical contact, and I wanted to show my friends that played little league football that I was just as tough – in fact *tougher* – than they were.

I hated the fact that my mother would never let me play little league football, and her decision left a scar of resentment that lingered for years. It wasn't that my mother was against sports, it's just that she had a disdain for what she perceived to be the inherent violence of football. She signed me up for soccer when I was in the first grade, and I was a natural. My speed gave me a decided advantage, and the sport came easily to me. But as much as I enjoyed soccer, I wasn't passionate about it. I grew up in an era when soccer was never seen on TV in America. I knew who Pele was, and I always made sure that my coach let me wear number 10 in honor of him; but that was about all I really knew or cared about soccer.

Football was what I watched, loved, and desperately wanted to play. I wanted to throw like Roger Staubach of the Dallas Cowboys; I wanted to catch like Lynn Swann of the Pittsburgh Steelers; I wanted to run like Georgia Tech's Eddie Lee Ivery; and I wanted to tackle like Alabama's Jeremiah Castille. I fell asleep at night with a football in my arms, my football cards spread around my bed, and beseeching God to please let me be a pro football player when I grew up.

But sometimes you just can't overcome your parents' decisions or your parents' genes. I was an elementary school playground superstar. But somewhere during my middle school years, puberty, natural selection, and the laws of the universe cruelly rendered me smaller and weaker than many of the peers over whom I had formerly excelled athletically. During the 6th and 7th grades many of my friends grew hair in strange new places, and this strange new hair somehow made them magically bigger, taller, and stronger than me. I prayed to acquire this gift of strange new hair that would also grant me new athletic superpowers. My prayer was slowly and only partially answered. I did eventually receive the gift of strange new hair; but for some reason, the whiskers with which God finally blessed me weren't accompanied by any athletic superpowers. I was still smaller and weaker than most of my fellow competitors.

So I learned to play basketball, a sport where mastering the fundamentals could give one an advantage over more physically gifted opponents. I mastered the art of using my left hand as deftly as my right hand. I carried my basketball everywhere I went, dribbling up and down stairs, learning how to go between my legs and behind my back. I forced myself to develop the proper shooting technique, shooting hundreds of free throws every day in my driveway. I got pretty good, very good in fact. And nothing gave me more pleasure than beating guys who were taller, stronger, more athletic (and hairier) than I was. I couldn't control natural law, but I could prove that even the capriciousness of nature must sometimes bow to the disciplines of human fundamentals. I had found a new love. And like most other loves in my life, it would eventually and frequently break my heart. But I'll save the cruel love story of basketball for another day.

Football had been my first suitor. And now at the age of 14, in my freshman year of high school, I finally had the opportunity to truly experience the sport I'd always dreamed of playing. My mother, in a decision which I'm sure she believed to be a protective one at the time, had sent me off to a "reform school for troubled youths." Thus I suddenly found myself in an environment where I was surrounded by criminals, pedophiles, and drug addicts – and where, alas – I was now able to play organized football for the very first time. I'm sure the irony of this will not be lost on the reader.

So here I was, finally playing my dream sport at this "reform school for troubled youths" called *Anneewakee*. And I was excited. Sort of. For some reason, nature was still dragging her feet regarding my physical development. I was a scrawny kid on a team full of guys for whom puberty was a distant memory – some that had committed armed robbery, and many who'd had sexual intercourse by the age of ten. This was a whole new playground, and my basketball fundamentals were not much use here. To sum it up, I was scared shitless.

But still, I was finally playing football. Or at least I was finally on a real football team – a *high school* football team. And as scared as I was, I was also thrilled. I was finally wearing a helmet and pads, and football (not soccer) cleats. I was now a real football player!

The problem was that I wasn't playing the position for which I was best suited. Our head coach, Coach Mackentire, had assured me that I would be a wide receiver. He had watched me run, noticed my speed, and had thrown passes to me during tryouts. Even though puberty was taking it's time, I was still fast. And I'd always had good hands. Coach had thrown me twenty passes in a row – post patterns, slant routs, bullets and bombs. And I hadn't dropped a one. So he told me that I would be a receiver in the fall. And I was happy about that. I didn't have any fear about running in open space, dodging defenders, diving and laying out to make a spectacular catch. Hell, this is what I had been doing all my life – in backyards, neighborhood streets, and schoolyard playgrounds. So what if everyone else on the team was bigger, stronger, and meaner? I could still outrun them, I could still get open, and I could still catch the damn football. I was Fred Biletnikoff and Lynn Swann rolled into one, and all the Mean Joe Green's in the world couldn't stop me from catching every pass that would be thrown my way. At least that's what I thought of myself. I may have been scared, but I was ready to be a wide receiver!

But then Coach changed his mind and decided to make me the backup quarterback. And as much as my childhood was filled with visions and prayers of growing up to become the next Roger Staubach, I had no desire to play that position now. Being smaller and weaker than everyone else on the team – and considering this was the first time I'd ever donned football armor – I lacked the requisite confidence and leadership that are essential to being a high school quarterback.

During practice I was relegated to leading the second team offense against the first team defense. I would crouch under center, calling out the signals as my hands trembled and my voice quivered. My tentativeness disrupted the rhythm of my cadence, causing the second team center to invariably hike the ball at the wrong moment. And the result was that the first team defensive line would usually arrive before the snap did, and in violent fashion. I would be ruthlessly hit just as the ball hit my hands. So I would fumble. And the defense would pounce on the fumble and then high five one another in celebratory fashion. And Coach would get mad. And he would throw his clipboard. And he would say run the play again. And I would tell our backup center to snap the ball more quickly this time. And the same thing would happen again. And Coach would yell again. And I would get up, brush myself off, and call the same play again (as Coach instructed, which of course gave the defense an even greater and ridiculously unnecessary advantage). And I would again plead with the center to *please* snap the ball faster this time. And I would then "bark" out the signals with my voice shaking even worse than before. And once more I would get pounded to the turf as the ball flew out of my hands and the defense pounced on it and celebrated as if they had won the Super Bowl. And Coach would cuss again. And he would take off his watch and tell me to hold it along with his clipboard. And then he would waddle up under center to run the second team offense himself. And then *he* would fumble as the defense actually tackled *him*, slamming his corpulent middle-aged torso into the Florida Bermudagrass turf. And then the defense would celebrate again like they had just won the Super Bowl. And Coach would dislodge the partially swallowed whistle from his throat and unleash a tirade of profanities that defied the laws of reason, anatomy, and the English language.

The whole thing was embarrassing. Downright humiliating. And it was also physically painful. I had always loved to throw the football. I'd thrown thousands of spirals on playgrounds, parking lots, and suburban cul-de-sacs. But how could I throw a spiral now if I couldn't even get the snap? And since most players on the team played both ways (offense and defense), that meant the first team offensive line was also the first team defensive line. And Coach Mackentire didn't feel the need to adjust things so that I could run the second team offense with the protection of at least a few of the starters on the offensive line. So nothing got accomplished. The first team defense never improved because they were never challenged, and the second team offense never got any better because we couldn't even execute the center to quarterback exchange. Whatever grandiose notions I had about being a football player were quickly disabused. I came to despise my first love. I hated football now. And I hated the fact that I now hated it.

But at least there was Tom.

Tom Braxton was not only the best player on the team, not only a great quarterback and a great leader, but he was also my best friend. At this "reform school," where I was truly surrounded by truly troubled teens, Tom was an oasis of normality, a beacon of light in a literal wilderness of fear and uncertainty. Neither of us belonged at *Anneewakee*, and as soon as we met we bonded over this unspoken but obvious truth. But besides that, Tom was one of the few people there who actually understood anything about sports. It was incredibly refreshing to be able to talk to somebody who knew as much about sports as I did. And yet our friendship revolved around much more than that. Tom's intellect, loyalty, and encouragement helped me to endure two of the most difficult years of my life. We had both been unjustly thrown into a sea of madness, and we found brotherhood in helping each other keep our sanity.

And the fact that Tom was such a great quarterback also caused me to look up to him. At practice he took me under his wing, teaching me everything he could about the position. He constantly encouraged me. He convinced me that I was actually capable of leading the team if he should ever become injured. Even though it wasn't true, Tom made me believe that I was actually a good quarterback. Rather than being embarrassed by me, Tom stood up for me. Tom commanded the respect of the entire team, and since he accepted me everyone else accepted me too (or at least they didn't fuck with me.) Such kindness, loyalty, and leadership are rare things in this world. Believe me.

Tom also helped save my life, or at least my health. During practices I always dreaded the one-on-one "shotgun" tackling drills that the coaches would arbitrarily decide to conduct. The team would be divided into two opposing single file lines, with twin "dummy bags" set two yards apart in between. A coach would toss the football to one player, who would then try to run directly over the opposing player, who would simultaneously attempt to slam the ball carrier directly on his back. Since the "dummy bags" were set up only two yards apart, there was no way to rely on speed or agility to dodge the tackler or to tackle the ball carrier without making full-fledged contact. This drill petrified me because the smallest guy on the team could wind up going against the biggest guy on the team. And since the drill was designed specifically for contact and power, my maneuverability gave me no advantage. Being the weakest guy on the team, I was always significantly outmatched.

I no longer possessed the bravado of my elementary schoolyard days. I was terrified of this segment of practice, and I always tried to find a way to get out of it. There was only one hope of evading it. Whenever I sensed that the tackling drills were approaching, I would ask one of the coaches if Tom and I could go warm up our arms. And since the tackling drills were always the last thing we did before we scrimmaged, the coaches would usually think this was a legitimate and natural request. This scheme worked for a little while, but not for long. It soon became obvious what I was up to, and that made the coaches all the more determined to toughen me up by making me participate in these God-forsaken gladiatorial contests. So I started asking Tom to ask the coaches if we could loosen up our arms, because I knew the coaches would respect Tom. And that worked for a little while, until the coaches figured out that I was employing Tom as a surrogate, which made them even more determined to include me in every tackling drill possible. After all, it wasn't like there was any real need to preserve the health or life of a 5'11," 150 pound second string QB with the heart of the cowardly lion – a kid who was obviously of no significant use to the team in any way, shape, or form.

So that's what all my childhood football dreams had become – a miserable existence of simply trying to endure each practice with my bones intact and my cognitive faculties relatively unaltered.

But as cowardly as I was, I was still an athlete, a competitor, a skinny kid who may have hated tackling drills but who would prove his mettle elsewhere. So I would try to win every sprint. I would try to be first whenever we ran laps. And I would do my best to embarrass anyone I could in any drills that involved pure skill rather than head to head contact. But rather than ingratiating me to my teammates, this only made them more determined to kick my ass when it was time for tackling.

And so it went, practice after practice – praying each day that the coaches would decide not to conduct tackling drills that particular afternoon. And amidst the terror I would find moments of joy whenever Tom and I were allowed to warm up our arms, when I would then just be a kid again, throwing spirals with my best friend and pretending I was Roger Staubach. And Tom would make me believe that I *could* be Roger Staubach.

And then there were the games. There were those mystical Friday night lights. There was a football field bathed in an effulgent flood, a radiant oval island in the middle of a black Florida panhandle wilderness. There were the glistening helmets and the freshly manicured grass that shimmered in the nighttime anticipation of the oncoming dew. And there were the bleachers, which held no more than a few hundred people on a good night. And we would gather in the end zone, behind a large paper sign that read: *"Go Warriors!"* And we would run through the sign. And the night was brighter than noon. And we were football players. And *I* was a football player. And God how I loved that part of it.

And tonight we were playing *Academy Prep*. And they were good. Damn good. Better than any team we had played before. And we hadn't won a game all season. And we hadn't even been close to winning a game all season.

And opposing teams always seemed to be possessed of extra motivation when they played us. They all seemed to relish beating the crap out of us, even though doing so was really no great feat. Coach Mackentire finally explained why these teams were so motivated to humiliate us. You see, our competitors were told that our school was basically a juvenile detention center, and that we were all criminals and rapists and drug addicts and essentially the scum of the earth – which of course was only partially true. So the opposing coaches would tell their teams that we were dirty players, that we were horrible human beings, and that we deserved a good ass kicking on the field. And since this was long before the prevalence of the internet the opposing players had no way to verify whether or not any of this was true. And the aggressive nature of football being what it is, I don't think any of the opposing players were too concerned about dispelling the information their coaches were feeding them. As far as they were concerned, we were the bad guys and we deserved what was coming to us.

And on this particular Friday night it was apparent that *Academy Prep*'s coaches had really driven the point home in their pre-game pep talk. They were undefeated, and they had a running back that would eventually play football for the *Naval Academy*. We were woefully outmatched, even more so than usual. Their team was playing with viciousness, as if they were fighting a holy crusade where one's heavenly crowns were determined by the amount of pain one inflicted upon the infidels. Tom could barely execute a handoff, much less have time in the pocket to pass. They were killing him. They were killing us. And they were deriving sadistic pleasure from it.

I watched helplessly from the sidelines, as always. But there was something about these actual games that neutralized my fear, at least to a degree. I wanted to play. I wanted to get in the game, at least for a few snaps. And I would usually sidle up to Coach about once each quarter and ask: "Coach, do you want me to go in and give Tom a rest for a few plays?" And sometimes, since there was never any real chance of us winning anyway, Coach would actually send me into the game for a play or two. And since I would receive the snap from the starting center and have the protection of the first string offensive line, then I would have no trouble executing one of the routine handoffs that was always called when I was in the game. And as simple of a task as it was, I nevertheless enjoyed it. To command the huddle, to call the play, and then to execute that play in a real game – as simple as it may have been – well, this always made me love football again.

But Coach would never let me do more than hand the ball off. My favorite play was the option, and I begged Coach to let me run the option play just once. Growing up, when I wasn't Roger Staubach throwing touchdown passes to Golden Richards, I pretended to be Walter Lewis running the Wishbone option offense for the Alabama Crimson Tide. And I knew I could run the option in a real game. The option played to my strengths – speed and agility. I knew how to fake the handoff to the fullback, read the defensive end, feign and juke, and either pitch or keep the ball. I wanted to run the option play so badly, just once, in real time. But Coach Mckentire always said no. (What is it about parents and coaches and teachers that cause them to never give you a chance to do the very things they're supposedly preparing you to do?)

I also wanted to throw a pass in a real game. So on one occasion that's exactly what I tried to do. We were losing to some team by four touchdowns, and Coach Mckentire put me in to give Tom a break. He told me to call "right 22 blast," a routine run play where I would simply hand the ball off to the tailback. But I had other ideas. I decided I would catch the defense and everyone else off guard by throwing a deep post pattern from a play action fake. No one would expect it. I would throw a touchdown pass and be a hero, at least for a moment. So in the huddle, instead of calling "right 22 blast," I called "right 22 blast, play action post." Then I broke the huddle by saying, *"ready...!"* And nine others responded *"break!"* And we sprinted up to the line of scrimmage. I was poised to throw my TD pass.

But something wasn't right. I didn't see our fullback behind me. Where was he? What the hell was he doing? And then I saw him running toward the sidelines, frantically signaling for a time out. And then I heard the referee blow his whistle. And then I saw our fullback pointing at me and yelling, "Coach, he was calling the wrong play! He was trying to change the play Coach! He was changing the play Coach!"

The son-of-a-bitch. Yeah, I was changing the play. I was trying to score a damn touchdown! There were three minutes left in the fourth quarter. We were losing by 28 points. What the hell did it matter if I was changing the play?!

But Coach didn't yell at me. He just took me out and put Tom back in. It's funny how you can come so close to realizing visions of glory only to have some jackass fuck it all up. But sports are a microcosm of life, and excuses are as valuable as fool's gold. Perhaps I would somehow have another chance to do something worthwhile in a football game. I could always hope. But hope is a dangerous thing.

So on this particular Friday night – as *Academy Prep* beat us up and down the field, and as I watched by best fried valiantly pull himself up from the turf time and time again – I sidled up to Coach and asked: "Coach, do you want me to give Tom a breather?"

He shoved me out of the way. "Sit down son!" he yelled, loudly enough for everyone to hear. "They're a pack of wolves! They'll eat you alive, son! They'll eat you alive! Take your helmet off and go sit down!"

My teammates snickered, stifling their guffaws only because they didn't want to invoke the ire of the assistant coaches. People in the stands laughed raucously. Everyone had heard it. They were slapping their knees and pointing at me, asking one other if they'd heard what Coach had said. It was a grand joke, and I was the butt of it. I was humiliated.

In the locker room, at halftime, the "trainer" walked around offering us cups of Gatorade from a tray. Coach Mckentire came in and knocked the tray out of his hands, sending a shower of Gatorade across the room.

"You all don't deserve any goddamn Gatorade!" he said. "You're playing like a bunch of pussies! They think you're criminals but you're just pussies! I wish I *did* have a team of criminals right now! But all I have is a team full of worthless pussies!"

I hadn't done anything to deserve or not deserve Gatorade. But I couldn't really see why my teammates didn't deserve any. I mean, they were out there truly doing their best against a private prep-school football factory whose players had obviously been led to believe that this was not so much a football game as a battle of good against evil, right against wrong, God against the devil. And if *Academy Prep* represented justice then the universe was more than just bending towards justice, it was downright prostrating before it.

Coach Mckentire's motivational halftime speech didn't seem to help much in the second half. We continued to get our asses kicked. And although Tom continued to take a beating, I didn't dare ask Coach if I could relieve him for a few plays. So I just stood on the sidelines, contemplating the unfairness and cruelty of life.

I think the score was something like 38-0 about midway through the fourth quarter when Coach Hennings, the special teams coach, came over to me.

"Do you want to return the kickoff?"

"Sir?"

"Do you want to *run back the kickoff?!* I'm not gonna ask you again!"

"Yessir! I can do it!"

"I know you can son. Just do two things, *two things…*"

"Yessir!"

"First of all, *catch the ball*. Secondly, *don't fumble the ball*. And other than that, just use your speed and run like hell!"

"Yessir!"

I couldn't believe it. Was this assistant coach playing a joke on me? I'd never even considered the possibility of running back a kickoff. But hell, I could do this! I *was* fast, and I wasn't scared of confronting bigger, stronger, but less agile tacklers in open space, where I could use my speed and quickness to at least ensure they wouldn't get a solid hit on me.

"When do I go in Coach?"

"Now son, right after this two point conversion."

I was too excited to even consider the fact that *Academy Prep* had been going for two all night long. Up by five touchdowns, and here they were again, still going for the two point conversion instead of kicking the extra point. Talk about disrespect! But this insult by their team was a million miles from my consciousness at the time. I was about to return the kickoff, and I was fully committed to the task at hand. I was either gonna score or be carried off the field on a stretcher. And I didn't care which, as long as I didn't fumble. This was my moment.

"Now coach?!"

"Yes! Now! Get in there! Don't fumble! Use that speed and do what you know how to do!"

I sprinted from the sidelines, mouthpiece in place and chinstrap fastened. This is how heroes are made. My heart was racing. My mind surged with visions of glory: I was going to receive the kickoff, tucking the ball in my arm and then deftly eluding potential tacklers as I raced 80 or 90 yards for a touchdown. It wouldn't matter that my touchdown would have little bearing on the outcome of the game. What would matter is that my teammates would pile on top of me in congratulatory celebration. I would earn their respect, gain their approval, prove that I was not a coward after all. And even if I didn't reach the end zone, I would run with courage, securing the ball without fumbling as I was crushed to the turf. Either way I would prove that I was indeed a *real* football player.

These were the thoughts that flooded my soul as I raced onto the field. Whatever fears I had were surpassed by the thrill of the opportunity that lay before me. This was something I could do! And I was all too ready to do it!

And that's when I heard it. As I was halfway onto the field, sprinting to the spot from which I would launch my run to glory, coach Mckentire's stentorian voice once again echoed through the Florida night for all to hear:

"What the hell is he doing?! Get him off the field! Who sent him out there? They'll kill him! They'll kill him! Get his goddamn ass off the field! Get him off the field!"

I ignored it. After all, Coach wasn't even talking to me; he was talking to somebody else – *everybody* else. But he wasn't specifically addressing me. So I kept running onto the field to take my spot. The way I reasoned it, Coach Hennings was the one who had given me the instructions, and I was going to follow those instructions. I couldn't disobey a coach.

And then I heard it again: "What's he doing?! Get him off the field! Get his ass off the field! Now! They're wolves! They're a pack of wolves! They'll kill him!"

I looked to the sidelines and saw Coach Hennings waving me back over. In fact, it seemed like everyone present that night was waving me back over – teammates, coaches, fans, and anyone within the glow of those field light beams. It seemed like the entire Florida panhandle was screaming at me in unison: "Get off the field! You're not a football player! You'll get hurt! You're wasting our time! GET OFF THE FIELD!"

I had endured embarrassment, disappointment, and shame on this football team. And I don't mean *collective* embarrassment, disappointment, and shame – I mean *personal* embarrassment, disappointment, and shame. And there is a significant difference, I can assure you. The thing I had once loved most had now been tormenting me in unimaginable ways. And this was the lowest moment of all, the worst humiliation, the cruelest disappointment. Love will indeed break your heart.

You do your best to control what you can control, to give yourself a fighting chance, to maintain hope that an opportunity will come your way. And then life and the bastards of life strip it all away from you. At least that's how it feels sometimes. And that's certainly how I felt right then, at that moment, on that Friday night under those unremitting lights.

So I jogged back to the sidelines and took a seat on the bench, watching the final minutes tick away, wishing I was invisible. I was no longer just disappointed; I was pissed off. I was sick and tired of being treated like this. I was sick of the fact that these coaches were more than happy to subject me to their sadistic tackling drills but they weren't willing to let me see real playing time in real games where I might actually have a chance of making a positive contribution. I was seething inside. I was fed up. But I was also helpless. There was absolutely nothing I could do about it. I could only sit there on the bench, stewing in rage, wallowing in self-pity and despair, wishing I could crawl away somewhere and hide.

Suddenly, I noticed a commotion on our sideline. I stood up to see what was happening. It was Coach Mckentire. He was apoplectic, scurrying up and down the sidelines screaming instructions to each and every player:

"*DO NOT* SHAKE THEIR HANDS! *DO NOT* SHAKE THEIR HANDS! GO STRAIGHT TO THE LOCKER ROOM! *STRAIGHT* TO THE LOCKER ROOM! *DO NOT* SHAKE THEIR HANDS! DO YOU UNDERSTAND?! *STRAIGHT* TO THE LOCKER ROOM!!! IF THEY WANT TO GO FOR TWO EVERY TIME THEN THEY CAN KISS MY ASS! *DON'T SHAKE THEIR HANDS!*"

Coach Mckentire was right. That was pretty unsportsmanlike of them to go for two after every touchdown. In fact, it was *really* poor sportsmanship, even if they did think we were criminals. And sportsmanship was very important to me. My little league soccer coaches, my coaches at basketball camp – and most of all, my father – had always emphasized the importance of principle, virtue, fairness, and integrity in athletic competition. If sport wasn't about sportsmanship, then what was the point? And if sports didn't teach you about life and how to live it, then what was the purpose of all the sweat and struggle and heartache and pain?

So there I was on the sidelines, seething in self-pity as the seconds ticked off the clock – full of resentment, bitterness, and rage. I had been a laughingstock on more than one occasion, and tonight I had experienced the ultimate disappointment and despair. But what was worse was that nobody seemed to care. My feelings didn't seem to matter. My very existence didn't seem to matter.

And as I watched Coach Mckentire's red-faced jowls spew "*DO NOT* shake their hands," I suddenly knew exactly what I would do. I would march across the field and shake hands with those motherfuckers. I would show *Academy Prep* – and more importantly, I would show Coach Mckentire and every teammate and every fan and everyone else who laughed at me or ignored me – what true sportsmanship is. This was one play that I could call all by myself, and nobody could blow the whistle or call a time out to stop it. Fuck all of y'all! I'll show you!

And that's just what I did. The clock hit zero and my teammates headed straight for the locker room. And I headed straight across the field to shake hands with the *Academy Prep* bastards that had beaten us to a pulp and rubbed our faces in it all night long. And as I walked towards them, with my helmet still on to hide the tears that were streaming down my face – tears of frustration and anger and guilt and shame – they started running towards me. At first I thought they were about to kill me, beat me unconscious, the one criminal they could lay hands on and exact vengeance from. But suddenly they were hugging me, patting me on the back, trying to lift me up on their shoulders.

Their whole team was gathering around me, and all I could say through my tears was, "I'm sorry. I'm so sorry."

"You're the best player on your team!" said one *Academy Prep* player. "You're a hero! You're the greatest player on your team! You're the greatest player on your team!"

"I'm so sorry," I stammered. "They didn't mean it. I promise you they didn't mean it. I'm so sorry."

I doubt if anything I said was intelligible to them through my sobs. And I wondered why in the hell I was apologizing to these bastards that had taken such great pleasure in pulverizing and disrespecting us for the past three hours.

And before I could make any sense of what I was saying or doing, or what they were saying or doing, my head was suddenly wrenched around by my facemask. Coach Hennings was jerking me away from the *Academy Prep* players and dragging me off the field as he shouted in my ear: "We're a *team*! A *team* goddammit! You do what the *team* does! Do you understand me! Who in the hell do you think you are?! You do what the *team* does!"

He dragged me into the locker room and that was it. Nobody said anything to me, other than a couple of guys who walked by and snarled the same sentiment as Coach Hennings, "This is a *team*! You let down the *team* man. You let down the *team*!"

I still don't know how to describe what I felt as I showered and changed clothes in the locker room that night. I guess I knew that I had done the right thing, but I also knew that I had done the right thing for a lot of the wrong reasons. And if you do the right thing for the wrong reasons, how right can it really be?

I don't know why I didn't think about Tom throughout the ordeal. He was certainly there when it happened. He was the leader of our team. He was my best friend. But I guess some things you just have to do on your own, and you have to live with the decisions you make by yourself. Maybe Tom knew that it was just something that I'd had to do alone. Maybe he knew that he had to sit back and let me act this one out all by myself. Or maybe, knowing me as well as he did, he knew that my actions were tainted with vengeance, pride, self-righteousness, and hypocrisy. And perhaps, understandably, he didn't want anything to do with my moral grandstanding.

I've only had a few truly great friends in my life (I can count them on one hand), and they're all able to sense my bullshit from a mile away. I hate them for it, and I love them for it. Tom has remained one of my best friends throughout the years; and his loyalty, kindness, and encouragement have helped me make it through many other difficult times in my life. He will always be as close as a brother to me.

At practice the following Monday, Coach Hennings came up to me and apologized:

"I'm sorry for what I said, and for what I did. I was wrong, and what you did was right. And I want to tell you something: *Always* follow your convictions. *Always* follow your convictions. Remember that."

I always appreciated what Coach Hennings said, and I have remembered it – even if I haven't always heeded it. I never harbored any ill will towards Coach Hennings. He was simply caught up in a moment of passion, as was I. And we each reacted the only way we knew how to at the time.

There is no glorious ending to this tale. I never got to run the option play or throw a pass in a game. I never got to return a kickoff. I never became a great football player. And unlike H.G. Bissinger's story of *Friday Night Lights*, mine is not a story of valiance in defeat. I just kept going to practice, kept trying to evade the tackling drills, and kept handing the ball off on the rare occasions when Coach decided to put me in a game. And I never played football again after that one season.

*   *   *

Years later, when I had dropped out of college and was floundering between dead end jobs, dead end relationships, and living a dead end lifestyle, I received this letter in the mail. It was from the parent of one of the *Academy Prep* football players:

Dear Sir,

I am a Sunday school teacher. I am also the father of one of the Academy Prep football players that played against your Anneewakee Warriors team a few years ago. I have often talked about your example of courage, integrity, and sportsmanship in my Sunday school class. I hope that the young people I teach will be inspired by the brave stance you took when you crossed the field alone to shake hands with our team. I can tell you that I and many of the other parents in the stands that night had tears in our eyes after watching what you did. It was one of the most inspiring things I've ever witnessed. I wanted to write to you and thank you for your wonderful example. I hope that life is treating you well.

Sincerely,
Allen Owen

I don't know how Mr. Owen found my address or why his letter arrived to me at that particular time in my life. But I wept when I read it. (Yes, I've cried a lot in my life.) I wept with guilt and shame, not only because this dear man had no idea what my true motivation had been when I crossed the field that night, but also because at the time of receiving his letter I was using drugs, selling drugs, getting girls pregnant, and basically doing everything that a Sunday school teacher should tell their students *not* to do.

But I also wept because I realized that his precious letter had come from God. Amazingly enough I was actually a professing Christian at the time – albeit a woefully fallen Christian. And Mr. Owen's letter was a divine voice that reminded me that my life still had value, that my life could still serve a purpose, that my life could still somehow touch others in a positive and meaningful way.

So I sat there that afternoon and read that letter over and over again. And I cried, and I prayed, and I writhed in guilt and hope and shame and faith and sorrow and gratitude. I was flooded with emotions. But mostly I was overwhelmed because somebody saw something good in me and had cared enough to take the time to let me know it. Somebody had shown me that my existence actually mattered after all.

The truth is that I had basically forgotten about what had occurred that night on that high school football field in Florida. But someone had remembered, and for some reason they had chosen to remind me at a time in my life when I desperately needed reminding. I saved that letter. And from time to time I pull it out and read it again, because sometimes I still need to be reminded that my life matters.

So that is the story of a paper hero – the story of a boy who prayed to become a football player, and who became a Christian instead, and who then became an even greater sinner, and who was then reminded that he was created for good, and who has struggled ever since to live accordingly.

God is present in friends, and strangers, and letters, and foes. God is present in disappointments and defeats and broken hearts. And God is present with paper heroes that fight windmills under Friday night lights.

By
GEBRE MENFES KIDUS
QB #15

[This story is dedicated to my dear friend and brother, Thomas Braxton Bryant IV, QB #12]

216. ~WAR IS HELL ~

You held no malice
For those you killed
It was simply honor
Your duty to fulfill

But they still haunt you
Those stares of death
Those anguished faces
Those dying breaths

If only they knew
You killed without hate
They might forgive you
From beyond the grave

But children are fatherless
And widows now grieve
You slaughtered their loved ones
For god and country

In weeping and wailing
All joy has been drowned
Because you followed orders
And shot them down

But your bullets weren't hateful
So please sleep well
And if they still haunt you
Just tell them, "War is hell"

217. ~ CHILD ~

I saw a little boy today. He was such a happy little boy. I guessed him to be about three years old. He was ambling around the restaurant where I sat reading and sipping my tea. He made the happiest sounds. Not screaming or yelling or crying. Just happy sounds of wonderment and excited curiosity. Sounds of joy. I smiled at him and waved, and he laughed and ran and hid behind his father's leg.

I couldn't stop watching that little boy. And as I watched him, I noticed after a while that there were tears on my face. I didn't know why at first. But then I realized I was crying because for that innocent child the world was still good. Life was still full of hope and promise and happiness and contentment. And I didn't want anything to corrupt such pure joy and pure love. I feared for him. My heart broke for him. Why couldn't life always be this way for him? Why must such innocence and peace be inevitably assaulted?

So I prayed to God for that small boy. I prayed that his happiness would always be preserved. I prayed for God to protect that little boy's heart, mind, and soul from all the evil that this world will throw at him. I prayed for that little boy with tears on my face, and in doing so I prayed for all children everywhere. I prayed for all humanity in fact, because somehow I saw all mankind wrapped up in that single child.

Perhaps I also recognized myself in that little boy. I too was once like him – happy and curious and invulnerable in my Papa's protective presence. And oh how badly I want to still be a little boy, untainted by sin and evil and heartache and loss and disillusionment and guilt and death. But alas, we must grow up. I don't know how any of us do it really. I guess I'm still trying to grow up. I guess I'm still fighting *having* to grow up. And as I fight the inevitable, my own children are growing up right before me; and it seems that the evanescence of their youth is even more fleeting than was my own.

Oh how thankful I am for Our Father in heaven who loves all of His children. In God's presence that's all we need to be: children clinging to Him – finding uncorrupted security, wonderment, and joy in His loving embrace. This is the only truth I know that enables me to understand anything else. It's the only truth that preserves my hope. It's the only way I can make any sense out of the juxtaposition of such innocence with such cruelty.

I think about how much Jesus loved the little children. Whatever I felt today as I watched that dear little boy was but an infinitesimal fraction of the divine pathos that Christ feels for us all. So I wept for the child, I prayed for the child, because I am the child.

218. ~ RELIGION ~

Religion is an interesting thing: powerful, beautiful, and saving when true – but destructive, divisive, and deadly when false.

219. ~ PRAGMATISM and PACIFISM ~

Ideals are rarely practical; but when we discard ideals because they aren't practical, then we succumb to the weak-mindedness of pragmatism. And the strongest evidence of pragmatism's folly is the ironic fact that it simply does not work.

Pacifism is ridiculed and dismissed as a naïve ideal that is neither realistic nor pragmatic. But as a pacifist, I simply ask: "How successful have violence and war been? Has violence brought an end to all wars? Has war brought an end to all violence?"

In reality, what one usually means by "impractical" is that it is *very difficult*. And all truly noble ideals are difficult to maintain and achieve. So, those who espouse the ideals of pacifism are not naïve, but instead courageous and resolute. And those who ridicule pacifism as unrealistic are either lazy or uncreative; or, perhaps even worse, they are evil.

The pragmatism of Machiavelli has only brought suffering, chaos, and cruelty to the world. But the nonviolent witness of the early Christian martyrs inspired the spread and growth of the Christian Faith. And the two greatest revolutionary social movements of the twentieth century were modeled after the nonviolent example of Our Lord Jesus Christ: Gandhi's nonviolent revolution that led India to independence from British rule, and the American Civil Rights movement which was guided by Dr. Martin Luther King's philosophy of nonviolent direct social action.

In following Christ we do not ask, *"Is it expedient? Will it work? Is it feasible? Is it safe?"* Instead we simply ask, *"Is it Christian?"*

220. ~ LIGHT and DARKNESS ~

Light does not coexist with darkness. Any attempt to mix light with darkness only brings cloudiness, haze, distortion, and confusion. The Light of God came into the world, but the world preferred the darkness. (St. John 3:19) Light will either draw you to it or repel you from it. Light is pleasing to some and offensive to others. But one thing about light is that it will always find you out. A person who closes the blinds and draws the curtains tight doesn't make the sun go away; they only deprive themselves of the sun's benefits. And the Light that is shunned today will become the fire that burns tomorrow.

"I am the light of the world. He who follows Me shall not walk in darkness, but have the light of life." [St. John 8:12]

"God is light, and in Him there is no darkness at all."
[I John 1:5]

"I came to send fire on the earth,
and how I wish it were already kindled!"
[St. Luke 12:49]

221. ~ TRUTH OVER CONFORMITY ~

Have the courage to accept the truth as it is revealed to you at different stages in your life. Choosing truth over the false security of conformity to the crowd, social acceptance, or financial/career stability is always a brave and difficult thing. But it is better to suffer in spiritual freedom than to be comfortably enslaved.

222. ~ THE STRUGGLE and RESULT of SPIRITUAL REVOLUTION ~

The *result* of spiritual revolution will be mental enlightenment, physical health, emotional peace, and social justice. But the *struggle* of spiritual revolution will be accompanied by pain, agony, frustration, and discouragement. 400 years of bondage. 40 years in the wilderness. 3 days in the grave. But in the end, eternal life!

223. ~ VAIN REBELLION ~

If your rebellion doesn't lead you to love God and love your fellow man, then your revolution is in vain. The wicked power structures of this world are sustained by useful idiots who steadily fortify Babylon's walls while believing they are engaged in revolutionary acts.

224. ~ AGAINST AN OSTENSIBLE PEACE ~

Any ostensible peace that relies upon the threat of violence is no peace at all. Violent power can sustain social order, but it cannot bring about societal peace. In an orderly manner, slaves were kidnapped and sold. In an orderly manner, Jews were systematically exterminated. And in an orderly manner, babies are routinely aborted.

But such orderly evils should never be confused for social justice and authentic peace. True peace often means – in fact, often requires – social disorder.

225. ~ CEASELESS LOVE ~

God never ceases to pursue those He loves. And He loves us all. He loves all of us all of the time. Regardless of how many times we scorn our Divine Lover, regardless of how often we are unfaithful to Him, regardless of how frequently we betray Him by running into the arms of idols – Our Lord nevertheless continues to reach out to us with eternal arms of unconditional love. We can never escape His infinite mercy. We can never flee from the presence of His grace. His love is always with us. Please know this. Please find comfort in this.

226. ~ IRREPRESSIBLE ~

Divine Truth cannot be suppressed; it can only be denied, ignored, and refused.

227. ~ WHY I BELIEVE IN GOD ~

I believe in God for the same reason that I believe in air. I breathe, so I know that air exists. I exist, thus I know that God *is*.

228. ~ SANITY ~

Not only is sanity not a prerequisite for sainthood, but it may actually be an impediment. If we can look at all the injustice, inhumanity, and evil in this world and not go a little crazy, then I doubt if we'll be at home in heaven. If this is a sane world, then I pray that God would grant me the blessing of insanity.

229. ~ THE LOGIC of JUSTIFIABLE VIOLENCE ~

"War and violence are not good, but they are sometimes necessary to secure peace and defend the innocent."

This is the fundamental mindset of those who argue that war and violence are sometimes justifiable.

But to be consistent one must apply this same reasoning to other moral dilemmas. For example, one could also argue that a man with starving children would be justified in murdering another person and feeding their body to his children if that were the only source of food that would preserve their children's lives. One could also argue that rape would be justifiable if rape were the only means of preserving and perpetuating the human race. One could also argue that abortion is justifiable in order to control the population and thereby prevent people from dying from starvation. (And in fact we see the abortion supporters making this very argument constantly.)

I think any true Christian would be appalled by these horrific justifications for evil. But for some reason, when it comes to war and defensive killing, we easily fabricate the same insidious rationalizations.

230. ~ "TROUBLED" ~

Growing up they said I was "troubled." They said I was "disturbed." And they convinced me that this was a bad thing. But thanks to God, I now know better; because those who can experience so much suffering and remain unaffected, those who can look at all the injustice in the world and remain undisturbed — well, I think they are the ones who are actually in need of psychological examination. If spiritual faith and a passion for justice mean that one is emotionally "troubled" or psychologically "disturbed," then I pray to God that I'm never cured.

231. ~ PRIORITIZING HIS WILL ABOVE OUR OWN WILL ~

As Christians, we too often concern ourselves only with the lawfully permissible rather than striving for the perfect will of God. We fall prey to a worldly mindset of "my rights" rather than adopting the Christian mindset of self-denial and sacrificial obedience. For example:

- "She was unfaithful in our marriage, so I had a right to a divorce."
- "He attacked me first, so I had a right to hit him back."
- "I would have died if I didn't have the abortion, so I had a right to kill the baby."
- "This is my country, and I have a right to join the military and kill my enemies."
- "We have a right to enjoy sex without having children, so we have a right to use artificial birth control."

We can always manufacture justifications to support our own welfare, our own pleasure, and our own will. And we can always find select Bible verses or Church laws that we can twist to support our own individual agendas. But such a mindset is rooted in self-centeredness and legalism. In calling us to take up our cross and follow Him, Christ calls us to prioritize His will above our own will. He calls us to deny ourselves for the sake of others. He calls us to forsake our own temporal rights in order to pursue the eternal kingdom of God.

It is no easy thing to be a Christian. (And I confess that I am a Christian more by profession than by practice. May God have mercy on me.) But we have to understand that it is impossible to follow Christ while clinging to our own self-interests and our own individual and collective "rights." The only rights we have as Christians are the right to love God with all of our hearts and to love our neighbors as ourselves. And our enemies are no less our neighbors than are our own friends and family.

The Gospel is not a blueprint for effective government, individual security, or social order. The Gospel is the radical and paradoxical truth that by losing our lives we will gain them, and that by dying with Christ we will be raised to eternal life.

232. ~ CASUALTIES ~

Justice and compassion are too often the casualties of comfort and convenience.

233. ~ EQUALLY LOST / EQUALLY SAVED ~

Let us not have the mind of the Pharisee, looking at others and thinking, "They are lost." Rather, let us have the heart of the Publican who beat his breast and cried out, *"Lord have mercy on me, a sinner." [St. Luke 18:10-14]*

The Gospel is not about saying, "I am saved and you are lost." The Gospel is about recognizing that we are all equally lost and yet Christ came to equally save.

234. ~ NEVER TRUST... ~

Never trust anyone who presumes to speak for an entire race, an entire gender, or an entire religion. Not all Black people support Barack Obama, not all women support abortion, and not all Christians support the Pope. Nothing is more condescending and prejudicial than politicians and media pundits assuming that an entire group of people shares a monolithic political or social agenda.

235. ~ THE CHOICE of SUFFERING ~

The suffering I endure is usually of my own making, not of my own choosing. If I would choose to suffer, perhaps I would find true peace and possibly ease the suffering of others. Shall I seek to be resurrected without being crucified? I am not greater than God.

"Lord Jesus Christ, Son of God, have mercy on me, a sinner."

236. ~ SPLINTERS and SCARS ~

They enjoy their celebrations and parties while their loved ones struggle. They live for themselves while their neighbors suffer. They tighten their fists and close their hearts, preserving their wealth at the expense of others. They forsake their own families for the pleasures of Babylon. They heap wealth upon themselves while heaping judgment on their brothers.

But we must love them; we must forgive them; we must pray for them; and yes, if they come to us we must embrace them. But we are not obliged to side with them; for we must attend to the laments of the poor, the oppressed, and the abused that suffer from the heartless negligence of those who have the means to help them but refuse to do so. (Cf. St. Matthew 25:40)

The uncharitable have chosen their reward, and we have chosen ours. Let them cling to their dollars until they become ashes in their hands. But let us cling to the Cross and trust that it will carry us into eternity. Let us not trade our splinters and scars for their profits or their approval.

Though we may always share their familial blood, they may not always share their love. And through much heartbreak and pain I have come to know this truth: there is a spiritual bond that is truer than DNA, and there is a brotherly love that is stronger than heredity. It is a painful truth to bear, but the crosses we gladly endure will inevitably bring us blessings.

"Do not withhold good from those who deserve it when it is in your power to help them." [Proverbs 3:27]

"Whoever has the ability to remedy the suffering of others, but chooses rather to withhold aid out of selfish motives, may properly be judged the equivalent of a murderer." ~ St. Basil the Great ~

237. ~ PREDATORS and PREY ~

Why do you elect predators and then complain when they make you their prey?

238. ~ SIGNIFICANT PROCLAMATIONS ~

I have been criticized for my unequivocal defense of pacifism. I have been criticized for my frequent condemnations of abortion. And I have been criticized for my proclamations of Orthodox truth.

Well, I'm only one voice. I'm just a pilgrim passing through this terrestrial vale. And I can't think of anything more important to speak of than Peace, Life, and the Orthodox Christian Faith. If you know of something more significant, please let me know.

239. ~ LOVE WITHOUT BLOOD ~

If there is no struggle, no suffering, no heartache, and no pain, then don't call it love. Love without blood is mere sentiment.

240. ~ HONOR ~

I honor Saints, not soldiers.
I honor the dead who live,
not those who live to bring death.

I honor martyrdom, not militancy.
I honor those who lay down their own lives,
not those who cut down the lives of others.

I honor prophets, not politicians.
I honor those who die for Truth,
not those who kill for lies.

I honor the Faith, not the flag.
I honor those whose arms carry the Cross of life,
not those who arm themselves with weapons of death.

I honor the Gospel, not the government.
I honor those who cling to Christ,
not those who cling to guns, bombs, armies, and war.

I honor peace, not pragmatism.
I honor that which conforms to life and love,
not that which is destructive, deadly, demonic, and dishonorable.

This is what I honor.
And for this I am called a "dishonorable man."

241. ~ CEMETERY BELLY ~

A healthy tree
bears beautiful berries.
Don't make a fruitful womb
a cemetery belly.

242. ~ DON'T DISMISS, DON'T DISPARAGE ~

Please don't dismiss the panhandler as lazy and irresponsible. Don't disparage the destitute, the drunkard, and the drug addict as indolent and immoral. Unless you have been forced to beg or forced to sleep on the street, then you don't know what hard work it really is. And if you have never had to struggle against the bondage of addictions, then you will never know what intense labor it truly entails. All of us have made bad choices in our lives, and the only reason we survived our mistakes is because of the love of true friends and family who helped us up whenever we fell. So let's be careful about judging our neighbors in their misery and suffering. Christ is no less present in the homeless man, the prostitute, or the addict than He is in the icons we venerate on Sunday.

243. ~ THE CONFUSION of MAN ~

Man lives according to his own desires and rationale, ignoring the Creator's commands to the detriment of his own soul. Seeking human solutions rather than spiritual solutions, humanity tortures itself. People wage war, enslave their fellow man, give themselves over to all manner of addictions, plunder and oppress, slaughter the unborn, gorge on luxury and greed, and defile and pollute both the planet and themselves in the process. And then they scratch their befuddled heads and act shocked at all the misery that they themselves have created.

244. ~ PRIDE and SHAME ~

The young unwed girl approaches her family with trepidation and fear and announces that she is pregnant. Her news is received with disappointment and sorrow. There is no rejoicing, no celebration, no praise. The family members hang their heads and try to hide the shame they feel. Observing the scene, one would think that this news of life was in fact news of a tragic death.

But the young girl's brother approaches the family with enthusiasm and pride and announces that he is joining the military and marching off to war. His news is received with great happiness. There is celebration, joy, and praise. The family members do not try to hide the pride they feel. Observing the scene, one would think that this news of violence and killing was in fact news of the birth of a child.

The unwed mother who brings forth life is somehow scorned with shame, but the young man who brings forth death is somehow praised. And far too many professing Christians contribute to this madness.

245. ~ PRAYERS and TEARS ~

Let us not sow prayers of condescension or shed tears of judgmental pity, saying, "Lord, help that poor lost sinner." Instead, let us sow prayers of mercy and tears of true compassion, realizing that every man's suffering is in some sense our own, that every person's pain and weakness are also ours. The sins of the world are our sins, and darkness and depravity are evidence of our own failure to love others as God loves us. To see Christ in all people, to truly love all men – this is salvation.

246. ~ HONOR, DUTY, SACRIFICE, SERVICE ~

Honor... duty... sacrifice... service.... Will you pursue these things as a soldier of Christ or as a servant of this world, as a soldier of peace or as a servant of war, as a soldier of life or as a servant of death? Do you want to protect, defend, and liberate your fellow man?

Then offer your life as the light of the Gospel, and fight to bring the dead to life rather than to make the living die.

247. ~ WE LIVE AS LAMBS ~

We live as lambs, knowing that even if the sheep are slaughtered our souls are protected by the Lion.

248. ~ THE WEAKNESS of A POWERFUL NATION ~

The biggest weakness of a powerful nation is that it is a nation based on earthly power rather than eternal principles. Earthly powers are always susceptible to external conquerors and internal corruption. But eternal principles are impervious to violent destruction and moral decay. You can conquer capitalism, communism, fascism, and democracy; but you can't conquer Christ.

249. ~ CONDEMNATION and TRUTH ~

We are called to speak the truth in love, as St. Paul said. (Ephesians 4:14) But a loving truth is sometimes harsh, abrasive, disruptive and confrontational. Some sins warrant a gentle rebuke, but there are evils that demand a provocative voice crying in the wilderness. Let us not confuse confrontation with a lack of love. If I didn't love my fellow man, then I wouldn't try to dissuade them from joining the military. If I didn't love him, then I wouldn't be concerned about him risking his own life and threatening the lives of others in the service of an unchristian and godless cause. If I didn't love innocent children and unborn babies, then I wouldn't condemn militarism and abortion. If I didn't love Christ, then I wouldn't be compelled to decry all the blasphemous violence committed in His holy name. Those defending abortion condemn me when I condemn abortion as murder, and the "Just War" patriots condemn me when I condemn war as unjust, unchristian, and inhumane. That's admittedly a lot of condemnation flying around on all sides. But if condemning the violent deaths of innocent human beings is a sin, then I'll take my chances with that on Judgment Day.

250. ~ MAKING EXCUSES for EVIL ~

There are many evils that accompany a fallen world. Until the Second Coming and the Day of Judgment, sin will always be present here in this life and here on this earth. But as Christians we are called and empowered to resist sin and to flee from wickedness, not to justify, excuse, or consider evil "unavoidably necessary." We don't make excuses for prostitution, sorcery, drunkenness, adultery, child abuse, and heresy by saying: "We live in a fallen world, so sometimes we Christians must sell our bodies, practice witchcraft, get drunk, betray our spouses, abuse our children, and deny the Faith." We would rightly consider such rationalizations to be ludicrous. But for some odd reason, when it comes to the evils of violence and killing, we suddenly equivocate with Our Lord's clear commands and make all manner of justifications for why shedding the blood of our neighbors is not only permissible, but also honorable.

Straining at gnats and swallowing camels produces strange doctrines indeed.

251. ~ THE PRIMARY PHILOSOPHICAL CONCERN for THE CHRISTIAN ~

Let the world rely upon its mortal philosophies of "Just War theory," "necessary evil," "justifiable homicide," "collateral damage," and "permissible killing." But the primary philosophical concern for the Christian is this: when we violently deny another person their life, then we violently deny them the opportunity of repentance and salvation. Is that really what we feel called to do as professing Christians?

Show me a single New Testament passage, a single New Testament verse, a single Orthodox Teaching or Church Tradition that commands us to take up the sword rather than the Cross. Prove to me from the example of Our Savior and the teachings of His apostles that we must defend our own lives and the lives of others by any means necessary. Demonstrate conclusively that violence is part of Christian discipleship and that killing is compatible with the Great Commission, and I will lay down my cross and take up arms tomorrow.

252. ~ BURDENS and BLESSINGS ~

A society that views children as burdens and guns as blessings will never be a peaceful society.

253. ~ TWO TRAGIC THEOLOGICAL MISUNDERSTANDINGS ~

Two tragic misunderstandings of the Christian gospel:

1. Affirming the truth of the Sermon on the Mount while denying that He who spoke this truth is Himself the Truth.

2. Affirming that Christ is the Truth while denying that He who is the Truth spoke the truth in His Sermon on the Mount.

254. ~ MEANINGLESS COMPASSION ~

Love, compassion, sympathy, and justice are meaningless apart from sacrifice, suffering, struggle, and pain.

255. ~ STRUGGLE, PAIN, SORROW, and FAITH ~

The fruit of life is nourished by struggle.
Flowers of joy have their roots in pain.
Trees of love are watered with sorrow.
The mystery of existence is solved...
by faith.

256. ~ HEXES and CURSES ~

Hexes and curses

Potions and charms

Ouija's and Tarots

Crystals and palms...

Won't conquer

The Cross

The Church

The Sacraments

and the Psalms!

257. ~ CONFRONTING the IRRATIONALITY of EVIL ~

One can never effectively confront the irrationality of evil with logical argumentation or reasonable actions. One can only rebel against evil with the absurdity of truth, the insanity of life-affirmation, and the folly of the Cross. That's why lunatics are prophets and the reasonable are presidents.

258. ~ FREEDOM and SICKNESS ~

As long as you think that individual freedom means the right to do whatever you please with the support and enablement of the government, then you will always be a slave. And as long as you think religious freedom means the right to carry your cross without getting splinters, then you will never really know Christ. I see Christians and pagans equally demanding that the government give them the "rights" they claim they deserve. They equally bow before the idol of politics and then complain when their god repeatedly lets them down. I have no sympathy for those who complain of sickness while deliberately drinking from a poisoned well.

259. ~ POLITICAL or SPIRITUAL INVESTMENT? ~

I often hear Christians say, "There is no perfect human government because all humans are imperfect."

Exactly. And maybe that's why Christians who understand their imperfection should stop trying to get involved in the affairs of human government. Instead of trying to be leaders of the godless, let's just focus on being followers of God. Then, perhaps, the godless will see true examples of Christian living and desire to emulate it. We will have a more profound spiritual influence on our society if we prioritize and invest in the eternal Kingdom of Christ rather than investing it the temporal kingdoms of this fleeting world.

260. ~ LAWLESS SPIRITUALITY ~

To side with the law of the land over the law of Christian compassion is a spiritually dangerous thing. Give to the needy, succor the suffering, liberate the slaves, and give voice to the unborn. Fulfilling the law of love will make us lawless in the eyes of Babylon. But Christ is our King, and His judgment is all that matters.

261. ~ RENDER UNTO CAESAR ~

"And Jesus answering said unto them, Render to Caesar the things that are Caesar's, and to God the things that are God's. And they marveled at him." [St. Mark 12:17]

So this means that we should pay our taxes and obey the civil law as long as our taxes and obedience don't conflict with God's divine law. There are two kingdoms: the kingdoms of men and the Kingdom of God. As Christians, our allegiance is to the Kingdom of God. It is not our affair to try to reform the kingdoms of men. Let the world be the world, and let us be Christians. And the more we focus on being the Church, the greater impact we will have on the kingdoms of the world.

262. ~ POLITICS and THE GOSPEL ~

Human legality and divine morality are often at odds. This American political system operates on the principles of pragmatism, compromise, power, and coercion – things that are all "legal" but are nevertheless fundamentally at odds with the commands of the Gospel. The principle of democracy is also contrary to the will of God. As Christians we pray as Our Lord instructed: *"thy kingdom come, thy will be done, on earth as it is in heaven."* The Kingdom of heaven is not a democracy, and God's moral and spiritual laws are not subject to human vote. Our Christian duty is therefore to live and proclaim divine truth, to bear the fruit of the Gospel, and to be a prophetic witness against anything that undermines and opposes Christian truth.

This American government and this American political system operate on essentially the same utilitarian principles as the Mafia. A Christian might decide to join the Mafia with the noble intention of doing some good and perhaps making the Mafia more humane. But I would not view such an act as compatible with a true Christian calling. The principles and values of the Mafia are inherently evil and contrary to the Gospel, and no Christian should willingly embrace such ungodly principles, regardless of good intentions. I really believe that politics is no different. But sadly, many professing Christians have idolized this American government, and therefore they are unwilling to consider that the principles upon which this government was founded and is sustained may be fundamentally at odds with the Kingdom of Christ.

I'm certainly not advocating that we stay out of all fallen situations. We live in a fallen world and we are called to be "salt and light." (Cf. St. Matthew 5:13-16) The question is: what are the most Christian and most effective ways to proclaim the Gospel, to liberate the oppressed, and to influence our society with goodness and truth? And I don't think embracing the Machiavellian mechanisms of politics is either truly Christian or truly effective.

I have seen far too many good Christian people forsaking prophetic proclamation in favor of political proselytizing. And rather than having a righteous influence on government, the government almost always has an unrighteous influence on them. These politically active Christians become divided amongst themselves, and instead of focusing on the Kingdom of Christ they become myopically obsessed with their own nation, their own political party, and their own political agenda. And they inevitably end up compromising core Christian values for political expediency, believing that the ends somehow justify the means.

263. ~ A LONELY EXODUS ~

The exodus from Babylon is a lonely voyage. But there have always been pilgrims marching on the road to Zion. In spite of how it may seem, we are never really alone. The Saints who went before us are with us now, and we are surrounded by a "great cloud of witnesses." (Hebrews 12:1) The angels are by our side, and the Holy Spirit empowers us. We trod the narrow road, seeking entrance through the small gate. (St. Matthew 7:13-14)

Our friends, families, and even many of our so-called brethren tell us that we're headed in the wrong direction. Who are we, they ask, to think that we know better than the masses? Who are we, they ask, to question the infallibility of democracy? Who are we, they ask, to preach anything contrary to the consensus of history and the tide of progressive enlightenment? Who are we, they ask, to contradict the status quo or question the established political order?

But this world is not our home, and we will always be unwelcomed guests in this terrestrial abode. We will never be comfortable in this life. And love compels us to disrupt the comfort of those who have wedded themselves to a damnable worldly contentment. We are revolutionary sheep, marching to slaughter and to salvation.

264. ~ NECESSARY EVIL? ~

To call evil "necessary" undermines the power of God. Evil is never unavoidable. It is never necessary. Evil is always the result of human choice. No Christian should embrace such a fatalistic philosophy. We must always resist evil with good. We must never say, "I sinned and committed evil, but I couldn't help it. I sinned and committed evil, but it was necessary." I don't think such excuses will exonerate us on Judgment Day.

265. ~ HEAVEN and THE CROSS ~

Many want to go to heaven; few want to go to the Cross. But you can't have one without the other.

266. ~ WEST ~

I drove west. Seeking refuge. Running from my sins and the confrontation of their consequences. Away from the oppressive Deep South humidity and judgment and Bible Belt condemnation. Away from my wife and children. Away from "responsibility" and "accountability" and all the other manipulative guilt trip bullshit that people were so eager to lay upon me.

I drove out from under the canopy of the Mississippi Magnolias, through the Louisiana bayous, into the naked Texas foothills, and on and on until the highway met the sky.

But the further I drove, the closer I came to my problems. And I knew it would be so. That's why I had to go. I needed to be alone. I needed to reckon with God. I needed to reckon with myself. I needed to be still and listen to the truth of the universe – as painful as it may be.

Somewhere in West Texas I began to see the edge. Crossing into New Mexico the world stretched endlessly before me. It was then that I began to breathe. There's no judgment in the desert, no condemnation where heaven meets earth. There's only awe.

But you can't escape sin – even in a mystical, purple orange, flame sky horizon. And although I could breathe, I couldn't forget. I couldn't undo the damage I had done. I couldn't erase the pain I had caused. I couldn't heal the wounds I had inflicted.

I crossed the "four corners," into Utah, and began driving northwest towards Idaho where my sister lived at the time. She had told me it was OK to come see her for a little while. Thank God for that. But she wasn't happy with me. Nobody was. And there is no lonelier feeling than knowing that even those who love you the most are angry, upset, and disappointed in you. And to know that you deserve it all only makes things that much worse. You can't find comfort in being the victim. You can't find sympathy in appealing to a just cause. You can't find solidarity or understanding in co-sufferers for the faith. You have fucked up, and now you are all alone. And all you can do is drive and pray and read the words of Eldridge Cleaver and Black Elk and your Holy Bible when you stop to rest. (It's amazing how you can remember what books you were reading during seminal periods in your life.)

The things I experienced and discovered and suffered during those weeks out West are so complex and amazing and intense that they deserve a book of their own. And eventually I may write that book. But for now, all I can tell you is that in my deep desert travels and in my deep spiritual pain I experienced the inexpressible love of a true friend, the unconditional acceptance of my sister, the inexplicable kindness of strangers, the glorious intensity of the universe, the tangible appearance of angelic messengers, and the omnipresent hand of my Lord Jesus Christ guiding me every step of the way.

Perhaps, in time, I will write about all of those things in detail. I will write about the love of friends and strangers and the love of the few true Christian brethren who helped me through my darkest hours. I will write about the angels that came to me and kept me from committing suicide. I will write about the highways that stretched forever before me, and about the sepia canyons and rainbow arches of Utah, and about the snow capped Idaho Sawtooth Mountains, and about the sights and smells and stories I encountered on the Greyhound bus rides that I took home after my car completely died in the Tucumcari desert.

I didn't find any new answers or new truth or new revelations out West. But I found some clarity about some things I already knew. Like the fact that life is real, and sin is real, and friendship is real, and pain is real, and love is real, and suffering is real, and redemption is real. And unlike in the movies, these things do not resolve themselves in a linear fashion. They all exist together, inextricably and incomprehensibly intertwined – like body and soul, heaven and earth, time and eternity. And while it sucks sometimes, there is incredible grace in it all.

That's what I realized out there in the desert and in the mountains and in the Albuquerque bars and on those Greyhound buses. And it's not necessarily comforting. But it's true. And after all, *"the truth shall set you free."* [St. John 8:32]

267. ~ PSYCHEDELIC DRUGS ~

I have seen truth via the lens of psychedelic drugs – beautiful and frightening truth. But I always advise others to seek truth only via the truthful means of prayer, meditation, biblical study, ascetic struggle, intellectual rigor, emotional vulnerability, human relationship, and authentic life experience. There are no chemical shortcuts to the Creator. Hallucinogens may indeed open up "doors of perception," as Aldous Huxley – drawing upon William Blake's poetic phrase – eloquently wrote about in his book by that title. But opening up those doors of perception will bring us no closer to God than landing on the moon. We may experience new visions and observe the universe from a new perspective; but unless our hearts are humbled and open to divine love and love for others, then it will merely be just another long, strange, mind altering trip to nowhere.

"I am not so foolish as to equate what happens under the influence of Mescaline – or of any other drug – with the realization of the end and ultimate purpose of human life: Enlightenment, the Beatific Vision." ~ Aldous Huxley ~

268. ~ VOTING TO ENSLAVE THEMSELVES ~

Inherent in the right to vote is the right *not* to vote. Too many people dishonor those who marched, struggled, and died for their freedom by volitionally enslaving themselves to political masters.

269. ~ HERE and THERE ~

"Where? Where?"
My children want me there.
"I am here," I say.
But here is not there.

I am "here" for them.
But I send them
into the world
alone.

They want me "there,"
but they never complain.
And I want to be "there"
more than anything.

But all I give them
is "here."

Help me God.

270. ~ TRUE THINGS ~

Rainbow skies
Children's eyes

Flame sunrise
Sad goodbyes

Grandma's smiles
Babies' cries

Lovers' sighs
Liturgical highs...

These are things that never lie

271. ~ SHEEP AMONG WOLVES ~

He sends us out as sheep among wolves, but we somehow seek a safe and secure Christianity. He calls us to take up our own cross and follow Him to Golgotha, but we somehow seek a comfortable and painless faith. He tells us that we will be blessed when we are persecuted, reviled, and maligned; but we somehow seek fair and just treatment on the road to salvation. He tells us to enter through the narrow gate, but we somehow seek a smooth path to paradise with no obstacles in our way. He calls us to love our enemies and lay down our lives for others, but we are somehow willing to kill our fellow man to preserve our own temporal welfare and mortal existence. He calls us to work out our own salvation with fear and trembling, but we proclaim a false and presumptive spiritual security by saying "we are saved, and all is well."

We have somehow inverted the Gospel of the Cross and turned it into a Crossless Christianity. We have exchanged the difficult and paradoxical struggles of authentic faith for easy and systematic belief systems. We have chosen convenient paths – broad, smooth roads that lead us away from the agonizing truths of Christ and towards the comfortable lies of hell.

[Scripture references: St. Matthew 10:16; St. Luke 9:23; St. Matthew 5:10-12; St. Matthew 7:13-14; St. Luke 6:35; St. John 15:13; Philippians 2:12]

272. ~ FLAGS I WON'T CELEBRATE ~

As a Christian I will never celebrate any flag that waves over the shed blood of my fellow man.

273. ~ CULTURAL DECLINE? ~

Our culture is not declining. It's been in the gutter from day one. America's evils have simply morphed and manifested from one form of injustice to another. Stop trying to save and preserve something that is rotten at the core.

Christ never promised to protect nations. But He did promise that the gates of hell shall not prevail against His Church. (St. Matthew 16:18) If we invest in a godless government and a manmade constitution, then we place our faith in something that God has never told us to trust. But when we invest in Christ and His Church, then we will be eternally preserved.

Professing Christians who attempt to conflate the kingdom of Zion with the kingdom of Babylon will only end up dividing their own souls. How long will we keep trying to sing JAH's praises to the devil's tune?

274. ~ PROTECTION AGAINST FALSE FUNDAMENTALIST DOCTRINES ~

It's a constant struggle to protect our families and children from false fundamentalist doctrines and heterodox Evangelical theology. But we have to be vigilant. We live in a society that is infected with the damnable doctrines of "faith alone," "the Bible alone," and "once saved always saved." And unfortunately, those who espouse these erroneous doctrines are often more vocal and aggressive in promoting their errors than we Orthodox are in promoting Christian truth. I love and respect my Evangelical Protestant brethren in many ways, but when they attempt to influence my own family and children with their perverse dogmas then the Lion in me is awakened.

It is imperative that we don't fall prey to a "Sola Scriptura" approach to theological issues. Almost every false Christian doctrine of the past 500 years has been the tragic result of basing Christian authority on the "Bible alone." We must read and study the Scriptures in and through the apostolic Orthodox Church — the Church which has settled and preserved that *"faith which has once for all been delivered unto the saints." [Jude 3]*

Evangelical heresies are always based on certain isolated verses and passages of scripture that are violently wrested out of the context of apostolic Teaching and Tradition. The Protestant approach to theology is to exalt oneself as the arbiter and authority on what the Bible teaches. The Orthodox approach to theology is to humble oneself before the authority of Christ's Church and the Teaching of His apostles. Those who really love the Bible will read and study it diligently while always allowing the Church to guide them in sound doctrine and a proper understanding of the Faith.

Many Evangelicals have made an idol out of the Bible. They have elevated Holy Scripture above the Church, and they have confused the "word of God" for the "Word of God" – who is Christ Himself. (St. John 1:1) They are fond of preaching about the centrality of the Bible, and yet they misunderstand central biblical teachings regarding Christ and His Church. The louder they scream and the more violently they pound on their pulpits, the more they reveal that their faith is not really in Christ or in Scripture, but rather in their own egos and in their own fallible interpretations of the sacred texts.

However, I am tempered by the wisdom of Thomas Merton, who wrote:

"I will be a better Catholic, not if I can refute every shade of Protestantism, but if I can affirm the truth in it and still go further. So, too, with the Muslims, the Hindus, the Buddhists, etc. This does not mean syncretism, indifferentism, or the vapid and careless friendliness that accepts everything by thinking of nothing. There is much that one cannot "affirm" and "accept," but first one must say "yes" where one really can. If I affirm myself as Catholic merely by denying all that is Muslim, Jewish, Protestant, Hindu, Buddhist, etc., then in the end I will find that there is not much left for me to affirm as a Catholic – and certainly no breath of the Spirit with which to affirm it."

275. ~ BOOKS and SPORTS ~

One reason I love books so much is that they don't break your heart like sports do. I have so many great books to read, but the game is on. Why do I forsake the comfort of the pages of these faithful friends, exchanging them for the agony and betrayal of my favorite teams? Why do we fall in love with those who have no love for us? Who knows the answers to these human mysteries? Perhaps that's why there are so many books written about sports.

276. ~ CLINGING to CERTAINTIES or CLINGING to CHRIST? ~

Feel free to cling to your infallibilities, your certainties, your logical syllogisms and empirical proofs. But such things are of no benefit to me on this road to salvation. You see, faith is fraught with failure, doubt, folly and fear. Faith clings to the Cross with all of its splinters and blood, agony and pain. Mortal certainties undermine divine faith and disarm eternal hope. So I have no interest in such burdens. My heart and mind must be free to cling to Christ.

277. ~ KILLING IS NEVER A SOLUTION ~

Life-affirmation, not Life-negation! Killing is never a solution. *Never*! Those who seek answers in war, abortion, and capital punishment will inevitably find that the blood they shed is the blood that poisons their own souls and haunts their guilty consciences.

"Be not deceived; God is not mocked: for whatsoever a man soweth, that shall he also reap." [Galatians 6:7]

278. ~ RETURNING to THE ROOTS of OUR FAITH ~

As an Orthodox Christian, I call my Orthodox brethren to embrace the pacifist roots of our beloved Faith. To follow Christ is to follow Him to the Cross. It's hard to die to Christ and suffer for the kingdom when we kill to preserve our own lives and welfare.

There are effective ways to defend the innocent without inflicting violence upon our fellow man. But ultimately, we must realize that God will avenge the innocent and raise His children to eternal life. So we don't need to preserve our own lives or the lives of the innocent at all costs. We are Christians, and therefore we are not guided by the mortal philosophies of pragmatism or utilitarianism. We know that Christ is Risen, and we look beyond this world to the kingdom that is to come.

"For here we have no lasting city,
but we seek the city that is to come."
[Hebrews 13:14]

"But our citizenship is in heaven. And we eagerly await a Savior
from there, the Lord Jesus Christ." [Philippians 3:20]

279. ~ REVOLUTION AGAINST LUNACY ~

Babylon is lunacy, and it's foolish to expect sanity from the insane. I won't lend my vote to Babylon's political system, because I believe the Democratic process is fundamentally flawed. Any rule by the will of the masses is never the rule of the Kingdom of God. That's why all of these power-hungry politicians demand that we vote. Don't you ever wonder why these political parties (which claim to be diametrically opposed to each other) all agree on demanding that everyone vote? They all want power, and we willingly cede it to them by our participation in this corrupt and putrid democratic process.

The only truly revolutionary thing to do is to refuse to vote, to refuse to join their armed forces, and to refuse to call a godless government a government of God. But as long as they can get us to accept their manmade constitution, as long as they can get us to participate in their armies, and as long as they can get us to validate their power with our complicit votes, then they can always rule and control us. Democracy is the most ingenious form of slavery. It enables people to enslave themselves while thinking they are free, calling darkness "freedom" while cursing the light of liberation.

280. ~ ATTACHMENT and DETACHMENT ~

Some attach themselves to everything and find harmony with nothing. Others attach themselves to nothing and seek harmony with everything. But the end of either extreme is emptiness. Christ calls us to attach ourselves to His Cross, to attach ourselves to our fellow man, and to attach ourselves to love and service and self-denial. He calls us to empty ourselves so that we can be filled with God.

The unattached branch does not suffer from the elements; it does not suffer from the cold or the heat. But neither does the unattached branch produce leaves, flowers, and fruit. Because it is dead, it does not suffer; and yet because it is dead, it does not live.

Therefore, the Christian doesn't seek detachment from all things; rather, the Christian seeks attachment to Christ – who fulfills all things. In Him we are not protected from hardship, suffering, and temporal death – things which always accompany divinely authored love; but in Him we are preserved unto eternal life, where we will bathe in the infinite joy of the presence of God.

"I am the vine; you are the branches. If you remain in me and I in you, you will bear much fruit; apart from me you can do nothing." [St. John 15:5]

281. ~ FORFEITING DIVINE JUSTICE ~

When we trust in the carnal sword of mortal violence, we forfeit the eternal blessings of divine justice. Christ is coming to cut them down. Let us not uproot the wheat with the tares, lest we ourselves become chaff for the flames.

282. ~ MEEK and MIGHT ~

Meek believed in peace,
but Might believed in war.
So Might said,
"Let's fight, to prove who's right."
But Meek said, "No more!"

So Might drew its sword
to smite Meek on the head.
But Meek turned its cheek
and Might struck it dead.

So it seemed that Might was right,
or at least that's what they say.
But Meek will conquer Might
on that glorious Judgment Day.

283. ~ DROP ~

Drop your guard
and let me in
and together we'll conquer
this hate and sin.

Drop your defenses
and make a truce
and together we'll defeat
these lies with truth.

Drop your gun
and hold my hand
and together we'll enter
the Promised Land.

284. ~ FIGHTING for THE KINGDOM ~

The kingdom we fight for in this life is the kingdom we shall inherit in the next. If we fight with mortal weapons for temporal kingdoms, then the victories we win will be eternally lost. But if we fight with spiritual weapons for the kingdom of God, then our earthly losses will be infinitely victorious.

285. ~ SPORTS and WAR ~

Sports reveal the human soul. They bring out the best and the worst in us. Sports are a microcosm of the world. The passion of the fans and the rivalry on the pitch reveal both horrific shame and poetic beauty.

Unlike war, there is redemption in athletic competition. One does not equate victory with killing. To compete is to acknowledge the humanity of your opponent. He is your rival, not your enemy. He is your physical, mental, and spiritual challenger; and although you may despise him, you nevertheless view him as your fellow man. And unlike warfare, rivals in sport often become friends over time.

There is a profound intimacy in the blood, sweat, and tears shared by athletes vying for victory. But I am not naïve. Sport has unfortunately, at times, precipitated violence. The infamous "Soccer War" between El Salvador and Honduras in 1969 is one tragic example. But would humanity not be better served if conflicts were decided on fields of play rather than on fields of blood?

286. ~ RELIGION of VIOLENCE / RELIGION of PEACE ~

Our society is so thoroughly inundated with the religion of violence that in the aftermath of violent tragedy the most obvious and common sense solutions are not even considered. In the wake of the recent Ft. Hood shooting, all we hear are the same tired political debates about gun control. But those on the Left and those on the Right are equally oblivious to one simple fact: there would have been no Ft. Hood shooting if there was no Ft. Hood to begin with.

You see, you never hear about monks snapping and shooting up a monastery. That's because monks are trained in spiritual warfare, not carnal warfare. Now, I realize that not all Christians are called to the monastic life, but all Christians are nevertheless called to spiritual warfare. And we cannot truly cultivate the weapons of the Spirit if we train ourselves in the weapons of the flesh.

The military trains people to kill, so I never understand why people are so shocked and dismayed when soldiers do what they have been conditioned to do. It is folly to think that violence can be tamed and controlled. Once violence is embraced, it becomes a cruel and capricious wind that knows no harness.

Violence is demonic, and those who rely upon it will be inevitably victimized by it in one way or another. This is why Our Lord commanded Peter to put away the sword, uttering a universal and prophetic condemnation of violence: *"...for all who live by the sword shall die by the sword." [St. Matthew 26:52]* Even though one might kill others without being killed themselves, they cannot escape the psychological, emotional, and spiritual trauma that visits all who intentionally shed the blood of their fellow man.

The fact is that nothing we truly need requires a violent defense. The only thing that will endure eternally is our souls, and nobody can destroy our souls with bullets or bombs. However, we can eternally scar our own souls by violently decimating the lives of those created in the very image of God.

"Christian violence" is an oxymoron that is as absurd as "honest theft." Let the world cultivate the religion of violence, and let the Christian cultivate the religion of peace. One has nothing to do with the other.

[And in anticipation of the typical objection that violence is sometimes necessary to defend the innocent, I will point out that history clearly demonstrates that violence has destroyed far more innocents than it has saved. There are proactive nonviolent methods and means of defending the innocent. Mahatma Gandhi, Dr. Martin

Luther King, Jr. and others have demonstrated that nonviolent activism is far more liberating than violence. As Christians we must not use evil means to accomplish noble ends. Mortal violence never establishes peace or brings about divine justice. It always leaves bitterness and hatred in its wake. And those bitter seeds of resentment and hate will eventually and invariably sprout their dark revenge. Never trust in anything gained by the sword of man. Trust in Christ, who told his disciples to "put away thy sword." And hear the words of Tertullian, who wrote: *"In disarming Peter, Our Lord disarmed every soldier."*]

287. ~ FORWARD CHRISTIAN SOLDIERS ~

Keep struggling. Keep fighting. Our doubts, fears, failures, and losses are not in vain if we recognize that there's redemption in the suffering. It seems so bleak at times, but there is a purpose to it all. He was crucified and buried, but we know that's not the end of the story. For the followers of Christ, even tribulation, suffering, and death are victories. So forward Christian soldiers! It may be Friday, but Sunday soon come!

288. ~ VIOLENCE IS of THE WORLD ~

Violence has its place in the world for those who are of this world. But violence has no place in the heart or the hands of the Christian who is not of this world. The Christian is a citizen of heaven (Philippians 3:20), and he strives to live by the Spirit and not according to the flesh. (Galatians 5:16; Romans 8:5-11)

289. ~ LOVE and TRUST ~

We will never know love unless we dare to trust. There is no joy apart from faith.

290. ~ HERETICS IN HEAVEN ~

Do not be surprised to see heretics in heaven who fell prey to unorthodox doctrines yet upheld the teachings of Our Lord to love our enemies, to bless those that persecute us, and to not return evil for evil. And do not be surprised to see "Christians" in hell who maintained Orthodox tenets but despised the greatest commandments to love God with all of our hearts and to love our neighbors as ourselves. If our faith is not rooted in peace and love, then our faith is not Orthodox.

291. ~ OBLIGING EVIL ~

When the accepted law of the land is diametrically opposed to the law of the Gospel, then the Church does not have to obey civil authority. In fact, the Church is obliged to oppose systemic evil, whatever the cost. Countless martyrs died because they refused to oblige the idolatry of the evil rulers of their day. The Church must not sit around and wait for hearts and minds to change; instead she must actively proclaim and live out the Gospel so that hearts and minds *will* change.

It is impossible to fully proclaim Orthodox truth without condemning unjust institutions. The light and love of Christ inevitably burns wickedness and condemns inhumanity, injustice, and evil. The Church, in her authenticity, is the most revolutionary organism in the world.

292. ~ WORLDLY PHILOSOPHIES and THE CHRISTIAN FAITH ~

Worldly philosophies exalt contradiction; but the Christian Faith embraces paradox. Worldly philosophies sow confusion; but the Christian Faith affirms Mystery. Worldly philosophies produce rational atheists; but the Christian Faith produces holy fools. Worldly philosophies declare, "God is dead;" but the Christian Faith declares, *"He is risen!"*

293. ~ THE GREATEST REVOLUTION ~

A closed fist can strike a mighty blow, but only an open hand can give and receive. Christ opened His hands to receive our nails and to give us eternal life. Redemption is the greatest revolution.

294. ~ WHY CHRIST DIED ~

Christ died so that man may live, not so that man may kill.

295. ~ A POWERFUL and BEAUTIFUL TRUTH ~

God loves us, *all* of us. This is such a powerful and beautiful truth. The world is in chaos because people don't believe that God truly loves mankind. It is impossible to hate our fellow man if we know the love of God. Authentic faith does not seek to prove its veracity by the violent oppression of opposing points of view. Those who truly trust in God do not burn Churches, betray their brethren, or forsake their friends over philosophical disagreements. They are consumed with divine love, and therefore they are never corrupted by demonic hate.

296. ~ THE FOLLY of THE CROSS ~

The folly of the Cross is what separates the Gospel from all other religions. The world exalts materialism and earthy success as the supreme aspirations of human existence. But Christianity teaches us to forsake the world and forsake our own lives in order to live eternally. And as long as we rely on the sword then we fail to rely on the Cross. Our Lord gave up His own life without taking up arms to defend Himself or others. The Messiah was rejected by those who expected a violent revolutionary who would defend the Jews against Roman tyranny. Today, many people are still looking in vain for such a revolutionary Messiah. And sadly, many professing Christians have rejected Our Lord's nonviolent teachings and example, refashioning Him into an idol of militant Christian zealotry. But Christ calls us to follow Him, without qualification. He did not say, "Take up your cross and follow me, but take up arms to defend yourself when necessary." Our Lord calls us to follow Him to the Cross. And how can we be crucified with Him if we violently resist those who would crucify us?

297. ~ HERESY ~

Pacifism is simply rebellion against the heresy of iconoclasm. If it is wrong to destroy icons made with wood and paint, then how can it be right to destroy living icons fashioned with the very breath of God? If condemning the destruction of living icons is unorthodox, then call me a heretic.

298. ~ THE FIRST STEP TOWARDS CHRIST ~

Sometimes the first step towards Christ is a rebellion against the many idols that are fashioned in His name.

299. ~ THE WEST HAS WON? ~

So they say the West has won
It has never seen the setting sun
Slavery, abortion, bomb and gun
But from the East shall come
The Risen Son

300. ~ THEOTOKOS: MOTHER of THE STREETS ~

Our Lady, the Theotokos,
"Mother of the Streets":

We pray for
the homeless
and the hungry
and the harlot.

We pray for the addict
the abandoned
and the abused.

We pray for all the rebel children
who fight for life
and for dignity
and for bread
and for peace.

Grant them hope and grace
and mercy and strength
in their revolutionary struggles.

In the Name of the Father,
and the Son, and the Holy Spirit, One God.
~ amen ~

301. ~ AN IMPOSSIBLE OVEREMPHASIS ~

It may be possible to overemphasize sin.
It may be possible to overemphasize hell.
It may be possible to overemphasize morality.
It may be possible to overemphasize fasting.
It may be possible to overemphasize spiritual gifts.
It may be possible to overemphasize divine judgment.
It may be possible to overemphasize asceticism.
It may be possible to overemphasize prophecy.
It may be possible to overemphasize miracles.

But it is impossible to overemphasize the love of God.

302. ~ DON'T CALL ME "MODERATE" ~

Call me "liberal" or call me "conservative," as long as you don't call me "moderate."

If "liberal" means compassion for the poor and the underprivileged, or if "liberal" means justice for the disinherited and the defenseless, then I pray that God would grant me a liberal heart. God forbid that I should I adopt a "moderate" view towards the injustices of racism, poverty, or the murder of defenseless unborn innocents.

And if "conservative" means the perpetuation of divine values, or if "conservative" means preservation of the family unit and adherence to immutable moral principles, then I pray that God would grant me a conservative spirit. God forbid that I should be "moderate" about the divine commands of *"Thou shall"* and *"Thou shalt not."*

I am an Orthodox Christian, and it seems to me that these liberal and conservative values are actually quite compatible with each other. But you wouldn't know that if your worldview is shaped by political propagandists and media pundits rather than by Christ, His Church, and a clear conscience.

There is plenty of room in the Christian heart for the principles of true compassion, authentic tolerance, human brotherhood, environmental stewardship, economic justice, the sanctity of life, religious freedom, and family stability. And as a Christian, there is frankly no place for equivocation, moderation, or compromise regarding any of these values.

Too many Christians have become "useful idiots" of both the political left and the political right. Too many of us have been brainwashed to be disturbed by the wrong things. We have succumbed to the demonic strategy of divide and rule. And therefore, professing Christians square off against each other in the public square – more loyal to their political affiliations, their social allegiances, and their racial identifications than to their own brothers and sisters in Christ.

But if we would only look to the saints and martyrs, to the disciples and apostles, and to Our Lord Himself, we would see clearly that love, mercy, justice, and peace transcend political, sectarian, and racial divisions. Politicians, creature preachers, and media whores profit from sowing discord and division in society. But as Orthodox Christians, we don't have to bow to Babylon's evil. We are not puppets on Satan's string. We are moved by the omnipotent hand of Our Almighty Creator, not by politicians' plastic smiles.

So the next time somebody asks you what your political affiliation is, simply tell them: *"I have no part in Babylon. I seek the Kingdom that is to come."* Tell them, *"My allegiance is to all mankind, and my loyalty is to Christ and His Church."* If they are liberals or conservatives – in the best senses of those terms – then they will honor you and they will become healers rather than dividers. And if they are "moderates," then remind them of the words of Our Lord:

"I know your deeds, that you are neither cold nor hot. I wish you were either one or the other! So, because you are lukewarm—neither hot nor cold—I am about to spit you out of my mouth."[Revelation 3:15-16]

303. ~ UNJUST CONDEMNATIONS ~

Slave owners condemned the abolitionists; segregationists condemned the freedom riders; and abortion advocates condemn the Life affirmers. And such unjust condemnations are often levied in the name of "liberty," "rights," and "choice." But truth, justice, and humanity always rise triumphant in the end. The oppressors are often on the right side of history, but they are always on the wrong side of eternity.

304. ~ LOSSES ~

I have lost friends because I refuse to support their politics. I have lost friends because I refuse to support their patriotism. I have lost friends because I refuse to support the legality of abortion. And I have lost friends because I refuse to support violence and killing committed in the name of God. But as heartbreaking as it is to lose one's friends, I will accept such losses so that others won't lose their lives.

305. ~ NONVIOLENCE and PEACEMAKING ~

I am wedded to nonviolence, but I still haven't learned how to be a peacemaker. It is one thing not to kill; it is another thing to truly spread peace and love. And sometimes the most difficult challenge is to be at peace with those who are closest to us. It's often easier to love an enemy from afar than to love our own Christian brethren or our own family members with whom we are intimately related. But what have we gained if we live our entire lives abstaining from violence while failing to bring peace and love to those around us?

306. ~ VILLAINS and VISION ~

Sometimes the worst villain is our own vision. And our perspective is always skewed when we ignore the beam in our own eye while searching for the speck in our brother's.

307. ~ PARENTAL PRIDE? ~

As a Christian parent, would you be proud if your child became a pimp, a prostitute, a pornographer, or a thief? Of course not! Yet you are proud when your children become professionally trained killers. The only difference is that the immorality of pimps, prostitutes, pornographers, and thieves is frowned upon by society while the iniquity of militarism is honored and esteemed.

308. ~ A REVOLUTIONARY EXAMPLE ~

Our Lord Jesus Christ was the most pro-active, nonviolent social revolutionary that ever lived. He conquered hate with love, He defeated violence with peace, and He destroyed sin and death with holiness and life. And yet we claim to worship Christ while manufacturing every conceivable argument against His nonviolent teachings and example.

309. ~ A MAN'S CONFESSION ~

A man went to Confession and said to the Priest:
"Father, I confess that I have an enemy that I cannot forgive. He speaks countless lies about me. He constantly tempts me with unspeakable sins. He brings misery and sorrow to my wife and children. I confess that I also judge him for being a great hypocrite,

because he claims to be a true Christian while he forsakes God by these very evils I have mentioned. Father, I confess that this man torments me so much that I am often tempted to kill him!"

Upon hearing his confession, the Priest replied:

"Whatever you do my son, please do not kill this man; for suicide is a greater sin than all the others you have mentioned."

310. ~ THREE THINGS YOU SHOULD NEVER JOIN ~

Three things you should never join: a gang, the mafia, and the military. They all operate on the same evil principle – offering you false security while paying you to kill.

311. ~ A SHARED PERVERSION ~

I've noticed that there is one thing that almost every nation, every religion, every race, every political party, and every philosophical ideology agrees upon: the belief that premeditated violence is sometimes necessary and justifiable. Stop and consider that for a moment. All these disparate and conflicting factions share a common faith in the ostensible necessity of violence. Imagine how different our world would be if the one conviction we all shared in common was the unconditional renunciation of war and killing.

312. ~ BLOOD and SPLINTERS ~

It is better to wash a stranger's feet than to shed a stranger's blood. It is better to bear the splinters of the Cross than to bear the stains of violence and killing.

313. ~ HOW? ~

How can I be a saint
when I'm a revolutionary?
But how can I be revolutionary
unless I become a saint?

How can I cultivate love
when I only see injustice?
But how can I cultivate justice
unless I first learn to love?

How can I heal an evil world
if I seek to burn it down?
But how can I burn down evil
unless I seek to heal the world?

314. ~ SPIRITUAL VISION ~

The spiritual mind...

Sees the ocean in a single tear

It sees a book in a single word

It sees a forest in a single tree

It sees humanity in a single child

It sees beauty in darkness
and hope on every horizon

The spiritual mind can see God in all things.

What separates a hero from the average human being? Not physical strength, intellectual brilliance, or unique talents. A hero may indeed possess such attributes, but those things are not what define heroism. Rather, the hero is a person who embodies certain intangibles, a person who fully embraces the spiritual and moral principles that weave the fabric of eternity.

Heroism is exemplified by an individual like Medgar Evers, a man who courageously chose to pursue truth and justice, freedom and humanity – regardless of the consequences. Heroism is not defined by fearlessness or certainty; it is defined by confronting evil in spite of fear, by embracing divine truth in the face of social upheaval and personal anxiety.

Medgar Evers grew up surrounded by the insidious evils of segregation and racism. He saw the horrors of racial violence and felt the sting of social injustice. It would have been easy for him to let fear dictate the course of his life. It would have been understandable if he had chosen to live by the natural law of self-preservation rather than the divine law of selfless and sacrificial intervention. But character is forged by choices, and Medgar Evers chose to live for humanity rather than to live for himself. He chose to live for justice rather than for safety and security. And ultimately, he chose to die for divine truth rather than to live by society's lies.

Medgar Evers labored to help James Meredith integrate the University of Mississippi, he worked to establish local chapters of the NAACP throughout Mississippi, and he consistently spoke out against a culture that was inherently unjust. And in all of these heroic endeavors, he never neglected to be a devoted husband and a loving father.

Medgar Evers was keenly aware that his activism placed his life in grave danger. In 1963, the year he was brutally murdered in cowardly fashion, Medgar Evers said:

"I'm looking to be shot any time I step out of my car. If I die, it will be in a good cause. Freedom has never been free. I love my children and I love my wife with all my heart. And I would die - die gladly - if that would make a better life for them."

Heroes are not born. They are not created by great education or strenuous physical training. Heroes emerge from a series of individual, volitional choices made throughout the course of one's life. Heroism is the result of the constant decision to choose truth over falsehood, peace over violence, good over evil, humanity over brutality, life-affirmation over death and destruction, and divine love over demonic hate.

Today we face the same choices that Medgar Evers faced. Circumstances are indeed different, and society has changed in many ways. But injustice and evil are no less present today than they were back then. The world is currently reeling from the evils of war, political divisiveness, religious intolerance, poverty, racism, bigotry, and the abortion of unborn innocents.

Medgar Evers was a hero because he chose to confront the evils of his own time, regardless of the cost. God has placed the same choices before each of us today. Will we choose to walk in Medgar's footsteps? Will we choose to confront evil and injustice, wherever it may be found? Or will we choose our own comfort and convenience, our own safety and security?

An evil man killed Medgar Evers, but Medgar Evers struck a mighty blow to evil. And as he famously said, *"You can kill a man, but you can't kill an idea."* Those are words that reveal the courage and consciousness of a hero.

MEDGAR EVERS: MEMORY ETERNAL!

+ 1925-1963 +

316. ~ ATTACK IDEOLOGIES, NOT INDIVIDUALS ~

The spiritual revolutionary recognizes that the real enemies are not people, but ideas. So he fights not with the weapons of the flesh, but with the weapons of the mind and the soul. Rather than attacking individuals, he attacks the ideologies and ideas that infect those individuals. He assails the evil system, not those who have been enslaved by the evil system.

When love is real, then it is inseparable from pain. The life of Our Lord bears witness to this fact. Yet we human creatures incessantly seek a painless love. We sacrifice love for security, comfort, pleasure, or a false tranquility. We do this because authentic love is never comfortable or convenient, and because love is often accompanied by agony, confusion, insecurity, and angst.

But the courageous spiritual soul accepts the disquieting trappings of love. They recognize that authentic love is invaluable and inestimable, worthy of the suffering that comes with it. I thank God for those rare brave souls who embraced love and its cost. I thank God for the Christian martyrs who embraced tribulation and torture because they loved Our Lord more than they loved their own lives.

Within the confines of mortal flesh and the constraints of temporal earth, love is too often ephemeral and evanescent. It intoxicates and then leaves us sick, so we decide to forsake it altogether. We despise it because we cannot tame it. We mock it because we do not understand it. We avoid it because we cannot calculate or control it.

Love is unpredictable and precarious, and therefore it is easier to settle for the security of predictability and restraint. But God is love. And God is unpredictable, uncontrollable, untamed, and unrestrained. Those who taste love experience God, and even the most fleeting moments of love point to the eternal Creator who is love. (I John 4:8) When we say "no" to love, we say "no" to God. And the world is in peril because it has abandoned love and abandoned its Divine source.

So, those that truly love will hurt because they dare to love. Their hearts are broken, their minds are tormented, and their souls ache. But at least they live an authentic life, free from the superficiality that permeates so much of human existence. And the greatest manifestation of love was Our Lord Eyesus Kristos (Jesus Christ), who proved through His life and death that love and pain are inextricably intertwined. What greater love and what greater pain were ever more present together than at the crucifixion of the Savior of the world?

Therefore, to pursue a painless love is an exercise in futility. But if we embrace love and its accompanying agony in this life, then we will be on the road to the painless love that awaits us in the next.

Love is suffering. Show me a person who has never truly suffered, and I will show you a person who has never truly loved.

"What is hell? I maintain that it is the suffering of being unable to love." ~ Fyodor Dostoevsky ~

318. ~ RATIONALIZATIONS of THE RICH ~

It's not that we *owe* our fellow man; it's that we have a *responsibility* to our fellow man. Many rich people look at the poor, and out of a guilty conscience they ask, "What do you want from *me*? What do *I* owe *you*?" And the poor answer them, "You owe us nothing. We only ask that you fulfill your human responsibility."

And what is our human responsibility but to fulfill the supreme commandment to love our God and to love our neighbors as ourselves? (Cf. St. Matthew 22:35-40; St. Luke 10:25-37)

319. ~ DON'T QUIBBLE WITH MYSTERY ~

Don't quibble with Holy Mystery. It transcends explanation and it needs no defense.

320. ~ FRIENDSHIP and FAMILY ~

In friendship and family there are no debts.

321. ~ WANT WITHOUT ~

We want flowers without dirt
and heaven without earth.

We want growth without struggle
and truth without trouble.

We want fruit without rain
and love without pain.

We want peace without justice
and brotherhood without service.

We want to be raptured
from the world to the sky.

We want to be born again,
but we don't want to die.

322. ~ TEARS ~

I cry and cry.
I'll weep until I die.
I shed tears to live
and I won't apologize.

I don't have time
for plastic smiles.
I don't have time
for empty laughs.
This one life is all I have.

I'm dying here,
and so are you.
So I'm crying and I'm asking:

What will you do?
What will we do?

Inhumanity, social injustice, and moral evil are ultimately spiritual issues. And as Christians, we are called to fight evil and injustice in our own hearts, in our own lives, in our communities, and in all the world. The Pro-Life fight has to be fought on many levels, with the love and power of God at the center of it all. But love is active, not apathetic.

Too many Christians today have embraced the erroneous notion that activism is futile in the fight against abortion. They say that we should simply focus on addressing the root spiritual and social factors that fuel the abortion rate. But this is a false dichotomy. Pro-Life activism does in fact address the spiritual and social factors that underlie abortion. Pro-Life activists proclaim the essential spiritual imperative of "Thou shalt not kill." They stand amidst a culture of death and proclaim the divine message of social justice and human rights.

And Pro-Life activists not only preach these truths, but they also provide tangible assistance and vital social services to people in need. Crises pregnancy centers, Christian charities, free medical care, adoption services, homeless shelters, and Church food pantries are just a few of the many works of service in which Pro-Life activists are involved. But along with these necessary and noble works, the clarion call of truth must also go forth. When human lives are being led away to slaughter, Christians must intervene to rescue them.

True Christian love does not turn a blind eye to systemic evils such as slavery, genocide, or abortion. If the abolitionists sat around and waited for the slave owners to develop a moral conscience, then slavery might still be legal today. And Moses didn't stand idly by waiting for Pharaoh's heart to change; rather, he stood before the callous tyrant and said: *"Let my people go!"*

So, as Christians, let's please abandon this absurd notion that Pro-Life activism is futile and ineffective. Instead, let's be honest with ourselves. We don't want to be active in this fight. We don't want to be scorned by polite society and looked upon as fanatics. We don't want to be marginalized and discarded as part of some "fringe element." So we have conveniently concocted these spurious and baseless arguments about how we need to forsake activism and wait for people's hearts and minds to change. We are cowards who would rather be acceptably Christian than prophetically Christ-like.

"Lord have mercy on us."

"Rescue those being led away to death; hold back those staggering toward slaughter. If you say, 'But we knew nothing about this,' does not He who weighs the heart perceive it? Does not He who guards your life know it? Will He not repay each person according to what he has done?" [Proverbs 24:11-12]

324. ~ PAINS of THE POETIC SOUL ~

I have been hurt deeply in my life. There have been times where I felt all alone, and it felt as if even God had turned His back on me. But I prayed through my tears and cried out to Him anyway. I read the Psalms and found comfort in their honest laments and hope filled praises. Sometimes all I could do was pray, "Lord, give me hope." And healing and hope always came, eventually. Sometimes hope came very slowly, but it always came. And hope is the precursor to healing.

I can relate to those who have poetic souls – those who are passionate, those who believe in love, nobility, and honor. Such people will perhaps be hurt more deeply and more often than others. But remember that King David had a poetic and passionate soul. He suffered greatly, both from his own sins and from the sins of the people he tried to lead. But God called him "a man after His own heart." (Acts 13:22)

"To love at all is to be vulnerable. Love anything, and your heart will certainly be wrung and possibly broken. If you want to make sure of keeping it intact, you must give your heart to no one, not even to an animal. Wrap it carefully round with hobbies and little luxuries; avoid all entanglements; lock it up safe in the casket or coffin of your selfishness. But in that casket – safe, dark, motionless,

airless – it will change. It will not be broken; it will become unbreakable, impenetrable, but also irredeemable." ~ C.S. Lewis ~

325. ~ THE WEIGHT of ENLIGHTENMENT ~

The weight of redemptive enlightenment is not an unbearable load. Nothing is heavier than the Cross, and yet nothing is lighter. Let us cast down the burden of easy sin and take up the liberation of struggle, suffering, and salvation.

326. ~ THE ART of WAR ~

The art of war is no art at all; and if it is, then it is the vilest, most uncreative, and loathsome form of art there is. As for myself, I refuse to call war "art."

327. ~ AMERICA'S TOLERANCE for CHRISTIANS ~

America has always tolerated Christians as long as they don't truly live and act as Christians. As long as we continue to be cogs in the wheel of the secular machine – by participating in politics, participating in war, accepting the murder of the unborn, and then going to Church on Sunday – then we have nothing to fear. But as soon as we stand *for* Christ and *against* the world, then we shall no longer be tolerated. The fact that Christians are so easily tolerated by American society should be a sobering indication that we may not really be Christians at all.

328. ~ BURNING BABYLON ~

Babylon cannot be reformed, renovated, corrected, or restored. She can neither be transformed by politics nor renewed by revolution. So rather than casting your feckless and futile political votes, cast the fire of prayer and the fuel of fasting. Chant down Babylon and watch her burn!

"And I heard another voice from heaven saying: Come out of her, my people, lest you share in her sins, and lest you receive of her plagues. For her sins have reached to heaven, and God has remembered her iniquities. Render to her just as she rendered to you, and repay her double according to her works; in the cup which she has mixed, mix double for her. In the measure that she glorified herself and lived luxuriously, in the same measure give her torment and sorrow; for she says in her heart, 'I sit as queen, and am no widow, and will not see sorrow.' Therefore her plagues will come in one day—death and mourning and famine. And she will be utterly burned with fire, for strong is the Lord God who judges her." [Revelation 18:4-8]

329. ~ THE IMAGE of GOD ~

We are all created in the image of God. (Genesis 1:26-27) What does this mean? My understanding of this concept has evolved as I have observed my children. My children play. They create. They laugh. They love. They are as all innocent children, still uncorrupted and undefiled by the ills and evils of society. For them, life and the world present wonder, joy, hope, and goodness. I know my children, and I see that their essence is the image of God. And God is good. Whatever this world does to them, or whatever sins and mistakes they commit in life, nothing can negate their essence. The divine spark that infused their conception can never be extinguished.

Regardless of this world's iniquity and evil, God's creation remains valuable, worthy, and deserving of dignity and respect. All of us were children once, and in the eyes of the Holy we remain children. There is nothing that others can do to us – or that we can do to ourselves – that can erase our value in the sight of God.

330. ~ GIVING and JUDGING ~

Give as if you were giving unto Christ, and let God do the judging. It's not our place to presume how the beggar will use the help we give him. If he abuses our charity, we are not cheated, for we loved our neighbor as we would want our neighbor to love us. But if we withhold help due to self-righteous judgment (which we conveniently like to call "discernment,") then we may have actually turned our backs on Christ Himself, and we risk being cast out with the goats on Judgment Day.

331. ~ LITTLE THINGS / GREAT LOVE ~

It is better to do little things with great love than to do great things with little love.

332. ~ KILLING TO PREVENT KILLING ~

Killing to prevent killing is using evil to prevent evil. We must only combat evil with good, as Our Lord taught and exemplified. Trying to conquer evil with war is like trying to illuminate darkness by extinguishing light.

"Do not be overcome by evil, but overcome evil with good."
[Romans 12:21]

333. ~ CHRIST IS BORN! GLORIFY HIM! ~

Simple shepherds stood amazed.
Wise Men prostrate fell.
Even the beasts bowed their heads.

The darkness of a humble cave
was illumined by the Light
of this newborn Prophet, Priest, and King.

God and sinners reconciled
through holy Incarnation.

This Christ child –
Who is fully divine and fully human –
what can separate His nature?

Even learned Magi
kneeled before this ineffable Mystery.

Great and small alike
worshipped at His nativity.

But there was no presence of the proud and the vain.

This seminal moment in eternal time
was beheld only by
the humble
the simple
the faithful
and wise.

Somehow, someway,
these men and beasts recognized
that this newborn Child
was Creator of the stars and Lord of the universe.

Christ is born!
Glorify Him!

334. ~ **PRESERVING FREEDOM?** ~

If we feel the need to kill our fellow man in order to preserve our own freedom, then we misunderstand what it means to be truly free.

335. ~ **GETTING and GIVING** ~

Most of our frustrations arise from our endeavors to "achieve" and our efforts to "attain." Everyone experiences failure and deficiency, and most people become enslaved by the futile desire to seek immunity from this inevitable condition of human existence. But our frustrations will diminish once we begin to change our focus from *getting* to *giving*. What we can *get* is often beyond our control, but what we can *give* is always within our power. So, as we focus on giving from our abilities, our resources, and our talents, then our frustrations will ebb and our peace will increase. And as we give, we will also help to alleviate the frustrations of those around us.

336. ~ **CRAZY PEOPLE** ~

I can deal with the crazy people. Hell, we're all nuts really. It's the people who think they're saner than the rest that you have to watch out for. You know, the ones running for office and trying to rule the world while the rest of us are simply trying to survive. I'll trust the fanatical ragamuffin on the street corner before I trust the silver tongued politician in his slick suit. Give me the impoverished prophets who share their bread rather than the wealthy blasphemers who steal my bread.

337. ~ GUILT and GOD'S LOVE ~

Guilt cannot exist in the certain remembrance of God's love.

338. ~ FIREWORKS ~

Not only do I find the sound of fireworks on the 4th of July extremely annoying, but I find it morally repugnant. Fireworks replicate the sound of the bloodshed, death, inhumanity, and destruction that were indispensible to the "founding" of America. And I personally find it impossible to celebrate these unchristian acts of war and killing.

So go ahead and enjoy your barbecues. But as you feast, stop and think for a moment about the burned flesh of innocent children who were scorched with American napalm. And pause to think about the innocent civilians who were gruesomely melted to death by America's atomic bombs. And if you want to justify such acts as the unfortunate "collateral damage" of war, then please explain why America murders its own unborn children with the same callous disregard.

Therefore, as you celebrate and extol your own "freedom," please think about the millions of innocent human beings who have been violently denied their liberty by the bombs and bullets you glorify and praise. That is, if you are a Christian or if you have a conscience.

339. ~ ALL LIFE ~

All human life is sacred. All human life bears the divine image. All human beings are living icons that have been fashioned with the very breath of God. The elderly, the unborn, the mentally ill, the physically disabled, the weak, the strong, the rich and the poor, the Black and the White, the Christian and the pagan, the heterosexual and the homosexual, the friend and the enemy, the sinner and the saint, the murderer and the pacifist – all are equally created in the image of God. Thus, to intentionally destroy human life for any reason is an act of blasphemy.

The Christian must refuse to embrace any action or ideology that violently undermines the sanctity of life or threatens the fundamental quality of life. The Christian must therefore oppose war, abortion, capital punishment, poverty, racism, and pseudo-scientific theories which teach that human life is the product of cosmic accident rather than the purposeful design of a loving Creator.

The Gospel of salvation is the glorious message that Christ died and rose again to conquer sin and death. So the Christian must never oppose the Gospel of peace by adopting anti-life philosophies and engaging in deliberate acts of violence, death, bloodshed, and destruction.

340. ~ SLAVERY ~

No one is more enslaved than those who believe that their oppressor is their liberator.

341. ~ "CHRISTIAN POLITICIAN"? ~

Show me one politician whose political platform is the Sermon on the Mount, and I will accept that he is a Christian politician. Otherwise, "Christian politician" is as much of an oxymoron as "altruistic pimp."

342. ~ AN EXHAUSTING DEFENSE ~

It gets exhausting trying to defend the sanctity of Life and the Christian imperatives of peace. I don't expect the godless to understand the humanity of the unborn or the importance of nonviolence; but it's tragic to see so many professing Christians actually argue on behalf of violence and killing. It astounds me to see the lengths some people will go to in order to reinterpret the Gospel and turn it into a message of militancy, politics, patriotism, and individual exaltation.

I have concluded that it really comes down to a simple choice: will we take Christ at His word and follow His example as He commands, or will we reject His clear teachings and example in order to preserve our own ideology, our own rights, and our own welfare? Do we love Christ and His Church (which means also loving neighbor and enemy as ourselves) or do we love our political, national, and denominational identity above the Lord we claim to serve?

When Jesus instructed His disciples to love their enemies, to bless those that persecute them, to turn the other cheek, and to put away the sword, He was not telling riddles, speaking in parables, or offering suggestions. He meant what He said. They are Christian commandments, not Buddhist koans. When Christ calls us to take up our cross and follow Him, He calls us to self-denial, suffering and death, not to prosperity, self-preservation and killing. We are not resurrected with Christ by killing for Christ. We are resurrected with Christ by dying with Christ.

So if you believe that it's ok to murder an unborn child, if you believe in exacting vengeance on your enemies, if you believe that it's permissible for Christians to kill other Christians in defense of the state, if you believe that spiritual weapons are ineffectual against sin and evil, if you believe that violence is a more holy approach to defending the innocent than the nonviolent approach of Christ, and if you believe that the sword is mightier than the Cross, then so be it. But please, I beg you: do not promote such beliefs in the name of Our Lord and Savior Jesus Christ.

343. ~ A SINNER IN HELL ~

A sinner in hell found himself surrounded by saints. "How is it that you saints are here with me in hell?" he asked. One of the saints answered him, saying, "We are not in hell, we are in heaven." The sinner was confused. "But I am in hell and you are here with me." The saint replied: "The love of God is everywhere, and all souls experience it. We are experiencing it as heaven, but you are experiencing it as hell."

344. ~ TRUTH and LIFE ~

The question of truth is a matter of life. The question of life is a matter of truth. Where truth prevails, life prevails. Where life prevails, truth prevails. When one opposes or denies life, he opposes and denies truth. And when one opposes and denies truth, he opposes and denies life.

That's why violence is always predicated upon lies. In order to destroy lives you must first subvert and suppress the truth. Systemic evil is invariably sustained by systemic lies. The incalculable blood that is shed by war and abortion flows from a foundation of falsehoods.

Our Lord said, *"I am the way, the truth, and the life, and no one can come to the Father except through me."* [St. John 14:6] To destroy life and to oppose truth is to thereby deny Christ. Where violence thrives, Christ is absent. But where life, love, and truth prevail, Christ is in our midst.

"There is a tragic clash between Truth and the world. Pure, undistorted truth burns up the world." ~ Nikolai Berdyaev ~

345. ~ BABYLON ~

Babylon: where they fight to keep lies in the schools and prayer out; where they fight to keep Mexicans from entering and babies from emerging; where war is an honor and peace is a shame; where profit is a virtue and poverty is a crime; where politicians are lawful and artists are outlaws; where fools are heroes and prophets are villains.

346. ~ THE IMPETUS of MYSTERY ~

The impetus of mystery resides in the reality of its ultimate truth. In other words, we are intrigued by mystery because behind it there is an answer. All riddles, puzzles, and mysteries convey inherent solutions, answers, and truths. We search, seek, and wonder because we intuitively sense a greater spiritual reality behind the material realities we observe. That's why the skeptic is a poor scientist and a poor philosopher. He forces himself to adopt an unnatural epistemology which states that radical doubt is the most objective foundation for the acquisition of knowledge. But from the moment we're born, we learn not by doubt but by curiosity. So we should wonder why we wonder. And our innate sense of wonder points to the reality of all things wondrous. And all things wondrous point to One who is ultimately wonderful.

347. ~ DEPTH, TRUTH, ETERNITY ~

There is depth in simplicity. There is truth in mystery. And there is eternity in the moment.

348. ~ TEACH ME TO PRAY ~

I know how to talk
I know how to eat
I know how to argue
I know how to drink

I know how to preach
I know how to write
I know how to judge
I know how to know that I'm right

But please Lord,
Teach me to PRAY!

349. ~ I WAIT ~

I could trust in bloodshed.
But I don't.
I could slit their wicked necks.
But I won't.

I could watch the evil bleed.
But I don't.
In their blood I could bathe my feet.
But I won't.

I could make them pay.
I could avenge, slaughter, and slay...

But I don't.
And I won't.

I have faith in Judgment Day.
So I leave violence alone.
I leave it alone.

And I wait.

I have received more than a few admonitions and rebukes from sincere people expressing concern over my "angry" words regarding the evils of politics, violence, and blind patriotic fervor. I have been told that my "awful" rhetoric and "hurtful" language is unproductive and unchristian. I have even been accused of cursing soldiers, which is simply not true. (I do not judge, condemn, or curse anyone; I simply condemn evil ideologies and evil actions.)

I am told that I will catch more flies with honey than with vinegar, and that it's better to light a candle than to curse the darkness. And while I agree with that, I also believe that awful things sometimes warrant an awful rebuke. Throughout the scriptures and throughout Church history, we see God using both gentle admonitions and harsh rebukes. We read that *"a gentle answer turns away wrath."* *[Proverbs 15:1]* But we also see God telling Ezekiel: *"When I say unto the wicked, O wicked man, thou shalt surely die; if thou dost not speak to warn the wicked from his way, that wicked man shall die in his iniquity; but his blood will I require at thine hand."* *[Ezekiel 33:8]*

We must always speak the truth in love (Ephesians 4:15), but we must not confuse harshness or anger for a lack of love. The man diving headlong into the consuming fire does not need a gentle word; he needs a life saving cry: *"Stop! Don't do that!"* Therefore, I try my best to provide a proper biblical and ecclesiastical balance in what I say and how I say it, although I'm sure I certainly fail in many ways.

The purpose of my life is not to please people, to get elected, to sell books, to gain a following, or to make everyone happy. The purpose of my life is to love God and to love my neighbors as myself. (St. Matthew 22:36-40)

When I proclaim Orthodoxy, I inevitably offend some of my Protestant friends. When I proclaim peace, I inevitably offend some of my military friends. When I speak for the unborn, I inevitably offend some of my "pro-choice" friends. When I point out the hypocrisies and evils of this American government, I inevitably offend most of my patriotic American friends – conservatives and liberals alike.

I do not wish to offend or upset anyone, but as Bob Marley (Berhane Selassie) said, *"The truth is an offense, but not a sin."* I don't speak *my* truth. I simply strive to point people to the life, teachings, and Truth of Our Lord Jesus Christ; for He alone is the Way, the Truth, and the Life. (St. John 14:6) I am sinful, erring, and fallible. So it's not my words that matter; it's His words that must be understood and followed.

People need to seriously think about the harsh realities of war, poverty, abortion, and slavery – as unpleasant as those realities may be. Those of us who call ourselves Christians should especially be voices of peace and life amidst the darkness and depravity of this nation, this government, and this world. If the children of God are afraid to point out these grim but necessary truths, then who else will?

Can we not love all our fellow men, regardless of their nationality? Can we not thank God for the blessings we have in America without turning a blind eye to this government's historical and current bloodshed and evil? Can we not decry injustice and inhumanity without being accused of bitterness and hatred?

It is love, not hate, which compels me to speak out against the violent death, the inhumane suffering, and the unjust oppression of my fellow human beings. If such love is wrong, then may God preserve my error.

351. ~ INSANITY and DIVINE LOVE ~

We are all sick, fallen, broken, desperate, and needy. We are all insane because we are all affected by the insanity of sin, and we all inhabit an insane world. And yet the glorious and mystical truth is that we remain the very image of God (Genesis 1:27). We are all fearfully and wonderfully made (Psalm 139:14). We are God's handiwork, created in Christ Jesus to do good works which God prepared in advance for us to do (Ephesians 2:10). And because we are His image, He became a man and suffered and died to redeem us. The love of God is the most insane thing in the world to those who are still of this world, to those who have not known divine restoration and redemption.

How can any of us truly understand or explain His love? But we must nevertheless trust in its incomprehensible mystery. And we see that those who truly live, demonstrate, and experience the love of God are often those that the world considers foolish, naïve, and insane. The world can't comprehend the love of God, and it still has no room for those who truly manifest such love. So it crucifies the God-bearers. It banishes the prophets and ridicules the saints. It rejects the innocent hope in a child's eyes in favor of a politician's cynical smile. It is more offended by the baby's gentle cry than by the chaotic cacophony of war.

Divine love is the greatest threat to evil. It is the most revolutionary force in the universe. May Our Lord grant us the strength to know and embrace such love. May He grant us the grace to accept our insanity so that we may find His peace.

"The time is coming when men will go mad, and when they see someone who is not mad they will condemn him, saying: 'You are mad! You are not like us!'" ~ St. Anthony the Great ~

352. ~ TWO KINGDOMS ~

The Christian must live with the tension of two kingdoms. We live in the world, yet our citizenship is in heaven. (Philippians 3:20) We must therefore navigate and engage a fallen world while having nothing to do with earthly kingdoms. Therefore we don't vote, we don't run for office, we don't join the military, and we don't get sidetracked and disillusioned by the ways and means of mortal governments and worldly affairs. And yet we must still "render unto Caesar." We pay our taxes, we obey the law, and we comport with society as long as that obedience and comportment doesn't compromise our obedience to Christ and His Church. And let's face it: it's not always easy to discern these matters. For example, should we pay taxes when we know that our taxes will be used to fund evils such as war and abortion? I would argue no, as I tend to adopt the philosophy of Henry David Thoreau in this regard. But we do have to honestly wrestle with these things. However, the main thing for Christians to understand is that our focus and allegiance is to the kingdom of God and not to the kingdoms of men. Therefore, we have no business taking oaths of allegiance to human governments, manmade constitutions, and nationalistic flags. As the apostle writes, *"For here we have no lasting city, but we seek the city that is to come." [Hebrews 13:14]*

I do not pretend or assert that pacifism is pragmatically effective for human governments which are based on the principles of power and expediency. The kingdoms of this world will always operate on a worldly ethos. I have no illusions that civil governments will become pacifistic and humanitarian. That's why I argue that Christians should never be involved in governmental affairs that require them to compromise obedience to Christ. We are to be salt and light, and we lose our flavor and dim our luminance when we divide our hearts, minds, and souls between the kingdom of God and the kingdoms of men.

"How does it become a man to behave toward the American government today? I answer, that he cannot without disgrace be associated with it. I cannot for an instant recognize that political organization as my government which is the slave holder's government also. All men recognize the right of revolution; that is, the right to refuse allegiance to, and to resist the government, when its tyranny or its inefficiency are great and unendurable."
~ Henry David Thoreau ~

353. ~ A FREE MAN in BABYLON ~

It is better to be a free man in prison than a slave in Babylon. And it is better to lose our heads than to lose our souls.

354. ~ PARADISE REGAINED ~

It's a beautiful world. A paradise lost but regained by Christ. We eat His Body and drink His Blood, then kill our brothers and wound the Church. We don't truly understand the love of God. If we did, then we would know how to truly love one another.

355. ~ ACCEPTABLE SERVICE ~

St. Paul writes:

*"Therefore, I urge you, brothers and sisters, in view of God's mercy, to offer your bodies as a **living sacrifice**, holy and pleasing to God—this is your true and proper **service**. Do not be conformed to the pattern of this world, but be transformed by the renewing of your mind. Then you will be able to test and approve what God's will is— his good, pleasing and perfect will." [Romans 12:1-2]*

Christ calls us to be *living* sacrifices. This is our acceptable Christian service. We lay down our own lives if need be, but we dare not destroy the lives of others. There are countless ways to serve God, to serve one's fellow man, and to serve one's country in a nonviolent capacity. Our Lord calls us to sacrifice our own lives, not to sacrifice the lives of others. Violent service is not Christian service.

356. ~ BLAMING GOD ~

It's easy to blame God for the sins we create ourselves. Many people endeavor to discredit divine revelation so they can avoid confronting their own reflection.

357. ~ HEART ~

A fragile heart is broken
and therefore it is healed.
A soft heart is molded
so the hand of God is revealed.

But the hard heart is worthless,
the shell of an empty soul.
It never suffers, never sorrows;
it is forever lonely, forever cold.

358. ~ PREACH THE GOSPEL ~

Preach the Gospel
in the Church.

Preach the Gospel
in the streets.

Preach the Gospel
to everyone you meet.

But make sure you know
that the Gospel means peace.

359. ~ SWORD and CROSS ~

When we meet the sword
with the Cross
Then though we are killed
we have not lost

360. ~ LIGHT and SIGHT ~

It is easy to see sin in man, but it is hard to see Christ in him. Sin is loud but feeble, conspicuous yet conquered. Christ is quiet but omnipotent, hidden yet victorious. The light of Christ illumines the world, but we focus on human darkness rather than on divine radiance. It is hard to gaze directly at the Son. The light of Christ blinds us in order to save us. Those who have been blinded by Eternal luminescence are unable to see man's sins; they see only Christ in all men. I see the darkness all too well. I am comfortable with my night vision. I do not want to be blinded by the light of Christ. But I pray for it.

361. ~ A BRIEF MESSAGE ON DR. KING'S BIRTHDAY ~
[1/20/2014]

Today, many will pay insincere homage to Dr. Martin Luther King, Jr. They will claim him as their hero while rejecting the values and ideals for which he lived and died. They will extol a prophetic King in the same breath with which they praise a presidential Pharaoh.

There will be parties and parades. There will be speeches from celebrities, politicians, and propagandists who profit from the very evils that Dr. King opposed. They will talk of his Dream while facilitating the nightmares of warfare, poverty, and abortion. They will pervert his message and legacy to suit their own self interests.

So I beg you: if you feel the need to rationalize and defend inhumanity, injustice and violence, please don't do so in the name of Dr. Martin Luther King, Jr. If you believe that patriotic identity trumps the brotherhood of humanity, if you believe that political affiliation transcends universal love, and if you believe that the right to kill overrides the right to Life, then so be it. But please don't misappropriate Dr. King's message of peace, justice, and divine love to support your putrid agendas of politics, war, and abortion.

The most effective way to marginalize the prophets is to turn them into symbolic icons and thereby dilute the truth and potency of their message. In other words, do with them exactly what the world has done with Christ. So we erect a statue of Dr. King, we declare his birthday a national holiday, and we call ourselves "Christians." But the last thing we do is take up our cross and lay down our lives for the poor, the oppressed, and the unborn victims of this nation's legislated slaughter.

Babylon's demonic spirit killed his body; but there is still a remnant that continues to carry the torch of Dr. King's peace and love, shining his light and echoing his truth.

We must remember that Dr. King was a disciple of Jesus Christ; and the Gospel will prevail eternally. These bloody swords will never conquer the Cross!

362. ~ NONVIOLENCE IS A METAPHYSICAL MORALITY ~

Nonviolence has no real power if it is merely a pragmatic strategy rather than a spiritually philosophical way of life. The nonviolent resistance movements of Mahatma Gandhi and Martin Luther King were effective strategies because they emanated from a metaphysical morality that adhered to spiritual power and divine truth. It is naïve to think that nonviolence will work only as a tactical scheme. Unless we are unconditionally wedded to the principles of peace, then our nonviolent maneuvers will not have enduring success.

The redemptive sacrifice of Our Lord was not a "strategy;" it was an inviolate example for all those who seek to follow Him. Only the Cross of Christ can save souls and redeem sinful men; but when we emulate Our Lord's example of unconditional love and sacrificial nonviolence, then we lead people to the Savior and we change the world.

363. ~ A DEARTH of CREATIVITY ~

It discloses a dearth of creativity when artists portray the lowest common denominators of life and justify it by saying that they are merely "reflecting reality." But this is the specious refrain that we often hear today from those in the entertainment industry. They somehow think that artistic authenticity means glorifying the seediest aspects of human existence and portraying the depravity of man at his worst.

But truly creative people are those that reflect the radiance of the Almighty Creator. Their artistic expressions stimulate the mind, the heart, and the soul. They are able to reflect the realities of life in ways that compel us to emulate life's goodness and beauty while warning us against its evils and horror. Truly creative works also awaken our own visionary energies when we encounter them, and they inspire us to use our own talents to enlighten human consciousness and uplift the human spirit. There can be no true creativity without a connection to the Creator.

"What is good in art has its beginning from God."
~ Clement of Alexandria ~

364. ~ CHILDREN TEACH US THE GREATEST LESSON ~

Children teach us the greatest lesson of all: the willingness to love and to be loved. And this is all that God really asks of us, that we love Him and that we allow ourselves to be loved *by* Him.

365. ~ LIES and TRUTH ~

There is no lie – regardless of how powerful and enduring – that can outlive the truth.

366. ~ REAL SOLUTIONS are SPIRITUAL SOLUTIONS ~

One cannot be truly free if they are illiterate, hungry, and paralyzed by fear. But one is not necessarily free just because they are educated, well fed, and isolated from violence and crime. Materialism, lust, and greed often constitute the strongest shackles of emotional, mental, and spiritual slavery. The oppressive systems of human history have been fueled by a materialistic worldview, and these systems have all viewed human problems and solutions through a materialistic lens. But the real and dire needs of humanity can only be fully met when approached from a metaphysical and spiritual perspective. Apart from God, there is no freedom. Apart from the Creator, there is no solution to the problems that plague His creation.

367. ~ BABYLON SLAVE ~

Babylon doesn't make you its slave; you make yourself a slave of Babylon, and then you curse the voice of freedom.

368. ~ DEFEATING EVIL ~

We do not oppose evil; we meet it with good. We do not acquiesce with evil; rather we manifest love. We do not tolerate evil, but we seek to suffer it as did Our Lord. And in this way, evil is defeated.

"Not by might nor by power,
but by my Spirit sayeth the Lord."
[Zechariah 4:6]

369. ~ SOLDIER ~

Soldier, I see pride in your eyes,
Masquerading shame
And hiding lies

Welcomed home to heroic parades
A uniform of medals
But a soul that's stained

Soldier, why are you mad at me?
Was it I that sent you overseas
To rob and kill
To steal and maim
All in the cause of a patriot's game?

Soldier, you were once a child
Quick to befriend and quick to smile
But now you're hardened
Been taught to hate
Trained to kill for god and state

Soldier, they demand I honor you
But I cannot honor what isn't true

And there is no greater lie than this:
That freedom is purchased
With a bullet's kiss

Soldier, I speak to you of peace and love
For there is no greater cause to serve

Trust no more
In the flag that waves
Send no more people to their graves

370. ~ AFRICA: THE ORIGIN ~

Africa is the origin. Africa is the continent from which all humanity emanated. The true spiritual and social condition of the planet is revealed in the spiritual and social condition of the African continent. Until Africa is free, the world will not be free.

"We look to the vision of an Africa not merely free, but united. We know that there are differences among us, but we also know that unity can be and has been attained among men of the most disparate origins. Differences of race, of religion, of culture, and of tradition are not impossible obstacles to the coming together of people."
~ H.I.M. Emperor Haile Selassie I ~
[From *Selected Speeches of Haile Selassie*]

"I want to talk about Africa. Each time I've gone there, the first thing my whole body is thirsty for is rhythms – to hear the music and see the dancers. It's about connections between us and where we came from. To this day, African music is my number one hunger. I can never get enough of the rhythms, the melodies, the second melodies, the colors, the way the music can suddenly change my mood from light and joyful to somber. If people ask me, I tell them that we play 99.9 percent African music. That's what Santana does. I wish there was a school that just taught one thing – how to have some humility and recognize that Africa is important and necessary to the world – and not just because of its music either." ~ Carlos Santana ~

371. ~ EVIL and LIES ~

Everything evil is based on a lie. Behind the linguistic euphemisms, behind the rhetorical obfuscations, behind the propaganda, behind the repetitive mantras of the politically monopolized masses, there is a truth that the devil fights to suppress. The very word itself is a lie: "Abortion" – an amorphous, innocuous term that masquerades the horror of the most unnatural, destructive, and violent practice ever conceived by man. Evil flourishes in the void of truth. Abortion is murder. We must speak this truth without apology.

But there is another evil that is also predicated upon a lie: the evil of *hopelessness*. The woman who murders her child through abortion is demonically assaulted with the lie that she is beyond forgiveness, that she has permanently severed herself from the love of God. Haunted with the reality of her irrevocable decision, she subsequently descends into guilt and despair. The demons convince her that God has turned His back; so she seeks solace in increasing sins, and her heart becomes increasingly hardened. And this works out well for the abortion industry, because most women who have one abortion will inevitably have another abortion. And make no mistake, there's a lot of money to be made from abortion. Despair leads to self-destruction, and abortion not only destroys an innocent child but it also destroys the spirit and peace of the woman who has aborted her child.

So the devil endeavors to keep women enslaved to the lies of abortion. First he convinces the woman that abortion is not murder. Then, after she has committed murder and *knows* that she has committed murder, Satan says, *"You are a murderer! God can never forgive you! There's no point in trying to repent now. You can't undo what you've done."*

There is an inextricable correlation between murder and lies. Our Lord said that Satan *"was a murderer from the beginning, not holding to the truth, for there is no truth in him. When he lies, he speaks his native language, for he is a liar and the father of lies." [St. John 8:44]*

So the Christian must not hesitate to speak the truth: abortion is murder. Period. But we must also speak the truth that there is forgiveness and healing for those who truly seek it. The Psalmist declares that *"The mercy of God endureth forever." [Psalm 136]* Whether you've had one abortion or multiple abortions, there is salvation in Christ, redemption in His Cross, and healing through the Sacramental graces of His Church. But as the prophet Jonah declared from the belly of the great fish: *"Those who follow vanity and lies forsake their own mercy." [Jonah 2:9]*

The tools of the devil are laughably weak. His greatest weapons are lies, and his lies are easily defeated by the simple proclamation of divine truth. I know many truly liberated women, and their liberation is predicated upon reliance upon the truth of the Gospel. They are strong women that rest in God's forgiveness, women that march in eternal truth and proclaim divine grace. I have also known many women that are in bondage to guilt, anger, and despair. They are angry at God and they rail against the very world to which they are enslaved. They are miserable because they choose to believe lies rather than the truth. But they too can be emancipated; for as Our Lord said, *"The truth shall make you free." [St. John 8:32]*

Evildoers are merely those who are enslaved to lies. Therefore, our duty as Christians is to liberate all people with divine truth. Our mission is to bring hope to the hopeless and light to the darkness. Abortion is the great lie of our time; and like Goliath, it too shall be felled with the sling of truth and the stone of the Gospel. No lie can endure forever. And where love abides, lies die.

"The Spirit of the Sovereign Lord is on me, because the Lord has anointed me to proclaim good news to the poor. He has sent me to bind up the brokenhearted, to proclaim freedom for the captives and release from darkness for the prisoners, to proclaim the year of the Lord's favor and the day of vengeance of our God, to comfort all who mourn, and provide for those who grieve in Zion— to bestow on them a crown of beauty instead of ashes, oil instead of mourning, and a garment of praise instead of a spirit of despair. They will be called oaks of righteousness, a planting of the Lord for the display of his splendor." [Isaiah 61:1-3]

372. ~ SEEKING CROWNS or SEEKING CHRIST? ~

Some seek heavenly crowns and heavenly rewards, but the true Christian seeks only Christ. If we do not experience His loving embrace in this life, then we will not experience His embrace in eternity. If we are crowned with all the stars of the universe but do not have Christ in our hearts, then we are crowned with chains.

373. ~ PRAY for THE PROPHETS ~

Keep the prophets always in your prayers, for they trod upon the path of greatest difficulty. And as you experience persecutions, setbacks, and hardships in your own life, remember that the sweetness of Zion awaits all those who endure the bitterness of living righteously in an unrighteous world. Remember also that upon Baptism all Orthodox Christians become prophets of Christ, His Truth, and His Church. As Bishop Kallistos Ware explains:

"The Church is not only hierarchical, it is charismatic and Pentecostal. 'Quench not the Spirit. Despise not prophesyings' (I Thessalonians 5:19-20). The Holy Spirit is poured out upon all God's people. There is a special ordained ministry of bishops, priests, and deacons; yet at the same time the whole people of God are prophets and priests."

374. ~ UNCONDITIONAL LOVE ~

Unconditional love is sometimes very painful. It is costly. It is epitomized by the Cross of Our Lord. But there is a mystical joy in the midst of our divine suffering, for St. Stephen radiated the luminescence of the Holy Spirit even as he was being stoned to death. (Cf. Acts 6:15; 7:54-60) It is a holy paradox that true and unconditional love often brings us deep pain as it elevates us towards God.

375. ~ THE ULTIMATE SPIRITUAL DELUSION ~

Pride is the ultimate spiritual delusion. Pride says, "I need no Savior, I am responsible for my own salvation." Pride says, "I am 'saved,' and therefore I need no Church, no Priest, no apostolic Teaching and Tradition to guide me." Pride says, "I can understand the scriptures on my own, because the Holy Spirit works through me independently of anyone else."

At one extreme, pride says, "I will ascend to heaven on the merits of my own noble works," and at the other extreme it says, "God has saved me and damned others, so I am above any need to struggle and work out my salvation with fear and trembling." Pride isolates and elevates the individual as his own spiritual, moral, and theological authority. Pride leads men to set their own course and violently trample over any opinions, authorities, and people that impede their own personal happiness and welfare. Is it any wonder that pride thus paves the wide and accommodating road to hell?

376. ~THE SPIRITUAL SEEKER ~

The spiritual seeker may often dance on the edges of orthodoxy, perhaps dangerously so. Compelled by his thirst for the Divine, he will perpetually question, challenge, and disrupt the status quo. And he will be ostracized for his failure to conform to those who have safely settled into a secure façade of faith that makes no demands and ignites no fires. The spiritual seeker is a revolutionary who refuses to allow the infinite truths of God to be reduced to impotent legalisms and cold, dead customs.

But apart from the loving, firm, and secure guidance of the Church, the most sincere spiritual seeker will at best ascend no further than himself; and at worst he will descend into a hellish fate. That's why the Saints and Fathers of the Orthodox Faith were the truest revolutionaries. Rooted in the unshakable foundation of apostolic Teaching and Tradition, they were constantly rebelling against the injustice of their own sins, condemning pharisaic religiosity that masquerades as piety, and perpetually illuminating the divine fires of forgiveness, love, mercy, and grace.

The world will always produce its various religious sages and shamans who offer esoteric insights devoid of any real spiritual substance. But eternal truth has always emanated from the mouths, pens, and lives of God's saints to transform the souls of men in every era of human history. St. Paul writes that the Church is the foundation and pillar of truth. (I Timothy 3:15) And therefore, apart from the Church there can be no transcendental and eternally victorious revolution. When we lay down our arms, take up our Cross, and allow Christ to change our own hearts, only then can we hope to change the world.

377. ~ THE HERESY of HOPE? ~

Because of the Cross, I am eternally hopeful. Because of God's enduring mercy, I have hope for my own salvation. Because of Christ's infinite love, I have hope for all creatures, all spirits, and all souls. Because of the omnipotent fire of divine love, perhaps even the devil himself may be saved. I dare not assert this as a certainty, but I can hope. And I can't think of anything more unchristian and contrary to the Gospel than to preach a message of hopelessness and despair. If hope is a heresy, then let me stand condemned.

378. ~ BEAUTY and HEART ~

If it is not born from the heart, then it cannot be beautiful. And if it does not suffer, agonize, doubt, and despair, then it cannot be of the heart.

379. ~ REVOLUTIONARY CONDEMNATION? ~

There is nothing original, insightful, or revolutionary about condemning organized religion because of the hypocrisy of the religiously organized. Condemning the specks in the eyes of the religious will not obviate the beams that impede the vision of the irreligious. There is more nobility in sinful Christians that feed the poor than in the self-righteous "revolutionaries" who condemn injustice in theory but ignore the presence of Christ in the reality of the suffering.

380. ~ FREE WILL and ETERNAL HOPE ~

Man's free will is not in bondage and powerless to respond to divine love; and it is not more powerful than the love of God that imbued it within us. The Cross has conquered sin and death, and the mercy of God endures forever. (Psalm 136) Therefore it is quite Orthodox and quite Christian to hope that all souls may ultimately be saved. The doctrine of undeniable universalism may be a heresy, but I find it even more heretical to find pleasure in the torment of the damned. I'm wary of any doctrine that negates hope. Because of the Cross, I believe hope is eternal and infinite. So we can and should hope for the ultimate salvation of all souls, just as we expectantly hope for the restoration of all creation.

"To hope for all souls is imperative;
and it is quite tenable that their salvation is inevitable."
~ G.K. Chesterton ~

"God will seek us – how long? Until he finds us. And when he's found the last little shriveling rebellious soul and has depopulated hell, then death will be swallowed up in victory, and Christ will turn over all things to the Father that He may be all and in all. Then every tongue shall confess that Jesus Christ is Lord, to the glory of God the Father." ~ Clarence Jordan ~

381. ~ MAMA ~

Mama,

We've been struggling from day one
When we both struggled to see me born
You gave me life and gave me love
We've tried and cried, but it's not enough

I've failed you in so many ways
To be myself, you feel betrayed
You turn your back because you care
But it gets too painful for me to bear

I still struggle towards the light
You still look at me with love and fright

I'm a work of art that you can't perfect
But I'm a work of art nonetheless

You gave me the colors
Now let me create
My failures are not your mistakes

We're as separate as sculptor and stone
Different as mother and embryo
And yet, always, forever, just as close

382. ~ LABOR and CAPITAL ~

Hammer and sickle
Dollars and cents
Labor and capital
Repent, repent!

383. ~ A PORTRAIT of THE GOSPEL ~

As I watch my wife breastfeed our infant daughter, I see a beautiful portrait of the Gospel. Our little baby is completely dependent upon my wife to feed and nourish her. My wife has everything our daughter needs for sustenance and growth. If my wife does not feed her, our infant will not survive. Yet our daughter must struggle to receive the milk from her mother's breast. I witness our little girl labor to latch on and nurse. I see her exert tremendous energy and effort to receive the life-giving nutriment she needs. But my wife initiates the feeding, cradling our daughter in her loving arms and coaxing her to drink the vital sustenance from her nurturing bosom. During the suckling process, I observe a profound oneness that occurs between mother and child – a mystical cooperation that results in our baby's physical and emotional development.

Similarly, God initiates and provides everything necessary for our salvation; but we must "latch on" and struggle to avail ourselves of the spiritual nourishment we desperately need. Our spiritual efforts do not earn us God's love any more than my infant daughter's efforts to nurse earn her the love of her mother. God loves us unconditionally; and He is ever reaching out to us, coaxing us, cradling us, calling us to exert all of our energy and strength in the effort to receive His divine sustenance. Our Lord never withholds His love, His mercy, or His grace. He offers it freely to all people – unconditionally and unmerited. But divine love is only received with the same faith, effort, and struggle of an infant child who is completely dependent upon its mother's sustaining breast.

As with mother and nursing child, the Gospel is a synergistic cooperation between God and man. We are completely dependent upon the grace of Christ, His Cross, and His Church. But this spiritual dependence involves striving, effort, cooperation, and struggle on our part. Certainly, when our efforts fail and we grow weak in our striving, the unconditional love and strength of God will preserve us – just as a loving mother preserves and protects her infant child. But although our redemption is freely given to us by God, we must cooperate and struggle to avail ourselves of His salvific grace.

I have never seen my wife happier than during the moments when she has nursed one of our infant children. And I have never seen my children more content than during those moments when they suckled from their mother's breast. In analogous fashion, God is never more glorified than when we cling to Him with all of our heart, mind, soul, and strength. And we are never more at peace than when we strive with all of our being to be at one with our God.

There is profound poignancy in the simple endeavor of a mother nursing her infant child. And through this vital act in the cycle of life, God provides a clear portrait of the mystical work of salvation. We are little children, completely dependent upon our heavenly Father. But we must labor with the faith, innocence, and effort of a newborn infant who clings with all of its essence to the vitality of its mother's breast. Surely this is what Our Lord meant when He said:

"Assuredly, I say to you, whoever does not receive the kingdom of God as a little child will by no means enter into it."
[St. Mark 10:15]

"Truly, I say to you, unless you are converted and become as little children, you will by no means enter the kingdom of Heaven."
[St. Matthew 18:3]

384. ~ LENTEN MESSAGE to MY FELLOW ORTHODOX CHRISTIANS ~

My dear fellow Orthodox Christians:

It is good that we confess the Nicene Creed. It's good that we uphold the doctrines of the Holy Trinity, the Incarnation, and the glorious Resurrection. It's good that we proclaim Orthodox truth and avail ourselves of the sacramental graces. It's good that we preserve the ancient Liturgy and worship in the manner of the apostles. All of these things are integral to our Orthodox Faith, and we dare not dispense with any part of them. But if we remain Orthodox in every aspect while supporting the deliberate destruction of human beings created in the image of God, then we have completely misunderstood the Gospel. If we do not love, forgive, and bless our enemies, then regardless of our profession or creed we are no different from the world.

Let us not be Orthodox Pharisees – straining at gnats and swallowing camels, perfecting the letter while forsaking the Spirit, praising the Prince of Peace while preparing for violence and war. God forbid that we should receive His Body and Blood, and then destroy the bodies of our neighbors and shed the blood of our fellow man. I'm not an Orthodox theologian, but I know there's nothing Orthodox about that.

So as we journey forward through Great Lent, let us commit to fasting from violence and bloodshed, death and destruction, vengeance and hate. Let us remember the words of our holy father St. John Chrysostom: *"Our warfare is to make the dead to live, not to make the living dead."*

"In peace let us pray to the Lord."

385. ~ LIFE IS LIBERATION ~

Pregnancy is not a disease. A fetus is not a tumor. A baby is not a punitive "consequence." Children are not burdens. And motherhood is not slavery.

Life affirmation, not Life negation! Life is liberation! *Embrace it!*

386. ~ POLITICIANS and THE MASSES ~

Politicians are too often showmen that pose as shamans, shysters that present themselves as sages. And the masses willingly consume their snake oil, foolishly believing that its intoxication is actually a cure.

387. ~ A GENTLE HEART ~

Lord, give me a gentle heart. I am too busy attacking in the name of "truth." I am too busy correcting error and disproving heresy (as if God needs my help). I am too busy cursing Goliath while neglecting to actually harness a sling and gather some stones. I am too busy cultivating a façade of righteousness while my heart withers from a lack of spiritual nourishment. I am too busy using my words to insult and offend; and thus it is not Goliath that is injured, but rather the cause of the Gospel.

I realize now that the most profound impact upon my life has come not from those who are "great," but from those who are gentle. My grandmothers, my father, my children, my father-in-law, and my forbearing wife – their gentle love has sustained me and led me to believe that life is really worth living.

So, please pray for God to grant me a gentle heart. For without such a heart, I will not only die, but I will most probably be damned.

388. ~ A TASTE and A FEAST ~

I have tasted the darkness, but I feast on the Light.

389. ~ POOR CHOICE ~

There are too many Christians who choose political proselytizing over prophetic proclamation. The problem with this is that they often end up becoming politicians and cease being Christians.

390. ~ WOLVES or SHEEP? ~

We are either wolves are sheep. We cannot be both. Sheep are not predators, nor do they slay the wolves that prey upon them. Sheep are not armed with fangs and claws. How then, one may ask, do the sheep survive without weapons of defense? The answer is simple: they stay close to the Shepherd. The Lion of Judah is their protector and avenger. Christians can no more be soldiers than sheep can be wolves.

391. ~ WHAT STRANGE FAITH IS THIS? ~

With boldness and clarity we preach the truth that because Christ's blood was shed, the blood of bulls and goats no longer need be spilled. And, yet, how blind we are to an even greater truth: the truth that because His blood was spilled, the blood of our fellow man no longer need be shed. What strange faith is this that has more mercy on dumb beasts than on human beings created in the image of God? The Gospel that reconciles man to God and man to man can never be reconciled with doctrines that justify violence, war, and killing.

392. ~ THE RICH LIBERAL ~

The rich liberal is full of rationales for his cruel selfishness and apathetic indifference to the plight of the suffering. The rich liberal is often an advocate of inept social programs ostensibly designed to help the poor, but which in actuality only perpetuate poverty. Instead of personally sharing his own wealth with those in need, the rich liberal simply boasts of his leftist politics. At cocktail parties, the rich liberal passionately articulates his insincere laments about poverty, racism, and homelessness. But when the poor knock on his door, he calls the police!

393. ~ WHO WON? ~

Who won your war sir?
Tell me
What did you kill for?
What did you preserve
by burying your brothers in the earth?

Who won your war sir?
Tell me
What did you kill for?
What flag still waves
because images of God were sent to their graves?

Who won your war sir?
Tell me
What did you kill for?
What ideal is now safe
because children were burned and women were raped?

Who won your war sir?
Tell me
What did you kill for?
What nation now thrives
from the bullets and bombs that poisoned the skies?

Who won your war sir?
Tell me
What did you kill for?
Is humanity now free
because of killing's misery?

Who won your war sir?
Tell me
No, I don't care
It matters not to me who won
Wars are waged and hell's seeds are sown

So go ahead and celebrate
Pin your medals and have your parades

But I will never rejoice with you
War is a sin
And that is the truth

394. ~ THE MYSTERIES of THE UNIVERSE DWELL WITHIN ~

I am the river
I am the mountain
I am the sand
and I am the sea.

I am lightning and thunder
sky and cloud.

I am moon and stars
sun and rain.

I am fire and ice
wind and rock.

I am movement, depth,
height, progress, and flow –
as are we all.

The mysteries of the universe
dwell within.

For we are divinely created
in the indelible image of Almighty God.

"God created man in His own image, in the image of God He
created him; male and female He created them." [Genesis 1:27]

"I will praise thee; for I am fearfully and wonderfully made:
marvelous are thy works, and that my soul knoweth right well."
[Psalm 139:14]

395. ~ SALVATION ~

Salvation is free, but not easy. It is completely dependent upon the grace of God, yet we must work it out with fear and trembling. It is given to all, but only a few find it. We are saved only by His Cross, and yet not without taking up our own.

396. ~ BRIEF THOUGHTS on THE FORT HOOD, TEXAS TRAGEDY ~
[4/2/2014]

My sincere prayers go out to the victims of the shooting in Fort Hood, Texas today. May God grant a merciful repose for those who were killed, and may He comfort and heal those who were wounded. I pray that Christ will bring peace to the families and friends of the victims.

Once again we have witnessed the reciprocal evil of a culture of violence and death. The media will struggle to find a reason, a cause, an answer for why this tragedy occurred. And there really is no answer that will bring any comfort to the relatives of those who were injured or slain. Precious human lives were violently cut down, and no explanation is sufficient for those who mourn the loss of their loved ones at this dark hour.

It may seem insensitive, but I cannot be silent about the inextricable correlation between violence sown and violence reaped. A society that trains men and women to kill and then gives them medals for killing cannot expect to be immune from such bloodshed and horror. A society insane enough to allow the daily slaughter of its unborn innocents cannot be shocked when 16 innocent people are suddenly shot down by an insane man.

Most of us don't want to reckon with these truths. But the law of the harvest is inviolate. The seeds that are planted will produce their inevitable fruit. And sometimes the cruel harvest comes unexpectedly; and although cruel it is not necessarily unjust. It comes to us from our own hands. It is the manifestation of our own making. If we send our sons and daughters off to war, if we send our women to abort the fruit of their wombs, if we cling to our guns instead of the Cross, then we saturate our society with seeds of destruction. These seeds of violence simmer beneath the soil, pregnant with bloodshed that is fatefully unleashed at unpredictable and awful hours. And just as the violence of war and abortion have no regard for the guiltless, so too the violent harvest that is reaped spares not the innocent.

The truth be told, we as a society are collectively guilty for the tragic events that occurred in Fort Hood. We have not only tolerated violence but we have encouraged, supported, and praised it. In the pretext of peace, freedom, liberty and rights we have sown violence, death, chaos, and destruction. And once again we have been visited by a harvest that will haunt us. But most of us will not have the courage to face these realities. Rather than repenting of our cooperative evil, we will probably cling even more obstinately to militarism and violence. We will continue to poison our own well and then curse the waters upon which we collectively choke.

Violence is such a heavy burden to bear. Why in God's name can't we forsake it?

"Lord have mercy."

397. ~ NO GREATER HERESY ~

As Orthodox Christians, we have been diligent in discerning and combating many of the demonic deceptions that have lured men away from Christ and His Church throughout the centuries. We have guarded ourselves against false doctrines and heresies. We have been resolute in resisting the tide of moral relativism, and we have rightly refuted subjective spirituality which masquerades itself as Christian faith. We have preserved our Divine Liturgy from the vicissitudes of cultural corruption, iconoclasm, and novel innovations. We have indeed retained our Orthodoxy – our correct worship and right belief – in many vital areas.

However, in spite of our diligence to remain uncorrupted by the world and impervious to the wiles of the devil, too many of us have nevertheless fallen prey to the satanic spirit of bloodshed, violence, destruction and death. While exalting the Cross with our words, we have forsaken the Cross with our lives. We have exchanged the Wood of redemption for weapons of retaliation. We have abandoned the Gospel of reconciliation and wreaked vengeance on our enemies. While preaching the good news of salvation, we have engaged in horrific acts of destruction. While claiming to worship the Prince of Peace, we have effectively served the violent agenda of the prince of darkness. We have spurned the folly of the Cross in favor of the wisdom and expediency of this world. We have forsaken the simplicity of apostolic nonviolence and justified the inexcusable evils of war. We have fasted from the humility of Christ and feasted on patriotic pride. We have ignored the Christian imperatives of peace and embraced the Machiavellian methods of militarism and might.

There is no greater heresy, deception, or blasphemy than to embrace violence in the name of Our Lord and Savior. And there is certainly nothing Orthodox about destroying living human icons fashioned with the very breath of God. I do not claim to have any divine visions or revelatory dreams, but I can imagine Christ saying to the Orthodox Church today:

"You have done well in preserving sound doctrine. You have done well in your prayers and fasting. You have done well in safeguarding the Liturgy and trusting in the sacramental graces. You have done well in refuting heresies and upholding theological truth. For these things I commend you. But this one thing I have against you: You have not forsaken the sword. You have failed to recognize My presence in your enemies. You have failed to understand that I have called you to the Cross, and that the Cross means offering up your own lives without destroying the lives of others. You have failed to separate yourselves from the world by renouncing the militaristic methods of violence. You have failed to trust in the spiritual weapons I have issued you, and instead you have trusted in fleshly force and carnal power. You have obeyed many of my teachings and instructions, but you have ignored my commands to love your enemies and to bless those that persecute you. Repent of violence and

put away the sword! My kingdom is not of this world, and it will be ushered in by prayer, not by bloodshed."

398. ~ A MESSAGE TO MY PRO-LIFE COMRADES ~

To all my blessed comrades working in the Pro-Life movement:

Please don't dilute and confuse the Pro-Life message by promoting a right wing political agenda. Conservative politics can no more bring about an end to abortion than liberal politics can bring about world peace. When you oppose abortion in one breath and glorify the military in the next, then you distort our Pro-Life cause. Our mission is to promote the sanctity of all human life, and therefore we should never support any ideologies or actions that facilitate the deliberate destruction of human beings created in God's image.

We need to stop addressing abortion as a political issue and instead address it as a *human rights* issue. And authentic human rights transcend the narrow ideological confines of liberalism and conservatism. When we allow our message to be co-opted and framed by political definitions, then we undermine the inherent power of our Pro-Life truth.

So for God's sake, please stop conflating the Pro-Life cause with pro-death political positions such as supporting militarism, favoring capital punishment, and opposing substantive social programs that assist the poor. All human life is sacred, and to be authentically Pro-Life is to be unconditionally nonviolent and consistently concerned for the welfare of humanity both in and out of the womb.

There is nothing pro-family, pro-Christian, or pro-life about abandoning one's spouse and one's children in order to go and kill people overseas. Instead of "supporting the troops," we should encourage them to repent of their militarism and enlist in the nonviolent revolution to end the slaughter of unborn innocents right here in America.

God can surely bring about an end to abortion, but He always uses the faith and commitment of His children to accomplish His will.

Until we decide to truly uphold the sanctity of Life by renouncing all violence, warfare, and killing, then we have no right to expect God to hear our pleas to stop the violence of abortion. As long as we cling to the sword, then we cannot expect to see peace in the womb or peace in the world.

The road to end abortion is paved with the consistent life ethic. But we have forsaken this road and gone astray on the divergent paths of feckless political idealism. And thus the unborn and their mothers continue to suffer.

"Kyrie Elieson."

399. ~ WHO WILL STAND? ~

Who will stand with the person of conscience and conviction? Who will stand with the person that is unmoved by society's seductions? Who will stand with the person that is guided by principle rather than by what is popular, pragmatic or profitable? Who will stand with the person that stands for Christ, even if it costs them their life? Will *you*? Will *I*? Will *we*?

400. ~ FIGHTING, DYING, KILLING ~

There are some things worth fighting for. There are some things worth dying for. But there is nothing worth killing for. As Albert Camus wrote, *"It is better to be wrong by killing no one than to be right with mass graves.*

401. ~ TWO GREAT TRAGEDIES ~

There are two great tragedies: one is to live a life ruled by the passions, and the other is to live a passionless life.

402. ~ MISSIONARY HARVEST ~

You brought them the Bible,
the Bread and the Wine.
You brought them Baptism,
and that was fine.

But you forgot to bring them Christ, you see.
Rather, in His name you spread misery.

You subdued them with your gospel
of slavery and guns.
And now they seek to convert you
in due return.

The law of the harvest
none can evade:
Judgment for all injustice
done in the Savior's name.

403. ~ QUESTIONS ~

I don't know if I have too much truth to tell
or if I have a little truth but I don't tell it well.

I'm not sure if I'm going insane
or my sanity amidst evil is the reason for my pain.

I can't tell if reality is my faith
or if my belief despite chaos is what keeps me safe.

But questions presuppose answers
and I ask quite a lot.
So I strive towards God
because He's all that I've got.

404. ~ HATRED for AMERICA? ~

I have often been accused of hating America simply because I am outspoken about her wicked foundations and her current injustices. But hatred for people is wrong, and I do not hate anyone. However, the love of Christ compels me to hate injustice and evil. And love compels me to speak the truth. The worship of God compels me to destroy idols, even if I am condemned and crucified by the idolaters. Those of us living in America should not be so blinded by her luxuries and pleasures that we cannot see her evils and sins.

Many of our so-called "founding fathers" claimed to be Christians while they owned slaves and used their power to keep slavery a legal institution. Well, call me judgmental, but I say those slave owners were followers of Satan rather than followers of Christ. And I will humbly accept the judgment of God; for Our Lord did not merely say "do not judge" (St. Matthew 7:1), but He also commanded us to judge righteously (St. John 7:24). In other words, our judgment must be without hypocrisy. That is, we cannot condemn others for the very sins that we continue to commit ourselves.

I am not holy. I am a sinner struggling to work out my own salvation with fear and trembling. (Philippians 2:12) But silence about injustice is contempt for our neighbor, and apathy towards evil is certainly no virtue. I do not hate America, but I hate its oppressive foundations and its continual oppression. However, I love the land and I love the people. And because I love this land and its people then I desire to see this land cleansed from the perpetual stains of innocent blood. And I desire to see all people – black and white, young and old, born and unborn – liberated from the shackles of political deception, social oppression, and spiritual delusion.

405. ~ NO EASY ANSWERS ~
[Reflections on the December 2012 mass shooting in Newtown, Connecticut]

Most of you know that I am usually quick to write opinionated social commentary on the various prominent issues of the day. So, many people asked me yesterday why I had not written anything about the horrific events that occurred Friday in Newtown, Connecticut. Upon hearing the news of that unfathomable tragedy, I could not jump to immediate conclusions or proffer easy answers. Like most rational people, I was paralyzed by this irrational act of evil. All I could do was tune into the various cable news shows hoping to learn some bit of information that would enable me to somehow comprehend the incomprehensible.

You see, evil cannot be understood. By its very nature, evil is contrary to reason; it is the antithesis of truth; it is the privation of goodness and light. The only way to make sense of evil is to acknowledge it as such. We can search for cause and effect, we can analyze motives, we can scrutinize psychological and sociological factors, we can agitate for political solutions, we can blame public policies – but we will still be left shaking our heads and lamenting the senseless evil that is simply that: *senseless evil.*

Unfortunately, but not surprisingly, some are already using this horror as a political football. People on the Left are using this tragedy to further their gun control crusade, and others on the Right are using this tragedy to argue for their right to own as many guns as possible of whatever varieties they choose. The gun control crowd says that guns kill people. The NRA crowd says that people kill people. I'm neither a liberal nor a conservative, but it seems to me that both sides are right. A *person* killed 28 people Friday, and he used a *gun* to do so.

Dangerous people are dangerous people, with or without guns. But it seems to me that they become much more dangerous when they do have guns. Yet I also understand the position of those who want to maintain their right to use guns to defend themselves against dangerous people with guns. Personally, I hate guns and would never own one. If I could wave a magic wand and eliminate all guns from the face of the earth, I would certainly do so. But alas, such is not in my power. All I can do is choose personally not to kill and choose not to prepare to kill. I entrust my body and soul to my Creator, and I strive to use my existence on this earth to affirm and promote life, not destroy it. I'm not sure where that lands me on the political spectrum, and I really don't care.

Another unfortunate but unsurprising reaction comes from the misguided souls who claim that this horrific act of violence was an act of divine retribution on a nation that has turned its back on God. Well, I don't know what false god these people worship, but the God of my Orthodox Faith does not punish innocent children for the sins of a godless society. A just and holy God does not kill innocent babies; unjust and sinful people do. A righteous and merciful God does not massacre innocent children; depraved and heartless people do. So anyone who ascribes to God the evils that are wrought by men commits egregious blasphemy. The wrath of God is reserved not for innocent children, but for those who would harm these little ones. As Our Lord said:

"Then said he unto the disciples, Because of this world, offences will come: but woe unto him through whom they come! It were better for him that a millstone were hanged about his neck, and he cast into the sea, than that he should offend one of these little children." [St. Luke 17:1-2]

I certainly agree that this nation has its back turned to God, but I also think that in many ways it has always had its back turned to God. Yes, we have taken prayer and the Ten Commandments out of the public schools. But do we forget the evils that were with us when those things were still an integral part of our children's education? Were we a more righteous and God-fearing country when we taught our children to pray and instructed them in the divine commandments while unapologetically practicing the evils of slavery and segregation? When Nat Turner soaked his avenging sword in the blood of his oppressor's children, was he inflicting the wrath of God or was he doing the devil's bidding? Well, I submit that neither Nat Turner's bloody revolt nor the unjust society that bred his terrible zeal was divinely inspired. The only difference between then and now is that today we are much more honest about our contempt for God and His laws. We no longer pretend to honor God in our public institutions. In fact, the only vestiges of God that remain publicly acceptable are indelibly inscribed on our coins and dollar bills, which *should* read: *"This currency is the god in which we trust."*

There are consequences for sin, and injustice sowed gives birth to evil reaped. And sadly, in an evil and godless society, the innocent sometimes reap a harvest they did not plant. Yet their harvest is temporal, not eternal. Those who righteously suffer in this life are crowned with eternal rewards. The cruelties endured by the innocent in this life will be healed by the infinite mercy of God in the next. God does not rain down His wrath on the innocent; He resurrects and heals those that have innocently suffered the wrath of evil men.

I would like to make one other observation. Politicians and media pundits are often quick to attribute violent crime in this nation to poverty and lack of education. We are deluged with voices that would have us believe that if we could only eliminate poverty and increase funding for education, then violence would drastically decrease. But what do we notice about the tragedies that occurred at Columbine; Pearl, Mississippi; Paducah, Kentucky; Aurora, Illinois; and Newtown, Connecticut? These evil acts were not committed by poverty stricken, uneducated "minorities." They were committed by young, middle to upper class white males of average to high intelligence. So while I am fully behind any and all effective measures to eradicate poverty and improve the quality of education, I also realize that these things are not a remedy for evil.

Evil will be with us until the return of Christ, and unless we recognize and identify it as such, we will only continue to fuel it. Evil is a spiritual reality and a spiritual problem. We cannot solve it with education or eliminate it with economics. But a nation with its back turned to God is a nation that eschews spiritual realities and scoffs at divine truth. A nation with its back turned to God is a nation that laments the murder of 20 innocent children while supporting the murder of fifty million unborn babies. But do not expect the media to identify and address such collective cognitive dissonance.

So, do my thoughts provide any answers? Do they offer any solutions? Can anything I say help make sense of what happened last Friday? No, I don't think so. I can only express my thoughts and opinions in the hope that they might help contribute to corporate and individual reflection. As I have said before, *"In seeking solutions, always start with self."* We may not be able to make sense of things. We may not be able to change things. But we can always alter our own lives, change our own attitudes, and conform our own responses and reactions to the will of God. And when our first response to injustice and evil is individual and collective repentance, then we can never go wrong. God is always near to those who sincerely seek Him. And as is true with individuals, a nation with its back turned to God can always turn around and embrace Him.

It may seem simplistic, but at least one thing seems pretty clear to me: We don't need more guns in our society, but we certainly need more prayer. Bullets can't raise the dead, but prayer can comfort those who mourn. Weapons can't heal the wounded, but prayer can mend hurting hearts. Guns may provide physical protection, but only prayer can protect the soul.

I can hear Rachel weeping for her children. But I know that the 20 precious children that were killed last Friday are now dancing in their Father's arms, joyously playing in the glorious Kingdom of Heaven. And I believe that they now intercede for all children – born and unborn – who remain behind, fighting to preserve their innocent existence in a world that wages war on them each and every day.

May the unfailing mercy of God comfort all those personally affected by this tragedy. And may the unfailing mercy of God enlighten all of us while there is still time to embrace it.

In the Name of the Father, the Son, and the Holy Spirit, One God, ~ amen ~

406. ~ CARNAL FORCE and SPIRITUAL FORCE ~

Violence, militarism, and political power can always be defeated by violence, militarism, and political power. But nonviolence, love, and spiritual power are impervious to such carnal forces. They are eternally victorious.

407. ~ FLESH TURNS TO SALT ~

Cemeteries in one eye
Karma in the other
The Father gave them life
But Babylon is their mother

Chasing elections
With war in their plans
Speaking of freedom
With blood on their hands

Tongues of deception
Souls that house lies
They rape the earth
They poison the skies

Shadows are their gods
Illusions they exalt
Their kingdoms shall burn
As their flesh turns to salt

408. ~ PUT DOWN YOUR GUN and PICK UP A SONG ~

Bullets kill
But notes heal

Put down your gun
And pick up a song

Don't pull the trigger
Strum a chord instead

War enslaves
Music liberates

It is with deep humility that I address these words to you. I have never been incarcerated, so I do not pretend to know your suffering, your pain, or your struggle. All I can do is attempt to imagine the difficulty of your circumstances, yet I know this alone cannot equip me to fully empathize with your situation.

However, I write to you because I know that I could very easily be in prison myself. In my own life, I have committed crimes that violated the laws of society. And, more importantly, I have often violated the spiritual and moral laws of Almighty God. So I address you as someone who may well deserve to be in your place, while you may very well deserve the physical freedom from which I currently benefit. Also, I am very aware that as long as I continue to write, speak, and act on behalf of authentic social justice and spiritual truth, I make myself an enemy of the power structures and forces of this fallen world. So I try to prepare myself for the consequences of my actions, which may eventually result in my own imprisonment or death.

I write to you regardless of whether you are innocent or guilty of the crimes for which the system has convicted you. I cannot change your circumstances; I can only offer these modest thoughts that I hope will contribute to your strength, hope, perseverance, and peace. I pray that my words do not appear condescending, as I realize that many of you who read this have already experienced spiritual knowledge and insights far deeper than anything put forth here. But even the simplest of truths are worthy of continual reflection, thus I hope that you will benefit from these humble words of spiritual encouragement.

The world, the flesh, and the devil are the three great enemies of man. (Cf. Ephesians 2:2-3) So whether we are victimized by worldly powers, by satanic forces, or by our own sins, it is important to remember that as long as life exists, the battle can be fought. Prison is not death, although it may often feel like hell. Yet God has often used the hellish circumstances of prison to accomplish His divine purpose through those who are in submission to His divine will.

So I offer the following examples and exhortations in the hope that they will assist in the cultivation of your consciousness and the strengthening of your spirit and soul:

1) Joseph, the son of Jacob, was betrayed by his brothers and sold into Egyptian slavery; and then he was subsequently imprisoned because of the false allegations of Potiphar's iniquitous wife. Although unjustly accused and wrongly sentenced, the hand of the Lord was upon Joseph. And Joseph remained faithful to his God. While in prison God gave Joseph prophetic dreams that convicted the heart of Pharaoh, and in time Joseph was made overseer of the affairs of Egypt. God used the plight of Joseph to restore the spiritual strength and hope of his family, and consequently all of Israel benefited.

2) Dr. Martin Luther King, Jr. wrote perhaps his most famous piece of literature from behind bars. His _Letter from a Birmingham Jail_ challenged religious leaders to shake off the shackles of apathy and admonished them to directly confront injustice. This prophetic letter has provided inspiration for liberation movements and freedom struggles across the globe. Had Dr. King not experienced the confines of jail, he would never have written the words that continue to inspire many advocates of peace, freedom, and human rights today.

3) The Apostle Paul wrote much of the New Testament from a state of incarceration. His imprisonment and persecution provided the spiritual insights and prophetic proclamations that forever changed the course of history. Many spiritual revolutionaries have studied and applied St. Paul's teachings in their own endeavors for human rights and social justice.

4) Nelson Mandela in effect ended Apartheid from inside the walls of prison. Twenty-five years of physical confinement could not thwart his righteous efforts and spiritual energies. Through faith, hope, and perseverance, he refused to allow his spirit to be broken. And when he eventually walked to freedom with his head held high, prison

guards who had once been unmerciful in their treatment of him were wiping tears of admiration and respect from their eyes.

5) Our Lord Jesus Christ experienced the suffering of imprisonment, torture, and capital punishment. But injustice, pain, and death were not the end of the story. Resurrection, triumph, and glory had the final say. So today there may be sorrow, suffering, agony, and perhaps even death; but resurrection, life, and joy will always be the ultimate and enduring fate of those who love God. Therefore, whether you face a sentence of a year, a decade, a life sentence, or even if you are awaiting execution, know that the Lord of Life, Justice, and Peace is your ever-present comfort and companion.

6) Contemplate the words of Henry David Thoreau, who wrote:
"Under a government which imprisons any unjustly, the true place for a just man is also a prison."

7) Understand that no physical bars or material walls can imprison your mind, your spirit, or your soul. The systems, governments, laws, and prisons of man are ineffective against the Spirit and power of God. In fact, God may be nearer to the prisoner than to those who are ostensibly "free" but are imprisoned by materialism, lust, perversion, greed, corruption, dishonesty, and demonic deception.

8) No crime or guilt is beyond the scope of the Creator's forgiveness, mercy, and grace. Nobody is beyond redemption. The great lie of Satan is to convince people that they have "gone too far," that they have committed the "unpardonable sin." But the condemnation and sentence of man is not the same as that of our merciful Lord. Repentance and submission to God always provide the access to forgiveness and salvation. In spite of the callousness of man, *"The mercy of God endureth forever." [Psalm 136]*

9) Although your conviction, sentence, or current circumstances may be unjust, know that the ultimate justice of God will prevail. By living justly in an unjust environment, you will gain the power and strength

of a just and holy God. And in time, all those who have been wrongly treated will be divinely recompensed and avenged.

10) Strive to make your cell a chapel and your prison a place of worship. Christ worshiped His Father in the manger, in the wilderness, in the Garden of Gethsemane, in Pilate's court, and even as He lay dying on the Cross.

11) Make every effort to see God in the presence of your fellow man. Whether they are an inmate, a guard, or a warden, they are still created in the divine image; therefore they too can be redeemed and changed. Nelson Mandela never allowed others to rob him of his dignity. But he also treated those around him with dignity and respect, even when they acted and behaved in ways that were not worthy of it. But over time, his self-respect and his righteous treatment of others had a profound and lasting effect on his captors.

12) Never give in to the negativity and evil of others. We cannot control our circumstances or the actions of others, but we can always control our own responses and reactions. Nothing or no one can break the spirit of an individual who lives in surrender and submission to God.

13) Consider Mahatma Gandhi's reflections upon his own time in jail:
    "To bear suffering is in itself a kind of happiness, there is no need to be worried by it. Realizing that our sole duty is to break free from our mental and spiritual fetters by enduring every hardship rather than remaining bound for life, I felt light in the heart and tried to instill courage in the others."

14) Realize that prison is in many ways a microcosm of the world. The strong rule the weak. Justice is perverted or ignored. Racism, division, violence, and discord permeate the environment. And the righteous are ridiculed while the cruel and corrupt go unpunished.

So, all of us in life have a choice: we can submit to the Creator's established will and order, or we can conform to the perverse morality of the ways of the world. Righteousness is often accompanied by pain, but remember that suffering for righteousness is always redemptive.

In conclusion, it is my hope and prayer that something I have written will uplift you and give you hope. Perhaps I will one day find myself in the position of consulting my own words in this particular context. Know that you have my deepest respect and admiration for the struggle in which you are engaged. As long as we fight the spiritual fight, then the battle is already won. Only when we refuse to struggle, only when we concede defeat, only when we allow our circumstances to conquer our spirits – only then will we have lost the war.

I leave you with these words of Holy Scripture:

"What shall we then say to these things? If God be for us, who can be against us? He that spared not his own Son, but delivered him up for us all, how shall he not with him also freely give us all things? Who shall lay anything to the charge of God's elect? It is God that justifieth. Who is he that condemneth? It is Christ that died, yea rather, that is risen again, who is even at the right hand of God, who also maketh intercession for us. Who shall separate us from the love of Christ? Shall tribulation, or distress, or persecution, or famine, or nakedness, or peril, or sword? As it is written, 'for thy sake we are killed all the daylong; we are accounted as sheep for the slaughter.' Nay, in all these things we are more than conquerors through him that loved us. For I am persuaded, that neither death, nor life, nor angels, nor principalities, nor powers, nor things present, nor things to come, nor height, nor depth, nor any other creature, shall be able to separate us from the love of God, which is in Christ Jesus our Lord." [Romans 8:31-39]

~ Amen ~

410. ~ KEEP LIVING! ~

They will pity you only in death, but never in life. So don't waste time seeking that which the world will never bestow. Though you try to kill yourself a hundred times, they will only view you as an attention seeker, an emotional coward, an inconvenient distraction from their materialistic productivity and worldly peace of mind. But when death does reach you – by whatever means it may come – they will gather with flowers and tears and speak of how much they loved and cared about you. Therefore, keep living. Keep living so that you can rob them of the smug satisfaction of their floral tributes and orchestrated sorrow. Curse Babylon by living for God! More Life!

411. ~ SPEAK of THE DEVIL ~

He will speak so eloquently of "compassion" that it becomes an idol for which they will torture and kill. He will extol the virtue of "tolerance" so that it becomes an ideal for which they will brutally silence any opposition. He will pontificate upon the value of "peace" until they wage barbaric wars in its very name. He will talk profoundly of "God" so that he can convince them to do the devil's bidding. And as he speaks his beguiling and insidious lies, the Antichrist may very well be using a teleprompter.

412. ~ CHANT DOWN BABYLON ~

Chant down Babylon with words of truth and Psalms of praise. Burn Babylon with acts of love and deeds of virtue. Conquer evil with good and defeat darkness with light. JAH warriors need no guns; we have the weapons of the Spirit. They can kill the body but they can't kill the soul. They can destroy the messenger, but they can't destroy the message. Peace and Love! This is our holy fire!

413. ~ MY REBEL SONG ~

This is my rebel song:
To speak peace and life
all day long.

This is my revolution:
To manifest love
as the only solution.

This is my battle cry:
To proclaim the Gospel
'til the day I die.

Some will fight me
and some will spite me,
but the real revolutionaries
stand beside me.

I have nothing to do
with politics, patriotism,
and swords.
I'm wedded to the Incarnate Word.

Born as a Lamb
returning as a Lion
JAH children burn Babylon
with the Light of Zion.

We lay down our arms
and take up the Cross,
following Our Lord
we count the cost.

All Christian soldiers:
it's time to unite!
With peace and love
We'll win this fight!

414. ~ RECONCILIATION in RELATIONSHIPS ~

How do we find peace and reconciliation with those who seem intent on remaining at enmity with us? How do we find agreement with those who refuse to make any efforts to find agreement? How do we restore friendships with those who demand that we compromise our convictions or acquiesce with their opinions in order to do so? How can we once again trust those who have constantly and publicly misrepresented our views and slandered our character?

We may really want to be at peace with someone, but they have hurt us so deeply and they show no willingness to make amends or find common ground. And yet they are perhaps family, a friend, or a brother in Christ; and therefore we feel great sorrow at the rift that remains.

I don't care what you believe or how strongly I disagree with you – the fact is that if you are my family, my friend, or my brother in Christ, then that bond takes precedent over all other philosophical or theological differences we may have. We can argue and debate passionately about various issues, but love and respect come before all of that. Unfortunately, not everyone feels the same way. And that is one of the great tragedies in life.

"As much as is possible, so far as it depends on you, be at peace with all men." [Romans 12:18]

415. ~ A THEOPHANY MESSAGE TO OUR ORTHODOX PATRIARCHS ~

On this holy day when we celebrate Theophany/Epiphany/Timket (The Baptism of Our Lord), I would like to send out this simple message to all Orthodox patriarchs – Eastern Orthodox and Oriental Orthodox alike:

+ Greet one another with a holy kiss. (Romans 16:15)
+ Wash each other's feet. (St. John 13:14-17)
+ Confess your sins to one another. (James 5:16)
+ Forgive each other. (St. Matthew 6:14)

+ Serve one another. (Galatians 5:13)
+ Show holy affection to each other. (I Peter 5:14)
+ Show deference to one another in love (Philippians 2:3)
+ Walk in truth together. (I John 3:18; II John 1:5)
+ And above all, have fervent love for one another. (I Peter 4:8)

Remember that the last shall be first and the first shall be last. (St. Matthew 19:30) Set aside your disputes and embrace each other as equals before God. Learn from the glorious example of Christ, who while Lord of the universe nevertheless humbled Himself to be baptized by St. John the Forerunner.

It is time for the shepherds to stop dividing the flock. Teach the Faith, administer the Sacraments, and stop the bickering. We beseech you in the name of the Father, the Son, and the Holy Spirit – One God, ~amen ~

With sincere prayers and deepest respect,
+ GMK +

416. ~ BOOTSTRAPS, SELF-MADE MEN, & SELF-SUFFICIENT SOULS ~

To all the "bootstraps," "self-made men," and "self-sufficient souls":

Congratulations on your success! I applaud your hard work and industrious spirit. You should be very proud. Not everyone possesses your intellectual prowess, your physical health, or your emotional and mental stability. So be proud that you are better than those of us who are so weak and dependent. Be proud that someone loved and cared enough to teach you early on to work hard, study hard, and make the most of your innate talents and abilities. Be proud that you are better than those lazy miscreants who were born into less nurturing environments. Be proud that you have never had to ask for a handout, because you always had the abundant support of invisible arms that enabled you to endure and achieve. Be proud that you need neither the government nor God; for you are blessed not to be crippled, and therefore you have the luxury of scoffing at such crutches. Be proud that you don't have to deal with those irritating pangs of conscience that prick the rest of us when we pass by the homeless, the hungry, and the destitute; for you know that it's simply their own fault. If they had only been as well born, well nurtured, and well supported as you had, then they wouldn't be out on the street hassling you.

So be proud of your self-sufficiency. Be proud that you did it all by yourself. I am truly amazed at your accomplishments, because as for myself, I am desperately dependent upon others.

I am dependent upon those who pick up my garbage, those who keep water flowing to my house, those who supply food to my local grocery store, those who make the clothes I wear, and those who grow the coffee I drink. I am dependent upon those who teach my children Sunday school, those who lead me in the Divine Liturgy, and those who worship with me and pray for me. I am dependent on those who love me, listen to me, and befriend me. I am dependent on those who give of their time, their love, and their money so that I can not only live but also live a life that's worth living. Indeed, I am desperately dependent upon my God and my fellow man.

I confess that I am no "self-made man," no "self-sufficient soul". No, not *this* sinner. I cannot boast of such a thing. I am far too reliant upon my family, my friends, and my Lord. There is nothing that I could do by myself, on my own – other than sin.

I remember the time I put on a pair of boots and tried with all my might to pull myself up by the straps. I promise you – and you may not believe this – but it's impossible! Really! I mean, I tried and tried, but I could not do it! But then again, that was only my own personal experience. Apparently, there are people who do it all the time. They tell me it's indeed possible, but I've yet to see it actually happen. I've heard a lot about these "bootstrap" people, but I haven't met one yet. But then again, I haven't been to the circus in years.

417. ~ BOW, PROSTRATE, HUMBLE, and FIGHT ~

Bow your head, but don't bury it. Prostrate your intellect, but open your mind. Humble your heart, but don't harden it. Fight injustice and evil, but know that repentance is the most profound form of rebellion.

418. ~ THE SPIRITUAL REVOLUTIONARY ~

The spiritual revolutionary is called "quixotic," "arrogant," "judgmental," "acrimonious," "self-righteous," and "troublesome." He suffers from the betrayal of family and friends as much as from the arrows of his foes. He lights fires to illuminate the truth, but he is called an "arsonist." He tears down idols and destroys lies, but he is labeled a "criminal" and accused of treason. He weeps for the innocent, but he is called "sentimental" and "naïve." He boldly proclaims peace, but his rhetoric is condemned as "violent" and "disruptive."

Yet the torch of the spiritual revolutionary is inextinguishable, and those that seek to silence his truth heap fire on their own recalcitrant heads.

419. ~ DEMOCRATIC COMPLAINTS ~

You can complain about the government all day long, but as long as you trust in the philosophy of democracy then you have nobody but yourself to blame. You wonder how Bush and Barack got elected? What do you expect when you allow "the people" to actually decide such things? These Democrats and Republicans vehemently fight each other, and yet they both trust in "the power of the people" to decide what's right. But the people rarely ever do what's *right*; they usually do what they *want*. Democracy is simply organized chaos that inevitably leads to destruction.

Message to my Christian brothers and sisters: The kingdom of heaven is not a democracy. And please remember that Our Lord taught His disciples to pray, *"Thy kingdom come, thy will be done, on earth as it is in heaven."* No Christian should ever lend credence, participation, or support to a governmental system that allows the immutable laws and truths of God to be subjected to mortal human vote.

There is no perfect form of human government in this world, but democracy (and its various manifestations) is in my opinion one of the worst.

420. ~ WHOSE SIDE AM I ON? ~

I don't side with Israel over Palestine or Palestine over Israel. I don't side with the rich over the poor or the poor over the rich. I don't side with the unborn over the born or the born over the unborn. I don't side with the Black man over the White man or the White man over the Black man. I don't side with gay over straight or straight over gay. I don't side with woman over man or man over woman. I don't side with Christian over pagan or pagan over Christian. I don't side with liberal over conservative or conservative over liberal. I simply side with my fellow man; and I seek to prioritize the poor, the suffering, and all those who are victimized by cruelty, injustice, sin, and evil.

And when I look around, I don't see anyone that's immune from suffering and sorrow. I don't see anyone that's not being victimized by sin and evil. Satan is an equal opportunity destroyer, the common enemy of us all.

There are too many people taking political sides, and not enough people taking humanity's side. Wake up people! *Love, live, pray, forgive!*

421. ~ IF ~

If your freedom is purchased
at the barrel of a gun
then it ain't freedom,
it's slavery you've won.

If your truth is preserved
by shredding flesh
then it ain't truth,
it's veracity's death.

If your glory is gained
by the killing you've sown
then it ain't glory,
it's shame you own.

If your justice is earned
by violence and war
then it ain't justice,
it's the devil's whore.

422. ~ BLINDED ~

I'm trying to see you,
but I have beams in my eyes.
So I'm blind to your pain
and I ignore your cries.
Only tears can clear my vision
and make me realize...
that your suffering is also mine.

423. ~ NEVER GIVE UP! ~

Never give up! Keep fighting! JAH will make a way. No judgment, no condemnation, no self-hatred. Divine love is all that matters. Morality can't heal. Religion can't heal. Politics can't heal. Philosophy can't heal. The unconditional love of Christ is the only thing that can heal any of our broken souls. Bathe in the fire of His love and let everything else melt away.

424. ~ OUR HOPE for THE WORLD ~

Just as we must struggle to cooperate with God in our own salvation, so too we must cooperate with God to usher in His Kingdom. But His Kingdom will not be ushered in by political reform or violent revolution. His Kingdom will be ushered in by the proclamation of the Gospel and by our love for our fellow man. It is a mystical paradox that as the world grows colder it also grows nearer to its redemption. Our role as Christians is to align ourselves with redemption, with His Kingdom, rather than with the fallen political structures of this temporal existence. This is our hope as individuals, and this is our hope for the world.

425. ~ THE QUIXOTIC PROPHET ~

They gather to mock the quixotic prophet: *"What a fool he is! Cursing the darkness and tilting at the machine!"*

They have lights for the night and the machine gives them food; but here is this madman condemning their welfare. He thinks he is a knight, with his Bible and tongue, out to slay a dragon that is really their friend. Even in their mockery, they pity him: *"Next he will tell us that the earth is flat and the sky is falling! How sad to be so ignorant and insolent."*

But he pays no heed. The windmill churns and he steadies his lance for another run.

"Look! Here he goes again! He thinks he can stop our machine! The fool!"

Headlong he rushes forward, and again he is thrown back – violently, callously, with brutal disregard. The people laugh. It is such a curious sight.

"See him! He thinks he can stop science with his sacred book! He thinks he can stop progress with his sacred truth! Well, let him keep trying. It is certainly amusing to watch!"

He brushes himself off, and stands back up. He is bruised, bloodied, and beaten. But he is no less determined. Occasionally, someone from the crowd approaches him sincerely:

"You are wasting your time and injuring yourself. I feel sorry for you. I don't want you to get hurt. Believe what you will, but you cannot destroy the machine. And the more you try, the more you just turn everyone against you. Go quietly and live your life as you wish. But this fool's errand is doing nobody any good. For your own sake, stop this madness."

But he looks at them and replies:

"Thank you. But perhaps if you will help me fight, we can indeed destroy this dragon. Will you help me please?"

"No! I won't join in your madness. I have tried to warn you of your error, but if you persist then I cannot help you. Be a fool if you wish, but I will not accompany you."

Then the person returns to the crowd and shrugs. *"I tried to tell the fool, but he would not hear of it. And he even asked me to join in his folly! Imagine that!"*

The crowd roars again with laughter. *"Look! Here he goes again!"*

The Quixote makes another launch toward the machine, and again it slams him ruthlessly to the ground. Some of the people don't laugh this time. They love the machine and they hate the fool, but now the machine seems needlessly cruel. But it is still their machine, and they must remain loyal in order to be fed. Surely what appears to be cruelty must really be love.

"Go home!" they say. *"You are getting hurt. You will die if you continue this insanity."*

But slowly, once again, he arises and eyes the beast. And it is indeed a beast. And he is willing to die to reveal this truth – the truth that their beloved machine is actually a beast, a monster, a dragon, perhaps the devil itself.

So again he charges forth.

"Here he goes! Watch! He thinks he can fight our education with his prayers. He thinks he can fight our politics with his prophecy! No wonder he is poor, broken, bloodied, and alone. No, we don't feel sorry for him! He is bringing this on himself. We laugh at him because he deserves it. If he would only quit this madness and join us in our collective security, then he wouldn't suffer so. We have tried to tell him. But he won't listen. He is a self-righteous fool who loves to play the martyr, and so he deserves what he gets."

And so he arose again and again, time after time, hurling himself into the jaws of the machine. Into the claws of the beast. Into the mouth of the dragon. Until he could no longer stand. Until he could no longer think. Until he could no longer breathe. Until his very life was spent.

And the masses were bored by his death. It was not amusing. It was simply pitiful. There was no joy or mockery to be had in it. After all, nobody wished him to die. The fool had entertained them with his zeal and his foolish resolve, but his death was uneventful. And only a few had actually rejoiced in it.

But soon another madman arose from their midst. And although he was quite different, he was just as amusing with his conviction and faith. He launched himself against the machine just as the previous fool had. And the masses gathered, just as before, to mock his efforts. And eventually he met the same fate. The beast slayed him. And the masses took no pleasure in it, nor did they have any pity for him. A foolish life deserves a fool's death they reasoned.

And this is what continues to happen throughout the course of human history. The people love the machine (the beast), and the masses mock the few fools who presumptuously dare to fight it. They find great pleasure in joining together to ridicule the outcasts and the insane. The masses live by certain maxims that bind them together in universal solidarity:

"A little religion is ok, but too much religion makes one a fanatic."

"It's fine to believe in God, but science and the state are the only real answers to the real problems of humanity."

"Morality is fine for individuals, but education is the only hope for all mankind."

"Peace and nonviolence are great ideals, but sometimes violence is the only practical solution."

And thus they believe and thus they live – comforted by their collective "wisdom" and their mutual condemnation of anyone who dares to challenge it. Until one day the fire comes. And the fire comes just as surely and just as thoroughly as the flood came all those millenniums ago. And the fire devours the beast and torments the masses who worshiped it. And the quixotic prophets ride on the wings of angels, weeping for those that mocked them.

426. ~ MY WAR ~

I have no part in your political wars, your culture wars, your religious wars, or your world wars. I am an Orthodox Christian, and the only war in which I am conscripted is the spiritual war of good vs. evil, the war of the Kingdom of heaven vs. the dominion of hell. My weapons are spiritual not carnal, and my greatest adversary is my own sin. My enemies are not liberals or conservatives, Muslims or Jews, Russians or Americans. My enemies are the devil and his demonic minions. With the power of the Holy Spirit and with nonviolent Christian militancy, I stand in opposition to all earthly wars, violence, hatred, and strife. I am a Christian; the Gospel is the cause for which I fight; and my weapons are peace, love, forgiveness, and truth. I am a weak soldier of Christ, but at least I know that I'm fighting the right war and fighting with the right weapons – spiritual weapons that shall eternally prevail. The Cross has conquered and Christ is risen! So as long as I fight according to these truths, then I can never lose this spiritual war.

427. ~ MISSIONARY LESSONS ~

Some of the greatest lessons I ever learned were in Bible College. It wasn't the doctrine or the theology (which was quite heterodox and fallacious in many ways); it was the wise and humble teachers whose sincere love for God and the Holy Scriptures left an indelible impression on me. They took the time to mentor me, to answer my many questions, and to encourage my zeal while gently rebuking my insufferable arrogance.

But most of all, I remember the Missions Conference that was held every year. Missionaries from all over the world came to tell us of cultures that we knew nothing about. These missionaries lived sparse lives and dedicated themselves to ministering to the people that God had compelled them to love and serve. They shared such amazing stories of adventure, hardship, victory, and struggle. I would spend hours and hours with these missionaries, absorbing all I could about their lives and their labors. I wanted to be a spiritual hero just like them. They weren't in the news, they weren't famous, but their lives were more fascinating than the greatest fictitious adventures of which any novelist could conceive. And yet they exuded nothing but humility and grace, kindness and compassion. Love poured from their countenances and their words.

There are living saints in this world – unknown, unrewarded, and yes, dare I say it, even unorthodox. I have met some of them. It is to my shame that I have not followed their glorious examples.

428. ~ LAY YOUR BURDEN DOWN ~

Peace is not a lot to ask
It's not as heavy as guns and flasks
Better to bear the weight of the Cross
Than to bear the guilt of life that's lost

Soldier, lay your burden down
Can't kill your way to heavenly crowns
Conscience weighted with the lead you bear
Haunted by the eyes of a dead man's stare

The harvest is plentiful, the laborers few
Can't reap souls from hate that's spewed
The earth is the Lord's and the fullness thereof
So why desecrate it with innocent blood?

Mash up your bullets, rend your guns
Come serve the Father, the Spirit, the Son
Life is for living, death is for hell
The angels are singing, of peace they do tell

Shake off the shackles of death and sin
Love your brother and be born again
No more killing for Uncle Sam
Come join the kingdom of the great I AM

429. ~ UNITY ~

"Them" are us
"They" are we
"I" am you
And "you" are me

430. ~ COMPASSION ~

To have compassion on anyone – no matter who they are or what they have done – is never wrong. Never.

431. ~ NO SUCH THING ~

There is no such thing as a "pro-choice" pacifist, and there is no such thing as a "pro-life" soldier. And in spite of all the rationalizations about how nobody's "pro-abortion" they are only "pro-choice," and how nobody's "pro-war" they are only "pro-defense," the reality is that to support the evils of war and abortion is to support the violent deaths of innocent human beings. Period.

432. ~ "IF THEY WOULD JUST COME TO JESUS" ~

I often hear Christians say:

"If they would just come to Jesus, they wouldn't have abortions."
"If they would just come to Jesus, they wouldn't be poor anymore."
"If the world just knew Jesus, there wouldn't be any more wars."

OK. Maybe so. But have we ever considered that people won't come to Jesus unless we actually bring Jesus to them? Have we ever thought that maybe instead of just preaching about Jesus we should actually minister to their needs in His name?

We recoil from Pro-Life activism and we self-righteously shun the beggar; but we enthusiastically support life-destroying and life-demeaning political policies, we encourage our children to join the military, and we praise soldiers who are paid to kill. And then we dare to lecture the impoverished, the brokenhearted, the suffering and afflicted about their need to repent and "accept Jesus." And we don't even consider the fact that our own apathetic indifference combined with our own pro-active evil is largely responsible for the suffering of those to whom we presume to preach.

I'm not sure what kind of sick, perverted, demonic religion would condemn money spent on the poor while praising money that's spent on war; but I can assure you that it's not the religion of Christ. I'm not sure what kind of sick, perverted, demonic religion would judge the homeless and the impoverished as "faithless" while praising the politician and the soldier as "faithful;" but I can assure you that it is not the religion of Christ.

But there are wolves in sheep's clothing, who in defense of their callousness love to cite the words of Our Lord: *"The poor you will always have with you."* *[St. Matthew 26:11]* But I wonder if they would derive the same apathetic indifference from Christ's words if He had said: "Riches you will always have with you." I wonder if we would therefore ignore riches the same way we currently ignore the poor. I wonder if rather than men standing on the corner begging for money, these same men stood on the corner offering us money. I wonder if we would still invoke Our Lord's words in the same manner, saying:

"No thank you. Keep your wealth. For Our Lord said that riches we will always have with us. I am not wealthy. In fact, I am poor. But I trust in Our Lord's words. Riches will always be with me, so I am content."

Would this really be our response? I doubt it. I seriously doubt it.

433. ~ WHY? ~

Why all these books on war, but no books on how to feed the poor? The first step towards literacy is the abolition of poverty. The people are eager to read, but it is cruel to demand they do so with empty stomachs. The end of ignorance and war begins with food and justice for all.

434. ~ ALL SINS MAY BE FORGIVEN, BUT NO SINS MAY BE JUSTIFIED ~

All sins may be forgiven, but no sins may be justified. Therefore, let us not seek premeditated justifications and premeditated forgiveness for the sin of killing, but let us predetermine instead that we will never kill. It is better to enter the Kingdom as victims, martyrs, and slaughtered sheep than to enter hell as conquerors, killers, and self-preserving wolves. It is better to enter heaven soaked in our own blood and washed in His than to enter hell ensconced in the shed blood of our neighbor.

435. ~ CREATIVITY and HARD WORK ~

Don't assume that creativity is not hard work. Don't assume that creative work is not "real work." Don't assume that artists, writers, musicians, and artisans don't work as hard as anyone else. Don't assume that unless someone punches a clock or receives a salary that they are lazy and unmotivated.

Don't assume that your paycheck makes you a harder working individual than the rest of us. Many of us create day and night, with little sleep, striving to use our creative talents to glorify God, uplift humanity, and heal the world. And for our efforts, most of us receive little more than an occasional word of encouragement and gratitude (which is always deeply, deeply appreciated.)

People pay good money for "arts and entertainments" that enslave the mind and scar the soul; but the revolutionary labors of prophetic creativity and artistic spirituality usually go unrewarded in our society. But as spiritual artists, we don't create for profit. We create because that's what we were born to do. It is the only life we know.

So we don't ask you to praise us, or even to like us. We only ask that you don't judge us. But if you truly do like or appreciate something we have created, it would be nice if you supported us the same way you support your local movie theater, your local cable TV service, your local newspaper, and your local bookstore.

Our words and our art may be provocative, radical, insensitive, and offensive; but we are only trying to make the world a better place. And we need all the prayers, love, and financial support we can get. Our works probably won't be promoted on C-SPAN or "Good Morning America;" but we are here, and if you know us please, please, please support us!

436. ~ EVIL CONTRIBUTIONS ~

Christians should never contribute to political division and nationalistic idolatry. God loves all people equally. Christ died for the Jew and the Gentile alike. This is the good news of salvation – that God so loved the *world*. (St. John 3:16) We disgrace the Gospel and we dishonor Christ when we side with one people over another. Christians should never do such a thing. Our citizenship is in heaven (Philippians 2:12), and we are called to be ambassadors of Christ to all people of all nations. It's quite appropriate – and in fact quite necessary – to align ourselves with righteous ideologies over evil ideologies. But we must never succumb to the demonic mindset of viewing one people as less human than another. So it's distressing (and sickening really) to see professing Christians aligning themselves with a baby-killing nation like America in support of a Zionist political state called "Israel" against our own Arab Christian brothers and sisters in the Middle East. If we are true Christians, we will condemn violence on all sides, and we will take no sides in any political war. Christ loves the innocent Palestinian as much as the innocent Jew. And, believe it or not, He loves the guilty too. The Christian must proclaim the love of Christ to all. To side with one segment of humanity against another is to side with the devil, and to condone violence is to side with hell.

437. ~ NO ROOM ~

If we have no room for the hungry stranger and the homeless man... if we have no room for the neglected orphan and the woman abused... if we have no room for those afflicted with AIDS, for lepers and drunkards, prostitutes and thieves... if we have no room for those unlike ourselves... if we have no room for the poor, for the beggar, or the prisoner in chains... if we have no room for the unwed mother and unborn child... then we have no room for Christ.

Our Lord has room in His heart for all. Do we have room in our hearts for Him?

438. ~ "HOW?" and "WHY?" ~

Those that only ask "how" will be easily contented, for "how" can always be answered with logical syllogisms and empirical demonstrations. But those that ask "why" are not so easily comforted, for the answers to "why" often reside beyond the secure confines of material and rational finitude. The scientist can always explain how the universe works, but he is powerless to explain why the universe *is*. He can explain the mechanisms of the "something," but he can't explain why there is something rather than nothing. The rationalist contents himself merely with questions of "how," and he discovers nothing beyond this material existence and his own logical understanding. But those who dare to perpetually ask "why" live with the angst of the unanswered and the unknown. Yet behind the why is a Who – Our Lord Jesus Christ, in whom and through whom are all the answers of eternal mysteries.

"For by him were all things created, that are in heaven,
and that are in earth, visible and invisible,
whether they be thrones, or dominions, or principalities, or powers:
all things were created by him, and for him." [Colossians 1:16]

"For from him and through him and for him are all things.
To him be the glory forever! Amen." [Romans 11:36]

303

439. ~ CAN WE LOSE OUR SALVATION? ~

There is a longstanding debate within Protestantism about whether or not we can lose our salvation. But Orthodoxy doesn't view salvation as something we can possess or lose. Salvation is not a cosmic lottery ticket. Salvation is the experience of Divine love that begins in this life and extends into eternity. How can we "possess" God's love? And how can we "lose" God's love?

So, for the Orthodox, the question of whether or not we can lose our salvation misses the point entirely. Those who know the love of family and friends do not worry about whether they can retain or lose such love. And if true human love endures unconditionally, then all the more does divine love endure unconditionally.

"God loves us more than a father, mother, friend, or anyone else could love us. He loves us more than we are able to love ourselves."
~ St. John Chrysostom ~

440. ~ LIES and THE CONSUMING FIRE ~

Where there is war, where there is poverty, where there is abortion, there will always be lies. Such evils are certainly not born from the light of truth; they are the poisonous produce of veracity's violent suppression. There is no more insidious lie than to bomb, starve, and abort innocent children in the name of freedom, truth, justice, and rights. The blood of innocents spills from mendacious minds, demonic hearts, and prevaricating tongues. We must therefore shine the light of divine truth, exposing the hellish deceits that undergird this damnable darkness of violence and killing. We must shine the light of Christ and let it burn anyone and anything that dares to stand in its way. Our God is a consuming fire, and those that destroy human lives in His holy name heap coals of brimstone upon their own depraved souls.

441. ~ SALVATION ~

I saw the light through the trees
In the fire I felt the breeze
Ensconced in lies, I felt the truth
Divine deliverance from the folly of youth

A spinning world was in your hands
As I was drowning in shallow sand
Demons screamed, but I heard your voice
A grace that conquered mortal choice

Salvation is found...
In the thunder and the rainbow alike

442. ~ FIGHT for FREEDOM ~

Fight for freedom
on your knees.

Work for justice
with prayerful pleas.

Speak the truth
with grace and love.

Seek your answers
from God above.

Increase your soul
destroy your guns.

Love your brother
We all are one.

443. ~ <u>**GEORGE AND THE DEVIL**</u> ~

(The following is a true story. Names have been changed to protect the identity of those involved. Please be forewarned that it contains graphic language and disturbing material. This story is not suitable for children. Please be advised.)

George and I dug up palmetto roots in the Florida panhandle wilderness, toiling together under the relentless midday summer sun. George had only been with us for a few days, recently sent to us from the E&O ("Evaluation and Observation Unit"), where one was initially incarcerated for approximately 3 months before being moved to an "outside vocational group." We were both patients/residents/inmates at a place called "Anneewakee," which was supposedly a Native American word meaning "land of the friendly people." There were indeed some friendly people at Anneewakee, but there were also monsters and demons that prowled too often undetected.

Our group of twelve was clearing an acre of hardscrabble palmetto and pine tree land in order to build wood cabins in which to live. In the meantime we slept in Camel tents, two people to a tent. So we were motivated to work hard and fast in order to achieve our goal of living in solid structures that would better protect us from rattlesnakes, wild boars, alligators, scorpions, and the capricious elements.

The Gulf coast was three miles to the south, and to the north lay nothing but swampy, dense, and uninhabited forest. No need for electric walls and razor wire. You could take your chances with the ocean or with the swamps. Or you could do the safer thing and steal a bicycle and ride down the lone two-lane road that led to Tallahassee 60 miles away. That's what one guy tried. Problem was, it takes a few hours to get to Tallahassee on a bike, and it doesn't take long to realize that somebody's gone. The police were alerted, and the poor guy was caught only ten miles away and shipped back to the E&O for another three month sojourn in padded confinement.

Most of the people at Anneewakee were "juvenile delinquents" sent there by court order. Others, like me, were sent by their parents for one reason or another. My crime was that I had been expelled from three different schools, and my psychiatrist persuaded my parents that living with hardened criminals under the authority of pedophiles would somehow motivate me to care more about math.

So here I was, pounding away at sand and soil with our new group member George. I had been in the group for almost a year, so I was pretty well acclimated to how things worked. You see, at Anneewakee there was no predetermined sentence. You had to earn your way out of the place. The more you complied, the more you "worked on your problems," and the more you demonstrated a willingness to obey authority and cooperate with the group, then the more privileges you could earn and the better chance you had of eventually "terminating from the program."

From day one, as I sat in the solitary confinement of my padded cell in the E&O, I decided that I would accept these conditions and do my best to adhere to them. I realized this was really my only choice. It was very clear: rebellion would keep me confined, and compliance might one day get me released. It was 1983, I was 14 years old, and the only thing I knew about Communism was that our USA hockey team had beaten those Commie Russian bastards a few years earlier in the winter Olympics at Lake Placid, New York. Of course, it never dawned on me that most people in Russia were much freer than I was at the current moment.

George had been quiet since his arrival to our group. He was large and slovenly, an oafish sort. He had clear innocent eyes that never quite met your gaze. He dug away with his flathead shovel, and I swung my pickaxe. I had earned the right to wield a pickaxe. George was new and so he was limited to the use of a flathead shovel. A spade shovel had to be earned. Every object at Anneewakee was considered a potential weapon, something that could be used to harm oneself or others. In the E&O it was a privilege just to wear a belt, to wear a watch, or to wield a pen. So the right to grasp a shovel was no small thing. The right to dig and hoe and saw and chop was a hard-earned privilege. At Anneewakee, shovels and wheelbarrows were status symbols that conveyed one's "growth" and "maturity." Tools came with trust, and while some of us could be trusted to dig, not all of us could be trusted with just any kind of shovel. The authorities had somehow determined that it was easier to kill someone with a spade shovel than with a flathead.

We dug and swatted at the variety of stinging, sucking, biting flying insects that pervaded the panhandle swampland. The layers of insect repellent were thick enough to permeate the air with a ubiquitous chemical sweetness, but they didn't do much to deter the mosquitoes and dog flies. We wore snake guards around our calves on account of the Eastern Diamondback rattlers that were prevalent in the area. Palmetto bushes are rattlesnake havens, and we were uprooting their territory with reckless abandon.

You have to talk when you're working. There's nothing else to do. Conversation alleviates the boredom and helps pass the time; and the more interesting the conversation, the better. In the E&O I quickly learned that there were plenty of fascinating conversations to be had with my comrades in consignment. As a virginal adolescent, I was fascinated by the boastful sexual exploits of a 15 year old guy who was locked up in my ward. We would play checkers in the afternoon and he would regale me with explicit accounts of his numerous sexual conquests. I didn't understand the mechanics or lingo of half of what he said, but I was enthralled nonetheless. It was obvious to him that I was quite wet behind the ears, so he was kind enough to balance his boasting with tutorial information without me having to inquire. Even so, I still didn't understand much. But I must confess that listening to his lurid stories was some of the best entertainment I've ever had to this day.

As George and I battled the palmetto roots and panhandle heat, I ventured the standard inquiry posed to all new blood, *"So what are you in here for?"*

"I don't really want to talk about it," George said flatly, without irritation or offense.

"I understand. That's cool. But one thing I've learned since I've been here is that the quicker you talk about your problems, the quicker you can get out of this place."

I had bought into the party line, even though I knew a lot of it was bullshit.

George kept his head down and scraped away the sand from the roots with his flathead shovel. *"Well, I'm from Los Angeles. I guess my home situation was kind of fucked up."*

"How so?" I inquired. *"If you don't mind me asking. I mean, if you feel like sharing."*

"I guess I got in some trouble, you know."

"Well, yeah, I can relate to that," I said. *"I got into trouble too."*

"Mine was different."

"Look," I began, *"you don't have to tell me anything you don't want to. But it's just you and me talking here. We might as well talk. It helps the time go by. My parents sent me here because I kept getting kicked out of school. I had this asshole psychiatrist who tried to put me on Ritalin and he convinced my parents to send me to this place. But I guess I needed it. I caused them a lot of problems, and I see that now. The group has really helped me, and I'm learning a lot and growing. But I still have a long way to go."*

I was sincere, but I was mostly naïve and mostly full of the propaganda that I had chosen to buy into out of self-preservation. Sure, I was truly interested in George, but I was also interested in passing the time and listening to some salacious stories that would take my mind off of the blisters and these accursed dog flies.

"Well, I guess my mom was a drug addict," George said, matter-of-factly.

"Damn, that must have sucked."

"Yeah. I came home from school one day and my mom started shooting at me. But she didn't mean to. She didn't know it was me. She thought it was her pimp coming to beat her up again."

George said all of this with no inflection in his voice. He spoke as if he were talking about the weather. I was shaken. I had never heard a story like this. I mean, my favorite TV show back then was *"Hill Street Blues,"* but this was some real shit that made Steven Bochco's world look like Disneyland.

"What did you do then? I mean, what happened after that?" I asked stupidly. I didn't know what to say. How do you respond to something like that?

309

"She apologized when she realized it was me. She didn't mean to do it. My mom's a heroin addict, and she doesn't know what she does a lot of times."

"Damn." I shook my head. Sometimes that's all you can do: shake your head and say *"Damn."*

But then, for some reason, I continued:

"Well, look man, there are a lot people here that don't deserve to be here. A lot of people are here because their parents are screwed up and stuff. The thing is to try and make the most of it. You know, just try to talk about stuff and work with the group. It can really help you."

I think I believed that. I think I meant well.

"No. I deserve to be here," George said.

"It doesn't sound like it to me," I replied. *"It's not your fault your mom is on drugs. And it's better for you to be here than to be home in that environment where you could be killed by a drug dealer or pimp or something."*

I wanted to comfort George, to let him know that he didn't deserve this fate. His mom was screwed up, but that wasn't his fault.

"You don't understand," he said.

"What do you mean George? What's up? What don't I understand?"

"I can't tell you."

"Look George, whatever it is, you can tell me. That's what we're here for, to talk about things, to confide in each other, to help each other. The more you talk about your problems, the quicker you can get out of here."

"Yeah, I know. But I can't tell you."

We kept uprooting the palmettos and tossing them into a pile that was now as tall as we were. The conversation had taken my mind off of the agonizing work conditions. I was absorbed in George's story. And the fact that he was holding back a piece of vital information intrigued me all the more. In the interest of his "therapy," I needed to get him to reveal his deep, dark secret. After all, talking about my own problems is what had earned me the right to use a pickaxe instead of a flathead shovel. So I was obliged to encourage George to make the same progress. After all, a flathead shovel is really no match for those damn palmetto scrubs.

"Like I said, you don't have to tell me anything," I reassured him. *"Just know that whatever you tell me stays with me."*

That was the truth. For all of my many sins and character flaws, I would never betray someone's confidence. At least I don't think I would. But then again, I may have done so over the course of my life. But I meant it with George, and I kept my word. I think.

"I feel like I should tell somebody," George replied. *"But I don't know how. I don't think I can."*

"I'm not pressuring you man. Just know that you can tell me if you want to. Hell, we're out here working and sweating in this heat with mosquitoes biting the hell out of us, and we're getting to know each other. We're in this same place and we're both trying to get out as fast as we can. Might as well come clean with each other and talk about shit. It's not like they can arrest you for what you tell me. Hell, you're already here!"

George kept digging, and as he dug he kept his head down and began to speak in the same matter-of-fact tone: *"Well, I was arrested see. Because I did something bad. I did something really bad."*

"We all did something bad man, that's why we're all here."

"Not bad like I did," George said. And then without any change of tone, expression, or demeanor he simply said: *"I raped my sister."*

I was fourteen years old. I had listened to the graphic sexual exploits of my buddy in the E&O, and I had a vague understanding of sex and what it entailed. I mean, as virginal as I was, I'd had numerous dalliances of petting with girls at the various schools I had been sent to prior to Anneewakee. When I was in the 6th grade, a pretty and fully developed 8th grade girl taught me how to kiss and showed me how to touch her breasts and fondle her genitals on the backseat of the bus every afternoon. If that sounds like every teenage boy's fantasy, I can assure you that it wasn't. I felt no emotional connection with that girl. Our make-out sessions made me physically aroused, but I also experienced deep shame and tremendous guilt afterwards. I never told anyone. I was embarrassed to even tell my friends. To "go with" a girl your own age was all the rage back then, but if any of my peers had known the things I was actually doing with a girl two years older than me, they would have called me a freak. My guilt was exacerbated later on when I finally told the poor girl that I couldn't do those things with her anymore. She cried and didn't understand. I guess she associated physical intimacy with emotional intimacy, whereas our sexually charged physical contact was way too much for me to handle at my age and stage of development. I felt guilty for doing the things I did with her, but I felt even worse when I decided to tell her that I couldn't be with her any longer. In her mind I was her boyfriend, and our make-out sessions were simply a natural expression of mutual affection. But I, on the other hand, felt intuitive guilt for indulging in desires and acts that from my standpoint had nothing to do with emotion, affection, or love. My experience with that girl set the precedent for a pattern of spiritually unhealthy relationships with the opposite sex that would haunt me until I got married, and even afterwards.

So as a virginal fourteen year old, George's revelation was hard for me to fully process. When he told me that he had raped his sister, I really didn't know the full import of the term. *Rape.* I just knew that it was something very violent, something sexual, something criminally and abominably awful. I was stunned by what he said, but my naivety protected me somewhat from the seismic reality of what I was actually hearing.

"Damn." Sometimes that's really all you can say, right?

"Yeah, but that's not the worst of it."

"It's not?"

"No. You see..."

George kept digging. The inflection of his voice never altered. He showed no change of emotion as he added, *"She was three years old."*

I vaguely understood the concept of rape, much less the concept of incest, much less the logistics of raping a three year old child. And the fact that George related this horror in such a nondescript manner probably helped me to absorb it as calmly as I did.

One thing we were programmed to do from day one at Anneewakee – from the moment we were thrown into the E&O – was *not to judge.* Who was I to judge anyone else's problems? We were all here together, and it didn't matter *what* we did to get here; the fact is that we *were* here. So who was I to judge George? My duty was to encourage him to share his problems with the group, because the group was omniscient. The group could solve any problem. The group was infallible. The individual must submit his will, his ego, and his opinions to the jury and judgment of the group. Whether somebody stole a biscuit from the dining hall or whether they raped their three year old sister, no one had the right to judge another. *Individuals* were simply supposed to encourage, support, and understand one another; the *group* would judge. And I learned that the group often judged lesser sins much more harshly than it judged greater sins. And time and experience have shown me that this same twisted dynamic also fuels the majority of human governments and political systems of this world.

So I received George's words with a spirit of non-condemnation. Perhaps I didn't really want to understand what he had said. Perhaps I deliberately ignored the specific reality of his words in order to retain my own sanity. I couldn't judge. It didn't matter what he did. He was here digging up palmetto roots, and so was I. The only significant difference was that I dug them up with a pickaxe and he dug them up with a flathead shovel. We were in this thing together, and I wanted to get out and I wanted to help him get out. That's all that mattered.

"Wow." I may have said *"Damn"* again, but I don't remember. It was *"Wow,"* or *"Damn"* or something like that. Hell, what else can you say?

Neither of us said anything for a while. We just continued to plumb the earth and let the reality of the revelation linger in the miasma of insect repellent and sun-baked, humid Gulf salt air. He had raped his sister. And she was three years old. And he had chosen to tell me. And I guess I was supposed to have some answers, since I had convinced him to tell me.

But I didn't have any answers. I still couldn't figure out why I was in this God-forsaken place digging up palmetto roots and fighting off every biting insect known to man. What answers could I give to George? Hell, I didn't even know if I wanted to give him any answers. How do you console a monster? *Should* you console a monster? And yet, as I watched him dig and looked at his oafish figure and his innocent eyes that were perpetually fixated on the ground, I couldn't help but to feel strangely sorry for him.

So I said, *"You have to talk about this in group meeting."*

*"I can't. I can't talk about it. I told **you**, but I can't tell the group. I can't."*

"Look man, you have to. I won't tell anyone. You don't have to do it tonight, but you've got to do it eventually. The sooner you tell the group, the quicker they can help you and the quicker you can get out of here. I won't let anyone judge you. We're all in here together man. Remember that. No one has the right to condemn you. Just express your feelings and the group will accept you and help you."

When all else fails, you can always fall back on the party line. I believed what I was saying, and I think I was right, as naïve as it sounded. That's the only advice I could come up with. I was certainly unequipped to counsel George about the rape of his three year old sister. I mean, if a licensed psychiatrist couldn't figure out that my problems in school were directly related to the dysfunctional alcoholic environment I had to deal with at home, then there was certainly no way I could figure out how to help George deal with this horrific situation.

The sun began to drop behind the Florida pines, and the pile of palmetto roots was now a small hill that was taller than both of us. We shared a mutual satisfaction in our accomplishment. Our pile was taller than everyone else's. We had worked hard, talked hard, and now it was time to eat, shower, and get ready for the nightly group meeting. I felt good knowing that I had helped our new group member open up about his problems. I patted myself on the back, because I had encouraged George to share his troubles with me. Now I could only hope that George would one day share his burden with the entire group.

After supper and showers we walked down the beaten trail back to the campsite, slowly and cautiously, many of us with long sticks, beating the brush on either side to scare off any rattlers that may be near. Even at night, the Florida panhandle was oppressively hot in the summer, but the Gulf breeze would often waft in and provide a modicum of relief in the evenings. The group logs surrounded the campfire, the size of which was determined by the seasons and the weather. On rare occasions, if there was no wind and the night heat was stifling, there would be no kindled wood, just a kerosene lantern set in the middle of the blackened ashy sand. But tonight there was a suitable breeze, and we made a small but firm flame. We took our places on the group logs around the fire, and it seemed that we all shared an unspoken satisfaction of a good day's work together. The supper at the dining hall had been good. We were clean from our showers. And some nights just seemed more conducive to opening up and sharing than others. This felt like one of those times.

But I was not expecting George to bare his revelation tonight. I thought it would take some time before he disclosed his secret to the group. And as much as I had coaxed him to reveal it to me, I wasn't about to pressure him to tell the entire group until he was fully ready. The group might be omniscient, but there's some knowledge that human omniscience can't even handle.

There is no thicker darkness than the nighttime of the Florida panhandle wilderness. Faces around the circle of fire become intensely clear and magnified against the curtain of blackness that stretches endlessly beyond them. A campfire in the midst of an endless pitch black expanse engenders a sense of solidarity and intimacy among those who share its offer of warmth and light. There is a shared vulnerability, a common awareness of mortality and finitude. All are equally subject to the terrible mysteries and unfathomable horrors that potentially lurk beyond its flickering flames.

We had all barely taken our seats when George began to speak:

"I guess I have something to share."

George seemed nervous, less matter-of-fact than he had been with me earlier that day. He looked down as he spoke. He fumbled with his hands and kicked at the sand.

"I'm not really sure if I should say it, but I guess I need to."

I was conflicted. On the one hand I felt great pride that I had convinced George to share his troubles with the group, but on the other hand I wasn't sure he was ready yet. Maybe he needed more time. Maybe he should tell our group leader first. ("Group leaders" were the ostensible "professionals" that were hired to be in charge of each group. None of them were licensed psychiatrists or psychologists, and it turned out that many of them were pedophiles and child abusers.) But if George felt the need to share with the group, then I reasoned that this was a good thing, right?

"The thing is... well...the thing is..." George stammered. *"I'm not sure if I should say this..."*

"Go ahead George... It's OK man, just talk to us... We're here to help man, just say it..." The group offered its sincere encouragement.

I was afraid for George to say it, but my voyeuristic side was quietly urging him on. I suspect that the entire group felt the same way I had felt earlier that afternoon. *What did you do?* It was the question that fascinated us all and somehow bound us together. We all wanted to know if the other's crime was greater or lesser than our own. A pissing contest, essentially. And I was the ultimate loser. I didn't have any crimes on my record, no jail time to boast of, no Judge that had sentenced me to this fate. I was the kid who got kicked out of Catholic school, got kicked out of boarding school, and got kicked out of reform school; the kid whose parents paid a shrink 80 dollars an hour to recommend that I be sent to this hellhole that my mother euphemistically called a "wilderness program." I looked at my comrades gathered around the fire and thought, *"You ain't gonna win this pissing contest; in fact, you're gonna wish you hadn't even entered it."*

"It's alright George... Tell us what's on your mind... We're here to listen... We're here to help... We're no different than you... We all have problems..." The group essentially echoed the platitudes I had spouted to George earlier that day.

"Well..." George began, his voice quivering a bit. *"The thing is... well..."*

He clenched and unclenched his fists. His knees popped up and down like pistons. His fingernails dug into his palms. He shook his head as if he couldn't believe what he was about to say.

"The thing is... I guess... well... you see, I raped my little sister. And she was only three years old. And I raped her! She was only three! And I raped her!! I RAPED HER!!!"

George was staring at the fire when he said it. Then his head suddenly snapped up and his eyes locked right in on mine. He had never looked me in the eye before. His eyes were no longer shy and innocent. They were different. Completely different. Then, staring directly at me, and with a voice that I can only describe as inhuman, he said:

"I should never have told you! I should never have told you! You motherfucker! Now I'll have to snap your goddamn neck! I'll have to kill you, you motherfucker. I'll have to break your neck! Why did you make me tell you?! You motherfucker! Why did you make me tell you?!!!"

Then his head snapped back and his gaze was on the fire. His face was taught and his eyes didn't blink. They couldn't blink. Spittle poured from his lips.

"I SEE THE DEVIL! In the fire! He's in the flames! The Devil is in the fire!!! I SEE THE DEVIL!!!"

George began to hit himself in the face. Violently. Uncontrollably. Blood gushed from his nose; his eyes rolled back in his head; he was foaming at the mouth. His arms launched a volley of fists that pummeled his own countenance, as if he were trying to viciously and permanently eradicate anything that could ever be recognized in the mirror again. He knocked two of his own teeth out.

Our group leader jumped up and commanded, *"Restrain him! Restrain him! Get on him!"* Everyone jumped on George and struggled to hold down his arms and legs. But I was paralyzed. I was terrified and shocked and immobile. There were at least 11 guys on top of George, and yet he still was not subdued. He was possessed of a maniacal strength that I had never seen before in my life and that I have never seen since. There was a cosmic battle taking place. And as much as I wanted to remain an innocent bystander, I was somehow intimately engaged, even though I couldn't move. I don't know how long it took. It could have been ten minutes or it could have been 45 minutes. All I know is that something inhuman or subhuman overwhelmed George, and it took every ounce of strength on everyone's part to get him under control.

Time stood eerily still during the struggle, but George was finally restrained; and whatever evil energy had possessed him seemed to finally be gone. As the fire crackled, I watched him lapse into a deep sleep. Somebody gently wiped the blood and sweat and tears from his face. We couldn't wake him and we all felt it best to let him rest. We put him in his tent, and then we all went to bed, oddly with no fear or trepidation. Looking back, I guess our lack of subsequent fear was because we had witnessed a catharsis. Without any substantial spiritual guidance to direct us, we nevertheless intuitively sensed that something had been necessarily expunged. George had come clean. He had unburdened himself. He had faced his devil, and he no longer had to carry that evil within him. Somehow we understood this expiation, even though none of us could articulate it; and we therefore retired to our Camel tents with nothing but our own desperate sleep in mind.

I was in that group with George for another six months or so. We never talked about his horror again – neither the evil he had committed nor the evil he saw in the fire that night. I don't know what happened to George, or if he ever saw the devil again. I can only pray that he found the grace and strength to deal with his many demons. We all have demons to fight, and George was no different from me in that regard. I wonder what happened to his drug addicted mother. I wonder what happened to his sister, that poor little girl. I wonder what happened to all the others who spent two or three years of their lives trying to survive at Anneewakee, "the land of the friendly people."

As my life has progressed, I've come to realize that there are people in this world much more evil than George, even though their sins are not as heinous. George was tormented by his actions, and that reveals the presence of a conscience. George was born into a dark corner of this world. He grew up in suffering and replicated that suffering. But somehow the knowledge of right and wrong, good and evil, was not completely erased from his soul. Yet the world is full of people who commit no crimes but inflict hellish suffering with calculated callousness. Legally and lawfully they murder, oppress, victimize and exploit. But instead of being called "monsters" they are called "CEO's" and "senators," "judges" and "presidents."

My time at Anneewakee and my friendship with George taught me a lot. It taught me that our world is "the land of the friendly people," full of villains and heroes and many monsters in disguise. The problem is that we usually confuse the heroes for the villains; and for whatever reason, we refuse to rip the masks off the monsters and expose them for what they really are. The monsters that ran Anneewakee had the power, and there's something about human nature that would rather submit to evil power than risk the suffering that might result from confronting corruption. Human history seems to bear witness to this.

We call the slave master's whip "necessary discipline;" we call Auschwitz's ashes a "cloudy day;" and we rationalize the decimated bodies of unborn children as the natural detritus of "reproductive choice." But because the pathos of conscience pulsates within us, we must find scapegoats for our moral affliction. So we ignore the systemic evils for which we ourselves are ultimately responsible, and we reserve our condemnations for individual monsters whose crimes transcend anything of which we believe we could ever really be capable.

George was a monster with a conscience. And his conscience forced him to confront his demons face to face. In doing so he seemed to find a measure of peace. And, at least while he remained at Anneewakee, he seemed to grow into a kind, sensitive, and good person. But as George was overcoming his own demons, Anneewakee was unleashing its own legions of hell. Rampant pedophilia, physical abuse, and psychological terror were forced upon countless innocent young men and women that were sentenced to live in that environment. And just like the world itself, the "good" people went about their way with their heads buried in the sand, refusing to expose and confront the evils in their midst.

I myself stood silently by and watched four grown men hold down one of my best friends as they methodically pulled out huge clumps of hair from his head. Another time, I saw the only African

American kid there being mercilessly beaten by a 350 pound man named Mr. Phillips.

"Who do you think you are nigger?! You're mine boy! Where you gonna run? You can take this beatin' or you can runaway into that theyah swamp and be food fa the gaytuhs!"

I saw the whole thing as I was taking out the trash one night. It terrified me. I had never suspected that Mr. Phillips was so evil. He always greeted me with a smile and a kind word. On occasion he would come by our group site to show us a freshly killed Eastern Diamondback that he'd recently shot. And sometimes he would bring us fried rabbit, gator tail, or wild boar stew that he had just cooked up. I perceived him to be a jovial "man's man" who protected the grounds and kept us safe. But that perception was immediately eviscerated as I witnessed his vicious brutality against that defenseless teenage boy. But I said nothing. I didn't dare to intervene. All I did was go back to the other side of the building and throw up. I was sickened by the evil of what I saw. Sick enough to puke but not sick enough to do anything. Not sick enough to say anything or do anything about it.

I have come to realize that such cowardice on my part is exactly what facilitates injustice and evil in the world. Edmund Burke famously said, *"All that is needed for evil to triumph is for good men to do nothing."* A great quote. But as someone once pointed out to me, good people don't *do nothing*. Good people *do something*. Goodness is not simply bothered by evil, goodness is disturbed enough to do something about it. In his book *People of The Lie*, M. Scott Peck, M.D. writes:

"Triggers are pulled by individuals. Orders are given and executed by individuals. In the last analysis, every single human act is ultimately the result of an individual choice... The plain fact of the matter is that any group will remain inevitably potentially conscienceless and evil until such a time as each and every individual holds himself or herself directly responsible for the behavior of the whole group – the organism – of which he or she is a part." (p. 215; 218)

I'm no psychologist, and my time at Anneewakee (which conveniently, for insurance purposes, had attained legal status as a psychiatric institute) conditioned me to be very skeptical of the fields of psychiatry and psychology. But I do believe that somehow George possessed the goodness to confront his own evil, to look squarely at his horrors and face the devil itself. Yet I saw the devil and turned away. And I've done so many times throughout my life. George did a monstrous thing, but he had the courage to reckon with it. Most of us don't do monstrous things, but we refuse to unmask the monsters among us. Who wants to look at evil? Better to call evil "good" than to look in the mirror and risk an honest reflection.

*   *   *

Years later I took my wife down to Carrabelle, Florida to show her "the land of the friendly people." Anneewakee had been shut down a few years after I left. "Doc" Poetter, the one-legged man in charge of the entire operation, had been convicted of pedophilia and child abuse and sentenced to prison. I wanted to show my wife the place where I had spent two of the most difficult years of my life. I wanted to show her the concrete and stucco buildings we had constructed ourselves, the cabins we had built, the beautiful football and baseball fields we had plowed and sodded by hand. We had been used as child labor to create Doc Poetter's pedophile paradise, but we had nevertheless taken great pride in what we had created with our cooperative sweat. Every brick, every nail, every coat of paint, every meal that was served, and every manicured blade of grass came from our own efforts and labor. As difficult and unfair as it was, we all felt very good about what we had built together.

The dirt road that led to the campus was gated and locked. There was a sign indicating that the property was for sale, along with a phone number. I called the number and explained to the man who answered that I had once lived here as a student at a place called "Anneewakee," and that I wanted to know if I could show my wife the campus. The man asked my name, and after I told him he said, *"I remember you well! I'll be there in 10 minutes."* "Mr. L" had been a group leader and one of my football coaches there. He was a genuinely nice man, one of the truly good guys at the place.

He showed up a few minutes later, unlocked the gate, and drove us down the dirt road towards the remains of the campus.

"They want to turn it into a golf course now," "Mr. L" lamented. *"Can you believe that? A golf course!"*

We turned onto the campus drive and approached a ghost town. The buildings were crumbling, the football field was overgrown, the cabins across the lake were falling apart. What had once been so efficient, so organized, so well-kept and well-run had now become a wasteland.

"After all the work you guys did," "Mr. L" said. *"Look at what they've allowed to happen to this place. After all the work you guys did. And now they want to make it a golf course."* He shook his head. *"They could turn it into a camp or into a school, or something that would preserve what you guys built. But they're gonna tear it all down and make a golf course!"*

It did indeed make me very sad. "Mr. L" led me on a trek back into the woods to show me the cabins and the group site that George and I had helped to build. The trail was barely traceable, and "Mr. L" beat back the bushes on either side with a long metal pole. I was scared to death of the rattlers that I knew were surely lurking nearby. I couldn't believe that I had actually once been acclimated to living in such a snake infested wilderness.

The group site we had built was completely overgrown, and our cabins were rotting and infested with cockroaches and spiders. This had been my home for two years, and now it was completely uninhabitable. I was flooded with a mix of emotions. I had hated this place. When I had lived here, all I could think about was getting the hell out of it. Now I was sad to see my erstwhile home so neglected and forsaken.

We wended our way back down the pine scrub path to the remnants of the main campus. It was the middle of summer, and just as hot as it had been on that day when George and I were digging up palmetto roots together. But there was no more work going on here now. No more group meetings. No more campfires. No more friendships being forged. No more children being abused.

A hawk circled overhead. A white crane glided up from the lake. The sun-baked air was silent and still. The only remaining inhabitants in the "land of the friendly people" were the ghosts and demons that we had long left behind.

444. ~ SAY A PRAYER ~

When you cry, say a prayer
When you laugh, say a prayer

When you fall, say a prayer
When you rise, say a prayer

When you work, say a prayer
When you play, say a prayer

When you struggle, say a prayer
When you rest, say a prayer

When you mourn, say a prayer
When you rejoice, say a prayer

With every breath, say a prayer

For every experience
is the proof of life...
the evidence of existence...
the unconditional offer
of divine hope

445. ~ DON'T TELL ME ~

Don't tell me you love the poor
Don't tell me you love your fellow man
Don't tell me you hate oppression
While you enable the abortionist's hand

Don't tell me you love justice
Don't tell me you love Our Lord
Don't tell me you hate war
While you sharpen the abortionist's sword

Don't tell me you love the homeless
Don't tell me you love peace
Don't tell me you love your neighbor
Unless you set the unborn free

446. ~ IF I'M DREAMING ~

If I'm dreaming, don't wake me,
although nightmares
may shake me.

There's too much good in my world,
so I'll endure
the absurd.

The horrors
are never as real
as the joys.

Demons scream at me
as I ascend
on the wings of angels.

Introduction

In defending Christian pacifism, I have sometimes been accused (and I believe unfairly so) of being disrespectful to Orthodox Priests who disagree with this philosophy. So I want to make it clear at the outset that I honor *Father "J" as an Orthodox Christian Priest, and therefore I will do my best to present this refutation in a respectful Christian manner. Sometimes bluntness is erroneously mistaken for rudeness, and I hope that those who read and hear this message will not fall prey to such a misunderstanding. Priests are fallible human beings with fallible human opinions. And as with all fallible human opinions, the personal views of Priests are also susceptible to examination and rebuttal. My own opinions certainly warrant equal scrutiny, and therefore I submit them to the correction and reproof of Orthodox Christian doctrine.

I would also like to say that while I have profound disagreement with Father J on this particular topic, I nevertheless appreciate his solid Orthodox teachings on many other subjects. Most of all, I truly appreciate his Orthodox Christian commitment to opposing the evil of abortion and affirming the life and dignity of the unborn child. I wish that more Orthodox Priests were as outspoken on that issue as he is.

*(I have withheld the name of this good Priest out of respect. I will therefore refer to him throughout as "Father J".)

Part I: Defining Pacifism and Dispelling a False Dichotomy

Father J's talk is titled: *"Jesus: Peacemaker Not Pacifist"*

To begin with, it's very important that we define the meaning of pacifism. There are actually various degrees and interpretations of pacifism. Webster's Dictionary defines pacifism as *"the belief that it is wrong to use war or violence to settle disputes; opposition to war or violence as a means of settling disputes; specifically a refusal to bear arms on moral or religious grounds; 2) an attitude or policy of nonresistance"*

There are many degrees of pacifism and various interpretations of its definition and application. So I will only speak for my own view of pacifism, which I define as *"the Christian imperative to actively oppose injustice and evil always and only with nonviolent principles and methods."* The power of Christian pacifism is derived from the fact that it is *Christian*. The Christian pacifist rejects the violent methods of the "god of this world," i.e. Satan (II Corinthians 4:4) and relies upon the spiritual weapons issued to us by God Himself. As St. Paul writes in Ephesians 6:

"Finally, my brethren, be strong in the Lord, and in the power of his might. Put on the whole armor of God, that you may be able to stand against the wiles of the devil. For we wrestle not against flesh and blood, but against principalities, against powers, against the rulers of the darkness of this world, against spiritual wickedness in high places. Wherefore take unto you the whole armor of God, that you may be able to withstand in the evil day, and having done all, to stand. Stand therefore, having your loins girded with truth, and having on the breastplate of righteousness; And your feet shod with the preparation of the gospel of peace; Above all, taking the shield of faith, wherewith ye shall be able to quench all the fiery darts of the wicked. And take the helmet of salvation, and the sword of the Spirit, which is the word of God: Praying always with all prayer and supplication in the Spirit, and watching thereunto with all perseverance and supplication for all saints." [Ephesians 6:10-18]

Authentic Christian pacifism is not a feckless idealism that imagines injustice and evil will vanish if we simply wish it away. The Christian pacifist is a soldier in this spiritual war, and he confronts evil with the militancy of prayer, love, and sacrificial nonviolent intervention.

So the fundamental problem with Father J's argument is that his entire premise is based upon a straw man, a gross mischaracterization of the Christian pacifist position. Father J presents pacifism as synonymous with apathy and cowardice. But there was certainly nothing apathetic or cowardly about the nonviolent sacrificial actions of Our Lord Jesus Christ. And there was nothing apathetic or cowardly about the pacifism of Mahatma Gandhi and Dr. Martin Luther King, Jr. – men who gave their very lives in the nonviolent struggle to confront and redress the great social injustices of their time. Father J has made the same mistake that most people make when they reject pacifism. He has confused Christian pacifism with a mentality of apathetic indifference to sin, evil, injustice and oppression. And this is a very unfortunate misconception, a misconception that I hope to correct with this humble and sincere response.

First let me address the title of Father J's talk: *"Jesus: Peacemaker not Pacifist."* The title is problematic because it presents a false dichotomy between pacifism and peacemaking. Pacifism is the unconditional commitment to nonviolence, and one cannot violently make peace. Violence can no more establish peace than theft can establish honesty. The simple fact is that it is impossible to make peace with somebody that you kill.

It's fine to philosophize and theorize about strong armies protecting national peace. But the grim realities of such militant "protection" reveal that the ostensible peace which violence provides is really no peace at all. As Dr. Martin Luther King, Jr. said, *"True peace is not the absence of tension but the presence of justice."* And nowhere is this truth more tragically evident than in the United States of America. We have the strongest military in the world, but it does nothing more than protect a superficial peace that obfuscates the violence of hunger, homelessness, poverty and abortion. Strong armies don't provide and protect the peace; they only preserve a façade of peace that makes the masses believe that their own manufactured violence is "law and order."

Part II: A Point by Point Rebuttal

Now, let's examine some of Father J's statements point by point:

1. Father J asks, *"Is there any spirit today that is unmolested by this nonsense of extreme pacifism?"*

With all due respect, I'm not sure what world Father J is living in. When I look at our world, I see rampant violence and discord everywhere. The spirit of warfare, division, sin, and oppression permeates the globe. Rather than extreme pacifism, I see extreme violence. In fact, violence is so prevalent that even the unborn child in the womb is not safe. The one realm of earthly existence where peace should be certain – the mother's womb – has become perhaps the least safe place of all. So to answer Father J's question: yes, the evil spirit of violence is all too prevalent and all too pervasive. I pray for the Spirit of pacifism to come quickly. But the Holy Spirit is not a molester; His peace is a choice that must be volitionally embraced.

2. Father J says, *"We live in a plague of pacifism."*

Now, as I stated at the outset, I'm sure Father J really means to say that we live in plague of *cowardice*. Surely he does not really mean that we live in a world plagued with peace and nonviolence. And surely he does not view peace as a "plague." But again I point out that he is erroneously confusing Christian pacifism with apathetic indifference to injustice and evil. The reality is that we don't live in a plague of pacifism; we live in a world plagued with violence.

He goes on to say, *"The Church has been plagued throughout her history with a false spirit of pacifism."*

That is a very troubling statement, because the Church honors and venerates countless Saints who submitted themselves to torture and martyrdom without violently defending themselves or others. Surely these Saints were not led by a "false spirit." Surely they are not to be condemned as cowards because they refused to injure or slay their oppressors. God forbid that we should make such an insinuation!

3. Father J then states, *"The pacifist believes that Christ conquered evil by submitting to evil on its own terms."*

This may be the most egregious misrepresentation of Christian pacifism that I've ever heard. Christian pacifism is not apathetic and passive acceptance of evil. Our Lord's sacrificial and atoning death on the Cross was the antithesis of submission to evil on its own terms. In fact, Christ confronted evil on *His* terms, not the devil's.

Our Lord refused to submit to the ideology of violence which dictates the retributive principle of "measure for measure." He refused to meet hate with hate. He refused to confound the calumniators with calumny. He refused to fight political powers with political machinations. He refused to destroy the lives of others in order to preserve His own life. By refusing to bow to evil, by refusing to acquiesce with evil, and by refusing to combat evil with the methods of evil, Our Lord provided salvation to all men and redeemed the entire world.

Christian pacifists simply seek to follow Our Lord's example to the best of their ability. The pacifist confronts evil directly and says: *"I refuse to allow you to dictate the terms of engagement. Do to me what you will, but I will not respond in kind. I will meet your violence with peace and your hate with love. I will resist your temporal evil with the weapons of eternal good. And even as you seek to destroy my life, I will seek to win your soul."*

As St. John Chrysostom said, *"Our warfare is to make the dying live, not to make the living die."*

4. Father J goes on to say: *"The pacifist believes that Christ's mandate to turn the other cheek means not resisting evil and allowing evil to do whatever it wants."*

Once again, this statement could not be further from the truth. For example, Dr. Martin Luther King, Jr. did not believe in allowing evil to do whatever it wanted. Instead, Dr. King was compelled by the teachings and example of Christ; so he confronted evil head on and declared, *"Thou shall not!"* He preached, marched, agitated, and offered up his very life in resisting evil. But he resisted evil nonviolently, lovingly, and only with the weapons and power of the Holy Spirit. And his pacifist resistance not only helped to change unjust laws, but it also changed hearts and minds.

5. Father J emphatically declares: *"Unfortunately today, our Orthodox Churches are filled with pacifists. Filled!"*

In the years since I have been a baptized Orthodox Christian, I have yet to meet another Orthodox Christian pacifist face to face. I have over 3,000 Facebook friends, most of whom are Orthodox Christians; and I would estimate that less than 5% of them are avowed pacifists. So I am simply baffled by Father J's statement here. I would love for him to tell me where these Orthodox Churches are that are filled with pacifists. I should like to send a letter of gratitude and encouragement to their priests and parishioners, for I continue to search for a solidarity of nonviolent Christian consciousness within my beloved Orthodox community.

6. Father J also takes a thinly veiled swipe at the **Orthodox Peace Fellowship**, a wonderful ministry that embraces and promotes the Orthodox patristic concept of the "consistent Life ethic." He remarks, *"We have this or that so-called 'Peace Fellowship' claiming to represent the Church, censuring the godly use of force at all."*

This statement is both unfair and inaccurate. It is unfair because it insinuates that the **Orthodox Peace Fellowship** is not really a fellowship of peace, but only a "so-called" peace fellowship. I have no idea why Father J feels the need to malign and impugn the **Orthodox Peace Fellowship** in this manner. And his statement is inaccurate because as I have already repeatedly stated (and will continue to reiterate throughout this refutation), Christian pacifism does not reject the godly use of force, but instead relies on the use of *godly* force. And the godly force that has been sanctioned for us as Christians is not the carnal force of violence, destruction, and killing. Godly force most certainly involves tremendous struggle, suffering, and self-sacrifice – but it does not involve the deliberate destruction of human beings created in God's holy image. As the angel declared to Zechariah the Prophet, *"Not by might nor by power, but by my Spirit declares the Lord God Almighty." [Zechariah 4:6]*

7. Father J also invokes the examples of Old Testament Saints as justification for the use of violence today. This is a common argument levied against the Christian pacifist. People will argue that since David killed Goliath, since the Israelites slaughtered pagan nations, and since Elijah slew the prophets of Baal, then violence is also acceptable for the Christian as well.

But there are some serious fallacies with this argument. For example, if the violent actions of saints in the Old Testament provide the standard for our behavior today, then why not take up arms and slaughter abortionists? Certainly we could save countless innocent unborn lives if we did so. Why not burn witches at the stake and kill the false prophets of our own day and time? If the militancy of the

Old Testament Saints is our standard, then we are most certainly failing miserably in our Christian duty.

But, of course, the reality is that as Christians our ultimate standard and model of behavior is Christ Himself. Therefore, the definitive questions we must ask are: how did Our Lord respond to injustice and evil? How did He respond to violence and oppression? In the debate over to kill or not to kill, the paramount question for the Christian is simply this: *"When Christ and His disciples walked upon the earth, facing violent opposition and witnessing tremendous oppression, did they respond with violence and killing?"* And the clear answer is a resounding and unequivocal *no!*

We must understand that Christ came to fulfill the law and the prophets. (St. Matthew 5:17) St. Paul writes that the law of the Spirit of life in Christ Jesus has made us free from the law of sin and death. (Romans 8:2) Just as we no longer need to offer animal sacrifices to atone for our sins, likewise we no longer need to injure and kill. Christ has liberated us from reliance upon weapons of fleshly destruction. He has commissioned us with spiritual weapons that are imbued with eternal power. (Ephesians 6) Our souls are redeemed by Him, and therefore we do not need to preserve our earthly lives by any means necessary. No weapon formed against us shall prosper. (Isaiah 54:17) Though our flesh may be destroyed, nothing can destroy our souls.

The Christian is not enslaved to the antiquated law of "an eye for an eye." In St. John 13:34, Our Lord gives His disciples a new commandment: *"A new command I give you, that you love one another, as I have loved you."* Christ is our Commander in Chief, and His orders are clear:

"Put away your sword." *[St. Matthew 26:52]*

"Do not repay evil with evil." *[I Peter 3:9]*

"Turn the other cheek." *[St. Matthew 5:39]*

"Love your enemies and bless those that persecute you." *[St. Luke 6:28]*

8. Father J says, *"Lots of Christians today see no place for the use of firmness or force in any sphere of life at all. Many say that you should never even spank your own children."*

I actually agree with Father J's statement here. There are many professing Christians today who unfortunately fail to stand up to evil, who fail to defend Christian truth, and who fail to discipline their children. But such failures are in no way reflective or indicative of the Christian pacifist position. The greatest Christian pacifist of the 20th century – Dr. Martin Luther King, Jr. – was a man who opposed evil, defended the Gospel, and by most accounts certainly disciplined his own children.

9. Father J brings up the tragic situation of Christian persecution in Syria. He says that according to pacifists, *"evidently the only appropriate response when violently attacked by Muslim Jihadis is to run, hide, or die."*

I will respond to this by first saying that there are never any easy answers in such horrific situations. Whether one espouses pacifism or some form of "just war" doctrine, the reality is that it's all theory until we are actually confronted with such evil ourselves. It's easy to advocate violent self-defense, and it's easy to say "turn the other cheek." But the nature of warfare and violence is chaotic, irrational, and unpredictable. All we can do is prayerfully prepare daily for the strength, courage, and grace to respond to violent aggression in the most Christian way possible.

But I must point out that while our Christian brothers and sisters are being persecuted in Syria, Egypt, and other parts of the world, we also have brothers and sisters who are being slaughtered by the thousands, daily, right here in America. There is no greater or more unjust violence anywhere in the world than the murder of unborn innocents that occurs with impunity in our own nation. So I find it oddly inconsistent when Christians argue for justifiable violence but refuse to take up arms to defend the most defenseless members of the human race. To be quite blunt, I can't think of anything more gutless or cowardly than demanding the right to violently defend oneself while refusing to violently defend innocent unborn children. Of course, as a Christian pacifist, I strongly condemn the use of violence in the Pro-Life cause. I am simply pointing out what I perceive to be a glaring inconsistency and gross hypocrisy on the part of those who rationalize violence for themselves but eschew violence in defense of the unborn.

When confronted with terrorism, aggression, and evil, Our Lord Jesus Christ did not run or hide. But He did die. And He did rise again. When confronted with terrorism, aggression, and evil, Dr. Martin Luther King, Jr. did not run or hide. But he did die. And as he eloquently stated, *"Truth crushed to earth will rise again."* When confronted with the terrorism, aggression, and evil of legalized abortion, there are countless Pro-Life activists who do not run and hide. They intervene nonviolently to reach out to pregnant women in distress and to give voice to voiceless unborn children. They endure insult and injury, curses and calumnies, and oftentimes jail or imprisonment.

So, once again I will respectfully point out that Father J has misrepresented the Christian pacifist position. We do not run; we do not hide; but we do indeed pray for the divine strength to meet hate with love, violence with peace, and death with dignity and grace. This is undoubtedly much easier said than done, but there is nothing easy or safe about the Cross.

10. Father J states: *"In the home, in the Church, and in the state there is a consistent drumbeat of nonresistance in the cloak of Christianity."*

I think I've been quite clear by now that Christian pacifism is not synonymous with nonresistance. We always resist evil and injustice, but we do so only with nonviolent Christian methods.

Let me also note that while the godless spirit of apathetic nonresistance may be infiltrating the home and the Church, the godless spirit of violence and killing permeates the state. From perpetual wars, to endless executions, to the abortion of unborn babies – our government is thoroughly saturated with the demonic spirit of death and destruction. Not only does this American state not resist evil, but instead it militantly resists righteousness. Under a government that ostensibly exists to protect the good, the good constantly struggles to protect itself from the government. Perhaps Father J and I have a fundamentally different view of the United States government. But that is a discussion for another day.

11. Father J recounts an incident where a Pro-Life activist was violently assaulted by an enraged man who had taken a woman in to have an abortion. As the Pro-Life activist was repeatedly hit in the face, he kept telling his assailant, *"There is forgiveness in Jesus. There is forgiveness in Jesus."* As he was attacked, there were other Pro-Life men who stood by watching and recorded the assault with their cell phone cameras. Father J asserts that these men should have physically intervened to stop the attack. He describes a thoughtful, well planned and calculated response to such instances of aggression. But the organized defensive scenario he describes is simply not realistic.

I spent three years as a Pro-Life sidewalk counselor, standing outside abortion clinics on a daily basis in order to deter women from the destructive and irrevocable decision of abortion. I can tell you that there is a spirit of darkness, hate, irrationality, and evil that pervades the atmosphere of an abortion clinic. There is nothing predictable or reasonable about what goes on there. The demonic presence is oppressively thick.

I was a committed philosophical pacifist back then, as I am now. But there was one time when I failed miserably to live up to my pacifist convictions. A dear Pro-Life lady was attempting to offer post-abortive healing literature to a woman who was exiting the clinic when the woman's boyfriend grabbed her by the arm and began to push her away. I instinctively ran down the sidewalk and shoved the man with tremendous violence and force. And in my rage I cursed the man and raised my fist to hit him again. He ran away like a frightened rabbit. The police came. I was very fortunate that I wasn't arrested. I felt tremendous guilt and shame. I had reacted violently, in anger, and there was nothing Christian about my actions.

You see, it happened in an instant. Violence is not something that can be predictably tamed or methodically controlled. The very nature of violence is contrary to reason and order. I am fortunate that the man did not have a gun, because he may have shot me. And if I had been someone who believed in carrying a gun myself, then I may have shot him.

So it's easy for Father J to lay out an ideal scenario for how such aggression should be dealt with. But these scenarios rarely jibe with reality. The Pro-Life victim Father J mentions simply responded to his attacker by saying, "There is forgiveness in Jesus." And in that particular response he demonstrated the power, truth, and nonviolent resolve of the Christian pacifist. I wish that I had been able to respond that way many years ago when I acted quite differently; but at the time I allowed my passions to overcome my Christian convictions. Violence always arises from the passions. And as Orthodox Christians, we must constantly strive to subdue the passions so that our souls can experience the eternal love of God.

During my years as a missionary to the unborn and their mothers, I experienced great failure and great success. I saw the depths of darkness, depravity, and despair; but I also saw many lives saved and many souls come to Christ. And as I reflect upon those difficult and tumultuous years of Pro-Life activism, I realize that the most powerful impact I had was when I was firm but humble, strong but loving, resilient but peaceful. Whenever I allowed my passions to dictate my words and actions, then I merely gave into the demonic spirit that was present. But when I remained prayerful, with my mind and heart fixated on eternal realities, then my efforts always had a much greater impact.

12. Father J states: *"The courageous and lawful use of force and discipline in appropriate defense of the innocent and their property, in parenting by what Solomon calls 'the rod,' the use of pastoral discipline in the Church and the vigilant guarding of the Mysteries from those who are not canonically prepared to receive them, and the use in the military and law enforcement of the justifiable use of force and even warfare is absolutely biblical and Christian and loving."*

The problem here is that Father J intertwines legitimacy with illegitimacy. He links truth with error, although I'm sure he does so

335

unintentionally. Once again I have to point out that the Christian pacifist is not opposed to force or discipline. As always, the issue is the *type* of force and the *method* of discipline.

As a Christian pacifist, I strive to defend the innocent, I strive to discipline my children, and I do my part in a lay capacity to affirm and protect the Sacramental Mysteries of the Orthodox Church. And I endeavor to do these things with vigilant nonviolence. In our home we choose to spank our children, and some may disagree with that. But I find it absurd to equate spanking one's children with the horrific violence that occurs in acts of war. I spank my children so that they may grow and develop as people and as Christians. That is discipline. But warfare destroys the development of lives and negates the opportunity for the killed to become Christians. War is not a Christian *discipline*; it is in my opinion a Christian *heresy*. It is easy to proclaim military violence as disciplinary and loving until you or your loved ones are on the wrong end of military violence. Then you would understand that there is nothing loving or Christian about it.

13. Father J says, *"The pacifistic spirit does not equal a peaceful spirit."*

Here is where I would like to take the opportunity to wholeheartedly agree with Father J. It is quite possible for one to be intellectually and philosophically wed to nonviolence while remaining completely devoid of the authentic peace of Christ. This is why I always qualify my pacifism as *Christian* pacifism. Apart from Our Lord Jesus Christ – the Prince of Peace – there will never be *true* peace. Even if wars ceased, poverty was eradicated, and abortion was outlawed, we still would not have peace apart from Christ Himself. We would perhaps have a less violent world (which would be wonderful), but we wouldn't necessarily have a peaceful world. We must never confuse the absence of violence with the presence of peace. But the absence of violence is certainly a wonderful starting point.

So I agree that not only is a Christless pacifist philosophy not synonymous with peace, but it is often quite antithetical to peace. Christian pacifism seeks to refrain *from* violence while actively working *for* peace. It is not rational to work for peace through violent methods, and it is not Christian to refrain from violence without actively laboring for justice and peace.

14. Father J states: *"These things go together: a soft heart, a great thirst for justice, and a courageous willingness to see it done."*

Here again, I am in complete agreement with him. The heart that is molded by Christ is a soft but resilient heart, and gentle but determined heart, a loving and active heart. The disciples of Christ were courageous in their confrontation of paganism, idolatry, injustice and evil. And their courage was not the absence of fear but the willingness to preach the Gospel in spite of their fear. They willed to see the Gospel preached to all nations, and their witness cost them their lives. They were courageous, active, and willing – but they were always *nonviolent*.

15. Father J says: *"Christ has brought peace to us through His Cross. But we only have this peace in our hearts after Jesus uses His strength to subdue us. He uses His firmness. His peace comes to us when we bow to Him as Lord and realize that He is the rightful governor of our lives and not we ourselves.... We see peace and strength together."*

Amen, amen, and amen. Here is another point upon which I agree with Father J. Our Orthodox theology teaches us that God honors our free will while also intervening to save us. This is one of the many holy paradoxes of our Christian Faith. We are autonomous human beings with the volitional capacity to choose good or evil, right or wrong, God or ourselves. And yet God works through His Holy Spirit to get our attention, to humble our arrogance, and to break through our hardened and obstinate hearts. But the choice is always ultimately up to us.

And this only serves to affirm the Christian pacifist position. We are not God. We are not the Holy Spirit. We have no right to force others to comply and convert. Our duty is to pray, preach, love, and serve. Our duty is simply to be ambassadors for Christ. (II Corinthians 2:50) We compel with truthful witness and loving service; we don't coerce with violence, manipulation, or militarism.

Peace and strength do indeed go together. In fact, as Christian pacifists we see no separation or dichotomy between peace and strength. Peace *is* strength, and this truth is most powerfully proven by the Cross of Christ.

16. Father J states: *"The Lord also established peace between us – between man and man. He brought all men into a unity in Himself. He broke down the barrier of the dividing wall. He established His reign within us, which we call 'His Kingdom.' And the hallmark of that reign within the Christian heart is peace... And our mission as Christians is to take this peace out into the world."*

Yes, this is great Christian truth – to take the peace of the Gospel into all the world! And how can we bring peace while bringing the violence of bloodshed, death, and destruction? How can we prove that the peace of Christ reigns in our hearts if we engage the world with the methods of the world, fighting carnal powers with carnal weapons?

St. Paul writes: *"Therefore, I urge you, brothers and sisters, in view of God's mercy, to offer your bodies as a living sacrifice, holy and pleasing to God—this is your true and proper worship. Do not conform to the pattern of this world, but be transformed by the renewing of your mind. Then you will be able to test and approve what God's will is—his good, pleasing and perfect will."* [Romans 12:1-2]

The apostle is clear: we must offer our own bodies as living sacrifices, not sacrifice the lives of others. Self-sacrifice is the true and proper worship – the antithesis of demonic paganism which exalts self-interest at the expense of the interests of others. The apostle is clear: we are not to be conformed to the pattern of this world, which extols violence as an acceptable method of conflict resolution. The apostle is clear: we must be transformed by the renewing of our minds, which means abandoning the fleshly mindset of violent self-justification.

Christ indeed died for all men, for all the world, and therefore we are reconciled – man to God, and man to man. Therefore our enemies are merely our lost brethren who are suffering from lack of the knowledge of salvation. Our mission is to rescue their souls with the hope of the Gospel, not to negate their lives with weapons of destruction.

The Christian Faith is the one authentic hope for human brotherhood and unity. And how can we achieve this brotherhood and unity if we pervert the Gospel and kill in Christ's name?

17. Father J says: *"In His own human life Christ constantly resisted evil men in stern word and deed."*

Yes, of course He did. And we must follow Our Lord's example in being equally stern in word and deed. But there is a grave difference between being *stern* and being *violent*. The disciples were certainly stern in word and deed, but they did not kill. And we have no divine dispensation to live and act any differently than the apostles. We are called to be fishers of men (St. Matthew 4:19), and we cannot win souls for the Kingdom if we violently cut down the lives to whom those souls belong.

18. Father J invokes Christ's participation in the feast of Hanukah as evidence that He condoned violence, since Hanukah is the celebration of the Maccabees' violent resistance to Greek polytheism and the imposition of Greek pagan life.

Well, by that logic, Jesus also condoned drunkenness and prostitution since He ate and drank with prostitutes and drunkards. It is quite a stretch to infer from Our Lord's company with soldiers, prostitutes, tax collectors, drunkards, and thieves that He condoned and blessed such activities. Jesus was a Jew, and therefore He participated in Jewish ceremonies and festivals. And yet as King of the Jews and Lord of all creation, Christ fulfilled all Old Testament laws, commandments, and customs.

Everything in the Old Testament is to be understood in the light of Christ's eternal Kingdom which has begun through the establishment of His Church. We are now citizens of heaven (Philippians 3:20), and Our Lord has taught us to pray: *"Thy kingdom come, thy will be done, on earth as it is in heaven."* [St. Matthew 6:10] No more animal sacrifices. No more stoning of adulterers. No more putting disobedient children to death. No more slaughtering one's enemy. No more violence and bloodshed. No more! No more! The blood of Christ has put an end to it! As He proclaimed with His dying breath, *"It is finished!" [St. John 19:30]*

19. Father J says, *"The Lord's acquiescence at the end of His ministry to evil men and to devils was the most brilliant of all military strategies. He performed the ultimate Trojan horse. He allowed them to crucify Him so that He could crucify the power of sin and death...*

I have heard this argument countless times, that Christ's ostensible nonviolence was merely a situational and pragmatic strategy that is not universally applicable for Christians today. But nothing could be further from the truth. If Our Lord's life, teachings, and atonement were merely pragmatic actions, then why did His disciples emulate His example? Why is the New Testament full of instructions and teachings about how to take up our cross, deny ourselves, forgive our enemies, and renounce vengeance? And why does the last 2,000 years of human history bear witness to the fact that victories won with the implementation of love, truth, and nonviolence are much greater and far more lasting than temporal victories gained through violence and bloodshed?

If Christ's entire life, ministry, and atonement were merely temporary mortal strategies to be jettisoned upon His death, then surely He would have let His disciples know. Surely the omnipotent, omniscient, omnipresent and Incarnate God would have left His followers clear instructions as to why we should *not* abide by His nonviolent example. Surely He would have spoken to the apostles through His Holy Spirit and let it be known that His crucifixion was not to be embraced as an example for us to follow. Surely the New Testament would be full of instructions on how to violently defend one's nation, one's family, and oneself. But this is not what we read. This is not the witness of the Word of God. Instead, the entire weight of the Gospels and New Testament epistles leads us in the total and unequivocal path of Christ. We are called to preach, to baptize, to heal, to serve, to take up our cross – and if need be – to die for others. But we are not called to kill.

Father J is mistaken when he states that Jesus acquiesced with evil at the end of His ministry. Our Lord never acquiesced with evil, and I believe that it's blasphemous to assert such a thing. In sacrificing His life on the Cross, Our Lord opposed evil in the strongest way possible. His death was not a relinquishment of righteousness, it was not a concession to injustice, and it was by no means an acceptance or acquiescence to the demands of hell. Instead, it was the militant, nonviolent, and spiritual defeat of sin and evil. I feel confident that Father J and I actually agree on this point, but I find problems with his statement that *"Jesus acquiesced to evil men and to devils at the end of His ministry."* Perhaps Father simply misspoke.

20. Father J states: *"The Prince of Peace is a warrior, and He establishes His peace within us by leading us in spiritual battle, by animating His own peace giving authority through the institutions which He created of the family, the Church, and the state. And to resist the use of authority in those realms under the cover of pacifism is to resist the means by which Our Lord promotes peace in this fallen world."*

Our Lord is a warrior indeed, and to Him alone belongs the battle. Through the power of His Cross and with His army of angels, Christ will forever vanquish the devil and his minions. Father J is absolutely correct that Christ leads us in spiritual battle. And the key word here is *spiritual* battle. We are Christian soldiers and Christ is our commanding officer. Our Lord has issued us spiritual weapons that are eternally efficacious. Therefore, to rely upon the feckless implements of carnal destruction is an unchristian and foolish endeavor. Why would we forsake heavenly power for earthly ammunition? Why would we trade the eternal power of the Holy Spirit for the ephemeral power of bullets and bombs?

And while I agree with Father J that Christ works in and through the family and the state (for in fact the omnipresent power of God is working in all the world), it is specifically in and through *His Church* that our spiritual warfare will be won. The Church is the only organism that has the divine promise that the gates of hell shall not prevail against it. (St. Matthew 16:18) Satan may overcome states, nations, families, and governments – but he will not prevail against the Church. And the power of the Church abides in her Sacramental graces, not in carnal militaristic power.

21. Father J concludes his talk by quoting from the 19th chapter of the Book of Revelation:

"And I saw heaven opened, and behold a white horse; and he that sat upon him was called Faithful and True, and in righteousness he doth judge and make war. His eyes were as a flame of fire, and on his head were many crowns; and he had a name written, that no man knew, but he himself. And he was clothed with a vesture dipped in blood: and his name is called The Word of God. And the armies which were in heaven followed him upon white horses, clothed in fine linen, white and clean. And out of his mouth goeth a sharp sword, that with it he should smite the nations: and he shall rule them with a rod of iron: and he treadeth the winepress of the fierceness and wrath of Almighty God. And he hath on his vesture and on his thigh a name written, KING OF KINGS, AND LORD OF LORDS." [Revelation 19:11-16]

*"**That** is Jesus Christ,"* Father J says.

And amen to that! That *is* Jesus Christ! And *we are not* Jesus Christ! We must come down from our own high horse and realize that Christ alone is worthy to ride the white horse of judgment and vengeance. We must subdue the vision of our passions and realize that Christ alone is worthy to have judgmental fire in His eyes. We must throw down our earthly crowns and hail the One who alone is worthy to wear the eternal diadem. We must preserve our own garments unstained with violence and acknowledge that God alone is worthy to wear vestures dipped in blood. We must wait upon the vengeance of *His* heavenly armies. We must wait upon the retribution of *His* divine sword. We must wait upon the revelation of *His* rod of iron. We must acknowledge that Christ alone is "King of Kings and Lord of Lords," and we are merely His servants.

Let not the sheep usurp the rod of the Shepherd. Let not the subject wrest the scepter from the King. Let not the creature assume the authority of the Creator. Let God alone separate the wheat from the tares.

I find it interesting that in quoting from Revelation, Father J failed to quote Revelation 12:19:

"Dearly beloved, avenge not yourselves, but rather give place unto wrath: for it is written, Vengeance is mine; I will repay, says the Lord."

Throughout the New Testament, Our Lord and His apostolic authors make it clear that violence, wrath, and divine retribution belong to God alone. When man presumes authority over life and death, he replicates the sin of Lucifer who attempted to ascend higher than God Himself. God alone retains the authority to create life and destroy life. And the entire impetus of the Christian Gospel is to preserve human lives and offer them the redeeming waters of salvation through Jesus Christ and His Church. Nothing interferes with this mission more than violence and killing. The simple fact is that we cannot lead men to salvation if we kill them. We cannot win souls while destroying bodies. We cannot offer the waters of redemption from a well that is poisoned with blood.

Conclusion

I believe that what Father J is really condemning – and rightly so – is apathy and cowardice within the Church. And if that's the case, then I will fully agree with him. The Church – the Body and Bride of Christ – is the most powerful spiritual, moral, and social force in the world. But instead of actively pursuing justice, confronting evil, and proclaiming the Gospel to all the world, we sit passively on the sidelines as our culture descends further and further into inhumanity, barbarism, chaos and evil. We go about our daily lives unmoved and unaffected by the slaughter of unborn innocents that occurs in our own backyard. We tepidly respond to the greatest moral evil and the most important human rights issue of our time – legalized abortion – with little more than an occasional Pro-Life sermon, an annual march, and our impotent votes. It seems that the only thing we are not apathetic about is demanding the right to violently defend our own personal safety and welfare. And somehow I don't think God is pleased or honored by such an attitude.

So in conclusion, if Father J wants to assert that Jesus and the Saints were not *passive*-ists, then I shall wholeheartedly agree with him. There was nothing passive about the life of Our Lord or the lives of the Saints. And there should not be anything passive about our own lives as Christians. In fact, the monastic life is the most active life of all, as monks devote their entire existence to ascetic rigors and ceaseless prayer. And true prayer is hard work, I can assure you.

But if Father J really means to say that the life, teachings, and example of Our Lord Jesus Christ do not point – without exception – to nonviolence, forgiveness, and unconditional love, then I must respectfully but forthrightly disagree with him.

Let us not forget that Our Lord was rejected and condemned by the Zealots because they expected the Messiah to be a violent political revolutionary. But Our Lord's revolutionary liberation was the salvation of the world – a salvation wrought by His ministry of healing, forgiveness, love, and atoning redemption on the Cross. Sadly, many professing Christians today reject the nonviolent teachings and example of Christ, just as the Zealots did back then. In the name of the Prince of Peace, Christians embrace the idols of patriotism, politics, war, and destruction. Rather than elevating the message of the Cross, we suppress it under the rubrics of Old Testament laws and human rationales. Rather than following Christ and heeding His words, we refashion Him into a god of our own making – a false god who tells us to preserve our own lives at the expense of others. We have inverted the Cross and refashioned it into a sword. In our zealousness for flag, country, and constitution, we have unwittingly crucified the message of the Gospel and blasphemed Our Savior.

There are Muslim terrorists who in the name of the "religion of peace" fly planes into buildings and behead those that refuse to convert to Islam. And as they commit these violent atrocities they exclaim, "Allahu akbar!" (God is great!) They greet one another with the words, "Asalaam alaikum" (Peace be unto you) as they conspire to murder those they consider to be "infidels." But as Christians we are set apart from the world because we are disciples of Christ. We do not kill in the name of our God. We do not make converts with violent force. We forsake bloodshed and embrace the folly of the Cross. We do not murder those who reject the Gospel. We love our enemies and bless those who persecute us. And such love and blessings are not issued with the blade of the sword or the barrel of a gun.

Finally, I would like to emphasize one very important point: Jesus Christ was crucified as a Lamb, but this crucified Lamb will be eternally revealed as the divine Victor who has redeemed persons of every tribe and language and people and nation. (Revelation 5) His Judgment will be complete and the forces of hell will be defeated. God is a *just* God, and His recompense will not be passive. Therefore it is important that we don't misappropriate His divine retribution. Whenever man presumes to use the sword to establish earthly justice and temporal peace, he invariably leaves a wake of innocent blood behind. So as Christians we must wait upon the Lord. *"They that wait upon the LORD shall renew their strength; they shall mount up with wings as eagles; they shall run, and not be weary; and they shall walk, and not faint."* [Isaiah 40:31]

We must have faith that injustice and evil will be divinely avenged in God's perfect time. We must sheathe our swords – yea, break them – so that Christ can turn our weapons of destruction into implements of healing.

Our God is not a tame God, and His justice will be perfect and pure. So we place our faith in Him, trusting that no innocent soul will slip through His merciful grasp. The blood of the martyrs and the butchered bodies of unborn innocents are not unseen by the eyes of divinity. Christ shall come again – riding with a sword in His mouth (Revelation 19:15) – and His harvest will be both terrible and sweet. But if we usurp His sword, then we inevitably cut down the wheat with the tares, and we slaughter the sheep with the goats.

Our Lord has therefore told us to wait upon *His* judgment. As the Psalmist declares, *"The evildoers shall be cut off: but those that wait upon the LORD shall inherit the earth."* [Psalm 37:9] And Our Lord echoed the Psalmist when He said, *"The meek shall inherit the earth." [St. Matthew 5:5]* So we wait for holy retribution, working out our own salvation with fear and trembling, as St. Paul instructs. (Philippians 2:12)

The Christian pacifist does not turn a blind eye to evil. He confronts evil directly, but refuses to reap a harvest that belongs to God alone. The Christian pacifist walks through the fields of this world, carrying his cross not a scythe, bearing the Gospel not a gun.

So, was Jesus a pacifist? Well, no philosophical term or ideology is sufficient to define the Lord of all creation. Jesus transcends the limitations of human definition. He transcends patriotic, ethnic, and religious identity. He is Lord of all. And Christ is no less God than the Father and the Holy Spirit. He is the same God who drowned Pharaoh in the Red Sea, and the same God who will return on the clouds wielding a sword of divine justice. But when He walked the earth in His humble but glorious Incarnation, His commands were specific, clear, unambiguous and firm:

"Put away the sword. Love your enemies. Turn the other cheek. Bless those that persecute you. And go into all the world and make disciples of all nations."

As Orthodox Christians, we reject the heresy of iconoclasm. But if we dare not destroy icons made with wood and paint, then why would we dare to destroy living icons fashioned with the very breath of God? When confronted with evil the Christian pacifist does not say, "Evil, have your way." Instead, the Christian pacifist stands nonviolently against evil and prays, *"Have your way O Lord." [Psalm 86:11; Psalm 25:4-5]*

Let us end by reflecting upon the words and example of St. Martin of Tours, who stood before Caesar and said:

"Hitherto I have served you as a soldier: allow me now to become a soldier to God. Let the man who is to serve thee receive thy donative. I am a soldier of Christ; it is not lawful for me to fight. If this conduct of mine is ascribed to cowardice, and not to faith, I will take my stand unarmed before the line of battle tomorrow, and in the name of the Lord Jesus, protected by the sign of the cross, and not by shield or helmet, I will safely penetrate the ranks of the enemy."

346

And once again let us recall the blessed words of St. John Chrysostom, "The Golden Mouth": *"Our warfare is to make the dead to live, not to make the living die."*

(If anything I have written has been disrespectful or contrary to the Teachings and Traditions of the Orthodox Christian Faith, then may God forgive and correct me. I kiss Father J's hand and ask his prayers for this sinner. And I encourage the reader to pray for Father J and for all of our Orthodox Priests who labor to shepherd us in the True Christian Faith. *"Lord have mercy."*)

"Blessed are the peacemakers,
for they shall be called the children of God."
[St. Matthew 5:9]

~ In peace let us pray to the Lord ~

448. ~ GIVE IT ALL AWAY ~

We drag these chains that suffocate our souls; but we polish them, we preserve them, we multiply them, and we adore them. We cannot fathom life apart from these burdens that we have confused for blessings. So give it all away. Give it all away so that you can truly keep all that's truly worth keeping.

449. ~ TOO DAMN REBELLIOUS ~

I don't care how much you hurt me, betray me, disappoint me, abuse me, or curse me – you won't drive me away from God. You will only drive me further into His arms. So go ahead world; try and make a doubter out of me. You'll just make me trust God's love all the more. The fact is: I'm just too damn rebellious to be an atheist.

450. ~ THOSE THAT DESTROY SERVE THOSE THAT CREATE ~

The poet's ink
is sacred blood.
The artist's brush
breaks soldiers' swords.

Children's songs
kill politicians' lies.
The light of angels
heals sin-scarred skies.

Governments drown
in philosophers' wells.
The truth of heaven
conquers lies of hell.

Demons are tamed
by a sanctified pen.
Beauty prevails
over the evils of men.

Love refuses
to bow to hate.
Those that destroy
serve those that create.

451. ~ A CHRISTIAN KINSHIP? ~

There was a time in my life when I felt an immediate bond of brotherhood and solidarity with anyone who professed faith in Jesus Christ. Regardless of differences of denomination or doctrine, I felt a close kinship with anyone who also accepted the salvation of Christ and His Cross.

But it is becoming increasingly difficult for me to feel this kinship with all other professing American Christians these days. Most American Christians will usually accept the fact that I'm Orthodox, and they will accept our profound theological differences. Most will usually accept my long hair, my beard, and my tattoos. Most will accept my interracial marriage and our dreadlocked children. Professing American Christians today seem quite willing to tolerate a variety of differences of opinion, style, and tastes among themselves. Apparently, as long as you profess Jesus Christ as your Lord and Savior, then you are part of the Christian club and most Christians will accept you as one of their own. And that's good.

However, if you dare to suggest that politics, patriotism, war, and killing are fundamentally antithetical to the Prince of Peace and the Gospel of salvation, then you are suddenly viewed as some sort of fanatical blasphemer. It seems that countless unorthodox beliefs are tolerated within the professing Christian community today. But if you actually proclaim the Orthodox Christian belief that the violent, premeditated destruction of human beings created in the image of God is unequivocally and inherently evil, then that is somehow viewed to be a wild perversion of the Gospel.

So I confess: I sadly no longer feel a Christian kinship with those who use the glorious name of Our Lord to promote, defend, justify, and excuse the evils of warfare and killing. Such professing Christians may be much less sinful and much more virtuous than I am, but if they do not honor the image of God in their fellow man – family, friends, Christians, pagans, and enemies alike – then I have no true fellowship with them. I will love them, I will befriend them, and I will pray with them. But as long as they use the name of Christ to support the evils of violence and killing, then I am afraid that they are worshipping another god.

I will never break fellowship with anyone. But those who believe that it's acceptable to break the lives and souls of their fellow man have already broken fellowship with me. What kinship can I have with those who rationalize killing in the name of Christ? It seems that we shall always be wedded to different Gospels.

452. ~ HOW THE PAGANS VIEW THE CHRISTIANS ~

There was once a time when idolatrous, bloodthirsty, self-loving pagans looked at Christians and said:

"Those people are not like us. They are different. They share their wealth equally amongst themselves, and they give feely even to strangers. They forgive their enemies. They love one another. They have no care for earthly kingdoms, for they believe in a kingdom that is to come. They have no swords, but instead trust in prayer. They do not seek to conquer anyone, and yet their numbers steadily increase. Amongst all people in the world, these Christians think, live, and act differently. We do not understand them, but we wish to know them."

But today idolatrous, bloodthirsty, and self-loving pagans look at Christians and say:

"They are no different than us. Their rich do not share equally with their poor. They refuse to help strangers. They take vengeance on their enemies. They do not truly love one another. They trust in politics and identify themselves by earthly nationalities. They join armies and learn how to kill. They think, live, and act like most other people in the world, and they rarely make converts. We understand them, but we do not wish to know them."

453. ~ HELP YOUR FAMILY, FRIENDS, and CHRISTIAN BRETHREN! ~

If you have friends, family members, or Christian brethren that need your help, then for God's sake help them! Don't wait for them to ask for help. Reach out to them and ask them what they need. Don't presume that everything is ok with them just because they haven't asked for help. If you are living well while your relatives, friends, or fellow Christians are struggling to make ends meet, then you should be ashamed.

Do you think that homeless people woke up one morning and decided to become homeless? Do you think that the man begging on the corner doesn't have a family? Do you think he doesn't have friends? Do you suppose he never went to Church? Do you suppose that it couldn't happen to you?

We love to rationalize our callous indifference to other people's suffering by saying that they made bad choices in their lives. Well, we've all made bad choices in our lives, but that doesn't mean we deserve to be cast aside like garbage by the people who are supposed to love us unconditionally and assist us in spite of our mistakes.

It's a shame that we have to ask for help. It's a shame that some of us find more aid and support from a godless government than from our own Churches, our own families, and our own friends. And I've found that it's usually the poor and the struggling that are often the most generous and loving.

Our Churches are full of the wealthy who worship next to the poor. We have millionaires praying beside folks who can't even pay their water bills. Something is drastically wrong here. It's disgraceful enough when family members forsake their own relatives, but it's even worse when Christians forsake their own Christian brethren.

So please reach out and ask people if they need help. As someone told me long ago, if you have to be asked for help, then you are already too late.

454. ~ SUPPORTING HUMANITY ~

I don't support states. I support humanity. Therefore, it's never a question of Israel or Palestine, Russia or Ukraine, the United States or China. It's only a question of humanity or inhumanity, violence or nonviolence, love or hate, justice or injustice, the Gospel or governments.

455. ~ A FLAWED THEOLOGICAL FOUNDATION ~

There is no clearer indication of a flawed theological foundation than somebody telling you that you're going to hell. Anyone who presumes such omniscience misunderstands God and misunderstands themselves. Jesus will judge the sheep and the goats. Our duty is to preach the Gospel and leave judgment to Him. Only God knows the hearts of men. Even those who appear to be the most wicked may actually be experiencing a conversion of the heart as we sit in judgment of them. Fundamentalism is a horrible disease, but Orthodoxy is a wonderful cure.

456. ~ CONFESSING OUR UNKNOWING ~

Only by confessing our unknowing are we able to experience Him who surpasses all knowing.

457. ~ HORROR and REDEMPTION in CHRISTIAN ART ~

The Christian artist does not hesitate to show the horror, knowing that the darker the reality the more radiant is the light of redemption. Nothing is more spurious, trite, and unrealistic than attempts to portray depravity while ignoring the redemptive aspects that reside amidst it.

458. ~ UNIVERSAL DEMANDS of THE HUMAN RACE ~

1. We – the collective voices of the conscience of humanity – demand an end to war, poverty, and abortion.

2. We refuse to lend our voices or our votes to any individual, corporation, nationality, or political party that seeks solutions through the violence of the ballot, the bomb, or the bullet.

3. We demand the peaceful settlement of disputes.

4. We reject any practice or policy that pits nation against nation, mother against child, and man against man.

5. We refuse to be used as pawns in the demonic game of "realpolitik."

6. We take no sides on the grounds of nationality, religion, gender, or race.

7. We represent one human family with the common interests of peace, love, and brotherhood.

8. We know that the earth and the fullness thereof abundantly provides for the tangible necessities required for us to live and thrive according to our divinely created nature. Therefore, we refuse to support any ideology or practice that rapes the earth and robs humanity of earth's natural resources.

9. We believe that to deprive anyone of food, water, and shelter based on their income is a crime against humanity and a crime against the indelible law of the universe.

10. With a clear and united voice, we proclaim and pledge allegiance to two divine and universal commands: *"Thou shalt not kill." "Do unto others as you would have them do unto you."*

459. ~ OVER THERE and OVER HERE ~

Those killers are terrorists
over there.
They are savages –
those fascists,
communists, and Muslims
over there.

But our killers are heroes
over here.
We are humanitarians –
our politicians,
generals, and abortionists
over here.

God save us from the evil
over there.
Lest we lose our freedom
to murder and oppress
blaspheme and sin
over here.

Kill their killers
over there
before they kill our killers
over here.

460. ~ HAMMER and NAILS ~

I am the hammer
The nails are my sins
Though I crucify Him
He still calls me "His"

461. ~ INDIVIDUAL and COLLECTIVE MORALITY ~

If it is morally right for individuals, is it not also morally right for nations? If it is morally right for persons, is it not also morally right for governments? If it is morally right for one human being, is it not also morally right for all humanity? Do we forget that nations, states, and governments are comprised of individual people? If the moral imperatives of peace, love, justice, and forgiveness are indeed universal, then they are equally applicable to the individual and the collective alike.

462. ~ PACIFISM and REVOLUTION ~

A pacifism that is not born from a revolutionary heart is nothing more than a feckless, cowardly philosophy that only protects one from the difficulties and dangers of truly confronting injustice and evil. But it must also be said that any revolution that is achieved through violence is nothing more than a replacement of one form of oppression with another. Love compels the true revolutionary to action; and love dictates that authentic revolutionary actions are predicated upon the divine values of nonviolence, self-sacrifice, forgiveness, and life-affirmation.

463. ~ SWORDS of JUSTICE? ~

Everyone thinks his own sword to be just and his enemy's sword to be evil. And so men perpetually slay one another in the name of God and country, faith and freedom. And the children's playground, which is the earth, becomes a field of blood in which the innocent drown. But in the name of such "justice" men still refuse to relinquish their swords. And with shameless blasphemy, many extol their killing in the name of Christ and justify their evil with the sign of the Cross.

464. ~ **THOUGHTS on THE PASSING of ROBIN WILLIAMS** ~
[8/12/2014]

Apparently, according to certain fundamentalist "Christians," Robin Williams is now burning in hell. They tell me that anyone who commits suicide while being "in their right mind" cannot be saved. Well, I'm no Priest and I'm no psychiatrist, but I don't think anyone who commits suicide is in their right mind. So I can never pass judgment on anyone who chooses to take their own life.

People tell me that suicide is the ultimate act of selfishness, and yet many of these same people defend the "right" of a woman to murder her own unborn child. How curious it is that we praise politicians and soldiers who kill children and civilians with dispassionate premeditation, but we condemn to hell those that are driven to suicide by hopelessness and despair. What a strange world this is.

The Orthodox Church is very clear that suicide is an egregious sin. However, the Church has also come to acknowledge the reality and severity of mental illness. Clinical depression, bi-polar disorder, and schizophrenia can actually incapacitate one's ability to make rational choices. So, if untreated, a person struggling with mental illness may not even be able to exercise the choice to continue living.

Therefore, our Orthodox Christian approach to suicide must be clear and twofold: 1) suicide is a grievous sin; 2) compassion and mercy must be extended to those that struggle with mental illness and suicidal inclinations.

We must encourage people to get psychological and medical help. For many people, it's not simply a matter of willing themselves through the darkness. It's not a matter of a lack of faith. It's a physiological and psychological illness that is as real and as severe as cancer or heart disease. We don't look at people who die from cancer and say, "If they'd only had more faith, then they would have survived." But for some reason, we view psychological illness as weakness, as a lack of faith, as a failure to exert the necessary will power to overcome one's problems.

Mental illness is a horrible disease, and it's sad that there is still such a stigma attached to it. My roommate in Bible College

356

committed suicide. It broke my heart. He was a devout Christian who loved the Lord and was passionate about the Gospel. I saw him battle depression, but I never understood at the time that he was battling a real disease that was beyond his control. I have no qualms about saying that his suicidal act was in no way justifiable while also saying that I have great confidence that Our Lord will embrace him in the Kingdom.

God alone will judge the souls of those who take their own lives. And I have hope in God's unfailing mercy. So let us condemn the act of suicide as clearly as we can, but let us not condemn the souls of those who succumb to a depression and despair that is beyond their control.

Now, while it may seem insensitive, I must also address an aspect of this tragedy that most people won't dare to touch:

Robin Williams and his girlfriend decided to abort their innocent unborn child in the 1970's (See the book, _"Robin Williams: A Biography"_ by Andy Dougan). Now, I'm in no way suggesting that his abortion experience caused Robin Williams' mental illness; but I _am_ saying that it certainly didn't help. Anyone who is involved in the deliberate destruction of human life will be deeply affected by it. Regardless of how much our society praises soldiers and extols the "freedom of choice" for women to slaughter their unborn babies, the fact is that killing always brings with it a cruel and inescapable reciprocity.

God is merciful, and through the Cross there is salvation for all who repent. But we have been conditioned by our culture to believe that we can "legally" kill without consequences. Yet violating the immutable laws of God regarding the sanctity of Life brings with it dire ramifications.

You won't see anyone in the media bringing up Robin Williams' involvement in the murder of his unborn child. They will only focus on the psychological problems he had. But if we ever hope to truly address human _psychological_ illnesses, we must also address human _spiritual_ illness. There is always a correlation. Killing begets killing, violence begets violence, and life begets life. Human beings may absolutely need psychiatric and medicinal help, but we also need Sacramental help. To treat the body and mind without treating the soul will never bring about authentic and holistic human healing.

America is full of scarred and broken people that have been deeply wounded by their involvement in the violence of militarism and abortion. Men are as deeply affected by abortion as women are, and women are as deeply affected by war as men are. But most people don't even connect the dots. We are told that abortion is simply a matter of "choice," and that war always involves a little "collateral damage." Therefore we have millions of people who are walking around with hollow souls, broken hearts, and damaged psyches; but they don't even understand why.

So I will continue to point out the correlation between death sowed and death reaped, between violence perpetrated and violence received. And I will continue to declare that it matters not what the laws of men say; what matters is the law of God. Scripture is clear:

"Put away your sword, for all who draw the sword will die by the sword." [St. Matthew 26:52]

"Do not be deceived: God cannot be mocked. A man reaps what he sows." [Galatians 6:7]

May God have mercy on all of our wretched souls. May He teach us to affirm and embrace Life, no matter how difficult or how desperate the circumstances may be. Killing is never a solution. Never! But I confess that I have much more sympathy for those who desperately choose to end their own lives than for those who premeditatedly choose to end the lives of others.

"Lord have mercy."

465. ~ TAMING BULLETS ~

Placing instruments of destruction in the hands of sinful human beings never leads to anything good. And sinful human beings always seem to think they can somehow manage and control these weapons of death. Stupid people trust in "smart bombs," and fools think they are wise enough to tame bullets.

466. ~ CAUSES and "SOLUTIONS" ~

Q. What do terrorists, police officers, abortionists, soldiers, the mafia, and most politicians all have in common?

A. They all believe that their cause is just and that violence and killing are "solutions."

Now, please understand, I'm not morally equating terrorists, abortionists, and the mafia with policeman, soldiers, and politicians. I am simply pointing out that they all truly believe their particular use of violence is justified and that their particular acts of killing are necessary solutions. And such misguided and unchristian convictions have only led to suffering, misery, and chaos in the world. Therefore, let the true followers of Christ heed the Savior's command to *"put away thy sword."[St. Matthew 26:52]* Our cause is His Kingdom, and His Kingdom needs no violent defense.

467. ~ SLAUGHTERING OUR OWN SALVATION ~

If the majority of the human population was comprised of people with Down syndrome, then I imagine we wouldn't have as much war, violence, and racism in the world. And yet, somehow these precious souls are viewed as less human than the rest of us. In their arrogance and ignorance, people self-righteously judge these innocent souls as "defective" and not deserving of the chance to be born. It's the tragic and timeless fate of humanity: mankind perpetually rejects, condemns, and slaughters his own salvation.

468. ~ BANK ROBBER ~

I'll rob a bank
But I won't rob you
That's not wrong
It's what I have to do

I'll take the loot
And do some good
I'll have some fun
And buy some food

I'll live a little
And I'll help the poor
I won't be sorry
I'll go back for more

I'll rob a bank
But without a gun
I'll do it honestly
Like a politician

I'll spend the money
However I please
And damn the rich
If they dare judge me!

469. ~ LOVE IS NOT BLIND ~

Love is not color blind,
but love is not blinded by color.
Love knows the brutality of history
but love refuses to hate another.

Love will always embrace
the beautiful distinctions of race.
Love has no time for division.
Love is too busy for prejudice and hate.

470. ~ SPIRIT of SATAN / SPIRIT of CHRIST ~

There is a spirit of self-righteousness, judgment, fear, cruelty, callousness, and pharisaical religiosity that lies at the heart of heretical theology and demonic philosophies. The spirit that leads one to believe that an innocent newborn baby is "totally depraved" and destined for the flames of hell; the spirit that leads one to have no sympathy for those who felt such despair that they ended their own lives; the spirit that leads one to sever relationships with those who dare to disagree with them; the spirit that leads one to invoke the name of God as they violently kill their fellow man; the spirit that leads one to rejoice in God's judgment but lament His mercy: this is the spirit of Satan, and it permeates our world.

And how do we overcome this evil spirit? We overcome it with the Spirit of love, with the Spirit of forgiveness, with the Spirit of humility, with the Spirit of compassion and understanding, with the Spirit of sacrifice and self-denial, and with the Spirit of authentic tolerance which is rooted in a faith so true that it is not threatened by differences of opinion. We overcome the spirit of Satan with the Spirit of Christ.

All sound doctrines and all true ideas are rooted in the Spirit of mercy. To plead God's mercy for our own souls and for the souls of all others – this is the desire and hope that binds us all together as human beings created in the image of God. He will judge us all, and that's why we must never judge one another. This is why the most common and frequent prayer of Orthodox Christians is:

"Lord have mercy on us."

471. ~ A DIFFICULT BUT CLEAR MESSAGE ~

The message of the Gospel is difficult but unambiguous. The teachings and example of Our Lord are challenging but clear. The Christian must never intentionally kill. In fact, while the Orthodox Church maintains a clear distinction between murder and defensive killing, the Church holds the sanctity of life in such high regard that it requires those who have killed even accidentally to confess and do penance before receiving the Eucharist. As a beloved Ethiopian Orthodox Priest explained to me:

"We ask the Lord to forgive us of our sins committed 'willingly' and 'unwillingly'. Thus both intentional and accidental killing are sins and must have confession, penance, and absolution applied before receiving the Holy Qurban (Holy Eucharist)."

Turning the other cheek does not mean that we do not resist evil. It means that we do not resist evil with evil, but rather we resist evil with good. Our Lord's death on the Cross epitomized the redemptive power of confronting evil with self-sacrifice and love for one's enemies.

Peace, nonviolence, love, and forgiveness are not options for the Christian. Whether or not we are all called to martyrdom is not the issue. The issue is that we are all called to deny ourselves, take up our cross, and follow Christ. And in following Christ we must be prepared for the reality of martyrdom.

God has equipped us with spiritual weapons that we are to employ in this spiritual war (Cf. Ephesians 6). So we intervene with our own lives on behalf of the lives of the innocent and the suffering, but we do not intervene by destroying the lives of others. No persecution or evil in the world today is worse than the persecution and evil that Our Lord's disciples and apostles faced. And how did they respond? They did not respond by taking up arms and waging a violent revolution. Instead, they took up the Cross and died leading others to eternal life.

Sadly, many within the Church today have strayed from the clear teachings of Christ regarding peace, nonviolence, and love for enemies. It seems to be a natural but unfortunate tendency for us to rationalize our way out of obedience to the difficult demands of following Our Lord. I for one certainly don't pretend that I have fully embraced these difficult demands.

May God grant us His wisdom, mercy, strength, and grace as we struggle to confront evil while conforming our lives and thoughts to His perfect will.

472. ~ TAKING UP ARMS ~

It is impossible to take up arms when our arms have taken up the Cross.

473. ~ THE CHURCH and THE POOR ~

So let me get this straight:

Socialism is "theft," but capitalism is "ambition." CEO's are "industrious," but the homeless are "lazy." Wealth is "earned," but poverty is somehow "deserved." Tithing is "stewardship," but charity is "enablement." The wealthy are "self-sufficient," but the poor are "dependent." And apparently, as I have sadly heard some of my fellow Christians assert, the man who desires another castle for his kingdom is no more selfish than the man who desires a cup of water to stay alive. It seems that the Church today has mastered the art of apologizing for the rich while abandoning her duty to defend the poor.

But the Christian commandments are simple and clear: we must love God and love our neighbors as ourselves (St. Mark 12:30-31). And to emphasize the imperatives of the Gospel, Christ said that our relationship with Him will be determined by how we treat the "least of these" (St. Matthew 25:31-46). God is no respecter of persons (Acts 10:34-35); the rich and the poor, the Black and the White, the male and the female, the born and the unborn all equally bear His divine image. However, the Gospel indicates that we have a priority to minister to the impoverished, the suffering, and the oppressed. *"The poor you will always have with you" [St. Matthew 26:11]* does not mean that we should not do everything we can to alleviate poverty and care for the impoverished.

It is a selfish, unchristian, and demonic mindset to say: "I have earned my own bread and my own wealth, and I am not responsible for the poverty and suffering of others. Let them work like I have and then they won't be poor."

Unshared wealth is nothing less than theft. If we have two coats and our brother has none, then we must give him one of our coats (St. Luke 3:11). And this principle applies to all wealth and capital. It is a sin to possess more than enough while our neighbor has less than enough.

Our Churches are full of the wealthy who worship next to the poor. One man owns three houses while his brother struggles to pay the water bill. A family of millionaires worships next to a family on food stamps. But do we not all tithe the same percentage? So why do some grow richer while others grow poorer? Does the poor man not work just as hard as the rich man?

It is tragic to see the deep divide of rich and poor in our society. Yet perhaps this is only to be expected from a culture that has yet to be redeemed by Christ. But for this same divide to exist within the Body of Christ is inexcusable. It is shameful really. Do we think that we will escape divine judgment for failing to love one another as Christ loves us?

"Lord have mercy."

474. ~ AUTHENTIC SOCIAL CONSCIOUSNESS ~

Authentic social consciousness does not begin with self, i.e. "my" freedom, "my" rights, "my" cause, "my" truth, "my" body, "my" choice, etc. Authentic social consciousness is *social* consciousness; i.e. it is concerned about freedom, justice, truth and rights for *all* people. That's why ostensible revolutionary movements that begin and end with a concern only for one group or one segment of humanity never bear lasting fruit. But when social movements are rooted in the genuine welfare of all humanity, in the affirmation of all human life, and in a witness to universal truth, then they become truly and enduringly revolutionary. The true revolutionary looks at the plight of poverty, racism, war, and abortion and sees the plight of the whole world. Therefore, in seeking to fill just one empty stomach, in seeking to dismantle a single bomb, in seeking to emancipate a solitary slave, and in seeking to save even one woman from abortion, the true revolutionary seeks to liberate the entire human race.

475. ~ FREEDOM ~

Some seek freedom in religion, others seek freedom in atheism. Some seek freedom in war, others seek freedom in peace. Some seek freedom in rules, others seek freedom in rebellion. Some seek freedom in morality, others seek freedom in licentiousness. Some seek freedom in piety, others seek freedom in sin. Some seek freedom in revolution, others seek freedom in obedience. Some seek freedom in laws, others seek freedom in anarchy. Some seek freedom in poverty, others seek freedom in wealth. Some seek freedom in indulgence, others seek freedom in abstinence. Some seek freedom in the expanses of the universe, and others seek freedom in the recesses of their souls.

What is freedom? Where is it to be found? I don't know. But I do know that all the questions of human existence are ultimately questions of human freedom. And apart from life, there is no existence and no freedom of which to speak. Therefore, it seems that the only real answer to these existential questions is to live, to choose life – both for ourselves and for others. At least with life there are questions, mysteries, struggles, and joys to experience. And I think that's worth honoring.

It takes great courage to live. And it sometimes takes great courage to let others live. Perhaps it is the courage of fools. But give me life – and all of its glorious folly – over death and nothingness. Give me life – and all of life's resplendent struggle – over death and the hell that may ensue. I don't know what freedom is, but I do know that freedom is predicated upon life.

476. ~ STANDING UP for RIGHTS ~

It seems to me that people do a pretty good job of standing up for their own rights. The problem is that people rarely stand up for the rights of others. And authentic rights are human rights, universal rights, rights that are equally applicable to all people – regardless of race, gender, religion, age, or birth status. Authentic human rights are defined by the Golden Rule. If you would not want to be oppressed, enslaved, or aborted, then don't oppress, enslave, or abort others. We are very "socially conscious" when it comes to our own welfare and interests, but we bury our heads in the sand when it comes to justice and rights for those that society deems less than human. But the real social revolutionaries are those that recognize and declare the rights of those whose humanity has been dismissed and denied by the political power structures of the contemporary day and age.

477. ~THREE PIECES of ADVICE ~

Recently, a young woman in her early twenties asked me what three pieces of advice I would give to a person her age. I had to think about it for a little while, but here's the advice I offered her, for whatever it's worth:

1. Do what you love, regardless of how profitable it is. As long as it's honest, positive, pure, and constructive – do what you love; and know that in doing so you will glorify God and make the world a better place.

2. Never abandon your faith. Even if you give up on religion, never give up on God, because God never gives up on you.

3. Don't look for love. Just love others – truly, selflessly, unconditionally, and sacrificially. Do this, and true love will find you.

478. ~ VICTIM or PILGRIM? ~

A victim views his circumstances as a prison; a pilgrim views his circumstances as a path. A victim may be placed on the path of salvation, but he only sees the rocks and hills that stand in his way. A pilgrim may be placed in a prison, but he views his cell as a ladder to God.

479. ~ I BELIEVE... ~

I believe that war today is a sin. I believe that involuntary poverty is a crime. I believe that abortion is the sacrament of Satan. I believe that all forms of injustice, violence, inhumanity, and oppression are diametrically opposed to the Gospel of peace, life, liberation, and salvation. Because I am a Christian, these are my beliefs. If such convictions are unorthodox, then I shall gladly abide in the company of heretics.

480. ~ NO GREATER EDUCATION ~

I wonder if the Wright brothers ever made paper airplanes during class. I wonder if Van Gogh ever drew sketches instead of doing his homework. I wonder if Rumi ever daydreamed while the teacher was lecturing. I wonder if Carlos Santana ever skipped school so he could go listen to the Blues.

There is no greater education than diligently pursuing your creative passion. It might not make you rich. It might not make you popular. But it might help you change the world.

481. ~ DREAM WARRIOR ~

When I sleep
I dream...
of lost lives
and lost loves,
of ocean waves
and giant snakes,
of grandmother's kiss
and the succubus hiss.

Sometimes I'm laughing.
Sometimes I'm crying.
Sometimes I'm falling.
Sometimes I'm rising.

But as I sleep
I'm always fighting,
and struggling to ascend
from darkness to light,
so that I will awaken
to serve my Lord another day...

I am a dream warrior.

482. ~ BABYLON FOURTH of JULY ~

The homeless cry
The unborn die
Bullets fly
And politicians lie
As fireworks adorn
The nighttime sky...

Another Babylon 4th of July

483. ~ WHY I LOVE ALABAMA FOOTBALL ~

I have always pulled for the "underdog," therefore it may seem strange that I'm such a huge fan of Alabama football. But my sympathies for the underdog go much deeper than sports. They are rooted in my passion for justice, equality, and truth. They are predicated upon my solidarity with those who thrive in spite of severe trials and persecutions. The people of the state of Alabama have suffered from the social upheavals of segregation, economic depression, and cultural prejudices; and their suffering has been compounded by unfair and misinformed stereotypes that are too often promoted by the national media.

As a state, Alabama certainly has its history of inhumanity, injustice, and sins. But to isolate Alabama as an island of social injustice amidst a shining sea of an otherwise utopian America is historically inaccurate and grossly dishonest. The people of Alabama – White and Black together – have collectively struggled to overcome the sins of the past. Through the cornerstones of confession, forgiveness, and unconditional love, Alabamians have demonstrated a spiritual and cultural resilience that is well represented by the statue of Vulcan (the Roman god of steel) whose cast-iron figure stands proudly atop Red Mountain, overlooking the city of Birmingham. And it is profoundly emblematic of the state's spiritual and cultural progress that 100,000 people of racial and socio-economic diversity now fill Bryant Denny stadium to passionately cheer for their beloved Crimson Tide – a football team comprised of both White and Black players and coaches.

The legendary Coach Paul "Bear" Bryant played no small role in Alabama's cultural transition. Bryant left his coaching job at the University of Kentucky because he abhorred its virulently racist basketball coach, Adolph Rupp. After coaching Texas A&M for a few years, Bear Bryant returned to his alma mater to take charge of the Crimson Tide football program in 1958. When asked why he left his success at A&M to come to BAMA, Bryant famously replied: *"Mama called. And when Mama calls, you just have to come running."* During the next three decades, he led the Crimson Tide to 6 National Championships, three of them with integrated teams.

369

Throughout the social turmoil of the 1960's, Coach Bryant refused to bow to the demands of racist politicians. He refused to allow the climate of segregation to determine his values or dictate his coaching ethics.

Against pressure not to do so, Bear Bryant recruited two African American players in 1970: John Mitchell and Wilbur Jackson. Mitchell was the first African American to play in a football game for the Crimson Tide, and Wilbur Jackson became one of the greatest running backs in Alabama history. Another little known fact is that Alabama's basketball coach at the time, C.M. Newton, had also recruited an African American athlete – Wendell Hudson – that same year.

But in spite of these realities, the media perpetuated the fictitious narrative that Coach Bryant did not want to recruit Black players until BAMA was easily defeated by Southern Cal in 1970. USC was led at the time by star running back Sam Cunningham, an African American, who rushed for 135 yards and scored two touchdowns against the TIDE. The media spun the opportunistic myth that after Bear Bryant witnessed Cunningham's prowess he decided that he needed to recruit Black players in order for Alabama to remain competitive. In other words, Coach Bryant was unfairly portrayed as a racially insensitive, amoral pragmatist that viewed Black athletes as mere commodities that could help him win football games. While this myth certainly weaves a provocative story and conveniently fits every negative stereotype about the state of Alabama, the truth is quite the opposite, and actually far more interesting.

As I mentioned, Bear Bryant recruited two African American players in 1970, and they were both members of the football team when BAMA faced USC and the great Sam Cunningham that year. The only reason they weren't on the field that day is because the NCAA ruled freshmen ineligible at that time. The truth is that Bear Bryant had not only already recruited Wilbur Jackson, but he had also convinced USC coach John McKay to schedule the game between the TIDE and the Trojans in order to help further race relations in Alabama. Coach Bryant presciently understood the power of football to help eliminate racial prejudices and accelerate social healing. This is the part of Bear Bryant's genius that is sadly overlooked, even by those who rightly acknowledge his unparalleled coaching skills.

Rather than allowing himself to be co-opted by political agendas, Coach Bryant instead focused on teaching core values that are essential for all people in all walks of life. Teamwork, brotherhood, individual and collective effort, discipline, preparation, and equality were the principles he imbued in his players, his coaches, and his teams. Rather than using football as a political platform – as political extremists on both the left and the right wanted him to do – Coach Bryant chose to simply be a teacher and a coach. And by being a teacher and a coach, Bear Bryant instilled indispensable principles that indelibly molded his players' character both on and off the playing field. The Bear famously said, "I don't have White players, I don't have Black players. I just have football players." Can there be a more succinct and profound statement of equality than that?

So, as someone who has always been endeared to the "underdog," I feel a profound allegiance to Alabama football. I have utmost respect for a football program that represents the heart, soul, and values of a collective people and an entire state. I have deep sympathy for a University, a culture, and a team that continues to be maligned, mocked, and disparaged for the sins of its past. And nothing is more indicative of true character than proving you can win in spite of the money, the media, and the myths that are levied against you.

Presently, we have a coach – Nick Saban – who embodies the principles and spirit of Alabamians. Coach Saban emphasizes discipline, honesty, work ethic, integrity – and perhaps most importantly – the two mantras that he echoes incessantly: *"Focus on the process,"* and *"overcome adversity."* And whether it's the process of forging iron in the furnaces of Birmingham's steel mills, or overcoming the adversity of segregation and racial injustice, Alabamians understand that their current football coach represents their values and struggles quite well.

Coach Saban came to Alabama in 2007, when TIDE football was at its ebb, when its fans were in the throes of despair. We were becoming the laughingstock of college football. We had been through scandals, losing seasons, and NCAA probations. Our once proud program was at its nadir. The BAMA haters were rejoicing. And it seemed as if the national media couldn't spend enough time discussing how Alabama football was finished, an irrelevant anachronism that had suffered the same final and just defeat as the Confederacy to which its state had once unfortunately belonged.

But there was one man who understood the pathos and ethos of Alabama football and the culture it represents. And that man was not even from Alabama. He was from West Virginia. But true and lasting values are not limited to locality; they are universal and timeless. Nick Saban was raised in West Virginia by the same values and the same work ethic that permeates the people of the Crimson state. The struggles of the Birmingham steel mills were the same struggles of the West Virginia coal mines, struggles that Nick Saban understood quite well. So he was up to the challenge; and he knew that his principles and standards would be welcomed in Tuscaloosa and beyond.

Nick Saban restored pride and dignity to Alabama football. In 2009, he brought Alabama its 13th National Championship in only his third season as head coach. In 2011 he led us to National Championship #14. And in 2012 he coached BAMA to its 15th National Championship, defeating The University of Notre Dame – another historical football powerhouse (and object of national media adoration). Winning three National Championships in four years, Coach Nick Saban served notice to all the doubters, detractors, deniers, and haters that Alabama is ultimately a winner – as a football program, as a university, as a state, and as a collective people.

The history of Alabama is a history of oppression – of both oppressing and having been oppressed. It is human history. It is the history of great sins and great forgiveness, of great evils and great good, of great horrors and great hopes. It is a history still in the making – like the lives of us all. Willie Morris once wrote, *"To escape the South – all of what it was and is – I would have to escape myself."*

I am a son of the South, and the South is still my home today. My roots began in the red clay of Milledgeville, Georgia. They gave birth to the fruit of my Atlanta youth. The Southern winds eventually took me Birmingham, and ultimately to Mississippi where I found a beautiful wife, had beautiful children, and put down roots that will produce fruits and fates of which only God can know.

My childhood heroes were Dr. Martin Luther King, Jr. and Muhammad Ali – two great sons of the South. Those men defined justice, character, perseverance, and grace. I am a "White" man who has been married to an African American woman for 16 years. We have three beautiful children. My late mother-in-law worked as Bear Bryant's secretary while she was earning her Master's Degree from the University of Alabama. My mother-in-law was a brilliant woman who was able to instinctively intuit someone's true character. She did not suffer fools, and she could not be conned. She told me that Coach Bryant was one of the finest people she had ever known, and that there was not a racist bone in his body. My mother-in-law was not prone to empty praise. Her respect was hard earned, and The Bear earned it – as I'm sure she earned his.

I loved Alabama football as a child, and admittedly for many childish reasons. I loved the Alabama uniforms. I loved the BAMA fight song. I loved their wishbone offense. But I also loved and admired Walter Lewis, the deftly skilled Alabama quarterback who was one of the few African American QB's playing in the early 80's. In spite of criticism from a few fans, Coach Bryant did not hesitate to make him the starter. As much as anything else, Walter Lewis is the reason why I'm an Alabama fan today. I coveted a #10 Alabama replica jersey when I was a kid. I wanted to grow up to run the wishbone like the great Walter Lewis.

There will always be those who prefer myth to fact. There will always be those who choose perception over reality. There will always be those who disparage excellence while they wallow in mediocrity. But I admire true winners – not because winning comes naturally to them, but because they are willing to embrace the principles, values, and character that are essential to enduring success both on and off the field. When a typically critical media once asked Nick Saban why he was so impatient and demanding, he simply replied: *"Mediocre people don't like high achievers, and high achievers don't like mediocre people."* His words could have just as easily been uttered by The Bear.

Alabama fans are not just fans. We are a family. We are one. We embrace each other and we love one another. We are Black and White. We are rich and poor. We are University alumni and we are blue collar diehards that have never darkened the door of a college. We know our past but we embrace our future. Our deep crimson colors represent the depth of our suffering, the depth of our struggle, the depth of our pain, the depth of our character, the depth of our resilience, and the depth of our indomitable spirit. We don't strive to win merely for "bragging rights." We strive to win in order to prove that the universal values of hard work, brotherhood, perseverance, and integrity can never be permanently extinguished.

It is impossible to have a tradition of excellence without tradition. And tradition stands the test of time because it is forged by timeless values. At Alabama we did not create our tradition; we gave birth to it through trials and tribulations, through blood and sweat, through tumult and tears, through failures and redemption. The TIDE may ebb and flow, but it can never be permanently repressed. Like the iron forged in the fires of the Birmingham steel mills, the people of Alabama will continue to grow tougher, stronger, and more resilient through every hardship that we collectively endure. Black and White, rich and poor, young and old, Democrat and Republican – we stand together in our solidarity and strength, perpetually echoing our mantra of victory: ROLL TIDE!

> *They got a name for the winners in the world*
> *But I want a name when I lose*
> *They call Alabama, "The Crimson Tide"*
> *Call me Deacon Blues*
> ~ Steely Dan ~

(This article was written in September of 2015. The landscape of college football is rapidly changing. College football is a big business now, and it has been for quite some time. And yet college football has nevertheless retained its unique passions and traditions. I am not so naïve as to believe that college football is pure, even at Alabama. But there are still certain standards, values, ethics, and principles that are necessary for enduring success and cultural longevity. Just as the dross of iron melts away to ruin, leaving the sculpted work to endure, so the dross of slavery, segregation, racism, cheating, scandals, and quick fixes will always melt away into the same ruinous gutter. I don't know what Nick Saban's ultimate legacy will be. I don't know if he will win more National Championships. I don't know if he will retire at Alabama. I don't know who his successor will be, or how successful his successor will be. I don't know if any scandals will be attached to Saban or to Alabama football subsequent to the time I am writing this article. Coaches are just people, and we should always be wary of elevating them to deific status. The horrific revelations that ultimately poisoned the legacy of Joe Paterno – fairly or unfairly – should sober us all.

But what I do know is that all true BAMA fans – those who truly represent the values and strength of the entire state – will always demand excellence from their football program: excellence of character, excellence of class, excellence of effort, and excellence of attitude. As much as we hate to lose, we'd rather lose with dignity than win with disgrace. And I am confident that this will always be true of the Alabama Crimson Tide – be it today, in the year 2015, or one hundred years from now.)

[In memory of my dear friend and brother: Christian Marshall Sheetz. Watching BAMA football will never be the same without you. Life won't be the same without you. Rest in Peace my friend.+++]

484. ~ GOVERNMENT PROTECTION ~

I've noticed that the rich think the government has a responsibility to protect them from the poor. But interestingly, they don't think the government has a responsibility to protect the poor from them.

485. ~ COME FOLLOW HIM ~

Throw down your arms
pick up your Cross
Seek peace and pursue it
No matter the cost

Lay down your guns
Lift up your brother
Bury your bullets
Love one another

Forsake abortion
Pursue salvation
No more politics
One world creation

Crucify pride
Cast away judgment
No more fear
No more punishment

Wide is the path
And broad is the gate
Of racism, violence,
Killing and hate

Narrow the path
And narrow the road
Is the way of the Shepherd
Who leads us home

Won't you come follow Him?

There is too much to say about my Papa. His life is worthy of an entire book. I often encouraged him to write an autobiography, or perhaps write some autobiographical short stories, but unfortunately life did not afford him more time to do so. The other day I discovered something he had jotted down in a small journal he had been keeping:

"I've been thinking about writing a book for years. I even have a name for it: 'It Was a Wonderful Journey'. I want to do it for my three grandchildren. I have been blessed with family, friends, and an exciting life of travel – over forty countries, five continents, and approximately a million miles in the air. I also want to include some humorous – and not so humorous – tales which I have mentally recorded. I just need to do it! There is so much to tell."

My Papa travelled the world, met fascinating people, and had some incredible experiences. Along the way he gained the admiration and respect of everyone who was privileged to know him. I wish that my thoughts were better organized, and there is much that I will probably forget to include; but I will try to say a few things about my Papa that I feel are important.

I was his son for almost 44 years – more than half his life – and yet I was constantly learning new things about my father. You see, my Papa was never one to brag about his importance or flaunt his erudition. Whenever I would remind him of his accolades and accomplishments, he would scoff and downplay their significance. Sometimes I would observe him in the presence of sophisticated company at dinner parties or social gatherings, and some pompous, self-aggrandizing individual would be dropping names and boasting about this or that, and my father would listen calmly and act very interested in it all. And I would be sitting there thinking, *"This person is an idiot compared to my father, and yet my dad is allowing this guy to think he's better than him. My father should start bragging about who **he's** met, and where **he's** been, and what **he's** done!"* But the thing is, my Papa never needed to feel more important than anyone else. He knew who he was, possessing that true self-confidence that results in humility rather than arrogance. Thus he could suffer highbrows, boors, and poseurs with amazing patience.

My father was an only child from Milledgeville, Georgia, raised by parents of humble status who instilled in him the values of hard work, integrity, and consideration for others. He was an Eagle Scout, he was the President of his ATO fraternity at Georgia Tech, and he became one of the most important and influential members of his consulting firm, **Kurt Salmon Associates**. He attended a military high school and served time in the Army, where he was a highly respected leader; and yet he never boasted in his military service. As I child, when I would ask him to tell me "army stories," he never would. My father always seemed to know that war and violence were not the answers to anything.

My father was also the "Best Man" at four weddings. That tells you how respected and admired he was by others. But his success in business, his social status, and his worldly experience never corrupted the ethos forged by his paternal and maternal genes, an ethos that gave birth to virtues as deep and intractable as the hardscrabble roots that plumb the red clay earth of middle Georgia.

Whether he was consulting an Egyptian textile tycoon or chatting with a waitress at the Waffle House, my Papa treated everyone with dignity and respect. He never approached people differently according to race or class. My father was willing to give everyone the benefit of the doubt, recognizing the humanity in all people. And yet it was not a conscious effort on his part; it was simply and naturally who he was.

My Papa made a very good living, but he lived simply and used his money to take care of his wife and children. We had all that we needed and plenty more, and yet my father never spoiled us. The materialistic mindset was repugnant to my father, and he eschewed opulence and ostentation. For all the money he made and all the experiences he had, he was essentially a man with simple tastes who was easily satisfied. He enjoyed a good barbecue sandwich as much as a Parisian Nicoise salad. He enjoyed his Levi jeans as much as his dark pinstriped suits. He loved the Andy Griffith Show as much as C-SPAN. He had cultivated tastes without any pretension. My father liked what he liked because he actually liked it, not because he was supposed to like it. There was no affectation with my Papa. He was who he was, authentically so.

My father did not display medals and awards, although I know he had them. The only thing my father ever seemed to want to show off was his "White Bug," the 1961 Mercedes Benz 190 SL that he drove everywhere. Rather than keeping this vintage automobile in the basement and preserving it at all costs, my father drove us all over town in it. When I was a little boy, as far as I could tell, God made Saturdays for one thing: riding around Atlanta in the White Bug with my Papa. He'd drive me to my soccer and basketball games in the White Bug, and afterwards he'd always take my sister and me out for Pizza. The White Bug also took us to countless Georgia Tech football and basketball games. But it really didn't matter where we were going or what we did, if Papa said, *"I've got to run some errands,"* I wanted to go with him. Riding to the cleaner's in the White Bug with my Papa on a Saturday morning seemed like the greatest thing on earth. Countless times as we were out and about in the White Bug, people would roll down their windows and ask, *"Hey sir, do you want to sell that car? I really want to buy it. How much are you asking? That's a great car! Are you sure you won't sell it?"* My Papa would just smile with pride and say, *"Oh thank you very much, but no, I could never sell this car."* In those moments, I would be the proudest little boy on earth! I felt like we were the center of the universe!

My Papa taught me many lessons that were – I am sad to say – not quickly learned. He taught me humility, class, and good sportsmanship. He taught me to be optimistic and to always see the positives in life. These were lessons that I was very slow to learn, but my Papa never gave up on me. I am ashamed to say that I didn't truly understand and appreciate these lessons until I was much older. And then, whenever I tried to express to my father how much I had learned from him and how much he had helped me, he truly seemed baffled. He really did not believe how much he had helped me and influenced me. But once again, that was his humble and gracious nature.

I remember the time I scored 9 goals in a little league soccer game. Our coach had promised us a Coca Cola for each goal we scored. Well, you better believe I was excited to get my 9 Coca Colas! The coach had to help me carry them to the car (yes, the White Bug) where my father was waiting for me. I just knew that my Papa was going to be so proud of me for scoring 9 goals and getting 9 Coca Colas! But when the coach and I told him why I had all those Coca Colas, my father looked disappointed. I didn't understand why, until he kindly and gently explained to me that I should be sharing those Cokes with my teammates. He was proud of me for scoring 9 goals, but he was disappointed in me for being selfish. I never forgot that. I would like to say that I learned right then and there to always do the right thing, to be humble and selfless, and to care more about others than about myself. But, alas, I continue to fall short. But moments like that set the standard for me, and whenever I have failed it is not for lack of example.

My father was not a saint, and I would not honor his memory by exaggerating his virtues or ignoring his flaws. He was quite human, and he was the first to admit his errors and weaknesses. I have no resentment towards my father, because he frequently apologized to me and often confessed that he agonized over certain decisions and actions that turned out to have a negative impact on me. I am now the father of three wonderful children, and I know how challenging parenthood is. There is no such thing as a perfect parent, and we learn as we go. But when a parent can look at a child and say, *"I'm sorry, I was wrong,"* or, *"I thought I was doing the right thing, but it may not have been,"* then that brings about a lot of healing and forgiveness. My father apologized to me many times and asked for my forgiveness, even when there was nothing to forgive. So, in spite of his mistakes, I know that he loved me deeply and always tried to do what was in my best interest. And I know that I certainly did not make it easy for him.

In the last few years, my father struggled with severe alcoholism. This was something that sneaked up on him over time and caught him unawares. He was never one to frequent bars or come home late in the evening intoxicated. He never set out to deliberately overindulge. But as with many things in life, that which we think we can control eventually begins to control us. It is something of which I must always be cognizant myself. However, I am happy and thankful to say that my Papa was sober for the last 10 weeks of his life. He chose to live with our family in our small home in Jackson, Mississippi for the last two and a half months before he passed. He didn't have to make that choice. But he did. And in making that choice, he demonstrated that he valued the love, nurture, and care of his family more than alcohol. I was so very proud of him, and I know that it was not easy. But his true strength and character once again prevailed, and I have great peace in knowing that my Papa died sober and of sound mind.

I told my father many times during the past few years that his love and support are what enabled me to have the wonderful family that I am blessed to have today. There were countless times when I disappointed my father. There were things I did that probably made him very ashamed. And although he always let me know that he was upset and bothered by certain actions or behaviors, he never abandoned me. He never gave up on me. He would always help me and support me as long as I was trying to do something worthwhile and productive with my life. It didn't matter if he agreed with all of my beliefs or understood all of my choices, as long as he saw me trying to do something positive he would support me and encourage me in my endeavors. In spite of all my struggles, failures, sins, and mistakes, my father always saw something good in me. He always believed in my potential, and he chose to invest himself in the glimmer of good that struggled to emerge from a son's soul that was often ensconced in negativity and darkness. That's unconditional love, and I felt it from my Papa all my life.

I have thought a lot about how to describe my father. It is not easy to do. He was a man of great depth, but it was difficult to peel back the layers. He was not emotional, and I only saw him cry a few times in my life. However, my father was very sensitive. He did not like to see anyone suffer in any way. If he could do something to help ease the suffering of another, he would do it.

My father was a man of great intellect, but beneath and beyond that he had an artistic soul. His passion was not evident on the surface, but it was revealed in his artwork and also in his love for music. Painting was merely a hobby for him, but I think his art was fantastic. I recently found something he wrote that discusses his approach to watercolor painting:

"When you face a sheet of watercolor paper – plain and white – it frightens you knowing that you wish to create something on it that others will enjoy. Once you dip the brush into the water and paint and then begin to apply it to the paper, it totally absorbs you. When you paint, try to evoke a feeling, because a photograph can capture the actual details better than an artist. The reason Van Gogh is my favorite artist is because he evokes feelings."

So, I would describe my father as a man who was both intellectual and artistic, although I think he trusted his intellectual nature much more than his artistic side. But one can tell a lot about him from his paintings. There is so much warmth and color and feeling in them, and even his pen and pencil sketches make you feel happy inside when you see them. They reveal his sensitivity. He never wore his feelings on his sleeve, but I think his love for art and music enabled his soul to breathe and revealed the beauty of his heart. Sometimes I think he relied too much on his intellectual capacities, and that he did so in order to protect his sensitive soul. But that's just an observation, an opinion.

I also have to mention my father's wonderful sense of humor. He loved to laugh, and I thought it was great that a man of his profound intellect could find humor in the corniest things. He loved the Andy Griffith Show, and he and I could watch episode after episode and love every minute of it. I will admit that I now judge people in part by whether or not they like the Andy Griffith Show. If they're too cool or too sophisticated to laugh at Barney Fife, then they're too cool for me.

I have so many wonderful memories of my Papa that I will cherish forever: The White Bug; all the Georgia Tech games we went to; the smell of his pipe that made me feel warm all over; the trip he took me on to Washington, D.C. for my 11th birthday; all the movies and sports we watched together; all the long talks we had about every topic imaginable; all the major events in my life that he showed up to and was present for; all of his encouraging words; all the meals he took us out to; the kindness and respect he showed to all my friends; the love he showed to my wife and children; his words of affirmation that made me feel that he was truly proud of me; the security I always felt while he was alive, and that I now fear I may have lost.

But God gave me my Papa for 43 years. There are many people who never get to know their father, and many people who have abusive or neglectful fathers. Some have wonderful fathers that they lose very early in their lives. My Papa lost his own father when he was only seventeen years old. So, my heart is full of gratitude and thanksgiving for all the years that I had with my father. I am thankful that our relationship grew stronger and stronger over time, and I am so happy that my Papa spent the last weeks of his life under our roof with his grandchildren, his daughter-in-law, and with me. I will always be grateful for that. I will cherish those few weeks for the rest of my life.

No words can accurately describe what I loved about my father and what I will miss. There is an essence of a person that transcends written or spoken words – a certain expression or trait, a particular scent, a gesture, a voice – these are things that are indelibly inscribed upon my consciousness, and they will stay with me always. My Papa will always be a part of me, and he will always be present in my mind, my heart, and my soul.

In less than two years time I have experienced the passing of our 11 week old daughter and now my 80 year old father. Life involves loss, and we only mourn the loss of those from whom we have gained so much. In spite of his imperfections, weaknesses, and flaws – which were few – my father gave me riches intangible and immeasurable. As with the spirit of my baby daughter, I will continue to feel the spirit of my Papa always and forever. There are only two people in this world who will know the power and love of the name "Papa," as we pronounced it and understood it. My sister and I will always know this particular power and love, and we alone are privileged to share it. We will miss our Papa so much, but we will always have him with us. God has been good to us.

For the past few years my father would often say, *"It's been a wonderful journey."* That would really annoy me, and I would respond, *"Papa, the journey ain't quite over yet. We'd like you to stick around for a while longer."* Well, now his earthly journey has finally come to an end; and I can certainly say that I have had a wonderful journey with him while he was here. He has left me with many indelible and wonderful memories. And as his soul continues its transcendent journey it will be accompanied by my love, my gratitude, and my prayers. I love you Papa, and I love you God for giving me my Papa. I don't know what else to say. My heart is so broken right now, and yet my heart is so full of gratitude.

487. ~ AN INVERSION of THE GOSPEL ~

Christ relinquished His heavenly abode and came to earth as a man. He endured ridicule, rejection, torture and death. He gave up His own life so that we may live eternally. This is the glorious news of the Gospel. But we invert the Gospel by preserving our own rights, our own welfare, and our own lives through the violent destruction of the lives of others. And yet we dare to call ourselves "Christians."

Although He possessed every eternal privilege and divine right, Our Lord never once uttered the words, "I have a right to…" But somehow, those of us who profess His holy name are always declaring our "right" to avenge our enemies and to violently preserve our own nations, our own families, our own lives, and our own welfare by destroying the lives of others. This is nothing less than a blasphemous perversion of the Savior's life and teachings. God forgive us!

488. ~ WAR'S VICTOR ~

In war there is only one victor: *death*.

489. ~ NEVER ENDING LESSONS ~

It could have been a piece of bread
That filled his stomach and kept him fed
But instead it was a piece of lead
That struck his brain and killed him dead

An enemy that could have been a friend
But instead we caused his life to end
And now his comrades rise again
To teach us lessons that will never end

490. ~ LOOKING for JUSTICE ~

You called the police, looking for justice.
You went to the judge, looking for justice.
You cast your vote, looking for justice.
You gave to the preacher, looking for justice.
You bought a gun, looking for justice.
You waved your flag, looking for justice.
You joined the cause, looking for justice.
You took up arms, looking for justice.
You said your pledge, looking for justice.
You supported the troops, looking for justice.

But when the beggar extended his hand,
you told him to get a job.

491. ~ DISHONORABLE ~

If it's dishonorable to steal another man's bread
and dishonorable to take another man's wife
then why do people find it honorable
to deprive other men of their lives?

492. ~ MEDITATION on THE EXALTATION of THE HOLY CROSS ~

Today, as Orthodox Christians exalt the glorious life-giving Cross, let us denounce every dishonorable weapon of death and destruction. The Cross has no companionship with the sword, and the Gospel will not accommodate those who endeavor to kill. It is impossible to follow the Savior while pledging obedience to destroyers. We cannot worship the divine Prince of Peace while taking oaths of allegiance to human armies. We shall either arm ourselves with mortal weapons or arm ourselves with the Cross. But we cannot carry both. One must choose between life and death, between Christ and Satan, between the Kingdom of heaven and the kingdoms of this world. The Cross is our salvation, but not if we are bent upon sowing destruction. We must trust in the Cross, cling to the Cross, and avail ourselves of its redemptive and atoning power. But how can we have faith in the Cross unless we forsake our reliance upon bullets, bombs, armies, and ballots? The Gospel is not about hedging our bets, saying, "praise the Lord and pass the ammunition." We cannot have one foot in Zion and one foot in Babylon. We cannot follow both Christ and Caesar. We cannot be equally allied with the God of heaven and the god of this world. We cannot march to the Promised Land while marching off to war. There is no greater blasphemy than to turn the Cross upside down and kill for states, nations, kings, and crowns. If we are Christians, then we are children, we are sheep, we are lambs; but we are not killers. It is either the sword or the Cross. The choice really is that simple. So exalt the Cross today! And as you exalt the Cross, throw down your arms, rend your uniforms, mash up your medals, and come follow Him!

493. ~ BROTHERS, SISTERS, NEIGHBORS ~

Christ died for all. The Cross has saved the entire world. Therefore we are all brothers and sisters. Just because many have failed to realize their salvation does not mean that they are not our family. In the light of the atonement and the glorious Resurrection, there is hope for human unity and the reconciliation of mankind. And it is up to those of us who cling to our salvation to manifest this truth to the world. We who call ourselves by the name of Christ must view all people as neighbors and brothers. We who claim to follow the Prince of Peace must never view our fellow man as an enemy in the crosshairs. Instead, we must view our ostensible enemies as inevitable children of the Cross. Whether you are Muslim or Jew, Christian or pagan, capitalist or communist, atheist or believer –you are my brother, my sister, and my neighbor; and I must treat you as such. For Christ died no less for you than for me.

494. ~ EDUCATION ~

The problem with formal education is that people who have been formally educated think that they are truly educated.

495. ~ RASTA and ORTHODOXY ~

Rastafari is not a "schism from Ethiopian Orthodoxy" as some people erroneously believe. The Rastafarian movement developed in Jamaica, not in Ethiopia. The religious and biblical tenets that were foundational to Rastafari were influenced more by evangelical millenarian theology than by Orthodoxy. As the movement grew and developed, more Rastas began to learn about the Orthodox Faith of Ethiopia and Emperor Haile Selassie. Eventually, more and more Rastas began to adopt Orthodox customs, and many (such as Bob Marley) became baptized converts to the Ethiopian Orthodox Christian Faith.

One of the difficulties about discussing Rastafari is the fact that there are countless interpretations and definitions of what it means to be a Rastafarian. So, there are many people who unfortunately condemn Rastafari out of prejudice and ignorance. If one defines

Rastafari as a religion based upon the worship of Emperor Haile Selassie, then one cannot be both Rasta and Orthodox. Our Orthodox Faith is very clear, and the words of His Majesty are also very clear: worship is due to the Father, the Son, and the Holy Spirit – One God, alone. Thus, there can be no theological compatibility between Christian worship and Emperor worship.

However, if one defines Rastafari as a way of life that seeks to follow the words and example of His Majesty regarding peace, unity, and adherence to the Orthodox Christian Faith, then there is no contradiction between Rasta and Orthodoxy. The largest Rastafari "mansion" is called the Twelve Tribes, founded by Dr. Vernon Carrington, aka "Prophet Gad." The Twelve Tribes adherents embrace Jesus Christ as God and do not worship Haile Selassie. Bob Marley (Berhane Selasie) was the most famous Rasta to identify with the Twelve Tribes before his Orthodox baptism.

The common denominators that unite all Rastafarians are things that are quite compatible with the Orthodox Christian Faith: 1) a love for the Holy Bible; 2) a profound respect for the sanctity of all human life; 3) an adherence to divine morality and the natural order of original creation; 4) a sincere desire for peace and human brotherhood; 5) an emphasis on positivity rather than negativity; 6) the belief in the power of prayer and chanted scripture; 7) the recognition of Africa as the blessed birthplace of all humanity; 8) the worship of One God.

So, while I primarily identify myself as an Orthodox Christian, I am not ashamed to also say that I am "Rasta." Apart from Rastafari, I would never have discovered the beautiful Orthodox Christian Faith. So how can I deny the path that led me to my spiritual home?

Peace and Love I-tinual!

496. ~ A DEMONIC MINDSET ~

"This violence is wrong! This killing is unjust! And we're gonna get violent to prove just how wrong violence is! And we're gonna kill to prove just how unjust killing is!"

This is the demonic mindset of the world today.

497. ~ THE GREATEST THREAT to AMERICAN LIVES ~

The greatest threat to innocent human lives in America is not ISIS, Al Qaeda, or the Taliban. The greatest threat to innocent human lives in America is legalized abortion. In fact, it's not a threat; it's a horrific, daily reality. But I guess it's easier to curse the enemy across the ocean than to confront the enemy in our own backyard.

498. ~ PROMISED LAND ~

The earth is conquered by the mighty, possessed by the rich, and raped by the greedy. But the earth shall be eternally inherited by the meek, the nonviolent, and the pure of heart. Castles of gold will become piles of sand, and the poor will arise with Christ to reap the Promised Land.

499. ~ UNCONSTRUCTIVE MASTERS ~

Those who have nothing constructive to offer themselves are quite adept at belittling the offerings of others.

500. ~ BRIEF NOTE on CAPITAL PUNISHMENT ~

The Orthodox Christian Faith does not teach retribution and vengeance. Our beautiful Orthodox Faith actually encourages quite the opposite. The staple prayer of all Orthodox Christians is, "Lord have mercy." And I certainly don't think this prayer means we are to ask God to be merciful to us while we refuse to be merciful to others. Nor do I think that God tells us to be merciful only to those who deserve it. In fact, the whole idea of mercy is that we receive an undeserved grace. As Orthodox Christians we are to desire the same mercy for others that we desire for ourselves. This is why capital punishment contradicts the Orthodox Christian spirit. When a murderer is executed, we have two human lives condemned to violent deaths by a lack of mercy: the innocent life of the victim and the guilty life of the victimizer. And between the innocent and the guilty, who is in more need of divine mercy?

"But what then is capital punishment but the most premeditated of murders, to which no criminal's deed, however calculated it may be, can be compared? For there to be equivalence, the death penalty would have to punish a criminal who had warned his victim of the date at which he would inflict a horrible death on him and who, from that moment onward, had confined him at his mercy for months."

~ Albert Camus ~

501. ~ IT'S HARD TO BE A CHRISTIAN ~

It's hard to be a Christian:

When we sin, we are called "hypocrites." When we try to do right, we are called "self-righteous." When we condemn immorality and evil, we are called "judgmental." When we fast and pray, we are called "holier-than-thou." When we turn the other cheek, we are called "weak." When we stand for Truth, we are called "divisive." When we love our enemies, we are called "fools." When we forsake politics, we are called "naïve." When we trust the Scriptures and the

Teachings of the Church more than the consensus of the world, we are called "ignorant." When we strive to honor Christ in every facet of our lives, we are called "fanatics."

Indeed, it is not easy to be a Christian. And yet it is so much harder not to be.

502. ~ TO FEEL IS TO LIVE ~

To feel is to live. That's why we are more alive when we are sad than when we are numb. Sorrow, mourning, and grief are not the enemies of life; they are the evidence of life. So let us give thanks to God for all things, rejoicing in every breath. The glory of divine comfort is discovered through pain of heart.

503. ~ MORE LIFE! ~

More Life = More Blessings! Life is mystery, depth, pain, struggle, beauty, agony, spirit, soul, and love. When you say "yes" to Life you say yes to all that accompanies it. And life is certainly not easy. But when you say "no" to life, then all you are left with is the easy emptiness of death – an easy emptiness that may simply be the prelude to hell.

504. ~ A BABYLONIAN EQUATION ~

Ego + authority + power + guns + a belief in the justification of premeditated violence = a dangerous and deadly combination. But somehow we have come to believe that this equation provides us with individual protection, community safety, and national security. Never underestimate the power of Babylon brainwashing.

505. ~ SHIP OF FOOLS ~

She thinks she's cute
In her Navy suit
Sailing away
Aboard a ship of fools

She loves the praise
And the pay is great
But war is hell
And she's paving the way

This glory and honor
Brings gore and horror
She's floating on lies
That will sink her tomorrow

It's "anchors aweigh!"
And the flag proudly waves
As she embarks upon death
Toward the depth of the grave

506. ~ ETERNAL MERCY ~

There are no injuries
that injustice can't invent

No limit to the sorrows
that sin can inflict

No impossible evils
that man can't commit

But Eternal mercy
heals all who repent

Christ does not need or require the violent defense of His Church. Violence might be effective in defending nations, religions, denominations, isms, and ideologies, but violence has no efficacious power to defend the Church. In fact, the use of violence in the ostensible defense of the Church only serves to contradict and undermine the teachings of the Christian Faith.

Extolling the use of violence in the name of Our Lord reveals a severe spiritual sickness. The message of the Cross is not only relevant for individuals; it is also relevant for the entire world. The truths of the Sermon on the Mount are as applicable to human governments as they are to human persons. Presidents, politicians, judges, and kings will be divinely tried by the same Gospel as saints, martyrs, priests, and monks.

If the incarnate God did not violently defend Himself and His disciples against the evils they faced, then who are we to think that our "cause" is more just and worthy than theirs? Who are we to presume that our own lives and the lives of our own brethren are more precious than the lives of Christ and His disciples? How dare we presume to tell Jesus that our cause is holier than His, that our situation is more dire than His was, that our world is more violent and evil than the world He inhabited? Who are we to accuse Christ of forsaking His own loved ones, of abandoning the innocent to the fate of evildoers because He refused to lead a violent revolutionary liberation movement? Who are we to take up the sword that Our Lord has unequivocally and universally condemned for His disciples (St. Matthew 26:52)? Who are we to invert the Gospel of love and forgiveness, manufacturing it into a doctrine of mortal retribution and violent self-preservation?

Promoting and defending violence in the precious name of Christ and His Church is simply demonic. But many professing Christians have fallen prey to the hellish spells of warfare, abortion, death, and destruction. This is a spiritual sickness that must be firmly addressed and exorcised with Gospel truth, sacramental power, and much prayer and fasting.

The only bloodshed that Christians must ever extol is the shed blood of Christ and the shed blood of the saints and martyrs who lived and died following His glorious example.

508. ~ GRACE ~

I truly appreciate proclamations about the grace of God. Really. I do. And often these proclamations are quite poetic. Usually they convey sentiments such as:

"My sins are deeper than the ocean, but God's grace is broader than the heavens." Or: "I am so unworthy, but His worthiness has erased my unworthiness and therefore I am now worthy in spite of my unworthiness."

And how can I argue with any of that? I have to say "amen."

But sometimes I wonder if these proclamations stem from a true understanding of divine grace. You see, the reality of grace is most profoundly revealed in the presence of excruciating suffering, depth of sin, and severe doubt. So if you want to truly glorify God and exalt His grace, then give me something real, something I can relate to. Tell me that you quit your job, cheated on your spouse, fell into the throes of addiction, abandoned your children, got excommunicated from your church, and repeatedly chose self-destruction over prayer, fasting, and sacramental communion. Tell me that you have been cruelly forsaken by family and friends. Tell me that you haven't had a truly restful night of sleep in months or years. Tell me that you sometimes struggle to maintain a desire to simply continue living. Tell me that hope is something that constantly seems to elude your grasp. Tell me that this is your life. Tell me that this is your reality. And tell me that somehow, in spite of your horrific failures and severe sufferings, you are nevertheless able to experience God's grace and feel His unconditional love. Then I will believe you. Then I will take you seriously when you preach the Gospel.

Anyone can proclaim grace from the Promised Land; but I need a grace that is preached from the belly of the whale. Anyone can preach grace on Sunday morning; but I need a grace that is preached from the agony of a Cross. Anyone can preach grace from the pulpit; but I need a grace that is proclaimed from prisons, from skid row, from abandonment, from the dark side of the rainbow.

509. ~ TO LIVE IS HOLY, and TO BE IS A BLESSING ~

The presence of every human life is precious. Our existence is important, and our lives are significant. To live is holy, and to be is a blessing. We must recognize the fact that God brought us into existence, and our lives are not accidental. Our worth as human beings has nothing to do with physical appearance, talent, or material wealth. We are valuable because the Creator has formed us, shaped us, and imbued us with mind, spirit, and an eternal soul. Those who fully realize this truth have profound respect both for themselves and for others.

510. ~ REVOLUTIONARY RHETORIC WITHOUT APOLOGY! ~

Since war, abortion, violence, and killing are justified and committed without moderation, measure, apology or shame, then I will not be moderate, measured, apologetic or ashamed in my condemnation of such evils.

I refuse to preach the Cross in moderation, for the Cross makes no compromise. We cannot be crucified with Christ while we are busy crucifying others.

Relentless violence must be fought with a revolutionary peace. Relentless lies must be opposed with revolutionary truth. Relentless hate must be confronted with revolutionary love. Relentless evil warrants a revolutionary rebuke.

So until innocent human lives are liberated from the politicians' wars and the abortionist's scalpel, I will continue to preach Our

Lord's message of peace, life, redemption and truth as provocatively, as forthrightly, and as bluntly as I can. And if the enemies of Christ are offended by the Gospel, then so be it.

I will be as careful with my rhetoric as you are with your drones and bombs. I will be as measured in my tone as you are in your wanton slaughter of unborn children. I will be as cautious with my words as you are with the lives of the innocent.

As long as there are captives to be set free, then I will speak provocatively on their behalf. When human beings created in God's image are being oppressed, enslaved, bombed, and aborted, then there is no time for manners or tact.

The Christian must not debate Pharaoh. The Christian must not plead with Babylon. The Christian must not acquiesce with the world in an attempt to reform the world. The Christian must simply preach the Gospel and live out its redemptive, liberating, and restorative truth.

Cease your killing, and let JAH children live!

511. ~ A STRANGE GOSPEL ~

They worship a false god who delivers them from their sins but cannot also deliver them from their enemies. They preach a feckless faith that proclaims a personal redemption that does not also extend to all the world. They rightly reject the necessity of human works in the atonement but somehow believe that mortal violence is necessary to assist God's saving arm. They want a Jesus who will grant them access to heaven, but they will kill their neighbor to preserve their existence here on earth. They cannot stop telling you that they are "saved by faith," but they apparently have no faith in Our Lord's commands to love our enemies and put away the sword. This is a strange gospel they serve, a strange gospel indeed. I love all my Christian brethren, but I confess that sometimes it seems we are professing a radically different Faith.

If the meek shall inherit the earth and the peacemakers shall be called the "children of God," then I tremble for the inheritance of the militant and the fate of the violent.

512. ~ EMBRACING LIES ~

Some people will embrace any theory, any philosophy, any myth, and any lie as long as it keeps them from having to acknowledge their Creator and fulfill their divine responsibility to their fellow man.

513. ~ VAIN IMAGINATION ~

Those who imagine that there is no God are really not very imaginative at all. But those who know their Creator are the most creative people in the world. "Art" that is designed to demonstrate that life has no designer is not only self-defeating, but it is also aesthetically impotent. But art that flows from God, through God, and to God is eternally transcendent.

514. ~ IRASCIBLE PACIFIST / DISPASSIONATE SOLDIER ~

I have more respect for the irascible pacifist who is angry, rude, and offensive than for the soldier who with dispassionate premeditation slaughters his fellow man.

515. ~ THE CROSS I LOVE ~

The Cross I venerate,
the Cross that I love,
the Cross I proclaim,
and the Cross that I wear,
is the Cross from which I often flee
and the Cross that I rarely bear.

516. ~ LET GO ~

Let go to receive
Let go to give
Let go to die
Let go to live

Let go to learn
Let go to grow
Let go to understand
Let go to know

Let go to forgive
Let go to trust
Let go to smile
Let go to love

"If you cling to your life, you will lose it;
but if you give up your life for me, you will find it."
[St. Matthew 10:39]

517. ~ A MILITANT RESPONSE TO A PERVASIVE VIOLENCE ~

The mindset of violence pervades our culture. From an early age we are inundated with the philosophy that violent force is necessary, noble, praiseworthy, and even glorious. We grow up playing with toy soldiers, water pistols, cap guns, and BB rifles. We play "Cowboys and Indians" and "War" in our backyards. From kindergarten on we are commanded to say the Pledge of Allegiance and ordered to salute "the stars and stripes." At sporting events we are instructed to stand up and sing exaltations to the glories of missiles and bombs. Our high school ROTC members flip rifles in artistic unison, making their weapons of death look like batons in the hands of circus jugglers. And our young, impressionable minds have hardly begun to contemplate the future and understand life when the military recruiters swarm down upon us like vultures, promising us adventure, college tuition, financial security, and an opportunity to see the world and "serve our country."

Patriotism and violence go hand in hand, and to question one is to question the other. Regardless of our political or religious affiliation, the one thing we are all supposed to agree upon is that America is the greatest country in the world and that we must love it (or leave it). And since this great and glorious nation was founded by violence and bloodshed, then it is only logical to assume that violence and bloodshed must not be necessarily wrong. In fact, violence and bloodshed must necessarily be right and good – at least in defense of our own cause and our own country. Killing is only wrong when others kill us. This is what we are taught, implicitly and explicitly.

These are the insidious ideas that poison our minds even during the innocence of childhood. They are so pervasive and so deeply rooted that even many who are transformed by the Gospel in every other facet of their lives still cannot forsake the idolatry of patriotism and the sin of the sword. They can forsake drugs and drink, fornication and debauchery, lies and lusts, passions and greed – but they cannot relinquish violence and killing. And although they may not be violent killers themselves, they gladly lend wholehearted support to those who violently kill on their behalf. They presume to pray to the Prince of Peace while praising soldiers of war and acquiescing with a government that is bent upon oppression and murder. The tragic fact is that in the minds and hearts of many Christians, the religion of violence still reigns above the religion of the Cross.

Most Bible colleges, Christian universities, and seminaries barely address the essential theological issue of nonviolence. The Gospel imperatives of peace are summarily dismissed with a cursory appeal to Romans 13, the selective highlighting of examples of divine violence in the Old Testament, and the specious and unorthodox rhetoric of "necessary evil." Of course, some of these institutions do specifically teach the "Just War" theory, but when they do so it is done without any serious logical, scriptural, or early Church critique of this demonic idea. The "Just War" theory is simply taught as a historically accepted and logically irrefutable concept that is unquestionably compatible with the Christian Gospel. However, nothing could be further from the truth. But the point here is that one of the most essential aspects of Christian theology – i.e., the sanctity of human life and all that this entails, such as love for enemies and affirmation of the image of God in all people – is not given the same logical, hermeneutical, and moral scrutiny that other peripheral doctrines of the Faith are given. There is something deeply wrong with Christian institutions that offer entire courses on eschatology (the study of the end times), hamartiology (the study of sin), and ecclesiology (the study of the Church) while offering no serious examination of Our Lord's teachings and example regarding peace and nonviolence.

This is why those of us who dare to question the compatibility of violent professions with Christian discipleship are often called "unpatriotic," "cowardly," and even "unorthodox." Society demands that we honor soldiers and praise their "service" as noble. Police officers demand that we unquestionably accept their authority and do what they say. We are conditioned to fear and obey those with uniforms, badges, and guns. And when we dare to suggest to "Christian" soldiers and "Christian" police officers that their professions are at odds with the Gospel, we usually receive visceral responses and emotional reactions condemning even the slightest consideration of such an idea. It's a spiritual sickness, a pathology that has so thoroughly saturated our cultural consciousness that people become irrational and sometimes even violent when we dare to speak the truth of peace.

Therefore, I feel the need to be forthright, provocative, and blunt in my condemnation of violence – especially when it comes to violence that is embraced, justified, and glorified in the name of Our Lord Jesus Christ. Since the philosophy of violence is aggressively and persistently thrust upon us by our culture, our government, and even by many of our churches, I cannot respond by compromising with death or tolerating perversions of the Gospel. I must condemn killing without apology or equivocation. I must condemn false gospels that ignore Our Lord's clear teachings regarding love for neighbors and forgiveness of enemies.

I break swords with rhetorical truth. I melt bullets with the words of Christ. I dismantle bombs with the prayers of the saints. I preach peace and let it burn anything in its way.

I am a militant pacifist, waging war against every demonic ideology that leads to the deliberate destruction of human beings created in the image of God. I am a soldier in JAH army – The Church of Jesus Christ – and I battle against anything that opposes His teachings and His truth. A pervasive evil warrants a militant response, and the Cross was the most militant response to evil that ever occurred. Therefore, as long as you preach violence in the name of my Lord, I will confront you with the Cross and conquer your destruction with His redemptive nails. The bloodshed you embrace will never overcome the shed Blood that saves.

"We demolish arguments and every pretension that sets itself up against the knowledge of God, and we take captive every thought to make it obedient to Christ." [II Corinthians 10:5]

518. ~ TRUE FAITH DOES not THREATEN with FEAR ~

Those who are truly secure in their own faith do not manipulate, threaten, scare, or intimidate others in order to convert them. They simply manifest the love of God and share the beautiful divine truths that they have been blessed to discover. Never trust anyone who presumes to know who is in hell. Only God is omniscient, and to Him alone belong the mysteries of eternal judgment. And let us remember that God's enduring mercies and unfailing love are not limited by time and space. The salvation of the Cross is vertically infinite and horizontally eternal.

519. ~ IGNORANCE, ARROGANCE, and the PILLARS of WISDOM ~

I am not really annoyed by ignorance, because we are all ignorant about numerous things. What annoys me is the arrogance that is too often wedded to ignorance. Humble ignorance can be educated and enlightened, but you can't teach an arrogant fool anything. So never presume to know what another person believes, what they think, or how they feel without first asking them. Set aside your prejudices and judgmental preconceptions. Begin by assuming that you *don't* know rather than presuming that you *do* know. Open up your heart and mind to the inestimable truths that God can teach you through all people. Humility, grace, and love are the three pillars of wisdom, reflecting the true fear and knowledge of God.

520. ~ THE SIMPLICITY of SHARING / THE BURDEN of GREED ~

Sharing is simple, safe, and ultimately self-beneficial. Greed is stressful, dangerous, and ultimately self-defeating. When individuals, societies, and nations feel the need to violently protect their resources and wealth, then those individuals, societies, and nations have far more than they truly need. And when individuals, societies, and nations feel the need to violently repel those who are knocking on their doors, then those individuals, societies, and nations are nothing more than robbers, murderers, and thieves.

Make no mistake: the impoverished of the world do not ask for charity; they only ask for what is rightfully theirs. The only reason that some do not have enough is because others have too much. And the nature of greed dictates that those who have an unjust abundance will oppress, enslave, murder and exploit in order to hoard the cornucopia that should rightfully spill into the laps of the poor.

There are no heavier burdens, and no crueler chains, than unshared wealth. Your wealth is theirs, but your life is your own. Give up what belongs to them so that you may preserve what is truly yours. We find our freedom in justly satisfying the needs of our neighbors.

"Those who love their neighbor as themselves possess nothing more than their neighbor; yet surely, you seem to have great possessions! How else can this be, but that you have preferred your own enjoyment to the consolation of many? For the more you abound in wealth, the more you lack in love. How many could you have delivered from want with but a single ring from your finger? How many households fallen into destitution might you have raised? In just one of your closets there are enough clothes to cover an entire town shivering with cold. You showed no mercy; it will not be shown to you. You opened not your house; you will be expelled from the Kingdom. You gave not your bread; you will not receive eternal life." ~ St. Basil the Great ~ *["On Social Justice"]*

"He has shown you, O man, what is good.
And what does the Lord require of you?
To act justly and to love mercy
and to walk humbly with your God."
[Micah 6:8]

521. ~ NO QUESTIONS ASKED ~

If you pray, I will pray with you
If you cry, I will cry with you
If you beg, I will beg with you
If you forgive, I will forgive with you
If you laugh, I will laugh with you
If you create, I will create with you
If you mourn, I will mourn with you
If you reach out, I will reach out with you
If you hope, I will hope with you
If you struggle, I will struggle with you...

No questions asked.

Whether you are Christian or Muslim,
Atheist or Jew,
Liberal or Conservative,
Black or White,
Man or Woman,
Gay or Straight –

I will stand with you
Whenever you stand
For justice and humanity,
Peace and love,
Life and truth.

I won't hate with you
I won't kill with you
I won't destroy with you
I won't tell lies with you

But when you choose to love,
I will always choose to love with you.

One planet, one people, PLEASE!

522. ~ GIVE ME A DOSE ~

Give me a dose
of holy love.
Fill my veins
with Jesus' blood.
Take me high
beyond this world.
I'll ride on clouds
and heal my soul.

Give me a dose
of heaven's truth.
Save me from
the sins of youth.
I'll kiss the Son
and feel His grace.
He'll wipe these tears
from my face.

Give me a dose
of night divine.
Get me drunk
on saving wine.
Feed me with
the bread of faith.
Because I'm lost
I know I'm saved.

523. ~ A MEDITATION on ELECTION DAY ~

[This meditation was written in the early morning hours of November 6, 2012, but I believe that its message is equally applicable to all subsequent American political elections.]

Today, many Americans will cast their votes and sow their political hopes. Tomorrow, some will celebrate a victory while others mourn a defeat. But those who gloat in their political triumph will inevitably be disappointed. And those who grieve their political loss will eventually realize that the realities of life are not fundamentally altered for better or worse by the vagaries of political tides. Regardless of who is elected, the capriciousness of nature will continue to strike its devastating blows; the injustice of man will perpetually rear its ugly head; and the physical, emotional, and spiritual challenges of daily life will remain ubiquitous obstacles that no politician can remove from our path. Our own sins will still be with us, and sin cannot be cured by political ideology or political personality.

People look at the world and see much that needs to be changed. They look at their country and hope that the next man they elect will provide answers to the problems that face us all. But the masses often institute "change" as the ends rather than the means, and they supplant authentic hope in God with a false god of "hope." In spite of the disillusionment, division, and disappointment it produces, the people nevertheless cling to the idolatry of democracy. When it works in their favor, people extol its virtues. But when democracy produces something contrary to the people's own egotistical desires, then they somehow curse its natural fruit as an unfathomable aberration.

In America, one person's "states rights" is in reality another man's slavery, and one person's "freedom of choice" is actually another individual's violent death. But the clever wording and "enlightened" idealism of America's so-called "founding fathers" have enabled injustice and inhumanity to remain indefinitely obfuscated by legal loopholes, political rhetoric, and unlimited constitutional interpretations. America's "founding fathers" ensured that slave owners and abolitionists, abortionists and unborn liberationists alike could invoke their words and ideals in defense of their own individual causes. But if this was the founding fathers' genius, then it hardly seems to be a genius born of God.

God does not obscure His clear truth in the deceptive mortal philosophies of the wisdom of this world. He did not anoint David to debate Goliath. He did not appoint His avenging angels to argue with the devil. He did not send Moses to negotiate with Pharaoh. Rather, He speaks through prophets who proclaim the unequivocal message of *"thou shalt"* and *"thou shall not!"* And Our Lord taught His disciples to pray, *"Thy Kingdom come, thy will be done, on earth as it is in Heaven."* *[St. Matthew 6:10]* I don't know how many times I have to point this out to my fellow Christian brethren, but the Kingdom of Heaven is *not* a democracy. The King is coming, and He won't be seeking your vote.

On Judgment Day, God will not ask us who we voted for. Instead, Our Lord will show us the hungry and ask if we fed them. He will show us the homeless and ask if we provided them with shelter. He will show us the brokenhearted and ask if we took time to help them heal. He will show us the prisoners and ask if we visited them in their confinements of despair. (Cf. St. Matthew 25:37-46) He will remind us of the words of His servant St. James, who wrote: *"Pure and undefiled religion in the sight of our God and Father is this: to visit orphans and widows in their distress, and to keep oneself unstained by the world."* *[James 1:27]*

I have many sincere Christian friends on all sides of the political spectrum. And in spite of my admonitions to the contrary, they will go out and cast their votes today. And I cannot pass judgment on them, for I am confident that they are acting in good conscience. Whatever happens in the next 24 hours, I will lose no sleep. I know Who sits on the throne, and I know in Whom I place my trust. But it will be sad to see so many of my Christian brethren once again being viscerally divided amongst themselves. It will be sad to see some of my brethren exulting in a hollow political victory and others despairing over an insignificant political defeat. And whatever this particular election produces, I doubt if it will produce healing, justice, peace, and love. How long will you dip your bucket in the harlot's well and then complain that you've been poisoned?

Nothing happens beyond God's control, and yet He affords those created in His divine image the ability to exercise free will. This reality is one of the great theological paradoxes. It is indeed a divine mystery. But some seek to resolve this mystery by attributing to God that which is due to the devil. God has indeed allowed America to establish its form of government, and He will allow Americans to choose their next president. But please do not be so foolish as to believe that God is for one of these candidates over the other. Choose your president, and place your hope in him if you dare. But do not ascribe to our Holy God the machinations of sinful men. God remains on His throne, and He has not anointed the ones who sit atop Babylon's idolatrous altar. God will let the people construct (and elect) their golden calves, but that doesn't mean He is blessing it.

Whatever happens today, regardless of who is elected, the divine imperatives remain unchanged. The solutions to the problems of life do not reside with any president, any Supreme Court, any congress or constitution. The answers lie within *us*. We must love our neighbors. We must love one another. We must serve our fellow man. We must do good to those who persecute us. We must turn the other cheek. We must seek peace and pursue it. We must cling to the Cross and invest in the Kingdom of Heaven rather than in the kingdoms of this world. If we do these things, then we do well, and our hope is not in vain. The battle is already won. But if we trade the life-giving commandments of Christ for political pursuits, then we shall inevitably eat the bread of sorrow tomorrow.

"Everyone thinks of changing the world, but nobody thinks of changing himself." ~ Leo Tolstoy ~

"Never let a politician grant you a favor. He will want to control you forever." ~ Bob Marley (Berhane Selassie) ~

"I owe no duty to forum, campaign, or senate. I stay awake for no public function. I make no effort to occupy a platform. I am no office seeker. I have no desire to smell out political corruption. I shun the voter's booth, the juryman's bench. I break no laws and push no lawsuits; I will not serve as a magistrate or judge. I refuse to do

military service. I desire to rule over no one – I have withdrawn from worldly politics! Now my only politics is spiritual – how that I might be anxious for nothing except to root out all worldly anxieties and care. " ~ Tertullian ~

"And I heard another voice from heaven, saying, Come out of her, my people, that ye be not partakers of her sins, and that ye receive not of her plagues. " [Revelation 18:4]

524. ~ SHAKE and QUAKE ~

Let the truth you speak shake the world, even if you are shaking as you speak the truth. There is nothing in Scripture that states that Jesus was eloquent in speech. We do not know how He sounded when He spoke; but we know what He said and we know that His words contain eternal life. The God that spoke the universe into existence may very well have been trembling of tongue when He spoke to the multitudes during His incarnate sojourn on this earth. So whether you are plagued with fear, trepidation, anxiety, or doubt, simply speak the truth and know that God accompanies you whenever you do so.

525. ~ HOW FREE ARE YOU? ~

It's a blessing to be free. I don't have a pulpit, so I don't have to cater my message to the sensibilities of a particular congregation. I'm not running for office, so I don't have to worry about offending people and losing votes. I'm not trying to make the best seller list, so I don't have to worry about writing to please people. I'm not a journalist, so I don't have to selectively choose politically correct issues to confront. I'm a free man, and therefore I can speak the truth to anyone, anytime, anywhere. The question is: how free are you?

526. ~ NO COERCION or PRESSURE in TRUE RELIGION ~

True religion and authentic spirituality are opposed to coercion and pressure. Our God is not a manipulative God. Our God does not make bargains with His children. Our God is not susceptible to bribery. The love of God cannot be purchased with tithes, deeds, prostrations, fasting, or Church attendance. His love extends to us unconditionally.

And yet true religion and authentic spirituality do involve tremendous struggle and great sacrifice. And all true Christians struggle and sacrifice in their own ways. Some are faithful in attending Divine Liturgy. Some are faithful in financial giving. Some are faithful in private prayer. Some are faithful in fasting. Some are faithful in ascetic disciplines. Some are faithful in deeds of charity and kindness. Some are faithful in labors of love. Some are faithful in artistic endeavors that glorify the Creator. Some are faithful in dispensing wisdom. Some are faithful in defending sound doctrine. Some are faithful in theological discourse. Some are faithful in preaching. And some are faithful in social activism.

Obviously, it would be ideal if every Christian could be faithful in all of these things. And we should all strive to develop a consistent commitment to Liturgical worship, theological truth, social justice, and lives of prayer. But we each possess different gifts, different strengths, different personalities and different passions. And it is important to remember that God is drawing all of us to Himself in His own way and in His own time.

He meets us where we are, as long as we seek to meet Him where He is. And He is omnipresent; He is everywhere.

So it is good and important – and even necessary – to worship Him in the Divine Liturgy, to receive Him in the Holy Eucharist, and to seek Him in prayer, in fasting, and in the needs of our neighbors. But there is no coercion or pressure in any of these things. The true worship of God, the true receptivity of God, and the true pursuit of God flow from hearts of desire, not hearts of obligation. Any form of worship that emanates from duty, guilt, or manipulation is no worship at all.

That's why the Orthodox Christian Faith is so beautiful. We all come with different sins, different failures, different weaknesses, and different strengths to receive the same Body and Blood of Our Lord Jesus Christ. And He receives the weakest with the same mercy that He receives the strongest. He embraces the one who comes at the last hour with the same love as the one who has been faithful from the beginning.

The glorious and liberating paradox of the Gospel is that while we are called to suffer and struggle, we are also promised divine comfort and rest. Hear the precious words of Our Lord:

"If any man will come after Me, let him deny himself, take up his cross daily, and follow Me." [St. Luke 9:23]

"Come unto Me, all who are weary and heavy-laden, and I will give you rest. Take My yoke upon you and learn from Me, for I am gentle and humble in heart, and you will find rest for your souls. For My yoke is easy and My burden is light." [St. Matthew 11:28-30]

527. ~ FAITH IS A CHOICE ~

Faith is a choice. Choosing to believe in spite of tremendous doubts. Choosing Life even when death seems like the easier option. Choosing to love when it's easier to hate. Choosing light when we are surrounded by darkness. Choosing hope when all we feel is despair. Choosing to trust God in spite of our fears. There is nothing easy about faith. But faith is our salvation.

"Lord I believe. Help thou mine unbelief." [St. Mark 9:24]

528. ~ SITUATIONAL FORGIVENESS? ~

We admire and applaud the African-American Christians in Charleston, South Carolina who extended love and forgiveness to the racist murderer who massacred their loved ones as they prayed in Church. We extol such courageous grace as the epitome of Christian virtue. But then we turn around and demand that our government violently retaliates against ISIS, Al Qaeda, and anyone else that threatens our personal welfare and national security.

But true Christian love, genuine Christian forgiveness, and authentic Christian mercy are not selective, situational ethics. For the Christian, they are not circumstantial options. God does not command us to love some enemies and kill others. Christ did not instruct His disciples to forgive certain offenses and avenge others. We are called – yea, *commanded* – to love all people, to forgive all offenses, to retaliate against no enemies, and to repay no evil with a reciprocal evil.

Love is our Christian weapon, and mercy is our divine duty. We may be considered fools in this life, but we shall be eternally victorious.

529. ~ IF THE CROSS IS MY SALVATION... ~

If the Cross is my salvation, then why do I need a gun? Why would I want to potentially send my enemy to hell in order to violently postpone my entrance to heaven?

530. ~ THE PATHOLOGY of PAPER ~

The pathology of our society is most clearly evident in the fact that we are willing to trade our food, art, crafts, skills, services, and souls for paper.

531. ~ REAPERS ~

Fire in the hills
Blood in the streets
Sky of ashes
Tears on our cheeks

Greed in our hearts
Lies in our souls
Truth in the grave
Ghosts of gold

Rivers run red
Trees turn white
We pray for darkness
In this nuclear night

The mountains melt
Birds fall like rain
We who sow violence
Reap our own pain

532. ~ HOLD MY HAND ~

A humble man I am not
A passionate man I am
A loving man I want to be...

Please Lord,
Hold my hand

533. ~ SENSE of JUSTICE ~

If you condemn those who break unjust laws in order to do just things like feed their families, rescue the unborn, and care for the poor, then your understanding of justice is woefully opposed to the justice of God.

534. ~ MEANS and CARING ~

It seems like the people who truly care don't have the means to help, and the people with the means to help don't really seem to care.

535. ~ PLEASE BE KIND TO THE OUTCASTS ~

I have great sympathy for the lonely souls who venture out into the streets to share the gospel, to preach repentance, to proclaim justice, to speak the message of peace, to plead for the unborn child, and to beg for money and food. I think it takes great humility, great faith, and great courage to do so. And most of these people receive nothing but insult and injury for their labors of livelihood and love.

So please be kind to the outcast fanatic who stands alone on the margins of society, crying for the inhumanity that surrounds him. Please be kind to the prophetic voice that is theologically illiterate and socially unskilled. Please be kind to those who hunger for food and for justice, who thirst for water and for life. Please be kind to those who have the spiritual courage to do what all of us should be doing, and who out of social necessity are doing what we all pray we will never have to do ourselves.

It is easy to embrace the incense, the icons, the chalice, and the homily. But it is hard to embrace the putrid piss and sweat and stink of the homeless drunk. It is hard to embrace the radical, unpolished, and unmannered voice of the stentorian Pro-Life revolutionary with his bloody signs of convicting truth. It is hard to embrace the androgynous street walker in search of authentic, unconditional love. It is hard to embrace the raggedy tweaker who hasn't eaten in four days but who would gladly pass up the finest gourmet meal for just one more hit. It is hard to embrace the sidewalk preacher who tells us that we're all going to hell (and yet who could possibly be lonelier?)

Christ is indeed in our midst. But we have dismissed Him as an indigent; we have mocked Him as a lunatic; and we have ignored Him as a stranger who might disrupt our comfort, our convenience, and our social status. If we are not careful, it might not be long before we crucify Him all over again.

"If you fail to recognize Christ in the beggar outside the Church, you will not find Him in the chalice." ~ St. John Chrysostom ~

536. ~ WHAT IS ORTHODOXY? ~

What is Orthodoxy?

Orthodoxy is the depth of spiritual mysticism with the restraint of divine truth.

Orthodoxy is the exaltation of individual freedom within the context of divine community.

Orthodoxy is the profound experience of grace amidst the arduous work of salvation.

Orthodoxy is the recognition of eternal beauty in a fallen, temporal world.

Orthodoxy is the impenetrable security of a Church comprised of sinful, erring, weak, and fallible human beings.

Orthodoxy is the knowledge of a God who transcends the limits of human knowledge.

Orthodoxy is the Sacramental grace that brings heaven to earth and earth to heaven.

Orthodoxy is the ultimate expression of God's unfailing mercy, unconditional love, and universal redemption.

In essence, Orthodoxy is the truest and fullest expression of the will and love of Our Lord Jesus Christ.

"And the Spirit and the bride say, Come. And let him that heareth say, Come. And let him that is thirsty come. And whosoever will, let him take the water of life freely." [Revelation 22:17]

537. ~ DIVINE AFFIRMATION CONQUERS DEMONIC GUILT ~

We seem to have no trouble believing that we're "worthless sinners," yet we struggle to accept the fact that we are divine poems created in the very image of God. But our perfection preceded our sinfulness, and we can't hope to fight sin unless we first understand our originally created nature. The devil's great lie is to convince us that we were created for darkness, guilt, judgment, and shame rather than for divine light, mercy, love, and grace. And because of this lie, the Truth was made incarnate. The Truth walked among us. The Truth healed us, forgave us, and loved us. The Truth allowed us to crucify Him. And the Truth rose again to prove that His love for us is immutably eternal. The Cross is the supreme act of divine affirmation for all the world. If only we would believe it!

"So God created human beings in his own image. In the image of God he created them; male and female he created them." [Genesis 1:27]

"For we are his workmanship, created in Christ Jesus unto good works, which God hath before ordained that we should walk in them." [Ephesians 2:10]

"For God so loved the world, that he gave his only begotten Son, that whosoever believeth in him should not perish, but have everlasting life." [St. John 3:16]

538. ~ LOSING and FINDING ~

You can never lose what's truly yours, and you can never truly possess what you don't already have.

539. ~ WHAT IS HELL? ~

What is hell? Is it real? Who goes there?

I don't know, and I don't really want to speculate. I'd rather lift minds and hearts toward heavenly realities. Damnation and demons are dissipated by the consummation of divine love. So follow Christ and leave the devil behind. Follow truth and let lies perish in its wake. Pursue positive vibes and let negativity burn to ashes. Embrace Life and know that the Resurrection has made death an illusion. Let love be your priority, your focus, and your path. And know that judgment, guilt and fear are eviscerated by the fire of God's eternal embrace.

540. ~ STEP TOWARDS REVOLUTION ~

The first step towards authentic revolution is the destruction of idols that obstruct the path to social justice and spiritual liberation. Religion without repentance is the spirituality of Satan. And peace without justice or justice without peace is the perpetuation of inhumanity, suffering, and evil. Therefore we must break the chains of social injustice and smash the gates of spiritual bondage. And make no mistake: the Gospel is no less social than it is spiritual. How we relate to "the least of these" on earth will determine how we will relate to God in eternity. So love your brother and step towards revolution!

They cry out. We hear, but we don't listen. Until it's too late. Then we pretend that we cared. But we will all cry out eventually – one way or another. Nothing can protect us from death and eternity. So we must listen now, while we can. We must attune our hearts to the suffering that is all around us, to the suffering that is right next to us.

Why should someone have to stand on the corner and beg for bread before we realize they need help? Why should someone have to walk into an abortion clinic before we realize how scared and desperate they are? Why should someone have to enslave themselves to addictions before we realize how badly they are hurting? Why should someone have to put a bullet in their head to get our attention?

So let's not weep for those who died from our own neglect. Let's at least honor their memories by admitting that we didn't give a damn about them while they lived. As the famous gospel song implores:

Give me my flowers
While I yet live
So that I can see the beauty
That they bring

Friends and loved ones
May give me flowers
When I'm sick
Or on my sick bed
But I'd rather have
Just one tulip right now
Than a truck load of roses
When I'm dead

Speak kind words to me
While I can hear them
So that I can hear the beauty
That they bring

542. ~ LIVE and LOVE, LOVE and LIVE ~

Live and love. Love and live. What is life divorced from love? And what is love divorced from life? You can no more separate life from love than you can separate water from the ocean, blue from the sky, light from the sun, or beauty from truth. Love is fruitfulness. Life is abundance. Enjoy it and embrace the fullness thereof!

543. ~ THE ESSENCE of REVOLUTION ~

The essence of revolution is destructive. Revolution is the tearing down of ideas, systems, values, and establishments that so offend a moral, intellectual, or emotional sensibility that the destruction of the present offense is prioritized above the rational planning of a future solution. But this is a natural thing, for cancer is only cured when a malignancy is destroyed, and a gangrenous appendage is amputated in order to save the body. It is a fundamental principle of both the physical and spiritual world that destruction is the precursor to healing. And there will never be spiritual healing apart from the revolutionary act of destroying individual and institutional idols.

544. ~ SHALLOWNESS and DEPTH ~

Shallow people need deep truth, and deep problems require simple solutions. We elect educated fools to solve the complexities that can only be remedied by obedience to divine simplicity. How long will we continue to seek answers from people who don't even understand the question?

545. ~ CORAZON ~

You welcomed me
with open arms,
in spite of
Cortez and Crocket,
Pope and Polk.

Freely you shared
your food and wine
your music and herb
your beauty and truth
your grace and love.

I climbed your pyramids.
I swam your oceans.
I tripped in your mountains.
I reveled in your Cervecerias.
I venerated the shroud of your Holy Virgin.
And my heart was both broken and healed
by your "morenas bellas."

Such unconditional love
and loyal friendship
from a country so wounded
and a people so steeped in suffering.

You are a land of passion,
a nation of joy,
a people of resilience,
a country of dignity and strength.

You gave me your heart,
and I carry it with me always.

Mexico...
If there is one word to describe you
Dios mio, it is "Corazon!"

546. ~ WHO CAN FIGHT THE DEMONS? ~

Who can fight the demons? The saints and monks and holy Priests, yes. But spiritual warfare is not only for the clergy, but for all children of Christ. We are all called to wage war against violence, sin, death, and the devil. Of course we dare not do so according to our own power or strength. But neither should we shrink from engaging the enemy out of cowardice or fear. We are militant sheep conscripted in the army of the Conquering Lion! So JAH children, arise and fight! Trust in God and fret not because of evildoers!

"Let God arise and let His enemies be scattered! Let those who hate Him flee before Him. As smoke is driven away, so drive them away. As wax melts before the fire, so let the wicked perish before God." [Psalm 68:1-2]

547. ~ THOUGHTS on the RIOTING in FERGUSON, MISSOURI ~
[November 25, 2014]

A justice system that is predicated on violent force will not produce justice or peace. A society that seeks to maintain law and order by violent force will inevitably produce anarchy and chaos. Using violence to stop violence only perpetuates violence. Violence is a sickness that cannot cure itself. Violence can only be cured with peace.

So here's Mr. Policeman with his gun, saying, "I'm gonna use this here gun to stop violence!" But for some strange reason, Mr. Policeman often does more to disrupt the peace than to preserve the peace. So then here comes Mr. Right Reverend Protester Preacher Man who says: "That policeman shot someone, and that wasn't peaceful! So we need to riot and loot and shoot in order to teach these policemen a lesson about peace!" And then more Mr. Policemans come running along with more guns, saying: "We're gonna use these here guns to stop this rioting and looting and shooting!" And on and on it goes.

There's nothing peaceful or just about a nation whose laws protect wealth and punish poverty. There's nothing peaceful or just about a society that disproportionately imprisons and aborts African Americans. There's nothing peaceful or just about a government that bombs innocent civilians overseas and legalizes the slaughter of its own unborn innocents right here in America. There's nothing peaceful or just about a legal system that prosecutes the poor and protects the prosperous.

And there's nothing revolutionary about rioting. When you riot, you play right into the system's hands. When you use violence to express your outrage at violence, then you merely perpetuate violence; and thus you increase the likelihood that you will continue to be victimized by violence. As Dr. Martin Luther King, Jr. said:

"The limitations of riots, aside from their immorality, is that they cannot win and their participants know it. Hence, rioting is not revolutionary but reactionary, because it invites defeat. It may involve an emotional catharsis, but it is inevitably followed by a sense of futility."

My heart goes out to the family of Michael Brown. I cannot imagine how devastated I would be if one of my own sons were violently killed. All violent deaths are tragic. And whenever a human life is violently destroyed, we are all in some sense responsible. Violence only occurs because we collectively embrace it, justify it, defend it, rely upon it – or at best – we are apathetic about it.

And when we turn a blind eye to the thousands of unarmed, unborn Black babies who are murdered every day in this country, then our outrage about the death of Michael Brown seems to ring hollow. If we remain apathetic about the millions of innocent children who are slaughtered in the womb year after year, then our moral indignation about anything else smacks of hypocrisy. If we cannot clearly see the evil of abortion, then our perspective of social justice is deeply flawed, and I doubt if God hears our laments or honors our tears.

Let us pray for peace in Ferguson, Missouri. Let us pray for peace for Michael Brown's family. Let us pray for peace in the womb. Let us pray for peace in the world. Let us pray for peace; let us work for peace; and let us commit to peace. Let us renounce violence at every turn, opposing injustice and evil only with the just and righteous methods of Christian power and Christian truth.

"Lord have mercy."

548. ~ TWO CONTRASTING VERSIONS of THE GOSPEL ~

There are two contrasting versions of the Gospel. One version says that God doesn't like you very much. In fact, He hates you and is poised to send down His wrath upon you. But for some reason, even though you don't deserve it, God decided to pour out His wrath upon His own Son instead of upon you. And after releasing His divine anger upon Christ, His wrath has been appeased and He now no longer hates you. And this version of the Gospel is somehow presented as a "gospel of grace and salvation."

Personally, I'm not too interested in a God who created me, then hated me after He created me, and then punished His own innocent Son in order that He may love me again. I'll leave such a perverse and capricious god to be worshipped by others.

But there is another version of the Gospel which says that God loves you. In fact, He loves you so much that He became a man, died, and rose again in order to liberate you from sin and death. You are not God's enemy, but rather His precious child who has been held captive by sin, death, and the lies of the devil. The wrath of God is not stored up for *you*, but rather for those principalities and forces that have barred you from your Father's loving embrace. (After all, hell was created not for man but for the devil and his demons. Cf. St. Matthew 25:41) And this version of the Gospel teaches that grace and salvation are supremely epitomized by the redemptive and sacrificial love of Christ on the Cross.

So, will you believe in a gospel that divides the Holy Trinity and has God punishing His own Son? Will you believe in a gospel that portrays a divine judge who cannot stand to look at you until a debt has been paid? Will you believe in a gospel that defines grace as a judicial transaction that has placated an angry god who would otherwise view you with disgust?

Or, will you believe in a Gospel that portrays the infinite, immutable, and unconditional love of the Father for His own children, a Gospel that is infused with the truth of the Creator's unfailing mercy which extends eternally to all mankind?

Our view of the Gospel determines how we view God, ourselves, and others. Healing, love, peace, and brotherhood don't flow from a doctrine that conditions people to believe that they are worthless sinners who deserve the wrath of a vengeful deity. And people who have such a perverse view of themselves and a perverse view of God usually tend to have a perverse view of others and a perverse view of life.

But those who understand their inherent worth as divine image bearers are inclined to worship the Father out of love rather than fear; and they are inclined to treat their fellow man with dignity, compassion and respect. Those who have a proper view of the Gospel don't burn heretics at the stake, they don't divide humanity based on doctrine and dogma, they don't feel threatened by those who have chosen a different path than their own, and they don't wage wars and kill those that profess a different religion or creed. Those who have truly found salvation in Christ understand that God has called them to simply love all men with the same love with which God has loved them.

God does not dangle you over the flames of hell as by the thread of a spider's web, as Jonathan Edwards declared. Rather, God descended from heaven to earth in order to embrace you in His forgiving arms and carry you with Him into eternal peace. Our Lord's outstretched, crucified hands were not an indication of a punitive, forensic transaction; they were proof of an infinite, divine love. This is the good news that can save the world.

549. ~ THE ONLY REVOLUTIONARY SOLUTION ~

You can't burn down injustice. You can't vote away injustice. You can't destroy injustice with bullets and bombs. You can't kill injustice with violence and hate. You can't eliminate injustice with politics. You can't stop injustice with militarism and might.

When you see injustice, get pissed off. Cry, shout, and lift your voice to the heavens. Organize, protest, march, and by all means let your voice be heard. But know this: the only thing that can truly conquer injustice is love. Love the oppressed and love the oppressor. Love your neighbor and love one another.

Love is the only revolutionary solution.

550. ~ CAST FROM THE MOUNTAINTOP ~

I am a romantic, and I suffer from the curse of being enslaved to the ideal. My understanding of faith and my understanding of love are precariously predicated upon the illusion of the mountaintop. As long as I can ignore the reality of the abyss below me, I can love and believe and preach and hope. But the abyss always beckons. And the winds of life inevitably knock me from my perch of peace and contentment. I tumble towards the darkness below. The mountain that I have adored from its peak now bruises and scars me as I fall broken upon its rocks. Now I curse the mountain. I can't see the light anymore. I no longer see the glorious view of life. I am beaten, I am tormented, and the abyss of darkness rises up to swallow me.

My faith and my love will now be revealed as either veracity or lie. Will I still believe? Will I still love? Will I cling to hope even as I am falling into despair?

I have mastered the art of preaching from the mountaintop. But I have no idea how to preach from the abyss. But life is comprised equally of darkness and light. If I can't believe and hope and love in my pain and through my crosses, then the Christ I proclaim is nothing more than a phantom, an absurd concoction of an accidental cosmic imagination.

So God keeps knocking me off the precipice of romanticism. This loving God is sometimes a cruel and clever devil. But I trust that there is purpose behind the pain God inflicts, whereas Satan would have us perpetually serve the gods of purposeless pleasures. I guess God breaks me to teach me the reality of faith. I pray for the strength and courage to keep learning these brutal lessons. But I really don't want to be a student anymore. I want to tell God to keep the damn degree and leave me alone! Leave me alone with my illusions. Leave me alone to bathe in my romantic fantasies. Don't disrupt my dreams with the realities of life. What good is my heart if it's continually broken? How much longer can a broken heart continue to beat?

Oh how badly I want a faith that doesn't require such suffering and pain! Oh how badly I want a faith that doesn't require a cross! But there is no such thing. That much I do know. My problem is that I want to idealize the Cross and make it aesthetically pleasing and spiritually comfortable. Let me venerate icons of the Cross. Let me wear a Cross around my neck. Let me preach the message of the Cross. Let me kiss the Cross and extol the Cross and tattoo the Cross on my body. Just don't let me have to pick it up and carry it! Just don't let the Cross give me splinters! Just don't let me be nailed to it! Allow me to romanticize the Cross, but please protect me from having to actually experience it!

But God isn't interested in my demands. He has other things in store for me. Will I love Him anyway? I must. How can I understand anything or love anything apart from Him? But I honestly don't know if I will make it this time. I will choose to believe anyway. I lay my sinful, broken, bleeding heart before Christ and ask Him to do what He will with it. Perhaps He will crush it. Perhaps He will heal it. But my heart is His, and that's all that matters. So the devil be damned! He will never take what belongs to God!

I am being cast from the mountaintop, but it is the hand of God that has sent me tumbling. And the hand of God is a nailed-scarred hand. And it is also a resurrected hand. So let His hand cast me into a divine darkness. How can we appreciate heaven without tasting hell? The divine hand that has thrust me on this descent is the divine hand that will also raise me up into eternity. I believe this. I know this. I must.

But hope is such a dangerous thing. I don't want to hope anymore. I am so tired of all this climbing and all this falling. Screw the view. Let me stay in the valley where there are no illusions and no disappointments. But I can't; because the same divine hand that casts me down is the same divine hand that pushes me to get back up and climb again. God how I hate it! And God how thankful I am for it!

551. ~ FREEDOM and SLAVERY ~

As long as you believe that you must kill to preserve your freedom, then you will always be a slave. Christ was imprisoned, tortured, and crucified; yet He was the freest man who ever walked the earth. Although He had the power to destroy his enemies, He responded to them only with love. And He beckons us to come and follow Him. But most would rather violently preserve the illusion of a carnal freedom than relinquish the sword in order to liberate their souls.

552. ~ HELP ONE ANOTHER ~

Life could be so easy if people just helped each other. So much suffering could be avoided, so much good could be preserved, so much joy could be produced, so much happiness could be found – if people just helped each other. But we are enslaved to conditions and judgments and grudges and demands. We justify the sin of selfishness with the sin of self-righteousness. God showers us with unconditional love, but we turn around and demand that others earn our kindness.

God forgive me for not doing more. God forgive me for not helping others more than I should. God forgive me for not sacrificing more in order to help those in need. I must have failed miserably. I guess that's why God has to keep teaching me through these sufferings. Sometimes I think it must be a blessing to have a heart of stone. Sometimes life just hurts too damn much.

And this is supposed to be such a happy season. But every year people suffer much worse than I do during Christmas, and I pay no mind. So shame on me for complaining. Who am I to grumble when I have so much to be thankful for?

All I want to say is that if you can help somebody today, please do so. Even if they have wronged you, hurt you, or failed you – even if they don't deserve your mercy – please, help them anyway.

Do you think the saints attained holiness on their own? They all had abundant help. We could all be saints if we loved one another more, if we helped one another along the way, if we forgave each other. I know it's not easy to love the unlovable. But if you loved us anyway, you might be surprised at what God can do with that.

553. ~ A GLORIOUS HOPE for SAINTS and SINNERS ~

Some seek answers in deserts, mountains, and caves – in ascetic abstinence and disciplined solitude. Others seek answers in cities, aesthetic pursuits, and epicurean delights – in pleasure and in the company of pleasure seekers. And the truth is always to be found in the middle. We cannot understand heaven unless our feet are planted on the earth, and we cannot understand earth unless our hearts cry out for heaven. We cannot know beauty apart from suffering, and we cannot understand suffering apart from beauty. God did not create man and remain aloof in His heaven. He became a man and walked the earth. He tasted and felt and desired and struggled and suffered and died and rose again. Herein is the truth: "Emmanuel" – God is with us. Heaven meets earth. Divinity meets humanity. A glorious hope for saints and sinners alike.

554. ~ BURN ELECTION DAY! ~

To Babylon kings
I'll never bow down
I trust no politician
White or brown

They ask for my vote
But they want my mind
Soul snatchers, vampires
Oppressing mankind

One Lord I serve
One God alone
JAH Kingdom come
Christ on the throne

I burn the White House
And Capitol too
With prayers of fire
Through and through

Chant down the system
Burn election day!
Christian soldiers arise
Don't vote…
Fast, prophesy, and pray!

555. ~ GIVE THEM LIFE ~

Give them life
Let them be born
Preserve their lives
Free them from war

556. ~ IDEOLOGY and FRIENDSHIP ~

If someone ceases to be your friend because of ideological differences, then that reveals both the insecurity of their beliefs and their ignorance of the true meaning of friendship.

557. ~ CHRISTIANS and GUNS ~

If we truly believe in the power and salvation of the Cross, then why do we need guns? The only answer is that we don't really believe in the power and salvation of the Cross. Instead, we believe that our temporal lives must be preserved and defended at all costs. We don't really believe in a just God who will welcome all the innocently and unjustly slain into His eternal comfort. And we don't really want to sacrifice our own lives to defend the innocent. We'd rather defend them with violence so that we won't have to suffer and die ourselves. It's easy to be noble and brave with a cross around our neck and our finger on the trigger. But it's much harder to confront injustice and evil with the Cross alone.

The bottom line is that reliance on premeditated violence is always contrary to the Gospel and contrary to the teachings and example of Christ. I don't care how many priests "bless" weapons of destruction; those weapons are not blessed by God. Perhaps the priests are praying for those weapons to not function, to not kill. Only in that case could I acquiesce with such a blessing of weapons.

As for hunting, I don't really see the need for it in today's world. I'm not opposed to hunting for food when absolutely necessary. And killing animals is certainly not the same thing as killing human beings created in the very image of God. However, I believe Christians should always err on the side of life affirmation. Christ came to conquer sin and death, and we should give witness to this victory of life over death with all of our actions and thoughts. Our Lord has redeemed all of creation. So even when we kill animals we are replicating our fallen state rather than our redemptive state.

People also need to remember that when they choose to keep guns in their homes then they are allowing for the possibility that those guns will contribute to accidental shootings or to suicides. As Christians, are we willing to take that risk? Is such a risk commensurate with our primary mission to bring salvation, healing, life and liberation to all men?

I am willing to trust God with my own soul and with the souls of my family members. I am willing to trust God with the souls of the guilty and innocent alike. I am therefore prepared not to kill, not to destroy, not to violently deny anyone their life for any reason. I pray for the strength and courage to confront evil and aggression only with my own life and only with the militant weapons of the Holy Spirit.

Guns ultimately only protect us from the Cross. And apart from the Cross we are damned.

558. ~ LUNACY, FANATICISM, SANITY, and REASON ~

Be careful about trying to heal lunatics. Be careful about trying to temper the zeal of fanatics. After all, they said that John the Baptist was mentally ill; so they cured him by decapitation. They said that Jesus was too radical, so they moderated Him with the Cross.

In the Orthodox tradition there have been many "fools for Christ." But I've never heard of any saint who was called "a sane and reasonable one for Christ." Not because sanity and reason are opposed to God, but because the truly reasonable and the truly sane are always opposed to the insanity of the world.

559. ~ ART IS NOT A COMPETITION ~

Art should never be a competition. What point is there in trying to judge what is more beautiful: a hummingbird or a rose, a sunset or a sunrise, the mountains or the sea? The Creator intends for us to appreciate them all. There is beauty in simplicity and there is beauty in complexity. There is beauty in darkness and there is beauty in light. There is beauty in life; and because of the Redemption, there is beauty even in death. Nothing negates the aesthetic sensibility more than turning beauty into a contest. True artists do not create out of a desire to defeat others. True artists create simply because their soul demands it.

560. ~ INCLUSIVE HEAVEN / EXCLUSIVE HELL ~

I have no problem believing in an inclusive heaven, because in the presence of God's infinite mercy all sinners will learn to love one another. Therefore I think that the best preparation for heaven is to learn to love one another here on earth. According the Gospels our entrance to eternal life will not be predicated upon our recitation of the Nicene Creed, upon our theological acumen, or upon whether or not we 'accepted Jesus as our personal Lord and Savior.' According to the Gospels our entrance to heaven will be determined by our compassion for the suffering, by our mercy for others, and by our love for our neighbors. It is hell, not heaven, that is exclusive. The devil will not accept the tolerant, the merciful, the kind and the just. Hell excludes the compassionate and the loving. But heaven welcomes all sinners who have the love of Christ in their hearts.

561. ~ CRIMINALS ~

When the guilty rule, the innocent are called "unruly." Under unjust laws the innocent are condemned as outlaws. When criminals are in power the powerless are considered criminals.

562. ~ THANKFULNESS ~

I have so much to be thankful for. But if I had to sum it up, I'd have to say that I'm thankful that God has blessed me with a life that makes it easy for me to be thankful. Many people in this world live without gratitude because they've never experienced the love, grace, kindness, and mercy that I have been blessed to experience throughout the years. So it's easy for me to say that everyone else should be grateful, because even in my darkest hours I know that I am loved by my family, my friends, and my God. But there are many people in the world who have been abandoned by family, forsaken by friends, and condemned by those who claim to represent God and His Church. So they live without gratitude because they struggle to find something to be grateful for. So let us be thankful for the gift of thankfulness. If our hearts are truly grateful today, then we are blessed beyond measure. The state of gratitude is a state of grace, a divine gift that we should continuously cultivate and never take for granted.

563. ~ PHILOSOPHY of LIFE ~

I support anything that affirms human life, protects human life, and enhances the quality of human life. I realize that such a philosophy is not politically expedient. It probably won't get you elected, but respecting *human* life is indispensable to *eternal* life.

564. ~ SALVATION IN, THROUGH, and FROM THE CHURCH ~

To be simultaneously saved in and through the Church as we are also being saved from the Church. This is our holy paradox.

In other words, the Church is full of sinners, full of problems, full of failure, and full of historical atrocities. The Church is not immune from fighting and conflict, corrupt clergy, division and discord. And yet only within the Church do we have the Sacramental graces, the sound doctrine, and the vital fellowship that we need to lead us to eternal life.

The Church is the Ark of our salvation, and within its confines there is a foul and obnoxious odor. But this Ark is leading us to heaven, and we dare not abandon ship. Perhaps that's one of the many reasons why we use so much incense in the Orthodox Church.

565. ~ DEHUMANIZING THE GOSPEL ~

Collectively dehumanize them, and then it becomes permissible to collectively kill them. Label them "commies," "fascists," "terrorists," "thugs," "criminals," "illegals," "animals," "fetuses," etc. Then it becomes quite easy to bomb, torture, execute, and abort them. In fact, it even becomes "honorable" to do so. But if we dare to look behind the façade of every dehumanizing label ascribed to people that interfere with our own welfare or comfort, we will see the countenance and image of Our Lord Jesus Christ staring back at us. The enemy aggressor and the innocent unborn child equally bear the image of God. Therefore to premeditatedly and intentionally kill another human being is nothing less than a heretical act of iconoclasm. When we kill, we crucify the image of God and invert the message of the Cross. And all the patriotic flag waving, anthem singing, pledge reciting, law invoking, nationalistic rationalizations will not excuse such blasphemy on Judgment Day.

566. ~ DIVISION IS EXHAUSTING ~

I've grown tired of viewing the world in terms of "believers" and "unbelievers," the "saved" and the "lost," the "righteous" and the "damned." The Lord will indeed separate the sheep from the goats in the end. But until that day, our duty is simply to love one another. If we truly look at humanity through the lens of the Gospel, we will only see images of God struggling in a fallen world just like we are. We are all in this thing together. It may be difficult to lift up your fellow man, but it's much easier than pulling up the wheat with the tares. There are too many people trying to preach people into heaven while they are content to let people suffer here on earth. Rather than helping their neighbors, they divide people into categories of "good" and "bad," "worthy" and "unworthy," "sinners" and "saints." But I have found such divisions to be utterly exhausting. That's why I prefer to leave division to God.

567. ~ ONE GOD, ONE PEOPLE, ONE FAITH, ONE LOVE ~

Who saves? God saves. Who is God? Who can know?

Many holy names. Many holy paths. But One God, One people, One faith, One love.

We must come to God only through Christ. (St. John 14:6) We must enter through the narrow gate. (St. Matthew 7:13-14) But we must understand that the love of Christ is far more comprehensive than we can ever imagine. And the narrow gate is infinitely broader than the judgments and prejudices of the human heart.

The path to heaven is paved with paradox. It is a narrow and difficult road, to be sure; and yet it may nevertheless prove to be all encompassing in the end.

568. ~ THE TORMENTS of WEALTH and POVERTY ~

Wealth discomfits the human spirit as much as poverty does. Man's soul is equally tormented by both the tragedy of desperate need and the tragedy of unshared abundance.

569. ~ SILENCE THE VIOLENCE ~

Silence the violence
It's time to pray
Silence the violence
Chase the devil away

Silence the violence
Hear the children sing
Silence the violence
Let the Church bells ring

Silence the violence
Politician, hush your lies
Silence the violence
There's peace in the skies

Silence the violence
Wars can't win
Silence the violence
Love rides on the wind

570. ~ NOW IS A TIME ~

Now is a time to fight
Now is a time to pray
Now is a time to stand
But now is not a time to hate

Now is a time to love
Now is a time to forgive
Now is a time to die
But now is not a time to kill

There was a time for wrath
There was a time for war
But when God became a man
He said, "No more. No more."

571. ~ NOTE on PEACE ~

Peace is not a liberal ideal. Peace is not a conservative ideal. Peace is not the product of political pragmatism or bourgeois "activism." Peace does not selectively condemn some wars and apathetically tolerate others. Peace does not pit rich against poor, nation against nation, mother against child, and political affiliation against political affiliation. Peace does not wave the party banner and use it as a weapon to destroy the opposition. Peace does not curse one presidential warmonger and then excuse the next. Peace does not affirm the rights of some to the exclusion of the rights of all. Peace is a divine imperative rooted in Our Lord Jesus Christ, "the Prince of Peace."

Peace begins in our hearts, extends to our homes, and flows through every aspect of our lives. Peace is always others-centered, never self-centered. Peace is the inviolate respect for all human life – in all of life's circumstances and throughout every stage of life's existence. Peace is inextricably bound to love and to God – bound to God who is Peace and who is Love. Peace is not a social cause. Peace is the indispensible spiritual foundation upon which the future of humanity is predicated.

"Peace I leave with you; my peace I give you. I do not give to you as the world gives. Do not let your hearts be troubled and do not be afraid... Peace be with you." [St. John 14:27; St. Luke 24:36]

572. ~ BLINDNESS and LOVE ~

Those on the right often seem blind to the reality of racism, and those on the left often seem blind because they can't see anything other than racism. Politics is poison people! Free your minds from political prejudices and look at life through the eyes of Christ. We will never bring love to the world until we see the world with a heart of love.

There is no justice in violence. There is no restoration in revenge. There is no redemption in retaliation. There is no solution in death. Hate won't cure injustice. Killing won't heal cruelty. And wrong will never recompense wrongs.

The apostle says: *"Be angry and sin not; let not the sun go down on your wrath." [Ephesians 4:26]* So don't forsake your righteous anger. By all means, let the fires of justice burn brightly. Let the flames of God incinerate everything that is opposed to truth and love, humanity and life. But know this: the divine fires are fueled by tears of compassion, hearts of forgiveness, and lives of peace.

"Do not be deceived: God is not mocked. Whatever a man sows that shall he also reap." [Galatians 6:7] Therefore let us have faith in the inevitable reciprocity of the divine harvest. We are not called to bear the scythe of violence; we are called to bear the Cross of peace and love. And as we bear the Cross, we know without a doubt that the Lord will soon return. He will indeed come riding – riding in glory – riding upon the clouds. He will come riding with a sword in His mouth. He will come riding to cut down all who without repentance, shame, or remorse cut down the innocent of the earth.

And do not be confused. When Christ said that *"the meek shall inherit the earth,"* He was not referring to the timid, the cowardly, or the weak of heart. He was referring instead to those who have every natural right to violently defend themselves but who choose to die rather than to kill. He was speaking of those who have the mortal means to avenge the innocent but who choose to sacrifice their own lives rather than to shed the blood of others. He was prophesying the blessed fate of those who relinquish finite, earthly, and physical strength in order to gain the eternal company of divine love. The "meek" are not the impotent and the feeble; the "meek" are those who volitionally forsake the power of temporal might in order to defer to the eternal power of divine justice.

Love is the only truly revolutionary weapon. Love exposes cowards. Love makes the demons tremble. Love dies without killing because it knows that it will forever rise again and again and again… Love willingly dies because it knows that it can never really be killed.

We live in an age where justice is rare and peace is rarer. We cannot escape the incessant mantra of the masses: *"No justice, no peace!"* But the masses don't understand that peace is always the foundation of justice. The pseudo-revolutionaries always invert the ontology of the divine moral imperatives, putting justice before peace and brotherhood before love. But apart from the divine pillars of peace and love, a "just brotherhood" will end up looking like Stalin's "Socialism in One Country" or Jim Jones' "Guyana paradise."

Love one another and be at peace. Do this, and justice will *"roll on like a river, righteousness like a never-ending stream!"* *[Amos 5:24]*

LOVE is REVOLUTION.

"Above all, love each other deeply,
because love covers over a multitude of sins."
[I Peter 4:8]

574. ~ NOTHING ELSE MATTERS ~

Love is just, and justice is peace, and peace is love, and love is life – always life, *always* life. Apart from life, nothing else matters.

575. ~ THERE'S NO SUCH THING AS A "NEGATIVE PEACE" ~

There is no such thing as a negative peace or a peaceful negativity. True peace is proactive, vigilant, sacrificial, and uncompromising. Peace is the active cultivation of positive thoughts, positive prayers, positive actions, and a positive life.

576. ~ PURITY, PLEASURE, LIFE and HOLINESS ~

To condemn romance, passion, orgasm, and ecstasy is to condemn life itself. Life would not exist apart from such pleasures and joys. When we reject those things which perpetuate life, enrich life, and sustain life, we are in some real sense rejecting holiness. Purity can be found in abstinence, but purity can also be found in indulgence. Some choose cavernous solitude, and others choose sensual companionship. What matters is not the act, but the intention. If it is done with love, purity of heart, and a conviction for life affirmation, it is indeed holy.

577. ~ TO BEAR THE IMAGE of GOD ~

To bear the image of God is simultaneously the greatest burden and the greatest blessing, the greatest agony and the greatest gift.

578. ~ POVERTY, BEGGING, and GIVING ~

Involuntary poverty is not a Christian ideal, and the Gospels never indicate such a thing. There are certain monks that take a voluntary vow of poverty in order to grow closer to God. But this is not a vow that all Christians can take. Most of us have families to feed and support, so we are not all called to the monastic life. But what we *are* all called to do is give to the poor, without condition, as we are able to do so. It is not our place to lecture the poor about "dignity," "work ethic," and "personal responsibility." We should simply see the face of Christ in the poor and do what we can to help them. And we should always know that we too could find ourselves stripped of our comforts, wealth, and possessions at any moment.

The Golden Rule is the standard. If we would want others to help us, then we should help others as much as we can. The hungry man is enslaved to hunger, and our job is to liberate him with food. The homeless man is enslaved to the elements, and our job is to liberate him with shelter. The sick man is enslaved to sickness, and our job is to liberate him with medicine and healing. We cannot presume to preach heavenly realities without meeting earthly needs.

Jesus said, *"The poor you will have with you always."[St. Matthew 26:11]* But that doesn't mean we shouldn't work to eradicate poverty and labor to change social structures that create such hellish conditions. We should always seek nonviolent Christian solutions to evil systems that perpetuate misery and suffering.

It requires divine humility to beg, and we should never be too proud or self-righteous to hold out our hands and request help. And we should never be too self-centered and self-righteous to refuse help to those that ask. As Christians we should be humble enough to beg and gracious enough to give. And in truly taking care of one another, we can be an example to the world.

"Brother Francis," I said, "All my life there's been something I've found perplexing. Enlighten me. Some people do not beg, and even if offered charity they refuse to accept it. Others accept alms although they do not beg. And still others beg actively. Which is right?"

"Holy humility," said Francis, "requires that you hold out your hand to beg and that you accept what is given you Brother Leo. The rest is arrogance. The rich have an obligation to the poor; let them fulfill their obligation."[From the book St. Francis by Nikos Kazantzakis]

579. ~ LAMBS and WOLVES ~

Because we are lambs governed by the Shepherd, we are ungovernable by the wolves of this world.

580. ~ A CONSTANT STRUGGLE or A DAMNABLE CONTENTMENT? ~

We pray to the saints for comfort, peace, and protection. And yet we know that even the saints were not protected from suffering, agony, and death. We know that we cannot evade the Cross, so our prayer is simply that God will enable us to endure it. Those that preceded us did not pave the way, they merely revealed the way. To know the path of salvation doesn't lessen the difficulty of the journey. And yet to not know is to always be lost. Many recognize the eternal highway, but they reject it because it's a rocky road; it's a bitter path to trod. Thus they prefer to amble down the broad and smooth roads that lead to nowhere. So remember that it's better to be found constantly struggling towards salvation than to be lost to an eternity of damnable contentment.

581. ~ PREPARATION and EXPECTATION ~

When you prepare for war, you must be prepared to be a casualty of war. Whether you flash a soldier's salute, a policeman's badge, or a gangster's colors, if you live by the sword you must expect to die by the sword. The violent death of any human being grieves me deeply. But when you make a conscious choice to trust in bullets and bombs, then why are you shocked when you reap the violent fruit of the violent path you have chosen?

A police officer killed in the line of duty is tragic; but it's no more tragic than the violent deaths of those on the receiving end of policemen's violence. A uniform and a badge do not magically make a person more human or more of a divine image bearer than anyone else. How long will we continue to mourn those slain in the "act of duty" while refusing to condemn these violent "duties" that perpetuate bloodshed and killing?

Put away your gun! Put away your badge! Take off your uniform and take up the Cross! Let us arm ourselves with the weapons of the Spirit, preparing to sacrifice our own lives without violently sacrificing the lives of others.

582. ~ LOOK OUT FOR JAH LOVE ~

Look out for JAH love,
It won't leave you alone.
Look out for JAH love,
A love that melts stone.

Look out for JAH love,
It's a consuming fire.
Look out for JAH love,
It transcends desire.

Look out for JAH love,
It will set you apart.
Look out for JAH love,
It will break your heart.

Look out for JAH love,
It crushes as it saves.
Look out for JAH love,
It points to the grave.

Look out for JAH love,
It comes for the weak.
Look out for JAH love,
It burns, but it heals.

Have you ever met a saint? I've met saints in books and dreams and scriptures and prayers. And you probably have too, even if you didn't know it. But I am truly blessed, because I have known a saint face to face, personally, in this world, in this terrestrial realm. And not only have I known him, but I have loved him and he has loved me. No one, other than my children, has shown me the pure love of Christ like this great man. I know that I shouldn't use the word "great" in reference to any human being. Only God is great. But my father-in-law is the greatest man I know. He is a living saint. And that's no exaggeration.

I have sometimes been asked this question: "If you could meet anyone in the world, who would it be?" I don't even have to think about the answer. I've already met him. I know him. He's my father-in-law, Mr. Toby Hite III.

I have spent thousands of hours sitting at his feet, listening to his wisdom, seeking his advice, and discussing every imaginable aspect of life. He tolerates my passionate views, he listens patiently to my ridiculous opinions, he endures my judgmental rants, and then he gently offers me words of truth infused with mercy and grace – words of necessary truth that are always packaged with golden-gilded kindness.

My father-in-law has been blind since he was six months old, but I've never met anyone who can see as well as he can. He grew up dirt poor in the Mississippi Delta. He experienced numerous prejudices thrust upon him because of race, "disability," and poverty. If any man has a right to be angry and bitter, certainly he does. And yet I have never heard him utter a single grievance, a single word of self-pity, or a single sentiment that would indicate that he blames anything or anyone else for the hardships he has endured and continues to endure. God how I wish that he would complain, just a little bit! How small I feel when I go on and on about my petty problems while he endures such trials with nothing but dignity and grace.

The man can discuss any subject you bring up – politics, sports, movies, books, art, philosophy, and history. History! My goodness, the man could teach history at any Ivy League school. And not only does he know the facts of history, but he knows the truth of history. And that's a rare thing, believe me.

He already knows more than you or I do. But what makes him brilliant is that he's not afraid to say that he doesn't know something. His profound intellect fuels a perpetual desire to learn. Unlike most of us, he's never trying to prove his mental prowess, he's never trying to win a debate, he's not trying to pass himself off as "enlightened" or "in the know." He loves learning new things, and his openness of mind emanates from the strength of his heart and the security of his soul.

God has sent me divine assistance throughout my life, but my father-in-law is my living guardian angel. If you ever want to make a pilgrimage to meet a holy man, find a way to make it to Hazlehurst, Mississippi and spend some time with him. He would think it absurd for me to say such a thing. He would reject everything I'm saying about his saintliness. In this world of self-proclaimed prophets and self-aggrandizing politicians, my father-in-law is an aberration. He cares nothing about prominence or praise. He is a humble follower of Our Lord Jesus Christ. And he would be the first to tell anyone to look to Jesus and not to him. But I have never known anyone who reflects the love and grace and truth of Christ like he does.

I have no excuse for my sins, because Jesus has met me face to face through Mr. Toby Hite III. I love you so much "Big Dad!" Words cannot express it. I hope that he knows how much I love him. It would make him uncomfortable for me to tell him face to face, although I have tried. I think he knows. I hope so. He has always been there for me. As Kierkegaard wrote:

"When the heart is full you should not grudgingly and loftily – short-changing the other – injure him by pressing your lips together in silence. You should let the mouth speak out of the abundance of the heart. You should not be ashamed of your feelings and still less of honestly giving to each one his due." [Works of Love]

I have had three fathers in my life: my biological father, my "Papa;" my father-in-law, "Big Dad;" and God the Father in Heaven. I guess Our Lord knew that I would need an extra helping of fatherly love and guidance in my life. And I am so very thankful for that.

Albert Camus wrote, *"There are people who vindicate the world, who help others live just by their presence."* Well, that's my father-in-law. He has more than blessed and enriched my life; he has helped me to live.

584. ~ DEMONIC LIES and DIVINE REDEMPTION ~

As long as the devil can convince us that we were born in sin, then we are defeated at the outset. Satan will do everything he can to convince us that we are worthless, hopeless, and destined to sin and failure. But the truth is that we have been created in the very image of God. As sinful as we may be, nothing can eradicate the image of God that is indelibly imprinted upon us. When the biblical writers stated that they were "conceived in sin" and "sinful from the womb," they were using hyperbole to express how deeply they felt their sinfulness and how deeply they felt the need for divine redemption. But these verses are by no means to be interpreted as a literal dogma that unborn babies, infants, and innocent children are "totally depraved." These verses by no means indicate that human beings were created inherently deserving of some sort of eternal hellfire. Our Lord himself said that hell was created not for man, but for the devil and his demons (St. Matthew 25:41).

This is why Orthodox theology is so important. Western Christian heresies have conditioned people to view themselves and others with judgment, condemnation, fear, and guilt. But if we were really born as inherently awful as Luther, Calvin, and their subsequent sycophants say we are, then I wonder why God felt the need to go through such pains to redeem us? Yes, we need the Cross. We need it desperately. But the fact that we need the Cross so desperately proves that there is something within us that is worth making the Cross necessary to begin with.

585. ~ GRATITUDE and THIRST ~

To thank God for water is the spirit of Christian gratitude; but to thank God for thirst is the spirit of the saints. When we realize that our greatest needs are our greatest blessings, then we will be saved. For in hunger and thirst and desire and pain, the soul is crying out for God. And the soul that cries out to God will undoubtedly be redeemed.

586. ~ PURPOSE ~

Many people squander their lives trying to figure out what their purpose is. Don't worry about what your purpose is, just know that your life has purpose. Once you realize that your life has purpose then you will live a purposeful life.

587. ~ TEACHERS and LEARNERS ~

We are all teachers and we are all learners. The problem is that those who are always learning don't realize how much they have to teach, and those who presume to teach don't realize how much they have to learn.

588. ~ THE FOCUS of TRUE BELIEVERS ~

Some presume to fly to heaven on the gossamer wings of their virtues. Some presume to be raised to heaven by virtue of their faith. And others seek entrance to eternity by the power of their confession or their knowledge of the Creed. But true believers are not consumed with thoughts of heaven and hell. They are too focused on loving God in this life, and they are too busy loving their neighbors here on earth.

589. ~ THE INSTRUMENTS of HELL and THE AIMS of HEAVEN ~

Violence can never be tamed or controlled. Once violence is embraced as a means to an end, there will be no end to the violent means that are used. Man throws a rock and complains when his enemy pulls out a knife. Man pulls out a knife and complains when his enemy pulls out a sword. Man pulls out a sword and complains when his enemy draws a gun. Man draws a gun and complains when his enemy throws a grenade. Man throws a grenade and complains when his enemy drops a bomb. Man drops a bomb and complains when his enemy nukes the world.

Violence knows no limits. It is foolish to think that you can rely upon the instruments of hell and accomplish the aims of heaven.

590. ~ THE TEMPTATION to READJUST TRUE THEOLOGY ~

All true theology is always easier to preach than it is to practice. But it is unorthodox to readjust theology in order to make it compatible with our comforts, desires, or perceived abilities. There is nothing easy about loving our enemies and blessing those that persecute us. There is nothing easy about sacrificing our own lives on behalf of others. There is nothing easy about truly and perpetually forgiving those that repeatedly hurt us. There is nothing easy about following Christ. There is nothing easy about the Cross.

There is always a great temptation to ignore, dismiss, or reinterpret the message of Our Lord in order to make it palatable to our own reasoning and will. There is a temptation to say: "Yes, Christ tells us to forgive, but surely there must be a limit. Yes, Christ tells us to serve our neighbors, but surely we must set some conditions. Yes, Christ tells us to love our enemies, but surely some enemies are so evil that they must be killed." But Christ doesn't give us such qualifications. His words are clear enough, and His example removes any ambiguity that we may try to impose upon the clarity of His teachings.

The Gospel is quite demanding, and yet it is the only thing that can truly liberate us and bring us peace. But we want a Gospel that gives us access to eternity while allowing us to violently preserve our mortal existence. We want a Gospel that comforts us with heavenly promises while allowing us to violently preserve earthly interests. We want a Savior who died to save humanity but who nevertheless sanctions our right to kill to save ourselves and others. But no such Gospel exists.

The Gospel is mystically paradoxical; for while Christ calls us to take up our cross and follow Him (St. Luke 9:23), He also says that His yoke is easy and His burden is light (St. Matthew 11:30). Through the hardships of forgiveness, through the struggles of love, through the sacrifices of service, and through the trials of nonviolence we will find peace, comfort, joy and salvation. Through the apparent folly of the Cross we may lose our lives while ultimately finding eternal life.

I do not pretend to have even begun to truly live out the Gospel. I do not pretend to have mastered Christian forgiveness, Christian service, and Christian love. I do not pretend to have learned what it means to truly be a peacemaker. And I certainly don't pretend that I have learned how to take up my cross on a daily basis. But I do know what Our Lord has commanded. And although I often fail to obey Him, I dare not dismiss His words or reinterpret the Gospel so that it accommodates my failures and sins.

"Lord Jesus Christ, Son of God, have mercy on me a sinner."

591. ~ THE TSAR, THE EMPEROR, CHRIST and THE STATE ~

I love the Tsar and I love the Emperor, but I love Christ much more. I love the land and I love the people, but the state can go to hell. The Prince of Peace is my only Lord, and my only allegiance is as a citizen of His kingdom. God bless those who preserve the Orthodox Faith with missions, charities, seminaries and Churches. But when they take up the sword in the name of the Cross, then they blaspheme the Savior and undermine the very Faith they claim to defend.

592. ~ LIGHT and DARKNESS ~

If we want to bathe in the light, we must learn to dance in the darkness.

593. ~ HOLINESS IS A JOURNEY ~

Holiness is not a divinely stamped legal transaction; it is rather a divinely authored spiritual journey.

594. ~ MY EXPERIENCE WITH ISLAM ~

I visited a Mosque for about a year during my years in between Protestantism and my journey to Orthodoxy. I was befriended by many Muslims there, and I found them to be very devout, peace loving people who shared many of the same cultural, social, and moral concerns as Christians. I never got the sense that this Muslim community was in any way "liberal" or "moderate." They were very serious and "conservative" about their faith, and yet they were equally serious about condemning terrorism. The community was comprised of African Americans and Muslims of Middle Eastern descent. Women were an active and vocal part of the community. They were modest, humble, deeply knowledgeable about their religion, and in no way felt oppressed or discriminated against. The Imam was African American. This was a Sunni Muslim community, not the NOI (Nation of Islam).

There was one occasion when a visiting Imam from Egypt came to speak. Before he began, he commanded all the women to be moved to a separate room. The women always sat and prayed behind the men, and they were fine with that, as this is the universal practice within Islam. But when this Egyptian Imam commanded them to go to another room, a few of the women protested. But the Imam refused to speak until they moved. So they just got up and exited the Mosque completely. That was interesting, to say the least. Most people – men and women – seemed to accept the situation, as this Egyptian Imam was considered a high authority on Islam. There was a slight controversy afterward, but most of the women chose to humbly submit to the minor request rather than rise up in rebellion and uproar. How Muslim women view and respond to Islamic teaching and worship is an internal issue within their own religion. As long as people are not being violated, oppressed, and abused then it is not for me to pass judgment on the faith practices of others.

I read the Qur'an a few times. I thought that for the most part it was full of good practical and spiritual wisdom. However, as a Christian, I found certain parts quite disturbing. I tried hard to reconcile Islam with Christianity, but there were just too many verses in the Qur'an that blatantly contradicted and undermined true Christian doctrine. And then there were the violent verses. Unlike the Bible, where the Old Testament is fulfilled and clarified by the New Testament, the Qur'an has no such delineation. The violent verses are not dismissed contextually or explained away as allegorical. They are an inherent part of mainstream Islamic theology and history. No way around that. It always struck me as odd that Islamic prayers and Muslim greetings are centered on peace and the mercy of Allah, but when it comes to infidels there is no peace and no mercy. Quite different from what Jesus says about loving our enemies and blessing those that persecute us. Of course, most Christians sadly embrace the philosophy of the sword just as much as Muslims do, which is tragic.

I was very moved by the Sufi tradition within Islam. Sufism is very mystical and very peace oriented. I found a lot of similarity between the Sufis and the Quakers. If I had ever been convinced to become a Muslim, it would have been the Sufis that persuaded me. But I guess in the end I realized that all true peace only comes from Christ and through Christ. How could I ever truly pursue peace by forsaking the Prince of Peace, the God who became man to bring man peace?

But I can definitely see the appeal of Islam. Its theology is much simpler than Christian theology. The Qur'an is a much shorter scriptural text than the Bible, and much easier to understand. There is less doctrinal division amongst Muslims, although the divisions that do exist are quite profound. In Islam, there is an emphasis on the universality of human brotherhood that is very appealing to those who have suffered from the evils of racism. When you walk into a Christian Church for the first time, you never know what you will find. But Muslims can enter a Mosque anywhere in the world for Friday prayer, and they will be welcomed regardless of race or nationality. They will know how to pray and what to expect. The worship is universally consistent, and Arabic is the universal language that unites all Muslims of all nations. The simplicity of it all is very attractive to people who believe in God and simply want to worship in peace with their fellow man. And there is a logical consistency to Islamic theology that makes it quite difficult for a Muslim to reject the Islamic view of a monotheistic God in order to embrace the Mysteries of Orthodox Christianity, such as the Holy Eucharist and the Holy Trinity.

Recently I ran into some old Muslim friends from the Mosque I once regularly visited. I told them that I had been baptized into the Ethiopian Orthodox Church, but that the important thing is that we all comprise one human race created by One God. They smiled and nodded their heads and said they were very happy for me. There are many good Muslims in the world. I am glad to call some of them my friends – and yes, even my brothers.

That is my limited experience with Islam.

595. ~ SNIPER ~

The sniper sights the image of God in his crosshairs, makes a conscious decision to dehumanize him, ignores the Cross that stares him in the face, then pulls the trigger and sends his fellow man to a violent death. Such actions may be compatible with a godless government, but they are by no means compatible with the Gospel of Jesus Christ. The sniper may not necessarily be acting like a coward (although in many cases he is), but he most certainly isn't acting like a Christian. And all the Hollywood glorifications, military medals, and presidential praises won't help these blood shedders on Judgment Day.

"You have heard that it was said, 'You shall love your neighbor and hate your enemy.' "But I say to you, love your enemies and pray for those who persecute you, so that you may be sons of your Father who is in heaven; for He causes His sun to rise on the evil and the good, and sends rain on the righteous and the unrighteous." [St. Matthew 5:43-45]

596. ~ DID YOU MAKE IT IN THIS WORLD? ~

Did you make it in this world? Neither did I. Will you be remembered by this world? Neither will I. Have you succeeded in the eyes of this world? Neither have I.

But I don't really mind, because I know that money and fame and glory and praise aren't true. I was born from clay and I will return to the clay. That's all I am – as worthless as the earth from which I was formed, and yet nevertheless the very image of God.

So whether you're rich or poor, weak or strong, praised or scorned, walk with divine purpose; because it matters not what this world thinks about you. Tread ever forward towards the Cross, and in eternity you will find yourself marching with angels.

"The world and its desires pass away, but whoever does the will of God lives forever." [I John 2:17]

597. ~ BECAUSE MAN CAN CHOOSE ~

The winter cannot put away its frost
Nor the summer its scorching heat
The fox cannot slake its thirst for hen
Nor the bear dull its vicious claws
The ocean's waves cannot be tamed
Nor the fires of hell be cooled

But the thief can become an honest man
And the harlot can be made chaste
The adulterer can return to fidelity
And the racist can learn to love
And the world can perhaps one day know peace
Because man can always choose…
To put away his sword

598. ~ PEOPLE STOP! ~

People, stop fighting
The angels are crying
There's blood in the streets
And children are dying

People, stop killing
The blood tears are spilling
We can stop this madness
If only we're willing

People, start praying
Repent of this slaying
Let's hear the Lord's words
Let's please start obeying

599. ~ WE ARE BROKEN PEOPLE ~

We are broken people with broken hearts, breaking the hearts of others in an attempt to heal ourselves. We hurt so badly that we inevitably hurt others in the effort to assuage our own pain and guilt. And in the midst of all our misery and suffering, our brutality and evil, our addictions and despair, our inhumanity and injustice, our ignorance and hardness of heart, Our Lord Jesus approaches us with open arms. It doesn't matter if we're the president or a prostitute, a preacher or a panhandler – we're all suffering together from sin and sorrow, heartache and pain. Oh how Our Lord loves us so!

The Christian who truly knows the love of Christ does not say, "It is us against them;" he says, "It is all of us together who equally need Him." Whether we're doctors or shaman or psychologists or priests, we are all in equal need of divine healing. And Christ is ever in our midst, with His outstretched, all embracing, crucified arms of unconditional love. At the foot of the Cross all sin and judgment and condemnation and guilt are eternally eviscerated. At the foot of the Cross all sinners are reconciled both to one another and to their God.

Our Lord suffered so much for us because He realizes how much we suffer.

600. ~ BRAVE INTOLERANCE? ~

I think it's ridiculous for people to talk about how "brave" it is to mock religion in the name of free speech. I'm all for people's right to do so, but I don't see anything particularly brave about it. In fact, I've always thought it to be quite cowardly. There's nothing brave about being rude, insensitive, and bigoted towards people of faith (or towards anyone else for that matter.) Nobody should be murdered for being a bigot. But intolerance has a funny way of breeding intolerance. And the irony is that intolerant folks often print offensive and intolerant material believing they are exalting tolerance in the process. And as foolish and as misguided as they are, they no more deserve to be murdered than people of faith deserve to be ridiculed.

The violence of the pen can be as evil as the violence of the sword; and Our Lord clearly said that those who live by the sword will die by the sword (St. Matthew 26:52). Violence, prejudice, bigotry and hate will inevitably yield the same. I take no pleasure in the cruel aspects of the law of the harvest. I simply acknowledge it as the inviolate law that it is.

601. ~ THE POVERTY of OUR OWN SOULS ~

Every human being deserves to have good food, clean water, decent clothes, and a roof over their head. It doesn't matter what choices they've made, what addictions they may have, or what lifestyles they choose to live. The fact is that all human beings are the very image of God, and therefore all human beings deserve the basic necessities of life. Sin is its own worst punishment, and we are all sinners who will face the Judgment of God in due time. There is nothing Christian about viewing homelessness, hunger, and destitution as some sort of divine reciprocity for poor choices and bad decisions. So the next time you see the beggar on the corner, don't pacify your conscience with the self-righteous assumption that he is there because he deserves to be there. Instead, thank God that He has graced you to survive your own sins and your own poor choices through the help and support of loyal family and faithful friends. The fact is that those who are desperate enough to beg are merely reflections of our own self-righteous, apathetic, judgmental indifference to suffering. In the faces of the poor we see the poverty of our own souls.

602. ~ CREATIVE ATTRACTION ~

I am constantly amazed by the talents and spiritual consciousness of so many of my dear friends. I rejoice in their successes, and I feel blessed to know them. They have all helped me and encouraged me in my own life, and I'd like to believe that I have somehow encouraged them along the way as well. Some of my friends are famous and successful, and others are struggling – as I am – simply to make ends meet. But all of my friends are equally creative, equally talented in their own ways, and equally passionate about glorifying God and serving others.

We attract that which we are attracted to. And when I take inventory of the friends that God has blessed me with throughout my life, then I realize I must be desiring the right things.

603. ~ I WILL NOT COMPROMISE ~

I will not compromise on peace, I will not compromise on life, and I will not compromise on love. If it is truly Orthodox then it will be truly nonviolent. If it is truly Orthodox then it will be authentically life-affirming. If it is truly Orthodox then it will be immovably rooted in love. Any doctrine that is truly divine and divinely true will conform to peace, life, and love. All other doctrines will be winnowed by the calescent winds of hell.

604. ~ YOU ARE NOT A FAILURE! ~

You are not a failure. You are a child of God. You might sin, struggle, stumble, and fall; but you are *not* a failure. You are the very image of God. You are so valuable that God became a man and died on the Cross for you. You are so precious in His sight that He extends His unfailing mercy and offers His unconditional love to you.

The judgments of society are not the judgments of Our Lord. The fickle loyalty of man is not the abiding love of God. The demands of society are not the peace of the Savior. The standards of the world are not the expectations of our Creator. Sometimes those who try the hardest are those who suffer the most. Those who strive to *"seek peace and pursue it" [I Peter 3:11]* are those who experience the greatest violence. Those who proclaim righteousness are those who may fall into the worst of sins. Those who desire holiness are those who may succumb to the foulest temptations. And those who truly serve a heavenly cause are those who may suffer the worst earthly hardships.

When people say: "His ministry failed;" "Their marriage failed;" "Their children failed" etc., they speak the words of the devil rather than the words of God. For *"Our Lord works all things together for the good of those who love Him." [Romans 8:28]* The works of true love and genuine service to others are never failures. Ministry and marriage are not businesses that predicate success upon financial gain, popular following, or longevity. What appears to be stable on the outside may be rotten at the core, and what appears to be broken on the surface may be rock solid underneath. There are angels among us disguised in rags, and many saints are hidden in destitution and homelessness. And there are true servants of God whose families have fractured, whose friends have forsaken them, and whose lives appear to be "failures" in the eyes of those that see not through the eyes of Christ.

So remember that God does not look at any of His children as "failures." His love is too pure, too great, too faithful and too profound. He looks upon us with unconditional love – not because we deserve it, not because we have earned it, not because we are "holy" and not because we are "wretched." God loves mankind because He is God and He has fashioned us with divine love. If we know this truth, we will rise up and march forward with faith and hope – regardless of our circumstances, setbacks, sins or mistakes. The love of God is ever faithful and ever sure. Let nothing cause us to think otherwise.

605. ~ DEPRESSION, ILLNESS, LIGHT, DARKNESS, LIFE & FAITH ~

When I was in the throes of depression I didn't think life was worth living. Then I had a heart attack, and I prayed that I would stay alive just to feel anything at all again. And God answered my prayer, and I lived; and I was so very thankful for life. And then life eventually hurt some more, and once again I wondered if death would be better than pain. I contemplated God's mercy and God's heaven and I thought that I would rather be there than here. And then I had another heart attack. And I thought about my children, and my wife, and my friends, and all the things I love so much – simple things like good food and good music and good beer and good books and good movies and playing my guitar and everything so mystical and sweet about the Divine Liturgy (even though I don't make it to Church nearly enough.) And I prayed to God that I would live a little bit longer. And He answered me again. And I was thankful for life again – until I got depressed again, and life hurt again. And then I longed for heaven so deeply, even though I doubted if I belonged there.

But the spring emerged, the honeysuckle sprouted, and life was intoxicatingly sweet once more. And I made my children laugh and they made me happy, as they always do. And my wife and I found our moments of love. And I remembered my true friends and I reached out to them and they were there for me, as always. And the reggae and Santana and the wine and a good smoke now and then helped me to remember that life is good. But the darkness still accompanies every day. This is true for all of us. And life is just so damn painful at times.

I had three more pre-emptive heart procedures after my first two heart attacks (angioplasties and stents). You would think that by now I would have learned to never desire death again. But my faith is weak. Very weak. I could never end my own life by my own hand. My philosophical and spiritual commitment to the sanctity of life is too strong. And if nothing else, my sinful pride would prevent me from allowing my enemies the pleasure of rejoicing at such an act of utter hypocrisy. But I confess that I vacillate between tears of gratitude for life's radiant blessings and tears of despondency over the darkness that sometimes threatens to imprison my soul.

I want to go to heaven, and yet I cannot imagine a heaven without my children. But I know that to be with Christ is all that matters. He alone is my salvation and my joy. This is what I know in my head. But my heart wants life here on earth, with all the blessings of Eden and none of the curses of the fall.

I have one daughter already in heaven, but three children are here with me now. My father and my grandmothers and my blessed mother-in-law are in heaven, and some departed friends too. And yet I have family and friends still with me in this life – living and struggling through dusk and dawn, striving as I am to endure sunlight hope and midnight doubts.

We are all co-laborers in this trod through creation. Christ is in our midst! He is and always shall be! He is risen! I know this. And yet His Cross beckons. We cannot escape it. If only we could purchase salvation with a bullet, a confession, a creed, or a sinner's prayer. But it will never be that easy. It will always be a struggle. And I guess that's the point. Struggle is salvation and salvation is struggle. What else did Our Lord mean when He said, *"Follow me"*? I don't want to struggle. I just want to be saved. I guess Jesus loves me too much to let me off that easily. And I am thankful for that. Sometimes.

"Wake up and live, y'all! Wake up and live!"
~ Bob Marley (Berhane Selassie) ~

606. ~ COMFORT, COURAGE, and PROPHETIC FIRE ~

The problem with most Christian leaders today is not that they preach to the choir, but that they don't preach the prophetic fire. Too many preachers are pursuing popularity, esteem, praise and success rather than speaking the disruptive, uncomfortable, and divinely disturbing truth. But the real prophets rarely have comfortable lives, secure careers, and huge followings. True prophets tend to receive ridicule, scorn, and bullets rather than the praise and honor of men. But such are the souls that God uses to further His kingdom. So be courageous Christian leaders! The Kingdom of Heaven will not belong to the cowardly or the weak of heart.

There is no shame in trepidation and fear, but there *is* shame in compromising truth in order to preserve our comfort, our status, and our standing in the world. In extreme anxiety and agonizing fear, Our Lord sweated drops of blood in the Garden of Gethsemane. But He went to the Cross anyway, without relinquishing His truth. So let us tremble and let us fear; but let us never bow to evil or cede the truth upon which our souls and the souls of humanity depend.

607. ~ AN ABSURD, EVIL, and IRRATIONAL LIE ~

The absurd, evil, and irrational lie of abortion: *"Life will ruin your life."* Only demons could convince people to view life as their enemy and death as their friend.

608. ~ FALSE RELIGION, LIES, and SERVANTS of HELL ~

Any religion that claims to have a monopoly on the Creator is a false religion. Anyone who claims to be the sole inheritor of divine truth is a proselytizer of lies. And anyone who kills in the name of God is serving hell rather than heaven.

609. ~ JAH FIRE ~

Love is fire. Truth is fire. Justice is fire. Christ is fire. So just preach JAH fire and let it do it's purifying, purging, redemptive and reconciling work.

"I have come to cast fire upon the earth; and how I wish it were already kindled!" [St. Luke 12:49]

"Our God is a consuming fire." [Hebrews 12:29]

610. ~ DOWNTOWN ~

Downtown, late at night
Vixens and vampires
Pleasure and fright

Downtown, late at night
Preachers and dealers
Salvation and plight

Downtown, late at night
Temptation and horror
Blindness and sight

Downtown, late at night
Sirens and rhythms
Lovers and fights

Downtown, late at night
Life and death
Wrong and right

Downtown, late at night
Parties and poverty
Depth and height

Downtown, late at night
Sin and Redemption
Darkness and light

611. ~ GET OUT of OUR WAY ~

If you won't help us
while you're livin' high
then don't tell us you care
as we suffer and die

If you won't serve us
then get out of our way
and if you can't love us
don't tell us you'll pray

Just live your life
and serve your gods
but we are suffering
from your hearts so hard

The diamonds and gold
that adorn your necks
are chains that bind you
and break our backs

So keep your riches
and turn your face
but in the name of God
stop preaching about grace

612. ~ THE BLESSINGS of THE JOURNEY ~

We often become so obsessed with the destination that we fail to realize the blessings of the journey. It doesn't really matter what we achieve, what matters is how we live. It's not the outcome of our lives that's important, it's our approach to life that God is concerned about. Too many people are waiting for their blessings to come when God is already blessing them right where they are. Sometimes the greatest blessings are the crosses that God gives us to bear, for in bearing our crosses we draw closer to Him. And what greater blessing is there than nearness to Our Lord?

Don't be deceived by the world's definition of achievement. What God values and what the world values are often two very different things. I have seen Christians lose their faith and lose their lives because they allowed human opinions and society's standards to dictate their definition of success. Because they failed to amass temporal achievements, earthly awards, social status and financial gain, they fell into despair, believing that God and life had forsaken them. How tragic!

So rejoice in the journey, regardless of the circumstances and difficulties of life. God is with us wherever we are, and His unconditional love is all the blessing we will ever really need. Strive toward heaven and let the world and its judgments go to hell.

613. ~ NUANCED PERSPECTIVES and GOSPEL VISION ~

I believe it's very important to listen to the opposition and consider different points of view. Peace and justice are too often the casualties of narrow minded intransigence. Life is full of nuance, and we are all prejudiced by our own perspectives. So trying hard to understand the opinions of others is a crucial step towards the realization of true brotherhood and authentic social justice.

However, when we're talking about issues of human rights, there's really not much grey area. Enslaving, bombing, exterminating, and aborting innocent human lives is either just or unjust, either violent or nonviolent, either right or wrong. Attempting to nuance our way around the clear issues of the sanctity of human life produces insane and horrific realities. It was "nuance" that led the Supreme Court to view Dred Scott as 3/5ths of a person. It was "nuance" that justified the American government's murder of over 100,000 Japanese civilians with atomic bombs. And it's "nuance" that enables otherwise rational people to defend the legality of slaughtering innocent children in the womb. (And regarding abortion, the "nuanced" cases of rape, incest, and risk to the life of the mother account for less than 1% of all abortions performed in this country. So let's not let these "nuanced" exceptions legitimize the rule of abortion on demand. Too many babies are being "nuanced" to pieces in the womb.)

People do indeed see things differently, but as Christians our vision should be shaped by the Gospel. Our vision should be shaped by love and compassion. And our vision should be keenly focused on "the least of these," for Our Lord said: *"Verily I say unto you, Inasmuch as ye have done it unto one of the least of these my brethren, ye have done it unto me."* [St. Matthew 25:40] If we cannot see the humanity of our brethren – regardless of race, religion, nationality, gender, age, sexual orientation, or birth status – then there is something woefully wrong with our vision.

I'm not willing to simply say, "Well, slave owners just saw things differently; pedophiles just see things differently; abortionists just see things differently; etc." Where human life, authentic freedom, and true human dignity are threatened, I must as a follower of Christ stand up and unequivocally proclaim the right to life, the right to liberty, and the message of justice and peace. I will listen to other perspectives and I will tolerate dissent; but I will make no concessions regarding human rights, nonviolence, and the sanctity of life.

614. ~ PEACE IN THE *WORLD PEACE* IN THE WOMB ~

If we cannot understand the fundamental necessity of peace in the womb, if we cannot understand and embrace the unity of mother and unborn child, if we cannot recognize the humanity of innocent and vulnerable unborn human lives, then it is disingenuous to pontificate about peace in the world. If we condone, defend, justify or ignore the cruel, bloody and violently unnatural division of babies from their own mothers, then how can we expect to see the end of violence, war, injustice and oppression in society? There can be no peace in the world until there is peace in the womb.

"The so-called right to abortion has pitted mothers against their children and women against men. It has sown violence and discord at the heart of the most intimate human relationships. It has derogated the father's role in an increasingly fatherless society. It has portrayed the greatest of gifts – a child – as a competitor, an intrusion, and an inconvenience. It has accorded mothers unfettered dominion over the independent lives of their physically dependent sons and daughters. And, in granting this unconscionable power, it has exposed many women to unjust and selfish demands from their husbands or other sexual partners. Human rights are not a privilege conferred by government. They are every human being's entitlement by virtue of their humanity. The right to life does not depend, and must not be declared to be contingent, on the pleasure of anyone else, not even a parent or a sovereign. I feel that the greatest destroyer of peace today is abortion, because it is a war against the child – a direct killing of the innocent child – murder by the mother herself. And if we accept that a mother can kill even her own child, how can we tell other people not to kill one another?" ~ Mother Teresa ~

615. ~ SIDING with THE DEVIL ~

I don't care whose side you're on: if you side with the gun then you side with the devil. And I will never side with those who side with the devil.

616. ~ VACUOUS SOLUTION ~

There is hardly a more vacuous solution to the problem of evil than "jobs and education." Some of the worst evils the world has ever known have been committed by PhD's and CEO's.

617. ~ NO GREATER BLASPHEMY ~

There is no greater blasphemy and no greater idolatry than rejecting the Body and Blood of Christ while trusting in the sin of war and glorifying the bodies and bloodshed that perpetuate war. Repent of this madness!

618. ~ OF CHURCH and CONSTITUTION ~

I'm not too worried about assaults on a human constitution that gave birth to a government that has perpetually assaulted humanity. I seek guidance and truth from the Scriptures and the Church, not from the Supreme Court or human presidents. So the vagaries, vicissitudes, whims, and tides of Babylon's fickle government and capricious juridical nature will not vex my heart or disturb my peace of mind.

Where there is violence and injustice, I will stand in opposition. Where there is righteousness and peace, I will celebrate and rejoice. I wish happiness for others as I wish it for myself; but any happiness that is predicated upon a contradiction of the divine will and order is a tenuous happiness that inevitably turns into misery.

Babylon's ostensible freedoms always come with heavy chains – "freedoms" that are as confused and contradictory as her "enlightened" founders who carried pens of liberty in one hand and whips of oppression in the other.

619. ~ WEEP and FIND JOY ~

Life is much too serious to take too seriously. Tears without laughter are streams of poison. So let us laugh a little bit every day, knowing that nothing can negate the divine love that smiles upon us. Even Jesus seemed to prefer the company of joyous profligates over the company of humorless Pharisees. We must weep for our sins, and then laugh at the rest of it. How can we endure the thorns if we can't find joy in everything else?

620. ~ PERSONAL RESPONSIBILITY? ~

I'm all for personal responsibility. But let's take personal responsibility for ourselves without self-righteously condemning those who might not be blessed with the same favorable circumstances we may have. By all means, let us pull ourselves up by our own bootstraps; but let us dare not scorn those whose feet have been cut off. It's fine to be self-sufficient and to be proud of oneself. But beware of being so self-congratulatory that you sit in judgment of your less fortunate neighbors.

I think that what many people miss in all their preaching about "personal responsibility" is the word "personal." Somehow they make the leap from taking personal responsibility for themselves to lecturing everyone else about personal responsibility. At that point it becomes less about "personal" responsibility and more about some sort of coercive collective ethos that seems to diametrically contradict the very small-government, conservative values upon which their "personal responsibility" doctrine is predicated.

621. ~ MANY REFLECTIONS, ONE SUN ~

There are many reflections of sunlight, but only one sun. The man who thinks that he alone receives the sun's rays is a fool, and so is the man who denies the sun altogether.

622. ~ VIOLENCE, ANARCHY, and DEMOCRACY ~

Guns and riots have not wreaked as much havoc as gavels and robes. All the canons of history have not caused as much chaos as that which is born in courtrooms. Judges and juries have done more violence than tyrants and kings. It is not anarchy, but "law and order" that murders truth and causes the blood of innocents to flow. Democracy is nothing more than the lynch mob of the masses, perpetually sowing the evil seeds of strange fruit. Babylon "legality" is a crime against Divinity and a war on humanity. And if we don't rebel we become companions of hell.

623. ~ POLITICAL CHANGE and SOCIAL CHANGE ~

Never mistake political change for social change. Political change merely replaces one evil with another evil; but social change replaces injustice with justice, lies with truth, and death with life. So don't get it confused. Peace and humanity are never ushered in with the bullet or the ballet; they are the result of compassion, mercy, sacrifice and love – values that politics and war must crush in order to thrive.

624. ~ ALIENATING OUR PRO-LIFE COMRADES ~

In the fight against abortion, we must not alienate our Pro-Life comrades. The religious and moral views that shape our commitment to the sanctity of Life should never be used as a wedge to drive away fellow Pro-Life advocates. The issue at hand is protecting women and unborn children from the evil of abortion. Let's not get distracted with sectarian religious debates or peripheral moral arguments about homosexuality or gay marriage. The unborn child who is about to be murdered doesn't care if his rescuer is Catholic or Protestant, gay or straight, atheist or Christian. Unborn children and their mothers just need somebody to speak up for them and intervene on their behalves. The sidewalks of abortion clinics are dark and lonely places. Pro-Life activists need all the supportive company they can get. The transvestite or atheist who speaks up for unborn children and desperate mothers may be closer to the Kingdom than the professing Christian who ignores their plight.

625. ~ CHRISTIANITY and HUMAN RIGHTS ~

No true Christian will ever be on the wrong side of human rights. A Christian may be deceived, confused, misguided, and wrong about many things, but he will never be wrong about the sanctity of human life and human liberty. I don't care how well they know their Bibles, how often they go to Church, or how loudly they profess the name of Our Lord – slave owners, warmongers, abortionists (and those that support them) are not disciples of the Prince of Peace.

626. ~ REFLECTIONS on MISSED OPPORTUNITIES ~

I sometimes reflect on all the missed opportunities I've had in my life, enticed by feelings of disappointment, shame, and regret. Why did I quit the basketball team during my senior year of high school? Why did I drop out of college and never finish? Why didn't I ever call that one particular girl who gave me her number (and unlike all the others, seemed to actually share so much in common with me?)

But then I think of the life I have now – with all of the trials and agony and struggles and pain that have accompanied it – and I realize that the divine hand was leading me all along. I now understand that those "lost opportunities" were actually blessings in disguise. They were all used by God to lead me to Christ, to lead me to my wife, to lead me to fatherhood, to lead me to Orthodoxy, and by His grace – to lead me to eternal life.

I believe in fairy tales, but I also believe in horror stories. And I've come to realize that the most productive human lives are forged by daydreams and nightmares alike. There is no Resurrection without the Cross.

So don't lament what you think you've missed. Rejoice in the reality that God is with you now, today, at this very moment. If we find our present joy in Him, then we haven't lost a thing. Heaven has no regrets.

627. ~ JUST A FEW MORE HOURS ~
[A meditation on the hours between Good Friday and Easter Morning]

Just a few more hours…

We know this. But the disciples did not know it then. I wonder where they went after He was laid in the tomb. Did they go off to weep? Did they go off to pray? Did they return to the world to annul their grief? Did a flicker of hope remain in their hearts, even though a darker day had never been seen? No one was there to tell them that it would be…

Just a few more hours.

We realize this, we who are Christ's disciples today. But they did not know it on this black night 2,000 years ago. I think of Peter, who had walked on water, confessed Christ as the Son of God, cut off the soldier's ear, and then denied Our Lord three times. What sorrows and doubts and shames and fears swirled within his heart? St. Peter's words comfort us today, but who was there to comfort him then? No one was there to tell him that it would be...

Just a few more hours.

We have this hope to guide us now. But those faithful women who anointed the tomb, they did not know it when they sprinkled the Myrrh. Christ was dead. What unimaginable grief they must have felt, those blessed women. Even the Mother of God could not know that hope would rise in...

Just a few more hours.

Oh how I wish I could have been there – knowing what I know now – to comfort the disciples, to encourage those women, to let them all know that victory is on its way. I wish I could have been there to strengthen them with the same words, the same truth, and the same prayers with which they now comfort us today. But alas, there was nobody to tell them the good news back then. There was no one to announce that joy was coming in...

Just a few more hours.

We struggle in our lives; but we are accompanied by a certain hope. But on this night 2,000 years ago, they struggled without the certainty we now enjoy. They struggled to make sense of the suffering and death and evil that seemed to have permanently conquered hope and life and joy. They had no way of knowing that it would be...

Just a few more hours.

But tonight, we do know. We understand that the Cross and the tomb were not the final say. So we press on with hope always before us. We know that in just a few more hours we will proclaim: Christ is Risen! Therefore we can endure the temporal darkness, knowing that our faith is not in vain. We can struggle and weep, pray and doubt, rise and fall; but we do so always with an ever present hope in our hearts. No matter what happens to us – regardless of how bleak, how empty, or how painful life may get – we know that compared to eternity, it's only...

Just a few more hours.

628. ~ BABYLON JUSTICE and CHRISTIAN HOPE ~

OK, listen to me dear Christian people. Let me help you so that you won't continue to be shocked, disillusioned, and heartbroken by the various judicial rulings of the Babylon system. Just think about the following for a minute, seriously:

Nine human beings actually have the hubris and presumption to allow themselves to be extolled as the ultimate arbiters of right and wrong, truth and error, life and death. These nine people allow themselves to be called the Supreme Court – the *Supreme* Court! Do you know what the word "supreme" means? Here is the definition from the Merriam-Webster dictionary:

"SUPREME":
1) highest in rank or authority <the supreme commander>
2) highest in degree or quality <supreme endurance in war and in labour
3) ultimate, final <the supreme sacrifice>
Synonyms: chief, commanding, first, foremost, highest, preeminent, premier, primary, principal, super-eminent, head, top

Now just think about that! Do you know any truly God-fearing, truly humble, truly righteous, and truly discerning person that would dare to elevate themselves above God, above Christ, above the Holy Scriptures, and above the Teachings and Traditions of the Church? Would any true Christian dare to usurp the role of God and call himself part of a "Supreme Court"? Hell no!

So my dear, dear fellow Christians – as condescending as I may sound – I must nevertheless strongly urge you to stop trusting in these arrogant, black robed buffoons who act as if their mortal judgments are superior to the eternal Judgments of God. How can you possibly be surprised that such pompous minds produce nothing but "laws" of chaos, confusion, abomination, and evil?

Stop trusting in this stiff-necked institution! Stop facilitating such imperious idolatry with your votes, your hopes, your trust, and your tears. Do not be deceived! God is not mocked. He will not share His glory with another. Let them bang their gavels, flaunt their robes, and exalt their twisted logic and convoluted decrees. But as for myself, I will only honor one Judge – the One before whom all Babylon judges will ultimately bow and be broken.

629. ~ BELIEVERS and UNBELIEVERS ~

I have more respect for those who say, "I don't believe in God" than I do for those who speak of God while they spit on their neighbors. I prefer the atheist who loves me to the "Christian" who scorns me. (Of course, I must say that I have personally been helped more by Christians than by atheists – although there are fewer atheists in the world than Christians, and the atheists don't pretend to have a divine mandate to help their fellow man.) On Judgment Day, we may be surprised to find out who the real believers are.

630. ~ A MYSTICAL SYMBIOSIS ~

Mother and unborn child are not enemies. They are mystically united by God, and both lives are intended to bless each other. Abortion is the violent division of a glorious, natural, symbiotic human dependence. Abortion is the sorrowful epitome, the tragic exemplification, of all the violence and oppression that afflicts the human race today. How can we cultivate justice and unity among men when we support the unjust divide of mother and unborn child? How can we hope to have peace in the world when we support violence in the womb? *"Lord have mercy."* +++

631. ~ LITTLE GIRL ~

Little girl:
You built sandcastles
You chased butterflies
You wished upon rainbows
And you knew...
That you were His

Little girl:
You fell in love
Your heart was broken
You wished upon sunsets
And you hoped...
That you were His

Little girl:
You looked for a prince
But met devils instead
You wished upon clouds
And you tried to remember...
That you were His

Little girl:
You gave it your all
Body, mind, heart and soul
You wished upon thunder
And you wondered...
Are you still His?

Little girl:
Sandcastles washed away
Butterflies became demons
Now you wish upon darkness
And you question...
Are you still His?

Little girl:
Lost and falling

Bitter and broken
Wishing upon nothing
But you are always and forever...
Still His!

632. ~ IF I HAD THE POWER ~

If I had the power
I'd use that power for love
I'd crush all weapons of war
I'd mash bullets into to dust

If I had the power
I'd use that power for peace
I'd break the chains of armies
All soldiers would be freed

If I had the power
I'd use that power for good
I'd transform abortion clinics
Into mansions for the poor

If I had the power
I'd let the children play
I'd let them rule the world
And their love we'd all obey

If I had the power
This is what I'd do
But perhaps I have the power
And all I need is you

633. ~ LOVE for HUMANITY is NOT HATE ~

Encouraging soldiers to repent of their militarism is an act of love, not hate. Just as encouraging women not to have abortions is an act of love, not hate. It is compassion, not condemnation that compels us to affirm the sanctity of human life and proclaim the divine message of peace. If we did not love you then we would not urge you to flee from the hellish gates of military bases and abortion clinics. If we did not warn you not to engage in acts that lead to the shedding of innocent blood, then the blood of the innocents would also stain our own souls. Call us "unpatriotic." Call us "misogynistic." Call us what you will. We will love you anyway. We value your life as well as the lives you are intending to kill. How can a love for humanity ever be considered a position of hate?

634. ~ JESUS SAVES ~

From the time I was a little boy growing up in Atlanta, I knew that "Jesus Saves." I knew this because throughout the years, the steeple of "Big Bethel A.M.E. Church" has illuminated the nighttime Atlanta skyline with this precise message. It has been a beacon of neon radiance amidst a city drowning in racism, promiscuity, violence, and addiction.

I spent innumerable hours prowling the nocturnal streets of my ATL – selling drugs, chasing (and fleeing from women), getting kicked out of bars, playing music (the one honest thing I did do), and indulging in all manner of sins. I reveled in hedonistic slop – like the Prodigal Son – ignoring the truth that shined above me in neon blue.

God usually sends His messages to me loudly and clearly. He knows how dense I am. Divine subtlety doesn't seem to get the attention of this ignorant sinner. Throughout my life, I've had to labor to dismiss His clarion call. But when it comes to sin and failure, I'm somehow able to summon the effort.

The stories of my depravity are too dark and sordid to share here. But suffice it to say that I have feasted on the devil's urban excrement while the message of salvation stared down on me from lights above. And as much as I'd like to say that I've been delivered once and for all, there's still too much sin before me to boast of such a thing.

"Jesus Saves": this is the simple and universal truth that has enlightened my consciousness and illuminated the city that shaped me. I may not agree with some of the unorthodox doctrines of "Big Bethel A.M.E. Church," but this Church has consistently perpetuated the neon message of Christ – speaking peace to my sinful heart, and radiating hope to a beautiful and dark city that desperately seeks its merciful redemption. And for that, I am truly grateful.

So never underestimate, ridicule, or mock the signs of salvation. There is redemptive power in symbolic truth. I thank God for the blue neon hope that always called me home.

635. ~ TOO ORTHODOX / TOO REVOLUTIONARY ~

If you're too Orthodox for most revolutionaries and too revolutionary for most Orthodox, then you're probably close to Jesus.

636. ~ THE ISSUE of PROSPERITY ~

The issue of "prosperity" is an important and necessary discussion for us to have as Orthodox Christians. True prosperity transcends material or financial abundance, and yet we must have certain tangible things in order to survive – such as food, water, clothing, and shelter. And there is something deeply and fundamentally unjust when a few possess an unshared abundance while the many struggle and starve. God created the earth for all of us, and no man has a right to horde God's blessings while others suffer. As Dorothy Day rhetorically asked, "Do you suppose that God created diamonds only for the rich?"

And yet there is nothing Christian about trying to remedy these situations through violent revolution. Such "revolutionary" victories inevitably bring about more suffering and problems in the long run. And there is also nothing Christian about a false gospel that leads people to believe that spiritual blessings are commensurate with financial success. The path to hell is equally littered with the materialistic lies of communism and capitalism; it is paved evenly with the demonic detritus of political socialism and prosperity gospels.

I really believe the solution begins with us – as Christians, the Body of Christ. We must take care of one another. We must share freely and equally with all. And we must do so without coercion, manipulation, compulsion, or force. It is shameful that a man with five houses worships next to his brother who ekes out a living from check to check. We curse our politicians and condemn the ways of the world, but we as Christians fail to set the right example. If there is inequity and injustice within the very Body of Christ, then how can we ever hope to see equality and justice in the world?

637. ~ ALL THE REASON YOU NEED ~

Don't do it because God asks you to do it. Don't do it because God commands you to do it. Do it because God loves you, and His love is all the reason you need.

638. ~ BULLETS and SEEDS ~

Fire your bullets and I'll sow my seeds. You'll reap blood and death, but I'll reap the multiplication of life eternal.

Andy was one of my dearest friends. I will always have wonderful memories of all the hours we spent playing Scrabble, drinking Guinness, listening to great music, and discussing theology. I will remember the many trips we took to New Orleans together – prowling the French Quarter, preaching the gospel in the Voodoo shops half drunk, and searching for the most authentic Gumbo we could find in the city. I will remember the time we took my infant son Noah and went to visit my mom for a week at her cabin in the Blue Ridge Mountains. Andy was a learned herpetologist and an intrepid searcher for snakes and all things reptilian. As we were driving down the mountain late one night, Andy started screaming at the top of his lungs: "Snake! Snake! Stop the car! Stop the car!" It was pitch black, and I don't know how he could see anything. But he jumped out, and sure enough he picked up a snake that was about a foot long. I was terrified of course, but he assured me that it was non-venomous. He was absolutely thrilled. That was Andy. Nothing made him happier than finding a snake.

My friend Andy was quite brilliant. His mind was incredibly sharp, and he was constantly reading and expanding his knowledge. I always learned a lot from being around him. We certainly didn't agree on everything; but he kept me on my toes, and I always came away smarter for having spent time with him. I remember one occasion when he came over and I gave him a rough draft of a new book I was working on. He read a page or two, through the manuscript down, cursed me and then stormed out of the house. Two days later he called me up as if nothing had happened: "Hey man! Are you up for some beer and Scrabble?!" That was Andy. It took me a while to understand him, but once I did I learned to really appreciate him.

I loved Andy's genuine heart. There were no false pretenses with him. He never put on airs or tried to be something he wasn't. And he didn't need to, because he was great just the way he was. Andy wasn't the most socially polished or tactful person, but who cares? What you saw is what you got. Andy was real, and real people are hard to find in this world. I think Andy was always looking to find out who was genuine, who was loyal, who would really love and accept him unconditionally. He made superficial uncomfortable, and I confess that I really admired that. I often wish that I could be so bold.

Andy loved to laugh, and he always let you know what he felt and what he thought. I loved that about him. He was a straight shooter. And I always found it ironic that Andy looked up to people who didn't know nearly as much as he did. Perhaps that's why the people who were supposed to encourage him, support him, affirm him, and lift him up seemed to always keep him at arm's length. Somebody who knows more than the preacher, who is bold enough to ask difficult questions, who speaks bluntly about his feelings and opinions, and who doesn't necessarily conform to church society's standards (or society's standards) of "success" is usually not wholeheartedly embraced. Oh, the Church loved Andy well enough – from a safe distance. But Andy loved the Church with all of his heart. He gave his heart completely and received only a half measure in return.

And my dear friend loved Jesus Christ with a passion that we all should have. There is no doubt about that.

I am honored that Andy was my friend, and I will miss him greatly. I obviously failed him. I should have been a better friend to him. I should have called him more often. I should have told him that I loved him more often. I should have listened to him more carefully. I should have sensed his suffering. But I didn't. I failed. There was so much about life that he loved. I wish I could have reminded him about all those things that made life worth living for him. But I didn't.

There was a huge turnout at his funeral today. There were some good words spoken. Lots of love and lots of tears. We all grieve and we will all miss him. But I wonder why we always wait until it's too late to show up and show our love. Where were we when he was here on this earth? Where were we when he needed us? We seem to do a good job of loving people in death. Why can't we love them in life? I let my friend slip into darkness without offering him any light. But I do know that the Light of Christ comforts him now.

I look forward to that day when we shall embrace each other in the Kingdom. I loved my dear friend Andy, and I still love him. The world just won't be the same without him in it. But the world is better, and I am better, because God sent him our way.

640. ~ WOMAN HELP ME ~

Woman don't push me. Woman don't pull me. You are my equal; so don't let me trample on you, and don't try to wear my crown. Walk beside me, and help me lead you towards the Lord of us both.

641. ~ TEARS and LAUGHTER ~

Laugh until you cry, and cry until you laugh. Live this way, pray this way, and be saved this way.

642. ~ WE REJOICE IN OUR SPLINTERS ~

Peace and love and patience and hope come with many crosses. True peace exists in the midst of tension. Real love is accompanied by sorrow. Patience is often born from pain. And hope rises from the ashes of despair. The things that truly make life worth living are only acquired through the hardships of life. So we cling to the Cross and rejoice in our splinters.

643. ~ SUMMARY THOUGHTS on THE SAME SEX MARRIAGE RULING ~
[6/27/2015]

I see life and love and beauty and joy; and yet I also see inhumanity, injustice, evil, and oppression. I want so badly to focus on the good, to accentuate the positive, to proclaim glorious truths rather than cruel realities. I live a beautiful life in a cold world, and I endure a cold life in a beautiful world. I am reminded of the paradox of the prophets who felt the pathos of the Divine as they identified with mortal suffering and human sin.

I am by no means a prophet, only a servant – too often a servant of self rather than a servant of God and my fellows. But I do feel a paradoxical angst that wreaks havoc on my soul, pulling it simultaneously towards light and darkness, virtue and iniquity. One minute my heart shouts to the world: *"Look at God! See His mercy! Know His love! Find His salvation!"* And the next minute my heart cries out: *"Stop this madness! Repent of this evil! What the hell is wrong with us all?!"* Back and forth I go, like the pendulum of my conscience – today an internet prophet, and tomorrow wallowing in a harlot's embrace.

So why do I say all of this? I say it because recently I have railed against Babylon like a madman, and perhaps rightly so. I have highlighted the darkness, bemoaned the impending doom, chastised and warned, mocked and scorned. Maybe God's hand was in some of that, but it was mostly my own fist flailing in the air. The cynicism of Diogenes, but without his wisdom. The zeal of Don Quixote, but without his courage. God forgive me.

And that's why I wish to end my jeremiads with my vision honed upon the positive, with my heart attuned to melody rather than cacophony:

Millions of homosexual people are happy today because the law now allows them to marry, to enjoy all the legal benefits of marriage, and to pursue the same monogamous betrothed love that heterosexuals have always enjoyed. And when I think of people loving one another, being happy with one another, pledging marital faithfulness to one another, and celebrating the fact that to do so is now legal, then I can't see anything but beauty and goodness in that. Whatever insidious political agendas may be at work behind all of this, I will choose to rejoice in the fact that mutual human love, mutual human relationship, mutual human affection, and mutual human fidelity are celebrated in a significant way today. I can see the beauty in that. And yes, I can see God in that. I think we all can, if we want to.

One Love always.

644. ~ THIS IS THE NECESSARY REVOLUTION ~

To cling to peace…
By any means necessary

To refuse to kill…
By any means necessary

To affirm life…
By any means necessary

To say no to war…
By any means necessary

To love all people…
By any means necessary…

This is the necessary revolution.

645. ~ RISING TIDE ~

Good times come and good times go.
Life is full of ebb and flow.

But character is forged in hardship.
And champions steadily rise…

*Like the **TIDE**…*
Unstoppable!

646. ~ KILLING INFIDELS ~

In order to prove that we are more civilized than those that kill infidels, we must kill the uncivilized that kill infidels. How else will those who kill infidels learn how evil they are unless we kill those who kill infidels to prove how righteous we are? This is what clearly separates them from us: they kill to teach infidels a lesson, and we kill to teach infidel killers a lesson. Infidel killers are barbaric, but those who kill infidel killers are civilized and holy. Or is it the other way around? I confess that I do get confused with it all.

647. ~ SUFFERING and SALVATION ~

Suffering is not necessarily an indication that we are far from God. In fact, it may be a divine blessing that keeps us close to God. After all, how can we be saved if we flee from the Cross?

Some suffer because they run *from* God, and some suffer because they run *to* God. What we do with our suffering, what we learn from our suffering, and how we use our suffering will determine whether or not our suffering will be a blessing or a curse.

"But even if you should suffer for what is right, you are blessed... For it is better, if it is God's will, to suffer for doing good than for doing evil." [I Peter 3:14-17]

648. ~ HEART of LOVE ~

We will never bring love to the world until we see the world with a heart of love.

God, how we crave contentment! If we could just be content in our relationships, content in our finances, content in our families, and content in our faith, then that would be such a blessing. Or so we think.

But contentment doesn't really produce anything worthwhile. Contentment doesn't produce the Blues. Contentment doesn't produce the art of Van Gogh. Contentment doesn't produce prophecy. Contentment doesn't produce romance, love, labor, and birth. Contentment doesn't produce revolution. Contentment doesn't produce the divinely voiced explosion of universal fire and darkness, chaos and order, beauty and horror that compose the prelude to an eternal symphony of peace. And contentment certainly doesn't lead God to become man – to suffer and die and rise again – in order to atone for humanity.

So as much as we long for contentment, I think it's actually quite overrated. In fact, contentment may be quite dangerous. The contented don't cry out for salvation. The contented don't beg for redemption. And who can be saved except those that are desperate enough to know they need saving?

Perhaps the secret of life – especially eternal life – is learning to be content in our discontent. Perhaps the safest place to be is in the belly of the whale, in the midst of the fiery furnace, on an ark tossed about by a raging sea, or nailed to a cross next to God himself.

Contentment hasn't caught me yet, and I've been waiting for it to find me ever since I was born. It seems we just aren't destined to meet. And I think I realize now what a blessing that is.

650. ~ CULTIVATING a VISION of LIFE AFFIRMATION ~

Let us see the humanity of all humanity. Let us recognize the life of the living. Let us acknowledge the value of "the least of these." Let us affirm the worth of "the wretched of the earth." Whether Black or White, rich or poor, gay or straight, citizen or "illegal" alien, capital or labor, man or woman, born or unborn – let us honor, respect, assist, and love all human life. And let us denounce violence and decry injustice – wherever it occurs, by whatever means it is perpetuated, and by whatever name it justifies itself. Whether the evil comes via a policeman's bullets, Obama's drones, a bully's fists, or an abortionist's scalpel, we must unequivocally denounce it and intervene with love, truth, and nonviolent sacrificial action.

We must stop viewing the world through the idiocy of ideology, and instead view the world through the enlightened scope of compassion, mercy, love, and justice – mercy, love, and justice for all people, everywhere. And we must especially attune our consciences to the cries of the suffering, the disadvantaged, the voiceless, and the oppressed.

Politicians will only tell you half of the story. So let's stop allowing them to tell us who we should care about; because implicit in their compassion for some is apathy towards and callous disregard for others.

Let us apply the Golden Rule, that timeless and universal law that when truly heeded yields true justice and true peace. If I am hungry, feed me. If I am being enslaved, emancipate me. If I am being oppressed, be just to me. If I am being discriminated against because of my race, religion, or sexuality, then love me and work to eradicate the prejudices that wound me. And if I am an unborn life in the womb, then let me live and speak up for my right to be born.

Peace and justice are predicated upon the "consistent Life ethic." We can't have world peace if we don't work for peace in the womb; and we won't stop violence in the womb if we aren't equally committed to stopping violence in the world. Let us cultivate a vision of Life affirmation. How can we recognize the problems or find solutions unless we first learn to see the value and sanctity of all human life?

Never accuse anyone of having a "victim mentality." Their struggles may be different than your struggles. Their wounds may be different than your wounds. Their strengths may be different than your strengths, and their weaknesses may be different than your weaknesses. If they are crying out, then there must be a reason. And even if their laments are nothing more than cries for attention, then consider how desperate someone must be to resort to such a thing. Are such souls not still in need of mercy and compassion?

Our duty is to console the suffering, to assists those in need, to love the unloved, and to give (as we are able) to those that ask. Life and sin, heartache and loss, and the evils of this world victimize us all. So let us offer compassion to those who cry out for help. God will judge their hearts. Christ alone retains the authority to separate the sheep from the goats, the wheat from the tares. Our job is to love, to serve, and to forgive our fellow man.

I've read in the Gospels where Jesus said, "Arise and walk," after He healed the lame man. I've read in the Gospels where Jesus said, "Go and sin no more," as He offered His forgiveness and compassion to the woman caught in adultery. I've read in the Gospels where Jesus said, "This kind only comes out through prayer and fasting," as He encouraged His disciples to engage in the struggle of spiritual warfare. But I never recall Jesus saying, "Just get over it." I never recall Jesus saying, "Stop acting like a victim." I never recall Him saying, "Pull yourself up by your bootstraps."

Jesus points us to our need for Him; and inseparable from our need for Him is our need for one another. We cannot worship God in a vacuum. We cannot truly worship Him alone. To worship God is to serve our brothers, and to serve our brothers is to worship God.

We do not deserve divine mercy, but it is offered to us freely. And yet we turn around and refuse mercy to others based on what we think they deserve.

God help us. And may God help us to help one another.

652. ~ SUFFERING and COMPASSION ~

Suffering is the soil that nourishes the flowers of compassion. But the weeds of bitterness also sprout from the same sod of sorrow. If we water the seeds of resentment, then our lives will be ugly and unfruitful. But if we nurture the seeds of compassion, then we will yield the beautiful harvest of brotherhood, justice, humanity, and peace. Suffering is the cradle of compassion, and compassion is the healing of humanity. If we uproot bitterness and nourish mercy, then our suffering will never be in vain.

653. ~ MY FLAWED HEROES ~

I don't apologize for having flawed heroes. My heroes aren't my saviors; they are people whose lives, words, and examples point me to *The Savior*. Regardless of their fallacies and failures, their courage and conviction inspire me to be a better person and a better Christian.

People tell me that Dr. Martin Luther King, Jr. was a socialist. They say that Thomas Merton was unorthodox. They reject Mother Teresa as a Papist. They accuse Marcus Garvey of fanaticism. They claim that Albert Camus was an atheist. They say Bob Marley was a womanizer. They accuse Dorothy Day of being a communist. They renounce Malcolm X as a militant. They call St. Francis of Assisi an idealist. They insist that Gandhi was a racist. They condemn Tolstoy as an apostate. They call Carlos Santana a hippie. They say I shouldn't admire Muhammad Ali, because he's a Muslim. And they tell me that Haile Selassie was a tyrant.

Well, I can't answer all of those criticisms. But such accusations won't negate the truth that my heroes spoke and the good that they did. My heroes affirmed life, worked for justice, and desired peace. Regardless of their religions, ideologies, or strategic philosophies, they never viewed war, abortion, or any act of intentional killing as solutions to the problems that plague humanity. They were all willing to grow, to change, and to conform their convictions to the will and truth of the Creator. Only Christ is perfect, and He alone is who I choose to follow. But my heroes all bear the reflection of Christ's righteousness, compassion, justice, and love in one way or another.

I admire these people, not because of their flaws, but because God was able to use them in spite of their flaws. And that gives me hope, because I know how severely flawed *I* am. My heroes let me know that God can use a crooked river to bring the water of life to thirsty souls. So I am thankful to have such conscious companions on this spiritual trod through creation. I don't know where I'd be without them.

654. ~ VICTIMS or EXECUTIONERS ~

We are either enslavers or liberators; we are either oppressors or the oppressed; we are either murderers or victims. There is no middle ground. We cannot stake neutral ground between justice and injustice, between humanity and inhumanity, between life affirmation and life destruction and think that we are any better than the executioners. We cannot vote for killers and think that we are any less guilty than those who pull the trigger.

"It is the job of thinking people not to be on the side of the executioners." ~ Albert Camus ~

655. ~ LOVE IS NEVER A HERESY ~

A god who demands that we torture, hate, divide, and kill in his name is a god that I refuse to worship. I serve the One True God – a God who is not only loving, but a God who *is* love. And I am willing to forsake all other ideologies, all other doctrines, and all other causes in the effort to remain faithful to the commandment and truth of love. If my theology is wrong, let it not be because I have justified violence, hatred, and death. If I err, I pray that I err on the side of life, on the side of peace, and on the side of mercy. Love is never a heresy.

Therefore I bow before Divine Love and ask Him to live in me and through me – now and unto eternity. Amen.

"Whoever does not love does not know God, because God is love."
[I John 4:8]

"Love the Lord your God with all your heart and with all your soul and with all your mind and with all your strength; and Love your neighbor as yourself. There is no commandment greater than these." [St. Mark 12:30-31]

"For in Christ Jesus neither circumcision nor uncircumcision has any value. The only thing that counts is faith expressing itself through love." [Galatians 5:6]

"Whoever claims to love God yet hates a brother or sister is a liar. For whoever does not love their brother and sister, whom they have seen, cannot love God, whom they have not seen." [I John 4:20]

"If I speak in the tongues of men or of angels, but do not have love, I am only a resounding gong or a clanging cymbal. If I have the gift of prophecy and can fathom all mysteries and all knowledge, and if I have a faith that can move mountains, but do not have love, I am nothing. If I give all I possess to the poor and give over my body to hardship that I may boast, but do not have love, I gain nothing. Love is patient, love is kind. It does not envy, it does not boast, it is not proud. It does not dishonor others, it is not self-seeking, it is not easily angered, it keeps no record of wrongs. Love does not delight in evil but rejoices with the truth. It always protects, always trusts, always hopes, always perseveres. Love never fails. But where there are prophecies, they will cease; where there are tongues, they will be stilled; where there is knowledge, it will pass away. For we know in part and we prophesy in part, but when completeness comes, what is in part disappears. When I was a child, I talked like a child, I thought like a child, I reasoned like a child. When I became a man, I put the ways of childhood behind me. For now we see only a reflection as in a mirror; then we shall see face to face. Now I know in part; then I shall know fully, even as I am fully known. And now these three

remain: faith, hope and love. But the greatest of these is love." [I
Corinthians 13]

656. ~ EVISCERATION of HUMAN JUDGMENTS ~

When we humble ourselves, we will be accused of arrogance.
When we act with love, we will be accused of hate. When we offer
wisdom, we will be called fools. And when we speak the truth, we
will be maligned with lies. But God knows our hearts. He alone is the
fashioner of our souls. So fret not when you are slandered unfairly.
Christ died for us, and His mercy endureth forever. In the light of this
eternal truth, finite human judgments are eviscerated.

657. ~ HELLISH GATES or HEAVENLY TRUTHS? ~

We have to remember that Christianity – *true* Christianity; i.e. the
Church – is not merely one religion among many that survives or
perishes according to its ability to preserve itself with gold and sword.
The Church cannot be defeated, extinguished, or annihilated by carnal
forces. However, as individuals, we can apostatize by our refusal to
obey Our Lords commands, by rejecting His example, and by
fashioning doctrines of violence that we justify in His holy name.

Our Lord promised that, *"The gates of hell shall not prevail
against the Church." [St. Matthew 16:18]* Let us be careful, lest by
our complicity in the evils of warfare and killing we find ourselves
aligned with hellish gates rather than heavenly truths.

The forcible displacement of human beings from their geographically or biologically native environments is an act of violence and injustice that will inevitably produce commensurate acts of retaliatory evil. Europeans violently enslaving and displacing Black people from the African continent... Nazis violently denying Jews their right to exist on earth... Zionists violently displacing the Palestinian people from their native homeland... abortionists violently displacing unborn babies from their mothers' wombs – such atrocities will always produce reciprocal horrors.

The first principle of human rights and social justice is simply to not violently interfere with the natural lives and indigenous lands of others. And the second principle of human rights and social justice is that peaceful but genuine reparations be made where an injustice has occurred.

Therefore, return the land to the displaced people, and make it possible for displaced people to return to their native lands. Feed the poor and house the homeless who suffer from the systems that create poverty and homelessness. And as for abortion: since it is impossible to return the aborted child to the womb of life, then those who have defended, supported and perpetuated abortion must make reparations by giving their time, their money, and their resources in the effort to ensure that the rights of the unborn are preserved and protected henceforth and until the end of time.

Freedom begins with the right to life and extends to the right to self-determination. And freedom is fulfilled when the poor are valued as much as the powerful, and when the weak are protected as equally as the wealthy.

It is unjust, inhumane, and evil to violently rob indigenous people of their native land. It is unjust, inhumane, and evil to violently deny human beings food, water, clothing, and shelter. And it is unjust, inhumane, and evil to violently rip innocent children from their mothers' wombs.

The oppressed can forgive the oppressor, and victims can choose to love their tormentors. But true peace will only come to fruition when those who have violated their fellow man truly repent. And repentance without reparations is an anemic sentiment devoid of any authentic spiritual substance.

"Atone for your sins with alms and your wrongdoings with compassion to the poor. Then, perhaps God will forgive your trespasses." [Daniel 4:27]

"Rescue the weak and the needy; deliver them from the hand of the wicked." [Psalm 82:4]

"He has shown you, O man, what is good. And what does the LORD require of you? To act justly and to love mercy and to walk humbly with your God." [Micah 6:8]

659. ~ REACTION vs. REVOLUTION ~

If we attempt to fight oppression with the same violent tactics as the oppressor, then we are merely being reactionary rather than revolutionary. The reactionary violence of the freedom fighter will inevitably be met with a greater reactionary violence from the freedom denier. Therefore, violent revolution is inherently self-defeating, empowering the victimizer rather than liberating the victimized. Violent revolt is not only spiritually impotent, it is also pragmatically ineffectual. Hatred, vengeance, and retaliation are not revolutionary principles. They only serve to strengthen rather than weaken the oppressor. But unconditional love, unmerited forgiveness, and the proactive nonviolent refusal to accept injustice are the three pillars of authentic social justice and true spiritual revolution.

660. ~ THE TRUE REVOLUTIONARIES ~

Who are the true revolutionaries? They are those that sheathe their swords and unleash their prayers.

661. ~ IF ONLY I COULD SEE THE SHORE ~

If only I could see the shore
I'd jump ship and swim.

But I can't see it yet.

I'm stuck aboard a nightmare
waiting for the seas to calm,
looking for a dove of peace
to bring me an olive branch.

How much longer?

I'm growing weary.

The sails are torn
so I have to row.

But the oars give me splinters.
These damnable splinters!

I'm getting nowhere.

The waters steadily rise.
Waves and winds assault me.

Maybe I should give up,
cast myself into the sea,
let it bury me
so I won't suffer anymore.

But a monster might swallow me,
preserving my pain
in its hellish belly.
God, I don't want to run the risk!

So I'll stay right here.
And I'll try to keep rowing.

I have no other choice.

And I'll keep looking

for that distant shore,
for that dove of peace,
for a rainbow in the sky.

I'll keep looking
and searching...
for hope.

And I'll keep trusting
that these splinters
and these waves
and these storms
and this suffering
will somehow be...
my salvation.

Lord, help me to endure!

662. ~ "THE PEOPLE of GOD?" ~

First we say, "We are the people of God." And that enables us to say, "Those people are not of God." And this allows us to commit unspeakable evils in the name of God. And then we dare to condemn the atheist who looks at us and asks: "If God exists, then how can God allow those who believe in God to commit such horrors in the name of God?"

663. ~ HISTORY, IDENTITY, and DESTINY ~

All people should know their history, embrace their identity, and fulfill their divine destiny. But nobody should pervert history, discredit their identity, and destroy their destiny by promoting racist ideologies, historical fallacies, and pseudo-scientific theories that undermine truth and perpetuate violence and division in the world.

True knowledge of self never leads to hatred for others; and true spiritual consciousness never leads to invidious attitudes of prejudice or demonic acts of racism.

664. ~ PEACE, JUSTICE, and REVOLUTION ~

As long as we keep thinking that peace is predicated upon justice, we'll never have either. Peace is not a situational ethic or a circumstantial social construct. Peace is a choice, a commitment, a state of mind and a condition of the heart. The true peacemakers are always the ones who bring about true justice; but those who eschew peace in the pursuit of justice inevitably perpetuate the social bondage and political corruption they seek to reform.

As long as we mistakenly believe that peace is the child and justice is the mother, then we will remain enslaved to violence and destruction. The false prophets fill our minds with the rhetorical refrain: "No justice! No peace!" And because we embrace this specious syllogism, we find ourselves with exactly that: no justice, and no peace.

We suffer as individuals and as a society because we have inverted cause and effect. We violently pursue justice in the absurd hope that this will somehow produce peace. But what we should do is vigilantly wed ourselves to divine peace so that we can reap the harvest of true social justice.

If history demonstrates anything, it demonstrates that any ostensible revolution that is won by violence can just as easily be overthrown by violence. So at what point do we wake up and realize that violence is not revolutionary at all?

In times of violence and conflict, our actions and voices will either contribute to reason, peace, and love or to insanity, destruction, and hate. Let us choose to act and speak in ways that will cultivate brotherhood and humanity rather than animosity and division. Let us extinguish the dark fires of evil so that the light of righteousness can prevail.

Beware! God is not mocked. Every evil word and every violent action will be divinely recompensed. Those who think that reactionary rioting is revolutionary are as ignorant and foolish as those who think that justice can be delivered with billy clubs, armies, bullets, and bombs.

True peace is truly revolutionary, and true revolutionaries are unconditionally committed to peace. Take off your badge, throw down your arms, drop your bricks, and love your brother. Now *that's* a revolution!

665. ~ LET US SEEK and LET US HOPE ~

Let us *"seek peace and pursue it." [Psalm 34:14; I Peter 3:11]* Let us *"love mercy and do justice." [Micah 6:8]* Let us cultivate a *"pure and undefiled religion, which is to care for orphans and widows in their distress, keeping oneself unstained by the world. [James 1:27]* Let us *"pray without ceasing." [I Thessalonians 5:17]* Let us nurture that *"perfect love which casteth out fear. [I John 4:18]* And by all means let us hope. Let us always hope! For a flicker of hope destroys despair.

"So we do not lose heart. Though our outer self is wasting away, our inner self is being renewed day by day. For this momentary affliction is preparing for us an eternal weight of glory beyond all comparison, as we look not to the things that are seen but to the things that are unseen. For the things that are seen are transient, but the things that are unseen are eternal." [II Corinthians 4:16-18]

"Blessed be the God and Father of our Lord Jesus Christ! According to his great mercy, he has caused us to be born again to a living hope through the resurrection of Jesus Christ from the dead." [I Peter 1:3]

667. ~ I'M NOT A PASSIVE PACIFIST ~

I'm not a *passive* pacifist. I'm a *militant* pacifist. Peace cannot be waged with apathy, indifference, or compromise with evil. The words of peace are not always peaceable words. Preaching *"Thou shalt not kill"* will always anger those who are paid to soldier, police, and politic. Condemning violence will always offend those who profit from bloodshed and destruction. Peace is not the absence of conflict and tension. Peace is the unconditional commitment to love our enemies; it is the unwavering affirmation of the sanctity of *all* human life in *all* situations. Peace is by no means passive. Peace is a metaphysical struggle, a cosmic battle, a spiritual war.

668. ~ PERSONAL SACRIFICE / SACRIFICING LIVES ~

I have more respect for an unwed mother raising eight children on welfare than I do for a rich married woman with a Master's degree who killed her unborn children on her road to "success." One sacrificially struggles in order to personally affirm life. The other sacrifices lives in order to avoid having to personally struggle.

669. ~ GOD IS LOVE ~

God is love. God is omnipresent. God is eternal. Thus His love is omnipresent and eternal. God cannot be separated from love, and love cannot be separated from God. Therefore, God's love is unlimited, ubiquitous, and infinitely omnipotent. The limitation is not with divine love, but rather with our human understanding, awareness, and experience of divine love.

670. ~ HAPPY TO OFFEND ~

I won't spit on your flag, I won't burn your flag, and I won't honor your flag. My allegiance is to Christ, His Cross, and His Church alone. I seek solidarity with Christians, not with countrymen. I seek unity with humanity, not with nationality. I refuse to value the constitution more than the Cross or the government more than God. If that is offensive, then I am happy to offend.

671. ~ THE REVOLUTION ~

The revolution is not about Black against White, rich against poor, male against female, gay against straight, or believers against unbelievers. The revolution is about suffering people against corrupt power. If you're wearing a soldier's uniform, a policeman's badge, or a politician's suit, then you're on the wrong side of this cosmic battle. Repent of your violence and join the side of humanity and peace. The love train is on the move. Get on board or get out of the way!

672. ~ CORRUPTION and COMPLICITY ~

Corrupt power depends on the cooperation and complicity of the people. Seeking to reform a corrupt political system by participation in that system is like attempting to purify poison by ingesting poison. Democracy is social suicide, and our votes are the daggers of our own destruction. Revolution and liberation begin with our resistance to and withdrawal from the political system that relies upon us being its participatory pawns. How long will we continue to vainly pursue freedom by voting to enslave ourselves to one master after another?

673. ~ MOTHER MARY: REVOLUTIONARY ~

Mother Mary
Revolutionary:
You fed the hungry
With Bread from your womb

Mother Mary
Revolutionary:
You liberated the oppressed
By bringing God to man

Mother Mary
Revolutionary:
You gave birth to Justice
Without shedding blood

Mother Mary
Revolutionary:
You revealed the Word
To all the world

Mother Mary
Revolutionary:
You defended humanity
By choosing Life

Mother Mary
Revolutionary:
What pierced your heart
Has saved us all

Mother Mary
Revolutionary:
The rich are empty
But the poor are full

Mother Mary
Revolutionary:
Hear our prayers. Hear our prayers.

674. ~ A SIMPLE LESSON LEARNED from TIME WITH MY DAUGHTER ~

Today I spent some simple but enjoyable time with Adayah, my 10 year old daughter, and I learned something very important from it. We spent about two hours at the coffee shop. I caught up on some reading, and my daughter wrote a letter and drew some pictures to give to my wife for Mother's Day. When I'm reading, I'm often inspired by thoughts and ideas that I try to jot down and expand upon at a later time. So Adayah asked me what I was writing, and I showed her my recently jotted note. She read the paragraph and said she didn't understand it because of some of the big words. So I defined the vocabulary, and then I asked her to try to understand the point I was trying to make. We ended up having a very good philosophical conversation that lasted about 20 minutes, and my daughter seemed pleased to actually comprehend the essence of what I had written.

Then, after we left the coffee shop, we stopped by to visit one of my spiritual heroes who is currently in physical rehab after having recently suffered a stroke. It was wonderful to see him, and he seemed very encouraged by our brief visit. So as we were driving home, I suddenly realized something that I pray I'll never forget, and I shared it with my daughter. This is what I said to her:

"Adayah, I really enjoyed our time together. And you know what? You did three things today that were very important. In fact, if everyone did these three things every day, they would be happier as individuals and the entire world would be a much happier place. And here are the three things you did:

1. You used your creativity in a positive way.
2. You spent time thinking about important ideas that deal with peace and the welfare of humanity.
3. You took time to encourage and uplift someone else.

And Adayah, you know what else? None of those things cost any money. Everyone can do all three of these things everyday for free. Isn't that cool?"

So, this is a simple lesson that I learned from spending time with my daughter today. I hope I don't forget these powerful truths. Let's all pray and strive to do these three things each and every day of our lives. If we are positively creative, thoughtfully engaged about peace and human rights, and actively endeavoring to serve others, then no day will ever be wasted and our lives will be profoundly meaningful.

I love spending time with my children, because I am constantly learning simply from being in their presence.

675. ~ "POWER TO THE PEOPLE!" ? ~

Yes, there is power in the people. But it's a power that can be used either for good or for evil. There is power in a hammer, but a hammer can be used to build a home or to bash in a man's skull. And historically, the people – the masses – have collectively wrought more horror than virtue. When Moses ascended Mt. Sinai to receive the Ten Commandments, what did the Israelites do in the valley? They fashioned a golden calf and reveled in idolatry. When Pontius Pilate allowed the crowd to decide who should be released and who should be crucified, who did the masses demand be freed? They shouted, "Free Barabbas! Crucify Christ!"

In fact, when the people do use their power for good, it is usually simply a corrective to the evil that they previously conspired to commit. So I'm not too interested in "power to the people." Such power is limited to worldly concerns, and therefore it tends to eschew transcendental truths in the pursuit of a secularly defined "justice." This "people power" too often tramples upon divine peace and violates Christian love in the vain collective endeavor to erect perpetual towers of Babel.

So what I'm genuinely concerned with, and what I'm truly inspired by, are people in obeisance to their Creator. Whether it's one individual in obedience to God or a million people in divine submission to Christ, that's *real* revolutionary power! The masses gave us Nazism, Communism, and abortion on demand. But one man on a Cross gave us salvation.

Think about it!

676. ~ NEUTRALIZING TRUE REVOLUTION ~

The most effective way to neutralize true revolution is to distract the masses from the real injustices by convincing them to rebel against lesser injustices. Use politics and the media to tell the people what to get mad about, and then you can keep them blindly oblivious to their own slavery. With diversion and distraction you can make them demand their own chains by convincing them that their bondage is actually their liberation. And before you know it, you can have the people mutilating their own bodies, murdering their own offspring, exploiting their fellow man, and waging war against people they don't even know – all in the name of their own "revolutionary freedom."

677. ~ FUNDAMENTALISM is NOT FAITH ~

Fundamentalism is not faith. Fundamentalism focuses on judgment, fear, punishment and reward. Fundamentalism is inherently legalistic, viewing God as a tyrannical judge who sends people to heaven or hell based upon either their deeds or their intellectual assent to some divine legal contract. In contrast, Orthodox theology emphasizes God's unfailing mercy and unconditional love. Orthodoxy is entirely predicated upon faith in God the Father who loves all of His human children. For us, the Cross is not some cosmic juridical transaction that placated the wrath of a vengeful deity; the Cross is rather the supreme act of divine sacrificial love that breaks the bonds of sin and death and enables all men to freely enter into the Father's loving, eternal embrace.

In the end, the only philosophy, doctrine, ideology, or creed that will matter is love. If we are right about everything else but we don't have love, then we will find ourselves estranged from the Kingdom. Yet if we are wrong about all else but we have maintained love, then we shall eternally experience the love of God. Obedience, holiness, prayer, faith, justice, asceticism, morality, and virtue are meaningless apart from love.

St. John the Evangelist says:

"Whoever does not love does not know God, because God is love." [I John 4:8]

And St. Paul writes:

"If I speak in the tongues of men or of angels, but do not have love, I am only a resounding gong or a clanging cymbal. If I have the gift of prophecy and can fathom all mysteries and all knowledge, and if I have a faith that can move mountains, but do not have love, I am nothing. If I give all I possess to the poor and give over my body to hardship that I may boast, but do not have love, I gain nothing. Love is patient, love is kind. It does not envy, it does not boast, it is not proud. It does not dishonor others, it is not self-seeking, it is not easily angered, it keeps no record of wrongs. Love does not delight in evil but rejoices with the truth. It always protects, always trusts, always hopes, always perseveres. Love never fails. But where there are prophecies, they will cease; where there are tongues, they will be stilled; where there is knowledge, it will pass away. For we know in part and we prophesy in part, but when completeness comes, what is in part disappears. When I was a child, I talked like a child, I thought like a child, I reasoned like a child. When I became a man, I put the ways of childhood behind me. For now we see only a reflection as in a mirror; then we shall see face to face. Now I know in part; then I shall know fully, even as I am fully known. And now these three remain: faith, hope and love. But the greatest of these is love." [I Corinthians 13]

678. ~ HYPOCRITICAL CONDEMNATIONS by THE RICH ~

The wealthy condemn the violence of the poor, hypocritically ignoring their own violence of possessing too much while their brothers have too little.

679. ~ THE NEW MIDDLE PASSAGE ~

We no longer hang strange fruit
from our Southern trees.
Instead, we butcher Black fruit
in the wombs of Black women,
lest their children rise up
and cut down our plans,
killing our oppression
and slaying our death
with their very lives.

So now we lynch them
before they are born,
before they have a chance
to live and fight and pray and revolt.
We will rape their mothers
with our abortionists' knives;
and we will do so in the name
of their ostensible freedom.

We will extract their money and blood,
their peace and their hope.
And we will give them
the liberation of lifelessness in return.

We don't need nooses
or hoods
or burning crosses.
Just elections and lies and political smiles
that stretch for miles...
across the new middle passage
from which few will make it out alive.

Last night I was returning from my father-in-law's house when I got stuck in traffic for an hour and a half. It was 1:00 a.m. and there was a complete logjam on the highway. People finally just turned off their cars, got out and milled around the interstate trying to figure out what the holdup was. I am a very impatient person, and my anxiety levels really rise in situations like that, where I have no control over the circumstances. There was no escaping the dilemma. We were all walled in on either side of the highway. Nowhere to go. With my history of heart disease, I kept thinking, what if I have a heart attack right now? I'd be dead. My car is trapped, and there's no way for an ambulance to reach me. And besides that, I was just getting really pissed off at the whole situation, because I couldn't understand the ineptitude of the people who were supposed to be resolving the issue. I mean, there was absolutely no movement for an hour and a half.

Well, anyway, to get to the point of this story...

After sitting there for over an hour – stressing, worrying, and getting pissed off – it suddenly dawned on me that there may have been a very bad wreck that had caused this traffic jam. Yes, that's me: so self-centered that it took me that long to consider that there may actually be people in a much worse situation than I was in. So that's when I decided to take out my prayer beads and pray for anyone who may have been injured or killed in a wreck. (Yeah, again, this was only after I had stewed in self-centered aggravation for an hour and a half.) So I began to pray the Jesus Prayer: *"Lord Jesus Christ, Son of God, have mercy on us."* And after I had prayed for only about 15 seconds, the cars began to move and the traffic immediately cleared up.

Coincidence? Perhaps. But I think not. Another lesson learned. My stress, worry, and anxiety usually result from an unhealthy focus on myself. But when I get my eyes off of myself and began to pray and act on behalf of others, then my anxiety usually decreases and the blessings inevitably flow. Prayer is a powerful thing, and I don't rely on it nearly enough.

I found out later that there was indeed a horrible three car accident that caused the backup. I wish I had begun praying from the moment I got stuck in that traffic. But since God is not bound by space and time, I trust that He still answered my feeble prayers for those that were involved in that wreck.

I hope that I don't forget what God showed me last night. But as stubborn and narcissistic as I am, I probably will. And I am confident that God in His abundant grace will surely remind me once again.

681. ~ BEAUTIFUL UNORTHODOX TRUTHS ~

One of the many paradoxes about my life is that I am constantly drawn to the beautiful truths expressed by certain unorthodox (and even non-Christian or agnostic) spiritual writers, and yet I nevertheless cringe at some of the unorthodox things they say. I am inspired by their passion, and yet I can see that their passion also led them into great errors. But I guess I am drawn to such writers – people like Huxley, Camus, and Tolstoy – because their truths and their errors seem to reflect the realities of life, and life is certainly full of truth and error.

As much as I cherish the writings of the saints and Church fathers, I sometimes feel so far removed from them that it's hard for me to relate. Their talk of sin and struggle often seems too generic for me. Hagiography reads like fairy tales, and yet I realize that fairy tales teach us some of the greatest truths.

I am drawn more to those that are not afraid to bare their souls, those who are willing to express the darkness as well as the light. How can I relate to those who speak of faith, grace, and hope if they have not also spoken personally of depravity, doubt, and despair?

Sunlight is not truly appreciated by those who have not at some point been imprisoned on the dark side of the moon; and the radiance of joy cannot really be experienced by those who have not been hostage to the long, cold midnights of life.

Huxley and Camus acknowledged their agnostic uncertainty, and yet they were somehow always able to express a deep affirmation of life. In spite of their cosmic doubts, they persistently acknowledged a transcendent hope. That's the stuff that resonates with my own conflicted soul, and it's the marrow that stimulates the universal palate of all those who read and think and pray and dream.

682. ~ WITH A LITTLE POLITICAL ACUMEN... ~

If you want to enslave, oppress, and control the masses, just tell them that you're a "liberator" not a conqueror, that you're a "revolutionary" not a tyrant. The people are quite willing to be manipulated and suppressed as long as you convince them that you have their best interests at heart. Just keep them so focused on the injustices of the past that they become blind to the sins of the present. Offer them rhetorical promises of "hope and change," and then tell them how 'free' they are as you enact policies and laws designed to keep them in bondage.

With a little political acumen, you can even get the people to fight, kill, and oppress each other while believing they are simply exercising their own individual liberties. And the worse that things get for them, the better things will get for you. Because the more the masses suffer, the more they will be willing to believe the lies that empowered you and enslaved them.

This, my friends, is the essence politics. And politics never has been – and never will be – about what's best for the people. But keep on voting if you want to.

683. ~ REVOLUTION and REDEMPTION ~

It cannot truly heal if it doesn't first terrify, convict, disrupt, and disturb. The agony of revolution is the requisite precursor to redemption. Salvation comes through the Cross, with blood and thorns and nails and tears. The cross is the paradoxical epitome of agony and conflict, peace and love.

684. ~ WHAT I WILL LOVE and WHAT I WILL NOT SERVE ~

I will love kings, princes, magistrates, and constables. I will love equally both those who preserve my own interests and those who war against them. I will love my brothers, my neighbors, my friends, and my enemies. I will love all people, for all people bear the image of God. I will love my fellow man – regardless of nationality, religion, philosophy, or ideology.

But I will not honor the cause of injustice; I will not serve the cause of violence; and I will not obey the laws of oppression. I will not side with nation against nation, government against government, or army against army. I am a citizen of heaven, and my allegiance is to the Kingdom of God alone. I am a Christian, and therefore I have nothing to do with your politics, your flags, your constitutions, and your wars. Earthly kingdoms rise and fall, and woe unto those who trust in such temporal powers.

I celebrate no "freedom" that results in the suffering of others. I rejoice in no victories that are won at the expense of innocent lives. American "justice" is the fruit of inhumanity, and the liberties of Babylon emanate from the chains of hell.

The Cross alone is my salvation; Christ alone is my Lord; and the Church alone is the indivisible, impermeable, and infinitely enduring Kingdom to which I belong. So let my soul be pierced with the splinters of the Cross, but let it never be stained with my brother's blood.

685. ~ A MISPLACED HOPE and AN UNACCEPTABLE PHILOSOPHY ~

I will never understand why professing Christians place so much hope in the American constitution, the American government, and the ostensible "individual liberties" that they claim to guarantee. The only freedoms the Gospel seems to give us are the freedom to die for Christ and the freedom to sacrifice our lives for others. I don't see any freedom of religion, right to self-defense, freedom to vote, right to bear arms, freedom of speech, right to abortion, or freedom to sin guaranteed to Christians in the New Testament. Yes, God gives us free will, and the disciple of Christ has a divine obligation – yea, a commandment – to use that free will to affirm the life, dignity, and human personhood of his fellow man. That is the essence of the Golden Rule. But a society that is founded on the political concept of secular democracy, which presumes to safeguard "individual liberty," is destined for chaos (and to be sure, secular democracy is the only kind of democracy, for God is a King and his kingdom is theocratic.) In a democracy – or any variation thereof – it is inevitable that one person's view of liberty will conflict with another's. So whose liberty is more important, and whose definition of liberty has the final say? It all comes down to whose voice is the loudest, who has the power, and who is in control. With democracy the masses ultimately decide, and thus we see the perpetual violent manifestation of the Golden Calf, the Tower of Babel, and "Free Barabbas! Crucify Christ!" A society established upon such an unjust and inhumane philosophy may be acceptable for the godless, but it can never be acceptable for the Christian.

686. ~ MERCY, GRACE, and FAITH ~

I have great faith in the mercy and grace of God, but I have no faith in the mercy and grace of men.

687. ~ GOD DOESN'T NEED A MARKETING STRATEGY ~

The prophets didn't have a marketing technique, a sales pitch, or a campaign strategy. All they had was the truth. The Gospel doesn't need advertisers, it just needs adherents. Jesus isn't asking for promoters, He's just looking for followers. If your god needs a marketing strategy, then you're serving the wrong god.

688. ~ THE VIOLENT REVOLUTIONARY ~

The violent revolutionary
Takes up the gun
To defend justice and peace
And to make right
All that is wrong

The violent revolutionary
For the cause of humanity
Sheds his brother's blood
To end oppression
And establish equality

The violent revolutionary
Always means well
But his violent actions
Inevitably produce
Another living hell

The violent revolutionary
Is no revolutionary at all
In the name of freedom
He perpetuates
The chaos of The Fall

True revolution is born
From the overflow of love
Not the spilling of blood

689. ~ PREACHING PEACE / PREACHING THE CROSS ~

If I could preach peace without preaching the Cross, or if I could preach the Cross without preaching peace, then I would do so. But I cannot proclaim false securities or false gospels.

690. ~ WORLDLY GOSPELS and ETERNAL MERCY ~

Keep your gospels of temporal wealth, mortal health, and earthly prosperity. We're trusting in the Gospel of Eternal mercy. You may have it good today, accumulating carnal comforts while we suffer and weep. But our struggles are not in vain. We're glad to forsake your worldly castles of sand for the Kingdom of Zion and the Promised Land.

691. ~ WEAPONS of DEATH or THE CROSS of LIFE? ~

Will we choose weapons of death or the Cross of Life? We cannot carry both. We are either on the side of the *crucifiers* or the side of the *crucified*. The Cross will never compromise with the sword. There is no compatibility between instruments of destruction and the instrument of salvation.

692. ~ I'M STILL HERE ~

I've dwelled in darkness – dodging bullets, evading the law, running from God and eluding/deluding myself. I've chased sin as rats literally licked my face. I've tiptoed on the edge of madness, dancing with depravity as I stared into the abyss of despair. I've sipped darkness from the goblet of iniquity – imbibing sorrow, misery, self-destruction, and woe. I've dined with demons as angels protected me from above. I've been lost and found more times than I can count. Like the prodigal in the pigpen, I've been so desperate that I envied the bellies of the swine. But for some reason I'm still here – fighting, struggling, failing, and praying. For some reason I'm still here – falling and rising, rising and falling, falling and rising... until God decides to take me home.

693. ~ CONTENTMENT ~

The Lord always provides what we need, but not always what we want. I'm still trying to learn this lesson myself. We have to remember that wherever we are or whatever our circumstances may be, God is nevertheless with us. If we can understand this truth, we will learn the meaning of contentment.

"Delight yourself in the Lord, and He will give you the desires of your heart." [Psalm 37:4]

"You have made known to me the path of life. You will fill me with joy in your presence, with eternal pleasures at your right hand." [Psalm 16:11]

694. ~ SEARCHING for ANSWERS in THE WRONG PLACES ~

We spend billions on military defense while refusing money to help the poor in our own backyard. We spend billions searching for life on Mars while refusing to acknowledge life in the womb. We spend billions on scientific research and technological advancement, but we refuse to help our own families, our own friends, and our own neighbors in need. We look for answers everywhere, in everything, and in everyone except for ourselves. As Tolstoy wrote:

"Everyone thinks of changing the world. No one thinks of changing himself."

695. ~ ECUMENICAL HEAVEN / EXCLUSIVE HELL ~

Heaven will accommodate those who love God and love man. Hell will reject those who love God and love man. Heaven is ecumenical; hell is exclusive.

696. ~ WHEN REVOLUTION WILL BE A REALITY ~

Revolution will be a reality when violence is no longer viewed as revolutionary. Revolution will be a reality when peace is not only the ends but also the means. Revolution will be a reality when truth is the force and love is the weapon. Revolution will be a reality when justice is not only what we demand, but more importantly how we live.

697. ~ TALKING ABOUT THE SAME GOD? ~

Etymologically we may be talking about the same God, but we are most certainly talking about different deities when some are worshipping a god who commands them *to* kill and others are worshipping a God who commands them *not* to kill.

Call me a heretic, but I say it's better to be killed for obeying Jesus than to kill others in betrayal of Jesus.

698. ~ SUBJECTIVE BEGINNINGS and OBJECTIVE ENDS ~

The man who thinks he can fly by leaping from a building and flapping his arms is trusting in his own subjective reasoning. But the man who thinks he can fly by boarding an airplane is also trusting in his own subjective reasoning. However, the significant difference is that the man who boards an airplane is acknowledging and trusting in an objective reality that transcends his subjectivity and thus protects him from the futility of his own independent efforts to fly apart from technological assistance.

This is analogous to the person who thinks he can fully and accurately interpret the Scriptures on his own and the person who realizes he needs the guidance of the apostolic Church to interpret the Scriptures. Both are trusting in their own subjective reasoning. But the person who relies on apostolic Teaching and Tradition is trusting in an objective reality that transcends his subjectivity and thus protects him from the futility of his own independent efforts to understand theological truth and sound doctrine apart from the divine assistance of the Church.

We all essentially start from a subjective foundation, because we are the subjects. But many people begin and end with themselves. They never get outside of themselves; they never go beyond themselves. Therefore they fall to their deaths thinking they can fly without planes; and they fall into heresies thinking they can understand God apart from His Church. But the wise person, although he begins with self, is able to look beyond self to objective realities that transform the self.

The Orthodox Christian does not remain mired in subjective and egotistical interpretations of the holy texts. The Orthodox Christian prostrates his subjective reasoning before the objectively transcendent truths of Christ, His Cross, and His Church. The Orthodox Christian allows God to transform his subjectively sinful beginnings into objectively holy ends.

699. ~ ART, TRUTH, and REVOLUTION ~

All art is revolutionary, because truth is always revolutionary; and art – if it is really art – cannot help but be true.

700. ~ VIOLENCE IS STRANGE ~

It's strange how people want to justify violence in the name of "defending the innocent" while meanwhile they do nothing to minister to orphans, widows, the unborn, and the poor. It's strange how people are willing to violently defend people on the other side of the world while they refuse to help the suffering in their own communities.

The mentality of violence is a very strange thing indeed. Violent philosophies are as untamed and irrational as the bullets and bombs that slaughter innocent children and wreak havoc on civilian populations.

Maybe, just maybe, that's why Jesus commanded Peter to put away his sword (St. Matthew 26:52). Maybe, just maybe, that's why Jesus commanded His disciples to love their enemies (St. Luke 6:27). Maybe, just maybe, that's why Jesus said *"Blessed are the peacemakers." [St. Matthew 5:9]* And maybe, just maybe, that's why St. Paul said:

"Leave vengeance to God. Leave room for God's wrath, for it is written: 'It is mine to avenge; I will repay,' says the Lord.'" [Romans 12:19]

701. ~ UNIVERSAL LOGIC and RATIONAL TRANSCENDENCE ~

I believe in the unalterable universal law that 2+2 = 4. I also believe that sometimes 2+2 = sunsets and shadows and nightmares and rainbows. I believe in the inviolate laws of logic, and I also believe in the mystical truths of the rationally transcendent.

702. ~ DON'T BE FOOLED ~

Message to my fellow Christian brothers and sisters:

Don't be fooled: the political left is just as venomous, divisive, and bloodthirsty as the political right. Let us eschew these warring political factions and place our hope in Christ and His Church alone. Let us comfort the suffering, let us minister to the poor, let us speak for the voiceless, let us labor for peace, let us liberate the unborn from the scourge of abortion, and let us show love to our neighbors, to our enemies, and to one another. Let us not fall prey to the lies, deceptions, violence, and divisiveness of politics. The Democrats and the Republicans are equally guilty of ignoring the imperatives of the Gospel. And the political "moderates" are hardly any better with their spineless, lukewarm, apathetic equivocations. Let us simply live and proclaim the Gospel. Politics is a demonic distraction from the Great Commission. Our Kingdom is not of this world. Don't get caught up in the ism/schism, divide and rule, play you for a fool, shell game of rightwing cons and leftist lies. We've got too much real work to do. Let's get busy!

"Kyrie Eleison" +++

703. ~ DEPENDENCE ~

I confess: I am a "dependent." I always have been. I was dependent on my mother and father for my very conception. In the womb I depended upon my mother for sustenance, warmth, and the necessities of life. I depended on my mother's sacrifice and love for the gift of birth. I depended upon my parents' nurture, provision, and protection from infancy to adulthood – and even beyond. I depended on the kindness and mentoring of certain teachers and coaches throughout my school years. And I am still dependent to this day. I depend upon the loyalty and fellowship of my true friends and my dear brothers in Christ. I depend on our Orthodox priests who offer me the sacramental graces necessary for my salvation. I depend upon the intercessions of the saints and monks who pray for me continually. I depend on the protection and guidance of the holy angels who minister to me day and night. I depend upon the love and encouragement of my wife and children. I depend on the kindness of strangers and on the consideration of my fellow man. I depend upon those who supply water, gas, and electricity to my home. I depend on those who pick up my garbage, those who bring me my mail, and those who stock my local grocery store. I depend upon my doctors and pharmacists who provide me with the medicine and care that keeps me alive. And yes, I even depend by default on certain conveniences, provisions, protections, and "safety nets" afforded me by a government whose laws are in many ways diametrically opposed to my Orthodox Christian Faith. So truly, I confess: I am a "dependent." And I pray that God would protect me from ever becoming "independent." I cannot imagine what a lonely, miserable existence that would be.

704. ~ THE IDOLATRY of CHRISTIANITY ~

To follow Christ – even to the extent that we're willing to forsake the idolatry of Christianity – this is salvation. We too easily trade the difficult but blessed community for the security of corporations that we erroneously call "churches." There is always a great temptation to abandon the agonizing road of eternal life for the comfortable road of earthly religiosities. Christianity is the greatest enemy the Church has ever known.

705. ~ FOOD and SALVATION ~

One man wants food but he doesn't want salvation. Another man wants salvation but he doesn't want to feed the poor. Both are equally far from the Kingdom. *I* am far from the Kingdom.

706. ~ IT COULD ALL FALL APART ~

Yes, it could all fall apart
Your picture in a frame
It might fall and it might fracture
It might dissipate like rain

Yes, it could all fall apart
But were you really whole?
Clinging to your feckless lies
Broken by the truth you know

Yes, it could all fall apart
The image you hold so dear
A carefully crafted idolatry
That you cling to out of fear

Yes, it could all fall apart
Your castles made of glass
Rising high upon the winds today
Tomorrow crumbling into ash

707. ~ MIGHTIER THAN LEAD ~

They said if I'd carried a gun
I'd have never bled.
But I trusted in the Cross
and picked up a guitar instead.
And though my fingers bleed
I've found that strings
are mightier than lead.

708. ~ HOW ELSE COULD I BE SAVED? ~

Like many families in America, we live month to month, check to check, with no financial security. We live in a neighborhood where burglaries are frequent and gunshots are a nightly occurrence. We've often had to choose between buying medicine and buying groceries, between paying the utility bills and paying for a doctor's visit. We have friends and relatives who are living in luxury as we struggle to survive. But we have other friends and relatives who are struggling just as much as we are, yet they graciously lend us tangible help and financial assistance.

Such is the way of the world.

But God has shown me that it's my duty to help others as much as I can rather than cursing those who refuse to help me.

The truth is that I am blessed beyond measure. Millions (maybe billions) of people around the world have it much worse than I do.

It's just painful when the people who claim to love you don't lift a hand to help you. And yet here I am – claiming to love peace, life, and humanity; but what do I *really* do to promote peace, to protect life, or to uplift humanity? Not much. Certainly not enough.

Family and friends may have failed me, but I have surely failed them (and my fellow man) much worse.

So I am thankful for my humble life. I am thankful for the struggles. I am thankful for the insecurities. I am thankful for the trials and pains and disappointments and fears. I am thankful for the betrayals. I am thankful that I have to wake up each day and rely solely upon God.

How else could I be saved?

709. ~ CHRIST DOES NOT CALL US TO CHANGE THE WORLD ~

Christ does not call us to change the world. He calls us by grace to change ourselves. And when people change themselves and follow Him, then the world will inevitably be transformed. We need to stop fighting militant wars, political wars, and culture wars. The only war that God calls us to fight is the spiritual war.

710. ~ "HONEST" HYPOCRISY ~

I have more respect for those who proclaim the truth but fail to live completely truthful lives than for those who justify their sins and excesses in the name of "honesty." The world is full of "honest" secularists who say:

"I don't pretend to be holy, in fact I don't even believe in holiness. So at least I'm not a hypocrite, which makes me better than you Christians who always fail to live up to the values you preach."

These "honest" irreligious folks scoff at objective moral codes while somehow upholding hypocrisy as the unpardonable sin, which ironically makes them... well... hypocrites.

711. ~ DON'T FEAR THAT WHICH IS WORSE THAN DEATH ~

There are things worse than death, such as suffering, madness, and despair. And yet the one who suffers, the one who despairs, or the one who goes mad has the hope that he will be transformed and renewed by his afflictions. But he who dies without having gone through the fire, such is the one to be pitied. The lunatic, the tortured, and the hopeless fool have gone through a door and tasted the torment. And thus they live with their souls perpetually crying out for salvation. They crave nothing but mercy and peace, and therefore they draw near to the Lord of Mercy and the Prince of Peace. But woe unto those who are so comfortable that they never cry out for healing. Woe unto those whose contentedness precludes them from fearing hell or desiring heaven. Woe unto those whose earthly securities give them no reason to need a saving and loving God. So don't fear that which is worse than death. Fear that which fails to prepare you for death.

712. ~ "WAR IS EVIL, BUT..." ~

I can't tell you how many times I've read quotes, speeches, and books by people who clearly and brilliantly articulate the horrors and injustices of war only to then say, "But I am not a pacifist." It's like people who clearly understand and decry the horrific realities of abortion and then say, "But I still believe abortion should be legal." I will never understand that. I mean, I can understand people who support warfare and abortion because they are completely ignorant about the evils of warfare and abortion. But when people clearly recognize and acknowledge the horrific realities of premeditated mass killing and then continue to defend its legality and ostensible "necessity," then they are either schizophrenic at best or downright evil at worst.

If it's evil then renounce it, condemn it, and flee from it. Don't justify and excuse it.

713. ~ A LESSER POISON? ~

The lesser of two evils is still evil. How can the Christian vote for evil – be it a lesser or greater iniquity? Would we drink a lesser poison if we had the option not to drink poison at all? Flee from the polls as if fleeing from poison!

People tell me that refusing to vote is ineffectual, that political abstemious would only work if everyone refused to vote. Well, that's sort of like saying that Christianity would only work if everyone was a Christian, or that nonviolence would only work if everyone was nonviolent.

The fact is that the world will always be the world. But the Christian is not of this world. We are not motivated by pragmatism, but rather by Gospel truth. Temporal expedience is not the ultimate standard. The standard for us is what is right, what is true, what is eternally profitable.

714. ~ LIFE and DEATH WAR ~

Make no mistake: there is a war between life and death. And because Christ is Risen, life has eternally prevailed. So don't be on the losing side. Align yourself with the eternal victories of peace, love, and Life-affirmation. If you insist on choosing militarism, hatred, racism, and abortion then you are waging war against the divine laws of the universe, and thus you are defeated at the outset. What do you expect to win with your bombs, your burning crosses, and your butchering of unborn babies? Will such violent evils bring you peace, joy, and salvation? Of course not. No matter how loudly you shout your mantras of death and echo your violent demands, you are fighting a war you will never win. Though you kill and kill, life will always rise up – like Christ – to conquer your death and destruction. But the Kingdom of God is open to all who sincerely wish to enter through faith, repentance, and the Life-giving Cross. Christ died so that you no longer need to seek peace in violence, so that you no longer need to seek salvation in killing. Life is reaching out to you with infinite hope. Embrace it! Choose Life and choose eternal victory!

715. ~ DEAR FELLOW CHRISTIANS ~

Dear fellow Christians: Let us leave swords and whips and judgment and bloodshed and fire and brimstone to God alone. How can we take up arms when our arms have taken up the Cross? How can we condemn the weakness of others when our own vision is obfuscated by beams of sin? How can we engage in the terrible works of violence if we are working out our own salvation with fear and trembling?

"Lord Jesus Christ, Son of God, have mercy on us." +++

716. ~ SPIRITUAL WAR and DEMONIC DISTRACTIONS ~

Evil is evil, regardless of the label or banner under which it is committed. Liberal evil is just as oppressive as conservative evil. Secular evil is just as corrosive as religious evil. Too many people are wrapped up in ideological wars, culture wars, political wars, and sectarian wars. The only war that matters is the spiritual war. Let us align ourselves with peace and life. Let us enlist in the cause of humanity and justice. Let us pledge our allegiance to serving God and our fellow man. If we do this we shall be eternally victorious. All other battles are merely demonic distractions from the ultimate spiritual war that we are called to fight. No time for division in JAH army!

"Finally, my brethren, be strong in the Lord, and in the power of his might. Put on the whole armor of God, that ye may be able to stand against the wiles of the devil. For we wrestle not against flesh and blood, but against principalities, against powers, against the rulers of the darkness of this world, against spiritual wickedness in high places. Wherefore take unto you the whole armor of God, that ye may be able to withstand in the evil day, and having done all, to stand. Stand therefore, having your loins girt about with truth, and having on the breastplate of righteousness; And your feet shod with the preparation of the gospel of peace; Above all, taking the shield of faith, wherewith ye shall be able to quench all the fiery darts of the wicked. And take the helmet of salvation, and the sword of the Spirit, which is the word of God: Praying always with all prayer and

supplication in the Spirit, and watching thereunto with all perseverance and supplication for all saints." [Ephesians 6:10-18]

717. ~ FANATICISM ~

Nothing is as dangerous as religious fanaticism, and therefore we will use the secular sword to fanatically root out all vestiges of religious influence upon the state. We are too enlightened to tolerate religious obscurantism, we are too scientific to tolerate religious superstition, and we are too tolerant to tolerate religious intolerance. Either progress with us or off with your heads! Your religiosity is a threat to justice and humanity, and therefore we will use injustice and inhumanity to preserve our secular utopian nightmare. We will silence your fanatical religious godliness with our fanatical governmental godlessness.

718. ~ BRAVERY ~

Anyone can be brave behind badges, bombs, uniforms, and guns. Anyone can be brave with the protection of governments, gangs, armies, and states. Anyone can be brave when they are protected by violent force. But personally, I don't view bullets as bravery. I think bravery is dying for truth rather than killing for lies. I think bravery is dying for God rather than killing for governments. I think bravery is sacrificing for Christ rather than slaughtering for kings.

719. ~ CHOOSE THE PATH of PEACE ~

If you choose the path of violent force, then you really have no right to complain when you are victimized by violent force. Whether you are a soldier, a gang-banger, a police officer, a terrorist, or a politician, you cannot evade the prophecy of Our Lord. If you live by the sword you should expect to die by the sword.

Those of us who choose to trust God rather than guns expect nothing less than suffering and death. But we prefer to die to gain eternal life rather than kill to preserve our temporal existence.

Choose this day who you will serve: demons of death or the Lord of Life. Choose the path of peace. Your salvation depends upon it.

720. ~ HOLY SIGN and UNHOLY SIGHTING ~

There is nothing holy about making the sign of the Cross and then sighting your neighbor in the crosshairs of your rifle scope. You cannot honor Christ while you prepare to kill. The Christian soldier is armed with the Gospel, not guns; he marches to the Kingdom, not to war. Those who get paid to slaughter their fellow man are serving the armies of Satan, not the army of God.

721. ~ APPETITES, PASSIONS, SIN, and JUDGMENT ~

Gluttony and lust are both sins. And yet apart from hunger and sexual desire humanity would cease to exist. Sorrow comes equally to those who are ruled by the senses and to those who lead sensitively detached lives. That's really all I know about such matters. These mysteries are too great for me to sit in judgment and condemnation of the appetites and passions of others.

722. ~ LOST and FOUND ~

It is better to be lost and searching for God than to never be lost and never be found by God.

723. ~ AMMUNITION ~

They condemn the man
who takes up a gun
to protect wife, mother,
daughter, and son.

But they praise the soldier
who shoots to kill
for flag, adventure
and the G.I. Bill.

To patricians and politicians
they give ammunition
while they disarm and oppress
the common citizen.

But some of us don't need bullets,
for we are Christians.

The Cross is our shield,
the Cross is our Sword,
and we are eternally defended
by the Incarnate Word.

So keep your bombs and tanks
and armies and guns:
such weapons will always lose.
You fashion your own noose
with the violence you choose.

724. ~ IF I COULD TELL YOU, I WOULD ~

If I could tell you the meaning of love, I would.
If I could tell you the meaning of suffering, I would.
If I could tell you the meaning of joy, I would.
If I could tell you the meaning of sorrow, I would.
But I can't.
I don't understand any of it.
But somehow I know – beyond reason and certainty and evidence and logic – that the Cross is the meaning of it all.

725. ~ HEROES and VILLAINS ~

Just so you know:
You don't have to wear a badge, carry a gun, or get elected to be a hero. In fact, true heroes are those who refuse to put on a uniform, refuse to obey unjust orders, refuse to perpetuate a godless political system, and refuse to kill their fellow man. True heroes stand firmly against racism, war, abortion, police brutality, and anything that facilitates these evils. It's the ones with the uniforms, badges, and guns that are usually defending the status quo and violently preserving an unjust social order. We're living in an age where villains are hailed as heroes and heroes are condemned as villains.

726. ~ WHAT IS and WHAT IS NOT SINFUL (JUST A FEW THINGS) ~

Being homeless is not sinful, but a culture that creates homelessness is.

Loving your enemies is not sinful, but killing them is.

Refusing to obey a godless government is not sinful, but pledging allegiance to that government is.

Being poor is not sinful, but a society that forces people into poverty is.

Being religious is not sinful, but despising your neighbor in the name of God is.

Begging is not sinful, but refusing the beggar is.

Ignorance is not sinful, but the willful rejection of divine truth is.

Unemployment is not sinful, but exploiting the employed is.

Unwed pregnancy is not sinful, but killing an unborn baby is.

Sacrificial giving is not sinful, but usury is.

Refusing to kill is not sinful, but being paid to kill is.

(That is, if I correctly understand the teachings of the Gospel and the teachings of the Orthodox Church. And if I am wrong about these things, then please don't correct me.)

727. ~ A SIMPLE CONCEPT ~

It's a simple concept people:

"Equal rights for all," which means that nobody has the right to violently interfere with the life of another. If your own "individual right" means the murder and oppression of other individuals, then it is not a right but a wrong. Just because you have the power to enslave, colonize, bomb and abort does not mean that you have the unalienable, universal right to do so.

Yes, we have all free will. Regardless of religious morality or civil laws, people will still find ways to sin and violate the laws. But that doesn't mean we shouldn't have any laws at all. That doesn't mean we should jettison nonviolent activism and righteous opposition to unjust laws that violate the sanctity of human life and human freedom. Should we have tolerated slavery and segregation based on the idea that to outlaw these evils would be tantamount to "imposing our Christian morality on unbelievers"? Thank God that the abolitionists didn't subscribe to such a feckless philosophy!

I think Dr. Martin Luther King, Jr. said it best:

"We cannot legislate morality, but we can regulate behavior. The law cannot change the heart, but it can restrain the heartless."

When it comes to the preservation of human rights, the law should not be determined by the arbitrary will of the majority or the arbitrary will of the individual. The principle of human rights is a universal principle that is divinely authored. No one should have the right to violently interfere in the life of another. It is indeed a simple concept – a concept that, sadly, this sinful world inherently rejects.

Let us pray: *"Lord have mercy."*

728. ~ CAPTIVE of BABYLON ~

I am a third world man struggling with first world problems. I am a first world man burdened with a third world consciousness. I am a deracinated native and a descendent of those who profited from the deracination of the natives. I have the blood of Adam, the life of Eden, the soul of the universe – the spirit of all humanity and all the earth – flowing through my veins. And yet I too often choose to be a captive of Babylon.

729. ~ PREACH the GOSPEL, LIVE the GOSPEL, and LEAVE the REST to GOD ~

We only hurt our Pro-Life cause when we infect it with judgmental condemnations of other people's souls. Our Lord was very clear that what we do unto the least of these we do it unto Him (St. Matthew 25:40). According to the standards articulated by Christ, there may be more hope for the atheist who defends the unborn child than for the professing Christian who turns a blind eye to the murder of the innocents. Let us work out our own salvation with fear and trembling (Philippians 2:12), never presuming to know the fate of the souls of others. Preach the Gospel, live the Gospel, and leave the rest to God.

730. ~ COUNTER-REVOLUTIONARY ~

Hate is the most counter-revolutionary emotion, and violence is the most counter-revolutionary force. Peace and Love are not empty ideals; they are the indispensable foundations of authentic revolutionary change.

731. ~ THE CHURCH is A MISSION FIELD ~

Sometimes the Church is the greatest mission field. Sometimes professing Christians are those most in need of hearing the Gospel. So please: keep preaching the peace, hope, and divine social imperatives of the Good News to me. I need to be reminded daily.

732. ~ MILITANT SHEEP ~

We are the militant sheep: armed not with fangs and claws but with justice and truth. We are the militant sheep: we do not roar but neither do we retreat. We are the militant sheep: we neither kill our enemies nor flee from their threats. We are the militant sheep: protected by the Lion who will avenge His children with the swords of His teeth. We are the militant sheep: trusting in a God who will repay all evil and eternally right all temporal wrongs. We are the militant sheep: waging our Gospel war with meekness and faith, with love and peace. Yes, we are the militant sheep: oppress us today and reap hell tomorrow.

733. ~ RIGHT and WRONG THEOLOGY ~

If theology confuses the mind, then you're probably doing it wrong. But if theology convicts the heart, then you're probable doing it right.

734. ~ AN UNTAMED PEACE ~

We are not quiet. We are not tame. We are not compromised. We are not subdued. Ours is a confrontational peace, a militant nonviolence, an agitating truth, and an active love. Do not mistake our pacifism for weakness. Do not confuse our refusal to kill for our refusal to fight. Your bullets and jails and governments and armies will not subdue God's Spirit, God's Church, God's power or God's truth. Kill us and we shall simply rise from this world, with imprecatory prayers that comfort the oppressed and afflict the oppressors. The blood you shed only poisons your own souls. You can never destroy what Christ has preserved.

735. ~ "ENABLING" ~

They tell me that we shouldn't enable the poor with food stamps or support them with welfare programs, because that just makes them "lazy and dependent." But then they tell me we should enable politicians with our votes and that we should support the military with our tax dollars.

Apparently, according to the worldview of many, the right to vote and the right to kill are far more important than the right to eat and the right to human dignity.

736. ~ KILL ME COURAGEOUSLY ~

If you want to kill me, then don't be a coward about it. Come up to me, ask me my name, shake my hand, look me in the eye, and then shoot me if you still want to. Perhaps I deserve to die. But if you're man enough to put on a uniform, wear a badge, and tote a gun, then be man enough to get to know me before you violently end my life. Kill me with courage, not cowardice. (I realize this goes against everything they teach you in your armies, police academies, and gang initiations.)

If indeed I must die
from your violence and lies,
then do me one favor:

As you kill me,
please have the courage
to look me in the eye.

737. ~ HERETICAL RELIGION and DISHONEST TRUTH ~

Religion that needs to be preserved by violence is heresy, and truth that demands bloodshed is a lie. There is no need to kill for a Church and a Faith that are eternally indestructible.

738. ~ "A NATION of LAWS" ~

"We are a nation of laws" is a logically feckless and morally irrelevant argument. Every nation is a nation of laws. Nazi Germany was a nation of laws. North Korea is a nation of laws. South Africa during apartheid was a nation of laws. So when people attempt to make some sort of moral argument by saying, "America is a nation of laws," it really doesn't mean much. This "nation of laws" mantra was used in the past to justify slavery, segregation, and "manifest destiny," and it is being used today to justify police brutality, religious intolerance, and abortion on demand. So if you want to make a reasonable moral argument, please come up with something more substantive than "we are a nation of laws." History clearly demonstrates that the "laws of the land" are often the greatest impediments to peace, justice, humanity, and truth.

739. ~ WE ARE THE FEW ~

It's sad – quite tragic really – that some people are so poisoned by politics that they will actually support an evil simply because their ideological opponents are opposed to that evil. But there are a few of us who are actually free from all of this political enslavement. There are a few of us who truly stand for peace and life across the board.

We don't care *who* is opposing war, *who* is opposing the death penalty, *who* is fighting poverty, or *who* is denouncing abortion. If you are promoting peace, then we stand with you. If you are agitating for justice through nonviolent means, then we are your allies. If you are on the right side of life, then we are your comrades. We don't care about your political ideology: if you are working to uphold the sanctity, dignity, and quality of human life, then we'll gladly encourage your endeavors. There are a few of us who are free enough to look past politics and stand with anyone, anywhere, at anytime as long as they are standing for peace, justice, and life-affirmation.

But sadly, we are indeed only few.

We are the few who are driven neither by rightwing fundamentalist moralisms nor leftist partisan idealisms. We are the few who are truly free to think for ourselves. We are the few who conform all of our convictions to the Consistent Life Ethic, which is why we tend to offend those who are still enslaved to political propaganda and media manipulation. We are the few who understand that every individual human life is sacred, and that nobody has the right to discard a single human life with premeditated violence – for *any* reason. We are the few who will therefore continue to expose the hypocrisy and inconsistency of anyone who claims to be "pro-life" or "nonviolent" and yet supports militarism, the death penalty, capitalistic exploitation, or organizations that profit from killing unborn babies.

We are a rebellious and unpopular few. We don't run for office, so we don't really care about popularity or praise, criticism or condemnation. We are the obstinate few who instead care about the sanctity of humanity, about actions and ideas that correspond to life affirmation, and about peaceful means of enhancing the quality of human personhood and restoring human dignity. We may be few – perhaps sometimes as few as one – but we're full of love and we're armed with truth.

And we're coming for you!

740. ~ HOW LONG? ~

How long will we try to placate, tame, and seek compatibility with the damnable beast of a godless secular government? How long will we seek divine blessings from the idolatry of democracy? How long will we try to renovate and reform that which was born in hell?

Yes, we can certainly maintain hope – in fact, we *must* maintain hope – that through prayer, activism, repentance and faith we can profoundly change our society and our culture. Truly the Kingdom of God is among us (St. Luke 17:21), and His Kingdom has no end (Isaiah 9:7; Nicene Creed). But we must not confuse the Kingdom of Heaven for the kingdoms of men. We must not forsake our Gospel duty for political aspirations or military solutions. Authentic hope and enduring change come from true love for our neighbors and true submission to our Creator.

Let us not trade eternal hope and divine change for democracies of despair and political chains. Those who are secure in the Cross will never be secure in this world, and those who place security in this world will never know the security of the Cross.

741. ~ THERE WILL BE KILLING TODAY ~

There will be killing today
But I won't stop it
I'll just preach and plead
As they suffer and bleed

There will be killing today
But I won't stop it
I know when and where
But I'll only offer up a prayer

There will be killing today
Behind this gate
Upon this hill
Lives will be dashed
And blood will spill

There will be killing today
The cars will roll in
As women stumble out
And I'll raise my feeble shout

There will be killing today
But I won't stop it
I'll be a sidewalk prophet
But no, I won't stop it

There will be killing today
But how will I respond?
Coward that I am
Coward that I am

There will be killing today
And I wonder what I would do
If I truly valued their lives
As much as my own?

742. ~ "BLACK LIVES MATTER" / "ALL LIVES MATTER" ~

Yes, *Black Lives Matter!* And yes, *All Lives Matter!* But when one segment of humanity is disproportionately affected by violence and oppression, then it's only right to highlight the lives of those who are suffering inordinately. To do so is not discriminatory or racist. It is simply reflective of the natural cry for justice that beats in every human breast.

Of course, anyone who truly cares about Black lives will not fail to decry the unjust slaughter of innocent Black lives in the womb. We don't know when or where the next innocent Black youth will be shot down by a racist cop, but we do know when and where innocent unborn Black babies will be murdered by abortionists. So if you want to know who truly cares about *all* Black lives (not just the select lives that the media and the politicians tell you to care about), then look for those who are equally consistent in condemning police brutality, war, poverty, racism, and abortion.

Yes, the sad truth is that society seems callously indifferent to the murders of young Black men by bloodthirsty cops. But it is also a sad truth that many of those who exclaim *"Black Lives Matter!"* really don't give a damn about the sanctity of Black human life. If they did, then they would be demanding an end to the systemic murder of helpless unborn Black children. Not all cops are killers, but all abortionists are. An innocent Black youth may survive an encounter with a racist police officer, but an unborn Black baby in the womb will never survive an abortionist's "surgical" weapons.

I learned a long time ago that most people's social convictions are shaped by politics and the media rather than by divine truth and true human compassion. That's why most people demonstrate a selective moral outrage and a superficial social consciousness. Their view of society is shaped by their television screens, their definition of justice is dictated by political propaganda, and their understanding of human rights is determined by narrow *self-interest* rather than broad universal *human interest*.

And this is why politicians get elected while revolutionaries are killed. It's why monuments are built while poor people starve. It's why mountains are renamed while Black children die. And it's why the masses embrace lies while they crucify the Truth.

Such is life in Babylon, where Life really doesn't matter at all.

(Also see text #990)

743. ~ POLITICS ~

Politics is nothing more than people arguing about whose policies of violence, inhumanity, and injustice are better than the others' policies of violence, inhumanity, and injustice.

744. ~ CONFORMITY and CAPTIVITY ~

Whether it's conservative conformity or liberal conformity, it's all counter-revolutionary acquiescence, ideological brainwashing, the perpetuation of the status quo, the proliferation of evil disguised as political progress. The system doesn't give a damn whether you're a Republican or a Democrat, a right-winger or a leftist. All the system wants you to do is pay your taxes, support the troops, pledge your allegiance, and march to the polls like bovine to the slaughter. Far from changing the evil system, your liberalism and conservatism actually cooperate to fuel the evil system – like the slave and the prisoner who argue about how to humanize the slave trade and reform the penal code rather than rebelling against their captors and working to liberate one another.

You've been convinced to kill your brothers in the name of "patriotism;" you've been taught to pass judgmental condemnation on your neighbors in the name of "values;" you've been led to believe that religious persecution is "social progress;" and you've been persuaded to murder your own unborn children in the cause of "liberation and equality."

The system doesn't care about the ideology for which you discriminate and kill, just as long as you discriminate and kill. It matters not whether you are liberal or conservative, as long as you facilitate death, division, and destruction in one form or another, as long as you conform to the system of violence and oppression with your votes, your complicity, your acquiescence and your political obeisance.

America is a land of captivity, where the masses perpetually vote to enslave themselves in the name of liberty, progress, hope and change. America is a land of violence and oppression, where the masses perpetually conform to bloodshed and bondage in the name of freedom, justice, equality and peace.

"Emancipate yourselves from mental slavery,
none but ourselves can free our minds."
~ Marcus Garvey ~ / ~ Bob Marley (Berhane Selassie) ~

745. ~ COMPASSION ~

Compassion leads me to believe that the right to make a profit is not more important than the right to food, clothing, housing, and healthcare.

Compassion leads me to believe that the laws of the government are not more important than the rights to freedom and liberty.

Compassion leads me to believe that the right to national defense is not more important than the sanctity of all human life.

Compassion leads me to believe that the rights of men are not more important that the rights of women, and that the rights of women are not more important than the lives of unborn children.

Compassion leads me to believe that the words of constitutions and kings are not more important than the words of Christ and the Gospels.

The law of compassion also leads me to believe that selective compassion is often the greatest cruelty. To preserve the rights and lives of some at the expense of the rights and lives of others is conquest, not compassion.

And you won't find a platform of consistent compassion from any of these political candidates on either the right or the left. They all eschew the consistent life ethic, and they all support the deliberate destruction of human life in one form or another. So don't be fooled by political rhetoric that extols the virtue of compassion while masking policies of callousness and cruelty.

746. ~ CHURCH, COMMUNITY, and SOCIAL ANXIETY ~

There are many factors that cause people to shy away from community. Not everyone who eschews Church does so because of the hypocrisies and failures of those of us within the Church. Some people have social anxieties or other health and psychological issues which are beyond their control. I think we need to be sensitive to that. Many people would love nothing more than to come to Church, to be a part of the Church, and to receive the blessed Sacraments and holy fellowship that the Church provides. But they suffer from mental and physical issues that preclude them from doing so.

So rather than always telling people to come to Church, we need to take the Church to them. There are many people who are desperately lonely yet who also desperately fear social situations. We need to find creative and loving ways to minister to such people wherever they are in life. After all, Christ did not command His disciples to call the world to come and hear them preach; rather, He commanded them to go into all the world and preach the Gospel. (St. Mark 16:15; St. Matthew 28:18-20) And I think we too often forget this.

747. ~ BRIEF THOUGHTS on REPARATIONS ~

Yes, I definitely believe in the concept of Reparations. In fact, I believe that reparations are a must. This is a serious issue. Unfortunately it has become a pawn for political fodder, and few approach this topic with seriousness and wisdom. But all people of morality and good will must at least consider the justice and necessity of reparations. The principle of reparations is not rooted in politics, but rather in biblical and spiritual history. Moses demanded reparations from Pharaoh; and although what was returned to the Israelites was hardly able to recompense the grave injustices that had been committed by the Egyptians, it was nevertheless right that these reparations were demanded and subsequently given.

I personally think that there are many forms and means of reparations that should be discussed and debated. I believe that reparations should incorporate the material, social, economic, and psychological aspects of life that are essential to human personality and human dignity. But we cannot really make reparations for past injustices until we first eradicate the injustices of the present.

There are three points I would offer up for consideration in this important matter:

1) I don't think White people as a whole owe reparations; but the American government most certainly does. Not only did many White people not own slaves or benefit from slavery, but they suffered and died to help free the slaves. It is always a dangerous error to condemn an entire race of people for the crimes committed by some. But when we look at the systemic evils of this American government – historically and presently – (and the financial profit the government has accrued from these evils), then there is no question that this government owes a great debt to those who suffered and continue to suffer from its oppressive laws and policies.

2) I think it's important to make sure that reparations are truly reparative. For example, this Babylon government made ostensible reparations to Native Americans by giving them land (reservations) and economic opportunity (in the form of casinos). And these

"reparations" have effectively decimated Native Americans spiritually, economically, and psychologically. So be careful when Babylon pretends to throw you a lifeline; there may be a noose on the other end.

3) The first step towards authentic reparations should be the cessation of the current violence committed against African Americans in the forms of police brutality, mass incarceration, forced mis-education, exploitative taxation, and legalized abortion. This Babylon governmental system is tricky. Everything good they pretend to do is designed to ultimately control and oppress in the long run. (E.g. give the people a Black president who will support the murder of Black lives in the womb. Give the people "free" education designed to teach them that their oppressive government is actually their benevolent benefactor. Give the people charismatic figureheads and token policies that will lead them to believe restoration and progress are underway, while in reality these figureheads and policies lead the people into deeper bondage and greater suffering.)

So I am a firm believer in the principle of reparations, but I want to make sure that the reparations are truly reparative and not ultimately destructive. And I certainly don't trust Babylon to be an honest broker in the deal. So let the revolutionaries, the prophets, and the righteous voices that arise from oppression dictate the terms of the reparations. Don't trust the politicians to do it.

That's just my two cents on a controversial but very important issue.

748. ~ A SIMPLE CONCEPT ~

While my Orthodox Christian Faith deeply shapes all of my moral and social convictions, my primary argument against the evils of warfare, slavery, poverty, abortion (and anything else that devalues and destroys human life) is essentially a universal human argument. Regardless of our various religious views – or lack thereof – what we all share in common is our mutual human conception and our mutual human existence. There is no debate about that. What matters is that human life exists, and thus I argue that human life should be valued across the board. This is the only thing that really binds humanity – our common *human reality*. We can argue about God, religion, philosophy, politics, etc. We can all hold differing views on such matters. But what we all undoubtedly have in common is our *shared humanity*, our *shared life*, our *mutual human existence*.

Regardless of race, religion, gender, sexual orientation, socio-economic condition, politics, or birth status, the fact is that human life is *human life*, and therefore it should be protected rather than callously dismissed or violently discarded according to relativistic philosophical opinions or situational ethics. You don't need to be religious to recognize that once the value of human life is relegated to subjective definitions of personhood, quality, etc. that our own lives then cease to have any objective worth.

If we will allow one segment of humanity to be enslaved, then we have no objective moral basis to prevent our own enslavement. If we will allow some people to starve, then we have no objective moral basis to demand our own nourishment. If we will allow one group to be oppressed and violated, then we have no objective moral basis to prevent our own violent oppression. And if we are willing to destroy innocent lives in the womb, then we have no objective moral basis for protecting our own lives outside of the womb.

It's a simple concept, a concise universal axiom stated by someone much wiser than me: *"Live, and let live."*

Perhaps it's time to try it.

749. ~ OBSCENITIES ~

I confess that I'm not always a "proper" or "tasteful' Christian. And to be honest, I'm not sure I really want to be. Profane evils sometimes warrant a profane rebuke, and the struggles of the soul sometimes need to be expressed with viscerally honest language. The

Scriptures warn us about an unbridled tongue, and as Christians we must always strive to season our speech with grace and truth. But there can be grace in catharsis, there can be truth in pathos, and there can certainly be redemption in cursing idolatry and exposing evil with harsh (and even scatological) language. Too many people are more disturbed by the fact that I say "Fuck War" and "God Damn Abortion" than they are by the actual obscenities of war and the horrific realities of abortion.

750. ~ REVOLUTIONARY CREATIONS ~

Put pen and ink to paper today. Strum your fingers on some strings today. Splash colors across a canvas today. Make love and make a baby today. Create something beautiful and positive today.

Whether you build a sand castle on the seashore... whether you give birth to a song in your soul... or whether you sow seeds of life in the one you love... rejoice and sing praises to JAH! And know that in the process you are doing something truly revolutionary.

Today is your palette, and you are the artist. May the Master's hand guide your righteous creative intentions.

751. ~ I SAW GOD TODAY ~

I saw devils today
in the faces
of the human race.
And I also saw
in this human gaze
the very faces of God.

752. ~ LOVE ~

Love is the beginning. Love is the end. Love is the destination, the journey, and the path between the infinite and the eternal. Love shall remain when all else fades. Are we willing to forsake everything for the pursuit of love? What else can sustain us? What else can satisfy? All that is not of love is merely an ephemeral illusion that withers in the winds of eternity. Every truth, every right, every cause, and every endeavor is futile if it is not rooted in, established upon, and fulfilled by love. God is love; and to love God is to love one another.

Love is a dangerous thing. It will crush you if you trust it. But without it you can never be whole. Love crucifies, but love saves. We will either be saved together with love, or damned alone without it.

753. ~ HOW DO WE LOVE THE WICKED? ~

How do we love the hateful, the wicked, the shameless and unapologetic workers of iniquity? We may be able to theologically understand that the rapist, the racist, the pedophile and the abortionist nevertheless bear the image of God. We may be able to intellectually comprehend that Christ commands us to love the evildoer as much as the innocent and the victimizer as much as the victim. But how do we take this knowledge from our heads to our hearts? How do we cultivate a love for the wicked that moves us to weep for them as we weep for those who suffer at their hands? How do we learn to love the purveyors of evil as much as we love ourselves?

We must pray for the grace to find such love. We must always remember our own capacity for evil. We must see our own sinfulness in the horrors of the oppressor, recognizing that sin is the indiscriminate enemy of us all. We must see the icon of Christ that is extant even in living portraits of abomination and injustice. We must consider the injuries and wounds that we have inflicted on others by our callous actions, insensitive words, and apathetic indifference.

Perhaps we ourselves have not murdered, raped, aborted, or enslaved; but what have we done to stop murder, rape, abortion, and slavery?

I have railed against injustice and evil while too often forgetting the violence that I myself have wielded against the innocent and the suffering. I have found it hard to love the warmonger and the slave owner, yet I ask that Christ love this broken man who once perpetuated the slavery of addiction and the suffering of chemical bondage. I have found it difficult to find mercy for the abortionist, yet I plead the mercy of God for this sinner who once poisoned mother and unborn child with the sale of crack cocaine.

Perhaps I find it hard to love the evildoer because I don't truly understand the love of God myself. So it is easier to curse the clarity of evil than to strive towards the Mystery of divine darkness that will illuminate my mind and redeem my heart.

So how do we love the wicked? I don't know. But I know that it all begins with the knowledge of God's love for us. If we truly understood the love of Christ, we would forgive all men for everything. I confess that I still do not understand the love and mercy of Our Lord. It is too great a thing for me to comprehend. May He grant me the grace to know it.

754. ~ TRANSCENDENT TELEOLOGICAL BLESSINGS ~

I've heard the tears of angels dripping from Carlos Santana's guitar. I've seen the colors of heaven swirling in Van Gogh's art. I've felt the Creator's caress in my children's embrace. I've tasted the nectar of paradise in my Grandmothers' cooking. I've known the goodness of God through the honeysuckle's scent.

I've experienced beauty too profound, love too rich, and joys too inexpressible to doubt the glory and greatness of Our Lord. And I've also experienced sorrows and pains that are just as deep.

But no matter how bad things get, God will always comfort me with His transcendent teleological blessings. Sometimes you just need to put on some music, drink some wine, play with your children, or go outside and imbibe the aromas of the universe.

And always, *always*, pray and give thanks to the Creator for all things.

755. ~ "FREE" EDUCATION in BABYLON ~

They want to give you free education, so that you will be brainwashed, so that you will continue to empower the very politicians and the very system that keep you enslaved. As long as they can send you running to their colleges, joining their militaries, and scurrying to their voting booths, then they can continue to manipulate and control you. The freest people in Babylon are those who refuse to vote, those who refuse to kill, and those who refuse the propagandistic indoctrination that's disguised as education. And if they can't control you with politics, militarism, and mis-education, then they'll do their best to send you to prison. And that's why some of the strongest, freest, and wisest among us are actually those that society has locked up behind bars. The only things that are truly free in Babylon are those who are truly free from the manipulations of Babylon.

756. ~ MISINFORMATION in THE "INFORMATION AGE" ~

In spite of the fact that we are living in the so-called "information age," most people are still grossly uninformed (or misinformed) about the horrific realities of war, capital punishment, and abortion. Why? Because with deft deliberation – and in the name of "free speech," "journalistic investigation," and "objective neutrality" – the media diverts our attention away from the gruesome realities of these human atrocities with false flags, manufactured outrages, and peripheral political distractions. The last thing the media will ever do is show you the burning bodies, the smoking skulls, and the decimated bodies of human beings violently killed by soldiers, executioners, and abortionists. It's a basic principle of media marketing: ratings will drop if the news disrupts people's "happy hour" or disturbs their dinner. Just give them selective information that won't interfere with their digestion or kill their buzz.

757. ~ WE ARE THE CHRISTIAN QUIXOTES ~

We must speak for the voiceless, even if the whole world shouts us down. We must proclaim peace and life, justice and truth, even if we literally lose our heads for doing so.

The Gospel is not practical. The Cross is not expedient. The narrow road of salvation leads not to earthly prosperity and temporal comforts, but rather to our own suffering and death. And, yet, at the end of this narrow road there is resurrection and life everlasting.

So when they tell us that we're wasting our time agitating for justice, protesting war, and fighting abortion, we'll just keep our eyes on Christ and continue to raise our voices for the innocent and the oppressed. For we understand that we shall ultimately be judged by how we treated "the least of these."

We are the Christian Quixotes, perpetually raising the Cross against the windmills of violence, bloodshed, injustice, and evil. We struggle to build the Ark of Life while the world looks on with ridicule and scorn. But we know the rains are coming soon.

"I know that the prophetic vision is not popular today in some spiritual circles. But our task is not to be popular or to be seen as having an impact, but to speak the deepest truths that we know. We need to live our lives in accord with these deepest truths, even if doing so does not produce immediate results in the world."
~ Daniel Berrigan ~

758. ~ WE FOLLOW A NEW LAW ~

We are followers of Christ, preaching His Cross and serving His Kingdom. We have no desire to rule, punish, break, or subdue others. We defend the weak and protect the innocent by offering up our own lives, but never by destroying lives. The Incarnation, the Crucifixion, and the Resurrection of Our Lord changed everything. We are no longer slaves to sin, death, vengeance, and hate. We follow a new law that compels us to love our enemies and to bless those that persecute us. We preach the Gospel, we forsake the sword, and we leave vengeance to God alone.

(I tremble at my own words, because I am perhaps the biggest coward that ever walked the earth. I fail to simply treat even those I love with the love they deserve; so how will I possibly be able to sacrifice my very life for another? And yet, as a Christian, this is what I must prepare to do. But I fear that I won't do it. In fact, I don't do it. I know that innocent people are being unjustly slain all over the world, and I do nothing about it. So it's easy for me to preach the message of the Cross, but it's much more difficult for me to truly live it. God help me.)

759. ~ CONFESSIONS of AN "ABSOLUTIST" ~

Yes, I confess: I am guilty of being an "absolutist."

I absolutely believe that no man should enslave another.

I absolutely believe that the strong should not oppress the weak.

I absolutely believe that no man should accrue wealth at the expense of another's poverty.

I absolutely believe that to destroy the earth is to destroy ourselves.

I absolutely believe that war cannot establish peace.

I absolutely believe that hate cannot cure hate.

I absolutely believe that violence cannot heal violence.

I absolutely believe that abortion is not the answer to rape, incest, or unwanted pregnancy.

I am absolutely committed to Our Lord's inviolate instructions given in the Sermon on the Mount.

I am absolutely committed to peace, life, justice, and humanity. And I absolutely believe that if everyone on earth were absolutely committed to the same, then our world would surely be healed.

So yes, I am indeed an absolutist, without apology.

760. ~ BRIEF REFLECTIONS on ALDOUS HUXLEY ~

Aldous Huxley was a true intellectual, in the sense that he never allowed philosophical or political ideology to interfere with his pursuit of truth. In Huxley we see a man whose relentless pursuit of knowledge led him naturally from agnosticism to a deep faith in God. The man literally had an encyclopedic mind (he edited the fourteenth edition of the Encyclopedia Britannica.) Along with numerous other religious studies and metaphysical interests, Huxley was a serious student of the Orthodox saints and Church fathers.

Although Huxley never officially embraced the Orthodox Christian religion, his views on God and faith nevertheless drew heavily from Eastern and Oriental Christian thought. All of Huxley's empirical experiments and existential inquiries led him to the ultimate realization that there is an inextricable link between spiritual transcendence and the immanent imperatives of human compassion and human service here in the terrestrial realm.

Huxley was a true mystic, a true intellectual, someone who understood that all spiritual and philosophical questions are answered by life affirmation and humanitarian love.

"The law which we must obey, if we would know God as love, is itself a law of love. We cannot love God as we should unless we love

our neighbors as we should. We cannot love our neighbors as we should unless we love God as we should. And, finally, we cannot realize God as the active, all-pervading principle of love, until we ourselves have learned to love Him and our fellow creatures."
~ Aldous Huxley ~ *[The Divine Within]*

761. ~ GAZING THROUGH THE FISH TANK ~

I gazed at her through the fish tank. A blurred beauty obfuscated by rectangle water, elevator music, and the weed that warmed my mind. Was this a mermaid goddess or a schizophrenic nymph? Or was she both? She stared back at me, through the aquatic bubbles; or so I thought. I wanted to reach through the glass, past the goldfish, to touch her hand, to caress her soul on the other side. I could solve her problems, and I knew she could solve mine. Or at least we could run away and be healed, together, if only for a day.

But then my name was called. The door opened. The psychiatrist smiled his plastic smile. And I turned my back on the promises of life to enter an antiseptic office of deception and despair. And although I was only 12 years old, I knew I was making a huge mistake. Which is why I never took the goddamn Ritalin.

762. ~ A STRANGE and SAD SELECTIVITY ~

When we speak out against war, poverty, and the death penalty, our friends on the left express their solidarity and approval while our friends on the right say we're "impractical" and "naïve." And when we speak out against abortion, our friends on the right express their solidarity and approval while our friends on the left tell us that we're "tilting at windmills."

I find it so strange and so sad that so many people are so selective in their affirmations of life, their understanding of justice, and their advocacy of peace. It's quite tragic that people view social justice and human rights through the bifurcated lenses of political ideology rather than through the unobstructed vision of a compassionate heart.

763. ~ BEAUTIFUL and BLESSED / UGLY and UNHOLY ~

It's a beautiful and blessed thing when Christians unite with each other to worship and pray. It's an ugly and unholy thing when Christians unite with governments to kill and destroy.

764. ~ DESIRING DIVINE GRACE ~

We must not despair because we seem to lack grace. The desire for divine grace is itself a divine grace. The fact that we long for repentance, long for mercy, and long for the comfort of God is evidence not of our separation from Him but of His nearness to us.

765. ~ WHAT IF WE DARED to SUGGEST A GOSPEL of THE CROSS? ~

What if we dared to suggest that faith is not an isolated momentary decision in one's life, but rather a lifetime of persistent and conscientious struggle? What if we dared to preach that salvation is not predicated upon a onetime "acceptance of Jesus," but rather upon a lifetime of actually following Christ? What if we called people to "come to Jesus" while also telling them to "prepare to be crucified"? What if we dared to actually suggest a Gospel of the Cross?

Well, we probably wouldn't elicit many mass conversions. We probably wouldn't be putting many notches on our "discipleship belt." But we'd actually be preaching an authentic Christian Gospel –

an ancient and consistent Orthodox Gospel taught by Our Lord and His apostles.

I've seen too many people abandon their faith because their faith was predicated upon the false doctrine that salvation hinges upon a single moment in time, upon a single confession of faith, upon a single "sinners prayer." And then afterwards, when they still face the severe trials and tribulations of life, or when they continue to stumble and fall in their sins, they can't understand. They were led to believe they were "saved," so they have difficulty reconciling their "completed salvation" with the daily struggles and failures they continue to face. They are told: "You are *positionally* righteous, but you still need to be *sanctified*." But they intuitively realize that such an explanation is mere sophistry. It doesn't add up. It leads either to self-righteousness ("I am sanctified!") or to complete despair ("How can I be 'saved' and still sin and suffer so?")

The truth is: the Gospel is not a panacea for hardships or an anodyne for pain. On the contrary, the Gospel calls us to suffering. Our Lord clearly told His disciples: *"If anyone would come after me, he must deny himself and take up his cross daily and follow me." [St. Luke 9:23]* So we see that salvation is a daily endeavor, a daily decision, a daily choice to follow Christ and endure the struggles that accompany the narrow road which leads to the Kingdom. (Cf. St. Matthew 7:13-14) Contrary to the grossly redacted versions of the pop "gospels" of our contemporary age, salvation cannot be cheaply purchased by a momentary intellectual acquiescence to some false legalistic narrative disguised as the Holy Gospel.

However, the good news is that while Christ calls us to suffer and struggle, He nevertheless promises to be with us in our pain – comforting us during all of our trials, failures, heartaches and woes. For He also spoke these words of divine consolation:

"Take My yoke upon you and learn from Me, for I am gentle and humble in heart, and you will find rest for your souls. For My yoke is easy and My burden is light." [St. Matthew 11:29-30]

We all feel good when crowds stand together and corporately profess a "decision for Christ." It's good theater. And it's certainly a huge ego boost for the preacher. And there's not anything necessarily wrong with that. In fact, it may be a very legitimate and important beginning on the lifetime road to salvation. But it's really a crime (and "crime" is not even a strong enough word in this instance) to lead people to believe that some sort of mass recitation – or individual confession – of a "sinner's prayer" will magically punch their tickets to heaven. The Gospel is much deeper, much richer, much more demanding, and much more liberating than that.

And just so you know, I'm saying all this as someone who hasn't even begun to truly take up my cross. I neither presume to be "saved" nor do I fear "losing my salvation." So I judge no one. My sins are too strong, and my virtues too weak. I plead the mercy of God every day. That is my only hope. I rest in the unfailing love of Christ, and yet I must nevertheless continue to struggle.

This is our Orthodox Christian paradox. And a blessed paradox it is. We must embrace the Cross – with both its earthly horizontal anguish and its eternally vertical hope.

766. ~ THE EARTH IS A TIME MACHINE ~

The earth is a time machine, spinning us toward the future, propelled by the past, guided by an Eternal hand. No need to go backwards, no need to go forwards. Just hang on and ride through life one day at a time. All the answers to human suffering and worldly ills are presently before us. Let us love one another today, right now, truly and wholly – as we orbit toward the Kingdom.

767. ~ "PROLETARIAT UPRISINGS" ~

"Proletariat uprisings" orchestrated by blue blooded aristocrats are in reality counter-revolutionary bourgeois attempts to establish an elitist oligarchy that will profit off the backs of the people. The countenances of the real revolutionaries will not adorn the T-shirts of Ivy League frat boys.

768. ~ REFLECTIONS on HELL and DIVINE LOVE ~

While I do believe in hell, as the Church teaches, I am no longer convinced that hell is a place of literal, physical torment. In fact, I am no longer convinced that hell is a physical *place*, and I am no longer convinced that hell will be eternal.

"The mercy of God endures forever." *[Psalm 136]* God's love is omnipresent (because God is omnipresent and His nature cannot be separated from His being), which means – by extension – that the love of God extends even into the depths of hell. St. Isaac the Syrian wrote that *"the love of God is the fire of hell."* In other words, hell may simply be the experience of the rejection of God's love. Those who spurn the love of God in this life may experience the love of God as torment in the next life. I emphasize *"may."* I dare not proclaim this as a certainty. I'm only referencing the holy perspective of a saint here. (And please defer to the teachings of the saints and Church Fathers on this matter over the opinion of this fallible sinner.)

I also see no reason – based upon either scripture or Church Tradition – to believe that our free will is negated by physical death. Therefore, even if one's earthly choices lead them to a state of postmortem hell, there's no reason to assume that they can't still choose to respond to God's love even in such a hellish condition. But again, I'm only speculating. Trust the Orthodox Church over anything I say on this matter.

Many will cite Our Lord's story of the rich man and Lazarus (St. Luke 16:19-31), pointing out the great unbridgeable chasm that exists between those who live on earth and those who dwell in the "fire" of the hereafter. But there is nothing in Our Lord's account to suggest that such a "fire" is comprised of literal flames, or that those who experience this "fire" cannot still choose to embrace the love of God from whatever agonizing state in which they may find themselves. To the contrary, this story clearly shows that the spirit of human volition is still at work even after physical death.

And it is also hard to imagine that anyone suffering the excruciating torment of having their flesh literally burned with unquenchable fire could have the conscious wherewithal to utter even a single coherent sentence. So it is quite likely that the rich man was expressing a hyperbolic lament rather than a dogmatic statement regarding the specific nature of hell.

There is debate amongst biblical scholars as to whether St. Luke 16:19-31 is a *parable* of Jesus or an *actual historical anecdote*. But regardless of which one it is, it should nevertheless chasten and sober us. We should not take this earthly life for granted. We should not refuse to help those in need. We should not amass wealth at the expense of our neighbors. And we should not presume to bathe eternally in a divine love that we rejected, mocked, ridiculed, and spurned while we lived in this terrestrial realm.

And yet, I have hope that the love of Christ will overcome even the most recalcitrant of human hearts. If I am forced to place my bet on the power of human free will or the power of unfailing divine love, I will bet – without hesitation – on divine love. And, although in this temporal earthly vale, human volition and God's love may appear at times to be mutually exclusive, I am confident that they will harmonize in eternity. After all, *human* free will is a gift from the *divine* free will. And I doubt that the gift will prevail over the Giver.

I think that all true spiritual faith is the result of love, not fear. The demons have a fear-based faith (Cf. James 2:19). They believe in God, they tremble at God, and they hate God. I think that a lot of fundamentalist movements share this demonic "faith." Those who have never come to trust and know the love of God will always be preaching the wrath and fear of God. No one is more in need of the Good News of salvation than fundamentalists who are trapped in their heretical view of an angry, anthropomorphic, and vindictive deity.

I also think true morality and authentic virtue stem from love, not trepidation. For example, while my children know that I will discipline them, they strive to please me out of love rather than fear of my wrath. If I had children that obeyed me perfectly merely out of terror, then I would not be truly honored as a parent and they would not be truly happy as my children.

Whatever the reality, nature, and endurance of hell may be, hell was never intended to be the abode of human beings created in the image of God. Our Lord said that hell was prepared for the devil and his angels (St. Matthew 25:41).

I have hope that perhaps, ultimately, the love of God – as most powerfully expressed through the Cross – will eternally overcome the forces of sin and hell. I can't say for sure, but I dare not put any limits on the power and efficacy of the Cross. And what I can say for sure is that any theology that causes people to live in debilitating fear rather than in the joy of the certain knowledge of God's love is a doctrine of demons and a theology of the antichrist.

"There is no fear in love. But perfect love casts out fear, because fear has to do with punishment. The one who fears is not made perfect in love." [I John 4:18]

769. ~ MISSION STATEMENT of AN ORTHODOX CHRISTIAN PACIFIST ~

I believe nonviolence is the Christian way.

I believe with the Orthodox Church that while there are significant moral differences between murder and defensive killing, all killing of human life is nevertheless sinful.

I believe with the Orthodox Church that war is always evil in this Christian age.

I reject the Just War theory, for nothing that involves the killing of innocent human beings – be it intentional or ancillary – can ever be just.

I believe with St. Basil the Great that, *"Although the act of violence may seem required for the defense of the weak and innocent, it is never justifiable."*

I believe with Tertullian that, *"In disarming Peter, Our Lord disarmed every soldier."*

I believe with Father Stanley Harakas that: *"There is no ethical reasoning for war in the writings of the Greek Fathers. The Fathers wrote that only negative impacts arise from war. Even in unavoidable circumstances, the Fathers thought of war as the lesser of greater evils, but nonetheless evil. The term "just war" is not found in the writings of the Greek Fathers. The stance of the Fathers on war is pro-peace and an Orthodox "just war" theory does not exist."*

I believe in the admonition of St. Hippolytus: *"A Christian is not to become a soldier. He is not to burden himself with the sin of blood. But if he has shed blood, he is not to partake of the mysteries, unless he is purified by a punishment, tears, and wailing. He is not to come forward deceitfully but in the fear of God."*

I believe that the Sermon on the Mount is to be literally embraced and not rationalized away as mere metaphor. (St. Matthew 5:3-12)

I believe that when Our Lord said *"love your enemies,"* He actually meant it. (St. Matthew 5:44)

I believe that God commands us to fight injustice and evil, and that He has equipped us with spiritual weapons that are much more powerful than the carnal weapons of the flesh. (Psalm 82:4; Ephesians 6:10-18)

I believe with St. John Chrysostom that: *"Christians above all men are not permitted forcibly to correct the failings of those who sin. In our case, the wrong-doer must be made better, not by force, but by persuasion. The Christian's labor is to make the dead live, not to make the living dead."*

I believe that our diligent, nonviolent, sacrificial confrontations with injustice and evil will never be in vain; for although the innocent may still suffer and die, God will avenge them in eternity. (Psalm 58:10)

I believe in a God who will recompense all evil, vindicate all righteousness, and reward both the wicked and the just with divine due. (Galatians 6:7)

I believe that whenever mankind attempts to establish justice by the use of violence, he inevitably slays the wheat with the tares and leaves a wake of innocent blood in the process. (St. Matthew 13:24-30)

I believe that killing is fundamentally opposed to the propagation of the Gospel, for the Christian is called to lovingly win the enemy's life for the Kingdom not violently deny it the opportunity for repentance.

I believe that violence cannot coexist with the Great Commission (St. Matthew 28:18-20); for the Christian seeks to save the lost not subdue them.

I believe in Our Lord's command to the apostle, to which He attached a divine universal prophecy: *"Put away your sword, for all who live by the sword will perish by the sword." (St. Matthew 26:52)*

I believe that the Cross negated and nullified the believer's dependence on violence just as it negated and nullified the believer's dependence on animal sacrifices. The shedding of blood that was permissible in the Old Testament was but a shadow of the final, atoning, sacrificial blood that was shed by Our Lord. Therefore, I believe that reliance on violence for temporal salvation is as unchristian as reliance upon the blood of bulls and goats for eternal salvation. (Hebrews 10:1-10)

I believe that all human beings are icons of God, and therefore nobody has the right to violate and destroy God's holy image. (Genesis 1:27; Ephesians 2:10)

I believe it's tragic that some Christians would reverence icons made of wood and paint while arguing that it is permissible to destroy icons infused with the very breath of God. (Genesis 2:7)

I believe that peace is the Christian path and that nonviolence is the Christian imperative. But I also believe that although we may reject the use of injurious force and refuse to kill, if we have not truly loved our neighbors as ourselves then we are still guilty of violence.

This is what I believe, and if I am accused of sin or error for such convictions, then I will take my chances with that on Judgment Day. Until then, I will continue to chant with all my fellow Orthodox Christian brethren:
"In Peace Let Us Pray To The Lord."

770. ~ RESTLESS RIVERS / SHALLOW WATERS ~

There is no shame in suffering and struggle. There is no weakness in failure and loss. There is no defeat in loneliness and sorrow.

God treasures our tears. God honors our pain. He is present in the anguished mind. He lives in bowed and broken hearts.

The deepest truths and the greatest beauty are born from conflicted, fragile, and honest souls. Restless rivers flow to the ocean of heaven, but shallow waters are a stagnant hell.

771. ~ OUR FALLING ENABLES US TO RISE ~

We have to persevere. We have to press on. We have to keep fighting this spiritual war. We have to know that our struggles are not in vain as long as we don't give up.

Sometimes we need to stop trying to make sense of it all. Sometimes we have to stop trying to understand. Evil is irrational. Injustice is opposed to reason. Sin is oppressive. And sometimes life just seems to hurt for no reason at all. Heartache, depression, and anxiety cannot be cured by logical syllogisms or systematic theological paradigms. God does not call us to philosophical certainty; he calls us to faith. So when everything crumbles around us, we just have to pick up our cross and march forward – or crawl forward – with faith, hope, and love.

If only we understood that our falling is what enables us to rise to eternal life.

772. ~ OURS IS A JOYOUS REVOLUTION ~

Fight for peace with love and truth. Work for justice with brotherhood and prayer. Trust the unfailing mercy of God, and fret not because of evildoers. God is love, and those who love God will be eternally victorious. Ours is a joyous revolution, for we know that we cannot lose.

773. ~ OF SNAKES & WAVES, NIGHTMARES & DREAMS, INSOMNIA & THE NAME of JESUS ~

Some seek solace from the realities of life in somnolence and dreams. But not me. In spite of the pains and difficulties of the daily conscious struggle, I am nevertheless afraid to fall asleep. And yet I long for respite, for slumber, for the necessary rejuvenation of body, mind, and soul. But sleep too often eludes me.

And, yet, I'm not sure whether my insomnia is a blessing or a curse. For on those rare occasions when my body finally rests, when my eyelids finally shut, and when my mind finally drifts into the consciousness of Nod, I find myself in a world of horrors and delights and lusts and torments over which I have no control. And these dreams all seem truer to me than the realities of my wakened existence.

The nightmares are excruciating, and yet even the pleasant visions are so vivid that they, too, often terrify me. All I can do is struggle to navigate each phantasmic encounter with whatever semblance of awareness I still possess in those rare states of slumber. It is as if I enter another life when I sleep, and that life is a full-scale dream war. Like Dorothy in the Land of Oz, I have no control over my circumstances or surroundings. But even as I sleep, my free will is still awake. Thank God for that.

And then there are the snakes! Always with those damned snakes! They are ubiquitous lurkers. They invade even the most innocuous of my sleep visions. They do not strike, but they are often there – dormant and sluggish, but pervasive, invading, and capable of destruction. Their presence mocks me.

But sometimes I do dream of the water and of the waves. And those dreams are always good, absent of confusion or terror. Those ocean waves, clear and blue, strong and untamed, but ever so beckoning. And I immerse myself in those waves, and they are indomitable, and yet I love them and I am never afraid. I give myself to their power, body surfing, gliding with their strength, not resisting but letting them have their way with me. They play with me and then propel me safely to the sandy white shore. And I stand up and look around at paradise. Then I cast myself back into the ocean to play some more.

I love those dreams. But they don't come as frequently as the snakes. I wonder why. I wish they would.

Perhaps God doesn't want me to get too comfortable with sleep. Perhaps He wants me to be awake because there's too much work to do in this physical world. But oh how I long to sleep, soundly and peacefully, undisturbed by these nightmares and visions that seem more real than my conscious daily realities.

Yet, for the Christian soldier, there is no rest. We cannot escape the spiritual war. Neither food nor drink nor drug nor slumber can protect us from the battles to which we have been divinely called. And Christ is with us, always.

The snakes never touch me. They frighten me, yes. But they never touch me. I've noticed that. Unlike the waves, which wrap their arms around me and play with me and comfort me and show me their incredible power and force. The snakes would perish in those waves. It would be no contest. But I am always so alive in those mighty waters.

So I will fight when I am awake, and I will fight when I am asleep. And I will struggle to find sleep, and I will struggle to embrace sleep. Such is the battle for some of us. That's why I carry the Cross with me day and night. And it's why I carry the name of Jesus with me even into my dreams.

"Into your hands, O Lord, I commend my soul and my body. Bless me, have mercy upon me, and grant me life eternal."

"Lord Jesus Christ, Son of God, have mercy on me a sinner."

774. ~ A CRAZY IDEA ~

I'm not a politician, so forgive me for suggesting this crazy idea:

Perhaps we should spend less money funding institutions of death and destruction (for example, the military and Planned Parenthood) and more money on social programs to help those in need. But I guess I'm being naïve; because, you know, I guess we have to let people go homeless and hungry in order to fight terrorism and protect women's "right to choose."

775. ~ "SOCIAL GOSPEL" ? ~

There is no such thing as a "social gospel." There is just the Gospel. And the Gospel is inherently social. Salvation does not occur in a vacuum. An individual cannot be saved apart from love, mercy, and compassion for his fellow man. We cannot love Christ if we do not love others. We will not experience the peace and joy of heaven if we turn a blind eye to the violence and pain in the world. Those who preach eternal salvation while ignoring temporal suffering are preaching a doctrine of demons.

776. ~ DIVIDED SOUL ~

There is no division
of Holy Trinity or Holy Church.
There is no division
of the one united nature of Christ.

There is no division
of fire and heat
of truth and love
of justice and peace
of sun and light.

But there is a division
within my soul,
tormenting my conscience
and rending my heart in two.

How will this double-minded man be saved?

Lord have mercy on me,
a perpetually divided sinner.

777. ~ FISTS for ALL THE FLOWERS ~

We are fists for all the flowers
and flowers among the fists.
Swords of peace we sharpen
as violence we resist.

We raise our hammers of love
and sing our rebel songs,
carrying the Cross before us
as night turns into dawn.

We shine the light of Life
until darkness is no more.
With the bullets of the gospel
we shall win this war.

778. ~ IS YOUR GOD SO WEAK? ~

If your religion needs to be defended by politics, then politics is your religion. If your faith needs to be defended by violence, then violence is your faith. Is your God so weak that he needs your political protection and violent defense?

779. ~ ART, REBELLION, CREATIVITY, and THE CROSS ~

Art, when it is good, when it is real, is simultaneously an act of rebellion and an act of submission. It is rebellion against the stale, uninspired status quo that oppresses the human spirit and poisons the human condition. And it is submission to the metaphysical creativity that is latent within us all. Great art horizontally confronts sin, pain, injustice, and angst while vertically reaching towards transcendent truth and heavenly beauty. This is why the Cross was the truest act of rebellion, the greatest act of submission, and the most profound work of creativity that ever occurred. We mourn its agony, we embrace its hope, and we stand in awe of its mystery. Art, when it is good, when it is real, elicits from its beholder the same response.

780. ~ HELLISH SPECULATIONS ~

I think it's unhealthy to concern ourselves with speculations about hell. Let us focus on the love and mercy of God. Let us bathe in His love, preach His love, and live His love. Why focus on the domain of devils when Christ tells us to focus on the Kingdom? Why preach hellfire and damnation when we can preach mercy and love? Fear is a feckless apologetic, but love will save.

"The mercy of God endureth forever."[Psalm 136]

"There is no fear in love; because perfect love casteth out fear."
[I John 4:18]

781. ~ ENMITY with OTHERS / ENMITY with GOD ~

Those at enmity with others are often also at enmity with God. A nation that wages war against its own poor, its own "minorities," and its own unborn children cannot expect to live in peace and security. Those who sow violence and oppression will inevitably reap violence and oppression. The greatest threat to American security is not terrorism; the greatest threat to America is her own injustice, immorality, and evil.

"When the ways of people please the Lord, He causes even their enemies to be at peace with them." [Proverbs 16:7]

782. ~ TIRED CONDEMNATIONS ~

I am tired of condemning Protestants, Catholics, Muslims, homosexuals, and heretics. I am tired of condemning people. Period. Condemnation is laborious work. It wears me down. I can no longer condemn my fellow man. I am not God. Judgment of the person belongs to Him alone. But what I will continue to do is condemn actions and ideologies that undermine human personhood and destroy human life. So I don't care what you choose to believe or what you choose to do. As long as you affirm the sanctity of human life and contribute to peace in the world, then as far as I'm concerned your religion is OK by me. If sound doctrine means justifying hatred, prejudice, violence, and killing, then I'd rather be a heretic than a saint.

783. ~ WILL YOU LOVE ME IF...? ~

Will you love me if I piss you off? Will you love me if I don't share your politics? Will you love me if I practice a different faith than yours? Will you love me if I don't share your patriotism? Will you love me if I am homeless? Will you love me if I am rich? Will you love me if I don't support all the ostensible "rights" you think you should have? Will you love me if I condemn your capitalism, your socialism, your militarism, and your abortion? Will you love me if I am an alcoholic, an adulterer, a murderer, and a heretic? Will you love me even though I fail to love you? Will you love me with the true love of Christ?

If not, then I don't blame you. I struggle to love me too.

784. ~ COMFORTING SINNERS ~

Christ has comforted this sinner through the hands of many other sinners. Therefore, who am I not to also comfort sinners?

785. ~ CONQUERING EVIL ~

You can't conquer evil with bullets, but you can conquer it with love and prayer. You can't conquer injustice with bombs, but you can conquer it with truth, righteousness, and sacrificial service to your fellow man.

786. ~ ONE NIGHT DOWNTOWN ~
(The following autobiographical story contains graphic content, sexual references, and profane language. Please be advised.)

One night many years ago, I was partying with my girlfriend in downtown Atlanta. We were at a bar called the *Stein Club,* and Monday night was two dollar pitcher night. We were Monday night regulars. She and I had nothing in common really, other than a mutual physical attraction and a common interest in hedonistic pleasures. And even though she professed her love for me, I really couldn't stand the poor young woman. We had first met at this same dive, and our relationship seemed metaphorically bound by its dank, stale walls.

On this particular summer night I had begun to feel sick, having smoked too much weed and imbibed too much cheap beer. She, on the other hand, was feeling just right, lavishing me with her lustful affections in the dim barroom corner. But I was too wasted to be enticed by her advances. A sinner's misfortune. However, she was determined to prove that her charms could overcome the nausea in my gut and the swirling in my head. But her seductions only exacerbated my confusion. So I pushed her away and went outside to clear my head, hoping to calm the dizziness by inhaling the warm, still, night city air.

I sat down on a wall in a back alley and pulled out my harmonica. (I always carried a harmonica with me back in those days. I played harmonica in a couple of Blues bands at the time, and I was constantly trying to hone my chops.) I thought I could relieve the spinning in my head by sitting alone and playing some Blues, hoping that by focusing on one note at a time I could make everything stand still again. And so I tried. But the more I played, the sicker I felt. I tried to stop the carousel in my soul by looking up into the night sky, but I couldn't see any stars. All I saw were the massive downtown buildings closing in around me – giant, taunting windmills, with their superficial lights burning in the eternal blackness. I was really messed up: too sick to screw and too sick to play the Blues. And since that's all I really lived for back then, I was in pretty bad shape.

And just when I thought things couldn't get any worse, I saw this sodomite approaching me. And yes, sadly and to my shame, that's exactly what I thought at that time: "Why is this fucking *sodomite* approaching me?!" He was a gay prostitute. Downtown Atlanta was rife with prostitution in those days – gay hookers, straight hookers, and hookers that embodied everything in between. And since I was too drunk to have anything to do even with my own girlfriend, I certainly wanted nothing to do with a gay hooker.

"Are you ok?" he asked, with a pronounced lisp.

"Yeah. I'm cool."

"I like your harmonica playing. It sounds really good."

"Thanks."

"You don't feel too good do you?"

"I'm alright. I just needed some fresh air."

"Do you need something to drink? I can get you a Coke or a Sprite or something."

"No. I'm ok. Really. Thanks. I just need to be... just leave me alone..."

And then I puked. And I puked right all over the poor guy. But not on purpose.

"I'll go get you something to drink. You need some water. Hang on. I'll be right back," he said.

"I'm sorry man. I'm really sorry..."

"Don't worry. I know how it is. I've been sicker than you plenty of times."

So I sat there, with vomit on my clothes and my shoes and my breath. But I had made sure not to puke on my harmonica. I was glad about that at least. But I didn't even really care at the moment. I just felt like I would puke again if I didn't drink some water. I felt like I was about to dry heave. And I wanted some water so badly. I didn't want beer. I didn't want weed. I didn't want pussy. I didn't want Blues. I just wanted some water to saturate my throat and fill my stomach. Fun times, right? The price of partying. You have to pay your dues.

Soon he was back.

"Here you go. Drink this. It will help. This is water, but I got you some Sprite and Gatorade also. I didn't know what you preferred. But drink the water first. If you want me to get you something else, I will."

"Thanks." I took a sip. "Thanks so much."

The water felt cold and clean and pure as I drank it down. It may have been the sweetest water I've ever tasted. I felt better as soon as it hit my stomach. Then I sipped some of the Gatorade and some of the Sprite. The electrolytes and carbonation were manna from heaven.

"I think you're gonna be ok," he said. "And you really play that harmonica well. I mean it." And then the gay prostitute was suddenly gone, before I could thank him again.

I drank the blessed libations with slow deliberateness, making sure that I was cured of my nausea. I finished all of the water and all of the Gatorade and most of the Sprite. And in time the city stopped spinning and I remembered the lascivious vixen waiting for me inside. Perhaps now I could somehow summon the strength.

I cleaned myself up as best I could, and then I went back into the bar where she was waiting for me. She put her hands down my pants and whispered depraved things in my ear. Really depraved things. I told her to stop. I told her that I just wanted to go home and go to sleep.

"I just puked outside," I said.

"I don't care."

"Don't you get it? I feel like shit. I'm too wasted to fuck you."

"We'll see about that."

"You're a sick girl."

"Yes, I am."

And so I forced myself to rise to the iniquitous occasion.

That is a typical and uninspiring story of human sin. There I was, strangely revolted by a gay man who brought me the graces of compassion and mercy, but perversely drawn to a straight woman who offered me nothing but depravity and lust. And as for "sodomy," I certainly had no right to judge. By the strict definition of the term, I was guilty on multiple counts.

And yet I still haven't learned the divine lesson. For now I find myself more sympathetic to the gay stranger than to the girl I was dating at the time. What was her sin? What was her crime? That she wanted to be loved? That she looked for love in me? Who am I to pass moral judgments on gay prostitutes or promiscuous women? I am the sinner, and without sinners there would be no prostitution or promiscuity.

The more I reflect upon my life, the more I realize that I am too often the occasion of sin. I am too often the stumbling block. I am too often the deceiver. I am too often the cause of offenses and the conduit of error.

What did I do when that same girlfriend begged me to accompany her to her college senior Formal? I lied and promised her I would do so. But I had absolutely no intention of it. And I didn't even have the courtesy to call her and tell her ahead of time. I simply stood her up. She was devastated and pissed off and wounded just like any human being with a heart would be pissed off and hurt. But instead of leaving me, she wrote me a love letter. I scoffed at it at threw it in the trash.

Months later I had a crisis of conscience. I knew I needed to stop my sinful ways and end this unhealthy relationship. So I called her and broke up with her over the phone. She cried. She called me again and again asking for another chance. At one point she told me she had found Jesus and was attending church. After all, I had told her that "Jesus" was the reason I had to end the relationship. But I remained callous, curt, and firm:

"Stop calling me. This is over. Our relationship was always terrible, and I never loved you and you don't love me. You're just insecure and needy and you don't know what love is. I hope that you have indeed found God and found peace in your life. But don't call me anymore. I mean it. We're through."

Yeah, that was the essence of what I said, believe it or not. And I actually had "Christian" people telling me that what I did was exactly the right thing to do: break somebody's heart, dispose of them like garbage, cut them out of your life like a gangrenous appendage, and don't worry about what happens to them afterward. The most important thing is to do whatever you need to do not to ever have sex with them again – because sexual intimacy outside of marriage is somehow a greater offense to God than treating another human being like a cancerous tumor.

That's what I was taught and so that's what I did – even though I knew in my soul that there had to be a better way, even though I knew that my treatment of this young woman was anything but righteous and godly.

But she seemed to get the message. She stopped calling. I had successfully cut the tumor out of my life. I was healed. Except that instead of a tumor, something else was growing. After a couple of months, she called me out of the blue:

"I'm pregnant. I'm going to have an abortion. I don't want any money, but I want you to be there with me."

"You're not pregnant. I'm sterile. I've never gotten anyone pregnant in my entire life. You're really sick to try and pull this crap on me. Don't you ever give up?"

"You're an asshole" she said. "I didn't even have to tell you this, but I told you because I love you and I thought you'd care and at least would maybe want to be there with me."

"Look: if this is true – and I know that it's *not* true – then have the baby and give it to me and go live your life. I don't believe in abortion and I won't ever contribute to abortion in any way. I take responsibility for my actions. So if you are pregnant and it's really mine – which again, I know that it's *not* – then have the baby and I'll raise it myself. Otherwise don't call me again with this manipulative nonsense."

And then I hung up. And that's the last I ever heard from her. And I was glad about that. Except that now I have to live the rest of my life wondering if I lost a child (or children.) Because, as I later found out, I'm actually *not* sterile. Because in spite of my hard-heartedness, cruelty, and profligacy, God still saw fit to give me a wife. A wonderful wife. And that wonderful wife has seen fit to give me four children. So now I'm haunted by the thought of how many children I may have conceived before I was married, children that may have been denied life because their mothers wouldn't dare risk giving birth to babies who would be cursed with an asshole father like me.

So I think the gay prostitute that night in Atlanta saw me for who I really am: a perverse, drunk, sinner searching for peace in the night lights of this fallen world. And he came simply bearing the mercy of a cup of cold water – with no judgment, with no ulterior motive, with no seduction. He saw a fellow sinner in his sickness, and he sought only to offer me comfort. I think he was a Christ bearer. And I think my girlfriend at the time was also a Christ bearer. And I think that my wife is a Christ bearer. And I think that we all are Christ bearers.

Which is why I want so badly to learn to truly love others – all others – as Christ loves me. I think there are only enemies and sinners and heretics because we have been taught that there are enemies and sinners and heretics. Don't misunderstand: I certainly still believe that enemies and sinners and heretics exist; I'm just learning that they don't exist outside of me.

787. ~ FOLLOWING CHRIST ~

Following Christ is not about asking what is permissible, what is legal, what is pragmatic, or what is justifiable. Following Christ is simply about following Christ: loving as He loved, forgiving as He forgave, preaching what He preached, and perhaps even suffering as He suffered. The Cross is not about temporal expedience; the Cross is about eternal life.

"For what will it profit a man if he gains the whole world and forfeits his soul? Or what will a man give in exchange for his soul?" [St. Matthew 16:26]

"Whosoever shall seek to save his life shall lose it; and whosoever shall lose his life shall preserve it." [St. Luke 17:33]

788. ~ SAINTS and SAINTLINESS ~

Let us remember that not everything the saints did was saintly. When their actions and words conformed to the teachings and example of Christ, they were reflecting theosis. But when their words and actions contradicted the teachings and example of Christ, they were reflecting their common human need for divine redemption. For example, we should embrace St. Cyril's Christology while rejecting his reliance on the sword. We should cling to the theology of St. Nicholas, but we shouldn't go around slapping heretics. We should affirm the Orthodox opinions of Origen, but we shouldn't castrate ourselves.

789. ~ RUNNING INTO SALVATION ~

I ran from God and ran into myself. I ran from myself and ran into God. There is no escape. But this is our salvation.

790. ~ KISSING PARADISE ~

I see peace in the sky,
but the earth cries.
So take me high
above all this sin,
where angels dance
on the heads of demons.
But I have no wings,
so here I dwell.
And earth is heaven,
and earth is hell.
These dreams and devils,
hopes and fears,
angels and flames,
are all of my own making.
So I bow to the dirt
and kiss the paradise
that it soon will be.
In this mire
and in this mud
I taste His Body
and I taste His Blood.

791. ~ DEMONIC DREAM ATTACKS ~

The demons attacked me in my sleep again last night. They always assault me with their horrors and confusions and incessant lies. Once again I woke up shaking and sweating. The battle is fierce. But JAH is with me even in my dreams, just as He is always with me when I'm awake. Our Father will never leave me; He will never forsake me. (Hebrews 13:5)

When nightmares haunt me, I try to make the sign of the Cross. But the demons restrain my arms. I try to wake myself up, but the devils keep me in a state of slumber. I try to fight them, but they seem to overpower me. But the Name of Jesus is in my heart, and I call upon Him with unquenchable prayer: *"Lord Jesus Christ, Son of God, have mercy on me a sinner."* And the precious Name of Jesus sends these emissaries of hell scattering back to the hellish depths from whence they come!

I constantly struggle to find sleep, and then I seem to struggle even more when I finally do lapse into an exhausted state of slumber. But this is simply part of the spiritual battle. And so be it, for I'll rest forever in the Kingdom. Until then, I am called to fight this hell with the forces of heaven.

So do what you wish to me you cursed devils. But you'll never pry the Name of Jesus from my soul! And even though you seek to lead me to damnation, I will pray even for your salvation.

"And the seventy returned again with joy, saying, 'Lord, even the devils are subject unto us through thy name.' And He said unto them, 'I beheld Satan as lightning fall from heaven.'" [St. Luke 10:17-18]

792. ~ ABORTION and the "SELF-CONTROL" ARGUMENT ~

When promoting the Pro-Life cause I don't like to use the "self-control" argument. We all fall prey to various temptations from time to time. So I don't think we should just go around lecturing women about self-control – especially as men.

However, I do think we should unequivocally declare the profound difference between sins that result from a moment of weakness or temptation and the iniquity of calculated, premeditated murder. I've met many promiscuous, single mothers who succumb to sexual temptations but who would never consider murdering their unborn children. I have great respect for them. In spite of the fact that they know society will condemn them as "sluts" or "whores" and label their children as "illegitimate," they nevertheless embrace and affirm the sanctity of life. They gladly choose social ostracism over the evil of premeditated death and destruction.

Condemning single mothers and women who have sex out of wedlock is not compassionate. It doesn't help to save babies. And it's simply not Christian.

We need to say: "Ok, so you made a mistake. You were weak. You had sex and got pregnant. I can understand that. It's not the end of the world. God has given you the blessing of life even through your weakness. So embrace life and rejoice."

But condemnation and judgmental finger pointing doesn't seem to work very well. I know it sure doesn't work when that approach is used with me. And I'm a man. And the repercussions of my own sexual indiscretions – as severe as they have been – have nevertheless been much less consequential than what women face.

793. ~ POLITICS and THE KINGDOM ~

Personally speaking, I think Christians should refuse to participate in the corruption and divisiveness of politics. Our votes only enable and perpetuate the violence of democracy, capitalism, war, poverty, and abortion. Let us never cease to labor in the world on behalf of the poor, the oppressed, and "the least of these." Let us continually strive for the peaceful realization of social justice and human brotherhood. But let us pledge our political allegiance to the Kingdom of God alone.

794. ~ NONVIOLENCE is NOT SYNONYMOUS with APATHY ~

The common mischaracterization of the Christian pacifist position is that pacifism = "passive"-ism. But nonviolence is not synonymous with apathy. Christ certainly wasn't apathetic, and He certainly wasn't violent. Do we dare accuse Our Lord of standing idly by and allowing the innocent to suffer because He did not use violent force to defend them? Let us not forget that the Zealots rejected the Messiah precisely because He was not a violent revolutionary.

Let us also understand the historical examples of nonviolent activism that saved innocent lives and revolutionized social structures: e.g. the nonviolent activism of many abolitionists, the nonviolent activism of the Civil Rights Movement, and Gandhi's nonviolent struggle to lead India to independence from British rule.

Yes, life is full of awful choices; but authentic Christianity is not about situational ethics, utilitarian expediency, or Machiavellian pragmatism. Christianity is about choosing the Cross and being obedient to the example of Christ, even if that choice appears on the surface to be foolish and ineffectual. We must be prepared to offer our own lives in defense of the innocent, but we must never prepare to kill another.

On a Friday afternoon 2000 years ago the Cross appeared to be the epitome of folly and failure. But we know that the crucifixion was not the end of the story. Christ is Risen! And God will soon judge the living and the dead. Let us carry the Cross and relinquish the sword. Jesus does not call us to be crusaders; He calls us to be disciples.

"The chief difference between violence and nonviolence is that violence depends entirely on its own calculations. Nonviolence depends entirely on God and God's word." ~ Thomas Merton ~

795. ~ PLEASE DON'T TRY TO HEAL US ~

We are simple people. We have no fans, no disciples, no following. We write what we write, we say what we say, and we create what we create – not because it will bring us wealth, fame, or earthly esteem, but simply because we don't know how to live any other way.

And God preserve us from worldly success! We don't need to be corrupted any more than we already are.

There is no comfort, no respite, no temporal ease for the spiritual revolutionaries. We will always be in the trenches. And we have made our peace with that.

Our creativity, our beauty, and our truth emanate from our suffering. So please, don't try to heal us.

796. ~ RELATIONAL MINISTRY ~

A dear friend of mine who is a Presbyterian minister is writing a book about "relational ministry" and "relational evangelism." He asked me to offer some personal insights about these vital Christian principles, so here are a few of my thoughts on the subject:

First of all, I think relational evangelism and relational ministry always prioritize *relationship* above *evangelism* and *ministry*. In other words, the Christian simply builds friendships, loves others, ministers to their needs, and treats all people as equals. And without any ulterior agenda, the Christian simply trusts that God will work through these relationships to mutually edify and bless both parties. The relationship is the evangelism. The relationship *is* the ministry.

And this is exactly how my dear friend has ministered to me over the years. He's never tried to lecture me, preach to me, convert me, or rebuke me. He has simply been a faithful friend whose words and actions toward me have exuded the love and truth of the Gospel.

For example, when I was in college and succumbing to loneliness, temptations, and a host of negative habits and behaviors, I often went to my friend's dorm room to find solace and encouragement. No matter how busy he was or regardless of his plans, he would always stop what he was doing and talk to me – sometimes for hours. He never judged me. He never condemned me.

He never acted disappointed in me. He just listened to me. He just loved me. And I always left feeling like I could overcome my sins and struggles because I knew I had a true friend and loyal brother in Christ by my side.

That is relational ministry.

When – in spite of a deeply tumultuous relationship – I finally decided to elope with the girl I loved, my dear friend was the only one who came to the courthouse to support our nuptials. When everyone else criticized my decision and told me that our marriage was destined to fail, my dear friend demonstrated faith in a God who is bigger than human opinions. He was there for us, supporting us, and rejoicing with us. I'm sure that he too had great concerns about how things would turn out for us. But as a man of authentic faith, he was led by hope and trust rather than criticism and doubt.

That is relational ministry.

When – early in my marriage – my negative habits and behaviors continued to resurface, my dear friend never allowed his disappointment to affect our friendship. Because I knew that he cared about me, he didn't have to spell things out with finger pointing and shame. *He* knew that *I* already knew what I was doing wrong and what I needed to change. While others that barely knew me at all were casting stones and lecturing me with a self-righteous tone, my dear friend just continued to love me and listen to me and pray for me. He simply reminded me of the grace and love of Our Lord Jesus Christ while actually demonstrating true Christian grace and true Christian love.

That is relational ministry.

A couple of years after I was married, I went to my dear friend (who had by that time become a pastor) and told him that I had committed adultery. I expected him to finally wash his hands of me. After all, how much mercy and grace can you give someone before you finally put your foot down and say "enough!" But without condoning or excusing my actions, my friend's primary focus was helping me salvage my marriage. He knew I was a broken and despondent man, and his priority was to make sure I knew that I had at least one true friend and one true brother in Christ in this world. He didn't try to exploit my suffering as an opportunity to get me to come to his Church. He didn't try to jump in and offer us marriage counseling. He didn't try to give me a theology lesson on how my sin was related to erroneous doctrines and unorthodox beliefs. As always, he just listened to me, loved me, and prayed for me. And not only that, but he also gave me tangible assistance that enabled me to get through one of the most difficult times in my life. And I can honestly say that his unconditional love was instrumental in not only the *survival* but also the *blessed renewal* of our marriage.

That is relational ministry.

During the three years that I stood on the sidewalks of abortion clinics – praying and pleading for Life – my dear friend was one of the few Christians who actually came out to pray and plead with me. I cannot overstate how much his presence encouraged me and how much my spirit rejoiced whenever I saw him approaching. Those were such lonely, depressing years – standing daily in the shadow of death and destruction, trying to stem the tide of innocent blood with my finger in the dyke. But my friend supported my efforts in numerous ways. Not only did he come out to stand in solidarity with me on many occasions, but he also invited me to speak to his Church about the urgent plight of the unborn. He was also one of the few people to contribute financial support to my Pro-Life ministry. His love for Christ, his love for the unborn, his love for the suffering and oppressed, and his love for me helped to save countless lives from imminent destruction.

That is relational ministry.

My dear friend and I spent countless hours playing basketball, throwing the Frisbee, eating lunch, drinking beer, and going to movies – the simple pleasures of life that form lasting bonds. And during and in between it all were deep theological discussions, philosophical pursuits, and many brotherly prayers. In Christ we had all things in common, and in Christ we could strive together for a greater understanding of His will and His ways. My friend spent time with me because he valued relationship, not because he felt a need to "minister" to me. And nothing has ever ministered to me more than true friendship.

That is relational ministry.

When I was finally baptized into the Orthodox Christian Faith, my dear friend (who is a lifelong Evangelical Presbyterian) wrote me a beautiful letter expressing his sincere joy regarding my conversion. He had seen me meandering for years in a theological wilderness; and rather than chastising me for my many doctrinal diversions, he chose to see me as a Christian nomad who was constantly being led by the hand of God. And now he was rejoicing that Our Lord had finally led me to my true Orthodox Christian home. While many other Protestant acquaintances expressed disappointment and concern over my conversion to Orthodoxy, my dear friend expressed nothing but sincere happiness. I saved his poignant letter which I still keep next to my baptism robe. I cherish it deeply, and I read it whenever I need to be reminded that God has not abandoned me.

That is relational ministry.

And yet – after all the years of his Christian loyalty, unconditional love, tremendous generosity, and true kindness – I am ashamed to say that I profoundly grieved my dear friend and brother in Christ. He was subjected to words of scathing condemnation from this overzealous convert who was filled with Orthodox triumphalism and obnoxious pride. As my writing took vitriolic aim at all things "Protestant" and "Evangelical" – excoriating all "unorthodox" doctrines as heretical and demonic – my dear friend must have been not only deeply offended but deeply hurt. Since he is by far my intellectual and theological superior (my friend has a doctorate degree from Princeton Theological Seminary), it would have been quite easy for him to embarrass me with his own eviscerating pen. And I would have certainly deserved the humiliation. But instead, my dear friend picked up the phone and called me to simply express his sadness at the tone of my arrogant and stupid words. Once again, he didn't chastise me, he didn't condemn me, and he didn't lure me into a debate (which he surely would have won). He simply expressed his sincere concern about our friendship, indicating clearly that what mattered most to him was the preservation of our bond in the Lord.

That is relational ministry.

I intended to include scriptural references throughout this meditation to support my view of "relational ministry." But I think the entire Bible actually supports my humble expressions here. God is love (I John 4:8), and to love God is to love others (I John 4:20). God created the universe in perfection, and yet He still saw that something was not good. Can you imagine that? God had created perfection, and yet something was not good in His sight? And what was it that was "not good?" He looked upon Adam, created in His very image, and said: *"It is not good that man should be alone." [Genesis 2:18]*

So God has not only ordained and blessed human relationship, but He in fact viewed His own perfect creation as lacking without it. Friendship, family, and fellowship are indispensable aspects of human existence and spiritual growth. We were born from human union, we were nursed by human care, and we survive and thrive by human relationship.

We can feed the hungry, we can shelter the homeless, we can preach to the lost, and we can lead social revolutions – but unless we love our neighbors, *truly love our neighbors*, we have not been relational and our ministry is in vain.

My dear friend has ministered to me in the greatest way simply by being my friend.

And that, in my humble opinion, is relational ministry.

797. ~ THE COST and VALUE of PEACE ~

Peace costs much less than war, but it's infinitely more valuable.

798. ~ "CONCIERTO DE ARANJUEZ" ~

If the universe was created with music, then it must have been created with the symphonic strains of Joaquín Rodrigo's *"Concierto de Aranjuez."* Herein we hear the sounds of creative glory and universal wonder. Herein we hear the sadness of the human fall and the laments of suffering and sin. Herein we hear the harps of angels and the promise of divine redemption. Herein we hear struggle and beauty, pain and hope, agony and peace. Herein we hear the gentle cry of a baby and the triumphant thunder of God riding upon His clouds. In three movements – reminiscent of the Holy Trinity – this piece of music expresses all the emotion, angst, and hope of the universal cosmos and the human soul. This is the music of birth, life, death, and salvation.

Rodrigo stated that he intended for the concerto to capture *"the fragrance of magnolias, the singing of birds, and the gushing of fountains."* Indeed, I think he captured the melody of Eden's innocence and the chords of the Kingdom's glory.

799. ~ SLAVERY, ABORTION, and AUTHENTIC EMANCIPATION ~

Legalized abortion by the American government is the most violent, destructive, and systematically oppressive practice ever perpetrated against the Black race. With chattel slavery, the insidious goal was to exploit, use, and cruelly capitalize on Black slave labor for the purposes of White economic empowerment. But with abortion, the goal is to literally destroy Black lives in a most violent, callous, and brutal fashion.

With slavery, the unborn child was at least viewed as a commodity, an asset, a tool to be used. As devalued and dehumanized as he was, the unborn child still had some semblance of worth. The full, ripe belly of the Black slave woman was viewed positively not negatively. As horrific and inexcusable as it was to reduce mother and unborn child to mere materialistic commodities, there was nevertheless an acknowledgement of some aspect of life's intrinsic value – as perverse and corrupt as that acknowledgment may have been. (As I often say, "Where there is life, there is hope." In other words, as much as you may hate or despise me, just let me live. At least give me a fighting chance.)

But with abortion, the American government has declared that the unborn Black child has absolutely no value, absolutely no worth, and absolutely no reason to exist or right be born. Dred Scott was at least considered 3/5ths of a person, as horrific as that ruling was. And even the most evil, racist, and hard-hearted slave owner could somehow still see value in the child that grew within the slave woman's womb. But that flicker of value has been snuffed out by this perpetually racist and violent American government.

Babylon has successfully adopted the psychological strategy of Willie Lynch: employing the black-fisted gavel of Thurgood Marshall and the silver tongued mendacity of Barack Obama to achieve its goal of violently uprooting the Black tree before it can bear more Black fruit. This systemic, racist, oppressive psychological warfare has been so thoroughly effective that strong, intelligent, and otherwise rebellious young Black men have been convinced to do the Master's bidding. Babylon has actually persuaded those who should give their very lives to defend and protect their children to pay to have their own children killed – an evil that even Willie Lynch himself could not have conceived. Nat Turner rose up and died fighting an entire nation in order to defend his unborn children. But today many young Black men pay to have their unborn children butchered by rich white people who profit from the shedding of innocent African American blood.

And these Babylon politicians have convinced the masses that the murder of 20 million innocent unborn Black babies somehow constitutes "empowerment" and "progress" – liberation through self-destruction, and freedom through the willful slaughter of one's very own progeny. The most effective way to further oppression is to convince the oppressed that their oppressor is their liberator. Convince people that annihilation is emancipation, and you can exploit, use, and control them forever.

The bottom line is that anyone who supports legal abortion – or the politicians and political parties that support it – is actively fighting against women's progress and effectively working against the welfare of the African American community. It doesn't matter what your intentions are. It doesn't matter what "other issues" determine your vote. If you support those who justify, support, or defend the deliberate, premeditated, and violent destruction of innocent unborn Black babies in the womb, then the blood is on your hands.

Personally, I prefer the white racist enemy who wears no mask to the friendly politician who slaughters Black babies while hiding behind brown skin and a plastic smile. And I prefer those that are sincerely misguided and misinformed about economic issues to those that with deliberate callousness stake their claim on the side of social injustice, inhumanity, oppression, and death.

Authentic emancipation begins with revolutionary education; and revolutionary education won't be taught in the schools. We need to pray, we need to read the scriptures, and we need to follow the prophetic voices rather than the prevarications of political pimps.

"He called a little child to him, and placed the child among them. And he said: "Truly I tell you, unless you change and become like little children, you will never enter the kingdom of heaven. Therefore, whoever takes the lowly position of this child is the greatest in the kingdom of heaven. And whoever welcomes one such child in my name welcomes me. "If anyone causes one of these little ones—those who believe in me—to stumble, it would be better for them to have a large millstone hung around their neck and to be drowned in the depths of the sea. Woe to the world because of the things that cause people to stumble! Such things must come, but woe to the person through whom they come!" [St. Matthew 18:2-7]

"Verily I say unto you, Inasmuch as ye have done it unto one of the least of these my brethren, ye have done it unto me." [St. Matthew 25:40]

800. ~ WORTHLESS TRUTH ~

If it's absent of joy, if it's absent of passion, if it's absent of love, then it's worthless. Truth that does not move us is a lie.

My Mama is an artist. She has a creative, complex, passionate, intense, and loving soul. I haven't always understood or agreed with her, and I doubt if anyone has. But I've come to understand that this is to her credit rather than to her fault.

My Mama has lived an unconventional and unorthodox life; and this has brought her both tremendous hardships and tremendous joys. I have seen her experience incredible suffering and immense happiness. I have watched life bring her severe pains and wonderful pleasures. I have seen her experience emotional torment and transcendent peace. I have seen her betrayed by many and loved unconditionally by a few. I have seen her both broken and blessed.

And somehow all of these trials and triumphs seem inextricably interwoven in her life. And the older I get the more I realize just how similar we are. And these similarities have often been difficult for both of us. How can two people who are so alike have so much trouble understanding each other? Or maybe the problem is that we understand each other all too well. I doubt if either of us will ever really figure it out. Growing up I saw more than I wanted to see, more than any child should see, but perhaps what I nevertheless needed to see. Because in my Mama's struggles I often now see my own.

My Mama has lived her own way, but compassion has always been an unremitting guide of her soul. Even when I thought her decisions were harsh, and at times downright cruel, I still believed she had my best interest at heart. I think she always acted out of love, even though I didn't always understand or agree with her expressions of it. But I have never doubted that she loves me, and that is a confidence and security that every child should receive from their mother. I am blessed to know such unwavering affirmation.

My Mama has instilled in me a great appreciation for the Creator and for the creation, and also for artistic expressions of such beautiful things. Thus I have always carried within me a deep love for the glories of birds and butterflies, for mountains and beaches, and for pen and paint and music and song that attempt to express such mysteries. My Mama has found great pleasure and great peace in the wonders of nature, in the joy of music, and in the unlimited possibilities of the artist's palette. And I will always be grateful that she imparted these joys to me.

But nature is not tame. And great music and great art are not tame either. And there is nothing tame about my Mama's volatile soul. She used to curse the Blue Jays because they were "bully birds." She hated the cats that crept into our yard to prey upon the Robins. She loved nature, but she hated the injustices that nature produced. She abhorred violence and guns, and yet she kept a BB pistol on the kitchen table to drive away the squirrels that stole food from her bird feeders. She practiced the classical guitar until her fingernails broke. She created artistic masterpieces with which she was never content. She sometimes pounded on the piano with the violence of a thunderstorm. My Mama has always been a force of nature, with all of the unpredictable tempest and peace and darkness and light that accompanies it.

My Mama has always wanted the world to be right – to be a just, tolerant, compassionate, and forgiving world. And she has sometimes tried to force it to be so. And that has caused many problems, both for her and for others – and also for me. And as I said, the older I get the more I realize just how similar we are.

I have seen both the depth of anguish and the height of happiness in my Mama's countenance. I have seen her eyes melt with the tears of falling stars. I have seen her expression radiate with the irrepressible light of sunflowers. I have seen her exhibit terrifying rage born from unimaginable pain. And I have seen a smile that shone from heaven. In my Mama I have seen all the beauty and struggle and pain and hope of the universe.

But most of all, I have seen that she loves me. And such true love cannot always be understood. It is not always pleasant or comfortable. At times it is downright unbearable. But I thank God for it. I thank God for my Mama. I thank God for her love. And I thank God that our souls will forever be intertwined.

There is a word for something greater than anything I will ever understand, a word for something beyond comprehension – something so inexpressibly deep and rich and glorious and good that all we can do is give it a simple name: *infinity*. And throughout my life – in spite of my many failures and sins and disappointments and mistakes – my Mama has constantly told me: *"I love you way past infinity!"* And I have always known that she means it. For as St. Peter writes, *"Love covers a multitude of sins." [I Peter 4:8]*

802. ~ PACIFISM is NOT in MY NATURE, BELIEVE ME ~

Pacifism is not in my nature. Believe me. I am inclined to fight. I want to exact justice. I want to set things right. I want to defend the weak and avenge the victim. I want to protect the innocent and bring the wicked to their knees. I am inclined to be a Quixote, tilting at windmills in my arrogance and folly.

But Christ has called me to be a disciple, not a knight. And humanity will be saved through prayer, evangelism, and Christian obedience – not crusades, chivalry, and conquests. It is only by divine grace that I don't drop the Cross and pick up the sword.

803. ~ WHO WOULD SAVE WHO? ~

I had my Bible and she had her legs. I had my message and she had her charms. I had my suit and she had her skirt. I had my judgments and she had her truth. I had my righteousness and she had her reality. I had my gospel and she had her grace. I was a street corner preacher and she was a street corner whore. I crossed the street with a mission in mind. She smiled kindly and said hello, with no mission in mind. Who would save who?

804. ~ BOXED IN BY BABYLON'S BALLOT BOX ~

The system has brainwashed people to believe that the only way their voice can be heard is through the ballot box. Babylon would rather keep you voting and remaining complacent than to have you not vote and lead a revolution. As long as you remain enslaved to the ballot box, then you'll never be free.

And please remember that those who suffered and died to give people the right to vote didn't suffer and die so people would become enslaved to voting. The right *not* to vote is just as powerful – if not more so – than the right *to* vote.

805. ~ LOVE and ATHEISM ~

The Bible says that *"God is love."* *[I John 4:8]* Therefore, in spite of what they may say, anyone who truly loves can't be an atheist.

806. ~ DIVERSITY ~

I hear a lot of talk about "diversity" these days. It seems to be a top priority for many. But I've noticed that those who preach racial, ethnic, gender, and sexual diversity often exclude or even oppose the diversity of ideas. But I think ideological diversity is actually the most important kind of diversity. What good is diversity if we paint with every color but replicate the same piece of art? What good will come from the rainbow masses that have a monolithic mindset? Cultural diversity apart from ideological diversity results in Black and White, rich and poor, male and female, gay and straight, citizen and immigrant all working together to build the same damnable tower of Babel.

807. ~ FEAR and KILLING ~

"I feel threatened. I am afraid. So I must kill. To end the threat. To eliminate my fear."

So says the politician. So says the soldier. And so says the woman who has an abortion.

"I feel threatened. I am afraid. So I must love. In spite of the threat. In spite of my fear."

So says the disciple of Christ.

"There is no fear in love. But perfect love drives out fear, because fear has to do with punishment. The one who fears is not made perfect in love." [I John 4:18]

808. ~ REDEEMED from MADNESS ~

War is one of the curses of the fall. But the Orthodox view of salvation offers hope for humanity. Christ died to conquer sin and death, and therefore we need no longer be slaves to war and killing. We can be restored by grace to our originally created nature, when brother loved brother and man loved God. Because of the Cross and the glorious Resurrection, sin is no longer inevitable and unavoidable. That is why no Christian should ever excuse, justify, or participate in war. We have been redeemed from such madness.

809. ~ YOU CAN'T REASON with DARKNESS ~

I've realized that there is simply no way to reason with people who value human laws, human governments, and human constitutions above human life and human rights. The only thing that will persuade those who can't see the humanity of the oppressed is a divine quickening of the heart. Those who justify racism, slavery, genocide, and abortion are trapped in darkness. And you can't reason with darkness. All you can do is blaze the torch of truth and pray that God will lead them to the light. In their blindness they carefully hone rationalizations for supporting injustice and evil, but oh how quickly they would change their tune if they found themselves on the wrong end of the oppression.

810. ~ CHRISTMAS ~

May we never become too holy to celebrate the birth of Our Savior! May we never become too holy to celebrate the Mystery of the Incarnation! May we never become too holy to offer simple gifts to those we love in honor of the saving love that Christ has given us. And may the joyful celebration of Christmas be something that we carry with us every single day of our lives. Christ is born! If this isn't worth celebrating, I don't know what is.

811. ~ DIVINE LOVE and THE COLDNESS of HELL ~

I'd rather be burned by divine love than suffer the coldness of hell. So I'll cast myself into God's consuming fire, letting the light of His grace incinerate my sins.

812. ~ ICONS ~

Nazis are icons. Communists are icons. Republicans are icons. Democrats are icons. Homosexuals are icons. Muslims are icons. Liberals are icons. Conservatives are icons. Abortionists are icons. ISIS terrorists are icons. The mirror is an icon.

When you understand this, then you will understand the doctrine of Orthodox iconography.

813. ~ JUSTICE WAS LONELY ~

Justice was alone and longed for love, but love remained aloof. Justice wondered why it could not woo love, so justice turned to God for an answer.

"Dear God, I am justice but I am lonely. Why won't love come and be my companion?"

God answered:

"You are lonely because you are not what you think you are. Love and justice have always been wed, and they shall remain inseparable. If you were truly justice, as you claim, you would have always known love. But instead you are vengeance, punishment, retribution, and wrath. And love and justice have nothing to do with you."

814. ~ THE WEAPON in THE MANGER ~

When the divine Baby wrapped in swaddling clothes is the only weapon you need, then you will understand what it means to be a Christian.

815. ~ ORTHODOXY and SUBMISSION ~

If the Orthodox Christian Faith means blind submission to popes, patriarchs, preachers, and politicians, then consider me the most unorthodox person in the world. But thank God, Orthodoxy means anything but.

Society says that being a "quitter" is one of the worst things you can be. But I've never bought into that lie. In fact, I think quitting is sometimes the most productive and powerful thing you can do. So I encourage you to be a quitter:

Quit sinful habits.

Quit wasting the value of today in pursuit of an unpromised tomorrow.

Quit idolatry.

Quit giving money to institutions and organizations that exploit your charity for their own expansion and control.

Quit the military.

Quit working for companies whose CEO's make millions while refusing to pay you a living wage.

Quit voting.

Quit obeying those in power simply because they have power.

Quit killing.

Quit living according to the expectations and demands of others.

Quit school and learn for yourself.

Quit worrying and start praying.

Quit living according to human judgments and start living in the light of God's unconditional love.

Quit trusting in violence and start trusting Christ.

Quit hating and start loving.

Quit complaining and start a movement.

Sometimes quitting is the most revolutionary act there is. So get busy quitting so you can get busy living!

817. ~ NO GUILT, NO SHAME ~

No guilt, no shame
don't play that game

JAH forgives
so do the same

Our divine reflection
remains unchanged

Live in mercy
and crucify the pain

The fire of God
melts hellish chains

Release regret
and let love rain

It is not Christ, but Satan that condemns. Sin has no sting apart from an accuser. And sometimes we are our own merciless prosecutors. So go forward and live without guilt today!

818. ~ WE are REVOLUTIONARIES, WE are CHRISTIANS ~

Our peace provokes.
Our love offends.
Our truth divides.
Our Cross prevails.

We are revolutionaries.
We are Christians.

Violence is the result of the fall. Thus, if violence remains in our souls it is a product of our fallenness not our redemption. And redemption and theosis are about restoring us to our pre-fallen purity when we enjoyed uncorrupted communion with our Creator.

We err when we attempt to invoke divine blessing on fallen ways. We suffer when we attempt to equate that which may be legalistically permissible with that which is truly holy and good. The fact is that we cannot attain union with God though the violence and division of the sword.

Christ has conquered sin and death, and this is the supreme reality upon which we as Christians must base all of our philosophies and all of our actions. Regardless of the particular ethical dilemma or situational conflict, the Christian must always think and acts according to eternal truth. For the disciple of Christ, sin is never an answer to suffering. Iniquity is never an answer to evil. And violence is never a solution to violence.

So let's not try to "Christianize" sin or its ramifications. Let's not try to put God's heavenly stamp of approval on ideologies and actions that are born in hell.

If we die by violence then we have gained the kingdom. But if we preserve our earthly lives by killing others, then we may end up losing our very own souls. Let us never confuse what is necessary for temporal survival with what is necessary for eternal life.

There are blasphemous religions that teach that paradise will be ushered in by the sword. God forbid! Let us never be accused of promoting such heresies!

"For what will it profit a man if he gains the world but loses his soul?" [St. Matthew 16:26]

820. ~ ETERNAL LIFE and A LIVING HELL ~

To live with wonder, to live with gratitude, to live with love: this is eternal life. To live with cynicism, to live with indifference, and to live with hate: this is a living hell.

821. ~ INDELIBLE IMAGES ~

The image of God cannot be erased from even the worst sinner. Where they reflect divine truth, acknowledge and honor it. Where they deny divine truth, reject and condemn it. A straight pen can write crooked words, and a crooked stick can draw straight lines.

822. ~ "MARK" ~

My neighbor, my brother, and my friend Mark sleeps tonight outside in the bitter cold – two blocks from me, in a urine stained alley, behind the convenience store.

Our landlord says he simply can't stay here with us anymore.

"Sorry brother. I wish there was more that I could do for you. It's just out of my hands. But I'll come get you for the BAMA games. And I'll check on you tomorrow. Here are some blankets, and a jacket, and few dollars."

"Thank God for BAMA fans! I always knew that being a BAMA fan would help me out someday."

"But I'm not really helping you." I said. "I wish that I could. But I don't want my family to be out on the street. And if our landlord kicks us out, I don't know where we'll go."

"I understand. You've helped me out so much already. I'm thankful I met you. It's always a blessing to meet another Alabama fan. Don't worry. I'll make it. We BAMA fans know how to survive."

"Do you need me to take you to the Salvation Army?" I asked.

"No. I'm not allowed there anymore. The captain banned me."

"Do you want me to speak to the captain and see if I can get him to let you back in?"

"No. Too many rules. And people pick on me over there. But I'm a survivor. I'll be OK."

"What about the shelter downtown?" I inquired. "Can I take you there?"

"No. The last time I stayed there I got bed bugs and a guy tried to beat me up. There are some crazy people there. You never know what will happen. I'm safer sleeping behind the gas station."

"Do you want me to drive you upstate to your sister's?"

"No. Her husband doesn't like me very much."

"Do you want me to call her, talk to her, and explain your situation?"

"No. She knows my situation. She thinks I'm an alcoholic. And she's right. I am an alcoholic. I stayed with her for a while, but I got drunk and her husband got mad at me. So I can't go back there."

"But you stayed at FOA (Friends of Alcoholics) for a while. Can I take you there?"

"I can't go back there until April," Mark explained. "I can only stay there for three months at a time, and then I have to wait three months before I can go back."

So I drive him around the corner. I drop him off. I watch him look for an unsoiled patch of dirt where he can lay down his blankets for the night.

A few hours earlier, as I was coming out of the convenience store with my own beer for the night, I had seen a guy walk behind the building to take a piss in the very spot where Mark would now be sleeping.

Mark is happy to have new blankets. He is happy to have a new jacket – and a BAMA jacket at that. (It was too small for me, which is really the only reason I gave it to him. So don't mistake that as an act of altruism on my part.) He is happy to have met our family – our family that stays just around the corner, in our little home that is always warm in the winter and cool in the summer (although we constantly complain about our lack of living space, the violent neighborhood, and a host of other inconveniences that we sometimes consider unjust and intolerable.) And Mark is glad that his sister can now use our address to mail him a little bit of money and a few clothes from time to time.

On this particular night, when I drop him off, he waves and smiles and yells: "Roll Damn Tide!"

"Roll Tide!" I reply.

We had just watched the National Championship together. And we were both overjoyed by the incredible BAMA victory. As Mark reminded me all season, "We're undefeated whenever I've watched the games with you!" (And he's right. I wish I had gone to get him for the Ole Miss game earlier in the year. We lost that one.)

And tonight, in spite of everything else, we're both equally happy. BAMA has won another National Championship, and all the cruelties of life can't negate that truth.

Mark will huddle in a cold, piss-soaked corner of this world, drinking his beer and trying to find solace and sleep as he reflects on Crimson glories. And I will sit in my warm, dry home, with my wife and children nearby, reflecting on those same Crimson glories. And as Mark struggles to find warmth, hope, and peace, I will type away here on my computer, drinking too much of my own beer, philosophizing about the plight of my fellow man – my fellow man who "rests" his head in the darkness of human indifference two blocks away.

I love Mark, and he loves me. But he knows, and I know, that this whole human situation – and this whole world – is really fucked up.

823. ~ **THE WORDS and WISDOM of DR. MARTIN LUTHER KING, JR.** ~

Apart from Holy Scripture, the words of Dr. Martin Luther King have influenced my philosophy and shaped my convictions more than any others. It's tragic that most people only know Dr. King as a cultural icon rather than as the profound Christian philosopher that he truly was. Yes, he was a great preacher and a courageous social activist who died as a martyr for truth and rights. But his sermons and activism were the products of a rigorous philosophical mind that constantly sought to apply the teachings of Christ to his own life and to the problems of society.

So, do yourself a favor and take time to actually read and study Dr. King's writings. He was masterful at conveying complex philosophical ideas with simple language that we all can grasp. I especially recommend his wonderful book, _Why We Can't Wait_, which contains his _"Letter From A Birmingham Jail."_ That book changed my life. It proved to me – both from scripture and from sound logic – that systemic evil can be successfully challenged and overcome with spiritual force rather than violent force.

Dr. King's message and example remain ever relevant to the problems we face today. His words remind us that the answers to all social problems and cultural ills are to be found in an unwavering commitment to peace, a constant affirmation of life, and an adherence to the gospel of Jesus Christ.

824. ~ REGARDING ETERNAL TORMENT ~

Why are we so determined to cling to a belief in eternal torment? I think the main reason is that we don't want to lead others to presume upon heaven if they reject divine love. It would be irresponsible and unloving to teach a doctrine that could potentially result in leading people to hell rather than heaven.

But can anyone really be saved by fear alone? Is theosis* ever the product of sheer terror? Will anyone truly love God simply because they fear His eternal condemnation?

I'm by no means an expert on it, but from my reading of the saints and Church fathers it seems that theosis is the process of drawing near to God's love rather than being paralyzed by fear of His wrath.

Is hell eternal? I dare not answer this question with certainty. But here's my humble speculation, which as always is subject to the correction of the Orthodox Christian Church:

Hell is the fire of God's love that torments those who reject His love. And, theoretically, hell may indeed be eternal, since one may conceivably reject the love of God forever. But hell is not the absence or negation of hope, because God is omnipresent and His love is therefore also omnipresent. Thus the love of God extends unconditionally to all souls, in all places, and at all times. As the Psalmist writes:

"Where can I go from your Spirit? Where can I flee from your presence? If I go up to the heavens, you are there; if I make my bed in the depths, you are there. If I rise on the wings of the dawn, if I settle on the far side of the sea, even there your hand will guide me, your right hand will hold me fast. If I say, "Surely the darkness will hide me and the light become night around me," even the darkness will not be dark to you; the night will shine like the day, for darkness is as light to you." [Psalm 139:7-12]

Perhaps some souls will forever reject His love, and therefore in that sense hell may be eternal. But I choose to hope that even the devil himself will ultimately repent and embrace the perfect love of Our Lord.

But these are great and holy mysteries, and it is dangerous to rely on mere human speculation regarding these matters. What is certain is what the scriptures urge:

"Repent ye: for the kingdom of heaven is at hand."[St. Matthew 3:2]

"Repent, and turn to God, so that your sins may be wiped out, that times of refreshing may come from the Lord." [Acts 3:19]

May God grant me the gift and grace of repentance, a repentance that desires His love above all else.

*Theosis – Theosis (or "deification") is the Eastern Orthodox Christian concept of the transformative process of becoming united, by grace, with God in His attributes and energies.

My dear friend Roy McMillan has gone home to be with the Lord. To say that Roy was a controversial figure and a unique character would be understatements. But Roy devoted *his* life to saving the lives of *others*, and such devotion cannot be effectively undertaken with half-measures, compromise, or a lukewarm heart. The prophets are gifted with a certain fiery resolve that is often unsettling to the rest of us. Their souls are not refined by social standards, and their temperament is not softened by polite customs. Their consciousness is attuned to divine truth and human suffering, and those of us that go through life half asleep do not always understand such personalities.

Many people will remember Roy as the solitary, stentorian voice of life that echoed on the dark peripheries of death and destruction. Many will think of him as that "crazy anti-abortion activist" who "held those awful signs" and was "always getting arrested." But those of us who truly knew him will remember him for much more.

Yes, Roy McMillan was a bold and courageous witness for truth and rights. Yes, he was a voice for the voiceless and a sacrificial intercessor for the helpless. And yes, Roy McMillan was arrested countless times in his life – not for committing any acts of violence or theft, but for "disturbing the peace." And Roy would always point out that when babies are being killed, there is no peace. He would say that if innocent lives are being unjustly destroyed, then the community shouldn't be at peace. And he would rightly tell us that as long as the most helpless among us have no voice, then the Church should not be at peace. So, like other heroes before him in the struggle for human rights, Roy was quite willing to go to jail for a just cause. The fact is that Roy didn't disturb the peace; he simply exposed the violence and inhumanity that occurs day after day with the protection of the law and the complicity of our apathy and silence. All Roy did was disturb the conscience of society. All Roy did was disrupt the façade of peace that disguises the horror of bloodshed and brutality in our midst.

And yes, Roy was fanatical in his Pro-Life endeavors – fanatical, but never violent. As Cicero said in ancient times: *"Moderation in the pursuit of justice is no virtue; extremism in defense of liberty is no vice."*

The history of the Church records examples of "fools for Christ" who lived out the Gospel to such extremes that they were ridiculed, mocked, scorned, and rejected by society. Those living in darkness always curse the light. As St. Anthony the Great wrote in the third century: *"The time is coming when men will go mad, and when they see someone who is not mad they will say, 'He is mad! He is not like us!'"* Roy was indeed a madman, desperately trying to save the rest of us from our sanity.

Unlike most people, Roy truly understood abortion. For most of us, abortion is merely a social and political issue upon which we take a particular calculated stance. We are either "pro-life" or "pro-choice." We choose a side and then lazily concoct a justification for our position. And then we pat ourselves on the back and feel morally superior to those on the other side, because we are either the ones who "respect life," or else we are the ones who "respect choice." And we conclude that anyone who thinks differently must be either evil or insane.

But while the rest of us see abortion through the lens of politics or social ideology, Roy saw abortion through the lens of humanity. Roy always saw the individual human lives that were being violently snuffed out by abortion. He saw the humanity of the women who suffered physically, emotionally, and spiritually from abortion. He saw the horrific specter of racism that undergirds the abortion industry. He saw the deleterious impact that abortion has on our society and our culture. You see, for Roy, abortion was not simply an "issue." It was literally a matter of life and death, and therefore he acted like it. And that's why Roy had such a difficult time understanding how a Church that professes the Gospel of Jesus Christ could turn a blind eye to the suffering of "the least of these" in her midst.

Many of us who sympathized with Roy's righteous indignation and just cause would nevertheless cringe at some of his words and tactics. It was easy for those of us on the sidelines to self-righteously criticize the solitary Quixote who confronted the darkness day in and day out. And often, just when I would think that he had gone over the top and crossed the line, his vituperations would prove to be ultimately effective. I've met many young women over the years who told me that Roy's harsh message and graphic signs were what ultimately persuaded them not to go through with their abortions. So while we "polite" pro-lifers were wincing at Roy's words, God was using those words to redeem hearts and save lives. Because of Roy McMillan, I try not to question the actions of the prophets anymore.

Roy will undoubtedly be remembered by most for his radical Pro-Life activism, and rightly so. But Roy was much more than a vociferous voice of truth echoing in the wilderness. He was a wonderful family man and a wonderful friend. Roy helped me frequently over the years. In fact, when I was going through one of the most difficult times in my life, Roy was one of the few people who extended compassion and forgiveness. When many other Christian friends had turned their backs on me, Roy showed me nothing but unconditional love and support. That's the side of Roy that many people don't know about.

Those who never really knew Roy will perhaps think of him as a judgmental, self-righteous moralist who was always yelling at people about abortion. But Roy was actually one of the most non-judgmental and truly forgiving people I've ever known. He didn't just preach about the sanctity of life, he actually lived it out. He and his wife, Dr. Beverly McMillan, have personally sacrificed to help numerous unwed mothers and strangers in need. You see, Roy didn't just care about unborn babies, he cared about people. He cared about humanity. He cared not only about helping save lives, but also about helping people live better lives.

Roy challenged me in many ways. He challenged me to see the urgency of human suffering and human cruelty. He challenged me to apply the imperatives of the Gospel to my neighbor in need. He challenged me to re-examine my theology and make it applicable to the suffering and the oppressed. He challenged me to cultivate a heart of mercy, compassion, and forgiveness.

Roy also challenged me with his deep Catholic Faith. The many long, in-depth theological discussions we had were instrumental in my journey from evangelical Protestantism to Orthodoxy. A few years ago, shortly after I had been baptized into the Ethiopian Orthodox Church, I ran into Roy in the grocery store. I told him I had recently been baptized into the Orthodox Faith. *"That's wonderful!"* he exclaimed. *"You're getting closer!"* That was Roy in a nutshell: always finding a way to encourage you and challenge you at the same time.

In spite of the tremendous discouragements he faced in the Pro-Life battle, Roy always maintained a positive attitude and a sense of humor. Whenever he saw me, he smiled and gave me a hug and took time to encourage me. Nothing ever kept him down. I'm sure he must have wrestled with tremendous doubts and fears. I'm sure he must have been deeply wounded by the constant barrage of insults and curses that were thrown his way. And I imagine his greatest discouragement must have come from those of us who called ourselves his Christian brothers and yet did so little to help and support him in the struggle. But, in spite of those discouragements, Roy always had a smile on his face and a positive word to offer whenever he saw you. Only the grace of God could enable a man who struggled so much to maintain such a positive and irrepressible spirit.

Regardless of what anyone thinks about Roy McMillan, this much is undeniable: Roy was on the side of the oppressed; he was on the side of the suffering; he was on the side of the voiceless; he was on the side of the victims. Roy McMillan was on the side of human rights; he was on the side of justice; he was on the side of Life.

One of his favorite Bible verses came from Amos the prophet:

"Let justice roll down like waters and righteousness like an ever-flowing stream." [Amos 5:24]

Thousands of people are alive today because Roy McMillan intervened to save them from imminent destruction. That is not an exaggeration. And countless lives have been sustained and improved because of Roy's intervention and influence. Can anything greater be said about the impact of one man's life?

I am tempted to say that Roy was no saint. But how do I know? Some of his stories and anecdotes may have stretched credulity. Some of his antics may have been more than just a bit crass. And some of his methods may have indeed been questionable. But there is no doubt that Roy was God's instrument, a divine messenger sent to proclaim light and life in our culture of darkness and death.

I have no doubt that the gates of paradise were opened wide to welcome my friend Roy McMillan. And I suspect that a choir of unborn innocents greeted him with joyous refrains of honor and thanksgiving.

I loved Roy McMillan. It was an honor to know him and to call him my friend.

"And the King shall answer and say unto them,
Verily I say unto you, Inasmuch as ye have done it unto one
of the least of these my brethren, ye have done it unto me."
[St. Matthew 25:40]

Roy McMillan: Memory Eternal!!! +++

826. ~ IF HE WAS A GOOD MAN... ~

If he was a good man, he wouldn't be begging. After all, scripture says, "I have never seen the righteous forsaken or his children begging for bread." If he was a good man, he wouldn't be living on the street. After all, only drug addicts and drunkards find themselves without family, friends, and a home. If he was a good man, he wouldn't be in prison. After all, only murderers and thieves and dope dealers get locked up behind bars. If he was a good man, he wouldn't be hanging on that Cross. After all, only the unjust, immoral, and ungodly could deserve such a fate.

827. ~ THEY DO SO FOR ME ~

Those who struggle, fast, and pray do so not merely for themselves; they do so also for me. And I am truly grateful. I must learn to return the favor.

828. ~ THE SIN of PATIENCE ~

Earlier tonight I read Dr. King's *Letter From A Birmingham Jail* to my children. It's a masterpiece that I've read many times and will certainly read many times again. Dr. King explains why the argument for patience and gradualism is both unchristian and downright cruel when human life and human rights are at stake.

By all means, let us be patient with the sins and shortcomings of others. We are all flawed. We all have beams in our own eyes. But for God's sake, let us never be patient with human suffering and human oppression.

This is why I have no tolerance for those who express selective moral outrage about certain social issues while remaining mute about the wanton murder of unborn innocents. If you can't speak out against the greatest human rights violation of our time – legal abortion – then why speak out about anything at all? I have about as much respect for your opinion as I do for 19th century fundamentalist preachers who decried the evils of alcohol and adultery while ignoring the systematic enslavement of their fellow man.

There is a time for patience, tolerance, and understanding. But God forbid that we remain patient, tolerant, and understanding when it comes to the evils, cruelties, and injustices committed against human beings created in God's very image.

If our own lives were being crushed beneath the wheels of oppression, would we want our liberators to remain patient in coming to our rescue? Would we praise people for addressing other "social issues" while our very own lives were being grinded by the machine of slavery and death? Would we applaud the masses for respecting a civil "law and order" that legally and methodically destroyed our own lives and our own freedom?

I doubt it.

And yet when it comes to the oppression and murder of others, we somehow remain ever so patient, ever so tolerant, ever so understanding. And like Dr. King, I think that's a great sin.

829. ~ NINEVEH, JONAH, ISIS, and US ~

Do you remember the people of Nineveh, that most exceedingly wicked city of old? They were so evil that God decided to take action. So He called His prophet Jonah to arise and confront them. But the Lord did not call Jonah to raise up an army, to take up a sword, and to go and fight evil with evil. Instead, God called Jonah to go to Nineveh and preach, to go and proclaim His divine and holy word. But Jonah did not want to do it. Jonah was terribly afraid of these evildoers. And not only was he afraid, but he could not understand why God should have mercy on such wicked people.

So Jonah tried to flee from the command of God. He even preferred to be cast into a raging sea – whereupon he expected to die – than to obey the Lord's call. But God got his attention, and Jonah – spat from the belly of the whale – proceeded to Nineveh to proclaim the word of the Lord. And do you remember what happened? Those wicked people repented and begged God for salvation. And God heard their cries, and He changed their hearts to righteousness. And Jonah, the reluctant prophet, was not entirely pleased about it.

Do you know where Nineveh is located geographically? Nineveh is part of Iraq. And Nineveh has been the home of Orthodox Christians for more than fifteen centuries. But today, these Christians are confronted with an evil similar to the evil that Jonah faced. Today, these Christians are faced with the same challenge that confronted God's prophet centuries ago. Just as Jonah faced the extremely evil and wicked city of the Nineveh of old, Christians in the Middle East today face the extremely evil and wicked people of ISIS. Like the

Ninevites of Jonah's day, ISIS is merciless, wanton, and irrational in their evil. Like the Ninevites, they cannot be reasoned with. Like the Ninevites, it appears that they are beyond any hope of redemption or grace.

And when we see our innocent Christian brethren being tortured, beheaded, and burned alive, then it's easy for us to share Jonah's sentiment. It is easier for us to beseech God's wrath upon the wicked than to pray for God's mercy to change their hearts. It is easier for us to think that we must conquer their violence with a mightier violence than to believe that we can conquer them with Christian love and Christian truth.

But Christ has shown us that although evil may temporally crucify, the crucified will forever conquer. Although demonic wickedness has the power to send people to their earthly graves, divine righteousness has the power to resurrect people unto eternal life.

So in these perilous times, when evil is rearing its ugly head, let us remember the prophet Jonah. Let us remember that God used a single man with a single message to transform the hearts and minds of some of the most evil people that ever existed. God did not need an army to subdue the Ninevites; He simply needed the obedience of a single servant who was willing to obediently proclaim His truth. And God is the same yesterday, today, and forever (Hebrews 13:8).

If God could use the witness of Jonah to redeem the wicked city of Nineveh, then God can use His witnesses today to transform ISIS from terrorists into saints. But we must be willing to heed God's call. We must be willing to obey Our Lord's commands. We must love our enemies and bless those that persecute us. We must approach evil and speak divine truth. We must pray for the salvation of the wicked. We must rejoice when they repent. And we must celebrate the mercy that God showers upon them as we celebrate the mercy that God showers upon ourselves.

If we meet their hatred with love, their violence with peace, their lies with truth, and their evil with good, then how can we lose? Yes, we may lose our heads, but we will win our souls. And in the process, we may win their souls as well. And isn't that what our Great

Commission is all about: to bring the good news of salvation to all the world, including the wicked? As our holy father St. John Chrysostom said, *"Our warfare is to make the dead to live, not to make the living die."*

The story of Jonah is as relevant today as it has ever been. Let us pray, and let us obey. Heeding God's call is no easy task; but the story of Jonah shows us that running from God is much more difficult.

"Lord have mercy."

830. ~ MY GREATEST CROSS and MY GREATEST SIN ~

I feel too much, and that is my greatest cross. But I act too little, and that is my greatest sin. To hurt so much while doing so little to lessen the suffering of others is simply inexcusable. God have mercy on my soul.

831. ~ A SUMMARY of THE CONDESCENDING "CHRISTIAN" OPPOSITION to PACIFISM ~

Here's a basic summary of almost every condescending argument I receive from professing Christians who reject my pacifist position:

"I agree with you that peace is a nice ideal. I agree with you that peace is generally a Christian principle. I agree with you that war and violence and killing are not very nice things. So I think it's sort of neat that you talk about peace, because peace is kind of important sometimes. But just don't take peace too far. Because, you know, sometimes you just have to kill your brother and slaughter your neighbor and wreak all manner of evil in order to save your own ass and protect your own loved ones (by killing the loved ones of others) and defend the sacred idol of your own nation. But it's nice of you to remind us that peace is kind of cool in general. Just don't become

some sort of heretic that actually takes Christ at His very word. I mean, if you had been properly educated in theology then you'd know that Jesus didn't really mean for us to believe what He said or to literally follow His example. But we still think you're a neat guy for talking about peace a lot."

This is the mindset that we Christian pacifists constantly confront. May God grant us the peace of patience!

832. ~ JUST DON'T ASK THEM TO HELP YOU LIVE ~

People will gladly show up to your funeral. Just don't ask them to help you live.

833. ~ A MOMENT of GRATITUDE ~

I am deeply thankful for all of the wonderful friends who offer me their words of encouragement, support, challenge, and chastisement. I need all of it. I am an opinionated, judgmental, self-righteous sinner who is grieved by the pain, injustice, and suffering that I see in the world and that I have endured in my own life. (And it's to my shame that I allow my own personal suffering to blind me to the suffering that I too often cause others through my selfishness, apathy, and callousness.)

I write from my own experiences, from my own sorrows, and from my own vision of life which I pray is shaped by the Gospel of Our Lord Jesus Christ. This means that my words are always tainted with the fallibilities of subjectivity and sin; but I hope that they nevertheless somehow point to eternal and holy truths.

So that's why I covet the confirmation and correction, the affirmations and rebukes of others who have my best interest at heart. It gets very lonely standing for peace, life, and Orthodox Christian truth. And to be honest, I'm not really standing at all; I'm simply struggling to get up on my knees where the battle is truly won.

That's why I'm thankful for those who take time to send me words of encouragement, for those who engage me in positive and constructive dialogue, and for those who let me know when they think I'm going off the rails. I hope my dear friends will keep loving me. I hope they will keep praying for me. And I hope they will keep challenging me when they think it's warranted.

I need all the help I can get. Believe me.

834. ~ THE POWER of THE WRITTEN WORD ~

Did you know that Henry David Thoreau's essay, _Civil Disobedience_ profoundly influenced Leo Tolstoy? And did you know that Mahatma Gandhi's pacifism was deeply influenced by Tolstoy's book, _The Kingdom of God is Within You_? And did you know that Dr. Martin Luther King's philosophy of nonviolent direct action was shaped by Gandhi's own writings on the subject? And did you know that all four of these men were influenced by the teachings of the Christian gospels? So never underestimate the power of great ideas and spiritual truth conveyed through the written word. The pen is indeed mightier than the sword.

835. ~ SIGNIFICANT DIFFERENCES ~

Christ calls us to make disciples of all nations (St. Matthew 28:18-20). But He does not call us to make subjects of all nations. And that is a significant difference.

St. Paul said that governmental rulers do not bear the sword in vain (Romans 13:4). But he did not say that Christians do not bear the sword in vain. And that is a significant difference.

Christ told His disciples to render unto Caesar that which belongs to Caesar (St. Mark 12:17). But He didn't tell His disciples to seek to become Caesars. And that is a significant difference.

We are called to go into all the world and preach the Gospel (St. Mark 16:15). But we are not called to go into all the world and conquer Muslims, kill communists, spread capitalism, and plant the seeds of the "American Dream" in every nation on earth. And that is a significant difference.

836. ~ WE ARE CHRISTIANS, NOT VAMPIRES! ~

What madness is this, that we who make the sign of the Cross day and night, we who constantly beseech God's forgiveness with the incessant prayer, "Lord have mercy on us," we who gather in love to receive Our Lord's very Body and Blood, would then turn around at the whim of a politician's promise or a president's decree and take up arms to mercilessly slay our neighbors!

I say without hesitation that it is better to deny the Holy Trinity, to deny the deity of Christ, and to deny the sacramental mysteries than to affirm all Orthodox doctrines while slaughtering our brothers. I say without hesitation that it is better to be a heretical peacemaker than an Orthodox blood shedder.

How can we drink the Blood of Christ while we shed the blood of others? We are Christians, not vampires!

837. ~ ST. JOHN: PRAY for ME ~

Pray for me, O disciple that Jesus loved.

Pray for me, O disciple that lay upon Our Lord's breast.

Pray for me, O disciple that wept faithfully at the foot of the Cross.

Pray for me, O disciple that ran with hope to the empty tomb.

Pray for me, O disciple that wrote epistles of love.

Pray for me, O disciple of revelatory visions.

Pray for me, O disciple of prophetic pen.

Pray for me, O son of thunder.

Pray for me, O St. John – "The Evangelist," "The Revelator," "The Theologian," "The Divine."

838. ~ POLITICAL PRISON ~

Politics is a prison in which you have willingly confined yourself, a slavery to which you have deliberately chosen to submit. You have embraced the bondage of conservative shackles and liberal chains; you have gleefully bowed to Democrat oppression and Republican deception. And yet you lament your captivity.

But how can the revolutionary free those that refuse to free themselves? How can the prophets liberate those that prefer self-enslavement to emancipation? How can enlightenment come to those that love darkness more than illumination?

Your prison bars are paper thin, and your shackles are formed with gossamer links. Freedom awaits you if you truly want it. But I can't want it for you; and even God can't want it for you. You and you alone are responsible for enslaving yourself to political idolatry.

How long will you curse the waters of liberation while continuing to drink from these poisoned political wells? As Bob Marley said: *"With an abundance of water, the fool is thirsty."*

So there's nothing more I can do for you. I'm no savior. I'm no prophet. I'm no saint. I'm just a weak and struggling messenger. You can lead a prisoner to freedom, but you can't make him drink. You can lead a fool to truth, but you can't make him think.

"I freed a thousand slaves. But I could have freed a thousand more if only they knew they were slaves." ~ Harriet Tubman ~

"Emancipate yourselves from mental slavery. None but ourselves can free our minds." ~ Bob Marley (Berhane Selassie) ~

839. ~ BLOOD ~

The blood of the poor is the rich man's wine. The blood of the rich is the poor man's bread. And so goes the inhumane cycle of capitalism and communism. So goes the clash of the classes. So goes the perpetuation of worldly injustice and suffering.

Politicians, soldiers, and militant revolutionaries seek solutions with violence, bloodshed, and lies. But Christ offers His salvation equally – His Body and His Blood equally – to rich and poor alike.

At the foot of the Cross, and in the Eucharistic chalice, all humanity shall find peace, justice, and reconciliation. But rather than trusting in the shed blood of God Himself, we trust in shedding the blood of our very own brothers.

840. ~ "IT COULD HURT YOUR MINISTRY" ~

I've frequently had professing Christians tell me:

"If you marry someone of another race, it could hurt your ministry."

"If you have too many children, it could hurt your ministry."

"If you are seen with sinners, it could hurt your ministry."

Well, any "ministry" that conforms to racism, any ministry that views children as a burden, and any ministry that doesn't associate with sinners sure ain't a ministry of Jesus Christ. I can promise you that.

841. ~ LAW and ORDER ~

Everyone praises law and order until they're on the wrong end of law and order.

842. ~ THE POOR and IVORY TOWER ECONOMICS ~

Capitalism is the belief that making the rich richer will somehow help the poor. Socialism is the belief that making the rich poorer will somehow help the poor get richer. "Trickledown economics" sends the poor crashing over the waterfall; and socialist economics leaves everyone drowning in a shallow, stagnant pool.

Conservative governments and liberal governments both propose all manner of economic solutions – anything other than actually getting off the backs of those in poverty. The poor have never been served by the ivory tower economic philosophies of either the right or the left.

Never trust the rich to speak on behalf of the poor. Never trust the oppressor to speak on behalf of the oppressed. Never trust those in power to tell you what's best for those without power. Never trust politicians to speak for the people.

The real revolutionaries never get elected. In fact, the real revolutionaries never run for office. They're too busy serving the sufferers.

843. ~ LOVE IS... ~

Love is suffering, and love is redemption. Love is agony, and love is peace. Love is beauty, and love is pain. Love is terrible, and love is true.

Love is a harsh thunder that precipitates a gentle rain.

But whatever it is, love is life. Without love, our existence is empty. Without love, life is stale. Without love, the hottest fires always leave us cold.

So let our hearts be broken, over and over again. For this is how we truly live – now and always and into eternity. Let us love with blood and tears and crucified hearts, knowing that Our Lord will forever cleanse our grief with His nailed-scarred hands.

Love is salvation.

844. ~ WE LOVE THEM in THE GRAVE ~

They cried out, in so many ways – with art and pen and heart and song. They cried out with their very existence. But no one listened. Until it was too late.

Why do we only give our flowers and our tears and our presence and our love to the dead? We're always too busy to love them in life, but God how we love them in the grave.

845. ~ TODAY and TOMORROW ~

Today you extract the blood, sweat, and tears of your brother. Tomorrow God extracts the payment of your soul.

846. ~ TRIALS and CROSSES and CURSES and THANKSGIVING ~

Every day I lament my sufferings, my struggles, my sicknesses, and my poverty. But without these trials I wouldn't be worth a damn to anyone. So I constantly curse my crosses, and yet I constantly thank God for them.

847. ~ THEY WILL RISE UP ~

The oppressed will rise up, one way or another. The voiceless will be heard, one way or another. The victims will resist, one way or another. The sufferers will revolt, one way or another.

The slave will inevitably rend his shackles. The prisoner will inevitably break through his walls. The poor will inevitably find their way to your table. The aborted unborn will inevitably be avenged.

So live at the expense of others if you dare. But your exploitation will surely return to haunt you – if not in this life, then most certainly in the next.

848. ~ AM I YOUR "MINISTRY" or AM I YOUR BROTHER? ~

What if I didn't want to be saved, but I still wanted to be helped? What if I didn't want a sermon, but I still wanted bread? What if you couldn't redeem my soul, but you could still give me peace of mind? What if I didn't want to go to your Church, but I still longed for your Church to come to me? What if I wasn't worried about heaven, but I just wanted relief from my living hell?

Would you still be willing to help me? Would your gospel still apply?

Am I your "ministry" or am I your brother?

849. ~ VOTING and PRAYING ~

Voting and praying for God to protect us from our evil choices is like going to war and praying not to get killed. There's no spiritual security in compromising the Gospel. It's irrational, futile, and unchristian to attempt to use unholy means to establish holy ends. Let us leave worldly things to the world and put our trust where it truly belongs. The Kingdom of Heaven won't be ushered in by the bullet or the ballot.

850. ~ "PACIFIED" CHRISTIANS? ~

The problem is not that Christians have become *pacifistic* (let us pray for the day when we can be rightly accused of such a thing!); the problem is that Christians have become *pacified* by the demonic anesthetizations of nationalism, militarism, and the satiating teats of politics and democracy.

We have become willing to kill for the right to wear and preach the Cross, but we no longer understand what the Cross means. We have traded the substantive commands of Christ for mere symbols that we confuse for Christianity.

In diametric opposition to the example of Our Lord and His disciples, we will take up the Cross and bash our Muslim brothers to death with it before we allow ourselves to be crucified. We are ready to defend our "Christianity" with violence and bloodshed, even if it means that we trample the Gospel underfoot.

We must ask ourselves if we are really any longer the "Church militant," or if we are merely a church that has been completely subdued by the hellish powers of patriotism, politics, hatred, and destruction.

851. ~ LIFE is FULL of PAIN and FULL of HOPE ~

Some people try to justify abortion by claiming that it will reduce poverty, that it will prevent "unwanted children" from coming into the world, and arguing that it's somehow a therapeutic remedy for rape and incest. Well, you know, decapitation also cures headaches. But I'm one of those "fanatical religious zealots" who think that people shouldn't permanently lose their heads trying to alleviate a temporary problem. Life is painful sometimes; but life is always full of promise and pregnant with hope. So keep your head on your shoulders, and nurture the life within you.

No life, no blessings. More life, more blessings!

852. ~ SERVICE, HONOR, FEAR, and OBEDIENCE ~

I serve no masters, I honor no lords.
I bow to no magistrates,
I fear no gods.

I am a Christian:
I obey One King, I worship One Lord.

853. ~ THE ABSURDITY of VIOLENCE (SWORDS WON'T SAVE YOUR SOULS) ~

Using violence to save unborn babies in America is somehow considered a great sin (and it is indeed a sin), but using violence to defend the legality of killing of babies in America is somehow worthy of Medals of Honor. That more than anything shows you the absurdity, the futility, the contradiction, and the insanity of violence. Your swords won't end abortion; your swords won't bring peace to your nation; and your swords certainly won't save your souls.

854. ~ TOGETHER WE SUFFER, TOGETHER WE ARE SAVED ~

The first step toward freedom is the realization that we are all enslaved. The first step toward liberation is the recognition that we are all oppressed. The first step toward redemption is the knowledge that we are all redeemable. And the first step toward revolution is the awareness that we are all brothers and sisters in the struggle.

Sin does not discriminate. Evil has no color. Satan is an equal opportunity destroyer. But God is One, and in God we are all united. Together we suffer, and together we are saved.

If you care, you will suffer. If you care, you will make mistakes. If you care, you will sometimes sin in your desire to make things right. If you care, you will be misunderstood. If you care, you will be called a fool. If you care, your heart will be repeatedly broken. If you care, you will be abandoned and betrayed. If you care, many will hate you. If you care, you will struggle with depression and despondency. If you care, you will have dark nights of the soul. If you care, you will sometimes do crazy things (because it's hard to react reasonably to an unreasonable world.)

But if you care, Christ cares with you. And if you care, you can actually change some things. If you care, you can perhaps save lives, inspire people, and uplift humanity.

If you care enough to compose a song, write a book, paint a picture, preach a sermon, shout on the street corner, get arrested, go to Liturgy, fall in love, have your heart broken, fall in love again, paint another picture, write another book, preach on the street corner some more, and hope that you won't get arrested this time – for any of it... well, God is somehow in all of that I believe. And I also think that God is just as present in those of us who do nothing more than turn on the news and weep at the horrors we see before us.

I guess what I'm trying to say is that as long as we care, then Our Lord is with us and there is hope for us all.

I've often thought that apathy is perhaps the greatest sin. I know that the Bible indicates that pride is the original sin, the root of all other sins. But pride has nevertheless produced some beautiful and awe-inspiring things. But what has apathy ever given to the world? At least pride is capable of thinking, "I can stop that evil!" But apathy doesn't even acknowledge that the evil exists. Beauty and goodness and justice and love emanate from suffering and struggle, pathos and pain.

Bad art may be forgiven; but to remain unmoved by beauty will not. Doubts may be forgiven; but a lack of wonder will not. Tilting at windmills may be forgiven; but allowing our neighbors to be grinded in the gears will not. Denying the existence of the Creator may be forgiven; but ignoring the glories and responsibilities of creation will not.

It's a horrible curse to care, and it's a damnable sin not to care. May God grant us the grace to care, even if it crucifies us.

856. ~ CHILDREN ARE HEROES ~

All children are heroes before they grow up. What are saints and martyrs and revolutionaries other than grown men and women who refuse to abandon the purity and idealism of childhood?

857. ~ "THE PROBLEM" ~

There are problems, human problems, complex universal human problems. But our fallen human nature demands that we must find a scapegoat. Some specific group of humans must be designated as "the problem." Get enough people to believe that a certain segment of humanity is "the problem," and you can eventually unleash unholy hell on "the problem."

But somehow, when the smoke clears and the ashes settle, the problem still remains. And then there will always be some other group of people that becomes "the problem": e.g., Jews, Muslims, communists, fascists, Blacks, Whites, women, immigrants, refugees, unborn children, etc.

So we keep trying to eliminate "the problem" with prisons and wars and executions and abortions and genocides and all manner of discrimination and oppression. And eventually *we* become the ones that are designated as "the problem." And suddenly we find *ourselves* on the wrong end of the gas chambers and ovens and nooses and chains and desperate desert-crossing deaths. And this is how history perpetually and tragically repeats itself.

"We" are *"them."* And until we realize it, we are all in peril.

858. ~ I CONFESS MY CONTRADICTION ~

I confess my contradiction: I am a Christian anarchist who nevertheless prays for the restoration of the Ethiopian Christian Monarchy. And I'm quite alright with that. I reject the violent laws of man, but I embrace the peaceful laws of God. Where human law parallels divine law, I will celebrate it. But where human law contradicts divine law, I will rebel against it. And I will never be able to perfectly reconcile the two. I will always be in some way guilty of contradictions, inconsistencies, and hypocrisy. But that's OK, because I've learned that the road to Paradise is paved with paradox.

859. ~ COUNTER-REVOLUTIONARY CONSCIOUSNESS ~

Nothing is more counter-revolutionary than embracing the ways of the oppressor as a means of rebelling against oppression. Babylon is happy to let you participate in her elections, die in her wars, and be brainwashed by her schools – just as long as you're embracing and participating in the system.

The oppressor always supports "progress and change" as long as "progress and change" means empowering the immoral, godless, and oppressive political structure created and sustained by racism and violence. But once you start doing things like feeding the poor, disrupting the military-industrial complex, and defending the lives of innocent unborn babies, then you become a real revolutionary and a true threat to the powers that seek to control you.

The oppressor winks with satisfaction when he sees you joining the army, saluting the flag, and electing Black politicians that perpetuate the suffering and exploitation of Black people. But that same demon trembles when he sees you resisting politics and raising hell about the oppression and death of the innocents.

Just think about it: No reparations for slavery. No real restitution to Native Americans. Increased racial and socio-economic division. No end to poverty. More wars. More executions. More violence in the streets. No right to life for the most innocent among us.

But Babylon satiates the people with symbolism over substance; and the masses willingly accept their slavery because there's an African American in the White House, a monument to Dr. King in Washington, and sexually objectified Black women gyrating at the halftime of the Super Bowl.

The counter-revolution is being televised 24/7, and the sheep are constantly being put to sleep. But a few of us are still awake out here. Our insomnia feels like a curse most of the time, but we understand that it's really a blessing. So please don't sing us any of your Babylonian lullabies!

860. ~ EDUCATION and ERUDITION ~

You can have a thousand books in your library, but if they all say the same thing then you will never really learn. And that's the problem with most "educated" people today. They surround themselves with choirs of books that sing praises to what they already believe. And thus they mistake their brainwashing for erudition.

861. ~ DON'T TELL ME THAT YOU'RE "PRO-LIFE"... ~

Yes, I want to overturn Roe vs. Wade. But I also want to overturn militarism, the prison industrial complex, and the entire godless political system that perpetuates war, crime, and abortion.

So don't tell me that you're "pro-life" as long as you vote for politicians that promote violence as a solution. Don't tell me that you're "pro-life" as long as you vote for politicians that view death as an answer. Don't tell me that you're "pro-life" as long as you lend participation and support to a political system predicated upon bloodshed and death. Don't tell me that you love unborn babies here in America while you support a government that bombs innocent babies overseas.

Abortion is merely another manifestation of the evil, injustice, and oppression upon which this nation was founded and is sustained. Politics is no more a solution to abortion than militarism is a solution to terrorism. Violence will never eliminate the evils that can only be erased with repentant hearts.

862. ~ GOD of RAINBOWS, GOD of THUNDER ~

The God of rainbows is also the God of thunder. So praise Him for the lightning as well as the sunlight. Praise Him for the earthquake as well as for the morning dew. Praise JAH name and know that He won't be tamed.

863. ~ GUERILLAS in THE REVOLUTION of THE RESURRECTION ~

So you'd rather we peacefully acquiesce with your violence than raise hell in pursuit of His peace?

Well, that ain't happening, we promise you.

As long as you seek salvation in oaths and pledges and armies and elections, then we will raise our voices of disruption and dissent. We will die rebelling against your allegiance to death; but we might save a few lives and liberate some souls in the process. And that's worth it all in the end to us.

We are provocateurs of peace, apostles of anarchy, revolutionaries of redemption, and liberators serving the Lord of Life. We will always be an impediment to your wars and politics and exploitation and abortion. Wherever the idolatry of violence is extolled, we will raise the hammer of peace against it.

You will never silence us, because our Christian truth echoes eternally. We are guerillas in the revolution of the Resurrection!

864. ~ GOD on THEIR LIPS and BLOOD on THEIR SOULS ~

To be honest, I'm not moved by eloquent prayers and rousing speeches delivered by those that murder, oppress, and destroy. Beware of those who have God on their lips and blood on their souls.

865. ~ PARENTING ~

There is no more difficult or more blessed work than parenting. It's a constant struggle, a constant challenge, and a constant reward. I may go to the grave broke as hell, but I'm investing in lives that will make the world richer in ways that truly matter. And parenting never ends. No matter how old my children get, I have to constantly encourage them, listen to them, love them, and pray for them.

Parenting is hard work. Really hard work. But the funny thing is, it never feels like work. It's a joy to be a father – the greatest joy I know – especially with children like mine.

866. ~ AMERICAN RESTORATION and HUMAN REDEMPTION ~

You see, some of us are not concerned with the preservation or restoration of America. We're simply concerned with the redemption of humanity. And that's the difference between patriots and Christians.

867. ~ REFLECTIONS on FLANNERY O'CONNOR ~

One of the many things I love about Flannery O'Connor is her deep respect for the eccentricities and absurdities of the Christian fundamentalist culture of the South. Unlike cynical, uninformed critics who think that great literature or great film is caricaturing devout but ignorant Southern Christians in the most disparaging manner possible, Ms. O'Connor always depicted the sincerity and passion that lay deeply at the heart of Southern religious fanaticism. Most people completely misunderstand Flannery O'Connor because they read her as someone who's simply making fun of rural Southern society and its many odd manifestations of fanatical Christian faith. But her writing actually demonstrates great honor and appreciation for fundamentalist zealotry, even as it simultaneously portrays its aberrant horrors.

O'Connor's stories articulate the mystery of religion and faith and passion and guilt, showing us that these things are inextricably intertwined. She didn't waste time writing about well-heeled Methodists and upper crust Presbyterians. To her, there was no real passion there, no oddities to be explored, no depth worthy of examination. So she wrote instead about the greatest religious mysteries she knew apart from her own Roman Catholic Faith. In her strangest and most horrific characters she shows us reflections of the mystery that is ourselves.

I love Flannery O'Connor.

"All boils down to grace I suppose. I am afraid of pain and I suppose that is what we have to have to get the grace. Give me the courage to stand the pain to get the grace, Oh Lord."
~ Flannery O'Connor ~

868. ~ REAL REVOLUTION ~

They don't mind you organizing. They don't mind you revolting. They don't mind you killing and burning and looting and voting. But when you start loving, when you start forgiving, when you start uniting, and when you start refusing to participate in their violence, then you become a true threat to the system that seeks to control, exploit, oppress, and destroy you.

Do you want to start a real revolution? Then lay down your arms, free your mind from politics, and learn to love your brother.

869. ~ GOD FASTED and PRAYED FOR US ~

God fasted and prayed for *us*. The Lord of the universe prayed with sweat and tears and anguish and blood – for *us*. Not because He had to. Not because He needed to. But simply because He chose to love us *that* much. The depth of God's love for humanity is a glorious, humbling, impenetrable, and incredibly hopeful mystery.

[Cf. St. Matthew 26:36-46; St. Mark 14:32-42; St. Luke 22:39-46]

870. ~ POLITICAL PREJUDICE ~

Political prejudice is just as demonic and dangerous as any other prejudice. I continue to see a nation of bigoted, prejudicial fools ready to tear each other apart in defense of their political idols. Leftwing prejudice and hatred are just as evil as rightwing prejudice and hatred. But those who are wedded to politics don't realize this, because politics has made them prejudiced. And when you mess with people's politics and prejudices, they may just get mad enough to torture, enslave, and kill you. So be careful.

871. ~ TIPS ON WRITING (FROM A STRUGGLING, BROKE AUTHOR) ~

First of all, if you want to be a good writer, be a good reader. Don't just learn to read well, but learn to read broadly. And never feel that you have to like what you read simply because others have told you that you're supposed to like it. If an author's words don't capture your imagination, stir your soul, challenge your prejudices, or prick your conscience, then don't feel that you have to plow through the rest of the tome. There are other authors and other books that are waiting to captivate your heart and mind.

Yes, sometimes it's important to discipline yourself to read long and difficult classics. For example, Dostoevsky is not easy reading, but it's important to read all the way through at least one of his novels once in your lifetime. But life is ultimately too short to waste time on books that don't bring you joy or conviction as you read them.

So read abundantly and read joyfully. And then, when you take up your own pen, trust that the influence of the authors you have admired will naturally influence your own work without interrupting your own voice. Don't try to emulate anyone else.

And don't try to be a "great" writer. Just write because you want to write, because you have to write, because your mind and heart simply cannot contain the ideas that flow through them. Write because your soul demands it.

Write one sentence the best way you can. And realize that sometimes one sentence is enough. Trust that sentence. And trust that brevity is often the greatest revealer of depth.

When you write, remember that it's *your* story and therefore you alone know best how to tell it. It's your own philosophy or idea that you are trying to convey, it's your own conviction or cause that you are trying to defend, and therefore you alone best know how to communicate it. So trust your own voice. Grammatical errors, typos, and stylistic faux pas can always be corrected and forgiven. But if your writing is not truly *your* writing, if your own authentic voice is not coming through your pen, then the words on the page will not truly matter.

Always be open to harsh criticisms and blunt critiques. And try hard to listen more to the criticisms than the praise (but don't pay attention to spiteful, negative, personal insults that have nothing to do with the actual substance or style of your writing.) And never assume that the insights of one person are more or less valid than the insights of another. Great books are not great because they receive the praise of academics, intellectuals, and corporately established publishing companies. Great books are great because they are able to reach a variety of people from a variety of walks of life. So, by all means, listen to your literature professor; but listen equally to the feedback of the neighbor next door.

And finally, don't ever measure the value of your voice by publication or financial remuneration. There are thousands of wealthy, published authors in the world whose books have nothing of substance to offer. So don't quit writing simply because you haven't been published or haven't been paid. Your voice matters; and somebody out there will find inspiration or joy from what you have written. So just keep on writing. And keep on writing what only you yourself can write. Write on!

(And one last small point: don't let anyone tell you that you're not an author if you haven't been published. As far as I'm concerned, if you're a writer then you're an author. So don't let anyone diminish your achievements simply because you haven't been published.)

872. ~ BEAUTY on A SUNDAY AFTERNOON ~

Sunday afternoon, after prayer, I'm sitting outside the café listening to the chatter of pretty young women at the table nearby. I'm intoxicated by their perfume and cigarette smoke and lipstick and skin that somehow blends beautifully with the gentle sunshine breeze of nascent spring. They are still young and still seeking and still unsure about life, but together they are confident and strong and invincible. But I am growing old. I no longer have the confidence of naivety. I envy it in them.

I am trying not to stare at the girl in the strapless black number with the beautiful tattoos. She is insecure about her dress. She is worried that it might make her look overweight. Her friends assure her that she looks beautiful. I would like to assure her that she is beautiful too. I find her fascinating.

I am not interested in flirting with her. I don't want to go to bed with her. I simply want to acknowledge the beauty of this day, the beauty of this young woman with the beautiful tattoos, the beauty of the naivety of youth, the beauty of these ephemeral and evanescent aesthetics that somehow point to eternal, indelible glories. But ultimately, I just want to sip my coffee, bathe in the lingering peace of the earlier morning's Divine Liturgy, and return to the words of Tolstoy that lay open before me.

But I am too curious about this particular creature. So I approach these young women and introduce myself. I tell the tattooed girl that I like her ink very much, and I ask her where she got her work done. She labors to repress a smile and answers my question with as much casualty as she can muster. She then pulls up her dress and shows me a brilliant black and grey portrait of Marilyn Monroe on her right thigh. She gives me the name of the tattoo artist. I thank her and return to my coffee and my book. Soon she comes over and gives me the name of another tattoo artist. I thank her again and pretend to write down the information she's given me.

My coffee time is over. Time to go home, and quickly! I am supposed to be a man, a grown man, a mature and seasoned man. But God how the passions of youth continue to haunt me!

There's so much beauty in the world, and sometimes it's difficult not to drink it all in to our own detriment and destruction. Maybe the key is to appreciate beauty, not worship it. And that's a very fine line sometimes. True beauty is worthy of veneration. But veneration is much different than worship. (But that's a theological discussion for another time.)

Beauty is a glorious and dangerous mystery. Perhaps beauty will save the world, as Dostoevsky wrote. But if we try to tame it, to subdue it, or enslave ourselves to it, then beauty will surely damn us. Thank God for beauty! God save us from beauty!

873. ~ GOOD ART and GREAT ART ~

Violence and lust and hatred and conflict are the themes of good art. But love and suffering and redemption and hope are the themes of great art. Show me depravity, but show me faith. Because one cannot be understood apart from the other.

874. ~ CHRIST CLARIFIES IT ALL ~

There are lots of disturbing and confusing passages in the Bible. But Christ clarifies it all:

- Love your enemies. (St. Matthew 5:44)
- Love one another. (St. John 13:34)
- Don't harm children. (St. Matthew 18:5-6)
- Don't trust in violence. (St. Matthew 26:52)
- Sacrifice your own life for others, but don't sacrifice the lives of others. (St. John 15:13)

It's pretty simple. Very difficult of course, but very simple.

875. ~ **RAPED** ~
(This story contains profanity and disturbing material. Please be advised.)

The blood dripped from her as he smiled.

"Fuck you," she thought. And "fuck your smile."

He had seemed so kind, so confident and reassuring. She had wanted to believe him. He'd asked her if she was sure that she wanted it. And she had assured him that she did. And she *had* wanted it. At least she had *thought* she wanted it.

He had said all the right things to assuage her ambivalence. He was a smooth talker, and she liked him for it. She was grateful for his charm. It was just what she needed. She wanted to be talked into it. And so she had submitted to him.

But it had hurt. Badly. And she sensed he had derived sadistic pleasure from the pain he inflicted. And now he smirked at her, with smug self-satisfaction, as blood ran down her legs and a tear fell on her cheek.

"Let's get some more gauze in here!" he barked. "This blood is a goddamned mess! Quickly! More gauze!"

"I can't stop bleeding," she said.

"You're ok. We're going to fix that." He smiled down at her. "This is quite normal."

She looked up at him, searching his eyes for the kindness, compassion, and reassurance that she thought she had seen half an hour earlier. But all she saw now was dark indifference behind that plastic bullshit grin.

The drugs and the trauma were rendering her semi-conscious. She felt herself drifting in and out of sleep, descending deeper into a nightmare. She tried helplessly to keep her eyes open, because whenever she closed them she saw rivers of blood pouring from her vagina and her nose and her mouth. She wanted to shake herself out of this horror. But every time she tried to sit up someone pushed her back down. She just wanted them to stop the bleeding. If someone would just stop the bleeding! But they appeared to just be standing there laughing at her.

"The drugs are kicking in. See, you can tell. Look at her. She's high as a kite! She's feelin' good. She's gonna be just fine now!"

The cackling voices seemed to mock her. It was all a big joke to them.

And where was he? Where had he gone? She tried to look for him, but all she saw were these green stethoscope women that hovered over her with their white laughing teeth and cold black eyes.

She didn't want to fall asleep. She didn't want to succumb to these dream terrors of endless blood. But it was too strong to resist now. So she just prayed for the bleeding to end. She would endure any nightmare, just as long as the bleeding would end. Please God, make it stop. But the blood kept coming. Pouring out from every part of her it seemed.

She felt blood flowing from her eyes. But when she wiped her eyes she realized they were only wet with tears.

"But why am I crying?" she wondered. "After all, this is what I wanted."

And still the blood poured out of her. And she knew it was unnatural for there to be so much of it and unnatural for it not to stop. And she realized that something deep within her was producing all of this blood. And she knew that she would bleed forever unless she could undo what she had done. But she couldn't undo it now. It was done.

"Drink this sweetheart," said one of the laughing green voices. "Sip on this juice and eat a cracker. It will help ease the nausea you feel."

She could barely open her eyes or her mouth. And she didn't want any goddamned juice or goddamned crackers. She wanted what had been taken from her. She wanted to have back what she couldn't have back. And she wanted the fucking blood to stop.

"Why don't they stop all this bleeding?!" she wondered. "And where is he? Where did he go? I need to speak to him. I need him to fix this!"

But she was too weak to say anything, too weak to do anything. She could no longer resist the nightmare she had chosen.

Her eyelids were lead curtains closing down on her soul. Her eyes shut and she saw a crimson river, steadily rising. It was rising too fast. And she saw a little girl on a merry-go-round, spinning happily beside this surging sanguinary tide. Soon the merry-go-round would be flooded, and the little girl would drown in blood. She wanted to warn the little girl, to save the little girl. She wanted to wake up and run and pick the little girl up in her arms and carry her to safety. And she knew that the little girl was her very own little girl. And she realized that it was now too late.

Too late. Too much blood now. Much too late now.

Then she heard a voice. It was his voice. She forced her own eyes open and searched for his.

"We've stopped the bleeding. You're fine. So you should be ok to drive home. And you're all paid up, so you're good to go now."

She looked up at his empty smiling face. And she looked up at the other vapid grins and lifeless eyes that surrounded her. And with every ounce of strength she could summon, she barely managed to whisper: *"Fuck you."*

876. ~ PROBLEM and ANSWER ~

If you think politics is the answer, then *you* are the problem. And if you realize that politics is the problem, then *you* need to be the answer.

877. ~ PROPERTY and PEOPLE ~

Babylon: where property is more important than people (unless you happen to be people with a lot of property.)

878. ~ WE ALL ARE ONE ~

The only reason that we are not all ONE is because we don't believe it and we don't act like it. We prioritize politics, religion, race, and ideology above brotherhood, peace, and love.

There is only One God, by whatever name we choose to call Him. And together we are all trodding through His creation, equally bearing His indelible image. But instead of acknowledging our common humanity and our common Creator, we war and fight and divide and conquer – and often in His holy name.

So God came to us, as one of us – loving us and healing us and even allowing us to kill Him – so that perhaps we might finally learn to love one another. But instead, we use the message of the Cross and the good news of salvation to perpetuate division, discord, and theological triumphalism. And I am as guilty as anyone in this regard. May God have mercy on me.

We strive to comprehend the inscrutable transcendence of God, but we fail to recognize the simple truths of His immanence. We "strain at a gnat but swallow a camel." (St. Matthew 23:24)

The greatest mystery of the Christian Faith is not the mystery of the Trinity, the mystery of the Incarnation, or the mystery of the Holy Eucharist. The greatest Christian mystery is simply the mystery of love: that we love God, that we love our neighbors, that we love our enemies, and that we love one another. Every Orthodox Christian doctrine and every Orthodox Christian sacrament points us to love: and not just love for our own, but love for all.

St. Paul wrote: *"Through Christ, God reconciled everything to Himself. He made peace with everything in heaven and on earth by means of Christ's blood on the Cross." [Colossians 1:20]*

So indeed, we are all one – *all of us* – Black and White, Muslim and Jew, gay and straight, Republican and Democrat, atheist and Christian, born and unborn, male and female (and all those struggling with their sexual identities.)

The only problem is that most people don't understand this good news of the Gospel, so they are lost in the darkness of division, prejudice, politics, and hate. And if we who profess to be followers of Christ don't preach and live the good news – the good news that *we are all truly one* – then what hope will humanity have?

"One love, one heart, one aim, one destiny!"
~ Marcus Garvey ~ / ~ Bob Marley (Berhane Selassie) ~

879. ~ JESUS and DEMOCRACY ~

We love Jesus as long as Jesus doesn't interfere with our democracy. We'll gladly follow Jesus as long as He doesn't interfere with our wars and guns and executions and abortions and capitalistic exploitation. As long as Jesus lets us fashion our golden calves and towers of Babel, then Jesus is the one we love. But if He starts messing with our idols, then we'll vote Jesus right on out and we'll vote Barabbas right on in. And that won't end up very well for Jesus, so He'd better not step out of line. (Of course, it will end up much worse for us. But we're too blind to see that.)

880. ~ CHRISTIAN ANARCHY ~

I used to think that anarchy meant chaos, violence, and disorder. But Leo Tolstoy, Henry David Thoreau, Nikolai Berdyaev, Ammon Hennacy, Jacques Ellul, and other Christian anarchists showed me that authentic anarchy means so ordering our lives in Christ that we inevitably rebel against all organized systems of violence, oppression, injustice, and evil. So, yes, there is indeed such a thing as "Christian anarchy;" and it's actually the root of all authentic rebellion.

"No matter what the motivation, I am against violence and aggression. Love is the way, not violence. But not using violence against those in power does not mean doing nothing. Christianity means a rejection of power and a fight against it." ~ Jacques Ellul ~

881. ~ JESUS WAS NOT A POLITICIAN ~

Jesus was not a progressive. Jesus was not a conservative. Jesus was not a politician. Jesus is *Lord*. So please stop misappropriating the message of the Savior to advance your worldly political agendas. It's not only blasphemous, it's also just plain tacky.

882. ~ HUMANITARIAN VALUES and ETHICAL VIRTUES ~

The sanctity of human life is the foundational principle upon which all humanitarian values and ethical virtues are ultimately contingent. Truth, freedom, justice, liberty, peace, and choice derive their significance from the existence of life itself, upon which all these ideals are predicated. That's why all true revolutionary struggles for human rights and social justice uphold the sanctity of life as their fundamental principle. To exalt humanitarian virtues while denying the right to life is both ontologically irrational and inevitably self-defeating. How can you cultivate the fruit of freedom if you believe in killing the tree of life?

883. ~ ON VENGEANCE, JUDGMENT, and RECONCILIATION ~

I am trying hard to reshape my understanding of God's ultimate, eschatological justice. I'm trying to view His final Judgment as ultimately restorative and universally reconciling. But when I think of innocent children being abused, aborted, and sexually exploited, then I can't help but to yearn for the wrath of God to rain down upon those who victimize these little ones.

I guess I just haven't matured enough in my faith. I know I should simply focus on my own sins. I know that *I* certainly don't deserve God's mercy. So who am I to concern myself with the judgment of other sinners? But I just can't see how the brutality inflicted upon innocent children won't somehow be divinely avenged in due time. This is one of the many reasons that I'm a pacifist. I fear I would be very bad news for a lot of very bad people if I wasn't. (And that's by no means the right Christian motive for nonviolence. So there's still a lot of spiritual growth that needs to take place in my life. I confess that.)

And yet, the truth is, I still would not wish a literal and eternal hellfire on abortionists and child molesters. I wouldn't wish such horrific suffering on Hitler himself. In fact, I have come to believe that true faith in the love of Christ is completely incompatible with belief in a divine judgment of literal and eternal flames. (That is simply my own opinion. I don't presume to speak for the Orthodox Church on this matter.) However, something within me nevertheless seems to demand that some sort of divine wrath be executed against those who inflict torture and pain upon the innocent.

But when I think more deeply about it – and pray more deeply about it – I realize that what I really want is for these injustices to simply *stop*. I just want there to be an end to all of this pain – an end to my own pain as well as an end to the pain inflicted upon others. And I think that Jesus came to put an end to all this suffering. And I think that through His suffering on the Cross, all suffering will thus be eradicated in eternity.

It shouldn't matter to me whether or not rapists, abortionists, and child abusers escape some sort of divine punishment. All that should matter to me is that God will put an end to all injustice, that He will heal all wounds, that He will dry every tear, that He will turn all suffering and sorrow into peace and joy.

If, in paradise, the lion will lay down with the lamb, then why should I not hope for the abortionist to hold hands with the aborted? Why should I not hope for the abuser to praise God along with the abused? Why should I not hope for the slave owner to be reconciled with the slave?

So I don't think it's actually hell or wrath or vengeance that I crave (although it certainly feels like it.) I think it's simply *justice* that my soul cries out for. And I think that God will surely execute His complete and final justice in due time. And I also think that His perfect and holy justice might look completely different from our fallible and cruel *human* justice. And I think that maybe all of humanity will somehow link arms in heaven and offer praise for a divine universal justice that is inseparable from a divine universal love.

Is this not the glorious hope of the Gospel: that God and sinners will be reconciled, that all things in heaven and earth will be reconciled, that the guilty and innocent will be reconciled, that even the abuser and the abused will be reconciled? Perhaps reconciliation *is* the the final Judgment and the ultimate justice.

In the meantime, all we can do – and all we should do – is beat our swords into plowshares, love our neighbors as ourselves, pray without ceasing, and thank God for His unfailing mercy. But I admit: when I see the innocent being victimized, it takes great restraint to forsake the sword and trust in the Transcendent.

"Lord have mercy on us all."

884. ~ HEAVEN, EARTH, and SALVATION ~

We try to pull God down from heaven because we need Him here on earth. But God already came down to earth. And when He walked the earth we crucified Him and sent Him back to heaven. I guess we all want salvation; we just don't want to follow the Savior.

885. ~ WE REFUSE ~

We refuse to be patient with violence and killing. We refuse to support ideologies, individuals, and organizations that perpetuate counter-revolutionary evils that masquerade as progress, hope, and change. We refuse to acquiesce with any inhumane ethic that rationalizes the murder and oppression of some human beings ostensibly for the benefit of others.

We refuse to compromise any human lives for any reason. Every life is sacred, and therefore we refuse to accept any philosophy or political platform that promotes death and destruction as humanitarian solutions.

Cut out our tongues so we can no longer speak. Cut off our fingers so we can no longer write. Throw us in prison so we can no longer protest. And kill us if that's what you must finally do to silence us. But as long as we trod through this terrestrial vale, then we will remain revolutionary agents of peace, love, and life.

Ideologies and movements that are built on death will meet their own inevitable and logical deaths. But the cause of life can never die. It will live eternally. So why fight it?

To side with life, to affirm life, to honor life, and to simply live life is the truest rebellion, the most powerful resistance, and the greatest revolution.

886. ~ THE OFFENSE of THE CONSISTENT LIFE ETHIC ~

When you preach the "consistent Life ethic," you will inevitably offend people who are wedded to death. And most of these people don't even realize they are wedded to death. And they get really upset when you point out that they are wedded to death. You see, they are somehow blind to the fact that promoting death as a solution to death clearly discloses their love for death. They tell you that war will bring peace, that violence will establish justice, that exploitation will eradicate poverty, that execution will preserve life, and that abortion will bring healing. And when you explain the insanity of such godless and inhumane notions, they will rise up and kill you to prove just how opposed to violence and death they really are.

887. ~ ONE GOD, INFINITELY UNBOUND ~

There is only One God, One Creator, One Savior, and One Lord. And God is too big, too infinite, and too eternal to be limited or confined by the narrow, sectarian definitions of finite human logic.

I am an Orthodox Christian, and by the grace of God I will defend and proclaim the mystical doctrines of the Orthodox Faith with my dying breath. But I will never presume that God is bound by my mortal rationale; I will never presume that the Holy Spirit is working only in my own small corner of the world; I will never presume that Christ is not also somehow living in the hearts and minds of people of other faiths or religions.

Where love is active, where life is affirmed, and where peace prevails, I am confident that God is present.

Perhaps some people will think I'm going to hell for asserting such a thing. But because of my faith in the Cross and my faith in the unfailing mercy of Our Lord, I nevertheless look forward to meeting them in heaven.

"Not everyone who says to Me, 'Lord, Lord,'
will enter the kingdom of heaven, but he who does the will
of My Father who is in heaven will enter." [St. Matthew 7:21]

"God is no respecter of persons:
But in every nation he that fears Him, and works
righteousness, is accepted with Him." [Acts 10:34-35]

"Whoever who does the will of my Father in heaven
is my brother and sister and mother!" [St. Matthew 12:50]

"The world and its desires pass away, but
whoever does the will of God lives forever." [I John 2:17]

888. ~ JESUS DIDN'T COME TO SAVE AMERICA ~

Jesus didn't come to redeem America (or any other nation state). And America is not the redeemer of the world. Jesus is the Savior, and Jesus came to save the entire human race. That's why all of your militaristic and political efforts to preserve and restore the USA will ultimately be proven futile. The "land of the free and the home of the brave" will inevitably crumble like every other earthly kingdom. It will crash like the tower of Babel. It will fall in a single hour like the great city of Babylon (Cf. Revelation 18).

So, dear Christian: why do you persist in forsaking the Lord in order to divide and kill and hate and conquer for the glory and preservation of a temporal kingdom that was built upon blood-soaked sand?

889. ~ ANARCHY and CHRISTIAN RESISTANCE ~

Obedience to the righteousness of Christ and His peaceable kingdom inherently entails rebellion against the evil and violent kingdoms of this world. Christian anarchism is not resistance to peace and order; it is simply resistance to rulers, institutions, and authorities that perpetuate violence and injustice in the name of peace and order.

890. ~ THE RARE MAJESTY of RAINBOWS ~

Beauty, peace, love, and life are born from suffering and struggle. Some people trade transcendent joy for temporal pleasures; they forsake ineffable beauty for a painless but colorless life. But as far as I'm concerned, the rare majesty of rainbows is worth the frequent pain of rain. So I must remember to thank God for the hardships in my life, because such trials are often the seeds of unimaginable blessings.

891. ~ WHO WOULD WANT to WORSHIP SUCH A GOD? ~

Who would want to worship and obey a god that torments infant babies in literal flames for all eternity? Who would want to worship and obey a god that rewards the righteous with the joy of seeing the damned burn in agony forever? Hitler himself was not so monstrous as the god depicted by those whose theology leads them to exult in the eternal torment of their fellow man.

892. ~ ABORTION and PUNISHMENT ~

Regarding the questions of *if* and *how* women who have illegal abortions should be punished if abortion ever becomes outlawed:

First of all, for true Christians, the question is moot. We are ambassadors of the Gospel (II Corinthians 5:20), and therefore we have nothing to do with violence and punishment. Those are worldly methods, and we are not of this world (Cf. St. John 17:16; Philippians 3:20; Hebrews 13:14). Our mission is to proclaim the good news of salvation: the love of Christ, the reconciliation of God and sinners, and the reconciliation of man with man. Therefore we do not pursue retribution and vengeance.

However, that does not mean that we hesitate to call abortion "murder." In proclaiming peace and life we must condemn with precise language any actions or ideologies that are violent, unjust, inhumane, oppressive, and murderous. Therefore, we do indeed pray and labor through Christian means to see abortion outlawed. And we also prayerfully work through nonviolent means to restrain murder, to promote peace, and to preserve human life.

But as servants of the Gospel we have nothing to do with punitive measures. Our desire is to liberate unborn babies, their mothers, and all those trapped in the evil system of the abortion industry. As Christ came to save us, we therefore also seek the salvation of all people – victim and victimizer, oppressor as well as the oppressed.

Of course, politicians, policemen, judges, and soldiers follow a different spirit. They live and move and act according to worldly values and worldly methods. In spite of what they may verbally *profess*, their vocational *professions* demand the acceptance and use of violent force, punitive measures, and deadly restraint. So they can never be truly pro-life or pro-peace. And they can never offer true Christian solutions to the evils that confront us. And therefore they will inevitably stumble and stutter and contradict themselves when challenged with such questions regarding the harmony of peace and life and justice.

But for the true followers of Christ, the answers are always as simple as what Our Lord taught and demonstrated:

Do not kill.
Leave vengeance to God.
Love your enemies.
Love one another.
Sacrifice your own lives, but don't sacrifice the lives of others.

But don't expect to see any politician running on a platform based on those principles. The Sermon on the Mount will never compromise with "realpolitik."

893. ~ THE BATTLE IS INTENSE ~

The battle is intense. I want to rest. I want to sleep. I want to be free from conflicts when I'm awake and horrors when I dream. I want to lay down the Cross and live without struggle.

Won't God love me anyway? So why subject myself to these travails when God will save me in the end? I don't want to fight anymore. But I'm not fighting just for myself. I'm not in this spiritual warfare alone. Others depend on me, just as I depend on them. I may be the weakest soldier in the battle, but I can't quit.

Damn these splinters! Damn these crosses! Damn these demons! And yet I thank God for all of these graces. My torments are the path to paradise. So I rejoice in my sickness, I rejoice in my heartbreak, I rejoice in my insomnia and insanity. Let me lose it all if I can gain Christ.

But perhaps my biggest problem is that I think I have to suffer to know God's love. Maybe I've suffered enough. Maybe we've all suffered enough. Maybe we just need to truly trust that God loves us – right where we are, just as we are. Maybe we drive ourselves crazy because we think we are somehow unworthy of the love of God – this God who created us with love, who redeemed us with love, and who will restore all things with love. Maybe all these demons are hallucinations that stem from the simple failure to believe – to *truly believe* – that God *truly* loves us.

I'm beginning to understand that this is the greatest spiritual battle, the truest spiritual warfare: to strive to know and understand and rest in the unconditional love of God. This requires faith. And, after all, we are saved by faith.

May God help me to know His love, to trust His love, and to manifest His love. This is the answer to it all. I think. Now if I can just have the faith to truly believe it and to truly live it. But when my faith fails, God's love prevails. This is the good news that I will cling to eternally. And this good news is the weapon with which I will continue to fight all darkness, all lies, all demons, and all despair.

894. ~ PREACH and PRAY ~

Preach the unconditional, unfailing, eternal love of God. Preach the victorious, saving, redemptive peace of the Gospel. And pray for the grace and strength to bathe in His love and live out His peace.

895. ~ I WISH THAT I COULD WISH ~

I wish that I could wish in dreams
to wish away these painful themes
of hunger, war, and things obscene.

But if I wake or if I sleep
nightmares haunt me as I seek peace.

So I fall down upon knees
I cross myself: God help me please.

And I know that He will.

896. ~ IF I COULD SING A SONG ~

If I could sing a song,
I'd sing a song of peace.

If I could sing a song,
I'd sing a song of hope.

If I could sing a song,
I'd sing a song of beauty,
and I'd sing of heaven above.

But if I only had one song to sing,
I'd sing of God's mercy, God's grace,
and most of all, His love.

Regardless of what some assert, rebellion is not contrary to the Christian Gospel. In fact, the Cross was the apex of insurrection. The Gospel compels us to oppose evil, to fight sin, to uplift humanity, and to confront injustice. The prophets, apostles, and Christian martyrs were the ultimate spiritual revolutionaries, condemning idolatry and offering up their own lives in resistance to the wickedness of this world. When Christ stretched out His crucified arms He embraced the suffering, the weak, and the oppressed. And when He rose on the third day He conquered sin and death. Christianity is therefore the epitome of rebellion. It is militant suffering and militant hope. It is righteous recalcitrance. It is agitation against iniquity. It is the cosmic confrontation of everything unholy and inhumane. It is the ultimate revolution: opposing lies with truth, evil with good, violence with peace, and hate with love. So don't ever let anyone tell you that rebellion is antithetical to the Christian Faith. Complacency and conformity have little to do with the Cross.

898. ~ **THE PARADIGM of PARADOX** ~

If you are seeking a rigidly consistent religion or worldview, then don't look to Christ or to the Gospel that He preached. The Cross is painfully paradoxical – full of agony and suffering, but giving us peace and hope. To follow Jesus is to live with the angst of tension – to be *in* this world without being *of* this world, to shape politics without being political, to submit to certain civil laws while preaching the Kingdom that needs no laws.

To be a Christian is to suffer in order to be healed, to resist through submission, and to die so that we may live. To accept and embrace these divine contradictions is the essence of true faith. Attempts to violently eliminate the paradigm of paradox inevitably result in theological heresies and social injustices.

We must ascend to heaven on the ladder of the crucifixion, which is infinitely vertical and eternally horizontal. And yet we keep trying to refashion the Cross into a construct that we can rationally understand and physically endure. But the Cross will not be bent or bowed or broken. It is we who must be bent and bowed and broken by the Cross.

"Lord have mercy on us." +++

899. ~ TWO ERRONEOUS EXTREMES ~

There are two equally erroneous extremes to which many Christians fall prey:

On the one hand, there are strains of "liberation theology" that politicize the Gospel to the expense of spiritual truth, thereby perverting the Gospel entirely. On the other hand, there is the "pie in the sky" mentality that ignores the tangible needs of temporal existence, forsaking the Gospel imperatives of social service and human liberation.

Some people have their heads so far up in heaven that they ignore the suffering here on earth, and others have their heads so deep in the world that they can't see the hope of heaven. But the Gospel is both spiritual and social. It is Christ centered and humanly focused. To love God is to love our neighbors, and to love our neighbors is to love God. Eternal life begins here in this life. Heaven begins here on earth. The social is inextricably linked to the sacred. As Jesus said: *"The Kingdom of God is among you."* [St. Luke 17:21]

900. ~ MERCY and JUDGMENT ~

As with all things that are truly of Christ, it's best to err on the side of mercy rather than punishment. For God's mercy will exceed His wrath. The Psalmist did not declare, *"The wrath of God endureth forever,"* but rather, *"The mercy of God endureth forever."* [Psalm

136] And after all, our staple Orthodox prayer is not, *"Lord bring judgment,"* but rather, *"Lord have mercy."*

901. ~ QUIXOTIC QUESTIONS ~

Are we truly voices crying in the wilderness or are we mere quixotes tilting at windmills? Are we prophetic witnesses or merely prideful provocateurs? Are we spiritual revolutionaries or worldly reactionaries? Are we agents of authentic change or activists of empty activism? It's hard to know sometimes. And anything we do will inevitably be criticized by those who do nothing. Which, I guess, is why most of us don't do anything at all.

902. ~ IGNORANCE that PASSES for CHRISTIANITY ~

There's so much ignorance that passes for Christianity these days. It's exhausting trying to convince some of my fellow Christians to renounce violence. It's frustrating enough trying to convince unbelievers to forsake the sword, but nonviolence should be a given for those of us who profess to follow the Prince of Peace. There's nothing easy about living out the Cross, but it's certainly not hard to understand. Better to confess our weakness and pray for strength than to embrace violence and killing in the name of faith. God help us!

903. ~ CARRY ON WITHOUT ME BABYLON ~

The Cross is my flag. The Gospel is my constitution. The Church is my country. So carry on without me Babylon. Your elections mean nothing to me.

904. ~ ONE DEATH, ONE SOLUTION ~

Anyone who seeks security, salvation, justice, and peace in the death of their fellow man does not understand the Gospel. There was only one death that was the solution to death, and that was the death of Christ.

905. ~ LOVE, FEAR, and GOD'S CHILDREN ~

Do I hope to make my children virtuous by constantly threatening to disown them, to inflict torture upon them, and by telling them that unless they respond to my love with their obedience they will suffer my indefinite wrath? No. I love my children because they are MY children, and nothing they can ever *do* or *not do* will have any bearing on my love for them. And who am I but a mortal, earthly, flawed, and sinful parent? Imagine then, how much greater is the love of our eternal Father in heaven!

906. ~ THROUGH IT ~

I've been through it. I'm going through it. And I'm gonna go through it. I just have to be thankful for whatever peace and joy I can grasp along the way. Life is a struggle. Always will be. But it wouldn't be worth much if I didn't have to fight for it.

907. ~ THE FALLACY of FIGHTING on THE ENEMY'S TERMS ~

When the enemy entices us to fight on its terms, then the enemy has won. The true Christian soldier carries no weapons of violence and death; he carries only the Cross of peace and life. We must pray for the Church to remain true to the commands of Christ. The *"Church militant"* does not mean the Church *violent*.

"The Lord will fight for you; you need only to be still."
[Exodus 14:14]

908. ~ VIOLENCE is A DISEASE ~

Not only does violence bring physical harm and death to its victims, but violence poisons the mind and soul of the one who inflicts it. Those who view violence as a solution will never be able to think or live correctly. Violence is insanity: war to stop war, killing to deter killing, death to preserve life, and abortion to bring "liberation."

Violence is undoubtedly a disease, but Christ is the cure.

909. ~ HELP, HEALING, and FAITH ~

Seeking help is not a lack of faith, but an act of faith. The demons always urge us to do it on our own, whispering their damnable lies:

"If you really had faith, you wouldn't need a doctor. If you really had faith, you wouldn't have anxiety. If you really had faith, you wouldn't be depressed. If you really had faith, you wouldn't need medicine or therapy."

But God is the Author of science and medicine, and He gave man the wisdom to heal and the knowledge to cure. And God also gave us one another so that we may find comfort and strength to endure our afflictions. There is no shame in admitting our suffering and asking for help. Medicine is not a spiritual crutch, it's a God given grace.

Yes, to be sure, as with all things in this fallen creation, there will be misapplications and abuses of divinely authored things. After all, even the scriptures themselves have been perverted, distorted, and misapplied to horrific ends. But we certainly don't jettison the holy texts simply because some have abused and corrupted the holy texts.

Similarly, we must not discard the salubrious mercies of medicinal science simply because some have misapplied and abused these blessings.

Many people limp through life crippled by their pride. They reject the help that is offered, and they refuse to seek the help they need. They profess to be independent and strong, but their weakness is evident and they evoke only pity. But the wise man knows he is weak, and he is not ashamed to flee towards help. Thus, having received the help he needs, he continues to live and glorify God – even though he carries many scars and wounds and bandages, and yea, even crutches. And in this way he is a Christ bearer, for even Our Lord Himself had help carrying His Cross.

Humility will save us. Pride will kill us. So, dear friends: if you are suffering in any way, don't be afraid to ask for help. We ALL need it.

910. ~ A SIMPLE and CONSISTENT CONCEPT ~

It's a simple concept called the "consistent life ethic." And it's not a Christian option; it's a Christian imperative. One cannot serve the Prince of Peace while participating in acts of violence, inhumanity, injustice, and militant force. The Gospel can never be harmonized with the sword. Whether you kill your enemy, slaughter your neighbor, slay your brother, or murder your unborn child, you are turning your back on Christ and following the path of Cain.

911. ~ WAR CRIMES ~

I pray for the day when we stop talking about "war crimes" and start realizing that war *is* the crime.

912. ~ STARRY NIGHTS and SEVERED EARS ~

We may never know our genius, our talent, or our strength until we are defeated, despondent, and broken. Creativity is more often the product of affliction than comfort. Starry nights are sometimes born from severed ears. There are no resurrections without crosses. God how I hate to suffer! But I wouldn't trade my splinters, thorns, and nails for all the pleasures and complacencies of hell.

913. ~ CHRISTIANS and CULTURE WARS ~

Christians have no more business taking part in culture wars than they do taking part in any other wars. We are not commanded to "win the culture;" we are simply commanded to preach the Gospel (St. Mark 16:15), to make disciples (St. Matthew 28:18-29), to love our neighbors (St. Mark 12:31), to love our enemies (St. Matthew 5:44), and to love one another (St. John 13:34-35).

This world is not our home (Philippians 3:20), and our salvation is not predicated upon political victories or the forceful imposition of cultural ideology. We are called to be salt and light (St. Matthew 5:13-14), and our society will be illuminated and seasoned not through our politics or cultural dominance, but rather through our true Christian love.

914. ~ CRUTCHES and WINGS ~

Lord, take away these crutches of sin and give me wings of healing. Cripple my despair so I can rise up and hope. And if I lose all else, please sustain me with the gift of faith.

God doesn't come and go. God *is*. His love is ever present. God is not a puppet that's manipulated by our emotions, our actions, or our lengthy prayers. Our worship, supplications, and repentance simply bring us into the awareness and experience of the divine love that extends to us with unconditional omnipresence.

Sometimes we feel close to God and sometimes we feel far from God. But that is simply due to the limitations and deceptions of our finite, fallen human perspective. It is important to know that God is never distant from us, and His love is never withdrawn from us. Let us rejoice when we feel close to God, but let us not predicate our spiritual health upon the subjectivity of our human emotions.

Human pathos is a divine gift, allowing our souls to express the lamentations and grief and sorrows that dwell within. But when we define our relationship to God or His relationship to us by pathos alone, then we are in danger of succumbing to a pathological spiritual despair.

No matter what you did or didn't do today, no matter what sins or what righteous deeds you did today, no matter how you felt today, God was present and His love was showered upon you. And it always will be.

God doesn't "show up" or "disappear." His love is ever present, ever faithful, and ever sure. Take hope in this truth.

"Where can I go from your Spirit? Where can I flee from your presence? If I go up to the heavens, you are there; if I make my bed in the depths, you are there. If I rise on the wings of the dawn, if I settle on the far side of the sea, even there your hand will guide me, your right hand will hold me fast. If I say, "Surely the darkness will hide me and the light become night around me," even the darkness will not be dark to you; the night will shine like the day, for darkness is as light to you." [Psalm 139:7-12]

Under no circumstances do I (or will I) vote. Period.

And don't tell me that unless I vote I have no right to complain. That's utter nonsense, another lie that too many Christians have blindly swallowed. I have every right to renounce evil and condemn injustice. And I have every right to refuse to participate in a political system that I believe is fundamentally unchristian and inherently antithetical to the divine will and order.

People argue that you can't change anything unless you participate in the political process. But how can you change a corrupt system that you continue to support? That's like expecting to find a faithful and virtuous relationship by perpetually sleeping with whores (and the analogy applies to both sexes.) Complicity with evil is the fuel of evil. So I refuse to comply with a political system that I believe is intrinsically corrupt and unjust. The first step to authentic change, spiritual prosperity, and social revolution is to renounce allegiance to political idolatry.

And please show me in Scripture or Church Teaching where God ordains and blesses democracy as His will for human government? Have you ever read the Lord's Prayer? *"Thy will be done, on earth as it is in heaven."* Remember that part? Well, the last time I checked, heaven is not a democracy. Democracy produced the Golden Calf, the tower of Babel, and "Free Barabbas! Crucify Christ!" And democracy (or variations thereof) has produced slavery, genocide, and abortion on demand. And this "democratic republic" has produced Bill Clinton, George Bush, Barack Obama, and now (as of the summer of 2016) Donald Trump and Hillary Clinton.

But I guess these are anomalies. Perhaps if we keep on voting we'll eventually usher in the Kingdom of God. I mean, this grand American experiment has to eventually produce righteousness, justice, and virtue – right? I mean, the "founding fathers" couldn't possibly have been wrong could they (you know, those slave owning, violent, conquering deists who based their philosophy on the secular ideals of the Enlightenment?)

As Christians, our government is the Kingdom of God, which has come to earth and walked amongst us. Christ is our Governor; and we are bound by His laws, not the laws of man. We obey civil laws and civil authority as long as they don't require us to compromise the will and commands of God.

Democracy is violence because it forcefully imposes the will of the majority on the will of the minority. Or, in our "democratic republic," it sometimes forcefully imposes the will of the minority on the majority. Either way, injustice is invariably done to some in the name of "justice for all."

Democracy is also antithetical to the will of God because it subjects divine morality and divine law to human vote. And no Christian should acquiesce with a political system that reduces eternal truths to the approval or disapproval of human consensus.

As a Christian I am commanded to forsake violence and live peaceably, as far as it depends on me, with all men (Romans 12:18). And even if I were to accept the principle of democracy as being compatible with the Gospel, I still could not vote for anyone who believes that violence and killing are solutions. I could never vote for anyone who supports abortion, militarism, or capital punishment. And I don't see any politicians who have made the Sermon on the Mount their political platform.

We may not be able to stop others from acting violently towards us, but we can make sure that we don't act violently towards others. And to vote for politicians that we know will execute violence is to act violently ourselves. There's no getting around that fact.

And by the way, to invoke Old Testament examples in an attempt to nullify the Sermon on the Mount and the example of Christ is horrible hermeneutics. I am often accused of ignoring the Old Testament. But I don't ignore the Old Testament; I simply understand and interpret the Old Testament in the context and clarity of the Gospel. "Love your enemies" is about as clear as it gets, and that command was spoken by God incarnate. So you really have to pervert and contort the scriptures to find a way to get out of obeying Our Lord's clear teachings and example regarding nonviolence.

Of course there are always those who invoke the specious argument: "But Jesus fashioned a whip and drove the moneychangers from the Temple." True. But He didn't fashion whips and pass them out to His disciples, and He didn't instruct His apostles to violently oppose blasphemers and sinners. So, let's leave whips and swords and violence and judgment to God alone. Ok? He doesn't require or command our violence. He will judge the wicked and recompense all evil in due time. Until then, let us follow what Our Lord commanded.

I don't know what the future holds for our country or for our world. I tremble at the violence, bigotry, discrimination, and evil that appears to loom on the horizon. The world is in turmoil. And yet the scriptures said it would be this way (I Peter 4:12-13). And yet Our Lord also said that the Kingdom of God is amongst us (St. Luke 17:21). I don't know if things will get better or worse. All I do know is that violence, war, and killing won't solve anything. We will not bomb, enslave, oppress, execute, imprison, abort, or vote our way to peace and Utopia. Of that, I am certain.

"Even so, come Lord Jesus." [Revelation 22:20]

917. ~ HONOR ~

Honor your soldiers. Honor your wars. Honor your militant victories and honor your militant deaths. Honor your flag, honor your constitution, and honor all the incalculable blood that was shed because of them. But please: just don't confuse such honor and glory for the honor and glory of Christ.

918. ~ POLITICIANS and HIPPIES ~

They gave out flowers and joints and beads and words of peace and lips of love and songs of freedom. And while politicians were plotting death and destruction and division and hate, those blessed hippies were changing the world.

919. ~ WHY DID YOU CHOOSE ME? ~

Why did you choose me God
to endure all this pain
and yet to see such beauty?

Why did you choose me God
to suffer these sorrows
and yet to know such joys?

Why did you choose me God
to feel this insanity
and yet to experience such love?

Why did you choose me God
to drown in a broken heart
while bathing in such mercy?

Why did you choose me God
to writhe in these agonies
and yet to rest in such grace?

Why did you choose me God
to taste of these hells
but to feast on such heaven?

Why did you choose me God?
I really don't know.
But I'm so glad that you did.

920. ~ MEMORIALIZING THE DEATH of WAR ~

Every Memorial Day I pray for the day when we will memorialize the death of war.

921. ~ HELL, NOW, and the HEREAFTER ~

I'm not particularly concerned about hell in the hereafter. I'm much more worried about those who create a living hell for themselves and others here in this life. It's shameful that we aren't as focused on bringing heavenly love to the hellish conditions of the world as we are about trying to preach starving people into heaven.

The Gospel is good news; and good news to the slave is freedom, good news to the oppressed is liberation, good news to the suffering is mercy, good news to the sick is medicine, and good news to the hungry is bread.

Don't get me wrong: I believe in heaven and hell, and I believe heaven and hell both begin right here on earth. The kingdom of God is among us (St. Luke 17:21). Christ is in our midst. And yet people are experiencing hell all around us. It's time to bind up the brokenhearted, to free the captives, to release the prisoners of darkness, and to do good to the poor (Isaiah 61:1).

It's utter blasphemy to threaten suffering people with eternal hellfire when they are begging us to ease their pain right now.

922. ~ "PAY YOUR TAXES" ~

Pay your taxes, so that you can have a strong military – a military that will protect you from the poor who threaten to rise up against you, because rather than giving to them you prefer to protect (at their expense) your own wealth and luxury that you confuse for "freedom."

923. ~ FRIENDSHIP and BROTHERHOOD ~

A true brother and a true friend will go toe to toe with you, challenging you, sharpening you, calling BS on you when you need it, and yet always loving and encouraging you above all things. Give thanks for true-hearted friends who know how to fight *with* you without fighting *against* you. That's a rare and blessed thing in this world. And in this regard I have been truly blessed.

924. ~ BE STILL and REST in GOD ~

Sometimes the best thing to do is to stop trying. Screw the puritanical work ethic. Just be still and rest in God. And that's hard to do sometimes, I know. I continue to struggle with doubts and fears and temptations and weaknesses that I wonder if I'll ever overcome.

But I think I'm learning that it's ok if I never overcome them. St. Paul prayed three times for God to remove the "thorn in his flesh," but God allowed it to remain. So don't assume that it's a sign of spiritual weakness to suffer with physical, emotional, or psychological problems. It sucks, but it's ok not to "succeed" in these struggles. God loves us just as much in our failures as He does in our achievements. In fact, we should actually be terrified of success, because success often has a way of making us think we no longer need God. Better to enter heaven crippled, broke, and insane than to enter hell in richness and health.

"In order to keep me from becoming conceited, I was given a thorn in my flesh, a messenger of Satan, to torment me. Three times I pleaded with the Lord to take it away from me. But he said to me, 'My grace is sufficient for you, for my power is made perfect in weakness.' Therefore I will boast all the more gladly about my weaknesses, so that Christ's power may rest on me. That is why, for Christ's sake, I delight in weaknesses, in insults, in hardships, in persecutions, in difficulties. For when I am weak, then I am strong." [II Corinthians 12:7-10]

A quote from a leader of the AHA movement (*Abolish Human Abortion*):

"It's a sin to deliberately destroy living images of God for any reason."

Later in the same speech: *"Capital punishment is appropriate justice for women who have abortions."*

Here we see another example of the contradictory and inconsistent reasoning of those who eschew the consistent life ethic. Violence and war and abortion and everything else that undermines and intentionally destroys human life is perpetuated by the refusal to acknowledge, affirm, and embrace the objective and inherent sanctity of every human life from conception to natural death. Once we begin to determine which human lives are worthy of preserving and which human lives are disposable based upon the subjectivity of our individual political, religious, or sectarian perspectives, then there remains no inviolate moral basis for the protection and preservation of our very own lives.

I applaud the AHA movement for their bold and unflinching agitation for the abolition of abortion. I appreciate their uncompromising witness against the greatest human rights atrocity of our time. The AHA movement is doing great work in clearly articulating the inhumanity, evils, and sin of abortion – as well as addressing the correlative sins that contribute to abortion. But sadly, their myopic view of the sanctity of *some* human lives has blinded them to the sanctity of *all* human life. If you are willing to intentionally and premeditatedly kill some images of God in the name of "justice" for other images of God, then you do not truly understand or recognize "images of God" at all.

Of course, the AHA crowd will invoke selective Old Testament laws and perversely extricate Romans 13 from the context of the entire New Testament as some sort of negation of Our Lord's clear teachings and example regarding nonviolence and love for enemies. And if that's their religious understanding, then I can no more argue with them than I can argue with ISIS. All I can do is point them to the peace, love, and life affirmation that was preached and lived by the Incarnate God who commanded His disciple to *"put away thy sword."* *[St. Matthew 26:52]* (And just as an aside: if you are Roman Catholic or Orthodox, then the AHA crowd thinks you are destined for the same literal hell that they believe ISIS will inherit. Never mind that they share much more in common with ISIS with their iconoclastic heresies than we Catholics and Orthodox do. But that's a discussion for another day.)

I pray for the abolition of abortion. But until that day comes, I wish to save lives – unborn lives, mothers' lives, Black lives, American lives, enemy's lives, Christian lives, Muslim lives, *all* lives. I will never be willing to violently sacrifice any human life for pragmatic ends or utilitarian expediency. I will never be willing to violently execute some human beings in the name of an ostensible "justice for all."

Unless you embrace the consistent life ethic, you are not truly Pro-Life and you are not truly helping to abolish human abortion. If you want to be a true abolitionist, then fight for the abolition of every law and ideology and rationalization and philosophy and mindset that justifies the deliberate destruction of any human life for any reason. Otherwise, sell your propaganda of death to someone else.

926. ~ WHO NEEDS SAVING MORE? ~

Who was holier: the one who washed Christ's feet with tears and perfume, or the one who cried out from his cross, "Lord, remember me in your Kingdom"?

Who was needier: the one who climbed a tree to get a glimpse of God, or the one who sat by the pool of Bethesda and begged for healing?

Who is "the least": the innocent shot dead by policemen's bullets, or the innocent who are cut down by the abortionists' knives?

Well, I don't know who is holier, who is needier, or who is "the least." But I think it's foolish to argue about such things. I just know that I need God, I desire to see God, and I want to be healed by God. And I think that in the depths of our souls we all want, need, and desire God.

So who needs saving more: the oppressed or the oppressor? I don't know. But I will fight to free the oppressed as I pray even for the oppressor to be saved. And in all of my writing and all of my rebellion and all of my activism and all of my apathy, I will constantly cry out: "Lord have mercy on *me*, a sinner. Lord have mercy on us. Lord have mercy, Lord have mercy, Lord have mercy..."

927. ~ IN THESE I WILL GIVE YOU CHRIST ~

Give me the mysticism of Huxley, the anarchism of Tolstoy, the existentialism of Camus, the nonviolence of Gandhi, the preaching of Dr. King, the service of Dorothy Day, the teachings of H.I.M. Emperor Haile Selassie, and the sacraments of Holy Orthodoxy – and in them all I will give you Christ.

928. ~ MY ALLEGIANCE ~

I am a Christian.
My ruler is Christ.
My citizenship is in heaven.
My constitution is the gospel.
My flag is the Cross.
My kingdom is the Church.
My politics is peace.
My weapon is love.
My allegiance is to truth.
My loyalty is to humanity.

929. ~ I WILL NEVER JUDGE ANOTHER'S ADDICTIONS ~

I will never judge another's addictions or another's pain. I respect those that have fallen time and time again much more than those that pretend like they could never fall at all.

930. ~ REPATRIATION ~

Repatriation begins in the heart; pilgrimage begins with the mind. We are all strangers in this fallen world, desperately trying to find our way back to the Garden. Many have found Zion in the concrete jungle while others have found hell in tropical paradise.

931. ~ 100% OF THE TIME ~

Life results in death 100% of the time. So let's get it right while we breathe so we can breathe eternally when our bodies cease.

932. ~ "ANTI-ESTABLISHMENT POLITICIAN" ~

"Anti-establishment politician" is an oxymoron. Any politician that promotes and utilizes the established political process to seek the power of political office is by definition "pro-establishment." How do people not understand this simple concept? An "anti-establishment politician" is like an "anti-pandering pimp." The label is self-contradictory and nonsensical.

Fools elect fools and then bemoan the fact that they've been fooled. But you can't help those who refuse to recognize the problem. Obstinacy is the greatest obstacle to spiritual and social revolution.

"Fools consider it an abomination to depart from evil."
[Proverbs 13:19]

Today I pray for everyone who's searching
for bread
for peace
for justice
for love
for happiness
for healing
for forgiveness
for health
for friendship
for hope
for mercy
for truth
for salvation
for grace
for brotherhood
for home.
Today, as every day, I pray for the world.
I pray for us all.
Please pray with me.
"Kyrie Eleison" +++

934. ~ RESENTMENT ~

Resentment is neither revolutionary nor redemptive. Resentment leads to destructive reactionary bitterness and dehumanizing divisiveness. The prophets spoke with the fire of righteous indignation and uncompromising rebuke, but their message always pointed to repentance and restoration.

When we have been wronged – either individually or collectively – let us be angry but let us sin not. Let us condemn the evils that have been committed against us, but let us forgive the evildoers. Let us hate the wrongs we have suffered, but let us nevertheless love those that committed the wrongs.

Peace and healing flow from loving truth, not bitter hate. Resentment is often the biggest impediment and the greatest obstacle to restorative justice. The fire of heaven purifies, but the fire of hell poisons. Let us be careful not to confuse the two.

935. ~ SAME ARGUMENTS for WAR and ABORTION ~

As I've often pointed out, the same arguments used to justify the evil of war are the same arguments used to justify the evil of abortion. Consider the words Alan Guttmacher, the director of Planned Parenthood in the 1960's, a man who himself performed many illegal abortions and who perhaps more than anyone else is responsible for the legality of abortion in America. In arguing for the legalization of abortion in 1961, Guttmacher said:

"I don't like killing. I don't like to do abortions, but many of you people probably fought in World War II and killed because you wanted to preserve something more important. I think a mother's welfare is more important than that of a fetus."

This quote is quite revelatory. Leaving aside the ludicrous implied comparison of innocent unborn lives to Nazis, this quote clearly demonstrates that those who promoted the legalization of abortion understood very well that abortion is an act of violence, an act of killing. And it discloses the insidious mindset of militarism: that the dehumanization and destruction of anyone who poses a threat to our comfort, convenience, and prosperity is somehow justifiable.

As long as we continue to seek our own welfare, security, and happiness by oppressing, torturing, or killing others, then we will continue to reap the cruel harvest of paranoia, terror, and reciprocal suffering. A society that violently discards its most vulnerable and innocent is a society that will inevitably be cut down by its own bloody sword.

936. ~ FOOD, PHILOSOPHY, LIFE, ART ~

Food is philosophy; philosophy is life; life is food. And they are woven together with art.

937. ~ SUCH MYSTERIES ARE ENOUGH FOR ME ~

I know nothing certain other than the mystery of life and the mystery of love. I dare not try to understand or explain these mysteries, but I have learned that God is to be found in them. I know nothing certain about God other than this. And I think that is enough for me.

938. ~ OUR HOLY PROVOCATION ~

We intend to agitate. We deliberately provoke. We want to offend and upset. We want to raise hell so we can expose it and then kick it back to the darkness from whence it comes. We love the confrontation. We relish the showdown. We are spiritual warriors, and Christ is our Commander in Chief. So assemble your earthly armies; build up your arsenals of lead; cast your feckless votes and elect your godless rulers. Levy all your carnal weapons against us. And if need be, nail us to the Cross. But we have already won, and you have already lost. So for us the battle is a blessing. We cherish it. You will never silence our holy provocation.

939. ~ THE THREE MOST BEAUTIFUL THINGS IN THE WORLD ~

The three most beautiful things in the world: young people in love, old people in love, and the life that is born in between.

I have many dear Muslim friends. Before I became Orthodox I used to join them frequently for Friday prayer at the local mosque here in Jackson, Mississippi. I heard many khutbahs (sermons) from the Imams. Never once did I hear anyone utter a single word of hatred, intolerance, prejudice, or violence. Terrorism was denounced vociferously and frequently as something completely antithetical to the Muslim Faith. I was never pressured or coerced to convert to Islam. I was welcomed by those devout people with sincere and unconditional love.

As an Orthodox Christian, I know how offended I am when anyone attempts to define the entire Christian religion by the bigotry and evil of perverse groups like Westboro Baptist church. So I know how my dear Muslim friends must feel when they hear ignorant people defining their entire faith by the intolerance, violence, and hatred of terrorists. I'm sure it grieves them deeply, to the core of their souls.

I have also known many homosexuals in my life. Some of them have been my friends. I have never known them to spew any hateful or violent words. And my homosexual friends would be deeply offended by any association with those who in the name of "gay pride" mock God, blaspheme Christ, and glorify unrestrained sexual licentiousness. Like Christians, Muslims, and everyone else, they are people created in the image of God who are struggling to understand and embrace the mysteries of life. They are not bad people. They are fallen people, like all of us. And, like most of us, they are trying to live good and meaningful lives.

I wish that I could say that I have never held a hateful or bigoted thought in my heart. I wish that I could say that I have never uttered ignorant and offensive words about Muslims and homosexuals (or anyone else.) But sadly, I cannot make such a claim. There was a period in my life (far too long a period) when I spouted the prejudices that were taught to me by my culture and by the version of "Christianity" to which I was first exposed. But in spite of what I was taught, I have no excuses. The law of God is indelibly inscribed upon the human heart, and it is a grievous sin to reject what the heart knows in order to cling to the lies of the mind. I am ashamed that I too often betrayed the truth of my soul in favor of the idolatry of prejudicial intellectual paradigms.

But our human brothers and sisters are our greatest teachers; and fortunately, the lessons never end. And if we truly listen we will eventually learn. If we look – if we really look – we will see both the image of God and our own reflection in every human countenance. And when we see ourselves reflected in the image of God in others then we cannot help but to repent of all of our hatred, all of our prejudices, all of our violence, and all of our self-righteous and judgmental certainties. And repentance is, after all, inseparable from faith.

God help us all. And God forgive me for the prejudices of my past (and the prejudices to which I still unwittingly cling.)

941. ~ DEHUMANIZING "LIBERATION" ~

I can't think of anything more dehumanizing than the insidious idea that peace and liberation will come through the masses punching a clock five days a week to produce capital for the privileged elite.

This is the condescending "solution" of the political mindset: Are the people restless, agitated, on the verge of revolt? Then build factories, and surround the factories with brothels and bars. Soon the people will be too tired, too drunk, and too anesthetized to think and to feel and to live accordingly.

But God did not create us to slave our lives away in pursuit of bread and happiness. Such a woeful condition was a curse of the fall. But Christ has broken the curse of sin and given us salvation. If Jesus freely offers us His own Body and Blood, then how dare we tell our neighbors to earn their bread by the sweat of their brow?

The fruit of the earth is abundant and plentiful, and no one should have to beg, steal, or borrow simply to live. If we all helped one another, if we all served one another, and if we all truly loved one another, then we wouldn't need to submit our peace to these bosses and businessmen and politicians and pimps.

942. ~ I DREAM TOO MUCH ~

I dream too much
please wake me up
Free me from
what I can't touch

If I can't feel
what I can see
then rouse me
from reality

Let me drift
to outer space
I'll kiss the stars
that warm my face

But save me from
these quicksand dreams
that sink me
in my silent screams

I'm too tired
to shut my eyes,
too scared to meet
the unconscious I

But if God wills it
so be it

I will praise Him
from nightmare depths.

943. ~ NOT EASY for ME TO SAY ~

Whenever I condemn the violence, hypocrisy, and evils of any politician, their supporters will inevitably respond: "That's easy for you to say. And the only reason you're able to say it is because of the freedoms you have as an American."

Well, leaving aside the fact that such a vapid response is by no means an argument for or defense of their beloved politician, let me nevertheless make something very clear:

My criticisms are *not* easy for me to say. It grieves me to the core to have to continue to speak out against war, capital punishment, abortion, and all other forms of premeditated, government sanctioned killing. And it pains me deeply to see people so blinded by political idolatry that they justify the murder of innocents. What *would be* easy for me would be to remain silent and not disturb and disrupt the status quo of violence, death, and destruction. But you need to know that I will gladly choose the discomforts of agitation over the anesthetization of apathy.

So, if I can offend you enough to awaken you from your political slumber, if I can upset you enough to open your eyes to the plight of the innocent, and if I can say something provocative enough to compel your consciousness towards compassion and peace, then I don't care what you think of me; I will have succeeded.

944. ~ UNDERSTANDING, LIVING, SUFFERING, and SALVATION ~

Just because I understand what true Christianity is doesn't mean that I live a true Christian life. But I'll keep preaching His Cross even as I continue trying to shrug off my own. Perhaps that's why my life has never been easy, and why it never will be. If I take up the Cross I suffer, and if I forsake the Cross I suffer more. And either way, through such sufferings my God will save me.

945. ~ A WORD ABOUT FATHERHOOD ~

Let me say a word about fatherhood:

Fatherhood is not about teaching, but about learning. My children are my teachers. Every day they teach me the most important lessons in life:

Unconditional love
A positive attitude
Kindness and respect for others
Sacrificial obedience
Unwavering faith in Christ and His Church
Humility and grace
A passionate love for life
Patience in difficulty
A forgiving spirit
Enthusiasm and joy
A non-judgmental attitude
An unwavering commitment to peace

Whatever my children may learn from me, I can assure you that I learn much more from them. Fatherhood is the greatest gift any man could ever receive. If the whole world were to turn against me, my children would still be by my side. I know the love of God because I have experienced the love of my children. I am truly blessed.

946. ~ IF SOLDIERS LAID DOWN THEIR WEAPONS ~

I am often asked: "But what will happen if soldiers laid down their weapons?"

Well, what happened when Christ and His disciples laid down their weapons? I'll tell you what happened: horrific things happened, like crucifixion and other unimaginable tortures and violent deaths. And yet the Gospel flourished, souls were saved, the Church was strengthened, and the Kingdom of heaven prevailed.

For those who know not Christ, this earthly existence is the end all be all, and so they kill and slaughter and torment their fellow man in order to preserve this fleeting temporal existence. But we are Christians. What have we to do with such godless insanity?

We either believe the Gospel or we don't. If we think we must bomb, shoot, and slaughter our neighbors in order to preserve our own nations, our own democracies, or our own lives, then we know not the Prince of Peace.

947. ~ BROKEN REVOLUTIONARIES and PIOUS NAVEL GAZERS ~

I respect the flawed, sinful, and broken revolutionaries more than the pious navel gazers who do nothing to change the world.

948. ~ LIBERAL, CONSERVATIVE, and THE GOSPEL ~

I really believe that Christians should strive as much as possible to avoid labels like "liberal" and "conservative." What matters is good and evil, right and wrong, truth and falsehood. I've been alternately accused of being a "flaming liberal" and a "rabid conservative," depending on the particular issue at hand. And I've learned that as soon as we attach an ideological label to someone, then we become inherently biased against all of their views and positions. But when we assess every social, moral, and political issue purely through the lens of the Gospel, then we will probably come down on the liberal side of some things and the conservative side of other things.

But politics has poisoned people's minds, dividing the Church and pitting brother against brother. So I refuse to judge anyone by whether they are liberal or conservative. Such labels no longer mean anything to me. I simply strive to consider the merits of someone's position based solely upon the truth of the Gospel. And most importantly, I strive to make sure that my own views and opinions reflect the love, peace, and truth of Our Lord Jesus Christ.

949. ~ REVOLUTIONARY REFLECTION ~

Diogenes trod through Athens with his lamp, searching in futility for one honest man. I trod through Babylon with a lamp of my own, searching for one true revolutionary. But until I examine myself I will always be searching in vain.

It truly does begin with us. Let us turn our lamps upon our own souls, illuminating our own reflections. Whatever evils we curse, whatever injustices we lament, whatever sins we condemn, whatever horrors we decry, let us realize that revolution always begins in the mirror.

950. ~ ONE IMMUTABLE LAW of SEX and WAR ~

There is one immutable law of sex and war: somebody always has a bigger gun. If you trust in your sword, you will inevitably end up with a broken heart and a broken soul. Love is the only enduring solution, the only lasting victory, the only force that will eternally conquer.

951. ~ NO ESCAPE ~

I bet you've been told many times by many preachers that you cannot escape the Judgment of God. Well, I'm no preacher; but I'm here to tell you that you cannot escape the Love of God! So stop running.

952. ~ WEALTH, POVERTY, FAMILY, FRIENDSHIP, THE CHURCH, & SHAME ~

If you feel ashamed to ask your family or friends for help, then there's something equally wrong with both you and them. And it is also worth questioning whether a Church that replicates the disparity of wealth in society is any Church at all.

Shame belongs not to the poor, but to the rich who exploit, ignore, and refuse the poor. But while forsaking the stranger in need is a grievous sin, I think it's a much worse sin to forsake one's own family and friends. There is no greater pain than to be refused by your own loved ones or to be denied by your own brethren.

I pray that my three children never turn their backs on each other. I pray that if one of them becomes wealthier than the others that they will share their wealth equally with their siblings – freely, joyously, and unconditionally. I pray that if one of them ever has a need (or even a want) that they will be able to freely ask and receive from another. I pray that regardless of whether they are wealthy or poor, that they will always use whatever money they have to help each other and to help others. I am trying to raise them right in this way; but it's an uphill battle in this materialistic, self-centered, prideful, and bootstrap shaming culture of ours.

953. ~ THE LENS of THE CROSS ~

When we view every human issue and every human being through the lens of the Cross, then the shackles of political, social, and spiritual bondage are broken. But when we elevate politics, race, and religion above love for God and love for one another, then we strengthen the chains of the very things that seek to enslave us all.

954. ~ SO, WHOSE SIDE ARE YOU ON? ~

When they brandish the sword, we brandish the Cross. When they pull out their guns, we pull out the Gospel. When they fight with the flesh, we fight by faith. When they unleash carnal weapons, we unleash our spiritual war.

We are the true spiritual revolutionaries, serving the Conquering Lion whose battle is already eternally won. We are a Church militant, but never a Church violent.

So, whose side are you on?

955. ~ THE GREATER SIN ~

The greater sin is not the failure to recognize injustice, but rather the refusal to confront injustice by those who clearly acknowledge it.

956. ~ THE BEAUTY, TRUTH, and ENDURANCE of MYSTERY ~

Everything that is beautiful and true and enduring is infused with mystery. And that's why everything that is beautiful and true and enduring involves such an agonizing but glorious struggle. We are fools when we attempt to reduce the sacred to the substance of what we can fully understand. Religion, sex, beauty, and love are best left in the realm of reverence – where mystery works its invariable magic as we remain perpetually in awe.

What a blessed thing it is to live with wonder; and what a tragedy it is to reduce transcendence to our own feeble and subjective mortal rationalizations. May God ever lead us in the glory of mystery, and may God protect us from jaded souls.

957. ~ SUCH IS NOT THE WAY of CHRIST ~

Believing that guns will stop violence is like believing that pornography will cure lust. It makes me so sad whenever I see professing Christians counseling their brethren to take up arms and train for bloodshed. Such is not the way of Christ or the path to genuine security and true peace. The Gospel is our only salvation, and love is our only weapon. As I will continue to proclaim: it is impossible to take up arms when our arms have taken up the Cross.

We cannot escape the prophecy of Our Lord: *"All who live by the sword shall die by the sword." [St. Matt. 26:52]* Why would we presume to know better than Christ how best to resist evil and preserve the good?

958. ~ BOB MARLEY and MUHAMMAD ALI ~

The two most recognizable figures in the entire world are Bob Marley and Muhammad Ali. People in almost every country on every continent know who Bob Marley and Muhammad Ali are. Their lives, their messages, and their meaning resonate with people of all races, all religions, and all walks of life. They changed the consciousness of humanity – uplifting the downtrodden, inspiring the hopeless, bringing joy to the sorrowful, and spreading faith in the Creator through their courageous actions and inspirational words.

They were two transcendent souls who spoke to the collective heart and collective spirit of the human race. They were two people who sacrificed and suffered for the truths they held dear. They were two charismatic figures with irrepressible spirits that proved that in spite of life's cruelties, life nevertheless has meaning and purpose.

Bob Marley and Muhammad Ali were the antithesis of politicians whose actions are always calculated to enhance their own personal power and prestige. Unlike the Clintons, Trumps, and Obamas of the world, Bob Marley and Muhammad Ali followed the Creator rather than political expediency or personal profit. And that's why they resonated so strongly with people across the globe.

They were truly revolutionary figures because they were truly authentic and truly genuine souls. They were both flawed and fallible, broken and fragile, and yet they were always able to transcend negativity and failure through positivity and faith. They showed us that strength is not the absence of weakness, but the courage to persevere in spite of weakness.

Bob Marley and Muhammad Ali proved that the most profound spiritual and social impact comes not through voting, running for office, getting elected, or accumulating power and wealth. Rather, they demonstrated that real and lasting revolutionary change is achieved through lives devoted to peace, love, justice, and faith. They taught us that a single soul filled with divine conviction can transform the world more positively and effectively than all armies, congresses, and governments combined.

Bob Marley and Muhammad Ali illuminated the universe with redemptive truth and revolutionary love. Their light will never be extinguished.

959. ~ IN THE VOICE of THE PEOPLE I HEARD THE VOICE of GOD ~

I stopped talking to God because I couldn't hear Him anymore. But I started talking to the people; and in the voice of the people I heard the voice of God speaking to me again. And I've been talking to God ever since.

960. ~ YOU and THEM ~

If you can't see the God who loves *them*, how can you see the God who loves *you*? And if you can't see that God loves *you*, then you will never truly understand that God loves *them*.

961. ~ I LET GO ~

I let go,
because
I'm no longer in control anyway.
Never was,
and never will be.

So why fight it?

I give myself to God:
surrendering to His justice
and His wrath
and His truth
and His love...

His love...
His love.

I let go.
I ride the insane
and uncontrollable waves
of His divine will.

Salvation is a roller coaster.
Let go and be crucified.
Be crucified and be saved.

962. ~ "SPEAKING TRUTH to POWER" ~

You can't speak truth to power or condemn corruption if you allow yourself to be conscripted and co-opted by power and corruption.

963. ~ "POLITICAL REVOLUTION" ~

"Political revolution" is an oxymoron. The only things politicians change are the means of injustices and the manifestations of evil. True revolution is spiritual, social, sacrificial and selfless – attributes that are all antithetical to the narcissistic, self-aggrandizing, Machiavellian machinations of political expediency.

Do you really want peace and justice? Then rise up and revolt against the political system that keeps you pacified with the ballot. Rise up and revolt against the system that keeps you anesthetized with political pied pipers that lead you to your doom.

964. ~ ON RACE and SUFFERING and POLITICS and REDEMPTION ~

I appreciate and respect the perspective of those who have suffered from systemic injustices and racist brutality. I would like to say that I too understand their perspective, but only those who have experienced a particular hurt are qualified to say they understand such hurt. We should never be dismissive about the suffering of others. We should never diminish the insights of those who speak from a place of pain. We should also remember that pain and suffering are human conditions with many manifestations and various effects. I may not understand your suffering, and you will probably never understand mine. But we both have suffered, and we would both be wise to listen to one another so that we can help one another heal.

I'm married to a woman who was terrorized by racists when she was a seven year old little girl. Taking a stroll around the lake with her mother one summer afternoon in their little town of Hazlehurst, Mississippi, three white men approached them on horseback. "Look at that cute little nigger girl! We oughta string her up and watch her swing!" She also witnessed the Ku Klux Klan parading through her town when she was around the same age. Those experiences scared her to death. I will never really know how deeply they affected her, what pain they left on her soul, what scars were embedded on her psyche as a result.

But I got a glimpse when we were kicked out of a restaurant in downtown Jackson many years ago, while we were dating. In the middle of our meal we were suddenly asked to leave. I asked why. The owner said that we were "loitering" and that no loitering was allowed. I was confused. Truly confused. We weren't being loud. We weren't dressed inappropriately. The restaurant wasn't crowded, and nobody was waiting for a table. So it didn't make sense. But we left.

I got into the car and looked over at my wife (girlfriend at the time). I saw tears streaming down her face. And suddenly the reality hit me. We had just been kicked out of a restaurant because she was Black and I was White. And this wasn't in the 50s or the 60s. This was in 1996. But she didn't cuss or yell or go on a rant about how unjust and wrong it all was. She just cried. And all I could do was cry with her.

I've thought about that incident a thousand times. And I've thought a thousand times of all the different things I wish I would have done, and what I *should* have done. I've thought about how I wish I would have realized what was happening as it was happening. I've thought about how I wish I would have sat there and sat there and sat there some more until those bastards called the cops or did something to literally force us out of their goddamned restaurant. But I didn't even understand what was really taking place. Until it was too late. Until I saw those tears rolling down her beautiful, brown, broken face.

My father-in-law grew up in the Mississippi Delta, born into dire poverty. He was afflicted with blindness when he was three months old, the result of a severe fever that completely burned out his retinas. He grew up suffering not only the scourges of racism but also the cruel prejudices hurled at him because of his blindness. (And I must tell you that it's not accurate to say that my father-in-law is "blind." And it's not accurate to say that he's "visually impaired." And it's not accurate to say that he's not "sighted." He has more vision and sight than anyone I've ever met in my entire life.)

But my father-in-law is a revolutionary of love. In all the years that I've known him, I've never heard him utter a single complaint about anything at all. Due to a number of economic (and other) injustices, the man is still working the night shift at the age of 80. Without any bitterness. Without any hate. Without any self-pity. He's the smartest man I've ever known. Pure brilliance, but he's too humble to flaunt it. I have to force it out of him, because I want to learn everything I can from him while I have the opportunity.

I could also tell you about my late mother-in-law, who spent her entire life helping and serving others – as a teacher, as a minister to the mentally disabled, as a mother that raised five incredibly talented, God-fearing, and hard working children, and as a devoted wife to the aforementioned wonderful man. A woman who did not suffer fools, but who knew exactly how to put them in their place with dignity and tact. A woman who constantly sacrificed her own comforts and desires in order to care for others. A woman who died after an intense battle with lung cancer – not because she ever touched a cigarette, but because she spent years working in an environment that was ensconced in second-hand smoke. But throughout all her suffering she never complained. She never cursed God or cursed others or cursed her circumstances. She endured her life and her death with sacrifice, dignity, gratitude, and grace.

So my wife and her father and her mother know more than just a little bit about suffering. And they know more than just a little bit about racism, injustice, and the pain and cruelties of prejudice. And because they know so much about such things, they would never vote for anyone who supports anything that perpetuates the suffering of others. Because they understand severe economic, physical, and psychological hardship, they would never willingly enable anything that contributes to the economic, physical, and psychological hardship of other human beings. Because they understand the pain of cruelty and death, they would never support the cruelty and death of defenseless unborn babies. Their own suffering has led them to oppose any and all suffering inflicted on anyone else for any reason whatsoever.

My father-in-law is my hero – more than anyone in this world. A true Christian. A true spiritual revolutionary. My best friend. My mentor. The clearest reflection of Christ that I've ever seen. And my wife is also my hero, the love of my life. For her to endure a life with me is a suffering in and of itself. And my blessed mother-in-law was the epitome of womanly virtue and heroic strength. She was the personification of authentic female dignity and female empowerment.

So when people tell me that I must vote, or that I must vote for a certain political party, then I have no tolerance for such inane and condescending ignorance. And when people tell me that they've personally suffered and therefore that's why they vote, then I'll kindly remind them that other people have suffered too – like my father-in-law and his wife and my wife – and that their suffering has led them to truly love others *so much* that they refuse to vote for anyone who would perpetuate the suffering of others. And there's not a single American political party today that doesn't perpetuate the suffering of human beings in one way or another. There's not a single American political party today that doesn't promote some manifestation of inhumanity, injustice, and evil.

So, while I will always respect someone's perspective as an individual or their perspective as a member of a particular race, gender, or religion, I will also point out that their perspective is just one perspective among many. We must be cautious about making universal truths out of our own subjective opinions. As I have learned not only from the objective teachings of the Holy Gospel, but also from the examples of my beautiful wife and her parents, we should always allow our own personal and subjective suffering to cultivate universal and objective compassion for every human being and every segment of humanity. We must never discount or disregard someone else's pain. And we should never assume that our own pain – either individually or collectively – is worse than another's.

Our social convictions and spiritual consciousness should never be based solely upon our own individual experiences, our own relativistic desires, or our own independent needs. Every injustice we suffer, every pain we endure, and every evil we encounter should compel us towards objective universal compassion, objective universal justice, and an objective universal affirmation of all human life. And then – and only then – we can experience the glorious mystery of our personal suffering being transformed into something universally redemptive and eternally restorative. Otherwise we will merely repeat the tragic cycle of replacing one evil with another evil, one injustice with another injustice, and one war with another war.

If we begin and end only with our own pain, then we will replicate the horrific error of the exaltation of some human lives at the expense of the extermination of other human lives. But if we allow our own pain to enlighten us to the pain of others – not just some others, but all others – then we will cultivate a revolutionary consciousness that will compel us to truly revolutionary action: actions of compassion, actions of love, actions of mercy, and actions of healing. And through such authentic revolutionary acts we can hope to find true human unity and true human restoration.

965. ~ "VOTING MATTERS" ~

Voting matters. Which is precisely why I don't vote. When you vote you empower evil. And a "lesser evil" is still evil. So don't let anyone tell you that your vote doesn't make a difference. Without your complicity in the political process, evil would not be empowered. Without the ballot box, the political wolves would not be able to continue devouring the sheep.

If you had the choice of drinking 12 ounces of poison, 6 ounces of poison, or not drinking poison at all, which would you choose? Would you deliberately choose to drink 6 ounces of poison as you justified your decision by saying, "6 ounces of poison is less toxic than 12 ounces of poison"? If you did, I'd call you a damn fool. And there wouldn't be much I could do to save you. So go ahead and drink the political venom if you want to. Just know that when you vote you commit social and spiritual suicide by empowering an inherently unjust and godless political system designed to enslave you with the cooperation of your own volition.

But, *"as for me and my household, we will choose to serve the Lord." [Joshua 24:15]* We will choose the waters of life and the Cross of salvation over the idolatry of democracy and the poison of politics. And the good news is that you are free to choose the same.

But the Savior will not force you to follow Him. You are always free to continue poisoning yourself, dying your slow death as you desperately seek to elect some false political savior that you think will liberate you.

Indeed, voting makes a difference. And the difference is literally a matter of life and death. I urge you to stop voting and start living.

(And by the way, please know that the same people who fought and died for our right to vote also fought and died for our right not to vote. The Civil Rights freedom fighters did not suffer, bleed, and die so that we would become slaves to the ballot box and obeisant servants to political masters.)

"Never let a politician grant you a favor;
they will want to control you forever...
Emancipate yourselves from mental slavery.
None but ourselves can free our minds."
~ Bob Marley (Berhane Selassie) ~

966. ~ TOO DEEP ~

If it's too "deep" or too complex for the common man, then it's not art, it's pretentiousness. As Tolstoy wrote: *"To say that a work of art is good, but incomprehensible to the majority of men, is like saying that some kind of food is very good but that most people cannot eat it."*

967. ~ VOTE or REVOLT ~

There are two types of people: those that vote and those that revolt. Revolution won't take place at the ballot box, and the kingdom of heaven won't be ushered in by democracy.

968. ~ THE CONTROVERSY of THE CROSS ~

The Cross will always be controversial, and you can't be a Christian theologian apart from a theology of the Cross. The Cross will always be a confrontational offense to evil powers, demonic dominions, and systemic injustices. Show me a theologian that has never preached or written anything controversial and I will show you a lukewarm Christian in danger of being spewed out of Our Lord's mouth.

"For the message of the cross is foolishness to those who are perishing, but to us who are being saved it is the power of God. We preach Christ crucified: a stumbling block to Jews and foolishness to Gentiles, but to those whom God has called, both Jews and Greeks, Christ the power of God and the wisdom of God. For the foolishness of God is wiser than the wisdom of man, and the weakness of God is stronger than the strength of man." [I Corinthians 1:18, 23-25]

"I know your deeds, that you are neither cold nor hot. I wish you were either one or the other! So, because you are lukewarm—neither hot nor cold—I am about to spit you out of my mouth."
[Revelation 3:15-16]

969. ~ THE MYSTERY of THE MOMENT ~

To live in the moment is to live for the infinite. The linear restraints of past and future are swallowed up by eternity; and thus to live completely, wholly, and uncompromisingly for the now is to live by faith in the divinely enduring. So love now, forgive now, rejoice now, and live now! The mystery of eternal life is revealed in the mystery of the moment.

970. ~ THEREIN IS THE TRUEST REVOLUTION ~

If you're an artist, paint! If you're a writer, write! If you're a preacher, preach! If you're a ditch digger, dig! But whoever you are and whatever you do – be all and do all for the glory of God, for the welfare of humanity, and for the benefit of the Kingdom. Therein is the truest revolution.

"So whether you eat or drink or whatever you do, do it all for the glory of God. [I Corinthians 10:31]

971. ~ ON READING ~

Don't try to be a "voracious" reader, an "avid" reader, or a "devour" of books. Words are not prey, they are life. Respect them as such. Read respectfully and read fully. If a single word or a single sentence moves you, then pause and read it again. And then read it once more. Read it over and over, and underline it if you wish. Absorb it.

Books are not trophies. Books shouldn't be notches on your belt that validate your erudition. Books should be vessels of wisdom, agents of inspiration, provocateurs of consciousness, and vehicles of joyous escape.

If an author's words are too pretentious, too stale, or too uninspired for you, then put their book aside and find a book that challenges you, moves you, or quickens your imagination. And when you find yourself captivated by the pages, then caress those pages, take time with those pages, and if need be, wrestle with those pages.

But don't rush it.

Books are like many mystical pleasures in life: you may never fully understand them, but if you take your time with them you will experience inexpressible joys.

It is better to read one unforgettable book than to read a thousand books that you never remember.

972. ~ BE QUICK to LOVE ~

Be quicker to listen than to correct. Be quicker to pray than to react. Be quicker to forgive than to condemn. And above all, be quick to love all. Revolution is forged with bended knees and outstretched arms.

973. ~ LOVE PEOPLE ~

Love people.
Because God loves people.
All people.
Unconditionally.
"For God so loved the world, that He gave his only begotten Son, that whosoever believeth in Him should not perish, but have everlasting life." [St. John 3:16]
His mercy endures forever. (Psalm 136)
Jesus died for sinners, and we are all sinners. So love sinners, because while we were still sinners Christ died for us. (Romans 5:8)
God will separate the wheat from the tares. (St. Matthew 13:29-30). In the meantime we are to love our fellow man, even our enemies. (St. Matthew 5:44)
Preach the truth, rebuke sin, call evil "evil" and good "good" (Isaiah 5:20); but love all people without condition or qualification. And then welcome people into the fold when they are drawn to your true Christian love.
After all, love covers a multitude of sins. (I Peter 4:8)

"Whoever claims to love God yet hates a brother or sister is a liar. For whoever does not love their brother and sister, whom they have seen, cannot love God whom they have not seen." [I John 4:20]

"Hatred stirs up conflict, but love covers all wrongs." [Proverbs 10:12]

974. ~ BLOOD ~

Blood is beauty
Blood is pain
Blood is fire
And blood is rain

Blood flows
To let you in
Breaking virginity
But cleansing sin

Blood hurts
But it also heals
Blood saves
Even as it bleeds

Blood is terror
And blood is nice
Blood is death
But blood is life

975. ~ RUNNING TO IDOLATRY ~

The system tells you to vote, and you run to the polls in obedience. God tells you to love your neighbor, and you run to the polls in rebellion. Politics is idolatry.

976. ~ ACTION and THOUGHT ~

Think as a person of action and act as a person of thought.

977. ~ PROTEST and PRAYER ~

If our protests are not rooted in and sustained by prayer then at best they remain impotent gestures, and at worst they descend into the same unjust, violent, and evil behavior they seek to redress. Before we can truly take a stand we have to fall on our knees. Before we can effectively confront oppression we have to cultivate a genuine love for the oppressor.

When prayer and love are our weapons, the walls of Babylon will fall. With prayer and love as our pillars, our protests will become truly prophetic, divinely effective, politically transformative and socially redemptive.

978. ~ THE POLITICIAN and THE REVOLUTIONARY ~

There is no reconciliation between the politician and the revolutionary. The politician always perpetuates the systemic order of injustice and evil – be it a conservative order or a liberal order. But the revolutionary always disrupts the godless system, revolting equally against right wing injustices and left wing inhumanities. The politician constantly tries to compromise the revolutionary by offering him political payments, political positions, and political prominence. But the true revolutionary can never be bought or sold. The true revolutionary would rather suffer for the truth than profit from a lie.

And every person must ultimately choose a side: we are either with the politicians or we are with the revolution. And if you are confused about which is which and who is who, just remember that the revolutionaries never ask for your votes; they simply ask for your sacrifice and service. They never ask for you to elect them to power; they simply ask you to help them confront systemic power. So make no mistake: when you vote for oppressors, warmongers, and blood-shedders, you actually betray the revolution and you sell your soul to the status quo.

979. ~ TRUTH IS A DANGEROUS THING ~

Truth is a dangerous thing. You have to get close to understand it, but if you get too close you die. But if you die for the truth you live forever.

980. ~ DOGMATIC DENUNCIATIONS ~

I'm always amused by dogmatic denunciations of dogma.

981. ~ MY POLITICAL CHOICE ~

To choose not to choose evil will always be my political choice. The philosophy of supporting a "lesser evil" only perpetuates evil. And the machine of this godless political system is fueled by the willingness of the masses to embrace evil in the name of good. People continue to feed the very beast they bemoan while cursing those of us who refuse to help them nourish it.

982. ~ CHRISTIANITY and ART ~

As a Christian I tried to be an artist, but as an artist I became a Christian.

983. ~ "GOVERNMENT," "BUSINESS," and "POLITICS" ~

When the oppressed take up arms to liberate themselves it's called "terrorism," but when the oppressor takes up arms to subdue the oppressed it's called "government." When the poor steal from the rich it's called "communism," but when the rich steal from the poor it's called "business." When the weak make demands of the strong it's called "insurrection," but when the strong make demands of the weak it's called "politics."

984. ~ WORDS ~

There are those who say: "Words are meaningless. Action is all that counts." But consider that every great truth, every great idea, and every great revelation came into the world through words. God Himself spoke the universe into existence. And then God came to earth, born as a man, as the Incarnate Word. The Bible itself is a compilation of the written word; and its words have not only inspired revolutions of peace, love, and human rights, but verily, they have led men even to eternal life.

It is a mistake to equate words with inaction. To preach is an act; to prophesy is an act; to write is an act; to speak out against evil and injustice is an act. In fact, righteous words give birth to righteous deeds. Truthful words precipitate truthful movements. Beautiful words yield beautiful lives. Profound words form the foundation and impetus of profound actions.

So don't diminish the power of words. Don't assume that those who wield the pen are less influential than those that take to the streets. Revolution is sown with ink and blood, and the two are inseparable.

985. ~ NO SUCH THING ~

There is no such thing as a successful liar, a successful thief, or a successful killer; for if they succeed they are called barristers, bankers, politicians and presidents.

986. ~ OUR ONLY POLITICAL CHOICE ~

As Christians we are citizens of the Kingdom of Heaven (Philippians 3:20). And the Kingdom is our only politics. The Machiavellian machinations of political pragmatism have nothing to do with the Gospel. Our Lord does not instruct us to choose some "lesser evil." He simply says, *"Follow Me."*

Babylon is falling all around us. The mission of Christian discipleship is not to preserve Babylon, but rather to call people to enter into the Kingdom. So we love others, we serve others, we show compassion to others, we prophesy to others, and we serve the Kingdom of Heaven as best we can in the midst of Babylon. But we do not adopt the methods of Babylon in some vain attempt to preserve, restore, or save Babylon.

Ultimately, there is only one political choice: Jesus or the world.

987. ~ BIG WORDS ~

"Peace," "life," "love," "brotherhood," "justice," "truth," "God"… these are big words. Very big words. But not nearly big enough. They can't really be defined; they can only be lived.

988. ~ NO MONOPOLY on SUFFERING ~

No single race, gender, religion, nationality, or individual has a monopoly on suffering. Suffering is a universal human condition, the result of the fall, the common curse that plagues us all. Suffering is perpetuated and exacerbated by attempts to alleviate it at the expense of others. Man suffers and then seeks to eliminate his pain by inflicting pain on his fellow man. Man hurts and then seeks justice by inflicting hurt on someone else. This is the sad and sordid cycle of the human condition.

The truth is that we will never really know the pain of others, and others will never really know our pain. The question is: we will allow our own suffering to cultivate compassion and mercy, or will we allow our own suffering to foster bitterness and hate? We can't evade suffering, but we *can* determine whether our suffering will be redemptive or destructive.

989. ~ A CONSUMING FIRE ~

God is a consuming fire. And His fire is love. Be consumed!

"God is a consuming fire." [Hebrews 12:29]

"God is love." [I John 4:8]

990. ~ MORE on "BLACK LIVES MATTER" / "ALL LIVES MATTER" ~

If you feel the need to criticize the truthful phrase "Black Lives Matter," then you are the problem. And if you feel the need to criticize the truthful phrase "All Lives Matter," then you too are the problem.

I will personally proclaim "Black Lives Matter" without apology. I will not cease pointing out the racist violence in society that destroys Black lives with police brutality, military recruitment, capitalistic exploitation, and abortion on demand. I refuse to allow politics, the media, or my friends on either the right or the left to dictate which forms of racist violence I should oppose and which forms of racist violence I should ignore. These issues are all inextricably linked, merely different manifestations of the bloodthirsty, inhumane system that has plagued this nation from its inception.

I will also proclaim "All Lives Matter," because that is equally true. And I refuse to allow politics, the media, or my friends on either the right or the left to silence or quench my unequivocal proclamation of the *"consistent Life ethic."* The lack of respect for Black lives in America is inextricably linked to a lack of respect for human life in general.

So, I will not apologize for saying "Black Lives Matter," and I will not apologize for saying "All Lives Matter." And I will say both with equal clarity and equal conviction. I will not compromise the truth for the sake of popularity or political ideology.

I refuse to be part of the problem. What about you?

(Also see #742)

991. ~ REFLECTIONS on THE MUSIC of CARLOS SANTANA ~

How do I describe the greatness of Carlos Santana? Well, his playing is infused with mysticism, fire, funk, rhythm, passion, melody, and flow. Carlos is a guitarist that takes us to the edges of the universe without ever losing the groove. Hendrix sometimes went too far, and others never go far enough. But Carlos reaches out to kiss the stars while keeping his feet firmly planted in the streets.

Carlos brought the barrio to Woodstock and Woodstock to the barrio. His music emanates from Mexico, but it channels Africa. It expresses the age old struggle of colonizer and colonized. It enlightens us with the mystical mushrooms of the Chiapas jungles while feeding us with the grit of Tijuana slums. It is San Francisco psychedelic rock rooted in Chicago Blues (and with Santana that is not a cliché.) His transcendental guitar runs are always harnessed by irrepressible conga rhythms and incandescent timbale flourishes – lest we all drift so far that we forget the realities of earth and our responsibility to our fellow earthlings.

From the deeply spiritual (*"Flame Sky"*) to the socially conscious (*"Life is For Living"* and *"Free All the People"*) to pure unadulterated down home funk (*"Fried Neck Bones and Home Fries"*), Carlos is always on a soulful journey. But wherever his soul may venture, he makes sure that he never leaves us behind. And that, in my opinion, is his genius – as is the genius of every great artist: giving us a glimpse of God while connecting us to ourselves and to humanity.

(And like all great artists, Carlos Santana is fallible and flawed. I do not pretend to like all of his music, and I don't pretend to agree with all of his spiritual and political views. But I would be very worried if I ever encountered anyone with whom I agreed 100% on everything. All I know is that Santana's music and philosophy have brought me great joy, great pleasure, and great peace throughout my life. And for that, I am deeply thankful.)

992. ~ TO DANCE WITH DEATH... ~

To dance with death is artistry. To make peace with death is mastery.

993. ~ THE "IMPOSITION" of CHRISTIANITY ~

Christianity has never been imposed on anyone, anywhere, ever. Anything imposed by coercion, compulsion, violence, or force is *not* Christianity. Swords and shields and shackles and chains have nothing to do with the Cross. And if there truly is a hell, then I suspect it shall be inhabited by those who oppressed, enslaved, and slaughtered others in the precious name of the Prince of Peace. But I have faith, that in the end, the unfailing mercy of God shall save even the oppressors.

994. ~ "POLITICAL CHANGE" ~

The one thing that both the political left and political right agree upon is the belief that you have to work within the system to change the system. And that's why rather than producing revolutionary change, politics merely produces the metamorphosis of one form of systemic injustice into another. The left and the right both bring about a semblance of "change," but they never bring transformative truth or spiritual hope.

"Political change" is merely the rearrangement of the status quo from time to time. There is no such thing as political revolution. True revolution is spiritual; it takes place in the human heart, not in the voting booth. And the spark of revolution that ignites the human soul cannot be quenched by political lies and political poison.

995. ~ DON'T PRETEND ~

You cannot claim to love peace or be a champion of human rights if you vote for politicians who support militarism, economic exploitation, abortion, or capital punishment. If you believe in violence, then at least be honest about it. But don't pretend to condemn those who pull the trigger when you pull the lever for those who bomb, execute, oppress, and abort.

996. ~ "TOLERANCE" and "LOVE" ~

If you are so "tolerant" and "loving" that you hate anyone who disagrees with your narrow definition of tolerance and love, then you are actually guilty of the very bigotry you claim to abhor.

997. ~ MY PAPA, MY TEACHER ~

My Papa used to say, in a loving and light-hearted manner:
"I wish I had it all figured out like you do. But I don't understand it all. I wish I did. But I pray for you often, even though I doubt if my prayers get very far."

My Papa didn't read the Bible, he rarely went to Church, and he never professed to worship Jesus as "the only way." But he loved me. He loved others. He used what God gave him to help people and to make the world a better place. And as erudite and worldly-wise as he was, when it came to matters of the transcendent he erred on the side of deep humility.

My Papa was always the smartest person in the room, but he went to great lengths to disguise that fact.

I now realize what an Orthodox soul he had. I miss him every day, but I feel his presence with me always. He is still teaching me, even though he has departed this world.

998. ~ CHRISTIAN ANARCHY ~

Christian anarchy is not rebellion against law and order, but rather rebellion against the systemic evils and injustices that masquerade as law and order. We rebel against evil precisely because Christ orders our lives towards good.

"There are different forms of anarchy and different currents in it. I must say very simply what anarchy I have in view. By anarchy I mean first an absolute rejection of violence." ~ Jacques Ellul ~

999. ~ TRUTH and TACT ~

I refuse to allow truth to be enslaved by tact. Manners too often masquerade lies, and morality is too often the casualty of decency.

1,000. ~ **BLOOD ON THE MOUNTAIN** ~
(Please be advised that this story contains disturbing material.)

The boy awoke with excitement in his heart. It was his 11th birthday, and a wonderful day had been planned. Papa and Grandmother were taking him to "Ghost Town In The Sky," an amusement park nestled high up in the beautiful Blue Ridge Mountains of North Carolina. It had been a great summer so far. He had spent two weeks at basketball camp where he won two awards and made a new best friend who happened to live in the same small mountain town where his family spent their summers.

The boy rolled out of bed, grabbed his basketball, and looked out of his upstairs window at the crystal clear mountain view that spread before his hopeful eyes. He was 11 years old. And he was happy. And great things lay ahead today.

"Ghost Town In The Sky" was about a two hour drive from their summer cabin home – a slow, winding, but scenic trip through dense mountain fog that eventually breaks to reveal blue dusted, smoky peaked ridges that rise majestically and stretch in endless expanse. Papa whistled as he drove, poorly but enthusiastically – *The Lone Ranger Theme (William Tell Overture)," "She'll Be Coming Round The Mountain," "Ramblin' Wreck from Georgia Tech," "Dixie."* Grandmother was happy but slightly nervous. Papa was driving too fast on the curvy roads she said. And she kept asking the boy about the skyline cable car that they had to take up the mountain to get to the amusement park. Was it safe? Had it ever broken? But other than that, Grandmother was happy and Papa was happy and that made the boy happy.

They arrived midmorning and got on the cable car that conveyed park goers slowly up the steep mountainside to the "Ghost Town" amusement park tucked atop the ridges above. Although the cable car was crowded the view from its windows was so gorgeous that Grandmother was calm. "Isn't this lovely?" she said. "Isn't this lovely?" And yes, it was lovely indeed, the boy thought.

The next few hours felt like a dream to him. He rode roller-coasters and watched a mock "Wild Western cowboy shootout" and repeatedly explored the "haunted house" and ate pizza and cotton candy and drank enough root beer to flood the French Broad River. He even convinced Grandmother to ride a small roller-coaster with him. And she had enjoyed it!

But the happiest moment was yet to come.

"Papa, there's a basketball shoot! Can I try?" the boy asked. "Just one time Papa! Can I try?"

"It's your birthday son, so yes, go ahead. It says three dollars for five shots, so here's three dollars. But that's all you get. Good luck!"

He paid the three dollars, stepped behind the line, and prepared for his first shot. He'd been playing basketball day in and day out all summer long, so he wasn't lacking for confidence. He believed he could make one shot in five tries, even though he knew the basket was rigged to make it higher and narrower than a regulation goal. The boy took a few dribbles, spun the ball in his hands, bent his knees and then lifted up on his toes to release the ball with his elbow in and with a flick of his wrist like he'd done thousands of times before at camp and in his driveway and on the schoolyard playground. And Papa and Grandmother and the mustachioed man with the cubicle of stuffed animals watched the basketball spin in a perfect arc – up through the clean Blue Ridge mountain air and down through the net with pure perfection.

The boy didn't need five shots. He did it with one.

And he surprised even himself. He looked first at his Papa, who was smiling with a pride that the boy had always wanted to see and would forever thereafter strive to see. And then he looked at Grandmother who was always proud of him and who didn't really understand sports but who nevertheless understood that something momentous had just happened in the little boy's life. And she was smiling and clapping and she was so proud of him. And even the jaded, mustachioed man who sold basketball shots for a living had a smile on his face too.

"You did it son. Nice shot! Take your pick. Whatever you want."

"I want the stuffed basketball!" said the boy.

"Are you sure? You can have any of these large stuffed animals. Anything you want."

"I want the stuffed basketball!" the boy said.

And so the boy got himself a stuffed basketball, about the same size as a regular basketball. And he was really proud of that stuffed basketball. And he couldn't wait to show it to Mama when they got home.

It had been a perfect birthday the boy thought. Better than perfect. Better than he deserved. And his heart was full of gratitude. As they rode the cable car back down the mountain slope, the boy gazed out the window and wondered what he had done to deserve such happiness. He couldn't find an answer. But why should happiness demand any answers?

On the drive home the boy stretched out on the back seat, cradling his stuffed basketball, replaying his winning shot over and over again in his mind. As the car meandered through the Blue Ridge hills back towards home, he struggled to keep his eyes open. The evening mountain fog filtered through the dusk light of the car window, and soon the boy was sound asleep. He dreamed of cowboys and cotton candy and a perfect basketball shot and a father's pride and a grandmother's love.

When he woke up it was dark and they were back at their summer mountain cabin. Papa and Mama had a party to go to at the art studio, and they were taking Grandmother along. So the boy was dropped off at a neighbor's who lived down the road. The boy ate a little supper (he was still full from the afternoon's pizza and cotton candy and root beer). He watched some TV, and then he soon fell asleep again with his stuffed basketball clutched in his arms.

Hours later Grandmother woke him up gently: "It's time to go. Just get in the car and go back to sleep and we'll be up the mountain and home in no time." The boy followed Grandmother out to the car, carrying his stuffed basketball. She got in the back seat with him and held his hand. Papa drove and Mama was up front in the passenger's side seat. The boy wondered why Grandmother was holding his hand so tightly.

"Just go back to sleep. It's ok. Just go back to sleep."

But he knew immediately that something was wrong and he didn't want to go back to sleep. The boy was worried about Grandmother because Grandmother was worried about something.

And Grandmother wasn't a worrier. Sure, she had been slightly nervous about the skyline cable car, but once she had gotten on it she had loved it. And she had also ridden a roller-coaster with the boy and even enjoyed the loud and raucous "Wild West showdown" acted out in the dusty main street of "Ghost Town." Grandmother was a tough woman. She was raised hard and she knew hard and she wasn't fazed by much. But the boy recognized that Grandmother was upset now. And the harder she held his hand and the more she tried to hide her concern, the more the boy understood that something was wrong.

Mama's breath reeked of alcohol. But the boy was used to that. He thought nothing of it. He hadn't yet fully made the connection that Mama became a different person, a different creature at night, after the bourbon had bitten her. She was just *Mama* – one person, a person who loved him deeply and a person he deeply loved.

At first it was just noise. Grownups arguing. And who knows what grownups argue about? And the boy was as used to the sound of arguing as he was to the smell of alcohol on his mother's breath. But the boy just knew that Papa and Mama were quarreling. And it was his birthday. And they shouldn't quarrel on his birthday. And they were making Grandmother upset. And this had been such a perfect day. And why were they disrupting that? "And forget my birthday," the boy thought. "Why are you upsetting Grandmother? What did *she* do wrong? Why are you all upsetting *her*?"

Papa drove up the dark dirt road toward the cabin. And Mama's voice got louder and louder inside of the car. The tension had long since been broken. The words were flying like bullets now – angry and hateful – fired with pinpoint animosity but careless aim. They were hurtful, incoherent, devilish words. The boy didn't understand any of them, but he felt them – even though they weren't meant for him.

The boy knew his words well enough. He read books and wrote stories and excelled in English even though he floundered in every other course in school. For the boy words had always made sense. He could arrange them, organize them, make them say whatever he wanted them to say. He found meaning in words. He found order in words. He found that words enabled him to create some small semblance of control in his life.

But the boy didn't understand any of the words that were being unleashed at that moment. They weren't words. They were profane syllabics that communicated wrath not reason. They were everything that words were not supposed to be – chaos, disharmony, confusion, hate. They were evil, irrational utterances that defied the very purpose of language itself.

As the cacophony increased Grandmother's grip grew stronger.

"You two stop it now. Now just stop this! Right now!"

But Mama didn't listen to Grandmother. An offense had taken root – whether real or perceived – and the bourbon would not allow her to forgive it. As Papa drove up the mountain he tried to quell the feud. "Not now. We'll discuss it tomorrow. It's the boy's birthday. Don't do this now. Please, let's not do this now."

But that only enraged Mama more. A tirade of expletives spewed from her mouth. Grandmother put her hands over the boy's ears, trying to shield him from words he had certainly heard and said in his life, but in an altogether different context. After all, boys will experiment with cussing even though they don't fully understand the logistics of the profanities they invoke. But the boy could still hear through Grandmother's hands, and everything he heard was trapped inside of that car. Mama's vitriol had no escape. Her wrath reverberated within those four doors. It fed upon itself, growing in violence and strength as the car slowly ascended the rocky, rut strewn road. Grandmother's hands were shaking now as she continued to try to muffle the boy's ears.

"It's ok. It's ok. Go to sleep now. It's ok."

But the boy was wide awake – too wide awake.

Papa finally pulled into the dirt driveway. The boy felt that if everyone could just get out of the car everything would be alright. Let whatever angry entity that had invaded be dissipated in the four winds of the mountain night air. An evil spirit had been trapped inside of the car, and it just needed to be released. That's what the boy believed. Or at least that's what he hoped.

So with his stuffed basketball in one hand and Grandmother's hand in the other, he got out of the car and went inside the cabin.

"Now let's go on up to bed," Grandmother said. But Papa and Mama were soon inside with them, and the kitchen room was quickly filled with the same spirit of chaos, confusion, venom, and hate that had been trapped inside of the car.

Mama was screaming things – vile, piercing, insane things – and Grandmother sat down and began to shake. The boy was terrified now, but not for himself. His Papa had already had one heart attack, and the doctor had clearly explained that any sort of stress could cause him to have another heart attack. The boy thought that his Mama was surely trying to kill his Papa, and maybe she was trying to kill Grandmother too.

But he was just an 11 year old boy. And he was facing something for which he had no answer. If he had a basketball and a hoop or a pen and some paper he could find a solution. He could practice and practice until he finally found a way to neutralize the opponent. Or he could read and write until he found an escape through books or through the words of his own imaginative pen. Three bucks for five shots and you win or lose. It doesn't determine your life. Write a story and it's your story, and some may like it and some may hate it. But it doesn't determine your life. But what does a boy do when his life is suddenly out of his hands, when he has no control of the situation, when peace and goodness and happiness and joy are being wrenched from his soul before his very eyes?

"I'm calling your mother," Papa said to Mama. "You're out of control and you need to go stay with her tonight and calm down."

He reached for the phone and that's when Mama launched. She dug her fingernails deep into his face and scratched until blood began to drip on the floor. Papa tried to push her away but her fingers were embedded in his flesh. The boy wanted him to hit her, to defend himself, to save his own life and also Grandmother's life. But Papa wouldn't. The blood ran down his face and then Mama released her grip to violently pull the phone cord out of the wall. And then she launched at him again.

And that's when the boy snapped. He charged at his Mama with curses and tears and fists flailing. He tackled her to the ground and spit on her and called her every goddamned name he could think of. And he looked her in the eyes and saw nothing but shock and confusion and pathetic dismay.

Then the boy bolted for the door, brushing past Grandmother, and ran down the dirt driveway and onto the mountain road and into the blackness. He ran hoping that death or oblivion or everything or nothing would swallow him up and consume him. He wanted to run into the darkness until he died. And then he realized that for some idiotic reason he was clutching his stuffed basketball. And now he hated that basketball, and he hated himself for still clinging to it.

He was still sprinting and he was halfway down the mountain road when the headlights caught up with him. He turned and stared directly into them. He knew it was his Papa. And he hated his Papa for letting this happen. He hated his Papa's weakness. He hated his cowardly tolerance. He hated him for allowing his Mama to ruin the best birthday he'd ever had. So the boy ran straight toward the headlights, hoping that his father would run him over accidentally and end the boy's life. He ran into those headlights and he threw his stuffed basketball at the windshield and he slung his little boy body onto the hood of the car.

But he was still alive. Not even injured. His stuffed basketball ricocheted off the car and into the mountain night. Papa got out and kneeled down and put his arms around the boy. There were no words said. The boy just cried and cried and shook his head and he didn't want any words. And his Papa didn't have any words to give him. But the boy got in the car and went back up the mountain with his Papa. And Grandmother was still sitting in the kitchen, still shaking. And she said to the boy, without any sense of judgment or rebuke: "I didn't know you knew such horrible words. I didn't know you knew such horrible words."

The bourbon had metabolized and Mama had fallen sleep. The storm was over. It was no longer the boy's birthday anyway. The midnight hour had come and gone. He went up to his bedroom and grabbed his real basketball, caressing it as he tried his best to fall asleep and forget what had happened. "Ghost Town In The Sky" was a fairytale land that he had visited lifetimes ago – its one tangible memory cast forever into the rhododendron, thistle, and Carolina hemlock night.

The sun came up the next morning, but the boy didn't notice. Something had broken inside of him and he would never completely trust life again. He understood now that happiness and hope were mere illusions that lured one into the cruel realities of disappointment, horror, and pain.

*   *   *

I see that little boy in the mirror every day. And I have to remind him that hope is not a lie, that happiness is real, that life in both its day and night, darkness and light is a journey worth the struggle. That little boy has experienced far too many blessings throughout his life, and the pains have been more than worth it.

There was blood and brokenness on the mountain that night. Demons were unleashed and they danced on a little boy's soul. But God put those demons back in their place. And that boy lived and grew and became a man and became the father of two other little boys who are now becoming men themselves. And what a beautiful and joyous experience that has been.

And I think the boy has learned to trust life now. But there may be more blood on the mountain in the future. He realizes that. But he also knows that on a blood soaked mountain 2,000 years ago salvation came to the world.

1,001. ~ DROWNING MAN ~

I am...
A drowning man
A dying man
A hungry man
A lonely man
A thirsty man
A suffering man
A desperate man
A praying man
A falling man
A failing man
A broken man

Please dear Jesus:
Take my hand.

Save me from others
And save me from myself.

I don't want to hurt anymore.

1,002. ~ NO WAY ~

Killing is no way to live
War is no way to peace
Violence is no way to love
Vengeance is no way to heal

1,003. ~ SUN TZU and LAO TZU ~

Some people study Sun Tzu's art of war, and others study Lao Tzu's art of peace. Not only will you become a master of what you study, but you will inevitably be mastered by what you study. I prefer to be mastered by peace than by war, and I also happen to think that peace is a much more beautiful art.

1,004. ~ THE LIGHT of CHRIST and THE LIGHT of HELL ~

The light of Christ will eternally conquer the light of hell. I believe this. And I believe it because the God I worship has defeated sin and death. The created fires of evil will be quenched by the uncreated light of God. But divine light, although saving, is nevertheless harsh. Divine light is an unremitting, purging fire. It burns away everything unholy. It will purify us all, but for many the purification will not be pleasant. And yet I am thankful for a God who loves me enough to save me even with fire.

1,005. ~ DON'T TAKE GOD TOO SERIOUSLY ~

One of the greatest blasphemies is to take God too seriously. Those who take God too seriously inevitably take themselves too seriously, and they end up taking life too seriously. God has a wonderful sense of humor, and He is glorified by laughter as much as by prayer. There is reverence in joy.

1,006. ~ NEIGHBORS ~

I have neighbors in prison, neighbors in poverty, neighbors in depression, and neighbors in despair. I have neighbors with wealth, neighbors with influence, neighbors with political power, and neighbors with nefarious intentions. I have neighbors that suffer in the streets and neighbors that bathe in mansions. I have neighbors struggling to survive and neighbors that profit at the expense of their neighbors. I have neighbors that are bombed and neighbors that do the bombing. I have neighbors with everything and neighbors with nothing. I have neighbors in the White House and I have neighbors in the womb.

And so do you.

1,007. ~ THE ONLY ANSWER to EVERY QUESTION THAT REALLY MATTERS ~

I don't have a theology degree. I don't have a philosophy degree. Hell, I don't even have a college degree. All I've got is my family, my friends, my Bible, my books, my prayers, and the Holy Sacraments of the Orthodox Church. And I've found out that's enough.

So take everything I write and say with a grain of salt. If you're looking for wisdom, truth, and profundity then don't look to me. Look to the innocence of children. My children have taught me more than all the teachers and tomes in my life combined.

So I won't try to outsmart you. I won't try to prove the truth by winning some debate. I will just try to love you. Because although I am an ignorant and uneducated man, I have learned that love is the only answer to every question that really matters.

1,008. ~ VOTING for CHANGE / BEING the CHANGE ~

As long as we keep voting for change rather than *being* the change that would negate any desire or need to vote, then we will keep having elections but we'll never have any change – at least not any real, authentic, social, spiritual, or revolutionary change. All we'll have is the vapid satisfaction that we've replaced another elephant with another jackass.

1,009. ~ IF YOU CAN'T PRAY... ~

If you can't pray, then just try to love. And if you can't love, then just try not to harm. I mean, if you can't bring yourself to believe in God and love your fellow man, then at least try not to rape and kill and abort and oppress. I really don't think that's too much to ask.

1,010. ~ SIN NATURE? ~

Sin is not our divinely created nature. Sin is a pathology we suffer from as a result of the fall. But this pathology is antithetical to our divinely fashioned nature, which is the very image of God. Sin is a disease that Christ came to cure and heal, not a guilt that earns us the wrath of some vengeful divine judge. We are not "sinners in the hands of an angry God;" we are sinners in the hands of a healing Savior. But in order to be healed we must acknowledge our sickness and run to the Holy Physician.

The guilty man runs *from* the law, but the sick child runs *to* his nurturing parent. As long as we view ourselves as guilty, we will always be running *from* God. But when we realize that we are sick, then we will finally run *to* God.

This is why our perpetual Orthodox Christian prayer is, *"Lord have mercy on us."* Because we know that God is merciful, and we know that He is eager to lavish mercy upon us. In fact, God lavishes His healing mercy on us even when we don't seek or deserve it. But we would be fools to reject the divine medicine that He freely offers us through His Cross, His Body, His Blood, and His Church.

Let us acknowledge the sickness of sin and flee to Our Father whose grace will heal us. God is not waiting to smash us with His cosmic gavel; He is waiting to embrace us in His crucified arms of unconditional love.

1,011. ~ HYPOCRISY and MORAL STANDARDS ~

No one can fully live up to their own rules except for those who declare that there are no rules. But even they fail to live by their own professed moral anarchy. For when their own personal comfort, security, power, or profit is threatened, they suddenly become the most vociferous voices of moral appeal.

It is better to exalt an objective moral standard that we fail to attain than to deny the existence of any objective standards at all. Hypocrisy belongs not to those that acknowledge right and wrong yet struggle to live accordingly; it belongs rather to those that deny right and wrong until a wrong is done unto them.

1,012. ~ A FEW THOUGHTS on THE RECENT PROTESTS of THE AMERICAN FLAG and THE NATIONAL ANTHEM ~
[8/29/2016]

1. Innocent people have been variously enslaved, oppressed, bombed, and aborted throughout the history of this nation. So I'm wondering why some people are suddenly bothered now? Why is it that certain athletes and celebrities (not many of course) are only just now deciding to protest by refusing to salute the flag and by speaking out against certain social injustices? And why are they so selective in their moral outrage?

But perhaps this is the beginning of their conscious awakening. Let's hope and pray that they begin to realize that the specific injustices they're currently protesting are inextricably linked to countless other historical American atrocities and evils.

2. For all those who demand that we salute the flag because of the freedoms that the flag represents: well, please understand that not all

of those freedoms are noble or virtuous freedoms. The freedom to accrue wealth at the expense of the poor, the freedom to produce and view pornography, and the freedom to profit from the sale of carcinogenic products, deadly food, and highly addictive pharmaceuticals are not freedoms that I will ever praise or extol.

3. People also need to know that there has never been a time in the history of this nation where all human lives have been granted full liberty, equal rights, and universal protection. This may sound harsh, but the fact is that the same American soldiers who kill to preserve our right to "free speech" and "religious liberty" are also preserving the right of mothers to murder their unborn children. So forgive me if I don't bow at the altar of a military that fights to protect child sacrifice (among many other social injustices and violations of human rights.)

4. Lastly, no Christian should ever salute a flag that proudly waves over the slain bodies of innocent human beings. And no Christian should ever join in the mass chorus of an anthem that glorifies warfare and bloodshed. So whenever you are asked to stand for the Pledge of Allegiance or the National Anthem, I encourage you to make the sign of the Cross and bow your head in prayer – not as a protest, but as a simple act of faith.

1,013. ~ UTILITARIANISM and THE GOSPEL ~

One of the many problems with the philosophy of Utilitarianism is that it sacrifices our neighbor who we are commanded to love right here and right now for a theoretical greater good in the future. The Utilitarian ethic would have us pass by those suffering on the Jericho road in order to pass legislation that would theoretically make the Jericho road safer. But the teachings of Christ and His Gospel compel us to prioritize the immediate needs of the individual neighbors in our daily path. We have no right to sacrifice a single human life today in pursuit of an idealized, future utopian humanity.

The world is constantly devising new political systems and mortal philosophies that presume to usher in social justice and world peace. Esteemed philosophers and political theorists have given us fascism and communism, democracy and tyranny, liberalism and conservatism. They have given us all manner of programs and paradigms and ideologies and governments – anything and everything other than, *"Love thy neighbor."*

1,014. ~ MIRACLES ~

We all experience miracles every day, but most of us are too blind to recognize them. We keep demanding that God reveal Himself; but all we have to do is open our eyes and look at creation, or close our eyes and look within. I've met devout people that have told me about the miracles they've experienced. And they all shared something in common: a deep sense of humility, a childlike faith, and a genuine love for other people. Miracles aren't experienced with the intellect. Miracles are experienced with the heart. May God open our hearts to see His glory.

1,015. ~ WHEN TO SIT and WHEN TO STAND ~

When Babylon stands the Christian must sit. And when Babylon sits the Christian must stand.

1,016. ~ BRIEF REFLECTIONS on KIERKEGAARD ~

A friend asked me why I am fascinated by Soren Kierkegaard. Well, there are so many reasons. But I guess I would say that Kierkegaard was a devout lover of Jesus who struggled mightily with doubt and angst and even despair. He was a passionate Christian who railed against the hypocrisies of institutionalized state religion. He was born in affluence, raised in a Christian home, granted educational and financial privilege, and yet he bore a soul of inexpressible suffering. Kierkegaard was a man who plumbed the depths of theology and philosophy but always came back to the purity and simplicity of love. He may not have been right about everything, but Kierkegaard is a man whose sincerity of heart I admire and trust.

And as impossible as it is to summarize Soren Kierkegaard, I will dare to summarize the essence of his paradoxical thought this way: Kierkegaard ultimately shows us that the realization of the objective truth of God can only come through the inescapable path of subjective experience.

1,017. ~ ONE MARK of A TRUE SPIRITUAL TEACHER ~

One mark of a true spiritual teacher: they never accuse you of being "unteachable" because you dare to ask questions.

1,018. ~ TWO KINDS of BOOKS ~

I have concluded that there only two kinds of books: readable and unreadable. And one of the great mysteries of the Bible is that it is somehow both.

1,019. ~ FAITH and FEAR ~

Because I have faith in water I drink, I bathe, I swim. If I feared water I would thirst, I would stink, I would drown.

1,020. ~ DIALOGUE WITH AN INSOMNIAC ~

"NORMAL" ONE: "You know, you could get so much more accomplished if you would just go to sleep at night."

INSOMNIAC: "But I can't go to sleep at night."

"NORMAL" ONE: "That's because you stay up all night."

INSOMNIAC: "Well, it's not really by choice."

"NORMAL" ONE: "You just need to get on a schedule."

INSOMNIAC: "Yeah, that would be great. But, you see, my insomnia sort of interferes with my ability to get on a consistent schedule."

"NORMAL" ONE: "That's why you've never held a job for very long."

INSOMNIAC: "Umm... yeah, that's one of the many drawbacks of insomnia. It sort of sucks to be broke along with not being able to sleep."

"NORMAL" ONE: "Your problem is that you worry too much. Stop worrying about things and just go to sleep."

INSOMNIAC: "Yeah, you're right again. Can't argue with you. I do worry too much. It would be nice to not have anxiety. Because if I didn't have anxiety then I probably wouldn't have insomnia. And if I didn't have insomnia then I would probably be able to hold down a job. And if I had a job and a steady income then I probably wouldn't worry so much. So yeah, it would be wonderful to be able to work and sleep and not worry. (And by the way, not that we need to justify any of this to you, but you should know that many of us who suffer from insomnia and anxiety also have severe physical health issues that compound our insomnia and anxiety. So be thankful that you don't suffer from these curses.)"

"NORMAL" ONE: "Well, what do you do with your life – staying up all night, not working, sitting around worrying all the time?"

INSOMNIAC: "Well, first of all, I do work. And I work very hard. I work hard at being a good father and a good husband. I work hard to use the gifts and talents God has given me for His glory. While others are sleeping and earning money, I am reading, studying, writing, creating, and trying to impart what little I've learned to my children so that they can engage the world and perhaps make it a better place."

"NORMAL" ONE: "But how does that pay the bills?"

INSOMNIAC: "Well, sometimes the bills don't get paid. But we survive, thanks to the love and support of family, friends, and the Church. But it is indeed a struggle."

"NORMAL" ONE: "But you're just making excuses. Everyone has it hard. You just need to pull yourself up by your bootstraps. Stop worrying, get a job, and go to sleep. Then you can make money and be successful like me. But you 'artistic types' just want people like me to foot the bill for your musings."

INSOMNIAC: "Well, we 'artistic types' do the best we can. And when your paycheck is spent and your money is gone, our words and our art and our books and our works will live on. And I am at peace with that, even if it keeps me up at night. As T.S. Eliot said: *'Anxiety is the handmaiden of creativity.'* But thanks for your concern."

1,021. ~ LOVE and SUFFERING ~

What is love? It is nothing less than the deepest suffering that the soul can know. And yet a life without love is an empty, joyless, meaningless existence.

1,022. ~ THE CHOICE ALWAYS HAS BEEN and ALWAYS WILL BE... ~

The choice always has been and always will be between good and evil, truth and lies, mercy and vengeance, peace and violence, life and death, love and hate. Regardless of the justice of the cause or the severity of the circumstances, if we choose lies, vengeance, evil and hate, then we choose the side of the oppressor and we act in a counter-revolutionary manner. But as long as we choose truth, mercy, peace, life, and love, then we cannot lose. As Our Lord promised, *"The meek shall inherit the earth." [St. Matthew 5:5]*

But do not think that the meek are cowardly or timid. It takes great strength and tremendous courage to truly love. The meek are not those who are afraid to fight, they are rather those who stand toe to toe with wickedness and love it to death. As Dostoevsky wrote: *"Love in reality is a harsh and dreadful thing compared to love in dreams."*

1,023. ~ THE MYSTERY of DEATH and LOSS and LIFE and HOPE ~

Sometimes it's so hard, this mystery of death and loss. Grief hits me in strange and unexpected ways. But when it hits me I embrace it. I am thankful for tears as I am thankful for the rain, thankful for a broken heart as I am thankful for the broken soil that receives rain's nourishment. Because through such brokenness I am compelled to cry out to God. I am compelled to proclaim that Christ is Risen! And that is the greater mystery, the conquering mystery, the triumphant mystery. The Resurrection is my hope, my truth, my salvation.

So I know that I will see my departed loved ones again. I will embrace them in eternity. Without my Jesus I would never survive this world. And I'm not sure if I would want to. But because of Him I have reason to live. I have reason to preach peace. I have reason to proclaim hope. And I have reason to militantly pursue Life. For all that I have suffered and will suffer, I have known love too strong to quit. Therefore I will go on, as long as I can, until God says otherwise. And I will rejoice in it all.

I feel better today. More hopeful. But tomorrow, who knows? Divine Liturgy this morning was very healing. I have learned that the devil will never sleep. He attacks in cruel and unexpected ways. Satan never fights fairly. His goal is to kill and destroy, to drive us to the point of an irrevocable despair. And he is all too willing to use those we love the most to accomplish his nefarious goals.

But this morning the Gospel reading was about forgiveness. And during his homily, our Priest explained how the world is in turmoil because people refuse to forgive one another. We will hate and kill and divorce and destroy before we forgive. And that is the tragedy.

But forgiveness is not a manipulative tool or a utilitarian strategy that produces intended results. Offering an apology and extending forgiveness yields nothing certain other than our own peace with God. Some people may never accept our apologies, and some people may never offer theirs. Yet we must apologize and offer forgiveness unconditionally, leaving it to God to work on the hearts of both those we have wronged and those by whom we have been wronged.

And as difficult as it may be, hope will always accompany our sincere contrition and our true forgiveness. Even if some of our human relationships are never reconciled, begging forgiveness and bestowing forgiveness will always keep us reconciled to God.

So be quick to apologize and be quick to forgive. The devil has a million tricks up his sleeve, but he is always defeated by genuine humility and unconditional love.

And know this too: although the devil is always busy, God is even busier. While the devil is constantly plotting evil, God is constantly answering prayers. So thanks to everyone who prays for this sinner. Please don't stop! Sometimes I feel like I'm not gonna make it. But my Jesus always pulls me through; and He does so with the participatory love and intercessions of the all saints and angels and brethren and sistren. So how can I possibly lose?!

1,025. ~ LIFE is NOT A COMPETITION ~

In spite of the godless cultural pressures and perverse societal standards that infect our consciousness, the truth is that life is not a game; life is not a sport; life is not a competition. Life is for *living*. Life is for *loving*. There are no winners and losers, for we are all equally destined for the grave. From dirt we were created, and to dirt we shall return. So don't ever let anyone tell you that you are a failure. Regardless of how "successful" some may be in the eyes of the world, they too will die like the poorest of the poor and the wretched of the earth.

Many people succumb to despondency and despair because they feel they have somehow "failed." Perhaps they didn't succeed in their business ventures; or perhaps their marriages didn't last; or perhaps their friends and family betrayed them; or perhaps their Christian ministries didn't produce tangible fruition. So they think that they have "lost." They believe the demonic lie that their lives are now worthless because they didn't succeed according to some meaningless human standard. And they hear the whispers, they hear the gossip. They feel the judgment, condemnation, and scorn of the self-righteous souls who will die just as surely as they will. But tragically, they allow the foolish opinions of these self-righteous voices to affect how they view themselves, how they view their own worth, how they view the importance and sanctity of their own lives.

I have lost dear friends to the tragedy of suicide – brilliant and creative and humble souls who were erroneously led to believe that they were failures because they didn't measure up to society's standards of "success." And what's even more tragic is that these friends were also devout Christians who suffered most severely from the cruel and harsh judgments of a "church" that was supposed to unconditionally and unceasingly love, support, and affirm their inherent human worth. But instead, the "church" judged them by the same superficialities of society and treated according to the same damnable lies of the world.

So don't ever let anyone tell you that you are a failure. Don't ever give up on life because of the smug condemnations and inane judgments of others. Life is not a contest. The earth will inevitably swallow us all. And afterwards there will be a divine resurrection and a divine Judgment. And then we will not be judged by our bank accounts, our family stability, our natural talents, or any other worldly measurement of success. We will be judged simply by our love for God and our love for others. That's it. That's all that will matter. So keep on living and keep on loving; and screw what anyone else thinks!

1,026. ~ LET THE WORLD CHOOSE AMONG DEVILS ~

The good news is that as Gospel believers we never have to choose evil. So just keep on choosing Jesus and let the world choose among devils.

1,027. ~ REVOLUTIONARY WANTS ~

I want...
revolutionary music
revolutionary art
revolutionary poetry
revolutionary song
revolutionary food
revolutionary sex
revolutionary thought
revolutionary activism
and revolutionary peace.

But I don't want
no revolutionary war.

For when killing begins,
then revolution ends.

1,028. ~ THE IMAGE of GOD ~

The image of God remains in all people – *all* of us – regardless of our sins and mistakes and iniquities and failures. We all suffer equally from the fall. We can either look at ourselves and others with judgmental disgust or we can look at ourselves and others as who we truly are: the very *image of God*. And I believe that if we all viewed every human being and all human life through the lens of God's unfailing love, then the world would no longer suffer from inhumanity and injustices.

As Christians, we of *all* people should manifest the love of God for *all* human creatures. Sin and Satan are the common enemies of us *all*, but the good news is that Jesus has saved us *all*. The image of God is never "disgusting" in His sight, and therefore we should never view ourselves or any other human being with contempt or scorn.

Yes, there are indeed violent and inhumane actions that are evil and disgusting, and we should condemn them as such. But the human being who commits those acts was nevertheless created by God and is nevertheless loved by God. And part of our Christian calling is to help them recognize this truth; for those who truly see God's image in themselves and in others will not rape, kill, hate, abort, or oppress. They will love, just as God intends.

Dear Lord, help us to always see You in our fellow man.

1,029. ~ DEEPER SHADE ~

Give me a deeper shade of soul
Give me a heavier peace of truth
And I'll wage this war of life
And with love I'll conquer you

1,030. ~ PATHOLOGY, CRIMINALITY, REVOLUTION, and DEMOCRACY ~

Our pathological society criminalizes, condemns, and cruelly confines those who remain maladjusted to its pathology. Visit a prison sometime. Get to know some of those that society has decided to lock away. You will discover that many of these "criminal misfits" are wiser, saner, and morally and spiritually richer than the politicians, police officers, and judges that have put them behind bars. And that's precisely what makes them so dangerous. Therefore the system must systematically suppress those who pose a threat to the system.

But it doesn't work. Because when you deny a man his food or deny him his freedom – and when you deny him these natural rights in the name of "law and order – then you create a revolutionary. And when you commit crimes against humanity and call it "government," then the winds of revolution will gather with gale force to smash the crooked pillars of this corrupt social experiment that you call "democracy."

1,031. ~ "LAW and ORDER" ~

As long as we continue to believe that we need "law and order" then we will continue to have evil and disorder. We will never have true peace or true justice until we put down our guns, take off our uniforms, throw away our badges, and truly love one another.

1,032. ~ MORAL and POLITICAL HYPOCRISY ~

The moral hypocrisy is equally rife among both Republicans and Democrats. The Republicans claim to be Pro-Life while they support militarism, capital punishment, and economic and social policies that crush the poor. And the Democrats claim to care about racism and poverty while they wholeheartedly support the racism of abortion and the violent destruction of the "least of these" in the womb. And what's tragic is that most people allow politics rather than the Gospel to shape their social consciousness. Thus, with their votes and political participation they perpetuate the evils and injustices of war, poverty, racism, and abortion – all in the name of fulfilling their "civic duty."

1,033. ~ FREE IN AMERICA? ~

So, you think you are free in America?
Well...
Try not paying your taxes.
Try not sending your children to school.
Try finding a cop to "protect and serve" you if you are the wrong race in the wrong place.
Try entering an abortion clinic and exercising your ostensible right to "freedom of speech" by proclaiming the words of peace and life.
Try to find food, shelter, and a place to sleep when you are hungry and homeless.
Try to find the right to life, liberty, and the pursuit of happiness if you're an unborn child.
Try seeing if the freedoms you enjoy as a rich man are still afforded you when you're broke.

You're not as free as you think you are. No one is more enslaved than those who celebrate their chains.

1,034. ~ ON CHRISTIAN ANARCHO-PACIFISM ~

Violence is never tamed. Violence cannot be controlled by violence. That's why we are pacifists. That's why we are anarchists. Governments and states and "law and order" always seek to control evil with the methods of evil. And that only produces perpetual evil. That's why we reject all endeavors of force and coercion.

When the law protects the good, we rejoice. But we also realize that the same law that preserves the good in one area also preserves evil in other areas. So we never celebrate law itself, because law is always predicated upon the sword. And the law is always a double edged sword, too often curing headaches by decapitation.

The anarcho-pacifist is able to equally condemn both slavery and the war that resulted in the end of slavery. The anarcho-pacifist is able to equally condemn both murder and the prison industrial complex that profits from murder. The anarcho-pacifist is able to equally condemn both the violence committed by the individual and the violence committed by the state. The anarcho-pacifist is able to consistently condemn any and all violence committed by anyone against anyone for any reason. We make no distinction between the rape, murder, and theft committed by individuals and the rape, murder, and theft committed by governments. It is all evil, and we condemn it equally and unequivocally as such.

Christian anarcho-pacifism is essentially a rejection of all violent human governments that seek to usurp the holy and peaceable governance of Christ and His Kingdom.

Of course, many will invoke Romans 13 in objection:

"For the one in authority is God's servant for your good. But if you do wrong, be afraid, for rulers do not bear the sword for no reason. They are God's servants, agents of wrath to bring punishment on the wrongdoer." [Romans 13:4]

Now far be it from me to quibble with the inspired words of St. Paul; but I will simply say that if there appears to be a conflict between the teachings of St. Paul and the teachings of Our Lord Jesus Christ (a conflict which is not actual but merely superficially apparent), then err on the side of Jesus. But a serious study of Romans 13 will reveal that there is no conflict between the apostle and the Savior. As author Ted Grimsrud explains:

"Nothing here speaks to Christians as participants in the state's work. When Paul mentions several functions in Romans 13:3-4, he

does not have in mind tasks that Christians themselves would accept. His readers may have things that are "due to the authority" (13:6-7), but none of these involve direct work for the state. Whatever it is that the state does, Paul is not endorsing Christians themselves having a responsibility to perform those tasks—especially if the tasks violate the call to neighbor love.

"Paul calls for discrimination. 'Pay to all what is due them' echoes Jesus' call for discernment. When Jesus stated, 'give to Caesar what is Caesar's and to God what is God's,' he meant: Be sure not to give Caesar the loyalty that belongs only to God. Paul writes in 13:7, 'render to all what is due them.' In the very next verse (unfortunately often not noticed when we quit reading at 13:7), Paul states "nothing is due to anyone except love." This is Paul's concern – is what Caesar claims is due to him part of the obligation of love? Only that which is part of the call to love is part of the Christian's duty.

"Romans 13 is consistent with the Sermon on the Mount. The logic that uses Romans 13:1-7 as a basis for participation in coercive practices relies on a disjunction between Romans 13:1-7 and the Sermon on the Mount. However, there is no disjunction. Both Romans 12–13 as a unit and Matthew 5–7 instruct Christians to be nonviolent in all their relationships, including the social. Both call on the disciples of Jesus to renounce participation in vengeance. Both call Christians 'to respect and be subject to the historical process in which the sword continues to be wielded and to bring about a kind of order under fire, but not to perceive in the wielding of the sword their own reconciling ministry' (John Howard Yoder, "The Politics of Jesus").

Romans 13:1-7, when read in light of Paul's overall theology, may be understood as a statement of how the revolutionary subordination of Christians contributes to Christ's victory over the Powers. Christians do so by holding together their rejection of Empire-idolatry with their commitment to active pacifism. Their most radical task (and most subversive) is to live visibly as communities where the enmity that had driven Paul himself to murderous violence is overcome – Jew and Gentile joined together in one fellowship, a witness to genuine peace in a violent world."

[Ted Grimsrud. *Arguing Peace: Collected Pacifist Writings, Volume Three: Biblical and Theological Essays. Peace Theology Books, 2014.*]

"Anarchism must be nonviolent since it is, by definition, opposition to coercion and force. And since the state is inherently violent, meaningful pacifism must likewise be anarchistic."

~ Leo Tolstoy ~

1,035. ~ A TRAGIC and BLASPHEMOUS PERVERSION of THE HOLY GOSPEL ~

If it is rooted in fear, guilt, shame, manipulation, coercion, or force, then it is not of God. The love of Christ is offered freely and unconditionally to all. To turn the good news of divine love into some sort of tyrannical cosmic guilt trip is a most tragic and blasphemous perversion of the Holy Gospel. The fear of divine judgment may be enough to keep us from sin, but only the realization of divine love can lead us to true righteousness. A child who obeys out of fear rather than love brings no real honor to his father.

1,036. ~ SELF-IMPOSED SLAVERY ~

You entrust the government with your health. You entrust the government with your education. You entrust the government with your nutrition. You entrust the government with your safety. You entrust the government with your peace. You entrust the government with your life. You entrust the government with your soul. You willingly enslave yourself to a master that you constantly curse while forsaking the God who alone can liberate you.

Dietrich Bonhoeffer was a fascinating man, someone I consider a hero in many ways. He was a committed Christian who truly sought to live out his faith, regardless of the personal or temporal consequences. For Bonhoeffer, the Cross was not merely a symbol of salvation, it was something that must be embraced and lived out in all of its tension and agony. I have great admiration for Bonhoeffer's courage to speak, live, and die for the Gospel as he understood it (and in my humble opinion, he understood the Gospel very well.) His differentiation between "cheap grace" and "costly grace," as profoundly articulated in his masterpiece *The Cost of Discipleship*, has had a profound impact on my own understanding of the Christian Faith.

Dietrich Bonhoeffer and Soren Kierkegaard are two of my favorite Protestant theologians. Both came from affluence and privilege, and yet they both suffered deeply as a result of their Christian convictions. Kierkegaard was a radical individualist while Bonhoeffer was always seeking the authentic Christian community. And as someone who personally rails against corrupt authority while desperately clinging to the accountability, encouragement, and fellowship of the apostolic Orthodox Church, I can certainly relate to the aspects they each emphasized.

Bonhoeffer's theology and life confront us with many uncomfortable paradoxes: for example, his articulation of a "religionless Christianity," his sincere solidarity with the suffering and oppressed in spite of his status of affluence and privilege, and his apparent decision to seek recourse in violence against his long held pacifist beliefs. But Bonhoeffer's philosophy and actions were deeply rooted in a theology of the Cross, and the Cross will always confront us with conflicts, agonies, antinomies, and tensions.

I confess that I am troubled by Dietrich Bonhoeffer's decision to ultimately act against his pacifist convictions (although there are good arguments to suggest that he didn't*.) And yet, if he did, I can completely understand his reasons. After all, we're talking about his attempt to assassinate Adolph Hitler, which at face value can hardly be considered an act of evil. But it still bothers me because of the unchristian precedent that I believe it sets and because of the erroneous implications that can unfortunately be derived from it (again, assuming that Bonhoeffer did indeed renounce pacifism and conspire to assassinate Hitler, which is highly debatable.)

In contemplating the writings and life of Dietrich Bonhoeffer, there are many questions that come to mind. But there are two in particular that I believe have not yet been adequately addressed by most contemporary Bonhoeffer scholars, two questions with which I think Bonhoeffer himself would want us to seriously wrestle:

1) What were the determining theological and philosophical ideas that caused Bonhoeffer to ultimately forsake his pacifist convictions; and was he right to do so (assuming he did)?

2) How can we apply Bonhoeffer's theology, philosophy, and resistance to the state sanctioned evil of his day to the social evils of our own day, most especially the evil of state sanctioned abortion?

Certainly, Bonhoeffer's understanding of human history gave him prior knowledge of the existence and capability of human atrocities. So his premeditated renunciation of pacifism surely wasn't based upon a naïve belief that the nonviolent teachings and example of Christ had somehow been pragmatically effective throughout history until Hitler suddenly came along. Of course, these issues are always merely academic until they are happening to *us,* or until they are happening to *our* neighbors in *our* midst. It is then that our theology is truly put to the test.

But Bonhoeffer was not driven by the capricious winds of existential subjectivity. He was always attuned to the objective Christian principle which dictates that love for God is inseparable from love and compassion for "the least of these." Whether it was the suffering of African Americans in the United States or the suffering of Jews in Nazi Germany, Bonhoeffer always felt compelled to offer a sacrificial solidarity with the victims of injustice and evil.

So while I disagree with Bonhoeffer's final course of action against the Nazi "final solution" (if indeed it is true that he was involved in a conspiracy to assassinate Hitler), I nevertheless respect and admire the fact that he truly cared enough to *do something.* I respect the fact that he loved the oppressed enough to attempt to liberate them, even though I reject the Machiavellian spirit of "liberation theology." We know that "liberation theology" is a theological construct that began to be prominently articulated only a few years after Bonhoeffer's murder. And many liberation theologians have used Bonhoeffer's apparent example as justification for their own violent revolutionary causes. In fact, I think an argument could be made that Dietrich Bonhoeffer was unwittingly the founder of "liberation theology," although I think he would be the first to denounce the perverse and violent interpretations of a false gospel perpetuated in the name of "liberation."

But what disturbs me so much about our admiration for Bonhoeffer is that a comparable evil is happening today, right now, in our own American midst. The ashes of slain unborn children rise from the chimneys of American abortuaries, but we don't do anything about it. And shame on those who invoke the specious and inane "Godwin's Law" "argument." That is no argument at all. The comparison here is more than valid. The reasons for the Jewish holocaust and the holocaust of the unborn may be different, but the fact is that our neighbors are being unjustly and systematically slaughtered all the same. And the same demonic spirit of dehumanization has been the impetus for the evils of slavery, genocide, and "abortion on demand."

And this is why I think Bonhoeffer's theology, thought, and actions are so important for us today. And this is also precisely why I am a pacifist. Because if violence is ever justified to save innocent lives, then surely it is justified to save the most innocent and defenseless members of the human race. If it is permissible to premeditatedly kill some lives in order to save other lives, then surely it is permissible to kill Hitler to save Jews and to kill abortionists to save innocent unborn children. But Christ says *"No!"* He says, *"Put away thy sword!"* [St. Matthew 26:52] And He didn't issue any qualifications or exceptions to that command. Christ was the most innocent and holy person who ever lived. He was God in the flesh. And yet He rebuked the one who sought to defend His innocent life with violent force.

It has been asked of me: "Well, if all of our reasons tend to go back to Christian language, then how do we make the case to a non-Christian that an unborn baby is a human life?"

And this is truly the crux of the issue, as it has always been with every human rights issue throughout the course of history. The philosophies of this world will always make distinctions between the "worthy" of humanity and the "disposable" of humanity. The godless will always promote specious and subjective determinations about which human lives are truly human and which human lives are not. Yet, for the Christian, all human life is sacred – from the moment of conception.

But more than being a matter of mere religious conviction, I would also point to clear biological evidence. You don't have to believe in God to believe in biology. And the biological fact is that at the moment of conception a unique and nascent human life comes into existence. Now, we can argue about the ethics, morality, and philosophy of whether or not that nascent human life deserves the same protection and rights as all other human beings; but there's no denying that biologically speaking a new human life exists from the moment of conception. And if we deny protection and rights to some human lives, then we have no objective basis to provide protection and rights to other human lives. And it seems that even atheists who have even a cursory familiarity with history can acknowledge that horrific social evils have occurred throughout the world whenever some human lives have been deemed to be less human than others. Which is why there are now more and more Pro-Life atheists. You don't have to be religious to understand the basic humanitarian principle of *"live and let live."*

Dred Scott was only considered 3/5ths of a person. Jews were considered to be vermin by the Nazis. And on and on, throughout history, we see the evils that result from the "legal" dehumanization of human lives. And today the unborn have been "legally" dehumanized. And no evil in history has destroyed as many innocent lives as legal abortion.

As I have written: *"With clarity and convenience people condemn the injustices of the past while they gladly contribute to the injustices of the present."* In other words, we all want to pretend that we would have been abolitionists during the days of slavery, that we would have been voices of resistance in Nazi Germany, that we would have opposed segregation in America and Apartheid in South Africa. But meanwhile, the unborn are slaughtered by the thousands daily, and in our very own cities. And those of us who are bothered by this evil do little to nothing about it, while most others wholeheartedly condone and support the legality of this horror.

We have always been a society of selective moral outrage and convenient social posturing. And whenever the prophets and abolitionists dare to arise in our midst, we do all we can to silence them. But God always sides with the conscientious few over the gutless many. The crowd may silence the prophets today, but the prophets shall have the last word in eternity. Although the Nazis unjustly executed Dietrich Bonhoeffer, his theological and social truth lives on forever.

Many have argued: *"Which is more effective, killing abortionists or trying to win hearts and minds? Killing abortionists would only make abortion stronger; indeed, it already has. So, we should reject violence against abortionists for both moral and strategic reasons. It does less good for the cause."*

Well, the problem with that argument is that it loses sight of the individual neighbors who are being led away to imminent death right here and right now. I imagine that Dietrich Bonhoeffer probably encountered similar arguments. I expect that some people believed that killing Hitler would only make him into a martyr and therefore ultimately strengthen the Nazi cause. But Bonhoeffer's main concern was to save his neighbors who were destined for imminent slaughter. Yes, Bonhoeffer was passionately wedded to the anti-Nazi cause, but his first priority was saving innocent lives. For Bonhoeffer, the ultimate question was not *"What is best for the cause?"* but rather *"How would I want someone to react and respond if I was being led away to a violent and unjust death?"*

And that's the same selfless and sacrificial mindset that some people, such as Paul Hill, use to justify killing abortionists. And the reality is that Paul Hill saved innocent lives on the day that he killed that baby killer. Innocent unborn babies were spared from abortion that morning. Who knows whether or not their mothers still had abortions later on? Perhaps they did. Perhaps they didn't. But Paul Hill's primary goal was to violently spare innocent lives that were being led away to violent deaths at that particular hour. And in that regard, he succeeded. He killed a life to save lives. That is the fact of the matter. And before we condemn his actions (or Bonhoeffer's), we should first ask ourselves how we would feel about someone who violently intervened to save our own lives from murder.

Paul Hill argued that, *"Whatever force is justified in defending the life of a **born** child is also justified in defending the life of an **unborn** child."* And upon his arrest he said: *"Now is the time to defend the unborn as to defend a slave that's about to be murdered."* Hill's last words before he was executed were: *"If you believe abortion is a lethal force, you should oppose that force and do what you have to do to stop it. May God help you to protect the unborn as you yourself would want to be protected."*

Now, do I agree with Paul Hill's violent actions? NO! A thousand times NO! Because his actions were not in line with the teachings and example of Jesus. And also because the abortionist, as evil as he may be, is no less our neighbor than the unborn child. And just as I would have argued with Paul Hill that the abortionist is our neighbor, I would have also argued with Dietrich Bonhoeffer that Hitler too is our neighbor. And therefore, killing abortionists or killing Hitler (or killing anyone else for any reason at all) is an unchristian act. But I would also adamantly argue that we should oppose evil, resist evil, condemn evil, and even sacrifice our own lives to stop evil; but we should never kill the evil person. Because the evil individual can always be redeemed.

The scriptures are replete with stories of the redemption of wicked men and wicked nations, (the Book of Jonah particularly comes to mind.) As Dr. Martin Luther King, Jr. said:

"The ultimate weakness of violence is that it is a descending spiral, begetting the very thing it seeks to destroy. Instead of diminishing evil, it multiplies it. Through violence you may murder the liar, but you cannot murder the lie, nor establish the truth.

Through violence you may murder the hater, but you do not murder hate. In fact, violence merely increases hate. And so it goes. Returning violence for violence multiplies violence, adding deeper darkness to a night already devoid of stars. Darkness cannot drive out darkness: only light can do that. Hate cannot drive out hate: only love can do that."

Now, to be fair, neither Bonhoeffer nor Paul Hill was motivated by vengeance or hate. They both made it very clear that their actions were purely defensive, not retributive. But again, we are confronted with Our Lord's response to St. Peter when he took out his sword to defend God in the flesh. Our Lord condemned his actions with an unequivocal and universal rebuke: *"Put away thy sword, for all who live by the sword shall perish by the sword." [St. Matthew 26:52]*

And this is the hard truth of the Gospel with which we have to wrestle. Our enemies are no less our neighbors than the innocent victims that they oppress and kill. Not to mention that killing the enemy doesn't destroy the enemy, it merely emboldens the enemy. But for the disciples of Christ, the pragmatic success or failure of loving our enemies is not the deciding factor. We are simply commanded to love *all*, regardless of the outcome. Our Lord did not commission us to love some more than others, and He certainly didn't commission us to kill some to save others.

And yet the devil is all too happy to have us embrace a righteous cause as long as we're willing to sacrifice innocent lives in pursuit of that cause. And that's the difference between the politician and the true spiritual revolutionary. The politician is willing to prioritize a social cause over the lives of innocent people, but revolutionaries prioritize the sanctity of human lives above all other social causes. Thus, beware of those who promote the "welfare of humanity" at the expense of individual human beings.

So, as Bonhoeffer rightly said, we must become "spokes in the wheel" in order to stop the wheels of evil, death, and destruction. But I would argue that we can become spokes in the wheel without violence and killing, as Gandhi, Dr. King, Dorothy Day, the Berrigan brothers, and many other less famous pacifists clearly demonstrated.

And at this point I must clearly reiterate: I *do not* agree with using violence to stop abortion! I cannot emphasize this strongly enough! I condemn violence against abortionists in no uncertain terms. I am simply trying to point out that until we personalize all of these various "social issues," then we will never really understand them. As long as the evil and injustice is happening to "them," then our response will always be inadequate. But once we realize that the "them" are us, then we will think and act and pray and respond differently.

And that's what Bonhoeffer and Paul Hill (and John Brown and Nat Turner and some of the Black Panthers and some of those in the "Black Lives Matter" movement) did. They personalized the great evils of their time. And then they acted as if their own lives were at stake. They believed they were loving their neighbors as themselves. And they were. The only problem is that again, as I have already pointed out, they failed to realize that the oppressor was no less their neighbor than the oppressed. And so they decided to kill one neighbor in an effort to save another neighbor. And while that makes sense on a purely human level, it diametrically contradicts the ethic of the Gospel.

So where does that leave us? How do we respond to the evil in our midst? How do we respond to the grave social injustices of our own day and age?

Well, first of all, we must personalize these issues, as the Good Samaritan did. We must identify ourselves with "them." We must view "their" suffering as our own. We must truly take the Golden Rule to heart: *"And just as you want men to do unto you, so do likewise unto them." [St. Luke 6:31]*

I am convinced that authentic Christian nonviolent activism can accomplish three things:

1) It can save and liberate human lives today, right here and right now.

2) It can help change hearts and minds, and it can shape the social consciousness of the culture in a positive way.

3) It can overturn evil hearts and redeem the souls of the oppressors.

There are two equally erroneous responses to the problem of evil: the first is *apathy*, and the second is *violence*. But Our Lord Jesus Christ showed us that with militant nonviolence and sacrificial love the gates of hell will be forever vanquished. So let's rise up and fight for justice and truth and peace, with the weapons of justice and truth and peace. And I feel confident that Dietrich Bonhoeffer would certainly be down with that.

"No one in the whole world can change the truth. One can only look for the truth, find it and serve it. The truth is in all places."
~Dietrich Bonhoeffer ~

"If the world refuses justice, the Christian will pursue mercy. And if the world takes refuge in lies, he will open his mouth for the voiceless and bear witness to the truth. For the sake of the brother – be he Jew or Greek, bond or free, strong or weak, noble or base – he will renounce the world. For the Christian serves the fellowship of the Body of Christ, and he cannot hide it from the world. He is called out of the world to follow Christ." ~ Dietrich Bonhoeffer ~

*"How does peace come about? Will it come through a system of political treaties? Will it come through the investment of international capital in different countries? Will it come through universal rearmament in order to guarantee peace? No. It won't come through any of these, for the sole reason that in all of these peace is confused for security. But there is no way to peace along the way of safety. So how will peace come? Who will call us to peace so that the world will hear, will **have** to hear? Only the one great ecumenical council of the holy Church of Christ all over the world can speak out so that the world, though it gnash its teeth, will have to hear, so that the peoples will rejoice because the Church of Christ in the name of Christ has taken the weapons from the hands of their sons, forbidden war, and proclaimed the peace of Christ against the raging world."*
~ Dietrich Bonhoeffer ~

* [See the book, *Bonhoeffer the Assassin?: Challenging the Myth, Recovering His Call to Peacemaking*, by Mark Thiessen Nation, Anthony G. Siegrist, Daniel P. Umbel, and Stanley Hauerwas.]

1,038. ~ **THE BEAUTY, BLESSING, and DIVERSITY of THE CHURCH** ~

In the Orthodox Church we have liberals and conservatives, Democrats and Republicans, socialists and capitalists, pacifists and "just war" theorists, ecumenists and fundamentalists. And I have learned to see the blessing and beauty in this diversity. If we seek a religion that caters to our subjective philosophical beliefs and our individual biblical interpretations, then at best we will flail in the stale waters of heterodoxy and at worst we will drown in the dark morass of cultic heresies. The Body of Christ has always been full of tensions and disputes and controversies and mistakes. But at the foot of the Cross and in the fellowship of the Holy Eucharist we all find unity, peace, and salvation.

1,039. ~ **SPEAKING and SILENCE** ~

Speak about politics and you will receive political responses.

Speak about religion and you will receive religious responses.

Speak about controversy and you will receive controversial responses.

Speak about justice and poverty and truth and rights and you will receive feedback on justice, poverty, truth, and rights.

Speak your opinion and you will receive opinions.

But whatever you do, *never* speak about your own financial hardships. You will receive nothing but deafening silence in return.

1,040. ~ **BABYLON CAN'T CONQUER ZION!** ~

Babylon can't conquer Zion! The devil is spewing his last gasp. The Kingdom of God is among us. We have hope. We have salvation. Let us proclaim it! Let us live it! And when we've said all there is to say, let us know that there is always more work to do. But let us ever labor with faith and joy in our hearts.

1,041. ~ CHURCH and STATE ~

When the Church supports the state, empowers the state, or cooperates with the state then it ceases to be the Church, because the witness of the Gospel is perpetually opposed to the machinations of violence, coercion, intimidation, and force. And whether the state is governed by the tyranny of fascism, the tyranny of communism, the tyranny of monarchy, or the tyranny of democracy, it is always governed by the sword. And the Blood of Christ shall always stand in opposition to the bloodshed of men. The true Church therefore has no more to do with the state than lambs have to do with wolves. It is not a matter of the separation of Church and state; it is a matter of the Church being a perpetual prophetic witness against the state.

[And I say this as a baptized Ethiopian Orthodox Tewahedo Christian. Ethiopia is a unique historical example in that it was a Christian monarchy for approximately 1500 years. In my first book, ***MYSTERY AND MEANING: Christian Philosophy & Orthodox Meditations***, I argued that the Ethiopian theocratic monarchy was God's intention for human government, and I saw many benefits and blessings that appeared to be associated with the Ethiopian monarchy. However, my thoughts have changed somewhat over time. Not that I condemn the Ethiopian monarchy, but I no longer view any human government that relies on the sword as compatible with the Christian gospel. I realize that this position puts me at odds with many, if not most, of my fellow Orthodox Christian brethren. And that's OK. Christians don't always have to agree on everything. His Imperial Majesty Emperor Haile Selassie will always have a special place in my heart. In many ways his teachings and example led me to the Orthodox Christian Faith. So I will always have deep respect and great admiration for him. But Christ alone is my Savior; and the teachings

and example of Christ are what I must embrace and follow above all
else.]

1,042. ~ IN POLITICS THERE ARE NO "GOOD GUYS" ~

In politics there are no "good guys." And the sooner you realize it
the freer you will be. Evil thrives on your naivety, and the more you
vote the more you enable and empower your own demise.

1,043. ~ MIRACLE WORKERS ~

God often uses His children to perform His miracles. After all,
the purpose of God's miracles is to reveal His presence and to
manifest His love. God sent me a miracle today – through the
kindness, generosity, and love of a friend who I've never even met
face to face. This miracle was an answer to the prayers of many other
people who have been interceding for me during a very difficult time
in my life. One of God's children listened to His voice and reached
out to bless me. And I received that blessing with humility, gratitude,
and faith. And I pray that I will now work harder to bless others in
whatever ways that I can.

Never hesitate to do good whenever you can for whoever you
can. And never underestimate the power of prayer and the power of
an encouraging word. My deepest gratitude to all those that have
prayed for me, that have offered me their words of strength and
peace, and that have reached out to me in whatever ways they could. I
give thanks for these miracle workers.

Tomorrow my soul may be again be filled with grief, pain, worry,
and doubt; but today I am filled with tears of gratefulness and a heart
of thanksgiving.

1,044. ~ UNKNOWN and UNNAMED ~

What are the names
of those unknown
who fought for truth
but all alone,
on playgrounds
and schoolyards
holding their own?

What are the names
of the little babes
who fought for lives
they couldn't save,
cut down
and silenced
with wombs for graves?

What are the names
of the pure and meek
who loved mercy
and peace did seek,
abused and killed
for the love
they preached?

The blessed unknown
the blessed unnamed...
these shall inherit
the earth all the same.

1,045. ~ **MY JESUS** ~

Who sent me angels?
My Jesus did.
Who sent me love?
My Jesus did.
Who sent me miracles?
My Jesus did.
Who sent me hope?
My Jesus did.
Who sent me manna?
My Jesus did.
Who sent me life?
My Jesus did.
Who sent me brotherhood?
My Jesus did.
Who sent me peace?
My Jesus did.
Who sent me truth?
My Jesus did.
Who sent me kindness?
My Jesus did.
Who sent me light?
My Jesus did.
Who sent me faith?
My Jesus did.
Who sent me mercy?
My Jesus did.

Yes...
Through many crosses
my Jesus has sent me abundant blessings.

And now He sends me to bless others.

Please Lord,
give me the strength to go forth and serve.

(Dedicated to all the people who have loved me and prayed for me and helped me in my times of need.
Please keep praying for this sinner!)

1,046. ~ KNOWLEDGE of SELF / KNOWLEDGE of OTHERS ~

While sincere introspection and deep personal reflection – i.e. "knowledge of self" – are vital, we must also know that Christ constantly points us toward others. We must strive to know ourselves so that we can effectively love and serve our fellow man. And in loving and serving our fellow man we will truly come to know ourselves.

"Love God and love others" – these are the two great commandments. True knowledge of self and true love of self are discovered in love for the Creator and love for all people created in His image. The deeper we look within, the more clearly we will see the needs of our neighbors. And the more we go out and serve our neighbors, the more clearly we will see and understand ourselves.

True mountaintop enlightenment will always lead the enlightened one back down to the streets. The saint who truly sees God will also see the suffering of his brothers and sisters. Those who are attuned to heaven will also be attuned to the human. Abraham, Moses, and Jesus spoke with God on mountains, but then they came back down to set things right. And it's worth noting that even Our resurrected Lord will come to earth again to perfect and restore all things.

True metaphysical meditation will always lead to true human mediation. To dwell in the Garden of paradise is to get comfortable with the grit and grime of the earth. The spiritual is inextricably linked to the social.

1,047. ~ UNLESS YOU CONDEMN IT ALL... ~

If you invoke the rhetoric of "all lives matter" in an attempt to diminish the injustices and pain suffered by one segment of humanity, then you don't understand what it means to be authentically Pro-Life. And, likewise, if your litany of social justice causes only includes some members of humanity but not all human lives, then you don't understand the meaning of social justice. I find it tragic that people are somehow able to make a false moral distinction between innocent

Black lives cut down by policemen's bullets and innocent Black lives murdered by mercenary abortionists. Unless you decry and condemn it all, I have little use for your selective political moralizing.

1,048. ~ SUPPLY and DEMAND ~

Supply and demand. It exists because you want it to exist. There is no circus without your patronization, and there is no political corruption without your electoral participation. So don't curse that which you willfully and obstinately contribute to. You're the one who votes for misery, and then you curse those of us who are trying to set you free.

1,049. ~ WITHOUT EXPECTATION ~

Speak words of peace, life, love, and truth. But don't expect to receive words of peace, life, love, and truth in return – at least not in *this* life.

1,050. ~ PERSONAL FAITH and POLITICAL CONVICTIONS ~

If your personal spiritual faith doesn't deeply shape your social and political convictions, then your faith is feckless and your convictions are hollow. Don't tell me how much you love God while you support the violent destruction of human beings created in His very image. But this is the specious refrain of the political wolves: *"I personally believe in what's right, but I can't impose what's right on others."* And then, once elected, they do everything they can to violently impose the wrong.

1,051. ~ HOW WILL I BE JUDGED? ~

Will I be judged by my kindness or by my callousness?

Will I be judged by the forgiveness I gave or by the grudges I held?

Will I be judged by my loyalty to the cause or by my betrayal of Christ?

Will I be judged by the lives I saved or by the lives I destroyed?

Will I be judged by my adoration or by my adultery?

Will I be judged by the Jesus I preached or by the junk that I sold?

All I know is that I will be judged by the fire of God's love. That is my hope, and that is my fear.

1,052. ~ ABORTION ~

Abortion is a very difficult issue to discuss. People get very emotional about it. Abortion has affected many people in our society, and not just the women who have abortions or the innocent babies that are violently aborted. It also affects men and fathers who have no say in whether their babies live or die. It robs grandparents of grandchildren and brothers and sisters of brothers and sisters. It also enables rapists and pedophiles to commit their evil deeds while covering up their crimes with a "legal" act of violence.

Abortion has not only murdered 55 million innocent unborn babies since it was federally legalized in 1973, but it has also irrevocably scarred and wounded the women who have had abortions. Many women have also died from these ostensibly "safe, rare, and legal" abortions. (And the only part of that equation that accurately applies is the "legal" part. Abortion nevertheless remains frequent and dangerous. And the capitalistic abortion industry doesn't care a whit about making abortion safe or rare. The more abortions the better, because more abortions means more profit for the abortionists.)

Abortion never solves or accomplishes anything, other than death. And how can we find peace in violence and death? Killing is never a solution to our problems.

Life is never easy. Life is indeed a struggle. But where there is life there is always hope. But the violent negation of life always leads to sorrow and despair. And this is exactly the devil's intention, for he was a liar and a murderer from the beginning. (St. John 8:44)

Pursuing peace, affirming life, and loving our neighbors – and even our enemies – are very difficult things to do. But it is a grave evil to oppress, violate, or kill another human being in order to advance our own interests and personal desires. My rights end where your life begins. True individual freedom never infringes upon the freedom or lives of others. It's a simple and age old concept: *"live and let live."*

I would also point out that the foundations of Planned Parenthood and the abortion industry are rooted in racism. That's why the majority of abortion clinics in America are located in "minority" communities. Abortion is the perpetuation of Margaret Sanger's eugenics nightmare, another manifestation of the systemic racism that continues to plague this wicked nation.

Every pregnancy involves at least three lives: the life of the mother, the life of the father, and the life of the baby. So abortion is not merely a "women's issue." Abortion is a *human* issue. And like all human rights issues, it affects the very soul of society. As Dr. Martin Luther King, Jr. said: *"Injustice anywhere is a threat to justice everywhere. Whatever affects one directly affects all indirectly."*

Therefore, I oppose abortion not only because it murders innocent babies, but also because it violates and scars the women who have abortions (and I have known many.) I oppose abortion not only because it violates the rights of the unborn, but also because it damages the social psyche of our culture. I oppose abortion not only because it contradicts the "consistent life ethic," but also because it is rooted in the insidious ideology of racism and discrimination.

In summation: I believe in peace, tolerance, and human rights; and abortion is the most violent, intolerant, and inhumane practice ever conceived by man.

"This day I call the heavens and the earth as witnesses against you: that I have set before you life and death, blessings and curses. Now choose life, so that you and your children may live." *[Deuteronomy 30:19]*

1,053. ~ THE ONE THING EVERY CHRISTIAN CAN DO ~

We might not be able to preach. We might not be able to fast. We might not be able to be missionaries or monks. We might not be able to feed the poor, shelter the homeless, or heal the sick. We might not even be able to go to Church. There are some things that even as Christians we just might not be able to do. But there is one thing that every Christian certainly *can* do, and that is *NOT KILL*.

1,054. ~ BORN IN THE GARDEN ~

I was born in the Garden
and I want to go back.
But Babylon is calling,
and I keep falling.
And I keep trying to stand
when I should be crawling...
towards the Cross,
towards the Tree of Life.

1,055. ~ DON'T PREACH THE CROSS ~

Don't preach against racism, because that might offend racists.

Don't preach against economic inequality, because that might offend the rich.

Don't preach against war, because that might offend soldiers.

Don't preach against abortion, because that might offend those who have had abortions.

Don't preach against politics, because that might offend politicians.

Don't preach against police brutality, because that might offend the police.

Don't preach against social injustice, because that might offend the unjust.

Don't preach against the government, because you might lose your tax exempt status.

So go ahead and preach, but don't dare preach the Cross. Because if you do, there might not be anyone left to preach to.

1,056. ~ AGAINST THE TROOPS / FOR THE PEOPLE ~

I am against the troops because I am for the people. And I will do all I can to persuade people to de-enlist from the military and enlist in the brotherhood of humanity. It is precisely because I love those in uniform that I desire for them to trade their badges and bullets for Christ and the Cross. How can I condemn war while supporting the troops that make war possible? How can I truly love soldiers unless I tell them to repent of their soldiering?

1,057. ~ BREAD, BULLETS, and FREEDOM ~

As long as anyone anywhere in the world feels the need to procure bread with bullets, then none of us are truly free or truly fed.

1,058. ~ A REFLECTION of THEIR OWN TORMENTED SOULS ~

God didn't suffer and die on the Cross for the "worthless." He died for human beings created in His very image. And we are all created in His divine image. So never let anyone make you feel less valuable than you really are. Regardless of your sins, your errors, your mistakes, or your crimes, God views you as more valuable than gold. Yes, cruel and hateful words do sting sometimes, but don't confuse such scorn for the truth. Forgive and love those that curse you. Their hatred is merely a reflection of their own tormented souls.

1,059. ~ THE MYSTERIES of LIFE and LOVE ~

Show me a person who has never known anger, and I will show you a person who has never known pain. Show me a person who has never known pain, and I will show you a person who has never loved. Show me a person who has never loved, and I will show you a person who has never truly lived.

Life hurts and love hurts, and sometimes unbearably so. But we keep on living and we keep on loving, because in spite of the pain, we find our greatest joy and our deepest peace in these glorious and agonizing mysteries of life and love.

1,060. ~ FREEDOM ~

Free from prison
But he's broke
And he's worrying
So he begs for work
But gets arrested
For loitering

1,061. ~ LAW and SUBMISSION ~

Every human law instituted by every human government in every human nation in every human era has been humanly "legal." So forgive me if I refuse to respect or submit to your damnable "law and order." I serve one divine King and one heavenly Kingdom, and that alone determines my obedience and submission.

1,062. ~ THANK GOD for THE CONSCIOUS ONES ~

Thank God for the conscious ones. There are many amongst us, believe me. Their voices are often drowned out by the cacophony of the politically brainwashed choirs, but their truth nevertheless remains unabated and unmoved. Consider the prophet Elijah, who thought he was the only one who had not fallen prey to idolatry. But JAH told him, *"I have 7,000 in Israel that have not bowed their knees to Baal." [I Kings 19:18]*

So don't despair over the voices of fools. Though they be loud and ubiquitous, they are empty and impotent. JAH's servants are holding firm, chanting down Babylon and watching her fall. The divine army is small, but it is eternally victorious.

"Fret not thyself because of evildoers, neither be thou envious of the workers of iniquity." [Psalm 37:1]

1,063. ~ BADASS ~

Any fool can be a badass with a gun in his hand. Put down your weapons and take up the Cross, and then we'll see how tough you really are.

1,064. ~ CONQUERING DEMONS ~

When we conquer the demons in the mirror, we conquer hell.

1,065. ~ POLITICS and THEOLOGY DON'T MIX ~

Politics and theology don't mix. What does Zion have to do with Babylon? What does Christ have to do with Caesar? What does the Kingdom of heaven have to do with the kingdoms of this world? Dear Christian, you cannot serve two masters.

1,066. ~ THANKFUL for THE PRIESTS & PROPHETS & PRAYER WARRIORS ~

I am thankful for all the priests and prophets and prayer warriors who faithfully intercede for me and hold me accountable in a non-judgmental and loving manner. I desperately need and appreciate their encouragement and rebuke. Please keep praying for this sinner. I am so weak and too often consumed by my passions. But the love of the brethren heals and strengthens me. May God help me to be more faithful in the life of corporate liturgical prayer and sacramental communion. How can I possibly hope to live without it?

1,067. ~ REVOLUTION ~

The revolution is ours for the taking,
but we're busier voting
than fasting and praying.
The revolution has already been won,
we will win with the Cross
but we'll lose with the gun.

1,068. ~ BRUCE ~

Let me tell you about a true hero. His name is Bruce Stuckey, and I am blessed to call him my friend. Bruce has been a Pro-Life activist for more than two decades. He has stood faithfully on the periphery of abortion clinics offering words of peace, life, love, and authentic Christian assistance – along with his constant prayers. In the face of death and despair and violence and evil, Bruce never loses his cool. He never veers from the path of love. He responds to insults and injury with compassion and grace.

I have stood with him on many occasions, and I have often lost my temper and allowed the words and actions of evildoers to elicit unchristian and uncharitable responses from me. The callousness and cruelty of misogynistic men dragging women into abortion clinics vexes my spirit, and I have not always been able to respond to such cowardice in a Christ-like manner. But I have never seen brother Bruce get out of the Spirit. Whenever I lost my temper, Bruce would always come and gently rebuke me, reminding me that Jesus is in control and that our job is simply to be ambassadors of Christ.

I have seen Bruce cursed and reviled and abused for simply trying to save lives and help poor women in dire need. But he never responds to evil with evil. Bruce is a true Christian warrior, fighting injustice and death and oppression with the weapons of truth and love and life. He is a genuine hero and a genuine friend. In the fight to save the innocent and bring an end to the scourge of abortion, Bruce Stuckey is an example that we should all follow. Please keep him and all other life-affirming, peacemaking activists in your prayers.

1,069. ~ KILLING TO MAKE A LIVING ~

If you have to violently destroy other human lives simply so you can personally make a profit, then your work and career are the labors of hell. Nothing is more demonic than killing to make a living. So don't enlist! Don't deploy! Better to be poor and enter heaven than to be cast out by the angels with your blood soaked riches. The military is the devil's domain, and Christ has nothing to do with it. Don't fool yourself.

1,070. ~ ELECTIONS or INSURRECTION? ~

Just know this: if everyone voted there would only be more elections, but if nobody voted that would be insurrection. And insurrection is not necessarily violent. To refuse to add fuel to the violent systemic order is the essence of nonviolent Christian rebellion. As long as they can keep us voting then they can keep us enslaved.

Most people in America will live and suffer and go to their graves voting for "change." How long will you continue to willfully participate in your own bondage? When you pull the lever in the voting booth, you become your own executioner. You're like the mouse in the maze that is rewarded with cheese but never escapes his cage.

1,071. ~ NEVER SHAME LIFE ~

Life is never wrong, never shameful, never a curse, never a sin. Life is always a blessing. Stop treating unwed pregnant women with judgment and scorn. The lives they bear are no less valuable than your own. Love them, support them, and give thanks to God for the fruit they are bringing into the world. Those who shame life dare to shame the Creator.

1,072. ~ WHAT IS REVOLUTION? ~

What is revolution? It is simply the refusal to hate and kill and oppress and conquer. It is rebellion against all forms of violence and imperialism. It is the rejection of the forceful imposition of the will of the powerful over the will of the weak.

Revolution is resistance to any philosophy that elevates the rights of some over the rights of others. This is why the true revolutionaries stand in militant opposition to the evils of racism, war, capitalistic exploitation, abortion, and sexual and religious discrimination. It is also why the true revolutionaries never attempt to set up their own violent, authoritarian governmental structures.

There simply is no such thing as a "revolutionary government." Those that overthrow one system of oppression in order to set up another system of oppression are not true insurrectionists. There is nothing truly revolutionary about little red books or little red stars on cute little black berets.

As soon as you make the conscious choice to shed blood or to cooperate with blood-shedders, then you become the very power against which the collective human soul intuitively and irrepressibly rebels.

1,073. ~ POWER and PROTEST ~

When those with power and privilege tell you that you're protesting the wrong way, then that's a great indication that you're probably protesting the right way.

1,074. ~ WHO'S TO BLAME FOR WAR? ~

Q. Who's to blame for war?
A. Those who justify, defend, and rationalize war.

Yes, it really is that simple.

The pain of sin and the consequences of evil are hell enough. No one escapes the judgment in this life. Do you suppose that the wicked are happy? Do you suppose that earthly riches and carnal pleasures can quench the fires that scorch the sinful heart? The fear of eternal hell is no threat to the soul that suffers in the eternal now.

Yes, our God is indeed a consuming fire (Hebrews 12:29); but His fire is love (I John 4:8). And His mercy endureth forever (Psalm 136).

So away with these demons of guilt and fear and damnation and wrath! The Cross has saved us all! Rejoice in the love and mercy of your Redeemer!

"The love of God is the fire of hell." ~ St. Isaac the Syrian ~

1,076. ~ A CONTEMPORARY TRANSLATION of FIRST SAMUEL CHAPTER 8 ~

So all the American Christian people gathered together and said: "We must vote for someone to lead us, such as all the other nations have."

But when they said, "Give us a president to lead us," this displeased the prophets. So the prophets prayed to the Lord. And the Lord told the prophets: "Listen to all that the people are saying to you; it is not you they have rejected, but they have rejected me as their ruler. As they have done from the day I brought them up out of bondage until this day, forsaking me and serving other gods, so they are doing to you. Now listen to them; but warn them solemnly and let them know what these politicians who will "lead" them will claim as their rights."

So the prophets told all the words of the Lord to the people who were voting for presidents and governors and mayors and senators. They said, "This is what your political rulers will claim as their rights: They will take your sons and daughters and make them serve their armies and wars while they themselves luxuriate in comfort and security. Some they will assign to be commanders of thousands and commanders of fifties, and others they will assign to build their prisons and jails, and still others will be appointed to build bombs and missiles and weapons of mass destruction. They will take your daughters to be their interns. They will take the best oilfields and goldmines and lands from other nations and declare them their own. They will take portions of your hard earned money and use it to enrich themselves and their friends. They will tax you and take from you and censor you and silence you until you become their slaves. And when that day comes, you will cry out for relief from the very people that *you* have chosen. But the Lord will not answer you in that day."

But the Christian people refused to listen to their prophets. "No!" they said. "We want to vote for a president! We want to be a democracy like the other nations, with someone to lead us and fight for us against our enemies." When the prophets heard all that the people said, they repeated it before the Lord. And the Lord answered: "Listen to them and let them go ahead and vote for their political rulers."

1,077. ~ THE ONLY RESPONSES TO EVIL? ~

If you think the only responses to evil are to either resort to violence or to do nothing at all, then you haven't read the Gospels. Jesus and His disciples and the apostles and the saints and the martyrs throughout history were neither violent nor apathetic. Those led by the Holy Spirit are the greatest revolutionaries, sacrificing their own welfare and blood and lives without destroying the welfare and lives of others. As Tertullian wrote: *"The blood of the martyrs is the seed of the Church."*

1,078. ~ "DISQUALIFIED"? ~

Anyone who tells you that you are "disqualified" for ministry is obviously not qualified to opine. The fact is that regardless of your sins and failures and mistakes, in the eyes of God you are never disqualified from praising His name and serving your fellow man. Any ostensible "ministry" that is predicated on anything other than loving God and loving others is not a ministry of Jesus. Yes, sadly, the arrogance and vanity of human opinions may lead you to believe that God can no longer use you. But that is a lie born from hell. If your "church" or your pastor or your organization or your "ministry" kicks you to the curb, know that God is still with you and He is still able to use you for the service of His Kingdom. So just shake the dust from your feet and keep on moving in the love and mercy of Our Lord Jesus Christ. You are always qualified to minister to your neighbor.

1,079. ~ WOLVES and SHEEP ~

Never trust wolves that tell you to fear the sheep.

1,080. ~ NOTHING OFFENDS THE FOOLISH MORE THAN THE ACTIONS of THE WISE ~

Those who build houses of straw curse those who build houses of sand. And those who build houses of sand curse those who build houses of straw. But they all join together to curse those that are building their houses upon the Rock. Because nothing offends the foolish more than the actions of the wise.

1,081. ~ REVOLUTIONARIES and CROSS-BEARERS ~

Revolutionaries and Cross-bearers will always suffer from opposition, betrayal, and splinters. In this criminal world, the righteous are considered criminals and the criminals are considered righteous. So keep fighting and agitating and praying for peace and love and justice and life to prevail. The Kingdom of Heaven is already among us (St. Luke 17:21). We need only to live it out.

1,082. ~ AFFLICTION and HEALING ~

The devil afflicts us with comforts and pleasures. God heals us with splinters and thorns.

1,083. ~ COMMUNION with THE CONDEMNED ~

Those that are condemned by society and laws and governments and rulers are the very ones with whom Christ calls us to have communion: the poor, the oppressed, the marginalized, and the dehumanized. To have fellowship with the community of the outcasts is to have communion with Christ. As Dietrich Bonhoeffer wrote:

"The exclusion of the weak and insignificant, the seemingly useless people, from everyday Christian life in community may actually mean the exclusion of Christ; for in them, Christ is knocking at the door."

1,084. ~ REVOLUTION IS... ~

Revolution is Black and White, young and old, clergy and laity, religious and secular, patriot and anarchist all rebelling in nonviolent solidarity against inhumanity, violence, oppression, and death.

1,085. ~ FLEE FROM THE IDOLATRY of THE VOTING BOOTH! ~

Flee from the idolatry of the voting booth! Resist the temptation to fuel Babylon's folly. Don't let anyone intimidate you, pressure you, or guilt you into voting. There is absolutely nothing in Scripture or Church Teaching that dictates that we must participate in these worldly political processes. In fact, the weight of the Gospels and the weight of apostolic Tradition urge us to trust not in politicians or worldly governments. As the Psalmist declares: *"Put not your trust in princes, in human beings, who cannot save." [Psalm 146:3]*

So stay away from the polls on Election Day, without apology. And instead of voting, go out and do some real good. Love your neighbors, serve your brothers, help the homeless, speak up for the unborn, feed the poor, denounce militarism and war, agitate for justice and freedom, and show these godless politicians that you don't need them to change the things that really need to be changed. Remember what Leo Tolstoy wrote: *"Everyone thinks of changing the world, but no one thinks of changing themselves."*

And if anyone dares to condemn you because you didn't vote, just ask them what they did that day to truly help someone else. And when they stumble to come up with an answer, then simply tell them to keep their mindless political slavery to themselves, because you are free and you intend to stay that way!

"Political violence is mob violence. The larger the crowd, the more anonymous its violence. And the impunity of anonymity, like the impunity of authority, unleashes man's capacity for evil. Under the shielding anonymity of the lynch mob and the voting booth, any atrocity is on the table... Democratic politics is a vital power ritual for the government. It makes the government all-important, all-relevant, all-preoccupying; this is especially so during election season. Each side's enemy candidate is demonized as an existential menace who can only be warded off by throwing all support behind your party's candidate. "Candidate X is not perfect, but we must stop Candidate Y!" If your candidate wins power, you become doubly loyal to the regime to keep the enemy herds down. If your candidate loses, you become doubly determined to help your tribe regain its

grip on the levers of power. Dismantling the machine is the last thing on your mind. Using democratic politics to foment civil strife is how the government divides and more fully conquers its subjects."

~ Dan Sanchez ~

1,086. ~ THE WRONG WAY ~

Putting people in prison, sending people to war, and giving people access to guns and pornography and abortion are not the way to cultivate a peaceful, just, and humane society.

1,087. ~ THE OFFENSE of TRUE PEACE ~

True peace is never the result of apathy and indifference. True peace does not magically ensue from the refusal to challenge evil and condemn injustice. Today, in the Church, we hear much talk about "not judging." But we forget what the Scriptures say:

*"Judge not according to **appearances**, but judge with **righteous** judgment." [St. John 7:24]*

"He that is spiritual judges all things, yet he himself is judged of no man." [I Corinthians 2:15]

We have confused compassion for a lack of confrontation and conflict. We have confused mercy and grace for a lack of proclaiming "thou shalt not!" But authentic peace is never born from compromising with evil. The peace of Christ is a militant peace. It is born from a Cross. It is inherently confrontational. It is neither violent nor cowardly. True peace is the proactive and provocative proclamation of justice, life, mercy, and truth. The true peacemakers are usually so offensive to the world that they are inevitably crucified. But because theirs is a real peace, a deep peace, a divine peace, then their peace reverberates eternally.

1,088. ~ RESTORATION, REVIVAL, and REDEMPTION ~

We need to stop asking God to restore, revive, and redeem our nation. Instead, we need to ask Him to restore, revive, and redeem our own hearts. And when our own hearts are restored, revived, and redeemed, then we will no longer place our hope and trust where they do not belong. We will no longer seek salvation in the idolatry of politics, patriotism, and human government. We will become citizens of the Kingdom of Heaven; and as Babylon crumbles all around us, we will rejoice rather than weep.

1,089. ~ "SUPERHERO" ~

You are my superhero
That's why I vote for you
You'll keep me safe at night
With armies, bombs, and nukes

You are my superhero
How else would I survive?
You'll live to protect me
With war, abortion, and lies

You are my superhero
Opposed to those evil beasts
That dare to speak of truth
And teach me love and peace

You are my superhero
And I will praise your name
Worthy! Worthy are you!
I'll elect you to my shame

1,090. ~ TERMINATIONS ~

Birth terminates a pregnancy. Abortion terminates a life.

1,091. ~ WHERE THERE IS LIFE THERE IS HOPE ~

Where there is life there is hope. The negation of life is the negation of hope. Life is never easy. It's always a struggle; but it's always a blessing too. I pray for the day when we will stop trying to bomb and execute and abort our way to peace.

1,092. ~ THEOLOGY TRANSCENDENT ~

Most true theology transcends rational explanation. And most heresies are born from attempts to reduce the infinitely transcendent to finite human logic. Always defer to sacred mystery.

1,093. ~ BABYLON DEMANDS ~

Babylon demands that we submit to her violence, worship her armies, salute her flags, vote for her rulers, obey her death, permit her poverty, bow to her badges, affirm her abortions, and acquiesce with her lies. And those that reject such idolatry are ridiculed, cursed, imprisoned, and shot – all in the name of "freedom and justice for all."

1,094. ~ OUR DAUGHTERS ~

Our daughters are delicate flowers that we must raise to be lions – gentle, graceful, meek, and kind, but standing firm as militant soldiers of Zion. Let modesty be their armor and submission be their weapon. And when the wolves of Babylon approach, then they shall rise up and roar and conquer!

1,095. ~ TO HELL WITH YOUR HELL! ~

To hell with your hell! Hell was created for the devil and his demons (St. Matthew 25:41). Hell is not our human abode. Hell is not our human destiny. We were created to know God and to love Him forever. Don't let anyone tell you otherwise. The fear-mongering of eternal flames and eternal torment and eternal suffering has nothing to do with the unfailing mercy of God (Psalm 136). There is enough hell here on earth to deal with. Anyone who seeks to scare you into heaven is echoing the father of lies (St. John 8:44). It is the love of God alone that compels and redeems and saves.

1,096. ~ "A MAN of THE PEOPLE" ~

Convince the masses that you are a man of the people, and there's no sin or crime that the people will not forgive. This is what the most successful politicians have always understood. As long as you can dupe the people into believing that you have their best interests at heart then you can exploit, manipulate, and abuse them, and they will actually praise you for it. This is why democracy inevitably gives birth to tyranny; and it's why the masses will tolerate all manner of oppression and evil as long as you allow them to choose it with the volition of their own vote.

1,097. ~ TRUE GUILT and TRUE GRACE ~

True guilt is hard earned. You have to really work for it. Which is why only true sinners can understand the ineffable mystery of true grace.

1,098. ~ LIBERATION THEOLOGY and THEOLOGY PROPER ~

We need not question if "liberation theology" is a proper theology. We need to simply understand that Theology Proper is inherently liberating.

1,099. ~ VOTING RIGHTS ~

Remember that inherent in the right to vote is the right *not* to vote. Anyone that tries to pressure, coerce, manipulate, or force you to vote is dishonoring those who suffered and died for your right to determine your own political beliefs and actions.

1,100. ~ TWO TYPES of PEOPLE ~

Some people derive pleasure from pulling you down, and others derive pleasure from putting you down. But a true friend and a worthwhile companion will always lift you up, help you up, and keep you looking up. There are two types of people in the world: those that try to drag you down to their level so they can say "See, you're no better than me," and those that say "Help me be a better me so I can help you be a better you."

1,101. ~ OUTLAWS ~

When we are ruled by Christ then we have no need for rules. And that's why those that follow the Prince of Peace will always be outlaws in this violent world of "law and order."

1,102. ~ A POST-ELECTION DAY MEDITATION ~
[11/9/2016]

My wife, in her wisdom and grace, rebuked me last night for reveling in the chaos and confusion of the election results. She asked me how I could take so much joy in it all when I'm constantly railing against politics. She told me that I should weep, regardless of who won the election, because it just means the perpetuation of more evil and injustice in one form or another. And I couldn't argue with her. She made me feel ashamed.

I confess that I do take pleasure in seeing people's idolatry become a bitter taste in their mouths. And as I've long said, I believe that all politics is idolatry and violence in one form or another. That's why I try to warn people against fueling these evil political systems with their participation and votes. So whenever one side loses, I take pleasure in the fact that idolatry has failed those that supported it, and I hope that their despair will lead them to forsake evil and cling to God.

But the truth is that I have many idols in my own life. And I often suffer from the reciprocity of my own sins. And I know that I wouldn't find it compassionate or Christian if people mocked and ridiculed me for suffering from my own misplaced faith and misguided hopes.

So this early morning, as the election results have now been determined, I should not laugh at those who are grieved to tears or filled with fear. Instead, I should offer them words of encouragement and hope. I should try to sympathize with their legitimate concerns. I should strive to understand why they voted and why they voted the way they did. That doesn't mean that I shouldn't disagree with them or continue to point out the idolatry of democracy and politics. But most of my friends who voted yesterday – on both the left and the right – did so out of a sincere desire to improve society and make this a better nation. Of course, sincerity is no substitute for righteousness and truth; but I do think it's important for us to understand that most people who participate in the political process do so out of noble intentions.

Regardless of who won this election, I was prepared to ridicule, mock, and demean both the winners and the losers. And because I am sinful and arrogant and opinionated and immature, I may still do that from time to time. But I am thankful for my wife's sagacious rebuke. While I'm busy writing and pontificating and ridiculing and mocking, my wife is going out every day living out the Orthodox Christian Faith and making a positive difference in the lives of countless people. She doesn't care about politics and she doesn't follow politics. And whenever I try to talk to her about politics, she's simply not interested. She's too busy doing the real spiritual and social work that makes a real positive difference in this world.

So I ask sincere forgiveness from those whom I may have offended with my sarcasm and ridicule regarding this election and its results.

Let me now offer some positive meditations for us to all reflect upon in the upcoming days and months. Regardless of whom you voted for or how you feel today, I encourage you contemplate the following truths:

1. God is still on His throne, and God is still in control. (As cliché as that sounds, it is a vital truth that cannot be emphasized enough.)

2. The hope for society and the hope for our world reside not with any president or politician. The hope resides with us. And our task is difficult but simple: "Love one another." [St. John 13:34] If we will just truly love one another – regardless of our racial, religious, political, and philosophical differences, we can truly transform our nation and positively affect our world.

3. Jettison fear and hate and negativity. Politics thrives on division. Politics preys upon our paranoia and our differences. Politics is fueled by our basest instincts rather than our highest divinely created nature. So whenever you encounter fear, hatred, and negative vibes, then simply sow peace and love and positivity. There is tremendous power in positive thoughts, positive words, and positive deeds. And this is not some "New Age" philosophy. This comes straight from Holy Scripture: *"Finally, brothers and sisters, whatever is true, whatever is noble, whatever is right, whatever is pure, whatever is lovely, whatever is admirable--if anything is excellent or praiseworthy--think about such things." [Philippians 4:8]*

4. Cultivate a spirit of forgiveness and healing. People on both the right and the left have sincere concerns about very real problems and vital social issues. The nature of politics is to divide people into ideological camps that pit some legitimate concerns against other legitimate concerns. So, in their desire to see the realization or preservation of one particular good they end up opposing another equally important and necessary good. And then people become embittered, angry, and vengeful if their own ideological agenda does not prevail. And as a result, humanity as a whole, and justice as a whole, and peace as a whole become the casualties. So we must learn to forgive each other. We must learn to work together to heal what we can heal, to unite where we can unite, and to realize that sin and evil are the common enemies of us all. As long as we continue to give our power to the powerful, to elect those who prosper by dividing and ruling us, then we will continue to suffer. But when we truly start forgiving each other and trying to heal one another, then we empower ourselves and we rob politics of its mastery over us.

5. The media will continue to tell us that this is a deeply divided country. And that narrative stirs up ratings and gives impetus to the politicians who thrive on pitting us against each other. But the Church is one (Ephesians 4:4-6), and the desire of Christ is that we be one (St. John 17:21). And even those who are not Christians are just as much the image of God as those of us who profess faith Our Lord

Jesus Christ. There is only One God and one human family. We are all brothers and sisters struggling together to make sense of our existence, to overcome our sins, to find peace and security and food and shelter and love. So let's get busy helping one another on this earthly sojourn.

"And I will give them one heart and one way, that they may fear Me always, for their own good and for the good of their children after them." [Jeremiah 32:39]

6. Politics is the devil's playground. And on his playground the demons stir up bullying and violence and intimidation and lies. There is no justice in that realm. The strong oppress the weak while the teachers look the other way. But the good news is that we don't have to play there anymore. We are free to leave Satan's domain and enter into the Kingdom of Christ where peace and justice reign forever. Truly, the Kingdom of God is in our midst. (St. Luke 17:21)

7. Finally, let's pray for all those in leadership and authority – not only in our own nation, but also for those in leadership and authority all over the world. May God bless them when they do good, and may He convict and chastise them when they do evil. And please pray the same for me. I need all the prayers I can get.

In conclusion, let me leave you with these verses of Holy Scripture to take to heart:

"Fret not yourself because of evildoers, neither be you envious of the workers of iniquity." [Psalm 37:1]

"He has stretched His hand out over the sea, He has made the kingdoms tremble; The LORD has given a command concerning Canaan to demolish its strongholds." [Isaiah 23:11]

"Perfect love casteth out fear." [I John 4:18]

"The gates of hell shall not prevail against the Church." [St. Matthew 16:17]

"For God hath not given us the spirit of fear; but of power, and of love, and of a sound mind." [II Timothy 1:7]

"Then the sovereignty, the dominion and the greatness of all the kingdoms under the whole heaven will be given to the people of the saints of the Highest One; His kingdom will be an everlasting kingdom, and all the dominions will serve and obey Him." [Daniel 7:27]

"The mercy of God endureth forever." [Psalm 136]

"The Most High is sovereign over the kingdoms of men and gives them to anyone He wishes." [Daniel 4:32]

"The nations made an uproar, the kingdoms tottered; He raised His voice, the earth melted." [Psalm 46:6]

"I make a decree that in all the dominion of my kingdom men are to fear and tremble before the God of Daniel; For He is the living God and enduring forever, And His kingdom is one which will not be destroyed, And His dominion will be forever." [Daniel 6:26]

"And Babylon, the beauty of kingdoms, the glory of the Chaldeans' pride, Will be as when God overthrew Sodom and Gomorrah." [Isaiah 13:19]

"If my people, who are called by my name, will humble themselves and pray and seek my face and turn from their wicked ways, then I will hear from heaven, and I will forgive their sin and will heal their land." [II Chronicles 7:14]

"Put not your trust in princes, in a son of man in whom there is no salvation." [Psalm 146:3]

"For whatever is born of God overcomes the world; and this is the victory that has overcome the world--our faith." [I John 5:4]

"These things I have spoken to you, so that in Me you may have peace. In the world you have tribulation, but take courage; I have overcome the world." [St. John 16:33]

1,103. ~ "RIGHTEOUS KILL" and "JUST WAR" ~

There is no such thing as a "righteous kill" or a "just war." The violent death of any human being for any reason is never righteous or just. There is no greater blasphemy than to ascribe righteousness and justice to the deliberate, intentional, and premeditated destruction of human beings created in the very image of God.

1,104. ~ DEFINITION of "POLITICIAN" ~

"POLITICIAN": 1) Someone who begs for votes while condemning those who beg for bread. 2) Someone who claims to speak for humanity while denying the humanity of the unborn. 3) Someone who runs on a "pro-life" platform while plotting new ways to execute, imprison, oppress, and kill. 4) Someone who speaks of peace while constantly preparing for war.

1,105. ~ THE CHRISTIAN NEEDS NO VIOLENT PROTECTION ~

The world will always militantly police the world. There is no earthly security in the Cross. Our Christian faith is not predicated upon the protection of violent force. I have no respect for soldiers and police officers who violently protect evildoers. "Yes," people say, "but those same soldiers and police officers also protect *you*!" Well, to admire those that protect injustice and oppression simply because I may also personally benefit is a selfish and unchristian perspective. Nazi soldiers protected German citizens. And sadly, many professing German Christians praised those soldiers just as many American Christians today praise the soldiers and cops that violently protect abortionists. Well, no thank you. As disciples of Christ we don't ask for your protection and we don't need your protection. This world is not our home. We'd rather be sent to heaven by the hands of the wicked than enter hell with their "protection."

1,106. ~ THE ESSENCE of ETERNAL LIFE ~

A loving Father neither justifies nor condemns His sinful child. But how the child responds to his Father's love is what determines whether they will be saved or whether they will suffer. The prodigal son suffered when he ran away from his father's love, but he was saved when he ran back into his father's loving arms. The love of God extends to all of us unconditionally, unaltered, ever-present and ever-sure. But divine love is never forced upon us. We can embrace it or we can reject it. To embrace the love of Christ is the essence of eternal life. Salvation is no more complicated than that.

1,107. ~ OUR HUMAN SUFFERINGS ARE INEXTRICABLY LINKED ~

Let me dispel the specious notion that unless you belong to a certain race, religion, gender, group, or nation then you cannot speak about the injustices and evils suffered by that race, religion, gender, group, or nation. As a member of the human race I cannot help but to identify with the suffering of any and all of my fellow human beings. Wherever and whenever people are being enslaved, oppressed, abused, and slaughtered, my soul and my conscience are aroused to indignation and action.

As human beings created in the indelible image of God, our sufferings are inextricably linked. As Dr. Martin Luther King, Jr. said: *"Injustice anywhere is a threat to justice everywhere. Whatever affects one directly affects all indirectly."* So don't let anyone tell you that you unless you belong to a certain segment of humanity then you can't speak to the universal issues of humanity.

Indeed, we must never presume to truly know the trials and pains of another. We and we alone know the sting of the injustices and evils that we have personally experienced in our own lives. So we must always listen to others when they express their own anger and hurt. And we must then seek to unite with them in human solidarity, working together to redress the injustices and evils that ultimately plague us all.

1,108. ~ FOREVERMORE ~

Give until it hurts, and then give some more. Love until you bleed, and then love some more. Cry until you laugh, and then cry some more. Laugh until you cry, and then laugh some more. Let play be your prayer, and let prayer be your play. Live until you die, and then live forevermore.

1,109. ~ REFORMATION? ~

Apostolic Teaching and Tradition do not need to be reformed by human opinion; our human opinions need to be reformed by apostolic Teaching and Tradition. People keep trying to change the Orthodox Faith rather than allowing the Orthodox Faith to change them.

1,110. ~ NUANCE and COMPROMISE ~

Life is full of nuance and compromise. But in order to properly negotiate these nuances, we must first begin with certain inviolate and universal principles. The problem is that we too often trample universal principles – such as liberty, justice, life, and peace – in the name of nuance and compromise. When we make nuance and compromise our first principles, then we end up jettisoning the divine principles that are paramount to a just and meaningful existence. The exception then becomes the rule and the rule becomes chaos and confusion.

1,111. ~ FEAR and LOVE ~

Fear is a feckless motivator. It can command one to obedience, but it can never compel one to love.

1,112. ~ THE FOUL FRUIT of DEMOCRACY ~
[11/10/2016]

With the election of Donald Trump we are once again witnessing the foul fruit that democracy produces. People love democracy when it yields what they personally want, but then they cry and complain when it results in something contradictory to their own selfish wills and impulses. And the masses rarely seek the will of God. They usually vote for their own vain desires (which are usually couched in the rhetoric of "freedom" and "progress") while cursing those whose vain desires happen to be different from their own.

And let us not ignore the fact that democracy (or a democratic republic) is forcefully implemented by the sword. Governmental democracy (and variations thereof) is enforced by the threat and use of governmental violence. So don't ever confuse democracy for the will of God or the peaceable Kingdom of Christ. I neither wept nor rejoiced when Obama was elected, and I neither wept nor rejoiced when Trump was elected. But I do mourn for the pitiful masses who continue to place their faith in worldly political philosophies and earthly rulers that cannot save.

1,113. ~ SITUATIONAL SUBJECTIVITIES and INVIOLATE IMPERATIVES ~

Situational subjectivities do not nullify or abrogate the objective and inviolate imperatives of Christ.

1,114. ~ CONVICTIONS and FRIENDSHIP ~

People with sincere and honest convictions will always love and respect you in spite of profound differences of opinion. If they don't value friendship and loyalty more than their petty political agendas, then they are weak, insecure, and vindictive people that you are better off without. It's very sad and very hurtful to lose friends over such foolishness, but it's not your fault. Just let them go and pray for them.

If their convictions aren't primarily based upon love and tolerance for others, then their convictions really aren't worth very much.

"Whatever town or village you enter, find out who is worthy and stay at his house until you move on. As you enter the house, greet its occupants. If the home is worthy, let your peace rest on it; if it is not, let your peace return to you. And if anyone will not welcome you or heed your words, shake the dust off your feet when you leave that home or town. Truly I tell you, it will be more bearable for Sodom and Gomorrah on the day of judgment than for that town."
[St. Matthew 10:11-15]

1,115. ~ ON FEAR, PARANOIA, and POLITICAL ANXIETY ~
[11/11/2016]

I've heard lots of talk about fear these past few days. Fear mongering is really being stirred up by the media and the political partisans on the losing end of this most recent election. People are lecturing me about how I should be sensitive to the fears that many people have because of the outcome. But I confess that I don't have much sympathy for those who allow their emotions and their thoughts to be dictated by the media and by political propaganda.

If you are truly fearful today because of some godless election results, then I encourage you to turn off your TV for a few days and pick up your Bible. Spend some time in prayer. Seek fellowship with some positive minded people. Go out and serve somebody in need. Get busy living and helping other people live.

Politicians and the media profit from keeping us fearful, angry, and divided. I'd probably be scared too if I believed everything I heard emanating from media pundits and politicians' lips. But if you're truly worried about your own safety and welfare, just stop for a moment and think about the homeless in our nation; think about the victims of our unjust American wars; think about the innocent young Black people that are cut down by the violence of gang warfare and policemen's bullets; think about the impoverished Mexican women and children who risk their lives to enter America so they can have access to clean water and the other basic necessities of life; and think about the unborn children whose lives are in constant jeopardy everyday in this land. Be afraid for *them*, because no matter who is president these are the people that will continue to suffer.

So stop feeling sorry for yourself because some politician that you don't even know and couldn't care less about you lost an election. Think about those in our society who are truly in peril every single day, and then go out and do something to help them personally. That homeless person you constantly pass by doesn't need you to vote, he needs you to help him yourself. Those innocent children who are murdered by bombs manufactured by Lockheed Martin, Boeing, and Northrop don't need you to vote for a "kinder, gentler machine gun hand," they need you to say NO to violence and killing; they need you to say NO to lending your votes to the election of one more murderous Commander in Chief who will perpetuate war so that munitions corporations can continue to make a profit. And those unborn children whose fate hinges on the whims of their mothers don't need you to vote, they need you to work and pray and agitate and plead for social justice and the sanctity of Life.

Fear is a natural and even healthy human emotion. But misplaced fear, paranoia, and political anxiety can be psychologically detrimental and emotionally crippling. So don't let anyone other than God tell you who or what to fear. Fear God first of all. Place your trust in Him alone. And let your thoughts, your actions, and your peace of mind be predicated upon His everlasting mercy, His divine will, and His unfailing love.

Here are some scriptures about fear, anxiety, and peace. If fear has truly struck your heart because of this recent election, then I encourage you to take solace and find comfort in the truth of God's word. Kingdoms rise and kingdoms fall. Rulers come and go. But Christ reigns with His Church and He reigns in our hearts, and His Kingdom shall endure forever.

"Do not be anxious about anything, but in every situation, by prayer and petition, with thanksgiving, present your requests to God.

And the peace of God, which transcends all understanding, will guard your hearts and your minds in Christ Jesus." [Philippians 4:6-7]

"When I am afraid, I put my trust in you." [Psalm 56:3]

"For God has not given us a spirit of fear, but of power and of love and of a sound mind." [2 Timothy 1:7]

"When anxiety was great within me, your consolation brought joy to my soul." [Psalm 94:19]

"The Lord is my light and my salvation—whom shall I fear? The Lord is the stronghold of my life—of whom shall I be afraid?" [Psalm 27:1]

"I prayed to the Lord, and he answered me. He freed me from all my fears." [Psalm 34:4]

"And fear not them which kill the body, but are not able to kill the soul: but rather fear him which is able to destroy both soul and body in hell." [St. Matthew 10:28]

"Fear of man will prove to be a snare, but whoever trusts in the Lord is kept safe." [Proverbs 29:25]

"And I am convinced that nothing can ever separate us from God's love. Neither death nor life, neither angels nor demons, neither our fears for today nor our worries about tomorrow—not even the powers of hell can separate us from God's love." [Romans 8:38-39]

"But even if you suffer for doing what is right, God will reward you for it. So don't worry or be afraid of their threats." [1 Peter 3:14]

"God is our refuge and strength, an ever-present help in trouble." [Psalm 46:1]

"Even though I walk through the valley of the shadow of death, I will fear no evil, for you are with me; your rod and your staff, they comfort me." [Psalm 23:4]

"Humble yourselves, then, under God's mighty hand, so that he will lift you up in his own good time. Leave all your worries with him, because he cares for you." [1 Peter 5:6-7]

"Peace is what I leave with you; it is my own peace that I give you. I do not give it as the world does. Do not be worried and upset; do not be afraid." [St. John 14:27]

"An anxious heart weighs a man down, but a kind word cheers him up." [Proverbs 12:25]

"The Lord is with me; I will not be afraid. What can man do to me? The Lord is with me; he is my helper." [Psalm 118:6-7]

"Fret not thyself because of evildoers, neither be thou envious against the workers of iniquity. For they shall soon be cut down like the grass, and wither as the green herb. Trust in the LORD, and do good; so shalt thou dwell in the land, and verily thou shalt be fed. Delight thyself also in the LORD: and he shall give thee the desires of thine heart. Commit thy way unto the LORD; trust also in him; and he shall bring it to pass. And he shall bring forth thy righteousness as the light, and thy judgment as the noonday. Rest in the LORD, and wait patiently for him: fret not thyself because of him who prospereth in his way, because of the man who bringeth wicked devices to pass. Cease from anger, and forsake wrath: fret not thyself in any wise to do evil. For evildoers shall be cut off: but those that wait upon the LORD, they shall inherit the earth. For yet a little while, and the wicked shall not be: yea, thou shalt diligently consider his place, and it shall not be. But the meek shall inherit the earth; and shall delight themselves in the abundance of peace. [Psalm 37]

1,116. ~ CHRISTIAN DISCIPLESHIP and POLITICAL IDEOLOGY ~

The Church must not seek to confront, condemn, or conform to liberalism or conservatism. Instead, the Church must simply be a prophetic witness *for* good and *against* evil. We must never confuse discipleship to Christ with political ideology. Our warfare is spiritual; and as children of the Kingdom we stand opposed to all evil philosophies, godless systems, and wicked structures – by whatever labels they manifest themselves.

1,117. ~ INDIVIDUAL AUTONOMY and HUMAN LIBERTY ~

If our personal choice violently silences another human voice, then that choice isn't liberty it's oppression. Our rights end where the lives of others begin. Everyone has a right to individual autonomy; but no one has the right to enslave, oppress, or abort another human individual.

1,118. ~ THE ONLY TRUTHS of WHICH YOU NEED TO BE CERTAIN ~

If you are unsure of the truth, then just try to be kind. If you are uncertain of religion, then just try to love. If you've never been loved, then just try to forgive. And if you've never been forgiven, then just know that God is love and that God forgives and that these are the only truths of which you need to be certain and sure.

1,119. ~ THE PEOPLE and THE MASSES ~

The needs of the suffering people are trampled under the political desires of the godless masses.

1,120. ~ **WHERE THE TRUTH RESIDES** ~

Between the fundamentalist that declares his truth and then condemns all who fail to adhere to it, and the cynic who denies the existence of any truth at all, resides the actual truth of mystery and paradox and eternity and God.

1,121. ~ **INSTITUTIONALIZED** ~

Politicians and cops and soldiers are the most institutionalized people of all. They don't even realize they are slaves. At least people in prison know they're in prison. And to recognize one's own bondage is the first step towards emancipation. That's why many incarcerated prisoners are actually some of the freest people in the world. And that's also why politicians, cops, and soldiers have to kill, coerce, intimidate, and oppress in order to preserve their own institutional slavery that they confuse for liberty. And that's what makes them so dangerous to those who are truly free, and that's what makes those who are truly free so dangerous to them.

1,122. ~ **"HUMAN RIGHTS ISSUES"** ~

"Human rights issues": let's understand the priority of the words in this phrase. Human rights are too often the casualty of people relegating them to mere "issues" while ignoring the reality of the actual human lives that are suffering and dying as a result of unjust laws and oppressive policies.

So let's focus first on the fact that our *human* brothers and sisters are being starved, bombed, shot dead in the streets, and aborted in their mothers' wombs. Then let's focus on the fact that our human brothers and sisters deserve the same *rights* that we do: the right to be born, the right to food and water and clothes and housing, the right to justice and equality and a living wage, and the right to authentic freedom and genuine peace.

Therefore, let us remember that 'human rights issues" are only issues because they involve real human beings. War, poverty, police brutality, racism, and abortion are not abstract subjects on which we should merely take some political position. Behind these "issues" are our brothers and sisters that desperately need our compassion, our love, and our sacrificial intervention on their behalf.

We need to stop talking about "issues" and start talking about people, about lives, and about the rights that every human being deserves from the womb to the tomb.

"Reverence for life means the removal of alienation, the restoration of empathy, compassion, and sympathy. And so the final result of knowledge is the same as that required of us by the commandment of love. Heart and reason agree together when we desire and dare to be men who seek to fathom the depths of the universe. Reason discovers the bridge between love for God and love for men – love for all creatures, reverence for all being, compassion for all life, however dissimilar to our own. I cannot but have reverence for all that is called life. I cannot avoid compassion for everything that is called life. That is the beginning and foundation of morality. Once a man has experienced it and continues to do so – and he who has once experienced it will continue to do so – he is ethical."
~ Albert Schweitzer ~

1,123. ~ POLITICIANS and PROPHETS, TRUTH and LIES ~

Politicians speak lies and call it the truth. Prophets live the truth and are accused of lies.

1,124. ~ RESPECT for INSTITUTIONAL OFFICE? ~

As a Christian I refuse to respect any institutional office that sows violence and war and oppression. I will always pray for these world leaders as we do in the Divine Liturgy. And I will respect them as human beings created in the divine image. And I will love them as such, as Christ commands. But I will not bow to their institutional office or accord it any respect. They sit on thrones of evil, and I will never call evil "good" or violent power "praiseworthy." It's an idolatrous blasphemy to give honor to an individual because of their political office rather than because they are simply the very image of God.

1,125. ~ PHILOSOPHERS, POETS, and CHRISTIANS ~

Philosophers speak of the love of truth, and poets speak of the truth of love. That's why every true Christian is both a philosopher and a poet, whether they realize it or not.

1,126. ~ MISTAKES ~

Don't learn to live *with* your mistakes. Learn to live *through* your mistakes.

1,127. ~ THANK YOU FOR YOUR SERVICE ~

Thank you to everyone who has served humanity, peace, and justice by saying NO to militarism, politics, and war. You are the ones who *truly* fought for me by refusing to hate and kill your fellow man. And for your service in the cause of peace, you received no medals or parades or holidays in your honor. Instead you were called cowards, traitors, and disgraces to your nation. But I will honor you, and I will salute you. And I will thank you for your service to the Gospel of Jesus Christ. You may be despised in this world, but your reward will be great in heaven.

"Blessed are the peacemakers, for they shall be called the children of God." [St. Matthew 5:9]

1,128. ~ THE MOST REVOLUTIONARY STATEMENT & THE MOST MILITANT ACT ~

The Sermon on the Mount was the most revolutionary statement ever made, and the Cross was the most militant act of resistance to evil that ever occurred.

1,129. ~ BLASPHEMING TRUTH ~

Let us not blaspheme truth by promoting our speculative and subjective lies in the name of truth's inviolate and objective sanctity.

1,130. ~ FOOLS and WISDOM ~

The sooner we realize that we are fools, the sooner we open ourselves up to wisdom.

1,131. ~ MOVED TO TEARS BY MY FRIENDS ~

Sometimes I am moved to tears when I think about all the wonderful friends I've had in my life. So many people have been so kind and so good to me along the way. To be sure, there have been many enemies and adversaries as well, but their hatred pales in comparison to the love and loyalty of all the good people I've known throughout the years.

I am a crazy, opinionated, arrogant, insecure, and sinful person. I've always been this way, even as a little boy. But for some reason God has always seen fit to send kind and accepting people into my life. They have shown me loyalty, generosity, and unconditional love. They have accepted me for who I am, and they have remained my friends in spite of all my flaws and offenses. And I imagine most of them don't even realize how much they mean to me.

I would not have survived all the hardships and pain in my life without the love, support, and kindness of so many very dear people. I hope they all know how much I love and appreciate them.

1,132. ~ IN A PATHOLOGICAL SOCIETY ~

In a pathological society modesty is considered "oppression," chastity is viewed as "prudishness," morality is condemned as "judgment," and virtue is perceived as an offense.

1,133. ~ "PRIVILEGE" ~

We all live in a fallen world, carrying the weight of sin, struggling to get back to the Garden from whence we came. Riches and laws and politics and prosperity cannot save us. In spite of how it may appear, none of us are truly "privileged." Death beckons each of us. And while we breathe, sin and Satan and evil and despair assault one and all alike. One fool thinks he is secure in his mansion, and another fool thinks he is damned in his poverty. The rich violently protect themselves from the poor, and the poor desperately seek justice from the rich.

But there is no real privilege in this world. Privilege is merely an illusion, a mirage, a conditional consciousness as fleeting as an orgasm or a satisfying meal. Desire is still our earthly master, and the grave is still our ultimate home.

Therefore, let us replace envy and hate with compassion and love. Let us strive to emulate the people of that first Christian Church who *"had everything in common, and sold property and possessions to give to anyone who had need."[Acts 2:44-45]* Let us forsake the violence of political coercion and governmental force and instead cultivate genuine mercy and sacrificial peace. For in this world we are all pilgrims without privilege, but in the Kingdom of God we are equal citizens of an eternal inheritance.

1,134. ~ RADICAL RELIGION ~

If your religion isn't radical then it's just a hobby. And I don't think God became a man, suffered, died, and rose again to give us another pleasant pastime to distract us from the realities of life.

1,135. ~ DEBATING THE DEVIL ~

Debate the devil and you will always lose. Love your brother and you will defeat the devil.

1,136. ~ CHRIST DOES NOT POSSESS US ~

Christ does not possess us, nor do we possess Him. He lives in us, and we live in Him. He is God and God is love. And love does not possess or own or enslave or control. Love offers itself freely, unconditionally, wholly, and irrevocably. Love is the antithesis of judgment, condemnation, and fear. Where love abides sin is vanquished. So we abide in Christ, and Christ abides in us. And this is freedom, this is peace, this is eternal life.

1,137. ~ I AM... ~

I am a Jew because I worship the God of Abraham, Isaac, and Jacob.

I am a Muslim because I seek peace through submission to the will of God.

I am a Rasta because I follow the teachings and Faith of H.I.M. Emperor Haile Selassie I.

I am a pacifist because I believe that violently destroying human beings created in the image of God is the ultimate act of sin and heresy.

I am an anarchist because human law and human government inevitably contradict and conflict with God's law and the government of His Kingdom.

I am a Christian because I place my ultimate faith in the life and death and Resurrection of Christ.

And I am Orthodox, because the Teachings and Traditions of the apostolic Faith are what formulate, shape, and inform all my convictions, all my actions, and all my beliefs.

1,138. ~ EXORCISING DEMONS ~

There are no demons that cannot be exorcised by love, humility, forgiveness, and grace. So be quick to apologize and quick to forgive, and thus disarm the devil.

1,139. ~ **LIES ARE NEVER REVOLUTIONARY** ~

Amidst political division, fear-mongering, paranoia, and strife, intellectual honesty is more important than ever. So state your case, make your argument, articulate your concerns, and lament your disappointments – but don't fuel hatred and fear by dishonestly demonizing those with whom you disagree. Peace and justice suffer when propaganda and lies are perpetuated as truth. So use your voice responsibly. By all means be provocative, be bold, be offensive and incendiary if need be; but don't compromise integrity for the sake of promoting your political ideology. Justice is served by adherence to truth, not by distorting the truth to further an agenda. Lies are never revolutionary.

1,140. ~ **NO COMPROMISE, NO MIDDLE GROUND, NO EQUIVOCATION** ~

One is either an oppressor or a revolutionary, a liberator or an accomplice, a prophet or a patriot. Where justice, truth, and life are at stake there can be no compromise, no middle ground, no equivocation. Peace makes its demand, humanity confronts our consciousness, and Christ calls us to the Cross. Contrary to what most people believe, hell is not the abode of fire and heat; it is rather the damnable condition of tepid apathy and lukewarm indifference.

"I know your deeds; you are neither cold nor hot. How I wish you were one or the other. But because you are lukewarm — neither hot nor cold — I am about to spit you out of My mouth!"
[Revelation 3:15-16]

1,141. ~ **SPIRITUAL VISION** ~

To see Christ in the poor, in the unborn, and in the marginalized and the oppressed – I think I have perhaps at least begun to have my vision sharpened by God to some degree. But to see Christ in the politician, in the abortionist, and in the rich who exploit and oppress the poor – well, I confess that my eyes are still closed. And if I can't see the image of God and the face of Christ in everyone, then I really can't see Him at all. I am just another prejudicial fool that speaks of Jesus while cursing my neighbors.

Dear Lord, please open my eyes and open my heart.

1,142. ~ DIVERSITY ~

If your "diversity" excludes, hates, and divides from those who believe, live, and vote differently than you do, then it's not diversity; it's just another form of bigoted, triumphal, prejudicial ignorance.

1,143. ~ REVOLUTIONARY THEOLOGY ~

A theology that is not defiant, confrontational, socially liberating and socially redemptive is nothing more than a human superstition with the name of God attached to it. Throughout the centuries the Orthodoxy of the apostles has been forged with sacrificial suffering and resistance unto death. The Cross not only bears witness to eternal salvation, it also presents itself as the most militantly efficacious weapon against social injustice, systemic evil, human oppression, and political sin. True theology is inherently revolutionary, and authentic revolution is inherently theological. One cannot love God apart from loving humanity, and one cannot truly love humanity apart from truly loving God. And love is never apathetic or indifferent to human suffering. Love binds up the brokenhearted, emancipates the enslaved, heals the hurting, and agitates for justice, truth, and human rights. That's why authentic Christianity is always accompanied by conflict and confrontation. As Bob Marley sang, *"Love would never leave us alone."*

1,144. ~ THE "RADICALIZATION" of DR. MARTIN LUTHER KING, JR.? ~

Contrary to a current and popular narrative, Dr. Martin Luther King Jr. did not become "radicalized" over time. The truth is that he was radicalized from the beginning. He always understood the Gospel as a radical call to sacrificial love, social engagement, and an unconditional commitment to peace. Dr. King was constantly criticized by people who wanted him to limit, temper, or pervert his broad and universal application of the Gospel of Jesus Christ. The Black Panthers criticized his commitment to nonviolence. The NAACP turned against him when he opposed the Vietnam War. And many who were focused on the issues of voting rights and segregation didn't understand why Dr. King got involved in the struggle for the rights of sanitation workers in Memphis, Tennessee.

But the Gospel compelled Dr. King to link the struggle of his own people to the struggle of all humanity. Therefore, wherever and whenever he encountered injustice, violence, and evil, Dr. King confronted it by elevating the Cross and sacrificially intervening to redeem the brokenness he saw before him. Because he was a disciple of Jesus Christ, he could not help but to be radical. And like so many other true disciples of Christ, he too was crucified.

1,145. ~ CROSS and CHAINS ~

Physical chains, mental chains, psychological chains, emotional chains, political chains, spiritual chains – the Cross is the hammer that breaks them all!

1,146. ~ BEGINNERS, QUITTERS, and LOSERS ~

A beginner can never be a loser. Only a quitter can be a loser. And even a quitter can begin again. That's why the Christian can never lose, because we are constantly being renewed, constantly being reborn, constantly rising from our sins and perpetually beginning our new life as inheritors of the Kingdom.

1,147. ~ OUR FIRST PRIORITY and OUR UNWAVERING PRINCIPLE ~

Whatever injustice we face, whatever evil we confront, whatever righteous cause we embrace, our first priority and our unwavering principle must be the refusal to kill.

1,148. ~ COMMUNITY ~

As much as I sometimes just want it to be about "me and Jesus," the truth is that the spiritual life cannot be lived in a vacuum. The disciples did not walk alone; they followed Christ together. God ordained community. The first thing that He ever declared to be "not good" was that *"it is not good for man to be alone" [Genesis 2:18]*. So God created woman for man. And Jesus called His disciples, anointed His apostles, and established His Church.

So we need community. We need one another. We need to struggle with and for – and sometimes even *against* – one another. At times it seems better that we should go it on our own. Community is burdensome. The Church can be awful. We Christians will annoy the hell out of each other sometimes. But Lord how we need one another! We simply cannot make it to heaven, or make it through this life, alone.

1,149. ~ COSMIC CONSCIOUSNESS ~

I have been to the edges of the cosmos and peered into hallways beyond. I have kissed the blackness of space; I have tasted the flames of the sun. I have danced on moonbeams and caressed fires that do not burn. I have faced the torment of demons as angels stood guard at my side. And yet I always returned to confront myself, to gaze into my own soul, to understand that my connection to the universe is vapid and meaningless apart from my connection to my fellow man. What may be discovered in the expanses of space, light years away, is nothing compared to the truth that may be discovered within. And truth that we discover within ourselves will always compel us to reach out to touch others.

1,150. ~ REFLECTIONS on THE DEATH of FIDEL CASTRO ~
[11/26/2016]

At first glance it is hard not to admire and sympathize with Fidel Castro in some ways. He led a revolution (albeit a violent revolution, which always ultimately turns out to be a counterrevolutionary endeavor; because violence always begets violence, and anything sustained by violence is susceptible to being undone by violence. However, that's a discussion for another day.) But the fact is that Fidel led an initially successful militant uprising which overthrew the corruption and immorality of the imperialist backed regime of Cuban dictator Fulgencio Batista. Castro orchestrated a well planned insurrection that effectively removed the stranglehold of American capitalism that was crushing and exploiting the Cuban poor. And he did so with a ragtag group of committed socialist guerillas who somehow managed to outwit and outfight the nationalist Cuban army, the U.S. military, the CIA, and the American imperialist president John F. Kennedy.

When Fidel Castro and Che Guevara rode victoriously into Havana sitting atop a tank and smoking cigars, the Cuban masses rejoiced. The banks were immediately nationalized, the casinos were shut down, prostitution was eradicated, and the national resources that had previously been siphoned off by America were now restored to the control of the Cuban populous. Socialism had prevailed. The poor were liberated. The power of the people had overcome the oppression of the American capitalist machine. At least that's what the people were initially led to believe.

But the socialist revolution quickly turned into a communist nightmare. And it did so almost overnight. Fidel and Che immediately let it be known that they were not at all interested in democratic socialism. Atheistic communism is what they espoused, and Batista's capitalist backed dictatorship would now be fully and thoroughly replaced by a repressive communist dictatorship. And when those who fought side by side with Fidel and Che – and who suffered and bled for the revolutionary democratic socialist ideal – dared to oppose the hard and drastic communist turn that Fidel and Che took, they were either executed or imprisoned.

So much for the power of the people, and so much for loyalty to those who fought for the revolution. No more democracy, no more Christianity, no more socialist solidarity. Fidel and Che set about killing and torturing and imprisoning anyone who opposed their efforts to immediately install an authoritarian communist regime.

Consider the life and fate of Huber Matos, who rode atop the tank alongside Fidel and Che as they triumphantly entered Havana. Matos was instrumental in overthrowing the Batista cabal. He was a devout Catholic and a committed socialist. He fought for the poor and sacrificed to liberate the Cuban people from the exploitation and excesses of Batista's American backed reign of corruption. And what was his reward? Well, because he dared to oppose Fidel and Che's efforts to turn the socialist revolution into an atheistic communist dictatorship, Matos was to receive either execution or imprisonment. Che favored execution, but Fidel decided on a 20 year prison sentence. Not because he was sympathetic to Matos, but because in Fidel's words, "I didn't want to make him into a martyr."

In his autobiography, _How Night Fell_, Huber Matos writes:

"Communist influence in the government had continued to grow. I had to leave power as soon as possible. I had to alert the Cuban people about what was really happening. So Fidel and Che debated whether to execute or imprison me. Che wanted to execute me but Fidel didn't want to make me into a martyr. So he put me in prison for 20 years. Prison was a long agony from which I only emerged *alive because of God's will. I had to go on hunger strikes, mount other types of protests. It was terrible. On and off, I spent a total of sixteen years in solitary confinement, constantly being told that I was never going to get out alive, that I had been sentenced to die in prison. They were very cruel, to the fullest extent of the word. I was tortured on several occasions."*

And Huber Matos was not the only comrade to be violently betrayed by Fidel's Marxist wrath. There are mysterious circumstances surrounding the deaths of Camilo Cienfuegos and Che Guevara, who both, unlike Matos, actually supported Fidel's hard turn towards communism. And in 1964, Castro admitted to incarcerating 15,000 political prisoners. In the name of the people, communism only has room for one authoritarian state ruler, and Fidel made certain that he alone would have the victory cigars and the sole platform to deliver his five hour speeches.

But Fidel was not content to merely eradicate God and Church from his own small island. As a crucifier of Christ, Castro sent his soldiers to assist the devil Mengistu who assassinated Emperor Haile Selassie and led the communist overthrow of the Ethiopian Christian Monarchy. You see, according to Fidel's depraved worldview, the only African nation to never be colonized somehow needed to be "liberated" from its Christian king and its Orthodox Christian Faith. And today, Mengistu is being given refuge in Zimbabwe by Robert Mugabe, who like Castro is another faux revolutionary who promotes communist ideology at the expense of his own people. And like Fidel, Mugabe also began his own ascent to authoritarianism by a legitimate resistance to British colonial power. But beware of a windswept house. The demon you scatter may be replaced by seven more, and the last condition will be worse than the first. (Cf. St. Matthew 12:43-45)

Castro's record of human rights violations was also horrific. Not only did he kill and imprison people who actually fought with him in the socialist revolution but resisted his atheistic Marxism, but he imprisoned and murdered homosexuals, Christians, and committed socialist dissidents who dared to speak out against his draconian and inhumane communist rule. Under Fidel Castro, the Cuban government refused to recognize the legitimacy of Cuban human rights organizations, alternative political parties, independent labor unions, or a free press. He also denied access to investigative international human rights monitors such as the "International Committee of the Red Cross" and "Human Rights Watch."

The Huffington Post stated: *"As a one-party communist state, Cuba often takes an authoritarian stance toward political opposition. The Cuban government recently detained some 50 opposition activists who had joined a peaceful weekly protest with the "Ladies in White," a group founded in 2003 to rally against the jailing of government opponents. They were among some 2,500 politically motivated detentions since the year's beginning, according to 'Human Rights Watch.'"*

So what is Fidel Castro's legacy? Well, like every other dictator who attains and maintains authoritarian power for a significant period, he too will be praised by some for "making the trains run on time." In Fidel's particular case, his apologists will point to Cuba's free health care, improved literacy rate, and most of all his perpetual David vs. Goliath posturing against the American imperialist behemoth. Castro was a real life political Robin Hood, and there is tremendous romanticism in his carefully constructed legend. But Castro's communist fairy tale was molded by the execution, repression, torture, and oppression of thousands upon thousands of human lives. And any ostensible revolution that must be sustained by perpetual executions is not revolutionary at all; and any "liberation" that is predicated upon oppression is nothing more than romanticized slavery.

We want so badly for the underdog to win, and we erroneously assume that the little guy is always the good guy. But in geopolitical realities, there are rarely any good guys. When it comes to Fidel vs. Kennedy, or communist Cuba vs. capitalist USA, there are only demons fighting demons, Babylon fighting Babylon. Yeah, the beards and the cigars and the berets sure look cool on T-shirts and college dorm room posters; but we have to be smart enough and wise enough and honest enough to look beyond the symbols and discern the substance of things.

So, as an Orthodox Christian, I will pray for Fidel Castro in his death. And I will pray for Cuba. I will pray for peace and prosperity and faith and healing to prevail in the hearts and minds and souls of the leaders and the people. And I will pray that the true revolution may now finally begin. Rastafari and Orthodox Tewahedo support neither communism nor capitalism. We never confuse politicians, soldiers, warmongers, and dictators for prophets and revolutionaries.

"Lord have mercy." +++

1,151. ~ THIS IS OUR DISCIPLESHIP ~

To side with life over death, peace over violence, liberty over oppression, truth over falsehood, right over wrong, freedom over bondage, good over evil, justice over corruption, prophecy over politics, brotherhood over division, love over hate, Christ over the world, Zion over Babylon...

This is our discipleship. And we may very well be crucified for it.

1,152. ~ WORK ~

If you want it to work, you've got to put in the work.

1,153. ~ THE TRUTH, TRIAL, and TRIUMPH of PEACE ~

The truth of peace is tested in times of conflict and tension. The Cross involves nails. We are nailed to the Cross with Christ. So those who have been crucified with Him cannot possibly take up the sword. His nails ensure that our hands remain open to love. And while hate may crucify love in this life, love will victoriously rise above hate in eternity. Therefore the Christian fights, and he fights with militant conviction. But the Christian does not kill. The Christian fights only with his own life, his own sweat, his own tears, and his own blood. And he does so not simply to gain a heavenly reward, but also to change unjust earthly realities.

"I have been crucified with Christ and I no longer live, but Christ lives in me. The life I now live in the body, I live by faith in the Son of God, who loved me and gave himself for me." [Galatians 2:20]

1,154. ~ BY THE SWEAT of THEIR BROW ~

There are many people who are unemployed that work harder than many people that have a job. So just keep that in mind. Be thankful for your paycheck, but don't lord it over your neighbor. That homeless person who begs for food day in and day out – standing in the bitter cold and in the relentless heat of the sun – is also earning their bread by the sweat of their brow.

1,155. ~ BURNING BABIES and BURNING FLAGS ~

I personally think that a nation that burns its own unborn babies doesn't have much moral authority to condemn those that burn its flag.

1,156. ~ OBJECTIVITY ~

If we want to be truly objective, we must first admit our own subjectivity. We are all burdened with prejudices, presuppositions, biases, and our own personal wills and desires. It is a natural tendency to seek opinions, politics, and "information" that affirms our own personal beliefs and our own preconceived convictions. That's why intellectual integrity and philosophical objectivity require tremendous effort and deep humility.

It's not easy to admit that we are not inherently objective. It's not easy to admit that we are naturally biased and prejudiced in many ways. It's not easy to confess that we might be in error, that we might need to learn, that what we have always believed might in fact be absolutely wrong.

That's why it's so important to understand that everything we read, everything we hear, and everything we view is tainted with an inherent bias and a subjective slant. And it's also important to understand that just because that information is biased and slanted doesn't necessarily mean that the information is wrong. That's another key to objectivity: the ability to recognize both the bias and the truth in the source of the information one receives.

But what's crucial is not to assume that the information is unbiased and objectively true simply because of the source. Instead, we should first assume that the information is biased, and then do our best to sift that information through the sieve of rigid logic, factual evidence, and historical truth. And this takes a lot of work, because our media outlets and scholastic institutions (and yes, even many of our religious leaders) often inundate us with half the story, grossly slanted perspectives, and outright political propaganda that's disguised as "information," "education," "news," and "gospel truth." And this is why we live in a society of educated fools, enlightened idiots, and jesters and jackasses that are extolled as sages and saints.

It takes a truly wise, humble, and righteous soul to see life through the objective lens of the Creator rather than through the lens of their own subjective creation. And the sooner we realize that we are not wise, not humble, and not righteous, then the sooner we will be able to discern things objectively and clearly.

1,157. ~ THE MOST EVIL and EFFECTIVE WEAPON AGAINST THE POOR ~

Legalized abortion is the most evil and effective weapon ever used in the war against the poor. Not only does abortion violently oppress and destroy the poorest of the poor (the defenseless and helpless children in the womb) but it enlists and employs the wealthy and the powerful to manipulate, coerce – and oftentimes even *force* – "minorities" and the impoverished to purchase the destruction of their own greatest assets: their very own children. The insidious mindset of those who promote abortion is the same as the mindset of the rich man who approaches the farmer and condescendingly says: "You don't need those cows, and you don't need that corn. Slaughter your cattle and burn down your cornfields. Those things are only burdens. You will be freer without them."

1,158. ~ IF ONLY WE COULD RESIST... ~

If only we could resist the political propaganda, the political fear-mongering, and the rampant political hyperbole with which we are constantly inundated. If only we could instead condemn the real evils that exist on all sides of the political spectrum. But what fun would that be? We'd have to then get busy doing things much more important and much more productive than voting and arguing and getting our kicks from the "news" on channel 666.

1,159. ~ TRUE STORIES ~

Every story, if true, begins with blood and water and is sustained by bread and wine. Every story, if true, is hellish and haunted and beautiful with mystery. Every story, if true, is agonizing and desperate, decadent but redemptive. Every story, if true, is ultimately both a human story and a Christian story.

I rode the waves as a little boy. And I've been riding them ever since, even though I'm far removed from the ocean now.

I've always wanted to go deeper, faster, higher – swimming to the edge of no return and then letting go, giving myself over to the power and the storm and the wrath and the safety of the biggest waves I could find. Because as long as I trusted them, they would always carry me to shore.

And somehow I have always known that out there in that vast tranquil sea – beyond the chaos of the crests and the crashes and the raging salt foam that fills your nose and forces itself down your throat and burns your eyes as you are held down on the ocean floor until you think you will be buried there – it's really out in the calm waters beyond that I have understood that death resides. While in the midst these beautiful, intense, dangerous, and unpredictable waves – it is here that life abides. (Salt is a mystical thing by the way. There is life in salt, and if we taste salt then we must be alive.)

You see, the waves make you struggle to survive. And apart from struggle there is only an inevitable and placid and uneventful death.

I dream of waves almost every night. I am a somnambulant surfer. I guess I dream of waves like I dream of God. Both are untamed. Both are dangerous. And yet they beckon us with their force and their awe and their promises of ineffable joy… if only we would give ourselves to them completely.

1,161. ~ DEAR CHRISTIAN: YOU are NOT THE PALE RIDER ~

Dear Christian: You are not the Pale Rider. You are not the angel of the Lord who alone is worthy to bear the sword. You are not the divine avenger. You are not David, anointed to slay pagan giants with a sling and a sword. You are not an Israelite sent to destroy godless nations. You are not God's vigilante commissioned to violently defend the righteous and slay the wicked.

No. You are instead a disciple of Jesus Christ. You are called to follow Him. You are commanded to forsake the sword, to love your enemies, to bless those that persecute you, and to lead men to eternal life not send them to earthly graves. You are commanded to take up your cross and go into the world to make disciples, not take up arms and go into the world to kill and destroy. You are called to sacrifice your own life to save others, but you are not called to sacrifice the lives of others – for any reason.

And this is the crucial and salient and significant difference between Christianity and Satanic religions: we do not engage in human sacrifice. We refuse to kill. We refuse to shed the blood of human beings created in the image of God. We pray and prepare to offer up our own lives to save another, but we never destroy the lives of others.

As St. John Chrysostom said: *"Our warfare is to make the dead to live, not to make the living die."*

[Scriptural references: Revelation 6:8; I Chronicles 21:16; Romans 12:19; I Samuel 17:51; St. John 13:35; St. Luke 9:23; St. Matthew 26:52; St. Matthew 5; St. Matthew 28:18-20]

1,162. ~ REPATRIATION ~

Repatriation is a must. We have to come out of Babylon (Revelation 18:4). First we must pursue a mental, psychological, and spiritual exodus; and then perhaps a physical and geographical exodus will follow. But if we merely change locations without changing our hearts, then we'll still find ourselves in the same old hell. The Zion train comes our way every day. But we must choose whether or not to get on board.

1,163. ~ PRO-LIFE HYPOCRISY? ~

Are Pro-Lifers perfect? No. Are we saints? Not many of us. Do we do all we can for everyone that we can? Probably not. Are there some people who claim to be Pro-Life only when it comes to abortion but not when it comes to war, capital punishment, poverty, or other issues that involve the sanctity and quality of human life? Yes, sadly there are indeed some people like that. But such folks have by no means cornered the market on hypocrisy and inconsistency.

If we are truly honest with ourselves, we will all have to admit that we fail both to hold perfectly consistent convictions and perfectly consistent lives that correspond with our convictions. But that doesn't discredit the truths we may espouse or negate the good we may do.

The defenders of abortion constantly attempt to discredit Pro-Lifers by stereotyping us as people who only care about life in the womb and not about human beings after they are born. But I would point out that it's Pro-Lifers who have established homeless shelters, adoption agencies, food pantries, crisis pregnancy centers, and that provide free life-affirming medical care to pregnant women in need. On the other hand, it seems the only things that abortion advocates offer are free condoms and free referrals for abortion "services" (which of course are never free.)

But as Alexander Solzhenitsyn pointed out: *"Violence has nothing to cover itself except the lie, and the lie has nothing to stand on other than violence. Once someone has embraced violence as his method, he must necessarily select the lie as his principle."*

So don't believe the anti-life propaganda. Any ideology that defends, justifies, excuses, or promotes the deliberate and violent negation of human life is a lie; and anyone who embraces such an ideology is an enemy of truth. Behind all the euphemisms, sophistry, and specious rationalizations there are real human lives, actual human beings, existent bodies, minds, and souls – at whatever stage or manifestation of development – that deserve to be recognized, honored, and granted the same fundamental protection and rights that we all dare to claim for ourselves.

As Dr. Martin Luther King, Jr. said: *"Injustice anywhere is a threat to justice everywhere. Whatever affects one directly affects all indirectly."*

We dehumanize ourselves when we dehumanize our neighbors. If we refuse to protect life in the womb, then we cannot hope or expect to protect our lives in this world. The legality of abortion places us all in peril.

1,164. ~ DAVID ~

David glorified God more with his harp than with his sword. David accomplished more with his Psalms than he ever did on the battlefield. David drove away more devils with his prayers than with his armies. So make music, not war. Sing praises to JAH, not hymns to the military. Put down your sword and chant down Babylon with Psalms and prayers and acts of love and words of truth.

> *Deliver me from the guilt of bloodshed,*
> *O God, you who are God my Savior,*
> *and my tongue will sing of your righteousness.*
> *Open my lips, Lord, and my mouth will declare your praise.*
> *You do not delight in sacrifice, or I would bring it;*
> *you do not take pleasure in burnt offerings.*
> *My sacrifice, O God, is a broken spirit;*
> *a broken and contrite heart you, God, will not despise.*
> *[Psalm 51:14-17]*

1,165. ~ AUTHENTIC REVOLUTION is PREDICATED UPON LIFE ~

There are those who fight for water, because we cannot live without it. There are those who fight for food, because food is the sustenance of life. There are those who fight for freedom, because without freedom life is despair. There are those who fight for peace, because violence is hell. And there are those who fight for justice, because justice is water and food and freedom and peace.

But let us first understand that all of these things – water, food, freedom, peace, and justice – are only meaningful because of *life*. If life is negated then nothing else matters. All values, morals, ethics, philosophies, and religions hinge upon the very existence of life.

Therefore, the first revolutionary principle is to recognize, affirm, protect, defend, acknowledge, and exalt the sanctity of human life. And the second revolutionary principle is to prioritize the needs of "the least of these" (St. Matthew 25:40). And by any objective, rational, biological, and sociological analysis there are no weaker, more helpless, and more vulnerable human lives than the precious unborn children who depend solely upon us to grant them access both to life and to the ideals that make life worth living.

It is both hypocritical and foolish to speak and preach and agitate for human ideals while ignoring or denying human life. Authentic revolution is always predicated upon life itself.

1,166. ~ ODD INVOCATIONS of THE OLD TESTAMENT ~

I always wonder why so many Christians invoke the Old Testament to justify war and killing, yet strangely, they don't invoke the Old Testament to justify polygamy. I find it odd that they are more disturbed by King David's adulterous, polygamous lifestyle than by his bloodshed and killing. And I guess that's because they haven't read their Bibles very carefully. Because when God prohibited David from building the Temple, it wasn't because of his sexual habits, it was because his hands were stained with blood. And the divine chastisement was not merely because David had murdered Bathsheba's husband Uriah. Because the scripture specifically states: *"You shall not build a house for My Name, because you have been a man of war and have shed blood." [I Chronicles 28:3]* And it's important to note that God did not qualify his rebuke of David because he had shed *innocent* blood or engaged in *unjust* war. God simply forbade David to build the Temple because he was "a man of war" who had "shed blood."

1,167. ~ LOVE, SALVATION, and COSMIC MYSTERY ~

As with theology, I've learned that there are no systematic answers to human relationships. We just have to love. And love doesn't make any sense sometimes. Hell, God died on a Cross for us. What sense does that make? And yet that is salvation. We just have to trust it. How? I don't know. It's a cosmic mystery. So in all of our human confusions and conflicts and controversies, we somehow have to summon the faith to simply love. How? I don't know. It's a cosmic mystery.

1,168. ~ DIVINE PURPOSE and POLITICAL DISTRACTION ~

As Christians, we have to remember that our government is the Kingdom of God. All these earthly human kingdoms will perish. Babylon will fall, and in a single hour (Revelation 18:2-10). Our commission is to make disciples and lead souls into the eternal Kingdom of Heaven. (St. Matthew 28:18-20). So we must not get distracted from our divine purpose by delving into worldly politics.

"Trust not trust in princes, in mortal man, in whom there is no salvation." [Psalm 146:3]

"When asked by the Pharisees when the kingdom of God would come, Jesus replied, "The kingdom of God will not come with observable signs. Nor will people say, 'Look, here it is,' or 'There it is.' For you see, the kingdom of God is in your midst." [St. Luke 17:20-21]

1,169. ~ I WENT TO WATCH A MAN DIE TODAY ~

*[This is not a true story. At least it's not **my** true story. But I suspect that it may be someone's true story. And I can only hope and pray that it will never be my true story.]*

I went to watch a man die today. He deserved to die, and I deserved to watch him die. I was invited to his execution, and I gladly accepted the invitation.

You see, this man – this monster – had killed someone I loved. And he had quite a lot of fun doing so, according to the testimony of his own words. He took his time with his killing. He didn't kill quickly or mercifully. He raped her and raped her and raped her again, and then killed her with more than 25 stab wounds.

This was not a human being. No human being with a soul could be capable of committing such an unspeakable and cowardly act of evil. And he had done this to my daughter. To my little girl. And she was just that – only a little girl. Not even grown yet. Just a 12 year old child who trusted the world and trusted me and trusted God and loved life and had a million dreams that she carried in her heart. And all of that was violently and suddenly taken from her.

As she was tortured and defiled and slowly murdered, she must have been thinking that her father was a liar, that life was in reality a cruel joke, that perhaps God was not real after all. I was supposed to tell her the truth and protect her always. She must have wondered where I was. She must have wondered why I was letting this happen to her. I will never know what she thought or what she felt in those agonizing moments of horror and death. I can only hope and pray that somehow God was with her, giving her the grace to endure her suffering and pain and death. I can only hope and pray that somehow she understood that it was not my fault, even though I will live the rest of my life believing that somehow it *was* my fault, that somehow I could have and should have been able to protect her.

So I went to watch her killer be killed – to watch her *murderer* be killed. And I wished that he could be killed the very same way he killed my daughter. His simple death would not be enough. To merely kill him would not be true justice. This was no "eye for an eye." This sick bastard had time to prepare for his fate. He would be served a last meal. He would have a chaplain or a priest or some minister come and pray with him before he lay down to die with anesthetics and drugs to send him to his grave as painlessly and comfortably as possible. But he didn't offer any of that to my little girl. He didn't kill her with compassion or mercy. So where is the reciprocal justice in killing him with all these amenities of dignity and comfort?

But I would at least be there to watch. And I would hope that as he died he might look into my eyes and see my hate and understand the pleasure I took in his life coming to an end. And I would watch him die, from my front row seat, for my daughter's sake. Because that's about as close as I could come to avenging her death. And by watching this monster die I could leave feeling certain that he would never do to anyone else what he did to my precious little girl. And that might not be much, but at least it would be something.

So yes, I went to watch a man die today. And I saw him die. And before he died I heard his words of apology and remorse. And I saw the fear on his face and the tears in his eyes as he was strapped down and injected with a series of drugs and poison. And he didn't die as quickly as I thought. So I watched him struggle and gasp for breath and gurgle and fight to speak. And I wondered what he was trying to say. And I wondered why I cared. So I sat and looked through the window as he was being killed. And I wanted to laugh at him. I wanted to see blood ooze from his eyes and mouth. I wanted to feel vengeance surging through my veins as death surged through his. I wanted to feel satisfaction and justice and peace.

But all I felt was sick. It only took a few minutes, but it seemed to take forever. Why did it take so long? And why was I bothered by the fact that it took so long? Why did I want it to be over so quickly?

So he died. He was killed. And I watched it. And he seemed to suffer throughout it all. But probably not nearly as much as my daughter suffered. And yet at the end of it all it didn't make any difference.

I left the prison and got into my car and tried to drive home. But I had to pull over so I could vomit. And then I cried. And I told myself that my tears were not for that son-of-a-bitch, but only for my daughter. But somehow I knew that I was crying and retching for all of us, for all of humanity. Somehow I knew that I was sick and despondent because of all the unnecessary death and evil and inhumanity that threaten each of us, not only from the depraved and the wicked, but also from the very institutions and people that presume to protect us from the depraved and the wicked. And I somehow knew that my tears and nausea emanated from my own hatred, from my own inhumanity, and from my own perverse desire to see my neighbor die.

And I just wanted to hold my daughter and love her some more and talk to her again. But she was still gone. And watching that man die his own cruel death did nothing to bring her back to me.

1,170. ~ THE MEDIA and MUSLIMS ~

The American corporatist media doesn't profit from promoting peace and brotherhood. The media doesn't profit from portraying devout Muslims in a positive light. The media has no vested interest in covering the countless righteous Muslims who condemn violence, terrorism, and prejudice in no uncertain terms. But in spite of what the media would have us believe, God is working mightily in and through people of different faiths and different religions and different lifestyles. Wherever people are preaching and living peace and love, Christ is in their midst.

1,171. ~ NEVER APOLOGIZE for YOUR OWN SUFFERING ~

Never judge the suffering of another. And never apologize for your own suffering. No one can truly understand someone else's pain. Depression and despair assault the wealthy and the poor alike. Loneliness and doubt are equal opportunity attackers. Anxiety and guilt prey upon people of all races, religions, and genders.

So when someone tells you they are hurting, when they express their worries and fears, when they plead for love and help, don't give them a lecture about working harder or a sermon about how they just need to have more faith. Just listen to them, and love them, and help them with whatever resources and means you have.

Today you may have your finances and your faith and your health and your mind all intact. And if so, give thanks and praise for those blessings. But know too that tomorrow you could lose it all – and not because you lacked trust in God, but because God calls us to the Cross and the Cross is unpredictable.

So if someone tells you they are suffering, don't assume they deserve it. Don't assume they are merely "looking for attention." Don't assume they are weak and need to just "toughen up." Instead, assume they are bearing their cross, struggling towards Calvary, bleeding with Jesus, and on the verge of death. And then come alongside them and help them carry their cross and help them live. Because regardless of how strong we may think we are, we are all dying anyway.

"If you get down and you quarrel every day, you're saying prayers to the devil, I say. Why not help one another along the way, and make life much easier?" ~ Bob Marley (Berhane Selassie) ~

1,172. ~ DOING THE OPPOSITE of THE CHRIST WE CONFESS ~

If we professing Christians were as eager to take up the Cross as we are to take up the sword, then the whole world may have been saved by now. But rather than saving souls we'd rather save our comfortable cultural customs that we blasphemously label "Christianity." And so we do the opposite of the Christ we confess: we kill our neighbors to preserve ourselves.

1,173. ~ NO VACANCY ~

No vacancy for Joseph and Mary
No vacancy for the incarnate unborn baby
No vacancy for the poor and the natty
In Babylon there's no vacancy
Only room for those with money
JAH have mercy!

1,174. ~ THE AGITATION of THE TRUE ABOLITIONISTS ~

Because their philosophy and actions are shaped by the Gospel of Jesus Christ, the true abolitionists agitate for the abolition of every institution, ideology, and practice that justifies the deliberate destruction and oppression of human life for any reason. Their commitment to the "consistent life ethic" leads them to clearly recognize that slavery, war, capital punishment, racism, poverty, police brutality, abortion, and the prison industrial complex are all inhumane evils that attack both the sanctity and the quality of human life.

The only way to truly abolish violence and killing is to remain unconditionally committed to peace and life. And the only way to truly abolish oppression is to refuse to cooperate with philosophies and systems that attack human existence and human freedom.

1,175. ~ NO MORAL GOVERNMENTAL AUTHORITY ~

A government that kills innocent people with bombs, drones, police bullets, and the legality of abortion has no moral authority to execute any criminal for any reason.

1,176. ~ ERR ON THE SIDE OF LIFE ~

Pregnancy is not a disease.
Children are not "consequences."
Babies are not burdens.
The unborn are not tumors.

Life is a miracle.
Life is healing.
Life is joy.
Life is a blessing.

Regardless of the circumstances, God has a plan for every life that comes into existence through the miracle of conception. I've come to believe that whatever the issue, whatever the debate, whatever the controversy, we can never go wrong by erring on the side of life.

1,177. ~ IT'S REALLY UP TO US NOW ~

In all of our brokenness and confusion, our religion and sin, our love and our heartache, our joy and disappointment, our expectation and sorrow – we all share a common human solidarity, dwelling together on this earthly ark that perpetually rotates through a cosmic sea. We are inextricably knit together in this terrestrial trod. But we make life hell because we fight and divide and hate and kill. Perhaps God will just let us keep on spinning in space until we decide to get our act together. After all, He came to earth to show us the way to eternal peace and eternal life, but we crucified Him for it. So what else is God supposed to do? I think it's really up to us now.

1,178. ~ THE GOSPEL and THE NICENE CREED ~

A friend once asked me to explain what I believe the Gospel is, and to include biblical references. Well, I simply believe that the Gospel is most clearly expressed and summarized by the Nicene Creed. So here is the Nicene Creed with scripture references attached:

I believe in (Romans 10:8-10; 1 John 4:15) One God (Deuteronomy 6:4, Ephesians 4:6) the Father (Matthew 6:9) Almighty, (Exodus 6:3)Creator of heaven and earth, (Genesis 1:1) and of all things visible and invisible; (Colossians 1:15-16)and in one Lord, Jesus Christ, (Acts 11:17) the only begotten (John 1:18; 3:16) Son of God (Matthew 14:33; 16:16) begotten of the Father before all ages; (John 1:2) Light of Light (Psalm 27: John 8:12; Matthew 17:2,5)true God of true God, (John 17:1-5) of one essence with the Father, (John 10:30) through Whom all things were made; (Hebrews 1:1-2)Who for us men and for our salvation (I Timothy 2: 4-5) came down from heaven (John 6:33,35)and was incarnate by the Holy Spirit and the Virgin Mary, (Luke 1:35) and became man. (John 1:14) He was crucified for us (Mark 15:25; I Corinthians 15:3) under Pontius Pilate, (John 1:14) He suffered, (Mark 8:31) and was buried; (Luke 23:53; I Corinthians 15: 4) He rose on the third day according to the Scriptures, (Luke 24:1; 1 Cor. 15:4) He ascended into heaven, (Luke 24:51; Acts 1:10) and He is seated at the right hand of the Father; (Mark 16:19; Acts 7:55) And He will come again in glory (Matthew 24:27) to judge the living and dead, (Acts 10:42; 2 I Timothy 4:1) And His kingdom shall have no end; (2 Peter 1:11) And I believe in the Holy Spirit, (John 14:26) the Lord (Acts 5:3-4) the Giver of life, (Genesis 1:2) Who proceeds from the Father, (John 15:26) Who together with the Father and the Son is worshipped and glorified, (Matthew 3:16-17) Who spoke through the prophets; (I Samuel 19:20; Ezekiel 11:5,13) And I believe in one, (Matthew 16:18) holy, (I Peter 2:5, 9) catholic (Mark 16:15) and apostolic Church; (Acts 2:42; Ephesians 2:19-22) I acknowledge one baptism for the remission of sins; (Ephesians 4:5) I expect the resurrection of the dead; (John 11:24; I Cor. 15:12-49) and the life of the age to come. (Mark 10:29-30)
~ Amen ~ (Psalm 106:48)

1,179. ~ THE ANARCHY of DISCIPLESHIP ~

Between us and the Cross there are countless authorities with their road blocks and detours and laws that demand we do anything and everything other than follow Jesus. The wide path to hell is paved with law and order and governmental rule, but the road to heaven is paved with the anarchy of discipleship.

1,180. ~ DIVERSITY and TRUTH ~

Diversity is a beautiful part of life. I celebrate it. The Church is full of diversity. But where there is diversity of doctrine there is also heresy and confusion. Diversity is most powerfully expressed within the context of truth. And those who walk in truth tend to exude a spirit of religious tolerance rather than religious triumphalism.

1,181. ~ GOD DOES not PUNISH THE INNOCENT BECAUSE of THE GUILTY ~

God does not punish innocent children for the sins of their parents. There are no "generational curses." God is holy and just, and there is nothing holy or just about tormenting the innocent as a judgment upon the guilty. Of course, people who believe in such a monstrous deity also believe in a God who punished His own innocent Son in order to appease His own insatiable wrath. But these are heretical and blasphemous notions, born from perverse interpretations of Scripture and blindness to the good news of the Gospel. So please, stop blaming God for the evils and horrors that are due to human sin alone.

1,182. ~ THE DIGNITY and WELFARE of WOMEN ~

Nothing is more demeaning and misogynistic than treating women like mere sex objects who can serve no other purpose than satisfying the male lust. Rapists, pedophiles, and women abusers love abortion because it allows them to control women and cover up their crimes against them.

I've seen countless women and young girls forced to have abortions against their wills. Where was their choice? And where were the "pro-choice" advocates to make sure their desire to give birth was affirmed and protected? They were nowhere to be found.

Women deserve better than abortion. Women are not animals that need to be sterilized with prophylactic chemicals. They are not pests that need to have their breeding controlled with abortion.
I've never seen a liberated woman coming out of an abortion clinic. I've only seen bloody, broken, weeping, and despondent women who paid to have some sadistic stranger violently suck the life out of them.

Surely we can do better than this as a society. Surely we can offer women healing, life-affirming, peaceful, and compassionate solutions to unwanted pregnancy. Nothing undermines the dignity and welfare of women more than the legality of abortion

I am Pro-Life because I am Pro-Woman.

1,183. ~ ALL THAT I REALLY THINK THAT I KNOW... ~

The older I get and the more I learn and the more clearly I see, the more I realize that we are all fools in one way or another. We're all just finite creatures in the hands of an infinite Creator, mortal dust fashioned by immortal divinity, struggling to make sense of our existence in this unfathomably vast universe. All that I really think I know with any certainty is that humility, peace, life, and love are the four pillars of a meaningful sojourn on this earth. If we can just love our God and love one another, then I think we will have understood all that is truly worth understanding. The rest of it is just cosmic static interfering with the divine frequency.

1,184. ~ THE BEAUTY and ABSURDITY of LIFE ~

Life is as absurd as it is beautiful and as beautiful as it is absurd. In fact, some of life's greatest beauty emanates from life's greatest absurdities. And I've learned that the absurdity is merely apparent but the beauty is real. The chaos and confusion and horror and pain can always be conquered by beauty and love and truth. It is only when we mistake the absurd for the real and the terrible for the True that we become victims of a nihilistic existence and a spiritual death. This is why as Christians we exalt the Cross but we bathe in the Resurrection.

1,185. ~ CONTRADICTION and PARADOX, COMMUNISM and THE GOSPEL ~

Communism is predicated in large part upon the philosophy of contradiction. Mao Tse-tung wrote a book entitled _On Contradiction_. And where contradiction prevails, anything can be justified. Evil is rationalized as a necessary dialectical precursor to good. Therefore it is permissible to kill, starve, oppress, and enslave today so that tomorrow all men will be liberated and fed.

And this philosophy is a demonic perversion of the Orthodox Christian truth of paradox. And paradox is much different than contradiction. Whereas contradiction is an irreconcilable logical opposite, paradox is a reconcilable mystery that transcends logic.

The nature of contradiction demands the violence of reason and violence against life, but the nature of paradox allows for the peaceful coexistence of human ideas and human beings that hold different ideas. This is why the sacraments of the Ethiopian Orthodox Church are called "Mysteries." They are neither irrational contradictions nor logical syllogisms that can be fully understood by mortal understanding.

Communism extols contradiction as a virtue, and thus "comrades" kill their neighbors in the name of "revolution." But the revolution of the Gospel extols holy paradoxes – the divine mysteries before which we prostrate ourselves in brotherhood and peace, loving even our enemies.

1,186. ~ A NATIVITY MEDITATION ~

This holy Nativity season, let us remember that Mary experienced an unplanned pregnancy. (Yes, the angel did indeed prophesy to her that she would conceive and give birth, but she was nevertheless surprised by the angelic news. And she surely experienced the same anxieties and apprehensions of any unwed pregnant woman.) But what she had not planned God had ordained.

And it is the same with every other pregnancy. Planned or unplanned, life is always a blessing, a gift replete with hope and promise and creative potential.

Imagine how different the world would be if our Savior had been aborted. And Herod certainly tried.

So as we meditate on the birth of God incarnate, let us also recognize and affirm the sanctity of all human life. Let us pray for the day when America is no longer a terror to unborn innocents.

Egypt once oppressed the people of God, but then Egypt became a refuge for the Son of God. And although America oppresses the unborn today, let us hope that it will soon become a refuge and safe haven for children in the womb.

"Lord have mercy." +++

1,187. ~ CHRISTIAN SERVICE NOT GOVERNMENT RULE ~

As Christians we serve society best not as magistrates or rulers or soldiers or enforcers. Rather, we serve society best as prophets, disciples, dissenters, and revolutionary agents of social justice and spiritual truth. We are not lawmakers or law officers. We are simply witnesses to the immutable divine law of the Gospel by which all men shall ultimately be judged. So let us be interested in Christian service rather than government rule.

1,188. ~ WHO ARE THE VISIONARIES? ~

Who are the visionaries?

The visionaries maintain faith when everyone else is in despair.

The visionaries preach peace when everyone else says kill.

The visionaries are wedded to life when everyone else is wedded to death.

The visionaries say "He is Risen!" when everyone else says "God is dead."

The visionaries sail forward when everyone else says they'll fall off the edge of the earth.

Because the visionaries realize that this too shall pass, that peace will prevail, that life conquers death, that the empty tomb is the greatest truth, and that even if they do fall off the edge of the earth they will nevertheless fall into the arms of a loving God.

1,189. ~ THE MANNERS and CIVILITY of THE RICH ~

The manners and civility of the rich would be quite admirable if they extended equally to the poor.

1,190. ~ FAITH WITHOUT LAUGHTER ~

Faith without laughter is nothing but fear cloaked in the feckless façade of certainty.

1,191. ~ CHEMICAL WARFARE ~

Your pill is a chain
That makes you a slave
Turning your womb
Into a grave

Chemical warfare
That's self-imposed
Killing yourself
With birth control

I think of all the life
Lost inside
Your cemetery soul

1,192. ~ MY PATRIOTIC PRAYER ~

I pray for the day when presidents and politicians will understand the words of the angelic hosts: *"Peace on earth, goodwill toward men." [St. Luke 2:14]* And I pray for the day when Americans will seek salvation in the manger rather than in the White House. This is my patriotic prayer.

1,193. ~ TRUE FREEDOM is ALWAYS ILLICIT ~

True freedom is always illicit. The world will tolerate a million forms of slavery, but it will crucify the one free man.

1,194. ~ THE MOST VIOLENT CENSORSHIP ~

There is no more violent, unjust, and inhumane form of censorship than legalized abortion. To decree that some human lives don't deserve to be born is the epitome of prejudice, bigotry, and judgmental intolerance.

1,195. ~ BEFORE I WRITE... ~

Before I write, I cry; and through my tears the words spill out. And before I write, I laugh; and through my happiness the type flows. And before I write, I curse; and with my vituperations I waste ink on paper and energy on windmills.

But whether I cry or curse or laugh, at least I am alive. At least I am feeling something, exalting something, condemning something, praising something, engaged in something. And when I can't feel anything at all, I write until I can. And if my pen is cold and my heart is stale, I let wine and music do the work. And with the right melody and the right drink and a simple prayer, I pour upon the empty page the reflections of my soul.

1,196. ~ THE GUILLOTINES of "POLITICAL PROGRESS" ~

A mob of murderers places a noose around my neck, and in the name of "liberation" it begs me to help them build my own scaffold. That is politics. And if I must be hanged it surely won't be because I acquiesced with my own destruction. I have no interest in cooperating with a bloodthirsty system in order to make my own death more palatable. I shall always eschew the guillotines of "political progress."

1,197. ~ TO ALL MY BLUE COLLAR BRETHREN ~

This one goes out to all my blue collar brethren – to all the proletariat, plebian hustlers and grinders who sweat and bleed and beg and scrap and fight and work to survive day after day. There is no rest for the common man – at least not in this life. So keep your head up, and keep sowing positive works and positive vibes. The Babylon system is cruel, but JAH is merciful (Psalm 136). Your labor is not in vain. The Kingdom of God is among you! (St. Luke 17:21)

"Therefore, my dear brothers and sisters, stand firm. Let nothing move you. Always give yourselves fully to the work of the Lord, because you know that your labor in the Lord is not in vain." [I Corinthians 15:58]

1,198. ~ SOCIAL CHANGE and POLITICAL CHAINS ~

As long as we accept the lie that the political process is the only method of social change, then we will forever remain enslaved to the chains of the political process.

1,199. ~ TO PRAY or TO DRINK WINE? ~

To pray or to drink wine? Well, rejoice and do both!

"Pray without ceasing." [I Thessalonians 5:17]

"So whether you eat or drink or whatever you do, do it all for the glory of God." [I Corinthians 10:31]

"Be joyful in hope, patient in affliction, faithful in prayer." [Romans 12:12]

"Give wine to those that be of heavy hearts. Let him drink, and forget his poverty, and remember his misery no more." [Proverbs 31:6-7]

"Go, eat your food with gladness, and drink your wine with a joyful heart, for it is now that God favors what you do." [Ecclesiastes 9:7]

"Too much wine and a man cannot see. Too little, the same."
~ Blaise Pascal ~

*"The Lord is near to all who call on him,
to all who call on him in truth." [Psalm 145:18]*

And know this: that while in wine there may be truth – *"In vino veritas"* – it is only when wine becomes Blood that we partake of *The Truth*.

1,200. ~ **OPEN MIND and UNLOCKED DOORS** ~

The mind is not opened by cynical doubt or rationalist skepticism; it is rather opened by the key of faith that unlocks doors of infinite wonder.

1,201. ~ **ON DIVINE LOVE, HOLINESS, and JUSTICE** ~

People will often say: "Yes, God is loving. But He is also holy and just." As if there is a distinction. As if there is some conflict within the nature of God. As if God wants to love us but His holiness and justice somehow prevent it, unless He tortures and kills His own Son in order that His justice may be satiated. Such a concept of God is downright blasphemous and heretical. The fact is that God is loving, and there is no "but" to qualify that truth. His love is holy, and His justice is love.

Walking the streets of Mexico City, carrying a bottle of Tequila and a freshly broken heart. Drowning in mezcal and the lost love of a Mestiza goddess. Blues on my Walkman – Little Walter speaking to me with bended harmonic notes and lyrical laments.

Side one of "The Best of Little Walter" ended. Time to pull out my Walkman and flip the tape.

I was in the barrio now, deep in the bowels of the most densely populated city on earth. Amidst a city of so many lights I had somehow stumbled upon a corridor of darkness. I had strayed from the floral fragrance of Gardenias and Dahlias Pinnatas into the bowels of stale beer, garbage, gang territory, and the raucous noise of impoverished "borracchos."

I was too drunk to care, but not drunk enough to forget my pain. As I was changing my Little Walter tape, I heard music: Mariachi music. And the music was emanating from a "cerveceria," a Mexican beer hall.

So I went inside.

And then everything stopped. The music stopped. The people stopped. And there were only men inside. No women. (And nothing more clearly indicates the state of male despair than the complete absence of women.) So I looked around and saw these Mexican men – dark and weathered, drunk and poor, desperate but full of life, strong and dignified and as recalcitrant as Aztecs in the face of Cortez and his Catholic conquerors. And I've never seen such faces. And they stared at me, at my gringo countenance, without judgment or condemnation or hate. They just looked at me with the most intense and serious and no bullshit sense of curiosity that I've ever encountered.

I was so far out of my cultural depth that I almost froze in the intensity of their collective gaze. Until I realized that I was just as drunk as they were. Until I realized that my heart, like theirs, was also broken – broken by experiences so vastly different and yet so profoundly common. Until I realized that right there and right then there was no escape for me or for them. They could have beaten me, killed me, inflicted upon this stupid "Yanqui" all the evils that my

European ancestors had inflicted upon them. And no one would have ever known. Just as the world knew nothing about them – nothing about their suffering, their anger, their frustration, and their sorrows. These men died a little bit every day, but the rest of the world didn't know and didn't care.

And I quickly understood that it didn't matter. We were just people here – people with the shared human afflictions of suffering and struggle, and a common human desire to escape our pain, however briefly. Through fermented swill, festive music, and the solidarity of human brotherhood we could perhaps find momentary collective respite. We were all nobodies, and we were nobodies together – with no cops, no politicians, no prostitutes and no priests to protect us or console us. We were, at that moment, alone together in the universe.

So I ordered a beer. And I beseeched a fellow "borracho" next to me (who spoke a little English) to ask the Mariachi band to play something in the key of E. And soon a Mariachi bass was thumping and a guitar was strumming and a trumpet was echoing its melody; and I pulled out my harmonica and started playing along in my own little world. And suddenly I was lifted up from my barstool and placed on top of a table. And then all these warm broken human faces were looking up at me and clapping and smiling and yelling and urging me on. And I played that damn harmonica like I had never played it before in my life. And I don't know how my blues harp worked with that Mariachi band, but somehow it did.

And that was one of realest human encounters I've ever experienced. And I've never felt closer to anyone in this world than I did to those strangers in that dark hole in the heart of Mexico City on that crazy night.

Mexico City... Natchez, Mississippi... Chicago, Illinois: love is love, heartbreak is heartbreak, humanity is humanity, drink is drink, and the Blues are the Blues – in any culture, in any language, in any tone, on any night, wherever you are.

1,203. ~ REVOLUTION and VIOLENCE ~

Any revolution achieved by the gun can just as easily be undone by the gun. That's why violence is never revolutionary. Bullets and bloodshed have no power to redeem hearts, persuade minds, and transform human consciousness. Those that have been violently defeated may be subservient today, but they are plotting to overthrow their conquerors tomorrow. Violence accomplishes no enduring victories. Truly revolutionary ideas do not need to be preserved with bloodshed and death.

1,204. ~ HUMANITY and HUMAN RIGHTS ~

If you are human then you have every right to address, opine, and agitate for issues of human rights and social justice. So don't ever let anyone tell you that unless you belong to a specific race, religion, gender, or political persuasion then you have no right to speak out about peace, truth, and humanitarian ideals. Nobody has a monopoly on suffering, and nobody has a monopoly on healing. If our neighbors are in pain, our own souls are also affected. Therefore, whenever anyone is being oppressed, enslaved, victimized, or aborted, we have every right to speak, act, and intervene to help them. As Dr. Martin Luther King, Jr. said: *"Injustice anywhere is a threat to justice everywhere. Whatever affects one directly affects all indirectly."*

1,205. ~ THE CHURCH and THE WORLD ~

A Church that is viewed as valid and unthreatening and compatible with an evil world is not the Church at all.

"If the world refuses justice the Christian will pursue mercy. And if the world takes refuge in lies, he will open his mouth for the voiceless and bear witness to the truth. For the sake of the brother – be he Jew or Greek, bond or free, strong or weak, noble or base – he

will renounce the world. For the Christian serves the fellowship of the Body of Christ, and he cannot hide it from the world. He is called out of the world to follow Christ." ~ Dietrich Bonhoeffer ~

1,206. ~ NO ROOM ~

No room for immigrants
Unless they are slaves
No room for the homeless
In this home of the brave

No room for justice
And no room for peace
Only room for politics
In this land of the free

No room for baby Jesus
No room in this inn
No room for the unborn
In our land of sin

1,207. ~ PROPHETS and PHARAOHS ~

Those whose hands work the soil, whose feet trod upon the ghetto streets, whose bodies sweat in sunburned fields and freeze in urban tenements – these are the souls that revolutionaries try to liberate and that politicians try to domesticate. These are the souls that prophets lead to rebellion while the Pharaohs lead their souls to bondage. Don't ever let a politician convince you that he's a "man of the people."

1,208. ~ SOCIETY'S OPPOSITION to THE GOSPEL ~

With war, society declares its opposition to the Gospel of peace. With capital punishment, society declares its opposition to the Gospel of forgiveness. And with abortion, society declares its opposition to the Gospel of Life.

1,209. ~ DON'T WAIT TO CREATE ~

If the saints waited until they became saints before they said anything, did anything, wrote anything, or created anything then we would never know that they were saints. They would have just lived quiet, isolated lives that touched no one, influenced no one, and benefitted no one.

So if you have something to say, then say it. If you have something to give, then give it. If you have something to portray, then portray it. Just do it all for the glory of God, trusting that He will multiply your beauty and truth, and trusting that He will forgive your errors and sins.

I would never trust the words or works of anyone who claimed to be sinless, perfect, or divine. Christ alone was the only perfect human being. He alone is God Incarnate. Anyone who claims perfection and holiness apart from Christ is a liar and a deceiver. And anyone who is truly united with Christ will never boast of their own holiness or virtue.

We all bear the indelible image of God, and therefore we were all created to create. And creativity is unlimited in its expressions and forms. So let us create with boldness, with confidence, and with humility – realizing that our creative potential is most fully realized when we create not for vanity or self-gratification, but when we create for the benefit of our neighbors and for the glory of God.

"For we are God's handiwork, created in Christ Jesus to do good works, which God prepared in advance for us to do." [Ephesians 2:10]

1,210. ~ SUICIDAL CONSIDERATION ~

He considered committing suicide to show them how much they had hurt him. But he realized that if he killed himself then he wouldn't be around to experience the gratification of the realization of their guilt. So he chose to live, so that through his own meager existence he would force them to reckon with the problems and pain of all humanity.

1,211. ~ LIVING and KILLING ~

Some people kill to make a living, and others live to make a killing. Either way they bring bankruptcy and death to their own souls.

1,212. ~ IF I MUST BE SENT AWAY AGAIN ~

I have frequent nightmares about being sent away from home as a child, being violently handed over to sadistic strangers and thrown into an empty cell of solitary confinement.

I will never really get over it.

But I am thankful for the experience. It will always haunt me, and yet I am stronger for having endured it.

But for God's sake: Parents, please don't ever send your children away without their consent! For a child to be violently wrenched from the security of their family and their friends and their natural home environment is an inexcusable abuse.

But I forgive my parents. Or at least I sincerely try.

They truly meant no harm. They knew not what they did.

And unlike my Jesus who suffered without any guilt, I know that the pain I caused my parents was worthy of the agony I was forced to endure.

And unlike the evildoers who crucified Christ, my parents truly believed that my nails and thorns were in my best interest. In fact, they were genuinely convinced that my torment was "treatment," and that breaking my heart was a benevolent act of love.

And perhaps they were right. So how can I blame them?

So I can't be bitter about those trials. I can only be honest. Because truth is the prelude to forgiveness; and forgiveness is the prelude to redemption; and redemption betroths reconciliation.

I know that I was crucified out of love rather than hate. And I can live with that. Because I have to live with the realization that I have crucified many others with my apathy and indifference and arrogance and evil. The sins of my parents were sins of weakness and ignorance and confusion and doubt. But my own sins have been much more deliberate, much more intentional, and therefore much more indefensible.

Yes, these nightmares still haunt me. I don't want to be sent away again! I still fear that some nefarious "they" will come to take me away, forcing me to wear a green hospital robe, placing me in a padded room, and declaring me a "criminal" or a "lunatic." And in a society run by the criminally insane, I realize that the truth tellers will always be considered outlaws. Incarcerate them, anesthetize them, mock them, and slay them – but by all means silence them.

But maybe these nightmares emanate from the large, dark beam that is firmly implanted in my own subconscious eye. Maybe my dreams still torment me because I have yet learned to truly forgive, to truly move forward, to truly bathe in the love and light of Christ. Most of all I am haunted by my own grudges. And I am too old to bear this weight any longer.

Please, Lord Jesus: take this yoke upon Yourself. I want peace with my family. And I really, really just want to get some sleep. And if I must be sent away again, Lord please, send me home to You.

1,213. ~ BLINDNESS and HUNGER ~

One man is blind because he is full; another is blind because he starves. When the full feed the hungry then both will see.

1,214. ~ CONSISTENCY and CHANGE ~

In consistency we may find the comfort of a stagnant security, but we won't find growth. There is one inviolate and consistent law of nature, and that is change.

1,215. ~ PILGRIMAGES ~

One man practices voluntary asceticism, takes a vow of voluntary poverty, lives in voluntary solitude, and people view him as a holy monk. Another man has asceticism, poverty, and solitude violently thrust upon him by society, and he is called a vagabond, a bum, a scoundrel and a tramp. We might do well to make fewer pilgrimages to monasteries and more pilgrimages to the streets.

1,216. ~ CHILDREN I'VE HAD, CHILDREN I'VE LOST ~

As far as I know, I've had six children. Three are still with me. One only lived for 11 weeks outside of the womb. Another was lost to miscarriage. The other was violently taken from me before she was born.

But I may have in fact fathered others – some that may have been cut down in the womb and some that may have been born but will never meet their father. I am haunted by the fact that I will probably never know.

Sex and love and lust and life are powerful and inseparable forces. With rubber barriers, prophylactic potions, and abortive bloodshed we try to entertain lust without love and sex without life. And with such futile endeavors we end up destroying the very images of God and the innocence of our very own souls.

1,217. ~ THE COMMON ERROR of ATHEISTIC MARXISM and THEOLOGICAL MILLENARIANISM ~

Atheistic Marxism and theological millenarianism both maintain the same fundamental error: they sacrifice the welfare and lives of present human beings in pursuit of a future humanistic utopia and a future heavenly kingdom. The Marxist views current human suffering as merely an inevitable and necessary stage in the dialectical equation, and the millenarian views current human suffering as merely a prologue to paradise.

But against these inhumane doctrines of both the religious and the irreligious, the Gospel interposes itself and compels humanity to love, serve, and heal humanity right here and right now. Christ proclaimed, *"The Kingdom of God is among you."* [St. Luke 17:21] And He clearly stated that all divine laws and prophetic utterances are summarized by two inseparable imperatives: *"Love the Lord your God with all your heart and with all your soul and with all your mind; and love your neighbor as yourself."* [St. Matthew 22:36-40]

There is no greater heresy than to tolerate and accept the present suffering of others in the name of some scientific sociological thesis or some eschatological expectation. The validity of any religion, philosophy, or social theory is determined by its concern with and action towards the human suffering of the present moment.

1,218. ~ GIVE ME THE COMPANY of THE MALADJUSTED ~

Give me the company of the maladjusted, the misfits, the outcasts and the insane. There is hope for them. The people I worry about are those that have sold their souls in conformity to a pathological society.

1,219. ~ PATIENCE and HUNGER ~

Patience is a luxury that the hungry cannot afford.

1,220. ~ HOPEFUL UNIVERSALISM ~

Who among us has the whole truth? Yes, as Christians we worship *The Truth*, but there is still no way that our finite minds and sinful hearts can fully grasp the eternality and holiness of the One we worship. I am a hopeful Universalist. It is only because the Orthodox Church forbids me to preach a dogma of certain Universalism that I refrain from doing so. But I really do believe that somehow, someway – in and through and by the Cross – all souls will ultimately be saved, perhaps even the devil himself. That is the faith, the confidence, and hope that I have in the unfailing mercy, the unconquerable grace, and the prevailing love of Christ.

"For God was pleased to have all His fullness dwell in Christ, and through Christ to reconcile all things to Himself, whether things on earth or things in heaven, by making peace through the blood of His cross." [Colossians 1:19-20]

1,221. ~ JUSTICE and TRUTH, LAW and ORDER ~

I've noticed that whenever the poor man speaks of justice and truth, the rich man speaks of law and order.

1,222. ~ BELIEVING MORE in DEVILS THAN in THE DIVINE ~

Since the religious cannot punish the devil, they often instead punish the devil's victims. Since they cannot punish sin they instead punish sinners. And in punishing sinners and Satan's victims, these religious people become Satan's greatest servants and themselves the most impious and unholy of human creatures. Through Inquisitions and witch burnings and heretic slayings and excommunications the "God fearing" prove they believe much more in devils than in the Divine.

Satan may turn out to be not God's created and fallen angel but rather the creation of humanity's own incarnational evil. And humanity constantly victimizes humanity in an effort to prove and punish the evil for which humanity alone is responsible. To save souls from the fires of eternal hell there are those who gladly subject souls to hell on earth. As long as we are killing and punishing people then we convince ourselves that evil is real and that we are righteously opposing it. And evil is indeed real, but it is we who have created it. And through our punishments and wars and executions it is we who suffer and we who die.

1,223. ~ A CLEAR REVELATION of WEAKNESS ~

Nothing more clearly reveals the weakness of your argument, your religion, your ideology, or your cause than the fact that you believe you must kill to defend it.

1,224. ~ SAINTS UPON MY WALL ~

Saints upon my wall
Praying as I sleep
From behind my piles of books
They keep their gaze on me
Whether I do wrong
Or whether I do right
They intercede from heaven
Throughout the day and night

Saints upon my wall
My blessed holy friends
Helping me to realize
I can overcome my sins
Sinners such as I
Embraced the Light of Christ
With such a cloud of witnesses
I pray to join my life

1,225. ~ BY BARING YOUR OWN SOUL YOU MIGHT HELP TO SAVE ANOTHER'S ~

In Romans chapters 7-8, one of my favorite passages of Holy Scripture, St. Paul uses the word "I" about 35 times (if I count correctly.) Shall we therefore accuse the apostle of narcissism, of conceit, of self-aggrandizement? God forbid! And yet, in the name of piety, many professed Christians will condemn anyone who dares to speak of themselves, of their own spiritual struggles, of their own encounters with divine grace.

But it's sort of difficult to personally testify to God's goodness and mercy without mentioning ourselves in the equation. And when we're suffering, it's sort of difficult to ask for prayers if we don't mention the fact that it's "we" who are suffering.

Personally, I am always blessed and edified when I read the honest, visceral, heartfelt, and personal words of my co-sufferers in

Christ. It makes me realize that I'm not alone in my struggles and pain. It helps me to realize that my own individual agony is inseparable from the agony of my brethren.

As I suffer, the Church suffers; and as the Church suffers, I suffer. As the Church corporately receives the Body and Blood of Christ, so I as an individual receive the Body and Blood of Christ; and as I as an individual receive the Body and Blood of Christ, so the Church corporately receives the Body and Blood of Christ.

In fact, if the prophets, saints, and apostles never talked about themselves at all, then the Bible would not exist. So yes, by all means let us strive to imitate St. John the Baptist who proclaimed, *"He must increase but I must decrease." [St. John 3:30]* And yet even in saying this, John the Baptist used the word "I."

So don't ever let anyone make you feel ashamed for expressing your personal, emotional, physical, and spiritual feelings and struggles. By baring your own soul you might help to save another's.

1,226. ~ FIRST and LAST "LAST SUPPER" ~

At the first Last Supper, Judas left early. But at the last Last Supper, I think Judas will stay and dine forever. I can't prove it. But I can hope for it. If Judas won't make it then I don't think I'll make it either. Judas only betrayed Jesus once. But I've betrayed Jesus too many times to count.

1,227. ~ WHAT IS A GREAT STORY? ~

A great story is an unbelievable story that resonates so profoundly with our common human condition that we know it is absolutely true. It might be a peg-legged sinner chasing a whale, or a reluctant prophet being swallowed by a whale. It might be primordial man relinquishing Eden, or space age man trying to reclaim it. It might be a girl reveling in a wonderland of madness, or a girl in a yellow brick dualistic dream struggling to return to reality.

Is a whale Satan or God? Is space heaven or hell? Is earth prison or paradise? Is an angel a demon or is a demon an angel?

We all carry witches and fairies, dragons and knights, trolls and lions within our consciousness. And we struggle to understand them, to separate them, to make sense of them.

Meister Eckhart wrote: *"The only thing that burns in hell is the part of you that won't let go of your life: your memories, your attachments. They burn them all away, but they're not punishing you, they're freeing your soul. If you're frightened of dying and you're holding on, you'll see devils tearing your life away. If you've made your peace, then the devils are really angels freeing you from the earth."*

The great stories are ultimately *our* stories; and in them we recognize our nakedness, our fears, our hopes, and our redemption. A great story reveals the conflicts and paradoxes of the human heart.

But great stories don't have to be intellectual to be enlightening or difficult to be deep. The episodes of *Sesame Street* and *Mister Rogers* that I watched at the age of five were as influential and moving as the novels of Hemingway and Dostoevsky that I read when I was 25.

The genius of all great stories is their ability to show how we all want to be loved, and how we all fail to love, and how we are all somehow loved anyway. And every great writer in every age has somehow been able to reveal – each in their own way – that the greatest tragedy in life is our failure to realize that we are truly loved.

In every great story the Gospel is profoundly present, although the storyteller may not even realize it – because the Gospel is indelibly imprinted upon our souls.

1,228. ~ TRUTH, FREEDOM, and THE SLAVERY of THE CROWD ~

The truth of a movement or the righteousness of a cause is not determined by the number of people that turn out to support it. While Noah built the ark, the masses gathered to mock him. While Moses talked to God alone on Sinai, the crowds in the valley were fashioning a golden calf. While Elijah and a remnant remained faithful, the majority worshipped Baal. While the lonely prophets preached repentance, the hordes gathered to build the tower of Babel. While twelve followed the Savior, the multitudes turned away. And while the Mother of Jesus pleaded for His life, the godless herds shouted, *"Free Barabbas! Crucify Christ!"*

So, with all due respect: I'm not interested with how many votes you get, how many people attend your marches, how large your congregation is, or how loudly you can get your orchestrated chorus to shout. If it's not based in truth, predicated upon peace, and cultivated by love, then I don't want any part of it.

I'm a free man. I refuse to be enslaved by your organized violence, your collaborative lies, your democratic division, and your coordinated political hate.

1,229. ~ CONSERVATIVES, LIBERALS, and MODERATES ~

"We will kill and rape and starve and oppress you. But don't worry, because we are *conservatives* freeing you from the evils of liberalism."

"We will kill and rape and starve and oppress you. But don't worry, because we are *liberals* freeing you from the evils of conservatism."

"We know that you are being killed and raped and starved and oppressed by both the right and the left. But don't worry, because we are *moderates* who stand in the middle and do nothing as people suffer all around us."

1,230. ~ ON COMFORT, THE CROWD, and SLAUGHTERHOUSES ~

I've always been more comfortable when I'm uncomfortable, when my opinion is not popular, when I stand against the crowd rather than with the crowd. And that's probably due more to obstinate hubris and sinful pride than to any sort of spiritual righteousness on my part.

Judas stood up and abandoned his brothers who were gathered at the table with Christ. Sometimes it is better to remain with good company than to "kick against the goads." As wise King Solomon wrote: *"There is wisdom in a multitude of counselors."* [Proverbs 11:14]

And yet I have always sensed great danger in the presence of the masses. Slaughterhouses do not exist for the single lamb; they exist for the extermination of the bovine herd.

1,231. ~ SLEEPING, DYING, DREAMING, LIVING ~

Some say, *"I'll sleep when I'm dead."* Others say, *"I'll dream while I live."* I see equal value in both perspectives.

1,232. ~ MORAL PROCLAMATIONS and HYPOCRITICAL CONDEMNATIONS ~

Preach your morality. Promote your morality. Feel free to argue and defend your morality. Hell, go ahead and shove your morality in my face. I'll respect you for at least having some passion and conviction. Just don't preach your own godless morality while hypocritically denouncing the God-fearing who preach theirs as being "self-righteous moralists." Because when you do that, then you actually become the very self-righteous moralists that you so smugly presume to condemn.

1,233. ~ TO HELL WITH YOUR "MAINSTREAM" EVILS! ~

When political ideologues condemn something or someone for being outside the "mainstream" just remember that slavery, segregation, Jim Crow laws, and lynchings were also once mainstream. Just like abortion is mainstream today. So with all due respect: to hell with your mainstream evils, by whatever political label you seek to perpetuate them.

1,234. ~ AN INCONSISTENT PACIFISM ~

I confess that my pacifism is full of inconsistencies. Although I am philosophically and theologically committed to nonviolence, I am nevertheless too often violent of heart and violent in speech. I am violent by my apathy and indifference to human suffering. I am violent by my cowardice. I am violent by my prioritization of defending an ideology over defending individuals. And while I refuse to take up the sword, I too easily wield a violent pen and a hurtful tongue. I have become a very thorough pacifist, but I still haven't learned to be a peacemaker.

1,235. ~ NUANCE ~

I'm all for nuance except when nuance leads to nooses and gas chambers and unborn babies being "nuanced" to pieces.

1,236. ~ REFLECTIONS on BONHOEFFER and SOCIAL ENGAGEMENT ~

Dietrich Bonhoeffer always urged the Church to be socially involved. I prefer the term "social engagement" to "political engagement," but I do agree that sometimes social action requires political involvement. And yet I also believe that one can be politically active without acquiescing with tyrannies, democracies, or dictatorships that are established upon unchristian principles.

So I agree with Bonhoeffer that social and political engagement is an essential aspect of Christian discipleship. The question then becomes how do we become socially and politically engaged in order to promote good without also promoting evil?

We have seen the problems of well intentioned Christian political movements such as the "Moral Majority" on the right and "Sojourners" on the left. Both movements began as a sincere attempt to make the Gospel socially and politically relevant. Both movements were spawned by a genuine desire to prioritize "the least of these." But the result of these movements was the perpetuation of political divisions that ended up doing more to divide the Church than to unite society. And in their efforts to redress certain social injustices their political allegiances facilitated the perpetuation of other injustices.

So these are questions and issues with which we need to honestly wrestle. Bonhoeffer's writings and legacy continue to remind us of the challenge at hand. May God lead and guide us in wisdom, peace, truth, and love. And may He grant us the grace of true courage born from true faith.

"I am guilty of cowardly silence at a time when I ought to have spoken. I am guilty of hypocrisy and untruthfulness in the face of force. I have been lacking in compassion and I have denied the poorest of my brethren. We, the Church, must confess that we have not proclaimed often or clearly enough our message of the One God who has revealed Himself for all times in Jesus Christ and who will tolerate not other gods beside Himself. The Church must confess her timidity, her evasiveness, her dangerous concessions. She has often been untrue to her office of guardianship but faithful to her office of comfort. She was silent when she should have cried out because the blood of the innocent was crying aloud to heaven. She has failed to speak the right word in the right way at the right time. She has not resisted to the uttermost the apostasy of faith, and she has brought upon herself the guilt of the godlessness of the masses. The Church

must confess that she has witnessed the lawless application of brutal force, the physical and spiritual suffering of countless innocent people, oppression, hatred, and murder, and that she has not raised her voice on behalf of the victims and has not hastened to their aid. She is guilty of the deaths of the weakest and most defenseless brethren of Jesus Christ. The Church must confess that she has desired security, peace and quiet, possessions and honor, to which she has no divine right. She has not borne witness to the truth of God. By her own silence she has rendered herself guilty because of her unwillingness to suffer for what she knows to be right."

~ Dietrich Bonhoeffer ~

1,237. ~ REVOLUTION, LEGALITY, and PROPHECY ~

There is no such thing as a legal revolution. The prophets are always outlaws.

1,238. ~ ABORTION IS NOT JUST A WOMEN'S ISSUE ~

Abortion is not just about women's rights. It's ultimately about *human rights*. Every pregnancy involves at least three lives: the life of the mother, the life of the father, and the life of the unborn child. Women cannot get pregnant by themselves; so it's ludicrous to demand that they should be granted the sole authority to determine the fate of the lives in their wombs, to demand the autonomous right to decide whether or not to kill the unborn child.

The "pro-choice" mindset is as old and as evil as slavery: *"My property, my rights!" "My body, my choice!" "If you're against abortion don't have one!" "If you're against slavery don't own slaves!"*

But no one should ever have the right to enslave, oppress, or abort another. Whenever issues of human rights are at stake, there are only two sides: the side of life and freedom or the side of death and oppression.

Abortion is a most insidious form of capitalistic exploitation, enriching large corporations like Planned Parenthood at the expense of poor, desperate, and disadvantaged women. Those who support legal abortion are counterrevolutionary conspirers with the same unjust and oppressive system that has always waged war against the poor, the vulnerable, the "minorities," and the weak.

Rather than empowering women, the legality of abortion empowers misogynistic men who want to control women and keep them reduced to mere objects for their own sexual gratification. Abortion allows rapists, pedophiles, and pimps to cover up their crimes and keep their victims silent. Abortion allows abusive boyfriends and husbands to force women to have abortions against their wills. Abortion allows adulterous men to violently cover up their sins so they can continue their infidelities. Nothing about any of this is empowering or liberating for women.

And what about the women who in a moment of panic and fear rush to have an abortion only to regret it for the rest of their lives? They get no refund. Or what about the countless women who are physically damaged beyond repair, or who die from these so-called "safe, rare, and legal" abortions? Not only can they never get the lives of their children back, but they can't get their reproductive choices back because their uteruses were ripped to shreds and their ability to conceive a child was destroyed forever. What a sad irony that this ostensible "reproductive choice" often destroys women's ability to ever again have a reproductive choice.

So as a man, as a husband, as a father, and as a member of the human race I refuse to let anyone tell me that I don't have the right to speak out about human rights, human life, and human dignity. I oppose abortion precisely because I care too much about women to perpetuate the lie that abortion is good for women. I oppose abortion because I care too much about freedom, justice, peace, and humanity to remain silent about this most destructive, demeaning, violent, and oppressive act.

Women deserve better than abortion. Society deserves better than abortion. We all deserve better than abortion.

As Dr. Martin Luther King, Jr. said: *"Injustice anywhere is a threat to justice everywhere. Whatever affects one directly affects all indirectly."*

It's time to put a stop to the injustice of abortion once and for all. God grant us the collective courage and social conviction to do so.

"It moves one's heart to think: Nine months before I was born there was a woman who loved me deeply. She did not know what I was going to be like, but she loved me because she carried me in her womb. And when she gave me birth, she took me in her arms, because her love was not just beginning – she conceived it along with me. A mother loves – and that is why abortion is so abhorrent."
~ Archbishop Oscar Romero ~

"When once a certain class of people has been placed by the temporal and spiritual authorities outside the ranks of those whose life has value, then nothing comes more naturally to men than murder." ~ Simone Weil ~

"Destruction of the embryo in the mother's womb is a violation of the right to live which God has bestowed upon this nascent life. To raise the question of whether we are here concerned already with a human being or not is merely to confuse the issue. The simple fact is that God certainly intended to create a human being and that this nascent human being has been deliberately deprived of his life. And this is nothing but murder." ~ Dietrich Bonhoeffer ~

"The propagandist's purpose is to make one set of people forget that certain other sets of people are human." ~ Aldous Huxley ~

1,239. ~ THIS HOLY NIGHT ~

I see my Jesus
In the womb
I pray for us
To make Him room

I see Him resting
On the hay
I pray that we
Would give Him way

I hear the Baby's
Gentle cry
And because of me
He soon will die

But heaven smiles
And stars are bright
For God is born
This holy night

1,240. ~ MYSTERIOUS SPELL ~

Harsh and hopeful
Painful but true
Sometimes warm
Sometimes blue
With thorns of blood
And buds that bloom
It's never too late
And never too soon
It can feel like heaven
And hurt like hell
Love is indeed
a mysterious spell

1,241. ~ OF BROKEN BARRIERS and DREAMS DEFERRED ~

In 1947, Jackie Robinson broke the "color barrier" and became the first Black man to play baseball in the major leagues. His courage, struggle, and heroism helped pave the way for racial justice and social progress. Robinson's nobility, skill, and grace – both on and off the field – inspired children of all colors. His example especially gave hope to African American boys and girls, inspiring them to believe that they too could rise to greatness and break new barriers. But 60 years later, Black children in the womb now struggle to break the "life barrier." They are victimized by a law that inhumanely condemns their very right to exist. Jackie Robinson endured horrendous insults and injuries in his lifetime, but he was at least afforded the opportunity to face such challenges. Yet today millions of Black children are not even afforded the right to be born, suffering cruel and vicious deaths at the hands of violent abortionists.

In 1963, Dr. Martin Luther King, Jr. stood in front of the Lincoln Memorial and envisioned day when "little black boys and black girls will be able to join hands with little white boys and white girls and walk together as sisters and brothers." His beautiful dream saturated our wounded nation with the healing tears of promise and hope. Dr. King made America believe that good could triumph over evil, and that justice could not remain dormant forever. But half a century later, little black unborn boys and girls have achieved the "equality" of being denied the fundamental right to life that is mutually denied to little white unborn boys and girls. The inestimable potential of choirs of children's voices that should reverberate across our land is muted by the silent screams of unborn innocents that are led away to daily slaughter.

So, it is in contemplation of broken barriers and dreams deferred that I compose this revolutionary statement.

As long as the color barrier that Jackie Robinson shattered remains supplanted by a legal barrier that shatters human Life, then I will not acknowledge any pretense of "progress." As long as Jackie Robinson's legacy is celebrated while our future heroes are denied the right to be born, to live, and to pursue similar greatness, then I will lend no credence to the hollow rhetoric of "hope and change."

I am a Christian, albeit an imperfect one. But a true Christian is a true revolutionary, rebelling against the sins in his own life and opposing the injustices and evils of this world. And as long as the fulfillment of Dr. King's dream remains impeded by the nightmare of abortion then I will agitate, offend, disrupt and disturb the status quo of systemic death and destruction.

I am neither a prophet, nor a hero, nor a saint. But a Christian need not be any of these things to proclaim *"liberty to the captives and freedom for the oppressed." [Isaiah 61:1]*

Therefore, I will continue to be a voice for the voiceless. I will remain unremitting in my condemnation of injustice and evil. I will not cede legitimacy to those who claim to care about poverty while they disregard the very poorest of the poor. I will refuse to say "peace, peace" where there is no peace. I will not cease to point out the pathology of a nation that sends a man to the moon but won't let a baby emerge from the womb. I will never conform to a culture that practices this wholesale act of barbarism which is euphemistically called "abortion."

I don't care if you stand to the left of me or to the right of me, if you don't stand for Life then I'll tell you to "get thee behind me Satan." Your politics, your religion, and your moral platitudes mean nothing to me if they do not fundamentally affirm the sacredness of human Life.

I write these words to honor Jackie Robinson and Dr. Martin Luther King, Jr. And I write these words to honor all others – past and present – who have ventured into the dark frontiers of social injustice with the lamp of truth and the light of Christ.

The battlefields change, and new weapons are constantly formed against us. But the war remains the same, and we recognize that the war is ultimately spiritual rather than carnal. So we fight for the sanctity of Life, and we oppose violence with peace. We wage our battles with the weapons of prayer, and we conquer the enemy with the power of love and the truth of the Gospel. But make no mistake: we do indeed fight, with a spiritual militancy that eternally prevails.

So, until the unborn are free to sing their cries of infant wonder, I will perpetually proclaim the revolutionary song – a song composed of the chords of peace, justice, love, and Life. And unpleasant, insistent, and inharmonious as it may sound amidst a culture of death, I will nevertheless sing this rebel song. I will sing this rebel song until either the unborn are free or until the society that condemns them condemns me to the same fate.

"Truly I tell you, whatever you did for one of the least of these brothers and sisters of mine, you did for me." [St. Matthew 25:40]

"In every man's chest there beats a heart...
Soon we will find out who are the real revolutionaries.
I don't want my people to be tricked by mercenaries...
Every man's got a right to decide his own destiny."
~ Bob Marley (Berhane Selassie) ~

1,242. ~ FASTING and KILLING ~

Better to eat and drink and refuse to kill than to fast from meat and slay our neighbors. Perhaps this Lent we should repent of militarism, soldiering, and the patriotic idolatry that fuels our bloodlust. Do we dare receive the Blood of Christ with hands which are stained with the blood of our brother?

1,243. ~ WHILE I STILL HAVE BREATH and SPEECH and INK in MY VEINS ~

I'm always honored and humbled when anyone takes an interest in anything I have to say. But I suspect most people are more intrigued by my insanity than by my insights (although I believe that madness is often the mother of enlightenment.)

But perhaps I am just a pompous jackass, which is probably the more plausible explanation for why some people read what I write. It's amusing to follow the rants of fools, and I guess I may at least be entertaining in that regard.

So please pray for this fool. And pray that I would be a fool for Christ rather than a fool for this world. And please follow the Gospel of Our Lord and the Teachings and Traditions of His Church above my own arrogant opinions. Because I can assure you that I am a broken man, clambering through the darkness, clinging to gossamer threads of hope. I'm just a Christian that tries to be a writer and a writer that tries to be a Christian.

If I am alive tomorrow with prayer still on my lips, then that is victory enough for me. So above all, love one another. Because more than anything else that is the message I wish to convey while I still have breath and speech and ink in my veins.

1,244. ~ SPLINTERS and SWORDS ~

With the splinters of His Cross, Jesus breaks every sword!

1,245. ~ ON FORGIVENESS and JUSTICE ~

There is freedom in forgiveness. Hatred and vengeance do nothing but enslave our own souls. But forgiveness is not apathy or indifference to suffering and injustice. Forgiveness is not weakness. It takes tremendous strength to truly forgive, and true forgiveness does not mean remaining silent about demands for restitution and reparations. Forgiveness does not mean acquiescing with evil or accepting injury and wrong. But it does mean forgiving even those that crucify us.

It is quite possible to forgive and demand justice at the same time. Forgiveness and justice are not in conflict with each other. True forgiveness is not blind to justice, and the truly just soul is a truly forgiving soul.

Christ didn't bow to wickedness. He made no peace with the devil. But He forgave those who drove the nails through His hands and feet. And by His refusal to neither compromise with evil nor hate those who did evil unto Him, Our Lord Jesus Christ conquered sin and defeated death and liberated all humanity to enter into eternal life.

May God give us grace and strength to do the same.

"We wish to recall here the spirit of tolerance shown by Our Lord Jesus Christ when He gave forgiveness to all including those that crucified Him... The preservation of peace and the guaranteeing of man's basic freedoms and rights require courage and eternal vigilance: courage to speak and act – and if necessary, to suffer and die – for truth and justice; eternal vigilance, that the least transgression of international morality shall not go undetected and without remedy." ~ H.I.M. Emperor Haile Selassie I ~

1,246. ~ THE GOSPEL FORMS MY RENUNCIATIONS ~

The Gospel of Jesus Christ leads me to renounce all violence and injustice done to anyone for any reason. Christian compassion compels me to love both mother and child, and to offer life affirming care that will help them both. Just as I believe that war will never bring about peace, I believe that abortion will never bring about healing or liberation. To oppress, harm, or kill one human being in order to bring peace, justice, and freedom to another human being only perpetuates the horrific cycle of misery and suffering in the world.

1,247. ~ WORSE BUT GREATER THAN WE REALIZE ~

Sin, violence, evil, and injustice are worse than we realize. And yet truth, love, peace, and hope are greater than we realize. The Cross was both the darkest and most redemptive moment in human history. Salvation comes not through mediating, ignoring, or obviating these tensions. It comes through living honestly and faithfully with them.

We must carry our own crosses, following Christ to His Cross, suffering as we are saved and proclaiming peace, love, and life amidst violence, hate, and death.

As William Stringfellow wrote:

"It is worse than you think it is, and yet you are freer than you think you are. The powers are raging beyond your control, and yet they are already overcome by Christ. The division is an uncrossable spiritual chasm, and yet through the Cross the chasm has been crossed. Death reigns and yet we have been freed from its bondage."

1,248. ~ HOW MEN are BROKEN by BOTH SECULAR and CHRISTIAN SOCIETY ~

Society is constantly blaming men, emasculating men, disempowering and disenfranchising men; and then men go to Church to look for comfort and grace only to have the yoke of burden and blame placed on them once again. And we wonder why there are so many fatherless children and single mothers in our culture.

Men are broken and destroyed by the undue pressures that society places upon them. Men have no say in whether their unborn children live or die, but if the mothers of their children grant them life then the men are forced to pay child support. Single mothers are financially supported by the government for each child they have, but single fathers are hunted down and treated like criminals unless they pay the fatherhood toll.

Men are constantly told that they are supposed to "provide." And in this capitalistic and materialistic society "provision" only means one thing: money. So when single fathers can't find work – or when the only work they *can* find won't pay enough to "provide" according to the standards of the government – then in a cruel twist of irony, men often turn to crime as a desperate measure to make enough money to stay out of jail. And how does this sordid cycle help anyone at all?

At one end secular society constantly lectures men about their evil "patriarchy," and on the other end Christian society constantly lectures men about their responsibility to "provide." At one end secular society views men as oppressive, authoritarian beasts, and on the other end Christian society tells men that they are "worse than unbelievers" (because apparently they think St. Paul was a capitalist who defined the meaning of "provide" in purely materialistic terms [Cf. I Timothy 5:8])

So where do poor, single fathers turn to for affirmation, support, encouragement, and strength? Who will value them for something other than the amount of money they can earn? Who will value them for all the countless things they can provide that are intangible but invaluable, spiritually indispensable but materially immeasurable?

Men have been beaten down, shamed, and guilt tripped to death by both the secular world and by the Church. And all this unfair and undue pressure has only served to weaken and break men rather than strengthen and inspire men. And women certainly do not benefit from weak, broken, and uninspired men.

Let me also speak a personal word to all the righteous, God-fearing, and true-hearted women out there:

We men can't be who we need to be without you being who you need to be. So strive to love us unconditionally just as you want us to love you unconditionally. Hold us accountable according to the standards of Christ rather than the standards of the world. Make us better men by believing in us, and by valuing us for who we are rather than by our material wealth (or lack thereof).

Jesus said, *"Foxes have dens and birds have nests, but the Son of Man has no place to lay his head... Come and follow me." [St. Matthew 8:20-22]* So we men – if we are to be godly men – must lead you towards salvation. And salvation involves nails and thorns and splinters and crosses. No honest Christian man can promise you earthly comfort or security. All we can promise you is that we will strive to always give you our love and loyalty and sacrificial devotion, that we will love and raise our children in the ways of the Lord, and that we will pursue the Kingdom of God above all else.

And those are no small things. But for many women in this society that is not enough – or more accurately, that's simply too much.

Our godless culture has pitted man against woman and woman against man. But God created woman from the side of man, to help man, to be equal to man, to love and affirm and assist and follow man as he leads her towards eternal life. But today we are fighting each other, making unfair demands of each other, oppressing and violating each other because we have lost sight of the Kingdom and instead desire earthly things above our own salvation.

So today men are reduced to walking ATM machines, and women are reduced to robotic creatures programmed to respond not to love or affection or righteousness or truth, but to mere material and financial compensation. Most marriages in our culture amount to little more than legalized transactional sex. And many professing Christians unfortunately warrant this same indictment.

Now, I don't expect society to ease up on men. The world will always be the world; and in the world's eyes a man's value is determined solely by the size of his wallet, by the size of his gun, or by his priapic prowess. But I do expect for the Church to be a refuge from the world, a witness against the world, and a bulwark of strength for both men and women who must live in and engage the world. And the yokes of pressure, guilt, manipulation, and shame will neither help men to be better men nor help women to be better women.

So please, give us men some grace. Because when men live in grace then women will benefit just as much – in all the ways that truly matter.

1,249. ~ REFLECTIONS on ALBERT CAMUS and ALDOUS HUXLEY ~

In my humble opinion, Albert Camus and Aldous Huxley were the two greatest non-Christian intellectuals of the 20th century. They were both men of tremendous intellectual prowess, and yet their intellect was always guided by a deep moral concern for human rights and a commitment to the sanctity of human life. Amidst a tumultuous sea of 20th century worldviews and philosophies, it was their sincere moral and ethical conscientiousness that set Camus and Huxley apart from the rest. Humanity was always at the heart of Camus's existentialism and Huxley's mysticism.

Camus diagnosed a similar problem with both Marxism and Christianity, pointing out that they both seek ultimate hope for humanity in future solutions. Marxism promises hope for humanity through a dialectical process that entails bloodshed and suffering in the here and now in order to pave way for a proletariat utopia down the road. And Christianity promises ultimate hope for humanity in an eschatological heavenly paradise. But Camus, as an authentic existentialist, argued that all we really know is that we exist *now*, and thus we must work *now* to stop human suffering. He didn't presume to say with any certainty that the hopes of Marxist dialectics or Christian eschatology were unfounded; he simply argued that to elevate and prioritize those hopes over and above the real existential suffering of the present moment is both a secular and religious blasphemy.

Aldous Huxley was not an existentialist, but a mystic. He was a passionate student of religion, a biblical scholar, a man who studied "enlightenment" and experimented with Eastern religions and hallucinogenic drugs. And throughout all of his academic studies and psychedelic experiences he always came back to the question and problem of his fellow man. He realized that while an individual can understand great and profound truths via academic education, hallucinogenic insights, or "mountaintop experiences," an individual still has a responsibility to his neighbor, to his brother, to his comrades in this mystical existence called "life."

The scholar has learned nothing if he hasn't learned to work to ease the suffering of others. The religious sage is in reality a fool if he doesn't teach respect for life and active compassion for the living. And if the "enlightened" soul ascends above the needs of humanity here on earth, then that soul is not enlightened but more likely damned.

So that's what I love about Albert Camus and Aldous Huxley. At the root of all their philosophical and experimental inquiries was a deep and passionate desire to respect life, to affirm life, and to ameliorate the suffering of human life. We Christians can learn much from both of them.

"It is better to be wrong by killing no one than to be right with mass graves." ~ Albert Camus ~

"The propagandist's purpose is to make one set of people forget that certain other sets of people are human." ~ Aldous Huxley ~

1,250. ~ VICTIMIZATION and REVOLUTION ~

We seem to constantly fight and argue over who is victimized the most in our society. There is a constant battle over whose grievances are the most legitimate and the most pressing, and politicians exploit this battle to keep us distracted and divided from the revolutionary work of brotherhood, justice, peace, and love. The fact is that we are all victimized by one common enemy: our own sins and the nefarious forces that prey upon our sins. And Satan and his political pawns love nothing more than for us to constantly condemn the specks in our neighbors' eyes while we remain blinded by the beams in our own eyes.

If we have been victims of injustice and evil, then the most powerful thing we can do to confront injustice and evil is to cultivate a spirit of tolerance and compassion for others. As we raise one clenched fist for justice, truth, and rights, let us extend our other hand in open service to our fellow man. When we get busy loving others then we go from being victims to victors, from being powerless to being truly empowered, and from being political reactionaries to spiritual revolutionaries.

There is no guarantee that others will ever treat us justly in this world. But we can always make sure that we act justly towards others. And if we focus our energies on that, I think it will make all the difference.

1,251. ~ CONVERSATION ~

Sometimes talking about something too much is just as problematic as not talking about something enough. It's not the quantity but the quality our conversation that matters. And quality conversation usually involves just as much listening as talking.

1,252. ~ "ILLEGAL" ~

Never forget that 2,000 years ago the infant Jesus was also considered "illegal" by the government of His time.

1,253. ~ THE TRUE MEASURE of FAITH ~

It's easy to love those who love us back. It's easy to be at peace with those who are peaceful. It's easy to be merciful with those who show us mercy. It's easy to be righteous and just with the just and the righteous. It's easy to give to those who reciprocate our kindness.

But the true measure of faith is a willingness to love even when we are hated, to remain nonviolent even when we are violently attacked, to be merciful even to those who are cruel, to be just with the unjust, and to give to others even when we know we will receive nothing in return.

To be a Christian means to be like Christ. And to be like Christ means to prepare not for wealth and war, but for crucifixion and eternal life. May God help us.

1,254. ~ THE STRENGTH to LOVE ~

Kindness is not cowardice. Forgiveness is not weakness. It takes tremendous courage and strength to love one's enemies. And love for the oppressor is not synonymous with acquiescing with oppression. As Dr. Martin Luther King, Jr. explains in his book, _Strength To Love_:

"I had almost despaired of the power of love to solve social problems. The turn-the-other-cheek and love-your-enemies philosophies were valid, I felt, only when individuals are in conflict with other individuals; but when racial groups and nations are in conflict, I thought a more realistic approach was necessary. But then I was introduced to the life and teachings of Mahatma Gandhi. As I read his works I became deeply fascinated by his campaigns of nonviolent resistance. The whole Gandhian concept of "satyagraha" ("satya" is truth which equals love and "graha" is force; "satyagraha" thus means truth-force or love-force) was profoundly significant to me. As I delved deeper into the philosophy of Gandhi, my skepticism concerning the power of love gradually diminished, and I came to see for the first time that the Christian doctrine of love, operating through the Gandhian method of nonviolence, is one of the most potent weapons available to an oppressed people in their struggle for freedom."

1,255. ~ ONE PLANET, ONE PEOPLE, ONE GOD, ONE LOVE ~

Regardless of religion or race, politics or nationality, gender or creed, we are all children of One God living together in this world that He created. Let us each believe freely, worship Our Lord as we are led, and be faithful to our righteous convictions. But above all, let us know that true religion is predicated upon two basic spiritual imperatives: _love God and love people._ If we would all heed these two basic commands, then we would have peace and justice in our world.

So it's really up to us. It starts with our willingness to respect, honor, and help each other in spite of our cultural, political, or religious differences. If we truly love God then we will truly love others. And love is really what it's all about.

This is the only life we have. Let's not waste it on violence and hate. Instead, let's get busy loving the Creator and loving one another. *One Planet! One People! One God! One Love!*

"Hearing that Jesus had silenced the Sadducees, the Pharisees got together. One of them, an expert in the law, tested him with this question: "Teacher, which is the greatest commandment in the Law?" Jesus replied: " 'Love the Lord your God with all your heart and with all your soul and with all   your mind.' This is the first and greatest commandment. And the second is like it: 'Love your neighbor as yourself.' All the Law and the Prophets hang on these two commandments." [St. Matthew 10:34-40]

1,256. ~ AUTHORITARIAN ASSAULTS on ART ~

The far right and the far left inevitably end up meeting in the same horrific authoritarian realm that stifles authentic individualism and artistic creativity. When life is reduced to "scientific" Marxist dialectics or materialistic capitalistic pursuits then the results are always uninspiring, unnatural, and inhumane.

1,257. ~ WHO WILL HONOR THE VETERANS of PEACE? ~

Who will honor the veterans of peace?

Who will honor those that refused to harm their fellow man?

Who will honor those that served the cause of truth rather than the lies of the state?

Who will honor those that chose Christ over country and Faith over flag?

Who will honor those that suffered torture, abuse, ridicule, and death simply because they rejected the idolatry of politics and patriotism, militarism and might?

Who will honor those that served the Spirit rather than the sword, the Gospel rather than the government?

Who will honor those that refused to submit to the sin of war, that refused to call good "evil" and evil "good"?

Yes, I ask you: who will honor the veterans of peace?

Who will honor those that are betrayed by family and friends, nation and church, simply because they heed the divine imperative of *"Thou shalt not kill."*?

I will. I will.

1,258. ~ WHERE THEN WILL I BE? ~

Today I betrayed Jesus.
Today Jesus forgives me.
Tomorrow I will sleep
while He sweats blood
and prays for me.
Friday He will be crucified,
and I wonder
where then will I be?

1,259. ~ IN RETURN ~

We will tolerate you on the slave ships. We will tolerate you in shackles. We will tolerate you as long as you provide us with your sweat and your songs and your servitude and your strange fruit.

Yes, we will even tolerate you in the White House. (In fact, that's where we like you the most. Because if we can trust you enough to let you run our hellish plantation, then we don't have to worry about you rebelling.)

But we will not tolerate your prolific procreation. We will not tolerate your devoted life affirmation, your natural familial bonds, your authentic African manhood and your genuine African femininity.

We will tolerate anything and everything except for your roots. We will tolerate any manner of your deeds as long as you don't plant your seeds.

We will give you education and lofty careers. We will give you political power and social prestige. And we will always pay you well to entertain us with the violent and dehumanizing stereotypes we foist upon you. (After all, we make a killing from your killing.) We will gladly give you a share in our godless Babylon kingdom... just as long as you give us the blood of your children – born and unborn – in return.

1,260. ~ WHETHER I SLEEP or DREAM or LIVE or DIE ~

How do you wake up from a nightmare when you can't even go to sleep? And how can you go to sleep when you're living a dream? I fear sleep more than life, and I fear life more than death. But whether I sleep or live or dream or die, I cling to the Cross of Our Lord. In all things I am being saved. And that is all that matters.

1,261. ~ SUBSTITUTING LAW FOR TRUTH ~

Humanity substitutes law for truth and thereby enslaves itself to systematic and orderly lies.

1,262. ~ MISSISSIPPI RIVER ~

Mississippi River
Deep and wide
Burdened with sins
Flowing with pride

Mississippi River
Thick with mud
Trying to outrun
Her stains of blood

Mississippi River
Lifeline and grave
Waters that haunt
Waters that save

1,263. ~ PRIDE KILLS. HUMILITY SAVES. ~

Even God Incarnate had help carrying His Cross. So who are we to think we can bear ours alone? Pride kills. Humility saves.

1,264. ~ CHOOSING to SEEK and ACCEPT THE MOST PEACEFUL and LOVING INTERPRETATIONS of ALL RELIGIONS and WORLDVIEWS ~

Every religion has a history, and a lot of that history is pretty awful. There will always be cosmic arguments regarding who and what determines the correct interpretation of religious texts and religious faith. But as a Christian my faith is in the Incarnate God, who lived and preached and died to teach us peace and love for all people – even our enemies. So I choose to seek and accept the most peaceful and loving interpretations of all religions and worldviews. Is my interpretation of the Gospel right? I don't know. But I do believe it is the Orthodox interpretation. Is the Orthodox interpretation the right interpretation? I don't know. But if the peace and love of Christ is heresy and error, then I would rather be wrong than right.

1,265. ~ THE MISTRESS of HOPE ~

Hope is a most dangerous and fickle mistress. She demands nothing less than complete loyalty; for one cannot hope halfheartedly. Hope is either fully embraced or fully denied.

So hope calls with siren song – alluring, enticing – offering promises that defy logic and reason, proffering betrothals that contradict intuition and experience. But she is a powerful seductress.

God how we want to believe! God how we want to trust! God how we want to cast ourselves into the arms of hope in spite of every cruelty we have suffered in life!

And God how viciously hope will turn on you! She will sink her fangs into your soul and suck the life out of you. If you let her.

But I refuse to accord hope such power. I refuse to worship this seductress. I refuse to hope for hope's sake. I refuse to make hope an idol before which I continually bow, an idol that continually breaks me. I refuse to hope in anything other than the bloody Cross and the empty tomb.

Because, over the course of my life, my heart has been shattered into a thousand pieces. My soul has been scarred beyond anything that this life can possibly repair. I have hoped beyond hope, over and over and over again. I have been bitten, infected, and irrevocably poisoned by this cruel and damnable mistress.

I made my bed with her, and I have only myself to blame. We are all victimized by our own idols. So I hope no more in hope herself. Hope will not save. Hope is not God. Hope is merely an instrument, a tool, something that will either be a vehicle to heaven or a vehicle to hell.

I have hoped in too many sunrises, only to learn that darkness inevitably comes crashing down. So I'll content myself with night noir and midnight melancholy. I'm comfortable here. It is in these nocturnal hours that I am most awake and most aware. When the vampires roam I shall stand vigil against them. Someone must be on guard. I am happy to do it. I've jettisoned all my expectations of warmth and light. So let darkness be my playground, and let me dwell in the shadow of raven wings. I will not be saved otherwise.

Hope was once my beloved mistress, but depression is the cross that I now wed; because I know that Christ is Risen, and thus I place my faith in nothing else.

O fickle mistress of hope: sell your seductions to someone else! My heart belongs to the Cross and the Resurrection. I give my soul to nothing more and nothing less. O fickle mistress of hope: I now gladly betray your deceptive leer for the crucified and risen Truth. I am your slave no more.

1,266. ~ DEPTH and SHALLOWNESS ~

Life is too big and too deep for small talk and shallow discourse.

"One of my good friends said, in a reggae riddim:
'Don't jump in the water, if you can't swim.'
The power of philosophy floats through my head
Light like a feather, heavy as lead."
~ Bob Marley (Berhane Selassie) ~

1,267. ~ CREATIVITY and CONSISTENCY ~

Consistency is the passion of the philosopher; creativity is the passion of the artist. I am persuaded that beauty and truth are born from consistent creativity and creative consistency.

1,268. ~ I TALK of GOD BECAUSE I AM FAR FROM GOD ~

I talk about God because I am far from God. The more we attempt to define the infinite, explain the ineffable, and defend the eternal, the more we demonstrate just how far removed we are from the divine experience. Lovers don't waste time trying to rationalize or justify their orgasms.

1,269. ~ THE HERESY of POVERTY ~

Where money is God the poor are condemned as heretics. But we are a "civilized" society, and therefore we don't burn our heretics at the stake. We simply banish them to lonely street corner destitution where they suffer in their heresies as we toss our Christian change at their feet.

It is important that our heretics be made to publicly suffer, otherwise the public may think it permissible to replicate the heretic's sins. And in America, it is clear that the greatest sin one can commit is to find oneself in poverty. Therefore our poor must be punished accordingly. It is the "god-fearing" thing to do. After all, there are many preachers who are quick to remind us that, *"If a man does not work he shall not eat." [II Thessalonians 3:10]*

So, by these preachers' twisted biblical interpretations, the beggar is a sinner, and nothing could be more unchristian than humbling oneself to beg for help. And thus we must never allow ourselves to fall so far from capitalism's idolatrous grace. God gave us the blessing of the profit motive, and unless we avail ourselves of this "blessing" then we have only ourselves to blame.

And yet everything in the writings of the Prophets, in the life and teachings of Christ, and in the 2,000 year old record of the saints and martyrs shows us that eternal salvation is in no way related to materialistic, financial, or earthly accomplishment. There is perhaps no greater heresy today than the blasphemous equation of worldly capitalistic "success" with authentic Christian faith. There is no greater sin than to oppress, kill, torture, or ignore the plight of our neighbors by appealing to the sacred Scriptures and the name of Christ. But this is exactly what we do when we put on our "Sunday best" and drive by the suffering and the afflicted on our way to worship the Lord who had no home during much of His time on earth.

1,270. ~ WAGING THE WRONG WARS ~

It is easier to condemn the enemies afar than to seek authentic peace at home. It is more convenient to bomb foreign "infidels" than to work for justice in one's own nation. It is safer to confront external devils than to face the demons within. We win these mortal battles but we lose our very souls. Through earthly warfare one may find temporal security; but it is only through spiritual warfare that one will find eternal life.

1,271. ~ AXE of LOVE ~

The tide of truth
the waves of peace
the forward surge
of irrepressible justice...

No evil can stop such good.

Rising from life
to give witness to life.
Flowing from the divine
to give voice to the human.
Bringing peace to sinners
and to the sinned against.

Governments and laws
and politics and hate will be felled
by the axe of our love.

1,272. ~ **BRAVE IN FLIGHT** ~

I'm told that they're the enemy
so I won't look them in the eye,
I'll just drop bombs on them
from a mile up in the sky.

If I happen to miss the target
and some children get blown away,
well I'm just following orders
and collecting a soldier's pay.

I'm a pilot in this war you see,
a patriot brave in flight,
setting fire to the flesh below me
and sleeping quite well at night.

1,273. ~ **MISSISSIPPI** ~

Faith healers
And bottle trees
Muddy waters
And Magnolia leaves

Columned porches
And delta blues
Cotton fields
And strange black fruit

Choctaw ghosts
And Jackson lights
Haunted pens
And Gulf shore nights

Bold new city
And blood soaked land
Shotgun houses
Mississippi: Goddam!

1,274. ~ "CHRISTIAN ARTISTS" ~

"Christian artists" are usually either poor artists or poor Christians. Attempts to make "Christian music," "Christian art," or "Christian movies" are as futile as attempts to make Christian food. If you are really a Christian – or if you are really an artist – then just do what you do: create from your heart and know that God is glorified through your honest expression and sincere effort. If you have to qualify your creativity with the adjective "Christian," then you have probably failed on both accounts.

(And I write this as someone whose first book is subtitled: *"Christian Philosophy & Orthodox Meditations."* So as always, I'm speaking to myself first and foremost here. Philosophy itself – as either an art or a science – needs no qualification. It may be true but not real, or real but not true. It may be deceptive or sincere, repulsive or redemptive, damnable or saving. And attaching the adjective "Christian" to it won't alter its essence. All philosophical ideas will be tried by the courts of temporal human opinion and the ultimate Truth of God.)

1,275. ~ PEACE and JUSTICE ~

If we seek peace we must pursue justice, and if we seek justice we must pursue peace. Peace and justice are as inseparable as fire and heat. There is no such thing as violent justice or an unjust peace.

1,276. ~ ART, REPULSION, and REDEMPTION ~

That which speaks to our hearts, that resonates with our souls, that illumines our minds and ignites our imagination is always that which is honest and real and naked and true – regardless of how absurdly abstract it may be portrayed or how simplistically mundane it may be conveyed. Whether cloaked in cubist contortionism or ensconced in impressionistic harmony, the truth is intuitively recognizable. Shapes and colors and mediums and forms are mere vehicles through which we recognize the ineffable and bow before the transcendent. And when art beckons – yea demands – that we go beyond ourselves, then we are confronted with things that are not always pleasant. But if it is true then it is redemptive, and therefore great art will sometimes repulse in order to save.

1,277. ~ A UNIVERSALLY SHARED HERESY ~

There seems to be one universally agreed upon philosophy, one universally maintained religion, one universally shared idolatry, one universally articulated blasphemy, one universally perpetuated heretical worldview by which humanity universally enslaves, condemns, and destroys itself – and that is the common belief held by almost every race, religion, nationality, and tribe that killing other people is not only sometimes permissible but also even noble. And what is the result of this common conviction? The result is perpetual war and perpetual killing, insatiable injustice and omnipresent oppression.

People will argue passionately over all manner of religious and philosophical ideas – and in fact they will even kill one another in defense of those ideas – and yet they will all agree upon the ostensible "necessity" and "justice" of bloodshed. They will all agree upon the "right" to slay their fellow man if the occasion so demands.

But against this universally held doctrine of demons Christ stretches out His nail-scarred hands and says, *"Forsake the sword and follow Me!"*

Yes, following Jesus may lead to our own crucifixion. And that certainly seems like a foolish path to take, which is why the road to heaven is a narrow road indeed (Cf. St. Matthew 7:13-14). And yet the world in its godless "wisdom" seeks peace and security in bloodshed and violence. So is it not better to be crucified and be saved than to kill and be damned?

1,278. ~ LIFE IS OUR COMMON ARK ~

We are all in the same boat together. Life is our common Ark. And together we shall all be saved, as long as we don't jump ship.

1,279. ~ SOLIDARITY ~

What do I value most in people? I've thought a lot about that. Certainly I find comfort and community with those who share my religious, political, and social views. Certainly I find comfort and community with those who share my aesthetic, artistic, and literary tastes. Certainly I find comfort and community with those who share my love for music (especially good music) and for sport (especially the right teams.) And, to be sure, I find comfort and community in the blood bonds of familial lineage and platonic camaraderie.

But *solidarity*? Where does one find that? I'm talking about that *real* solidarity, where you know that you are loved and valued and *taken care of*, in spite of your weaknesses and failures and sins.

Communists and fascists and nationalists and Republicans and Democrats and Christians and atheists and conservatives and liberals all offer a façade of solidarity. Agree with them, vote like them, preach what they preach, love what they love and hate what they hate – in other words, be loyal to the cause – and you will always be embraced. But God forbid that you even slightly dissent from the party line; for if you do, you will suffer either execution or excommunication.

I have sought solidarity in such superficial company. And I have learned that in such ideologies, isms, and cultural identities, true solidarity will never be found.

When I reflect upon my life, and when I meditate upon the genuine solidarity I have been blessed to find over the course of the years, I realize that true solidarity is predicated upon unconditional human brotherhood and unconditional brotherly love. I have found solidarity in unexpected places and with unexpected people. In fact, my closest friends, my deepest loves, and my most intimate connections are with people who probably disagree with many of my most cherished convictions and beliefs.

But they *love* me anyway. They *help* me anyway. They *encourage* me anyway. They *accept* me anyway. And I hope and pray that I do the same for them.

I have learned that in the revolution of true solidarity there are no deserters. Because true love, true loyalty, and true friendship will always hunt you down – not to convict you for your sins or execute you for your betrayal, but to remind you that you are forever loved and forever accepted in spite of your sins and betrayals.

And I know this truth because throughout my life God has showered me with the blessings of true people who have showered me with the blessings of true solidarity.

1,280. ~ COMPASSION IS THE KEY TO UNDERSTANDING ~

Compassion is the key to understanding. If we comprehend nothing else other than love for our neighbors, then we have recognized all the truth that truly matters.

1,281. ~ POLITICAL ECONOMICS ~

When it comes to political economics, I'm really not sure where I stand. I just know that I agree with the words of the Rastafarian Creed: *"Let the hungry be fed, let the naked be clothed, let the sick be nourished, let the aged be protected, and let the infants be cared for."* And I most certainly agree with the words of Our Lord Jesus Christ: *"I say unto you, whatever you did for one of the least these, my brothers of mine, you did also for me."* [St. Matthew 25:40]

I confess that I lean heavily towards socialism in many regards, precisely because the "haves" rarely give of their own accord to help the needs of the "have-nots." However, I don't think the Robin Hood philosophy is any more Christian than the Robber Baron philosophy.

So when it comes to these economic issues, I really struggle to know what the most Christian governmental solution is. And I guess I need to resign myself to the fact that "Christian governance" will always be an oxymoron.

Since we live in a secular society (and make no mistake, the United States is not a Christian nation, regardless of how desperately we wish it to be so), then I guess I would prefer for the government to tax the rich to provide for the poor. And since this American government is established upon the representation of "the people" (which itself is a godless and flawed foundation; but that's a discussion for another day), then whatever the government does is ultimately done with the consent and complicity of "the people."

The problem is that the poor are perpetually trampled underfoot of the rich. And somehow, even when the proletariat comprises the majority, the proletariat is nevertheless trampled by the "democracy" of the aristocratic minority.

But let's chalk this up to the fact that America is not a "pure democracy." We are actually a "democratic republic." And such semantic distinctions are very important in order to assuage our collective political and social conscience.

Perhaps America will perpetually fluctuate between the extremes of capitalistic exploitation and socialistic coercion – both of which are violent and thus antithetical to the ethic of the Gospel. And maybe that's as it should be in a secular and godless society. I really don't know.

But what I do know is that those of us who call ourselves by the name of Christ have done an awful job of taking care of one another. We vigorously fight over governmental economic policies while ignoring the gaping economic divides within the Church herself.

So let's start there – or more accurately, *here* – and let's take care of each other as we should, as Christ commands. I personally consider it blasphemy that millionaires are worshiping next to people who can barely pay the rent. That's a damn shame. Truly.

The world will always be the world – unjust, confused, broken, and cruel. And although we might not be able to fix the world, we can certainly give witness to the world. We can take care of each other – willingly and joyfully – and thereby be a light for society to follow.

For example, why does any Christian own health insurance or life insurance? Do we not trust the Body of Christ to collectively provide for our collective needs? How can we expect the world to take us seriously when we preach, "Place your faith in Jesus" while we place our own faith in capitalistic insurance companies?

The reality is that the current political debate about healthcare is merely a reflection of our own disgraceful failure as the Church. If we don't first get our own act together and truly care for one another, then we have no right to pontificate about the economic injustices of either the political left or the political right.

1,282. ~ IF THIS IS WHAT CONSTITUTES "LAW AND ORDER"... ~

The insanity and pathology of our society is most clearly revealed in the fact that in all 50 states it's legal to kill an unborn baby, but in most states it's a crime to smoke a joint. If this is what constitutes "law and order" then I pray for the courage to be a most disorderly outlaw.

1,283. ~ DISCOVERY of A SHALLOW MAN ~

I've tried to pray deeply when full and I've tried to pray deeply when fasting. Only to discover that either way I am a shallow man. I thank God for the intercessions of the holy.

1,284. ~ CHRISTIANITY and SUFFERING ~

Jesus didn't suffer so that we won't have to suffer. Jesus suffered to give us the grace and strength *to* suffer. Show me a Christian who hasn't suffered and I'll show you someone who isn't a Christian.

"If we suffer, we shall also reign with Him: if we deny Him, he also will deny us." [II Timothy 2:12]

"Whoever wants to be My disciple must deny themselves and take up their cross daily and follow Me." [St. Luke 9:23]

"Take My yoke upon you and learn from Me; for I am gentle and humble in heart, and you will find rest for your souls. For My yoke is easy and My burden is light." [St. Matthew 11:29-30]

"Let us then approach God's throne of grace with confidence, so that we may receive mercy and find grace to help us in our time of need." [Hebrews 4:16]

1,285. ~ INSANITY and ENLIGHTENMENT ~

There is a fine line between insanity and enlightenment. So don't be afraid to go crazy. We might have to lose our minds in order to save our souls. A true heart will be broken by a heartless world; a conscious soul will be condemned by a corrupt world; and a righteous mind will be crucified by an insane world.

1,286. ~ UNKNOWN TOMB ~

I've visited the tomb of the Unknown Soldier. But where is the tomb of the Unknown Peacemaker? I think it's somewhere in Jerusalem. And I think it's empty. But He is known by a few.

1,287. ~ SUFFERING, HEALING, and DEPENDENCY ~

Healing rarely occurs in an instant. And the deeper the wound the longer it takes to mend. And even then the scars remain. So stop shaming people for their "victimhood." Stop telling those who hurt to simply get over their pain.

We are all sick, wounded, and scarred by sin and by the cruel climate of our fallen world. And we all want to be healed, to be restored, to be forgiven and reconciled to our pristine, pre-fallen Edenic state. And by the grace of God and the power of the Cross we have tremendous hope. Our world will not always be this way. We will not always be this way. But the path of redemption is a constant struggle, a laborious process, an arduous and tumultuous journey.

So rather than judging others for their pain, their suffering, or their circumstances, we should strive to help them heal just as we ourselves seek to be healed.

I hear so much talk these days (and sadly often from Christian preachers) about "independence" and "self-sufficiency." As if the epitome of true Christian faith and genuine Christian virtue is somehow defined by self-sufficiency. Well, I confess: I can't really accomplish anything by myself; and I certainly can't heal myself or save myself. So feel free to put me in the "dependent" category. Feel free to label me "needy." Because I am needy and I am dependent. And I suspect that my neediness and dependency are the very things that might actually save me. God preserve me from ever becoming so self-sufficient that I no longer need Jesus or my fellow man!

And with all due respect, if you think you can make it through this life and into the next all by yourself, then you've got some very hard lessons in store for you. Job was a very rich and very righteous man, but consider the harsh and difficult truths that God taught him. And his "friends" offered him the same self-righteous, callous, and judgmental advice that is often preached from the pulpit today. So think about that.

1,288. ~ BABYLON and AFRICA ~

First they sent the slave ships, then they sent the colonizers, then they sent the missionaries, then they sent the communists, and now they send the abortionists. But the more Babylon tries to destroy Africa, the more Babylon only destroys itself.

1,289. ~ OUR MILITANCY ~

Love is our weapon. The saints are our comrades. Prayer is our power. The angels are our warriors. Peace is our militancy. Christ is our King. We cannot be defeated. For though you crucify us, we shall rise again with Him, in Him, and through Him.

1,290. ~ CRUCIFYING THE ONE WE PRESUME TO DEFEND ~

There were no swords in Eden, and there will be no swords in the Kingdom. And yet in our gardens of Gethsemane, as Our Lord prays for us to know the peace of His salvation, we still take up our swords in His holy name and crucify the One we presume to defend.

(Yes, we do read of the sword that guarded the Tree of Life and of the swords described in the Apocalypse. But these are surely metaphorical swords; and even if we interpret them as literal swords, they are swords wielded by God and His holy angels who alone are worthy to bear them.)

1,291. ~ REFLECTIONS on OUR OPPOSITION to THE DEATH PENALTY ~

In our efforts to repeal the death penalty we must not be guilty of turning a blind and callous eye toward those who suffer from murder, rape, and other unspeakable acts of violence. If we affirm the lives of the guilty but ignore the lives of the innocent then we are not truly promoting peace, justice, or life affirmation.

As we stand in solidarity with the living, we must also stand in solidarity with the dead. We must be voices not only for the voiceless murderers awaiting execution, but also for the voiceless victims who now lay silently buried in the earth.

Just as we know that sending murderers to their own violent graves won't resurrect their victims from theirs, we must also know that the Gospel of mercy compels us to recognize the suffering of the innocent. We must work not only to save the lives that are about to be violently victimized by the state, but we must also work to comfort those who mourn for the lives that they violently destroyed.

The Gospel commands us to love and forgive all people. And I believe that in our opposition to capital punishment we should be as concerned about bringing healing to the victims' families as we are with sparing the lives of those on death row.

True justice is always redemptive and restorative, not vindictive. So let us pray that the lives of those awaiting execution will be spared and redeemed by the blood of Christ. Let us seek to reconcile their lives with the lives of their victims' loved ones. Let us seek to reconcile their souls with the souls of those whose lives they cruelly ended.

And let us never forget that our "criminal justice system" has unjustly incarcerated and executed many innocent men and women. And let us also not forget that the guilty soul redeemed by Christ is now innocent in the eyes of God.

With one arm let us restrain the sword of the state, and with the other arm let us unite victim and victimizer. And with one voice let us affirm the sanctity, value, humanity, and right to life of both murderer and the murdered, of both the guilty and the guiltless.

And lest we self-righteously believe that we are somehow holier, more just, and less guilty than the murderers condemned to death by our government, let us consider these words of Holy Scripture:

"You have heard that it was said to the people long ago, 'You shall not murder, and anyone who murders will be subject to

judgment.' But I tell you that anyone who is angry with a brother or sister will be subject to judgment." [St. Matthew 5:21-22]

"Anyone who hates a brother or sister is a murderer, and you know that no murderer has eternal life residing in him." [I John 3:15]

And I don't know about you, but I know that I have certainly been angry with my brothers and sisters. And I know that I have certainly harbored hatred within my heart. So according my Lord Jesus Christ and His holy apostle, I am a murderer. So if murderers deserve execution, then let me be the first in line.

1,292. ~ ONE of THE MOST POLITICALLY POWERFUL THINGS WE CAN DO ~

One of the most politically powerful things we can do is refuse to lend our votes and participation to worldly political systems that wage war against the Kingdom of Heaven.

1,293. ~ FORGIVENESS ~

Forgiveness is hard. So hard. But there is no such thing as faith without it. "Seven times seventy" is what Our Lord said (St. Matthew 18:21-22). To forgive and forgive and keep on forgiving – even if those who abuse us, harm us, and repeatedly break our hearts show no ability or willingness to change. We forgive them anyway, because that's what it means to be a Christian.

And here is where we are tempted to insert the "but," as in:

"But surely God doesn't ask us to subject ourselves to continued abusE."

"But surely God doesn't tell us to keep on trusting and believing those who have proven to be disloyal and unfaithful."

"But surely God wants us to be discerning and not blindly risk being repeatedly hurt."

And I suppose all of those things may be true to some extent. But it seems that we have made a rule out of the clauses and thus perverted the divine imperative of forgiveness into some sort of situational ethic that is manageable and safe. But I don't think there's any such formula to forgiveness. Forgiveness is not easy. There is no comfort or security in it. True forgiveness may in fact get us crucified. But true forgiveness will also save.

Our Lord was very clear: *"If you do not forgive others their sins, your Father will not forgive your sins."* [St. Matthew 6:15]

And believe me, this is a lesson that I am still struggling to learn. May God grant me the grace to forgive others as much as He has forgiven me.

> *"And forgive us our sins, as we forgive*
> *those who have sinned against us."*
> *[St. Matthew 6:12]*

1,294. ~ BLOODY, GRUESOME, IMPOLITE TRUTH ~

I confess that I hate those graphic, bloody, gruesome pictures of aborted babies that Pro-Life activists enlarge and display on city sidewalks and college campuses. Those images are deeply disturbing, deeply offensive, and deeply disruptive to social tranquility. I find such public displays to be rude, insensitive, downright nauseating, and absolutely *necessary.*

As Bob Marley said, *"The truth is an offense, but not a sin."* And as Dr. Martin Luther King, Jr. said, *"True peace is not the absence of tension but the presence of justice."*

So if those horrific images really disturb us that much, then maybe we should do something to eradicate the unjust and inhumane realities they force us to acknowledge. The revolution of spiritual and social consciousness requires the confrontation of harsh, unpleasant, but redemptive truth. Prophets and revolutionaries have never been accused of being socially polished or culturally polite.

1,295. ~ NOT ENOUGH ~

I give it all, but I don't give enough. I never seem to be able to get out of the way of myself. So I hurt the ones I love the most. I'm always looking to be understood, but I'm always failing to understand – so desperate for mercy yet so full of judgment – constantly asking "What's wrong with *them*?" when I should be asking, "What's wrong with *me*?"

1,296. ~ DISPARITY of WEALTH ~

We criticize the disparity of wealth in society while we ignore or justify the disparity of wealth within many of our own churches and our own families.

1,297. ~ ABORTION, VIOLENCE, and LOGICAL CONSISTENCY ~

I've seen some of my anti-abortion comrades arguing that since abortion is murder then those who have abortions or perform abortions should be prosecuted, convicted, and executed for the crime of murder. They accuse those of us who are Pro-Life but are opposed to executing those who kill unborn babies of being philosophically and logically inconsistent.

Well, I will argue that the "consistent life ethic" is the most logically consistent worldview and the most authentically Christian philosophy. To affirm the sanctity of all human life – born and unborn, guilty and innocent, enemy and ally, Christian and pagan – is a most thoroughly consistent position to hold.

As Christians, we must recognize that all people bear the indelible image of God (Genesis 1:27), and therefore we dare not violently destroy these holy images for any reason. We must refuse to kill, either punitively or defensively or for any other reason. Our mission as disciples of Christ is to lead souls to eternal life, not send souls to their earthly graves. As St. John Chrysostom said: *"Our duty is to make the dead to live, not to make the living die."*

Yes, abortion is indeed murder, and we should never equivocate in saying so. And yet we must leave vengeance to God alone (Deuteronomy 32:35; Romans 12:19). Our goal is to seek redemption, reconciliation, and restoration for all people. That is the focus of the Gospel. (Colossians 1:19-20)

So I would argue that those who believe in the notion of justifiable violence are the ones who are ultimately inconsistent. In fact, nothing is more irrational and inconsistent than taking up arms to kill people on the other side of the world while refusing to violently defend the unborn innocents right here in America. But the very nature of violence is demonic (see Enoch 69:6-7), and thus violence is always inherently irrational and diametrically opposed to the ethic of Jesus.

So let us embrace the "consistent life ethic" and be therefore truly, authentically, and consistently Pro-Life. Let us embrace the "consistent life ethic" so that we may be truly, authentically, and consistently Christian.

1,298. ~ GETTING OVER PAIN ~

If God does not want us to get over His pain, then maybe He doesn't want us to get over our own pain. In the Orthodox Church we constantly meditate and reflect upon Our Lord's passion and death. We understand that His Cross is our redemption. So we never want to forget that. But we also know that the Cross was the precursor to the Resurrection. So the Gospel teaches us neither to deny pain, to ignore pain, nor to wallow in pain. The Gospel instructs us to embrace pain as part of the redemptive process.

Pain actually serves a holy purpose. So think about that before you tell somebody to simply "get over' their suffering. You may be advising them to forsake the very means of their salvation, essentially telling them to stop carrying their cross. And that's about the most spiritually unhealthy advice you could possibly give to someone.

Instead, what we should do is come alongside them and help them carry their cross – listening to them, weeping with them, struggling with them, bleeding with them, mourning with them – helping them anyway we can in the same way we would want to be helped ourselves.

Even Christ had help carrying His own Cross. And if God incarnate had help, then who are we not to help one another? If God doesn't ask us to overlook or dismiss His pain, who are we to dismiss and overlook the pain of others?

There is a significant difference between "getting over" pain and overcoming pain. We may never be able to get over our pain, but by the grace of God and the power of the Cross we can overcome our pain and turn our suffering into redemption.

"Those who do not co-suffer with those who live in great pain are suffering from the most fatal of spiritual illnesses: mercilessness."
~ Elder Paisios ~

1,299. ~ NO UPRISING ~

So much crying
But no uprising
Voting and marching
But truth denying

Political solutions
But no revolution
Educated fools
Teaching confusion

Bloody situation
But no confrontation
Innocents slain
In a brave, free nation

The Gospel compels us to engage society, because society is comprised of our fellow human beings. And loving our neighbors is a soteriological imperative. But the problem is that too many people have erroneously confused politics for authentic social engagement.

Sadly, we live in a society where people do little more than vote for some candidate or ballot initiative that they think will solve the problem. The mindset is essentially: "I'll cast my vote and let someone else deal with it. I'll love some of my neighbors enough to vote on their behalf (and in the process I'll be voting to oppress and murder some of my other neighbors that just don't mean as much to me.)"

And this is precisely why I advocate political divestment and genuine social investment. The Gospel is inherently political, because it proclaims the Kingdom of Heaven come to earth. And make no mistake, there is most certainly a political, social, ideological, and spiritual battle being waged between the Kingdom of God and the kingdoms of men.

To participate in the violence of democracies, to join violent armies, to militantly protect unjust laws, and to pledge allegiance to mortal flags and secular constitutions is to side with the kingdoms of this world against the Kingdom of Christ.

So, political *divestment* and Kingdom *investment*! This is how we will transform the world for Christ!

1,301. ~ HUMAN RIGHTS and ENVIRONMENTAL PROTECTION ~

Abortion is an environmental issue as well as a human rights issue. Human lives are part of the environment, and the reason we need to protect the environment is because a healthy environment is healthy for humanity. Destroying rain forests and destroying unborn children are therefore both unjust and inhumane acts of environmental violence. Protecting the environment means protecting human life, and protecting human life means protecting the environment.

1,302. ~ THE GRACE to BE VISIONIONARIES RATHER than REACTIONARIES ~

Those who have changed the world in positive ways – the revolutionaries, the prophets, and the saints – are people who refused to allow circumstances to affect their vision. Regardless of disappointments, setbacks, opposition, and adversity, they never lost sight of their purpose or their goals.

The devil tries to cripple our consciousness by convincing us to focus on our temporal circumstances rather on than honing our spiritual vision. Many people turned away from Jesus because the circumstances of discipleship were simply too difficult for them. But the disciples who remained faithful did so because they focused on the Author of the journey rather than on the circumstances of the journey.

So may God grant us the grace to be visionaries rather than reactionaries. May He give us the wisdom to keep our eyes focused on the Cross and our hearts fixed upon Him. While the world says, "there is no God, there is no hope, there is no meaning, there is no purpose; there is only misery and suffering and inevitable death" we as Christians must think and live and believe and love according the eternal truths and eternal hope that Christ has given us.

"Let us fix our eyes on Jesus, the author and perfecter of faith, who for the joy set before Him endured the Cross, scorning its shame, and sat down at the right hand of the throne of God." [Hebrews 12-2]

1,303. ~ TO SERVE ONE IS TO REBEL AGAINST THE OTHER ~

The gospel calls us to community, but it doesn't call us to democracy. The gospel calls us to social engagement, but it doesn't call us to vote. The gospel is inherently political, and yet the gospel stands diametrically opposed to the politics of this world.

The gospel is *"Thy Kingdom come, thy will be done."* It is not *"Our kingdom is and our will be done, by the violence of elections and wars and exploitation and oppression."*

One cannot be both a good citizen of earthly kingdoms and a good citizen of the Kingdom of Heaven. Babylon and Zion do not mix. To serve one is to rebel against the other.

1,304. ~ LOVE and SUFFER and LIVE ~

Let your heart be broken into a thousand pieces, a thousand times over. Love and suffer, because this is what it means to be truly alive.

1,305. ~ WHITEWASHING HISTORY ~

Those that whitewash the reminders of an evil history pave the way for that history to inevitably repeat itself. Let the gaping maw of the abyss stand nakedly before us, lest we fall into it again because we have pretended that it does not exist.

1,306. ~ NO ONE BUT YOURSELVES TO BLAME ~

Why are you perplexed? Why do you grieve? Why are you angry? Why do you fear? You are simply living out the repercussions of your own constitution, the manifestations of your own democracy, the fruit of your own political idolatry.

But rather than acknowledging your own blame and running to God in repentance, you project all the woes of the world onto a single political figure – a person who merely embodies the wickedness and folly that you have not only tolerated but wholeheartedly supported with your ideological partisanships, your patriotic poison, and your self-interested passions by which you justify the oppression of your neighbors.

So you want me to condemn the current president? Ok, I'll condemn him (or her), just as I always do. But know that those in power are the products of the kingdom you serve, not the Kingdom I serve. So you have no one but yourselves to blame.

1,307. ~ THE ONE GLORIOUS MYSTERY THAT INSEPARABLY BINDS US ALL ~

See life – in all of its glory and horror, joy and sorrow, hope and despair.

Live life – through all of its light and shadow, beauty and chaos, peace and pain.

Embrace life – with all of its sunshine and suffering, flowers and dirt, resurrections and crosses.

Live your life, and let others live theirs. Love your life, and love the lives of others. For God is the Author of life; and life is the one glorious mystery that inseparably binds us all.

1,308. ~ DAWN'S HOPE ~

The thick aroma of dew soaked grass fills my head in the approaching dawn. Trees drip gently from last night's rain. Birds arise with their morning songs. I drink deeply of the scents and sounds, the peace and hopes of life. I imbibe a remnant of Eden, evanescent yet eternal. The world changes with whirlwind speed; but the earth is the Lord's, and the fullness thereof.

1,309. ~ COUNTER-REVOLUTIONARY BLASPHEMIES ~

Make no mistake: violence and bloodshed – whether manifested by warfare or abortion – are inspired by the demonic not the divine. Nothing is more blasphemous than calling holy that which is born in hell. And nothing is more counter-revolutionary than invoking as a "right" that which is unjust, oppressive, intolerant, and inhumane.

"And the third demon was named Gadreel: this is he who showed the children of men all the blows of death, and all the weapons of death, and the shield and sword for battle. And from his hand they have ever since proceeded against those who dwell upon the earth... And the fifth demon was named Kasdeja: this is he who showed the children of men the demonic smiting of the embryo in the womb that it might pass away." [Book of Enoch 69:6-12]

1,310. ~ FALSE DICHOTOMIES ~

I reject the dichotomies of ethics and economics, of morality and progress, of facts and values, of the spiritual and the social, of the sacred and the practical. What is true is good and what is good is true. Holiness is not an impediment to social evolution and human enlightenment; it is the very foundation of evolution and enlightenment.

1,311. ~ RUNAWAY ~

You can run away from Jesus, but Jesus will never run away from you.

1,312. ~ SHARE YOUR WISDOM ~

Share your knowledge, share your wisdom, and share your convictions. If God is with you then you will not feel threatened, rejected, or offended if others do not receive the truth you speak. And never predicate "Love thy neighbor" on whether or not your neighbor agrees with you.

1,313. ~ THE PEOPLE of GOD ~

"We are the people of God."

These six words – when used as a statement of exclusivity, tribalism, and superiority – lead to the blasphemies of violence, hatred, and inhumanity. But when these same six words are used as a statement of universal brotherhood, universal humanity, and universal love, then they reveal the divine truth that leads to healing, unity, and peace in the world.

"We are the people of God" – **all** of us.

1,314. ~ LOVE THEM ~

Love them, even though they hurt you.
Love them, even though they betray you.
Love them, even though they disappoint you.
Love them, even though they hate you.
Love them, even though they kill you.

Love ain't easy. But love is our salvation.

1,315. ~ LORD HAVE MERCY on THE WORKING MAN ~

Lord have mercy
on the working man
with a broken spirit
and calloused hands

Lord have mercy
on the blue collar soul
who sweats to live
and bleeds for his dough

Lord have mercy
on the colony bees
that live and die
for the capitalist beast

1,316. ~ BLEED THE TRUTH in THE STREETS of BABYLON ~

Bleed the truth in the streets of Babylon. Confrontation is a must! Speak for the voiceless, live for the dying, rise up for the innocent, and chant down oppression. Revolt and rebel against systemic injustice and organized evil! Sabotage the demonic machine with body, mind, prayer, and peace. Subvert the violent system with paint and pen and prophetic witness. Disrupt the inhumane order with song and dance and revolutionary art. Be so creatively resistant that armies and governments and politicians and blood-shedders are brought to their knees in repentance and faith. Fight every manifestation of Babylon with the weapons of Zion. Rise up dear Christian soldiers! Trample down death with the life giving Cross! The battle belongs to the Lord!

1,317. ~ BULLIES and THE MEDIA ~

I despise bullies. I always have and I always will. And no tyranny, dictatorship, or malevolent monarchy has ever been as effective at bullying as the mainstream media has. And if you doubt me, just take some time to truly study human history.

Far from being an enemy of oppression, the media has historically too often been the facilitator and accomplice of oppression. So never, ever, let the media – be it rightwing media or leftwing media (or those who dishonestly claim to be neither) – make you believe they are victims.

In every other area of life people are held accountable for their duplicity, their crimes, and their violence. But the media can "report" falsehoods and distortions with impunity. And on the rare occasions when they're called to the carpet for their errors, the only justice they offer is a meaningless retraction on the back page after the damage has already been done.

The media can say and write and advance all manner of dishonesty and then simply claim it was an "innocent mistake" when their lies are exposed for what they are.

The media will gin up violence, instigate hate, foment social division and human discord, and then pretend to objectively cover the very unrest they helped to create. With microphone, pen, camera, and malicious bias the media sows as much violence as bullets, bombs, and terror.

So in this age of Babylonian confusion, discernment is a must. Half the story has never been told, and the half you are being told is most likely a lie.

1,318. ~ PASSING THROUGH ~

We are strangers in Babylon, pilgrims passing through this temporal vale – sowing seeds of light, love, and truth along the way. That's all we can do. We are marching towards heaven, inviting others to accompany us on the eternal journey. Our responsibility is no more and no less.

1,319. ~ LOVE IS THE GREAT MYSTERY of LIFE ~

Love is the great mystery of life. How to find it? How to give it? How to understand it? How to survive it?

Jesus taught and lived it best – perfectly in fact. And the apostles followed His example and wrote most eloquently about the meaning and truth of love. St. Paul's words in First Corinthians chapter 13 and the exhortations of St. John in his first two epistles are especially profound. And in the Cross, and in the words of the apostles, and in the lives of the saints and martyrs the notion of love as mere romantic sentiment is harshly disabused. Instead, love is revealed as something that suffers in order to survive, that hurts in order to heal, that sacrifices in order to save, and that forgives infinite offenses in order to prove its fidelity.

To be sure, love is also inextricably intertwined with visceral human passion and the emotional tapestry of the soul, which only compounds its mystery. If love was simply a logical syllogism or formulaic religious equation, then it would be difficult but manageable. And if love was simply an emotion, then we could ride its sentimental course until the feeling faded and then move on in search of the next romantic experience.

But love is not as easy as any of that. It is much more demanding and much more confusing. Love is excruciatingly mystical, beautifully painful, dangerously relentless but eternally rewarding. Love is neither tamed by human logic nor captured by human sentiment. Love is crucifixion and love is resurrection; and love is all the faith and truth and hope and pain that are endured in the shadow of Calvary and the light of the empty tomb.

"Choose love! Choose love! Enter the rose garden, let your soul make peace with the thorns." ~ Rumi ~

1,320. ~ I HEAR THE GRASS GROW ~

I hear the grass grow
I taste the nectar's sound
I smell the cosmic rhythm
I see the Creator's caress
I breathe what I touch
And I feel what I breathe
I am what is
And it all belongs...
To Him

1,321. ~ SO WHAT DOES THAT SAY ABOUT ME? ~

If my human talents, human abilities, and human worth were judged by my most offensive words and actions then I wouldn't stand a chance. We love to sing about grace being greater than our own sins, but we sure are harsh when it comes to the sins of others. Actors, comedians, and media commentators often get paid to make offensive remarks and insensitive jokes. But I've often made offensive remarks and stupid jokes for free. So what does that say about the pitiful condition of my own sinful heart?

1,322. ~ QUESTION THE "EXPERTS" ~

Always question the "experts" that claim to have a monopoly on expertise. They rely on your blind trust to advance their agendas. Your ignorance and obeisance are their profit. So never be afraid to challenge the teacher, the preacher, and the political creature. You are no less the image of God than they are, and you may actually be closer to the truth than they are. And never be cowed by the intimidation of the consensus. While the herd marches lockstep towards the slaughterhouse, it's the rogue bovine that runs in the opposite direction whose life is saved.

1,323. ~ THE SLAVERY of THE IDEOLOGY of FREEDOM ~

Underlying almost every individual and collective act of evil is the notion of "freedom." Lucifer rebelled against God in the name of freedom. The Southern Confederacy violently defended the evil of slavery in the name of freedom. Hitler exterminated Jews in the name of freedom. Communists murdered and oppressed millions in the name of freedom. Islamist terrorists kill innocent people in the name of freedom. Women abort their babies in the name of freedom. Every war that has ever been waged has been fought over the idea of freedom – each side viewing their own cause as a justified struggle for rights, liberty, and justice.

But Jesus didn't preach about individual liberty or political freedom. In fact, the word for "freedom" or "liberty" only appears 12 times in the entire New Testament, and never once in the four gospels, and never in the sense of individual autonomy or political rights. Instead, "freedom" is spoken of as liberation from the very ostensible "freedoms" that keep us in bondage – i.e. our own sins that we cultivate rather than crucify, that we exalt to our own depression and idolize to our own detriment.

In fact, Christ called His disciples away from the very things that we Americans idolize today: the right to make a profit, the right to kill our enemies, the right to violently repel our neighbors, the right to determine our own morality, the right to slaughter our unborn children, and the right to live however we please even at the expense of the rights and feelings of others.

We have made a god of freedom and in doing so we have only enslaved ourselves. But the Gospel of Jesus Christ confronts us with the paradoxical truth that the only way to be truly free is to truly become servants – to deny ourselves for the sake of others, to sacrifice our own preferred individual liberties in order to affirm the basic human rights of all, to crucify our own opinions and beliefs with trust in Christ and His Church.

St. James goes so far as to equate authentic freedom with obedient adherence to the divine law of the Gospel: *"But whoever looks intently into the perfect law that gives freedom, and continues in it – not forgetting what they have heard, but doing it – they will be blessed in what they do." [James 1:25]*

The United States was established on the flawed foundation of the irreconcilable attempt to combine individual liberty and divine faith. But between the vain inclinations of the human heart and the immutable will of God there can be no compromise, no harmony, and no peace. One is either with the Church or with the state, with the Cross or with the flag, with the Holy Gospel or with manmade constitutions, with compassion for "the least of these" or with the oppression of "the least of these. And foolish attempts to wed Zion with Babylon only lead to the evils and absurdities of Bible-quoting slave owners, clergy-blessed atomic bombs, and "Christian" abortionists.

1,324. ~ MOST of ALL I BELIEVE IN... ~

I believe in the Nicene Creed. I believe in the deity of Christ. I believe in the divine inspiration of the Holy Scriptures. I believe in the salvation of the life-giving Cross. I believe in the doctrines and sacraments of the apostolic Orthodox Church. I believe in the nonviolent imperatives of the Gospel of peace. But most of all I believe in love. And love is the most difficult of all Christian beliefs, practices, and virtues.

1,325. ~ STORIES I LOVE and STORIES I KNOW ~

The stories I love and the stories I know are not pretty stories. But they are beautiful stories – beautifully painful, beautifully real, beautifully deep, and beautifully redemptive. Every story I love and every story that resonates with my soul is essentially a true story, a story that reflects the Gospel story. And in spite of trite Sunday school lessons and vapid Hollywood depictions the Gospel story is actually a brutal story. The Gospel story is a horror story. It is a lurid story. It is an obscene and offensive story. The Gospel story is full of suffering and cruelty and torture and betrayal. It is full of death and the very smell of death. It is full of harlotry and drunkenness and whips and thorns and orgiastic crowds that cheer the violent condemnation of an innocent man. And at the end of the story the "good guys" remain just as politically, economically, and socially oppressed as before.

No, the Gospel Story is not a pretty story, regardless of how hard we try to make it so. But it is nevertheless a redemptive story. It is the truest story that has ever been told. And it is the one story by which all other stories are ultimately measured. Fear, mystery, drama, relationship, love, gore, heartbreak, suffering, miracles, death, and resurrection – do not all great stories contain at least some of these elements? Indeed they do. And every great story is a shadow of the truth of the divine story. So don't be afraid to write your own story. And don't be afraid to write it with all of its own naked horror and graphic pain. Otherwise it can never be truly redemptive.

1,326. ~ THE SIN of THE AMERICAN DREAM ~

The sin of the "American Dream" is that it equally deceives both oppressed and oppressor. It leads the oppressed to believe that salvation resides behind a white picket fence with a pool out back and three cars in the driveway. And it leads the oppressor to believe the same. Therefore the oppressed rise up in violent pursuit of the lie, and the oppressor violently suppresses them in order to preserve the lie.

1,327. ~ STILL STRUGGLING in THE MAGNOLIA STATE ~

We're still struggling here in the beautiful Magnolia State, where the specter of strange fruit drips like Spanish moss to mingle with the blood of unborn innocents. The gods of Abaddon once demanded the offerings of burning crosses and lynched human flesh. Today they demand the offerings of incinerated babies and dismembered fetal lives. But the real revolutionaries continue to rise up – confronting racism, injustice, inhumanity, and evil with the Gospel of peace and the life-giving Cross. Indeed, *"We shall overcome!"*

1,328. ~ BREAD AND SALVATION ~

One man lived for bread, and thus he starved his brothers and lost his soul. Another man lived for his soul, and thus he provided bread and salvation for his brothers.

1,329. ~ QUESTIONS for PLANNING RESISTANCE to BABYLON ~

Babylon is built upon violence and death, and white supremacy is merely one evil among many that exist in this systemic order of multifaceted injustice and oppression. Babylon doesn't care who's in power as long as those in power perpetuate violence and killing. Babylon will use Barack as easily as Bush to accomplish its nefarious ends. The war is not between white and black (as the system would like us to believe); the war is between life and death, humanity and inhumanity, justice and injustice, peace and violence, the Kingdom of Heaven and the kingdoms of this world.

So whatever the issue, fight, cause, or debate may be, simply ask yourself the following questions:

Does it affirm and side with life?

Does it affirm and side with humanity?

Does it affirm and side with justice?

Does it affirm and side with peace?

Does it affirm and side with the Kingdom of Heaven?

Consider these questions and then plan your resistance and rebellion accordingly. And as you become an authentic revolutionary who sides with truth over political tribalism, be prepared to invoke the condemnation and wrath of the politically brainwashed, myopic masses who serve Babylon's interests from both the ideological left and the ideological right.

1,330. ~ AMERICA'S "CRIMINAL JUSTICE" SYSTEM ~

America's "criminal justice" system is too rarely just and too frequently criminal.

1,331. ~ RESPECT and HONOR / INDIVIDUALS and INSTITUTIONS ~

You deserve my respect because you are a human being created in the image of God, not because you wear a badge, hold an office, don a uniform, or carry a gun. I have no respect for such symbols and instruments of Babylon's power and intimidation. I don't respect the military, I don't respect the presidency, and I don't respect the police force. But I do respect all my fellow human beings as human beings, regardless of which side of the law they're on. I honor individual images of God, not institutional structures that oppress, violate, and destroy the images of God.

1,332. ~ ON DEATH and KILLING ~

War, capital punishment, and abortion are not so much causes of death as they are symptoms of death. Those who are spiritually dead cannot help but to kill and do violence to themselves and to others.

Therefore, the most effective way to end the evils of violence and killing is to remain spiritually awake and spiritually alive ourselves, shining the light of life amidst our culture of death. People do not die because they go to war; they go to war because they are already dead. And the Gospel is all about resurrecting life from death. So let us preach it and let us live it!

1,333. ~ COURAGE, CONVICTION, and LONELINESS ~

Sometimes it takes more courage to sit rather than stand, to fall rather than rise, to be still rather than act. A soul of conviction is a lonely soul, condemned by the crowds for not engaging in their idolatry.

1,334. ~ IF I WROTE A HORROR STORY... ~

If I wrote a horror story it would be full of... well, horror. Terror would bleed from its pages, fear would grip your soul, insane realities would crucify your mind. It would be a story so replete with agony and pain and inexplicable cosmic metaphysics that you would be forced to reduce it to something less than the truth it really told. If I wrote a horror story it would be a gospel story. But that story already exists; and few of us actually have the stomach for it.

1,335. ~ OFF BALANCE ~

Whether you lean left or lean right, you're off balance. Politics will trip you up every time.

1,336. ~ CHRISTIANITY and COMMUNISM ~

Dorothy Day, Oscar Romero, and Martin Luther King, Jr. each denounced violence, poverty, and war in the name of Christ, and they were accused of being communists for doing so. Proof that true Christians will often be condemned as criminals by a criminal culture and accused of heresy by a heretical society.

"Alongside the condemnation of Marxism the Church now lays down a condemnation of the capitalist system as well. It is denounced as another version of practical materialism. Worldly interests try to make the Church's position seem Marxist when it is in fact insisting on fundamental human rights, when it is placing the whole weight of its institutional and prophetic authority at the service of the dispossessed and the weak." ~ Archbishop Oscar Romero ~

"Capitalism fails to realize that life is social. Communism fails to realize that life is personal. The good and just society is a society which reconciles the truths of individualism and collectivism."
~ Dr. Martin Luther King, Jr. ~

"When you feed the poor they call you a saint. When you ask why people are poor, they call you a communist." ~ Dorothy Day ~

1,337. ~ COMPLEXITY and SIMPLICITY ~

When others play a hundred notes then just play one. And play that one note with every ounce of your soul.

When others speak a thousand words then just speak a few. And speak those few words with all the conviction of your heart.

When others theorize about the human race then just point them to their human brothers. And tell them to dare not evade their hungry gaze.

When others study the cosmos then study the Creator. And pray for God to reveal Himself to you through His creation.

When others philosophize, idealize, and moralize beyond your comprehension or agreement, then just love them. And love them so truly and so deeply that love becomes their philosophy, their ideology, and their morality.

Never be intimidated by complexity. Just counter it with simplicity, knowing that truth is a well, divinely deep yet humanly accessible.

1,338. ~ A PRAYER ~

Dear Lord,

Please bless, encourage, and strengthen everyone who is
fighting for life
fighting for health
fighting for sobriety
fighting for peace
fighting for justice
fighting for forgiveness
fighting for reconciliation
fighting for truth
and fighting for hope.

Grant them the grace to struggle and the mercy to endure.

"But he said to me, 'My grace is sufficient for you, for my power is made perfect in weakness.' Therefore I will boast all the more gladly about my weaknesses, so that Christ's power may rest on me. That is why, for Christ's sake, I delight in weaknesses, in insults, in hardships, in persecutions, in difficulties. For when I am weak, then I am strong." [II Corinthians 12:9-10]

In the Name of the Father,
and the Son, and the Holy Spirit, One God.
~ amen ~

1,339. ~ CONFESSIONS of AN ARROGANT MAN ~

I am opinionated. I am arrogant. I am a hypocrite. I do not come close to living up to the ideals I espouse. I am quick to find the speck in the eye of my neighbor while ignoring the beam in my own. I am in desperate need of Christ Our Lord. The only reason I call myself a Christian is because I have no hope apart from Christ and His Church. So disagree with me, challenge me, correct me, and humble me; but please do so with a spirit of brotherly love and with the acknowledgment that Our Lord died no less for me than He did for you.

1,340. ~ GOVERNMENT and CHURCH ~

Government solutions are fundamentally violent solutions, which is why I never advocate political approaches to social and spiritual problems. The Church, when it is truly being the Church, is not a politically administrative institution; it is rather a living, vital, intuitively operative organism that instinctively addresses and meets the needs of both its own community and the society in which it finds itself.

1,341. ~ MESSAGE TO JAH SOLDIERS ~

In the name of freedom they assault our faith. In the name of progress they attack our God. In the name of justice they wage war on peace. And in the name of revolution they oppress and enslave. With politics and entertainment Babylon wages war on holiness and humanity, on liberation and truth. False prophets are extolled as sages while the real freedom fighters are ridiculed and mocked.

So stay awake out there dear people! Keep your conscience sharp and your consciousness keen. The road to Zion only goes one way – *forward*. And all of Babylon's evil designs are geared towards setting us back or keeping us stagnant. As long as they can keep us scurrying to the voting booths and running to join the military – enslaving us to the insidious cycle of voting and killing and dying and killing for the right to vote and kill – then they don't need whips and chains and shackles and Jim Crow laws. And as long as Babylon can keep us politically, racially, and religiously divided then they can corrupt and control us while telling us how free we supposedly are.

So fall on your knees conscious warriors! And then rise up with JAH's blessings and strength! We are guerilla soldiers in this spiritual warfare. We fight and run away and live to fight another day. And we have no illusions about "reforming" Babylon. We are fighting our way out of Babylon's hellish grip, and we gladly rejoice at her impending destruction. The more Babylon crumbles the closer we are to our salvation. So keep fighting with the weapons of the Gospel.

"Look up, and lift up your heads; for your redemption draweth nigh." [St. Luke 21:28]

1,342. ~ THE BLESSED COMMUNITY ~

"They devoted themselves to the apostles' teaching and to fellowship, to the breaking of bread and to prayer. Everyone was filled with awe at the many wonders and signs performed by the apostles. All the believers were together and had everything in common. They sold property and possessions to give to anyone who had need. Every day they continued to meet together in the temple courts. They broke bread in their homes and ate together with glad and sincere hearts, praising God and enjoying the favor of all the people. And the Lord added to their number daily those who were being saved." [Acts 2:42-47]

No state government. No violent ideology. No coercive political system. No utilitarian humanistic philosophy. Just the love of God working in and through the hearts of individuals living in blessed community. (And oh, by the way, Karl Marx plagiarized St. Luke –

stealing the divine ideal, depriving it of its authentic spiritual import, and attempting to violently impose it upon the entire world.)

So, do you want to spread the Gospel? Do you want peace on earth? Do you want true revolution? Well, here it is, from the words of the apostle, indelibly imprinted on the pages of Holy Scripture, divinely breathed from the mouth of God.

The question is: what will we do with it?

1,343. ~ SNAKE HANDLERS and GUN TOTERS ~

You know those misguided Holiness sectarians that pick up venomous snakes to prove their faith? They're pretty stupid to do that, don't you think? They're playing with death, and playing with death is no way to honor God.

And yet most people who rightly condemn those snake handlers somehow believe that taking up guns is a more righteous and less dangerous endeavor than handling poisonous serpents. But they're playing with death just the same; and I think that their actions are just as foolish and just as blasphemous as the snake handlers'.

You can have all the faith in the world, but no matter how much you think you might have mastered them, those snakes and bullets will eventually bite you.

And I realize that most people probably think they're the one person who's smart enough, faithful enough, and experienced enough to ensure that it won't happen to them. They have mastered their weapons. They are the responsible gun owner. They are that unique person who has somehow figured out a way to make sure that their guns and bullets will never do any harm to any innocent human being, ever. They have the same confidence as the experienced, faithful, intelligent snake handlers who keep their rattlesnakes "safely" and "responsibly" locked up inside their homes. But oops, somehow a snake got loose and bit little Jimmy Ray. And oops, somehow little Susie found Daddy's pistol and accidentally shot herself dead with it.

But, no, this could never happen to them. They're way too careful. Not like those other snake handlers and gun owners who weren't also trying to be just as careful.

You see, what we need to understand is that violence can't be tamed, any more than a venomous snake can be tamed. Just when you think you have it under control, it strikes and it kills. So the next time you mock someone for trying to prove their faith by handling deadly serpents, understand that when you handle deadly weapons you're being just as foolish; and when you brandish guns in the name of Jesus you're being just as heretical.

1,344. ~ PROFITING from PEOPLE'S NEED to EXIST ~

We have to purchase our food, buy our water, pay for our slice of earth, and vote for the right to life and the right to healthcare. And yet we somehow think we are free. There is no greater evil than financially exploiting and capitalizing on people's very need to live and exist.

1,345. ~ THE TRAGEDY of LIBERATION ~

There is a tragedy in liberation; and the tragedy is that when freedom is worshipped as God then those that finally attain it no longer know how to live. That's why the oppressor is happy to entertain violent uprisings, militant protests, godless political coups, and reactionary revolts. Because such things can be used to justify the oppressor's own violent and ruthless quelling of the revolutionaries. And even if such temporal rebellions succeed, the oppressor knows that in time they will inevitably self-destruct. The violent revolutionary becomes an unwitting pawn in the oppressor's game of divide and rule. And that's why the kingdoms and rulers of this world truly fear only one thing: people who are undivided in their loyalty and allegiance to the Kingdom of God. Because Christ's Kingdom breaks every throne and brings all rulers under His submission. Real revolution is always spiritual; and anything that produces positive and enduring change is always rooted in divine love and eternal truth.

1,346. ~ WEEDS AND WHEAT ~

Zion's weeds are better than Babylon's wheat.

1,347. ~ BEAUTY I SEE ~

Beauty I see
Beauty in we
Beauty in you
Beauty in me…
Beauty in all of our
glorious deformity

1,348. ~ PEACE, ANARCHY, and SOCIALISM ~

By *peace* I mean nonviolent resistance to injustice, inhumanity, and evil. By *anarchy* I mean the uncompromising rejection of the violence of the State. By *socialism* I mean a classless society where no one has political or economic power over another. And by *peace, anarchy,* and *socialism* I mean the organic and un-coerced spiritual community of human beings that adheres to and ushers in the Kingdom of Heaven.

1,349. ~ "I'M FREE!" ~

I'm *FREE!*

I'm free to say the Pledge of Allegiance, free to fly the American flag, and free to pay taxes.

I'm free to vote for my rulers and oppressors.

I'm free to join the military so I can bomb, shoot, and kill strangers that are my brothers.

I'm free to make a profit at the expense of my fellow man.

I'm free to have my children brainwashed by compulsory public school education.

I'm free to work and eat and live luxuriously while my neighbors suffer from poverty and hunger.

I'm free to worship God as long as God doesn't require me to violate the unjust and inhumane laws of the land.

I'm free to be "protected and served" by a police force that defends the interests of the wealthy against the interests of the poor.

I'm free to speak freely (in certain environments under certain circumstances according to certain laws in certain situations.)

I'm free to kill my unborn babies.

And I'm free to shoot off fireworks to prove just how free I am!

I'm a free American!

And don't you dare try to liberate me!

1,350. ~ ODE to THE RESCUER ~

You sow tears of Life, but you witness death.
You water with hope, and you observe despair.
You plant seeds of love, but you are met with hate.
You offer mercy, and endure condemnation in return.
You proclaim the truth, but you are showered with lies.
You labor in peace, and receive a violent response.
You offer wisdom, yet they call you a fool.
You are an ambassador of Christ,
but you are cursed as a criminal.

But please know this...
Your efforts are not in vain.
Your compassion is not unfruitful.
Your witness is heralded by the angels,
and the unborn innocents feel your presence.
The Author of Life smiles upon you,
and He who was crucified honors your struggle.
Today death stands before you and mocks,
but in eternity...
Life victorious for you and for those you seek to save.

+ *"Lord have mercy"* +

1,351. ~ "PRAISE THE LORD AND PASS THE AMMUNITION" ~

A Babylon army chaplain said *"Praise the Lord and pass the ammunition!"* Well, we soldiers in the army of Jesus say, *"Praising the Lord **is** our ammunition!"*

And your bullets won't stop our prayers.

1,352. ~ I NEED MORE NIGHTS LIKE THIS ~

Babylon 4th of July… my young conscious brother came over to fellowship with me. We cooked some food on the grill, reasoned about Rastafari and sacred scripture and Haile Selassie and Jesus Christ and the Holy Orthodox Faith – and about life in general – while listening to Bob Marley and roots reggae nonstop. Then we sat down and ate and watched the movie *Malcolm X* with my son and his friend.

I need more nights like this. With all the conscious vibes flowing, the fireworks didn't even vex me.

1,353. ~ TOGETHER ALONE ~

Together we live
Alone we die
Alone we suffer
Together we rise

1,354. ~ A REFLECTION on WILLIAM BLAKE'S PAINTING: "ALBION" ~

Here is Albion before the Cross, in all of his naturalistic and fallen glory, standing proudly before God. Naked and unashamed, with outstretched arms, he asks Christ: *"Why are you suffering for me? Do I look like I need saving?"*

And here is Our Lord, hanging naked and crucified above, stretching out His arms to unconditionally embrace His proud, rebellious, recalcitrant image.

Incarnate God dies to save dying man who thinks he's a god.

We are Albion. And God loves us, saves us, in spite of ourselves.

1,355. ~ TERRORISTS or DISCIPLES? ~

If we choose to protect our interests or impose our will by the use of bullets, bombs, and military might, then we are terrorists. And let's not kid ourselves about that fact. To make a conscious and calculated decision to defend our values, our loved ones, and/or our assets by threatening, and if need be, delivering bloodshed and death to those that threaten our values, loved ones, and possessions means that we are relying on terror for the preservation of something we cherish. And just like every terrorist that has ever lived, we probably believe that our cause is righteous and that our violence is justified.

But a revolutionary named Jesus unequivocally rebuked all violence, bloodshed, and killing. He told humanity to take up the Cross and put away the sword. And government sponsored terrorists crucified Him for it. But by His death He saved the world. And He rose again in eternal triumph.

So the question is: are we terrorists or disciples?

1,356. ~ FIRE, FIRE ~

Fire, fire
burning bright
Roaring lion
in the night
Brimstone flames
rise to slay
Babylon wolves
are Zion's prey

1,357. ~ RECONCILIATION and VIOLENCE ~

The essential theme, hope, expectation, and power of the Gospel is *reconciliation*. Through the Cross man is reconciled to God and man is reconciled to man. This is why violence and killing are the antithesis of Christian faith, and when committed in the name of God are the greatest blasphemies against Christian truth.

1,358. ~ OFFERINGS ~

When others bring terrible thunder, meet them with rainbow peace. When others bring gentle rain, give them some lightning fire. When others bring the hard facts, compliment them with poetic mystery. When others bring a flurry of notes and a multitude of strokes, offer them the mite born from your soul. You don't have to be a genius, an expert, or a supremely talented individual to penetrate human hearts and leave your indelible print upon the universe. Just bring the offering of your truest self and know that God will work wonders with it.

1,359. ~ WHEN NIGHT FELL ~

While the sun shone the sky looked empty. It was only when night fell that I saw how full the heavens really are. Sometimes darkness reveals more than light. We might have to suffer in order to see. We may need to be hurt in order to be healed. We may need to cry in order to understand. We may need to bleed in order to be born again. There are times when brightness blinds and darkness illuminates. So don't be afraid to cry and bleed and suffer and see!

1,360. ~ REVOLUTION and CREATIVITY ~

Revolution is born from creativity, and creativity apart from submission to the Creator is nothing more than rearranging clay.

1,361. ~ "THE TRIUMPH OF HUMANISM IS THE DEFEAT OF HUMANITY" ~

Never has so much suffering, violence, and division been perpetrated than in the name of "progress," "peace," and "unity." When the ideal of humanity is exalted as a god then human beings are inevitably sacrificed upon its idolatrous altar. The violation and destruction of human people becomes an acceptable means in the pursuit of the humanistic ends. Unique, living, actual individual lives are expendable in the cause of an idealized, potential, collective Utopian life.

And politicians have always persuaded the masses that their violent, divisive, and inhumane policies are actually somehow in their best human interest. "We must kill and oppress men today," they explain, "in order to protect and preserve mankind tomorrow." As Aldous Huxley wrote, *"The triumph of humanism is the defeat of humanity."*

1,362. ~ STARS ~

I see a billion stars
And I truly love them all
But like the tears on my cheek
I feel the ones that fall

1,363. ~ IF THE TRUTH NEVER SET YOU FREE... ~

If the truth never set you free, it's either because you never understood the truth or you never understood freedom.

I was born with pennies in my crib and a goldmine in my soul. Silver spoons surrounded me, but they never touched my mouth. I spent my childhood in a house on a hill, but it was never really mine. Before I could even grow old enough to truly disappoint I was banished from home, imprisoned in the solitary confines of a cold padded cell, and then spit into a hostile wilderness to struggle with co-sufferers of an unjust fate.

I have never experienced the peace of knowing there is a place that will always be my home, an abode of unconditional love, a constant refuge and safe harbor for a struggling, failing, but constantly striving sinner. I thought I knew such security as a child, but it was cruelly wrested from me – and made all the crueler because it was done under the guise of love.

To suffer from hatred, I could always understand that. But to suffer at the hands of those that love you... well, that is a mystery I have yet to grasp. And yet I tremble when I think of the suffering I have brought to those that I myself deeply love. But the child, regardless of his crimes, is always essentially innocent. The nascent clay is not responsible for how it is being molded.

No matter how thick the blood that binds, love in this world is always conditional. Obey; provide; measure up; and live to please. But don't dare disappoint and don't dare be a burden. In other words, if you want to be loved by this world then do anything but be truly human.

Jesus said, *"The foxes have dens and the birds have nests, yet the Son of Man has nowhere to lay His head." [St. Matthew 8:20]*

So I know that my anxieties are my blessings. My loneliness is my salvation. The betrayals have all been for my benefit.

The streets, brutally harsh but always true, may perhaps be my only real home in this temporal world. And that's ok. Because I was not born for this place, but for another.

1,365. ~ WRITING and DYING ~

Today I write and tomorrow I die. Or perhaps I die today so that I can write tomorrow. I bleed a little bit with each sentence that burns in my soul, demands a release, and spills forth through indigo pen.

But bloodletting is the writer's salvation.

Vampires live by sucking the blood of others, but writers live by bleeding their own souls freely upon the page. The succubus lives only to take, leaving nothing valuable or eternal in its soulless wake. But the writer – for good or for bad – leaves behind his heart and his mind and his humanity for others to feast upon (or choke upon.)

The writer is ultimately a giver. How people respond to his gift is not his concern. He bleeds with his pen because that's the only way he can truly live.

Perhaps that's what William Blake meant when he said: *"A poet, a painter, a musician, an architect: the man or woman who is not one of these is not a Christian."*

1,366. ~ TUMBLING DOWN ~

So you want to prove your manhood, test your mettle, engage in a struggle? Well God gave you mountains; He gave you oceans; and He gave you woman. But you can't conquer them, so instead you set out to conquer your fellow man. Many carnal kingdoms have been ruled by small men with small minds. And with just a little bit of love they all come tumbling down.

1,367. ~ MONSTER ~

He sliced the innocent man's flesh until blood began to ooze. He felt no remorse, no emotion, no sorrow. He continued to cut, deeper and deeper – taking no pleasure and feeling no pity. You may think he's a heartless monster; but beware lest you condemn the surgeon that might one day save your own life. The knife you view as "negative" might actually be the knife that positively heals.

1,368. ~ INSANITY ~

I've never met anyone in this world who sees clearly who isn't also deeply troubled. I don't trust anyone who thinks they're sane. People that can live amongst so much suffering and injustice and not go crazy, well, I consider them to be the real lunatics. So embrace your insanity, because by doing so you might actually help to heal the world.

"What I see around me would drive me insane, if I did not know that no matter what happens God will have the last word."
~ Elder Paisios ~

"The time is coming when men will go mad. And when they see someone who is not mad, they will say: 'He is mad! He is not like us!'" ~ St. Anthony the Great ~

1,369. ~ PRAYERS THAT I COVET ~

I seek the intercessions of the addicts, the drunkards, the harlots, the abused and the abandoned, the neglected and scorned, the disabled and deformed, the doubters, the lovers, the infirmed and insane, the truly faithful who lived life not with certainty but with desperation, clinging to shadows of hope, believing against belief, but always showing mercy to their neighbors. I covet their prayers, because in their lives I pray to see myself.

1,370. ~ FATHERS and CHILDREN in BABYLON ~

Countless fathers are behind bars because they didn't pay child support. Never mind that they supported their children with love and affection, time and teaching, inspiration and encouragement. Sorry kids. Daddy didn't pay the Babylon bill, so now he's in prison where he'll somehow learn to be a better father. This is another example of how the godless system supposedly puts "the children first."

1,371. ~ WHAT I DON'T TRUST and WHAT I DO TRUST ~

Here's what I *don't* trust: politicians, the media, the military, the police, academic propagandists, and judges and lawyers who protect politicians, the media, the military, the police, and academic propagandists.

Here's what I *do* trust: peace, justice, life, love, and the Kingdom of God and all those who serve His Kingdom through their commitment to peace, justice, life, and love.

1,372. ~ REFLECTIONS ON A SUICIDE ~

I just learned of another old friend that was lost to suicide. This life is so cold and so hard and so unforgiving sometimes. I don't have any answers. I'm not a Priest or a psychologist or a counselor of any sort. I just know that life can be unbelievably and unbearably difficult. I will never judge or condemn anyone for their weaknesses, addictions, failures, sins, or struggles. In fact, the more I see someone suffering the more I admire them, because I can relate to hardship. I can relate to doubt and insecurity and unspeakable temptations and depression and insanity. But I don't know how to relate to the comfortable, the well adjusted, the confident, and the certain. I love them and I am happy for them, but they are living an existence beyond my experience. And I'm not really sure that I want what they have. I might be damned if I didn't have to suffer and weep and cry out to God for mercy.

I wish all my dear friends could know how much I love them. I wish they knew they could reach out to me and find at least a listening ear. Lord knows, their love and encouragement have saved my life, probably more than once. I don't want to lose any more friends this way. And I don't want my friends to let me be lost this way either. But sometimes love is not enough, at least not in this life. But I know that love will carry us through eternity.

I can promise you that somebody out there loves you and cares for you deeply, more than you may realize. Life is worth fighting for. I truly believe that.

1,373. ~ THIS HOLY EXODUS ~

We can't tread *through* Babylon without treading *upon* Babylon. This holy exodus requires that we march and trample on the heads of many serpents. And sometimes we'll be bitten. But Christ heals the souls of those that suffer on the path to the Kingdom. So march on to Zion dear brothers and sisters! And help one another along the way, because we won't get there alone!

1,374. ~ WHAT TO DO? ~

What to do when all else has failed, when no argument will persuade, when reason does not prevail, when force and might and truth and logic cannot win the day?

What to do then?

Well, we should do what we should have done to begin with:

Love.

Love and love and love some more.

Love until it kills us.

Because love has already conquered.

1,375. ~ LIFE: BY ANY MEANS NECESSARY! ~

All violence is a form of desperation; and to rebel against the despair of violence – even when violence appears to be the only solution – is the most revolutionary act and the most positively militant endeavor of human existence. To live even when there seems to be no reason to live, to refuse to kill even when there seems to be every reason to kill: this is the rebellion that gives birth to reconciliation and redemption, social change and spiritual enlightenment. We refuse to shed the blood of others because Jesus' Blood is enough. We refuse to take our own lives because Christ gave His life so that we might live.

The real revolutionary says, "I will affirm life, by any means necessary!" The real revolutionary says with Albert Camus:

"There are causes worth dying for, but none worth killing for... It is better to be wrong by killing no one than to be right with mass graves... The most important thing you do every day is deciding not to kill yourself... It takes more courage to live than to shoot yourself... Live to the point of tears... If you trust life, life has to answer you."

1,376. ~ NO SUCH THING AS A SHALLOW DREAM ~

There is no such thing as a shallow dream. There is consciousness, there is the twilight and dawn of consciousness, and then there is the untamed well of subconscious, psychedelic, soul stirring realities.

And wells are deep and dark, yet full of life sustaining water. In the depth of our dreams we drown but we drink, we die but we live, we are terrified but we are born again.

We sleep next to death, and yet sleep lets us live.

Sometimes I would rather die than dream; but God has His reasons for all things. So we make the sign of the Cross, we close our eyes, and we enter into another dimension of the ubiquitous spiritual warfare that we can never escape. But we rise and fall and sleep and awake with one truth resonating in our souls: *Christ is Risen!*

1,377. ~ ACID DREAMS ~

Acid dreams are born
with flame skies
and fire dawn
dusk rainbows
and midnight sun
melted deserts
and Cross horizon...

Trip forward
into the arms of Jesus.

1,378. ~ APART from CALVARY ~

I want a peace I can feel
and a love I can see
a justice that's real
and a truth that sets free.

But I can't find it
apart from Calvary.

1,379. ~ UNBELIEF, APOSTASY, and PROVISION ~

If it is true that a person who does not provide for their own family is worse than an unbeliever (I Timothy 5:8), then I dare say that it is equally true that a Church which does not provide for its brethren is inherently apostate.

"Our life and death is with our neighbor. If we gain our brother we have gained God; but if we deny our brother we have sinned against Christ." ~ St. Anthony the Great ~

1,380. ~ THE COMPROMISE of CONSCIOUSNESS ~

The compromise of divine consciousness inevitably leads to the corruption of human creativity. Prolific art flows from those who prostrate their minds and hearts before the Creator. Those who believe in nothing will create anything and everything that reflects and accomplishes nothing. Nihilism cannot give birth to beauty, substance, inspiration, or healing. And those that labor to portray the meaningless of existence have contradicted their own worldview; for if life has no meaning then how can we even begin to understand the meaning of the meaningless they have attempted to portray?

1,381. ~ TO DENY LIFE IS TO DENY CHRIST ~

At the root of all heresy there is a disregard, disrespect, and devaluing of human life. Where the Gospel is truly preached, life is truly affirmed – not only life in its optimal circumstances, in its physical glories, in its romantic hopes and idealistic dreams – but also life in its horrors, deformities, struggles, and suffering.

From Mary's womb to Joseph's tomb, life is affirmed. From Eden's creation to Zion's redemption, life is affirmed. From Calvary's Friday to Easter Sunday, life is affirmed. The Gospel is always, forever, and eternally about life. To affirm life is to affirm Christ. To deny life is to deny Christ.

1,382. ~ THE GREATEST CURE FOR COWARDICE ~

Christian pacifism is truly the greatest cure for cowardice. Before I was a Christian (which inevitably led me to pacifism) I always predicated my confrontations upon whether or not I believed myself to possess superior strength, superior talent, superior intellect, or superior force. If I thought I could outwit, outsmart, outfight, or outgun my opponent then I was willing to be bold and brave. But if I calculated that I would lose a battle of mind or might, then I shied away from the conflict, even if I believed my cause to be right.

But Our Lord Jesus Christ showed me the ultimate fallacy and the inevitable failure of a mindset predicated upon faith in mortal strength and fleshly superiority. There will always be someone smarter, someone stronger, someone with a bigger gun and superior firepower (both in love and in war.)

And what will we do with our convictions then? If we have defended our truths and proved our "rightness" by humiliating and defeating those who challenge us, what have we really achieved? Will people believe in our cause because we have intellectually embarrassed them, physically dominated them, or emotionally eviscerated them? Will we lead souls to eternal life by shedding blood and destroying life on earth?

Jesus Christ shows me that I can speak the truth, live the truth, and confront the very forces of hell without physical violence, without intellectual prowess, and without conquering, defeating, or humiliating those that still await their redemption. I can stand toe-to-toe with anyone, anywhere – be it in the intellectual arena or the physical arena –and all I have to do is simply proclaim the Gospel.

And that is the only power and force that I need.

I know that I may be intellectually humiliated, physically dominated, and perhaps even crucified. But because I rely solely on the weapons of the Holy Spirit, I know that the faith and truth I proclaim will eternally prevail.

Am I afraid? Yes. Certainly. I don't pretend that I'm not. But I was much more afraid back in the days when I relied upon my own ability, my own strength, and my own prowess.

But now I am free to confront the cowardice, the lies, and the violence of Babylon and say:

"This is the truth. I am speaking it. Not by my own authority and not by the power of my own temporal might. Silence me. Imprison me. Crucify me. But the truth I proclaim shall live on forever. So outgun me, outsmart me, beat me to a pulp, nail me to a cross. Go ahead. Do what you will, but I will never stop confronting you with Truth."

And I have found that in clinging to peace I have become a much braver man than I ever was when I carried a gun.

"He said to me, 'My grace is sufficient for you, for My strength is made perfect in weakness.' Therefore most gladly I will rather boast in my infirmities, that the power of Christ may rest upon me. Therefore I take pleasure in infirmities, in reproaches, in needs, in persecutions, in distresses, for Christ's sake. For when I am weak, then I am strong." [I Corinthians 12:8-10]

1,383. ~ SEXUALITY ~

I pretty much have an opinion about everything. But one subject upon which I rarely opine is sexuality. Sex is one of the paradoxical mysteries of life: glorious and gut-wrenching, confusing and climactic, strangely simple yet deeply satisfying. Those who seek to conquer its mystery will never be fulfilled, and those that claim to have mastered it will always be empty.

Why is it that a thousand orgasms can't produce a single ounce of love, but love can produce a single orgasm that shakes the heavens? Why is it that so much of what we feel to be right and good and natural and unavoidable is actually spiritually detrimental and often physically deadly?

I don't have the answers to these questions. So I refrain from judging and opining on such matters (although I acknowledge that these very words are an opinion.)

I know what's recorded in the Bible about homosexuality, and I know what Jesus said about lust in general. And I've never met anyone in my entire life who claimed to be free from lust. (And if I ever did meet someone who claimed to be free from lust, I wouldn't believe them for a second.)

So here's my opinion on sexuality – heterosexuality and homosexuality and anything in between:

God loves you.

God wants you to love others.

Keep struggling.

Keep loving.

And that's all I really have to say about the matter. (And come to think of it, this should really be my only opinion on anything else and everything else.)

1,384. ~ THE MOST EFFECTIVE WAY to TRULY OPPOSE EVIL ~

The most effective way to truly oppose evil is to refuse to commit evil ourselves. God alone is the punisher and restrainer of the wicked (Romans 12:19). The Christian's duty is simply to intervene, interfere, and resist evil without resorting to the weapons or methods of evil.

"That is naïve!" says the Machiavellian cynic. "Your Christian philosophy only ensures that you and those you seek to defend will surely be killed. Your Gospel is a nice idea; and yes, how wonderful it would be if everyone embraced its irenic ethic. But this earthly existence will not be preserved by the meek. Evil will not be overcome by pacifism. The Gospel is fine for your Christian Church, but it won't work in the real world."

And to that we respond: "You may be right. This fleshly existence, fleeting as it is, perhaps will not be preserved by the peacemakers. The meek won't inherit this perishing world, but they will most certainly inherit a new heaven and a new earth (St. Matthew 5:5; Psalm 37:9; Revelation 21:1-4). So let the wicked enjoy their brief glories. Let the violent rejoice in their mortal conquests. But we will nevertheless be thorns in their sides – pricking their consciences, confronting their lies, and serving God's law of love and life in the midst of their earthly rules of violence and death. We will proclaim our loyalty to Christ's Kingdom alone, regardless of how desperately the world demands our loyalty to their dominions. And let them crucify us if they must; because beyond this temporal vale there is an eternal reality that we shall joyously possess."

As St. Paul wrote:

"The message of the cross is foolishness to those who are perishing, but to us who are being saved it is the power of God. For it is written: 'I will destroy the wisdom of the wise; the intelligence of the intelligent I will frustrate.' Where is the wise person? Where is the teacher of the law? Where is the philosopher of this age? Has not God made foolish the wisdom of the world? For since in the wisdom of God the world through its wisdom did not know him, God was pleased through the foolishness of what was preached to save those who believe. Jews demand signs and Greeks look for wisdom, but we preach Christ crucified: a stumbling block to Jews and foolishness to Gentiles, but to those whom God has called, both Jews and Greeks, Christ the power of God and the wisdom of God. For the foolishness of God is wiser than human wisdom, and the weakness of God is stronger than human strength." [I Corinthians 1:18-25]

"The Church is always authorized to complain, for the sake of this world, about the evils and injustices of this world. By the mercy of God, the inherent, invariable, unavoidable, intentional, unrelenting posture of the Church in the world is one of radical protest and profound dissent towards the prevailing status quo of secular society, whatever that may be at any given time, however much men boast that theirs is a great society." ~William Stringfellow ~

When I was a senior in high school I took a class called *"Creativity and Self Actualization."* (I went to a public high school in Atlanta, so yes, these types of courses actually existed there in the 1980's.) At the beginning of the year our teacher asked us to meditate and visualize Baba Ram Dass coming to speak to our school. Our textbook was Ram Dass's famous book, <u>Be Here Now</u>. So during the school year we would begin each class with a meditation and visualization session, with the hope of somehow getting Ram Dass to come and bless us with his wisdom. And sure enough, towards the end of the year, Ram Dass came all the way from his home in California to speak to our humble little high school in the middle of Atlanta, Georgia. And this was in 1987, long before the prevalence of cell phones and the internet. That experience taught me that positive vibes and a positive focus can indeed have a positive impact.

Ram Dass is not an Orthodox Christian, and like anyone else his words should be measured by the Teachings and Traditions of the apostolic Orthodox Faith. But he certainly has a lot of wisdom. And I will always remember him coming to speak to us those many years ago, and how our meditations and visualizations helped make that a reality.

One thing he emphasized that I will never forget – and which is actually quite compatible with Orthodox Christian theology – is that there are no shortcuts to enlightenment. Ram Dass cautioned us that it's very dangerous to seek God or mystical experiences through drug-induced altered states (and he said this as many of us in attendance were peaking on psilocybin mushrooms and LSD.) He explained that spiritual progress is hard work and that enlightenment involves effort. I have always remembered that.

Ram Dass was also friends with Aldous Huxley, whose book <u>Brave New World</u> made an indelible impression on me when I read it as a young teenager. And as an adult, Huxley's philosophical and spiritual writings have had an even greater influence on my life. Unlike many false prophets who exalt themselves and their own personalities at the expense of truth, Ram Dass and Huxley both exuded deep humility and a sincere desire to affirm human life and human peace.

From what I can tell, at the time of the writing of this book, Ram Dass is still going strong – living a humble, enlightened life that brings peace to others and peace to the world.

"We are all affecting the world every moment, whether we mean to or not. Our actions and states of mind matter, because we are so deeply interconnected with one another. I would like my life to be a statement of love and compassion – and where it isn't, that's where my work lies." ~ Ram Dass ~

1,386. ~ HOW TO FIGHT for TRUTH AND RIGHTS ~

Most certainly we should speak up for truth and rights; we should raise our voices for the voiceless; we should advocate for the victims of injustice and stand in solidarity with the oppressed. But we should never resort to wars and executions and violence to prove our point. We do God's work, but we dare not presume to execute God's vengeance.

"Where there is injustice I always believe in fighting. The question is: do you fight to punish or do you fight to change things? I believe that we are all such sinners that we should leave punishment to God alone."

1,387. ~ ART and LABELS ~

To label art is to misunderstand art. Let the colors and words and notes speak for themselves. Don't try to categorize them. Don't try to understand them. Just feel them and be transformed.

To hell with the "American Dream"! Live your own dream, and don't let the American nightmare get in your way.

1,389. ~ HOMOSEXUALITY, HUMANITY, and ABORTION ~

If you are more offended by gay weddings and transgender identity than you are by the deliberate, premeditated, and violent dismemberment of unborn children in the womb, then you're one of the reasons why the horror of abortion remains a legal reality. And by the way, "normal" heterosexuals are killing their unborn babies at a much higher rate than homosexuals. So let that sink in for a minute.

Abortion is not a "culture war" issue, a religious issue, or a political issue. Abortion is a *human rights* issue; and you don't have to be liberal or conservative, gay or straight, religious or irreligious to recognize and understand that the legality of abortion is the most barbaric and egregious human rights violation of our time.

Our individual human lives and our own human rights are inextricably linked to the rights and lives of others – *all* others, in all of their diverse human manifestations, nascent human stages, complex human confusions, various human struggles, and shared vulnerabilities, frailties, and failures. To deny the lives and intrinsic rights of the "least of these" in order to proclaim and avow our own lives and rights is the myopic hellish mindset that has facilitated inhumanity and injustice throughout the ages. As Dr. Martin Luther King, Jr. said:

"Injustice anywhere is a threat to justice everywhere. Whatever affects one directly affects all indirectly."

In other words, in biblical language, we are our brother's keeper. As long as we support the execution, torture, enslavement, bombing, imprisonment, discrimination, oppression, and abortion of our neighbors then we support our own vulnerability and victimhood. It is a maxim that a chain is only as strong as its weakest link; and it is equally axiomatic that humanity is only as strong as its weakest and most vulnerable members. If the innocent babe in the womb is not safe from society's cruel laws, then let us dare not think that we are somehow safe from those same cruel laws.

A society governed by violent and unjust legislation will invariably produce violence and injustice amongst its citizenry. We cannot escape being victimized by the seeds of injustice and evil that we ourselves sow and allow to grow.

How can we expect cops to treat us justly and peaceably when cops have pledged to violently uphold the violent and unjust laws that we support with our votes, with our civic compliance, and with our apathetic acquiescence? Why are we surprised when a cop shoots down an innocent unarmed Black man when cops get paid to protect the legal slaughter of unborn Black children in the womb?

So think about these things. Please. Not just for the unborn's sake, or for my sake, or for your sake, but for *humanity's* sake.

1,390. ~ LOVE IN ACTION ~

What do the prophets preach?
What does the beggar seek?
What fuels revolutionary speech?
What do the true saints teach?

Love...
and action...
and love in action.

1,391. ~ HERETICAL RELIGION and DISHONEST TRUTH ~

Religion that needs to be preserved by violence is heresy, and truth that demands bloodshed is a lie. There is no need to kill for a Church and a Faith that are eternally indestructible. Christ is the Way, the Truth, and the Life (St. John 14:6); and His divinely shed blood has nullified every justification and rationale for human bloodshed and killing.

1,392. ~ THE SEVEN STAGES of HUMAN CONSCIOUSNESS and HUMAN EXISTENCE ~

There are seven stages of human consciousness and human existence. The first stage is *Realization*. We realize that we are alive, that we exist, and correspondingly we realize that we live and exist in a fallen, unjust, and sinful condition.

The second stage is *Rebellion*. We instinctively revolt against this fallen, unjust, sinful condition, and we often do so in a manner that is just as fallen and unjust and sinful as the conditions against which we revolt.

The third stage is *Revelation*. We recognize that our finite individual rebellion against the universe is futile. We come to understand that there is a transcendent truth, a universal hope, and a divine reality that alone can heal the evils we both curse and contribute to.

And revelation leads to the fourth stage of human consciousness and human existence: *Revolution*. The individual who has received divine revelation cannot help but to live and think and move and act in a revolutionary manner. Divine revelation compels him to spiritual discipline and social activism. The revelation of divine truth never leaves one stagnant, apathetic, or indifferent. Revelation always precipitates individual, communal, prophetic, political, social, and cultural revolution.

And revolution leads to the fifth stage, which is *Redemption*. When individuals and groups of individuals are moved by divine revelation to repent of their sins, to redress social injustices, and to sacrificially intervene on behalf of the weak, the voiceless, and the oppressed then they imitate the Savior who brought redemption to the world. By preaching and living out the Gospel of Jesus Christ, fallen man is able to cooperate in the redemption of fallen humanity.

And redemption leads to the sixth stage of human existence and human consciousness: ***Restoration***. The person who initially realized the horror of existence and intuitively rebelled against it – often in all the wrong ways – now becomes a revolutionary agent of restoration. His life now brings healing, hope, and light to the darkness and despair around him.

And as he becomes an instrument of restoration, he experiences and manifests the seventh stage of human consciousness and human existence: ***Reconciliation***. This is the purpose and end of every revelatory idea and every revolutionary act. God and sinners reconciled. And sinners reconciled to God are sinners reconciled to each other. And in this ultimate reconciliation human beings find the fulfillment of their very existence and purpose.

"For God was pleased to have all His fullness dwell in Him, and through Him to reconcile to Himself all things, whether things on earth or things in heaven, by making peace through the blood of His cross." [Colossians 1:19-20]

But the tragedy is that most people never even awaken to the first stage of human consciousness: ***Realization***. They never realize their own sins, they ignore the groans of fallen creation, and they refuse the cries of their suffering brothers and sisters. They exist in that vapid and hellish condition of willful blindness to reality, thinking that peace and comfort will come from refusing to authentically acknowledge, confront, and engage themselves and their neighbors and their Creator.

1,393. ~ THE CHALLENGE of THE CHRISTIAN PROPHETS ~

The Christian prophets *challenge* the Church but they never *condemn* the Church. They recognize that the ark is severely worn and badly weathered; but they never abandon ship, for they know that in spite of the damage done to the vessel it nevertheless remains the very ark of salvation. And let us not forget that every baptized Orthodox believer is anointed and called to be a prophet. So let us prophesy with correction, not condemnation – plugging up the spiritual holes, bailing out the heretical water, and rowing together with all of our might toward "our redemption which draweth nigh" (St. Luke 21:28).

1,394. ~ IN THE NAME OF... ~

In the name of "national security" we fight to keep refugees from crossing the border. In the name of "law and order" we support a constabulary that violently enables the oppression of immigrants, the unborn, "minorities," and the poor. In the name of "choice" we slaughter human lives in the womb. And in the name of "liberty and freedom" our government bombs, imprisons, executes, and tortures those that dare to interfere with its systemic evils and injustices. And all this while having the audacity to inscribe *"In God We Trust"* on the blood-soaked currency we worship.

1,395. ~ THE POLITICIAN and THE ARTIST ~

The politician is a coward, a charmer, a charlatan who steals words, appropriates imagery, and manipulates the facts of history to advance his own feckless, mortal, solipsistic agenda. But the artist is a bold and unapologetic thief, a social offender, and a revolutionary who plunders from the well of universal truth in order to convict and inspire, to burn down and build up, to afflict and heal.

It is the nature of the politician to conceal the truth and deceive the people; but it is the nature of the artist to reveal the truth and bare his naked soul to the world. There may be an "art" to politics, but it is an art devoid of any aesthetic merit or redemptive potential.

The artist has no concern for pragmatic expediency. Unlike politicians who merely exploit existing social situations and historical circumstances for their own personal gain, the artist actually *creates*.

And the artist's creation may be beautiful or horrific, joyous or terrifying. But it is always real. And its creative honesty does more to positively change the world than any political platform or governmental legislation could ever hope to achieve.

1,396. ~ GOD'S WORK, GOD'S VENGEANCE ~

Most certainly we should speak up for truth and rights, we should raise our voices for the voiceless, we should advocate for the victims of injustice and stand in solidarity with the oppressed. But we should never resort to wars and executions and violence to prove our point. We do God's work, but we dare not presume to execute God's vengeance.

1,397. ~ ECONOMICS and SERVITUDE ~

Right-wing economic policies make people servants of corporate masters. Left-wing economic policies make people servants of the State. Stop enslaving yourself to politics. Be a servant of Christ and let His Lordship set you free.

"Do not make yourselves slaves of men." [I Corinthians 7:23]

1,398. ~ A MEDITATION from THE EMERGENCY ROOM ~

As I'm waiting here in the emergency room, praying for my own health and the health of all those around me – and contemplating the current political healthcare debate – these thoughts come to mind:

We are commanded to love our neighbors as ourselves. Why? Because our neighbors, like us, bear the very image of God, and as such they deserve our nurture and love as we deserve theirs. Whether such nurture and love – which involves active and sacrificial care for both body and soul – is a "right" or a "privilege" is a debate for politicians and ideologues. But for the disciples of Christ there is no debate. We love our neighbors as ourselves – physically, spiritually, socially, and politically. For us it really is just that simple.

Dear Lord, let us be healed so we may heal others. And dear Lord, let others be healed so they may also heal us.

1,399. ~ ARGUING ABOUT GOVERNMENTAL SOLUTIONS ~

Arguing about which governmental solutions are the best solutions is like arguing about which poison is easier to swallow. If we don't get busy loving and helping one another then we'll all be inevitable victims of the powers that seek to profit from our suffering.

1,400. ~ INHUMANE, UNJUST, and SELF-DEFEATING ARGUMENTS ~

Arguments for violence are ultimately inhumane, unjust, and inherently self-defeating arguments.

1,401. ~ ORTHODOX WORSHIP ~

King David danced before the Ark in a most "undignified" and "unorthodox" manner. And Michal, Saul's daughter, publicly condemned his actions as shameless and unbefitting for the King of Israel (II Samuel 6:14-16).

So while I shall always uphold and defend Orthodox Christian worship, I must be careful not to condemn those who express their sincere love for God in ways that I may not always understand or agree with. The word "Orthodox" literally means "correct worship," and those who worship God in Spirit and truth can never be wrong, no matter what society and churches may say.

"The wind bloweth where it listeth, and thou hearest the sound thereof, but canst not tell whence it cometh, and whither it goeth: so is every one that is born of the Spirit." [St. John 3:8]

"God is Spirit, and those who worship Him must worship Him in spirit and truth." [St. John 4:24]

1,402. ~ OUR ONLY POLITICS and OUR ULTIMATE REVOLUTION ~

To love our neighbors as ourselves: let this be our only politics; let this be our ultimate revolution.

1,403. ~ THE BLESSEDNESS of SUFFERING ~

Suffering is the common denominator of human life. It is the inevitable fate of all who live. But most of us revolve our lives around the avoidance of suffering. And ironically, the more we pursue pleasure the more pain we usually store up for ourselves in the long run.

No one enjoys suffering, and no one should deliberately seek to suffer out of masochistic motivations. But if we learn to understand and embrace it, then suffering can actually become a blessed gift. And as we learn to experience the blessedness of suffering, then we will also be able to ease the pain of those around us.

In order to understand and embrace suffering, we must first recognize and identify its causes. All suffering emanates from four primary sources: 1) suffering caused by our own sins; 2) suffering caused by others; 3) suffering caused by circumstances; and 4) suffering caused by the pursuit of righteousness. But regardless of what brings it about, how we respond to our suffering will determine whether it will be to our spiritual benefit or to our spiritual detriment.

Bitterness is the first obstacle we must overcome. Disappointment, heartache, frustration, and anger are natural responses to pain and suffering. And even when we acknowledge that our own sin is to blame, the consequences of our sin often seem more severe than we deserve.

So, how should we respond to **the suffering that we have brought upon ourselves through our own wrongful actions**? First, rather than cursing the consequences that we ourselves have manufactured, we must embrace the suffering rather than curse it. Anesthetization is never permanent; and unless we treat the disease that causes the pain then the pain will inevitably metastasize and proliferate. Therefore, as we experience the consequences of our own sin, we must recognize that our suffering is proof that God is just and that His moral laws are immutable.

And we can take solace from this realization, for the God that convicts is also the God that heals. The repercussive suffering that our own sins produce is actually an act of divine mercy; for if we embrace our temporal suffering in this life and allow it to drive us to repentance, then we will save ourselves from suffering in the life to come.

Physical pain is a natural warning that our bodies need mending, and the suffering we face because of our own sin is a natural warning that our souls need healing. And when the suffering we endure seems more severe than the sin we have committed, we should remind ourselves that it is better to be purified by the trials of life than to be purified by the fires of divine judgment.

This brings us to **the second cause of suffering: that which is caused by others.** Unfortunately, in this fallen and sin sick world, the righteous often suffer more than the wicked. There is tremendous suffering inflicted upon the innocent by cruel, callous, and godless men. The wicked prosper as their evil goes unrestrained. At times it seems that the God of justice is asleep. But King Solomon's insight is very instructive here: *"Because the sentence against evildoers is not promptly executed, therefore the hearts of men are filled with the* *desire to commit evil – because the sinner does evil a hundred times and survives. But indeed it will be well with those who fear God, for their reverence toward Him; and it shall not be well with the wicked man, and he shall not prolong his shadowy days." [Ecclesiastes 8:11-13]*

In other words, as Tolstoy wrote: *"God sees the truth, but waits."* Justice cannot long be evaded. The balance of eternity will set all things right.

Suffering is inflicted not only by the overtly wicked, but also by selfish and thoughtless individuals who cause misery by their sheer disregard and lack of concern for others. The routines and responsibilities of daily life are made more difficult simply because people have abandoned the basic habits of courtesy, consideration, and respect for one another.

How then should we deal with the suffering that is caused by others? Again, we must start by forsaking bitterness. We must not allow the urge for vengeance and retaliation to take root in our hearts. Our ability to embrace the suffering that is unfairly inflicted upon us by others will bring us closer to God if we allow it to. And as we endure suffering without hatred or retribution, we can also have a profoundly positive impact on those who caused our pain. Suffering embraced and endured is not only redemptive for the victim, but it is also potentially redemptive for the victimizer. In fact, the Cross of Christ is the greatest proof of this spiritual truth.

The prophets and saints of history have demonstrated the power of forgiveness. It is always a great temptation to avenge the wrongs done to us; but this never brings about healing or peace. The Incarnate God endured the sin and darkness of our defiled world, and He died the cruelest of deaths at the hands of sinful men. But Our Lord forgave even as He was being slain. He abdicated his divine right to save Himself, sacrificing His life for the sins of the world. The undeserved suffering of Christ provides the model for us to follow. In fact, Christ commands us to follow his example – in every way.

Many sages and spiritually minded social activists have emulated Christ by their embrace and endurance of unearned suffering. Their courage and consciousness helped to rectify social injustices and change the hearts of erring men. And their sacrificial suffering made the roads of life a little less rocky for the rest of us. So, whenever we suffer from the actions of others, we must remember that our response is critical to both the conditioning of our own souls and to the contribution of a healthy society. As Dr. Martin Luther King, Jr. wrote:

"My personal trials have also taught me the value of unmerited suffering. As my sufferings mounted I soon realized that there were two ways that I could respond to my situation: either to react with bitterness or seek to transform the suffering into a creative force. I decided to follow the latter course. Recognizing the necessity for suffering I have tried to make of it a virtue. If only to save myself from bitterness, I have attempted to see my personal ordeals as an opportunity to transform myself and heal the people involved in the tragic situation which now obtains. I have lived these last few years with the conviction that unearned suffering is redemptive. There are some who still find the cross a stumbling block, and others consider it foolishness, but I am more convinced than ever before that it is the power of God unto social and individual salvation. So like the Apostle Paul I can now humbly yet proudly say, "I bear in my body the marks of the Lord Jesus." The suffering and agonizing moments through which I have passed over the last few years have also drawn me closer to God. More than ever before, I am convinced of the reality of a personal God." [Pilgrimage To Nonviolence]

The third cause of suffering **is that which results from circumstances.** Sometimes this can be the most agonizing type of suffering. This agony stems from the acts of chaos, confusion, and senselessness that seem to permeate the planet. This global chaos seeps into our own small corners of the world, and none of us are unaffected by it.

But efforts to violently rearrange our circumstances never result in the satisfaction we seek. History is replete with examples of sociopolitical movements that sought to establish an egalitarian utopia but ultimately created only more misery and suffering in the end. And as individuals, we frequently fall into the same trap. We believe that more money, new relationships, a bigger house, or a better job will bring us the happiness we desire. In the futile endeavor to alter our circumstances we often starve our souls and cripple our spirits. And those who are spiritually anemic usually make life more miserable for those around them.

However, by understanding the fact that our world will never be perfect, and by realizing that life will always be accompanied by unfavorable circumstances, we can focus instead on the cultivation of a productive response to our difficulties and hardships. We will preserve our very sanity by accepting and embracing the reality of life's adversity, for many people drive themselves insane trying to change things which are beyond their control. Consider the words of Helen Keller: *"Character cannot be developed in ease and quiet. Only through experiences of trial and suffering can the soul be strengthened, vision cleared, ambition inspired, and success achieved."*

The fourth type of suffering is that which results from the pursuit of righteousness. It is an invariable truth that light and goodness will be opposed by the forces of darkness and evil. St. Paul says: *"Indeed, all who desire to live godly in Christ Jesus will be persecuted." [II Timothy 3:12]*

But those who willingly suffer in order to advance the cause of righteousness will always be blessed. The world is full of political movements and social organizations that do everything except suffer for the sake of righteousness. Yet Christ actually made suffering a prerequisite for following Him: *"If any man wishes to come after Me, he must deny himself, take up his cross daily and follow Me." [St. Luke 9:23]*

This does not mean refusing to resist evil or blindly accepting injustices done to us or to others. It simply means remembering that true spirituality involves choosing to bear the cross of suffering for the cause of righteousness. It means practicing those disciplines that contribute to the cultivation of our souls and the enlightening of our minds. It means pursuing Paradise rather than pleasure. Fasting, service to others, working for human rights and authentic social justice, prayer, worship, and self-denial are spiritual exercises that may involve suffering to some degree. These things do not earn us God's grace, but they develop our spirits and bring us closer to the God with whom we are already in relationship.

Our Lord taught: *"Blessed are you when they insult you and persecute you and utter every kind of evil against you because of Me. Rejoice and be glad, for your reward will be great in heaven. Thus they persecuted the prophets who were before you."* [St. Matthew 5:11-12]

St. Peter gives us this encouragement: *"Even if you should suffer because of righteousness, blessed are you... it is better to suffer for doing good, if that be the will of God, than for doing evil... As a result, those who suffer in accord with the will of God hand their souls over to a faithful Creator as they do good."* [I Peter 3:14, 17; 4:19]

And St. Mark the Ascetic said: *"Those who suffer for the sake of true devotion receive help from God."*

Suffering has many positive benefits. For example: It is *punitive*, pointing us to repentance. It is *healing* for those who understand and embrace it. It is *educational*, teaching priceless spiritual principles to those who are willing to learn. It is *productive*, bringing about spiritual growth. And it is *enlightening* for all those who accept the purpose and design behind it. Therefore, know that suffering always has a remedial and redemptive effect. If we view our trials and adversities from a spiritual perspective then we may find that suffering is in fact a blessing rather than a curse.

How sad it is that so many people spend their entire lives in the futile attempt to avoid suffering. In order to evade suffering they fall prey to materialism and carnal pleasures; and tragically, many resort to the exploitation and oppression of others in the process. The result of this is always the increase of suffering as addiction, disease, and the insanity which results from a perpetual violation of the conscience inevitably set in. The more that people try to elude the law of suffering, the more pain they bring to themselves and to the world around them.

Yet by understanding and embracing suffering, we can find hope and we can find God. This is the blessedness of suffering, and what a beautiful blessing it is! The Creator always presents us with a choice. Will we choose to suffer for righteousness? Will we choose to embrace suffering when we experience it as the result of our own sin? Will we choose patience and forgiveness when others have harmed us? Will we choose to embrace the opportunity to strengthen our souls when the circumstances of life are difficult and bitter?

All of us will suffer. This is an unavoidable fact of life. But the question is: how will we respond to the suffering that befalls us? The Creator has allowed us to determine whether our suffering will be for us a blessing or a curse. The choice is ours, and a wise response will bring blessed rewards.

Alexander Solzhenitsyn wrote: *"The happiness that comes from easy victories, from the total fulfillment of desires, from perpetual success, from feeling completely gorged – that too is suffering! That is spiritual death, a kind of unending moral indigestion. But if the heart grows warmer from the misfortunes suffered, if it is cleansed therein, then the years are not passing in vain."*

And let us consider the words of Dorothy Day: *"Why should I refuse what is the common lot of humanity? Why should I ask to be spared when I see the suffering of the family next door? Suffering borne with courage means to the devout mind a participation in the sufferings of Christ, and if bravely endured, can lighten the sufferings of others." [Dorothy Day: Selected Writings]*

And from the ancient Greek poet, Aeschylus: *"He who learns must suffer. And even in our sleep, pain that cannot forget falls drop by drop upon the heart, and in our own despair, against our will, wisdom comes to us by the awful grace of God."*

In conclusion, let us also find hope in the fact that the Christ who calls us to take up our cross is the same Christ who says:

"Come unto Me, all ye that labor and are heavy laden, and I will give you rest. Take my yoke upon you, and learn of Me; for I am meek and lowly in heart: and ye shall find rest unto your souls. For my yoke is easy, and my burden is light." [St. Matthew 11:29-30]

I leave you with these quotes from Blessed Father Seraphim Rose:

"Suffering is the reality of the human condition and the beginning of true spiritual life. If used in the right way, suffering can purify the heart, and 'the pure in heart shall see God.' [St. Matthew 5:8] The right approach is found in the heart which tries to humble itself and simply knows that it is suffering, and that there somehow exists a higher truth which can not only help this suffering, but can bring it into a totally different dimension."

"Pain of heart is the condition for spiritual growth and the manifestation of God's power. Healings, etc., occur to those in desperation, hearts pained but still trusting and hoping in God's help."

"Some people seem to have an 'easy' and uncomplicated path in life – or so it seems from the outside; while for others, everything seems complicated and difficult. Don't let that bother you. Actually, from the spiritual point of view, those who really have an 'easy' time are probably in spiritual danger! – precisely because without the element of suffering through whatever God sends, there is no spiritual profit or advancement. God knows each of us better than we know ourselves, and He sends what is needful for us, whatever we may think!"

"You must learn to suffer and bear – but do not view this as something 'endless and dreary.' God sends many consolations, and you will know them again. You must learn to find joy in the midst of increasing doses of sorrow; thus you can save your soul and help others."

"Spiritual life begins when things seem absolutely 'hopeless' – that is when one learns to turn to God and not to our own feeble efforts and ideas."

"Do not be depressed that there are people rising up against you. If everyone loved you, then I would say that there is some trouble there, because you are probably catering too much to people. Christ was also hated, and was crucified. Why should we expect everyone to suddenly love us, if we are following in the footsteps of Christ?"

"Indeed, how we all must learn and relearn that our pretensions and ideas must be tested by reality and forged in suffering."

"In spiritual life, it is often precisely in seemingly 'impossible' conditions that one really begins to grow."

"True spiritual life, even on the most elementary level, is always accompanied by suffering and difficulties. Therefore, you should rejoice in all your difficulties and sorrows."

"Everything you need to deepen your faith will come with suffering – if you accept it with humility and submission to God's will."

[Quotes from: <u>Father Seraphim Rose: His Life and Works</u>]

1,404. ~ CHRISTIANS, CAESAR, and THE POOR ~

If only we, as Christians, were as concerned about giving the poor their due as we are with giving Caesar his.

1,405. ~ REFLECTIONS on PROTESTS ~

It's not that people are protesting the wrong things; it's that they're not protesting the most important thing. It's great to tell our children not to eat too much candy, not to watch too much TV, and to go to bed on time; but if we ignore the fact that they're drinking poison then the rest of our parental instructions and admonitions are cruelly superfluous.

And that's similar to what is happening in our society today. There are lots of legitimate protests about many important issues, but if we fail to recognize and resist the systemic mass murder of innocent unborn children, then our other social protests will remain morally impotent and ultimately ineffective. Until we prioritize the rights and needs of the very "least of these" among us, then our cries and demands for justice will continue to ring hollow.

The damn house is burning down and we're busy trying to repaint the walls! If we don't first put out the fire, then we have no one but ourselves to blame if we're victimized by the very conflagration we refused to confront.

1,406. ~ THIS IS REVOLUTION ~

To keep on living when life seems hopeless... to refuse to kill when death looks like the only option... to affirm and cling to life in its nascence, its struggles, its pains, and its twilight... *This is revolution!*

1,407. ~ RETROACTIVE REVOLUTIONARIES ~

Evil cannot be excused by an appeal to "zeitgeist," i.e. arguing that those who defended or ignored the injustices of their time were simply prisoners of their own historical era. In every epoch of history there have been voices of conscience that decried the inhumanity and oppression of their day and age. These voices have always been in the minority, suffering the wrath and indignation of the masses for daring to proclaim prophetic truth to the herds that crucify them for doing so. Today we remember these heroes fondly with our tributes and memorials; but while they lived they were condemned as radical provocateurs that were disrupting "law and order" and posing a threat to "social stability."

And this is how human history always proceeds: people honoring the prophets of the past while mocking the prophets of the present, denouncing the injustices of yesteryear while heartily preserving the injustices of today.

Society is full of retroactive revolutionaries who shamelessly preserve the inhumane status quo of their own contemporary culture, boldly denouncing the crimes of the past while heartily condoning the crimes of the present.

Babylon is a chameleon – full of political changes and social transformations, but nonetheless remaining unalterably unjust, inhumane, and invariably oppressive.

1,408. ~ FROM YOUR SOUL ~

Give me something from your soul. Create brothers and sisters! Create!

Leave propaganda and practicality and politics to those who have nothing better to offer. Because I need you to feed my spirit. I need to bathe in your colors. I need to swim in your words. I need to ascend to heaven on the wings of your notes.

So don't sell out to temporal rewards. Be crucified by the explosion of your soul, and know that by doing so you will be caressing the cosmos and forever kissing God.

Give me art – naked, raw, honest, and true. Don't give me half measures because you're afraid of being obscene, and don't give me obscenities in the name of being "real." Just give your soul to the Creator, and I promise you that the soul of His creation will receive your offering.

We are all thirsty for revelatory expressions of our own angst and struggles and pains and hopes. So please, don't hold back. Speak to me through pen and paint and music and stage. Leave your agenda behind and let your work speak for itself.

Because if it's real it's true; and if it's true it's real. And anything more or anything less will never really matter.

It's easy to take a political, social, or moral stand when that stand is culturally popular and socially acceptable. It might in fact be the right stand to take, but it requires no real bravery, no true courage, no authentic conviction. But to speak clearly and boldly for life-affirmation amidst a culture wedded to death... now that takes real guts. To unequivocally proclaim "Thou shalt not kill" when politicians and pop stars and pro-abortion propagandists constantly demand the right to bomb and abort and execute anyone who interferes with their "manifest destiny," their "states rights," and their "freedom of choice"... well, that requires true spiritual integrity and authentic social consciousness.

So, where will you stand when the just and true cause is the unpopular and dangerous cause? Where will you stand when standing for what's right means standing in opposition to worldly profit and worldly praise?

Our society today is replete with pseudo-revolutionaries, hipster theologians, armchair activists, and "social justice" advocates who carefully calculate their convictions to make sure they're on the side of popular opinion rather than on the side of prophetic fire.

But the cosmic coals are already burning, and none of us can escape their eternal purgation. We will either participate in the winnowing redemption or we will be scorched by its divine chastening.

We won't be judged by our academic credentials, our social standing, or our political affiliation. We will be judged – individually and collectively – simply by how we treated the most helpless, the most vulnerable, and the most defenseless among us. The Jesus we profess to love while supporting ideologies, practices, and regimes that crucify Him with politics and militarism and abortion is a Jesus that will not know us on the day of divine reckoning.

"When the Son of Man comes in his glory, and all the angels with him, he will sit on his glorious throne. All the nations will be gathered before him, and he will separate the people one from another as a shepherd separates the sheep from the goats. He will put the sheep on

his right and the goats on his left. Then the King will say to those on his right, 'Come, you who are blessed by my Father; take your inheritance, the kingdom prepared for you since the creation of the world. For I was hungry and you gave me something to eat, I was thirsty and you gave me something to drink, I was a stranger and you invited me in, I needed clothes and you clothed me, I was sick and you looked after me, I was in prison and you came to visit me.' Then the righteous will answer him, 'Lord, when did we see you hungry and feed you, or thirsty and give you something to drink? When did we see you a stranger and invite you in, or needing clothes and clothe you? When did we see you sick or in prison and go to visit you?' The King will reply, 'Truly I tell you, whatever you did for one of the least of these brothers and sisters of mine, you did for me.' Then he will say to those on his left, 'Depart from me, you who are cursed, into the eternal fire prepared for the devil and his angels. For I was hungry and you gave me nothing to eat, I was thirsty and you gave me nothing to drink, I was a stranger and you did not invite me in, I needed clothes and you did not clothe me, I was sick and in prison and you did not look after me.' They also will answer, 'Lord, when did we see you hungry or thirsty or a stranger or needing clothes or sick or in prison, and did not help you?' He will reply, 'Truly I tell you, whatever you did not do for one of the least of these, you did not do for me.' Then they will go away to eternal punishment, but the righteous to eternal life." [St. Matthew 25:31-46]

1,410. ~ THE NIHILIST and THE REVOLUTIONARY ~

The nihilist, seeking to evade the evils and problems of existence, pretends to believe in nothing; and yet the nihilist has great faith in his own illusions. The revolutionary, on the other hand, believes very well in the problems of existence; but he refuses to accept by faith that such a problematic existence is a permanent and unalterable reality. That's why "Marxist revolution" is an oxymoron. Those that can see no further than the material realm can never be truly visionary, and therefore they can never be truly revolutionary.

1,411. ~ WE SIDE WITH LIFE – MILITANTLY SO ~

We will live and dream and sleep and wake and suffer and live some more. Through tears and pain and nightmares and despair we will keep living and revolt against it all.

We rebel against war and suicide and executions and abortion. And we rebel against a world that would have us believe that there are answers in war and suicide and executions and abortion.

We choose life, and this is our revolution. So to hell with your philosophies of death! We will live until we bleed and die and rise again.

We side with *life*. We side with *eternal life*. Militantly so.

1,412. ~ KINGDOM of GOD / KINGDOMS of MEN ~

Neutrality in times of controversy and conflict is never an option for the true Christian or the true revolutionary. Without apology, regardless of who it may offend, and in spite of the reprisals and suffering we may incur as a result, we must always choose to side with life, with love, with peace, with truth, with humanity, with justice, and with the Kingdom of Heaven against the kingdoms of this world. The Kingdom of God will never cooperate with the kingdoms of men. Politics and prophecy do not mix. There can be no harmony between Zion and Babylon. Choose this day which you will serve.

1,413. ~ THE INESCAPABLE HARVEST of INNOCENT BLOOD ~

As of the year 2015 there have been 55,000,000 innocent unborn children "legally" murdered since 1973. Until light, love, freedom, and peace come to the womb then we can never expect light, love, freedom, and peace to come to our world. Until we stop shedding innocent blood inside the dark walls of abortion mills, our society will continue to suffer from violence and bloodshed in the streets. Until we stop terrorizing the very "least of these" then we will never be safe from terror ourselves. Call it "karma," call it "reciprocity," or call it "the law of the harvest," but it is a universal and inescapable truth that a society will inevitably reap what it sows.

1,414. ~ YESTERDAY'S GRACE ~

Yesterday a prophet approached me at the coffee shop and asked me to interpret her dream. I told her to keep on prophesying and to please pray for me, a sinner.

Yesterday a beggar asked me for change. That's all I had. It's all I ever have. So I gave him a fist full of change, and his eyes lit up. "Quarters! Quarters!" he said. "I only needed 30 cents! Thanks man, thanks man!"

"Don't thank me" I said. "Tomorrow I may be asking you for change. Just pray for me."

Yesterday a sister in Christ called me with a burdened spirit. I had no answers for her, but my soul was lifted by her humility, grace, and wisdom. She called me with a broken heart, but it was my own broken heart that was healed by our conversation.

Yesterday I laughed with my children, I kissed my wife, I chatted with a very dear friend, and I felt the love of God.

Tomorrow may be hell, but I will remember yesterday. Hell is real, but heaven is forever. I choose to bathe in the grace of now. Because God is with me in the moment – in every moment – both horrible and hopeful.

It's not the circumstances but the Christ who is present in every circumstance that saves and heals and reconciles and redeems. I pray for the grace to share yesterday's grace to those who need it now and tomorrow and forever.

1,415. ~ FASCISM VS. PACIFISM ~

They tell me that words won't defeat fascism. Well, apparently war didn't defeat fascism either, since fascists are still running around today. And the fact is that I've never known any true pacifist who argues that the only response to evil and injustice should be mere words. What defeats hate and evil are love and truth sacrificially and boldly lived out. Nonviolence is not apathy and indifference to evil; it is rather vigilant confrontation with evil only by the methods of goodness and truth. Nonviolent warriors refuse to allow evil to dictate the terms of engagement. We look at evil and say: "We refuse to play by your rules. We refuse to accept your terms. We refuse to allow you to drag us down to your demonic mindset and your damnable methodologies. Instead, we are determined to literally love the hell out of you."

1,416. ~ THE POWER of YOUR WORDS, TEARS, SUFFERING, and HOPE ~

You will never really know the power of your words, the power of your tears, the power of your truth, the power of your suffering, the power of your prayers, the power of your struggle, and the power of your hope. You live and you love and yet you are rewarded with sorrow and pain. But what you don't see is the fruit of your efforts and the harvest of your faith. What you don't see is the eternal reverberations of a life-affirming soul that you were courageous enough to bare amidst a world of superficialities and death. If you give wisdom, if you give comfort, if you give forgiveness, if you give bread, if you give life, if you give anything of yourself to help another then you give to Christ; and in doing so you also receive Christ.

1,417. ~ FOR CHILDREN'S BROKEN HEARTS ~

I want to pray for every child's heart to never be broken. But I can't realistically pray for such a thing. This world is so merciless and cruel that it will inevitably break all hearts that beat long enough in its temporal realm. So I pray instead that every broken heart will become a Christ-healed heart, a redeemed heart, a heart whose wounds and suffering and scars will compel it to comfort and heal the hearts of others.

1,418. ~ EXTREMISM ~

I'm not interested in lukewarm philosophies, lukewarm worldviews, or lukewarm religions. Give me extremism, without apology. Whether I live or die, let me live and die for something real, something true, something that will endure forever – e.g. human rights, human freedom, human peace, and the divine principles upon which all such values are objectively predicated.

So whenever anyone tries to disparage an ideology or a movement by labeling it "extremist," the more inclined I am to actually take that ideology or movement seriously. Not because I value extremism for extremism's sake, but because extreme evils deserve extreme confrontation and extreme rebuke.

"I know your works, that you are neither cold nor hot: I wish that you were cold or hot. But because you are lukewarm, and neither cold nor hot, I will spew you out of my mouth." [Revelation 3:15-16]

1,419. ~ TERRORISTS, GOVERNMENTS, and THE MEDIA ~

I'm always amused when the media attempts to discredit some fringe social, political, or religious movement by saying: "And what's most frightening is that these people are willing to kill for their beliefs." As if these same journalists who pretend to be horrified by violence aren't also willing to kill for their own misguided beliefs.

After all, American journalists could not produce their propaganda and "reportage" without the protection and support of the most heavily armed state in the world.

I find it interesting (and disturbing) that armed minorities willing to die for their freedoms are called "terrorists," but armed majorities that kill to maintain control over minorities are called "governments."

1,420. ~ INSOMNIACS and VAMPIRES ~

If not for Christian insomniacs, who would be awake to fight the vampires?

1,421. ~ THE SIXTH and SEVENTH BOOKS of MOSES ~

Years ago I used to study the *Sixth and Seventh Books of Moses* and *The Magical Uses of the Psalms*. I was a Christian, and I thought I could sift through such occult materials without being deceived. The books were fascinating, and much of the information seemed to correspond with my Christian faith. But there were also things that made my soul recoil: pentagrams and symbols and esoteric formulas and incantations of "angels." Strange and confusing things; and God is not the author of confusion (I Corinthians 14:33).

Satan is a clever devil, always packaging his lies in the façade of truth. As my baptism into the Orthodox Church drew nigh, I realized that I needed to jettison these occult materials from my life. So I threw them out, along with my books on Voodoo that I had collected over the years. There are some things that we just don't need to know. Wise ignorance can save us, but educated evil can damn us.

In spite of the title, Moses the prophet did not write the _Sixth and Seventh Books of Moses_. The work is an 18th century text that combines influences of the Jewish Talmud and astrology while purporting to reveal spells that unlock the secrets of biblical miracles.

A Hebrew babe raised by Pharaoh's daughter, Moses was learned and adept in all the magic and sorceries of Egypt. He was a master of astrology and other arts of the occult. But His heart and soul belonged to God, and it was the power of God that enabled him to overpower and prevail against Pharaoh's sorcerers. And in the biblical Pentateuch, Moses – St. Moses – wrote down all that God wanted him to reveal to us.

So don't dabble with things that are not ordained by God and His Church, regardless of how spiritually fascinating they may seem. Remember that "Lucifer" means light, and Satan continues to appear to people as an angel of light (II Corinthians 11:14). In fact, Lucifer is more than happy to offer us "enlightenment" in exchange for our souls.

If you want holy, mystical, and spiritual literature, read the Bible – from Genesis to Revelation. And read the _entire_ Bible, which includes the book of Enoch and the book of Jubilees and the book of Sirach and the book of Maccabees (and many other sacred scriptures that are contained in the Orthodox canon but left out by the Protestant canon.) Read the Word of God that reveals Christ, the Word of God.

"By faith Moses, when he had grown up, refused to be known as the son of Pharaoh's daughter. He chose to be mistreated along with the people of God rather than to enjoy the fleeting pleasures of sin. He regarded disgrace for the sake of Christ as of greater value than the treasures of Egypt, because he was looking ahead to his reward." _[Hebrews 11:24-26]_

(A short story of demonic possession. Please be advised that this story contains some profanity.)

Through bloodshot eyes he stared at the blood moon and took another drink. The demons had not yet possessed him, but he was fully entertaining them now. What harm could they do that hadn't already been done? Fuck them. Let them enter. Let them come and possess and control and have their way with his soul. He was ready to dance with hell. Fuck it all. His life was already a spiraling abyss.

And besides, here was this glorious man speaking to him, to all of them – this wonderful, hopeful man, so full of charisma and intellect and presence. And this is what was needed today. No more fundamentalist preachers masquerading as politicians. No more politicians talking like preachers. What was needed was a man like this – a man with a polished tongue, deft with argument, cool and unflappable in the face of criticism. Here was a leader not too handsome, but just handsome enough – a leader who could make women swoon without arousing the jealousy of men – a leader who was ever winsome with wink and gesture and well honed smile. Here was a man of the world who could pass himself off as a man of the people – an elitist who could convince the masses that he was a man of the streets. It didn't matter what this glorious leader believed in – or if he believed in anything at all – it only mattered that he could make others also believe it or also not believe it.

God what a bull-shitter! But he was more than ready to go to hell with this bull-shitter, because life had already given him more hell and more bullshit than he could possibly take.

Time to win! Time to show the bastards who's in charge! And this was finally the right man to be in charge! This was the man to put all of these idiotic sons of bitches in their place! The political tables would turn now! About time! And he would gladly be damned in support of it!

So he took another swig from his blood drink, and he listened to the great man speak of promise and hope and humanity and a "new day." And he swallowed the rhetoric like he did the sanguine swill, knowing that though it tasted sweet and felt good it was actually killing him. But knowing he was being killed no longer bothered him. He embraced the pathology now, in all of its comforting, poisonous, destructively pleasing manifestations.

As long as he felt good he didn't care. He wanted to drown in the lies and the deception and the glorious intoxication of the crowd lust. He wanted to be seduced and used and ultimately destroyed by someone or anyone, by something or anything that would at least make him feel alive while he died.

And so the demons entered him, through the cheap wine and the cheap words of the charismatic man on the stage. And he submitted to the nefarious spirits. And the spirits were easy on him, patiently grooming him over the course of time.

And remarkably, the alcoholic man stopped drinking and his eyes became clear and he was suddenly able to look right into a person's heart while looking right past their humanity. And Satan placed his own hand upon his damned but sober soul. And in time he became an even more polished and deft and unflappable man than the one through whose words the demons had first entered. And then, in the devil's due time, he found himself prominently thrust upon the political stage himself, radiating the same superficial smile of hell, offering the same promises of one beautiful lie after another.

And now, although purely possessed, he suddenly cared about life again. And he became terrified of eternity. And then the demons began to torment and mock him. And his soul raged with the drunken power of the world and the eternal hell that beckoned day and night. And it became too terrible for him.

And he thought that since he had let the demons in then perhaps he could tell them to leave. But he knew he had neither the strength nor the authority to do any such thing. He was their slave now. And he had chosen this slavery.

Yet he remembered, somewhere in the depths of his possessed consciousness, that there was One who did have the strength and authority to cast these demons out. And so although he was unable to even hope or to even pray, his soul nevertheless cried out to God.

And I do not know how this story ends. I do not know what happened to the man's soul, because I fear too much for my own soul.

But I know that God is merciful. And God's mercy is the greatest truth I know.

Perhaps a blood moon viewed through bloodshed eyes hints at the blood of Jesus, the horrible and beautiful blood that's indelibly imprinted upon the universe and indelibly imprinted upon every human soul. The blood that terrorizes demons. The blood we must all reckon with, one way or another. The blood that saves.

1,423. ~ THEY CAN'T ROB US of OUR REBEL SOULS ~

From day one I've battled teachers and officers and soldiers and psychiatrists and politicians and all manner of "authorities" who presumed to know better than God what was best for me. Trying to force their lies and their pills and their laws and their propaganda upon my consciousness and my soul, they sought to mold me into the image of the godless world they served.

They robbed me of my childhood home. They robbed me of my youth. They robbed me of the security of family. They stole me from my friends. They took away almost everything that I loved and cherished. They tried to rob me of my faith and my hope. They tried their best to curtail the rebellion of a child who was crying out for freedom, justice, and peace. They wanted to break me, but the Holy Spirit has always been too strong for them.

I was a child, in a padded cell, with a broken heart and ceaseless tears. They thought they had won. But they didn't know the omnipresence of God. They didn't realize that within those walls, and forced to adorn their green robes, I became a monastic child. They threw me in their briar patch where my Jesus was waiting to embrace me. And rather than breaking me, those godless fools only strengthened me. In serving Babylon they only ended up serving Zion.

But they haven't stopped their assaults. I have learned that with age the battle intensifies rather than wanes. The demons never let up. Their hellish energy far surpasses my own mortal strength. So I do the only thing I can, the same thing I did when I was a childhood prisoner: I cling to the Cross and I pray, *"Lord have mercy on me, a sinner."* And I beg God to turn my own suffering into the fuel of compassion for others.

So, know this dear friends: the more the world assaults you with its lies, the more it reveals that you serve the truth. The more the world tries to fight you down, the more it reveals your divine strength. The more that devils and powers and evildoers and betrayers afflict you, the more it reveals that Christ is with you.

Stand firm, and keep fighting! They can't rob of us of our rebel souls!

(This one goes out to all my *Anneewakee* brothers and sisters. We alone know the struggle that we alone endured. Never give up!)

1,424. ~ THE ARTIST IS GOD'S SAGE ~

I believe in art, in all of its authentic manifestations. Art is not concerned with political agendas. Art is not calculated. Art is not paranoid. Art is not a means to an ends. Art is not beholden to anything or anyone other than the artist's own divinely shaped soul.

Art is revolutionary because it is revelatory. In revealing their hearts and minds and spirits, their agonies and their struggles and their hopes, artists reveal their Creator (regardless of whether or not they even intend to.) Even the artist that seeks to portray a nihilistic existence devoid of any divine Fashioner is nevertheless utilizing the elements and order of creation in their futile attempt to deny the purpose and meaning of creation.

When the universe doesn't make sense, when life seems empty, when everything that the true artists trust crumbles before them, they simply sit back and behold the glorious tapestry of Creation. And then they find comfort, they find solace, and they find that inexplicable and mystical peace which defies all rational explanation.

Because God *is*. And God is *love*. And that is all. And trying to explain it is a fool's errand. And amidst a world of educated and enlightened fools, the artist will always be God's sage.

1,425. ~ CEMETERY PRAYERS ~

My son and I went to say some prayers at Greenwood Cemetery this afternoon. It was a gorgeous day, and I felt a peace so deep that it could only be compared to the peace I experience during the Divine Liturgy.

Located in downtown Jackson, Mississippi, this historical cemetery is situated in the midst of a violent and poverty stricken neighborhood. But it felt like the Garden of Eden.

Cemeteries are great places to pray and meditate. They make you aware of the imminence of death, but also of the certain hope of the Resurrection. I didn't sense the presence of any ghosts or demons. I only sensed the insoluble bond of human community. Those of us who still walk upon the earth are not really different from those who are buried beneath the earth. After all, cemeteries will inevitably be the common home of all of us – at least for a time.

By His death, Christ has trampled death; and all those in graves and tombs today shall rise upon His expectant return.

I felt the prayers of the buried saints departed, and I also felt that those who are suffering in death were somehow grateful for our feeble but sincere intercessions.

So I encourage you to go visit a cemetery and read some scriptures and offer up some prayers. I think you will find that it really is a beautiful and blessed experience. Make peace with death while you live so that you will find peace when you die.

1,426. ~ UNBREAKABLE ~

Commandments, laws, rules, regulations... I break them. You break them. We all break them to one degree or another. But God's unfailing grace, His enduring mercy, and His unconditional love... those are impossible to break.

1,427. ~ HOW THE WEST WAS WON ~

They preached the Gospel
but lived by the sword.
They killed and conquered
in the name of the Lord.
They preached of Jesus
but lived by the gun.
And that my friend
is how the West was won.

1,428. ~ THE REVOLUTIONARY VICTORY of THE CHURCH ~

The victory belongs not to those who inflict evil but to those who endure evil. The Church is militant but not violent. She is peaceful but not passive. She is confrontational but not coercive. The Church will bleed and suffer and be crucified with Christ over and over again. And while the world laughs the Church will continue to triumph – eternally so. The Church is the most authentically revolutionary, rebellious, and radical force the world has ever known.

1,429. ~ ENTERTAINING ANGELS ~

Love your brother. Love your sister. Love your neighbor. Love the stranger. Entertain angels today!

"Let brotherly love continue. Do not neglect to show hospitality to strangers, for thereby some have entertained angels unawares."
[Hebrews 13:1-2]

1,430. ~ GUNS and LAW and JUSTICE and REBELLION ~

I'm not sure if more people have been killed with "legal" guns or "illegal" guns. And I'm not sure who gets to decide what is legal and what is illegal. But it seems that the people with the most guns always get to decide the matter. So I'm not sure if the problem is guns or the law. But guns and the law sure do seem to go together, murderously so. And the lawmakers with the guns never call their wars and executions and abortions and racist police brutality "murder." They always call it "justice." And whenever anyone challenges their "justice" they condemn it as "rebellion." Well, call me a rebel and shoot me dead. I know that my Jesus will raise me up.

1,431. ~ OUR BLESSED ORTHODOX PRIESTS ~

I love our Orthodox priests. They pray for us. They hear our confessions. They offer us the Body and Blood of Christ. They teach us through their homilies and writings and Bible studies. They forgive us and love us unconditionally. They rebuke us when we need it. And they faithfully and tirelessly lead us in the holy work of the Divine Liturgy.

And yes, because they are human, they sometimes become impatient with those like me who are unfaithful and arrogant and self-righteous and slothful. And yet, as representatives of Christ, they are always there to receive our confessions and to offer us the Sacraments of salvation.

So please pray for our blessed Orthodox Priests. Their calling is sacred and their labor is endless. They are on the front lines of spiritual warfare, fighting for the preservation of souls and vigilantly defending the true Christian Faith. And in today's world of manifest theological heresies and countless assaults on divine morality, their work is greatly intensified.

Offer supplications for them. And thank them. And encourage them. And do what you can to ease their burdens and let them know how much you appreciate them.

As for me, I need to begin by being more faithful in participating in the Divine Liturgy. Because I know that more than anything else, our Priests just want us to be there with them as they worship Jesus and receive and share His Sacramental blessings.

1,432. ~ FREE STATE ~

Any state that needs to be preserved by either military force or a "well regulated militia" will never be a truly free state. The only state that is truly free is that state of mind which is rooted in the truth, peace, and freedom of Jesus Christ.

1,433. ~ WHAT DO THEY HAVE? ~

What do they have – these "white privileged" souls who bleed and sweat and sacrifice their lives in coal mines and textile mills and iron-ore furnaces?

What do they have – these "redneck Republicans" who vote for values rather than economics, hoping against hope that the candidates who pretend to care about them actually will?

What do they have – this collective "poor white trash" that is mocked and disparaged and condemned and exploited by both the political left and the political right?

What do they have – these impoverished, viscerally honest, salt-of-the-earth souls who live simply to serve their God and their families and their fellow man?

What do they have – these desperate people with their coal-dust lungs and molten steel scars and constant accusations of racism and hatred and bigotry and "privilege"?

What do they have – these Church going, Bible believing, morality upholding, simple souls of faith?

They have salvation. That's what they have. And they're willing to suffer and die for it.

What about you? What do you have?

1,434. ~ MAY THE MELODY of MY SOUL NEVER HARMONIZE with THE CACOPHONY of BABYLON ~

Dear Lord: dash my ego and opinions and judgments and pride and sins against the rock of Christ your Son. Smash to pieces every thought and action and feeling that does not conform to your redemptive Truth. May the melody of my soul never harmonize with the cacophony of Babylon!

1,435. ~ GRACE FROM GEHENNA ~

Anyone can preach grace from the Garden, but I need a grace preached from the bowels of Gehenna.

1,436. ~ PHILOSOPHY, THEOLOGY, and CHILDREN ~

To philosophize is to both think and to feel. Thought divorced from emotion leads to knowledge without wisdom. And emotion divorced from thought leads to action without understanding and feeling without reason or purpose. Wonder leads to knowledge and knowledge leads to wonder; and perpetual wonder leads inevitably to reverence and worship. That's why the greatest philosophers are also theologians, and why the greatest theologians are also philosophers. And it's also why children are the greatest theologians and philosophers among us – because their wonder is never dimmed, and joy and thanksgiving are always in their hearts.

1,437. ~ PROPHECIES and FAITH ~

I've heard many fantastical and strange prophecies in my lifetime. But my weak heart, feeble faith, and lack of spiritual vision cause me to view such prophecies with skepticism and doubt. My instinct is to ask: "Where do you find that in scripture? What makes you qualified to predict the future? Why are you presuming to make such extra biblical proclamations?"

But I realize that God is not limited by my limited vision. So I have learned never to doubt any prophetic word that doesn't diametrically contradict Christ's word. I've learned never to question any prophecy that doesn't diametrically contradict Our Lord's Church or His teachings. I pray for the faith to accept and help manifest the word of the Lord whenever someone speaks it to me.

"Lord have mercy." +++

1,438. ~ IF YOU WANT TO PROVE YOUR COURAGE ~

Don't tell me how tough you are while hiding behind guns, uniforms, flags, and badges. If you want to prove your courage then stand up to guns and uniforms and flags and badges, armed with nothing but Gospel love and Gospel truth.

1,439. ~ ON KNEELING & STANDING & SOLIDARITY & THE STATUS QUO ~

It's easy to stand in solidarity with the status quo. It's much harder to stand in solidarity with the voiceless and the oppressed. It's easy to kneel on the bandwagon of popularity and praise. It's much harder to kneel beneath the weight of the Cross. So I don't care whether you stand or kneel; I only care about what you stand for and who you kneel to serve. I may stand with you and I may kneel with you; but I won't be standing or kneeling for the sake of patriotic flags, earthly politics, mortal agendas, or human kingdoms. But I will always kneel with you to help another human brother or sister stand back up on their feet. Because we all stand tallest when we kneel to serve our neighbors.

1,440. ~ RESIST, DON'T RUN ~

Resist,
don't run.
But never
use a gun.
Because
when you kill,
they've won.

1,441. ~ THE GREAT TEMPTATION for PEOPLE of CONSCIOUSNESS ~

The great temptation for all people of consciousness is to temper the rebellion, to reduce the revolution to that which can be managed and affirmed without sacrifice, personal bloodshed, and the pain of prophetic fire. The mindset is: "I will vote, and thereby my conscience will be appeased. I did nothing to really change anything, but at least I was *against them*. And even if I am on the wrong side of humanity, I will at least be on the correct side of the cocktail party."

This is the insidious seduction of politics; and those who are bewitched by its demonic spell will seek to crucify the life-affirming resistance and the revolutionary peacemakers with nails from both the ideological left and the ideological right.

1,442. ~ CLEAN HANDS and DIRTY HANDS ~

I prefer dirty hands that give me bread over clean hands that offer me nothing but pious platitudes.

1,443. ~ PACIFISM, ANARCHY, and THE STATE ~

Authentic pacifism leads inevitably to anarchism, and authentic anarchism is rooted in pacifism. Why? Because the laws of the state must ultimately be enforced by violence; and therefore one cannot rebel against the state without rebelling against violence, and one cannot rebel against violence without also rebelling against the state.

1,444. ~ SATAN and PRAYER ~

Satan is a firm believer in prayer – not because he loves prayer, but because he suffers from prayer. So say a prayer and burn the devil!

There are days when life hurts so much that all I want to do is die. And then there are days when life is so wonderful that I want to cling to this life forever. Most days are somewhere in between – stagnant, uninspired, gray days that I neither love nor hate.

But I'm learning it's the gray strokes that make the truth of black and white clearly stand out. And the joy of color can never be fully appreciated without the juxtaposition of its absence. We love sunrises and sunflowers and sunsets precisely because we endure rain and darkness and empty horizons.

So I cherish life, in all of its various shades, looking always to the Author and perfecter of my feeble faith (Hebrews 12:2). God is equally present in white cloud canvas afternoons and in black starless midnights. He is equally present in brilliant rainbow prisms and in colorless tunnels of despair. He is equally present in the radiant, effulgent joys of life and in the mundane grayness of existential ennui.

I am trying to embrace it all, to see my Jesus in it all, and to love all throughout it all. And love is not always colorful. In fact, love is most real when the feelings and colors and joys wane, and all we have is the immovable faithfulness of love itself – like the love of Our Lord that was demonstrated most clearly from the Cross of suffering.

1,446. ~ THE DIFFERENCE BETWEEN THE GOSPEL and POLITICS ~

Q. What is the difference between the Gospel and politics?

A. The Gospel compels us to prioritize our neighbors that are suffering, bleeding, and dying on the Jericho road. Politics compels us to ignore the plight of our neighbors in order to prioritize the improvement of the Jericho road infrastructure.

1,447. ~ DON'T COMPLICATE LIFE or THE WORK of LOVE ~

Life is difficult but not complicated. Whatever truly matters in life takes work, discipline, dedication and effort. Yes, talent certainly helps when it comes to temporal success; but the world is replete with talented, "successful" souls living empty and wasted lives.

So you don't have to be a genius to fulfill your purpose and make your life count. You don't have to solve the mysteries of the universe. You don't have to outsmart or outwit anyone. You don't have to "prove yourself" or validate your existence. You just have to live a life of love while doing what you love to the best of your ability. You just have to keep practicing, keep trying, keep praying, and keep forgiving.

Yes, that's difficult work for sure, but it's not complicated. Sometimes we have to stop trying to figure it all out and just work on loving more, loving harder, and loving in spite of everything else. Because talent won't last, and success won't last; and riches and fame and fortune and human praise won't last. But love will last. Love will last forever. And nothing is both simpler and more difficult than love.

The universe is woven with threads of complexity, but it is held together by the basic fabric of love. Many people get tangled up in dissecting the complex threads while others work on clinging to the plain fabric. Satan will deceive us with a million splinters, but Jesus saves us with one Cross.

So don't complicate the work of love, which is the work of salvation. Just work it out in all of its difficult but beautiful simplicity.

1,448. ~ REPARATIONS and THE BIBLE ~

The Israelites, led by God, demanded reparations from the Egyptians (Exodus 12:35-36). So if we dismiss, mock, or ridicule the concept of reparations we are dismissing, mocking, and ridiculing a divine biblical precedent. Let us heed the words of Daniel the prophet, who said to King Nebuchadnezzar: *"Atone for thy sins by* doing righteousness, and thine iniquities by showing mercy to the poor." [Daniel 4:27]

And let us individually and corporately cultivate the spirit of Zacchaeus, who said to Jesus: *"Look, Lord! Here and now I give half of my possessions to the poor, and if I have cheated anybody out of anything, I will pay back four times the amount." [St. Luke 19:8-9]*

1,449. ~ WORK ~

The work of forgiveness... the work of repentance... the work of peace... the work of unconditional love... the work of faith... the work of hope... the work of mercy... the work of remaining positive in a negative world... the work of living... This is *lifelong* work. And it never gets easier. But this is salvation. And make no mistake: salvation is work indeed. Yet God's grace is ever present in the work. So keep working and keep resting in His grace.

"Work out your salvation with fear and trembling."
[Philippians 2:12]

"But he said to me, 'My grace is sufficient for you, for my power is made perfect in weakness.' Therefore I will boast all the more gladly about my weaknesses, so that Christ's power may rest on me. That is why, for Christ's sake, I delight in weaknesses, in insults, in hardships, in persecutions, in difficulties. For when I am weak, then I am strong." [II Corinthians 12:9-11]

1,450. ~ WRITING and THINKING ~

I don't know how to think unless I write. In fact, I write not only to compose my thoughts but to compose my life. And I leave my compositions in God's hands, to do with them as He pleases.

1,451. ~ ANGER ~

Anger is as necessary as the thunderstorm. Thunderstorms stir up stale air, replenish rivers and lakes, and scatter seeds of fruition across the earth. Likewise, anger stirs up necessary controversy, awakens anesthetized consciences, and scatters seeds of action across the social landscape. It is not anger in and of itself that is bad; it is rather misplaced anger, misguided anger, and anger that leads to violence and hate that must be avoided.

Never trust anyone that tells you it is a sin to be angry about the evils of racism, war, poverty, or abortion. One cannot be a Christian without being angry about such evils and injustices. In fact, one cannot fully live without being angry about the inhumanities and injustices that undermine and diminish human life. Yet neither can one be a Christian without loving those who commit such evils and injustices.

As St. Paul wrote: *"Be angry, but sin not."* *[Ephesians 4:26]*

1,452. ~ ATHEISTIC REVELATIONS ~

Sometimes it is the atheist – in his articulation of the beauty, sorrow, and poignancy of life – who reveals the love and truth of God more than the Christian.

1,453. ~ PROBLEMS SOLVED ~

Love life,
and live to love.
This is how
all problems are solved.

1,454. ~ EVIL IS NEITHER LIBERAL NOR CONSERVATIVE ~

Evil is neither liberal nor conservative. Evil is evil, and it is equally at home in leftist illusions and rightwing dogmas. And as long as Satan can keep delusion warring with deception then he wins. Politics is hell's domain, and Mephistopheles is an ambidextrous devil. He will gladly drag you to the fire with either his left hand or his right. It makes no difference to him through which ideological gate you enter into the flames.

1,455. ~ QUICKSAND ~

You see the man
sinking in the quicksand.
You throw him a lifeline
and he says
"You've got a narrow mind!"
You beg him to grab hold
But he continues to boast:
"I'm free! I'm free!
I don't need your liberty!
This quicksand is saving me!"

1,456. ~ THE ANARCHISM of THE CHURCH ~

The Church of Christ is inherently anarchistic. While it oftentimes and variously manifests a hierarchy of priestly order and sacramental administration, it is nevertheless not bound by such temporal restrictions. There is indeed a priesthood of all believers (I Peter 2:5). And that's why the Church has not been and cannot be destroyed by political assaults upon ecclesiastic edifices and authentic Christian communities. And that's equally why the Church is not and cannot be preserved by political authorities and earthly armies.

And yet, as Orthodox Christians, we understand and value the divine spiritual order that Christ has ordained and established. We are not radical individualists, elevating our own will and understanding over and above God's will and truth. Because we *are* the Church we *need* the Church. We need the authority, the discipline, and the restorative community that Christ has instituted, ordained, and blessed.

But the divine holy order must never be confused for earthly political order. We must never confuse the Church for the state or the state for the Church. We must never think that the efficacy and preservation of our Holy Sacraments are contingent upon the protection of earthly political powers. They can destroy our buildings, they can desecrate our icons, and they can trample upon our Bread and Wine; but the Body and Blood of Jesus will still be offered to us – ever and always uncorrupted – through His faithful remnant.

1,457. ~ IF I CAN DIE THIS WAY ~

If I can die with gratitude in my heart and thanksgiving in my soul, then I will die a happy and "saved" man.

1,458. ~ "AGAINST THEM" ~

To be "against them" takes no courage, no originality, no real thought. Nothing is easier than serving up selective political condemnations to those one wishes to impress. Conformity is the endeavor of cowards and simpletons, the gutless abode of those that pontificate from their ivory towers in order to impress the esteemed and the elite. But to be *for* truth, to be *for* life, to be *for* peace, to be *for* justice, and to be *for* humanity – even if it means one may lose their academic, social, vocational, and financial stability – well, that's what makes one's theology real.

1,459. ~ I WILL BE WELL ~

Kill me today.
Slit my throat.
Send me to hell.

Crucify me
a thousand times,
and I will be well.

Because my Lord
is Risen!

1,460. ~ WE ARE INDEED REVOLUTIONARIES ~

Yes, we are indeed revolutionaries – revolutionary artists, revolutionary poets, revolutionary troubadours, revolutionary creators, and revolutionary lovers. But we are not revolutionary militarists, because we believe that violence – along with the hate that invariably spawns it – is the most counterrevolutionary force there is.

1,461. ~ CREATION, CORRUPTION, and THE LIE ~

Satan is not a creator; he is a corrupter. And since he can't create he perpetually seeks to corrupt, condemn, and pervert the original intent of God.

Communism is a corruption of human community. Capitalism is a corruption of human ingenuity and human resourcefulness. Politics is a human corruption of social cooperation. Law is a human corruption of the divine will and order. Government is a human corruption of the Kingdom of God.

We cling to the lie in pursuit of the truth. But if we would cling to the Truth we would be liberated from the lie. Yet the lie is so easy to believe. The lie is so easy to live; and to oppose the lie makes one a social pariah. So we hate and we kill and we divide and we scorn in order to comfortably conform to the lie that makes us feel safe, the lie that allows us to "belong." And because others affirm us in the lie we somehow think we are siding with truth.

But our own souls cry out against the betrayal. Our own souls demand a reckoning with reality. We intuitively know that the divine Judgment will expose all falsehoods.

Every mortal philosophy, every human ideology, every manmade theology, and every worldly methodology not rooted in the Gospel of Christ and the Kingdom of Christ will inevitably wither in the calescent winds of eternity.

So let the truth burn now – let it burn in us and among us and from us – so that its loving fire will save rather than damn.

1,462. ~ BY WAY of THE CROSS ~

Be as open-minded as the ocean, but as narrowly progressive as the River of Life. Let your consciousness absorb a billion stars while always bathing in One Son. Love all the world, but cling to the Kingdom of God alone. Know that there are countless paths to heaven, but they all proceed by way of the Cross.

1,463. ~ INFLICTION and AFFLICTION ~

Violence begets violence. A society that inflicts violence is a society that will be afflicted by violence.

1,464. ~ THE GOSPEL and THE SERMON on THE MOUNT ~

The Sermon on the Mount is not an idealistic aside to the Gospel, a poetic parenthesis in the Gospel, or an impractical philosophical addendum that Christ did not expect His disciples to actually live out. The Sermon on the Mount *is* the Gospel, and salvation and discipleship hinge upon its didactic imperatives.

1,465. ~ TEAR STAINED PILLOWS and BLOOD STAINED GARMENTS ~

Backseat fumblings, trying to undo things that can't be undone. Rites of passage leading to nowhere. False manhood and false womanhood, breaking barriers of innocent flesh. Conquered and the conquering, an adolescent dalliance that leaves the detritus of broken hearts and decimated souls in its wake. Tear stained pillows and blood stained garments. Teenage bravado masquerading all the pain and confusion and tumult of the universe. Forever trying to reclaim innocence. Forever seeking fidelity. Forever trying to be a real man. Forever trying to be a real woman. Forever seeking to truly love and to truly be loved.

1,466. ~ LET ME LIVE... ~

Caress my soul
until it bleeds.
Squeeze my brain,
and make me think.
Cut my heart
so I will feel.
Break my spirit
if it's not real.
Shake my life,
force me to live.
Let me live...
until it kills.

1,467. ~ INSEPARABLE ~

No separation
of tears and wood
Divinity and humanity
Body and Blood
Suffering and salvation
Three in One

1,468. ~ STORIES BEST LEFT UNTOLD ~

I have tasted blood. I have danced with demons. I have walked with ghosts. I have gazed into the abyss of hell, yet my spirit somehow remains attached to heaven.

I have stories to tell that are perhaps best left untold. They are too dark, too unbelievable. I am too afraid to tell them. I am too ashamed to tell them. But I carry these stories in my soul. I am haunted by them. I seek sleep to escape their horrors, yet I fear sleep because in my nightmares I confront their torments.

Every pain I suffer, every agony I endure, every injustice that befalls me is a mercy from God. I have done so much wrong in my life; I have hurt so many people; I have lived for myself at the expense of others. I curse the evils that befall me while forgetting the evils that I myself facilitated.

God knows my horror stories, and I think it's best to leave them with Him alone. His mercy endures forever. And I cling to it – even if that means I will only understand His mercy in the midst of my own thorns and splinters and seemingly unbearable crosses.

My instinct is to pray: "Save me God, but not like that." But I must learn to pray: "Save me God, however you choose."

And God will always answer: "I have saved you with the Cross and the Resurrection." I must understand that there is never one without the other. Suffering and hope are inseparably redemptive. I must also understand that the Cross of Our Lord and the Resurrection of Our Lord are the greatest evidence of God's unconditional love for potential demoniacs like me.

"Lord Jesus Christ, Son of God, have mercy on me a sinner."

1,469. ~ GOD and THE GOOD ~

If the good you seek to do is merely the result of some cosmic forensic transaction rather than the love of good itself, then you misunderstand goodness and you misunderstand God. God and goodness cannot be separated. To truly love what is good is to love God, and to truly love God is to love what is good. If you believe that God the Father needed to murder His own Son so that you can understand how good He is, then you blaspheme divinity and you grossly pervert the meaning of the Cross.

1,470. ~ THROUGH TEARS I AM SAVED ~

If I could smile
I'd smile down death.
If I could breathe
I'd give death breath.
If I could laugh
I'd laugh from the grave.
But I can only cry,
and through tears
I am saved

1,471. ~ FAITH and EXISTENCE ~

Could one paint sunsets if there was no sun? Could one paint colors if colors did not exist? Could one speak truth if existence was formed by a lie? Could one worship a risen Christ if Christ remained rotting in a tomb?

Faith does not mean believing in the absence of evidence; faith means living according to evidence that is deeper and realer than anything which can be proven by the measurements of temporal existence.

"Faith is being sure of what we hope for, certain of what we do not see." [Hebrews 11:1]

1,472. ~ SINGLE STEPS, SINGLE BREATHS ~

Sometimes one forward step is a greater achievement than climbing Mt. Everest. Sometimes one positive thought is a greater achievement than all of Einstein's brilliance. Sometimes one act of forgiveness is a greater achievement than all of the tribunals of worldly jurisprudence. Sometimes one word of kindness is more powerful than all the armies of militant violence. Sometimes one act of peace conquers every act of war. Sometimes one act of love conquers a million acts of hate.

Sometimes the choice to simply live – and to let others live – is the most revolutionary decision that one can make.

Life is lived with single breaths, with single steps, and with single beats of the heart. Let your lungs breathe peace, let your movement be positive, and let the metronome of your heart be tuned to love. The rest is in God's hands. And it is good to rest in Him.

1,473. ~ TEMPTED BY THE BULLET'S SMILE ~

I am tempted
by the bullet's smile.
And I'm not sure
if the enemy
is them or me.
Go away sweet bullet.
Your lead
won't set me free.

1,474. ~ BATHING IN DIVINE DARKNESS ~

As hope fades
I bathe
in shadows and shades.

Night rises
and I am at home
in the divine darkness.

1,475. ~ RADICALIZED ~

I'm not sure what it means to be "radicalized," but I'm pretty sure it means crucifixion. If our religion is not radically pro-peace, radically pro-poor, radically pro-justice, and radically pro-life, then our religion is nothing more than a superstitious hobby. Babylon will gladly tolerate our Christian faith as long as we don't truly live it out.

I confess that I am disturbed by the phrasing of Dorothy Day as having merely "regretted and moved past her abortion" (in the words of one Dorothy Day scholar.) This severely diminishes and downplays the fact that Dorothy Day repented of her abortion and spent the rest of her life prioritizing the plight of the weak, the poor, the defenseless, and the "least of these." There is a significant difference between repentance and mere regret, and it is clear from her own life and writings that Dorothy Day repented of her abortion and grieved over it for the duration of her years. In fact, her own abortion actually fueled her subsequent desire to sacrificially care for the downtrodden, the marginalized, and the oppressed. Her work for world peace and social justice was an integral part of the genuine contrition that followed her abortion.

The innocent unborn child in the womb was of great concern to Dorothy Day. Unfortunately, there are some who through their interpretations of her life seem to indicate (I hope unintentionally) that Dorothy Day's own abortion means that other women can also have abortions and then simply "move on" with their lives (as if abortion is an inconsequential "procedure" that doesn't violently destroy an innocent human life, as if it is something that doesn't leave deep psychological, emotional, and spiritual scars upon the mother who has the abortion.) And I think this grossly misrepresents Dorothy Day's own experience and message regarding the issue.

Dorothy Day was a woman who thoroughly embraced the "consistent life ethic," and we do an injustice to her memory if we focus on her love for the poor and her opposition to war while diminishing her opposition to abortion and downplaying her love for the innocent unborn life in the womb. Consider her own words: *"We are living in an age of genocide. Not only war, but the whole program of abortion."*

So if Dorothy Day recognized abortion as a form of genocide, then let us also recognize it as such. We cannot seek to herald Dorothy Day as a saint for her passionate social activism without realizing that her love for the unborn child was as integral to her spiritual and social consciousness as her love for all other oppressed members of the human race. For her, unborn victims of abortion also constituted the poor, the marginalized, and the suffering neighbor on the Jericho Road.

Not only that, but her deeply somber account of her own abortion reveals that she would never want other women to suffer from the same horrific experience. For Dorothy Day, opposition to abortion was actually a Pro-Woman issue as well as a Pro-Life issue. Mother and child are both victimized by the violence of abortion, and she opposed the unjust legality of this inhumane, destructive violation of the most sacred and natural of human bonds.

In fact, Dorothy Day's Pro-Life convictions were so strong that she even opposed birth control. Again, let us examine Ms. Day's own words:

"I'll never forget the time that I had to literally stand up against birth control. My sister Della had worked for Margaret Sanger, foundress of Planned Parenthood. When Della exhorted me that I shouldn't encourage my daughter Tamar to have so many children, I stood up firmly and walked out of the house, whereupon Della ran after me weeping, saying, 'Don't leave me, don't leave me! We just won't talk about it again.' To me, birth control and abortion are genocide. I say, make room for children, don't do away with them. The act that one is performing is for the purpose of fusing the two lives more closely together, and it so enriches them that another life springs forth from the union. Therefore, artificial prevention of conception and the aborting of a life conceived are sins that are great frustrations to the natural and spiritual order. No matter how cynically or casually the worldly may treat the birth of a child, it remains spiritually and physically a tremendous event."

Dorothy Day's life and writings challenge us all. Her life challenges anti-abortion folks on the political right to embrace the same concern for poverty, racism, and all other forms of violence and injustice. And she challenges those on the political left to understand that opposition to abortion is inseparable from working to eradicate poverty and laboring for authentic social justice in all other areas of life.

To downplay and diminish her deep opposition to abortion is to miss a crucial aspect of Dorothy Day's legacy and message. May we continue to be challenged and strengthened by Dorothy Day's true social courage, her sacrificial Christian compassion, and her "consistent life" convictions.

"The most effective social action we can take is to try to conform our lives to the folly of the Cross." ~ Dorothy Day ~

"Those who cannot see the face of Christ in the poor are atheists indeed." ~ Dorothy Day ~

"What confusion we have gotten into, when Christian prelates sprinkle holy water on scrap metal to be used for obliteration bombing, and name bombers for the Holy Innocents, for Our Lady of Mercy; who bless a man about to press a button which releases death on fifty thousand human beings, including little babies, the sick, the aged, the innocent as well as the guilty. 'You know not of what spirit you are,' said Jesus to His apostles when they wished to call down fire from heaven on the Samaritans." ~ Dorothy Day ~

"The final word is love. Love and ever more love – for the greatest and for the least – is the only solution to every problem that arises." ~ Dorothy Day ~

1,477. ~ FRIENDSHIP ~

Perhaps there are greater callings, nobler endeavors, and more virtuous pursuits, but I really can't think of anything holier than friendship. Friendship has not only saved me, but friendship has made me believe that life is worth saving. I thank God for true friendship, because through friendship I have truly found Christ.

Christianity without the honesty of gut-wrenching fellowship, mutual suffering, and common struggle is actually no Christianity at all. And I stand by these words, because God has showered me abundantly with loyal friends who verify this truth.

Whenever I've failed my friends, my friends have sustained me. Whenever I've betrayed them, my friends have been loyal to me. Whenever I have disappointed and abandoned and turned on them, my friends have somehow loved me anyway.

God how the love of friendship burns! And God how it saves! I know Jesus because I know my friends. And I know Jesus is the friend of this sinner because my friends have shown me the love of Jesus (even my friends who don't even profess to be Christians.)

"Friendship is one of the greatest gifts a human being can receive. It is a bond beyond common goals, common interests, or common histories. It is a bond stronger than sexual union can create, deeper than a shared fate can solidify, and even more intimate than the bonds of marriage or community. Friendship is being with the other in joy and sorrow, even when we cannot increase the joy or decrease the sorrow. It is a unity of souls that gives nobility and sincerity to love. Friendship makes all of life shine brightly."
~ Henri Nouwen ~

1,478. ~ APART from TRULY KNOWING that GOD TRULY LOVES US ~

Apart from truly knowing that God truly loves us we will never really get anything else right. We will never truly be able to love others. We will never truly be able to live holy lives. We will never truly know peace or truly be able to make peace.

Unless and until we truly know that God truly loves us, we will perpetually seek to fill the void with moralizing and activism and politics and philosophy and all manner of biblical expositions and interpretations that we confuse for the authentic theology that ushers us into the mystical experience of the Divine.

But once we truly realize that Our Lord truly loves us, then everything else will fall in place. But it won't be easy. In fact, life may become much more difficult in many ways. But we will endure the hardships and we will benefit from the pain, because we will know the eternal, unfailing, unconditional, omnipresent and omnipotent love of our Creator. We will suffer, but we will be ever comforted by the love that saves and redeems and leads us to eternal life.

1,479. ~ 10 CHRISTIAN RIGHTS GRANTED BY THE NEW TESTAMENT ~

1. ~~The right to kill.~~ The right to die for the sake of others. (I John 3:16)

2. ~~The right to worship freely and safely.~~ The right to worship in spirit and in truth. (St. John 4:24)

3. ~~The right to preserve our own lives.~~ The right to lay down our own lives. (St. John 15:13)

4. ~~The right to self-defense.~~ The right to self-sacrifice. (St. Luke 9:24)

5. ~~The right to earthly security.~~ The right to eternal life. (St. John 10:27-28)

6. ~~The right to bear arms.~~ The right to carry our crosses. (St. Luke 9:23)

7. ~~The right to make a profit.~~ The right to live and speak prophetically. (St. Mark 16:15)

8. ~~The right to shed our enemies' blood~~. The right to love our enemies and bless those that persecute us. (St. Matthew 5:44)

9. ~~The right to national security.~~ The right to heavenly citizenship. (Philippians 3:20)

10. ~~The right to Constitutional protection.~~ The right to spiritual protection and the right to live by the very Word of God. (Ephesians 6; St. Matthew 4:4)

War is hell. Don't go to hell.

1,481. ~ AT THE HOUR OF OUR DEATH ~

At the hour of our death, what will be our true regrets? Will we wish that we had worked harder, been right more often, argued better, or been more successful in the eyes of the world? I doubt it.

I think we will regret that we didn't laugh more, pray more, love more, and play more. If there's no suffering in our lives then we're not living right. And if there's no joy in our lives then we're living wrong.

1,482. ~ BLOOD and INK ~

I could write in order to eat, but if I did then my spirit would starve. So I write to live, even if it means my flesh suffers. The hunger of my soul fuels my pen, so I am thankful for the struggle. Blood and ink are inseparably linked within me. I write because my soul bleeds; and because my soul bleeds, I write.

1,483. ~ THE GOSPEL and SELF-PRESERVATION ~

If you're looking for a religion of self-preservation, the Christian gospel is not for you. There is nothing pragmatic, utilitarian, or expedient about the Cross. The Cross means suffering, betrayal, affliction, and death – everything that the philosophies of this world seek in vain to avoid.

The Gospel convicts, but it redeems. The Gospel kills, but it resurrects. The Gospel doesn't "work," but the Gospel saves.

1,484. ~ ELUSIVE STRUGGLE / BLESSED HOPE ~

Theosis is an elusive struggle, but a blessed hope. So keep struggling and keep hoping, because God's presence and mercy endure forever.

"Behold, a virgin shall be with child, and shall bring forth a son, and they shall call his name Emmanuel, which being interpreted is, God with us." [St. Matthew 1:23]

"O give thanks unto the Lord; for he is good: for his mercy endureth for ever..." [Psalm 136]

1,485. ~ DIETRICH BONHOEFFER, PACIFISM, and ABORTION ~

If one believes that Dietrich Bonhoeffer conspired to assassinate Hitler in order to save innocent people, and if one believes that he was justified in doing so, then one cannot condemn those who conspire to assassinate abortionists in order to save innocent unborn lives. I realize this is a provocative and controversial statement. But to praise violent resistance against the systematic slaughter of Jews while condemning violent resistance against the systematic slaughter of the unborn is to be logically, morally, ethically, and theologically inconsistent. Bonhoeffer would point out that to see the humanity of *some* while denying the humanity of *all* is one of the fundamental sins that lead to injustice, inhumanity, and evil in the world.

But contrary to the popular narrative, there is good evidence to suggest that Bonhoeffer in fact never did abandon his pacifist convictions. His resistance to Hitler and the Nazi regime was always nonviolent, and he died a martyr because of it. (For an in depth examination of the subject, I highly recommend the book: *Bonhoeffer the Assassin?: Challenging the Myth, Recovering His Call to Peacemaking* by Mark Thiessen Nation, Anthony G. Siegrist, and Daniel P. Umbel.)

Dietrich Bonhoeffer sacrificially intervened on behalf of his suffering neighbors, and he did so by emulating Our Lord Jesus

Christ who gave up His own life while refusing to destroy the lives of others.

Bonhoeffer denounced abortion as clearly as he denounced the Jewish holocaust:

"Destruction of the embryo in the mother's womb is a violation of the right to live which God has bestowed upon this nascent life. To raise the question whether we are here concerned already with a human being or not is merely to confuse the issue. The simple fact is that God certainly intended to create a human being and this new human being has been deliberately deprived of his life. And this is nothing but murder."

His words and example show us how we should fight and resist the evils of our own day and age. Bonhoeffer would certainly condemn violence against abortionists in unequivocal terms. Yet he would nevertheless urge us to intervene on behalf of our innocent unborn neighbors – sacrificially, urgently, practically, and always *nonviolently*.

There are two great tragedies regarding the interpretation of Dietrich Bonhoeffer and his legacy. The first tragedy is that people have been mistakenly led to believe that Bonhoeffer ultimately jettisoned his foundational theological pacifism in favor of the pragmatism of "Just War" philosophy. The second tragedy is that many who extol Bonhoeffer's sacrificial intervention on behalf of the oppressed of his time somehow turn a blind eye to the oppressed of their own time. They fail to apply Bonhoeffer's life and teachings regarding the Jewish holocaust to the holocaust of abortion today.

I think Dietrich Bonhoeffer would tell us that a theology which does not agitate and intervene on behalf of "the least of these" is nothing less than heresy. I think he would be grieved by those who study his life and yet miss the point of his life entirely. I think he would be equally grieved by those who kill abortionists and by those who justify, rationalize, defend, or ignore the inhumanity and evil of abortion.

I think Bonhoeffer would say that if there is any doubt or confusion about what he believed or what he did, we should interpret his life and works through the Gospel of Jesus Christ. I think

Bonhoeffer would say, "Above all, follow Jesus. And following Jesus means loving brothers, neighbors, and enemies alike – sacrificially so."

Others may interpret his life differently, but Bonhoeffer's writings and example make it clear to me that he promoted the inseparable values of justice, peace, and life-affirmation. As a true Christian and a true follower of the Gospel, he could do no less. And if we are true Christians and true followers of the Gospel, we too can do no less.

1,486. ~ REFLECTIONS on THE DEATH of CHARLES MANSON ~
[11/20/2017]

Charles Manson is dead, apparently of natural causes. He was 83 years old.

Charles Manson was an evil man, perhaps demonically possessed (but such evaluations are ultimately left to God alone.)

We find collective social comfort in despising charismatic, murderous bogeymen like Charles Manson, yet we vote for charismatic, murderous men like Bill Clinton, George W. Bush, Barack Obama, and Donald Trump.

Charles Manson was responsible for the barbaric shedding of innocent human blood, and he is without excuse. He will reckon with his Creator (and so shall we all.) Many will celebrate his death – *the witch is dead!* – yet they will continue to support politicians and a government and a military that make Charles Manson's cultish murders look quantitatively tame in comparison.

People contemplate Manson and his deluded followers and they wonder: "How in the world could anyone be seduced by such madness? How could anyone be brainwashed to commit such atrocities?" And I would ask these same people: "How in the world could anyone be seduced to vote for heartless killers that support the bombing, oppression, and aborting of innocent human lives? How could anyone be brainwashed to lend their complicity and support to global mass murder and abortion on demand?"

But we need our Charles Mansons and our Jim Jones and our Ted Bundys. We need our serial killers, our depraved madmen, and our maniacal lunatics to make us feel sane in comparison. We need to feel morally superior. We need to believe that we ourselves have nothing to do with the monsters we enable but despise.

Despite the unassailable record of human history, we as human individuals and we as a collective human society somehow believe we could never be so insanely cruel, insanely inhumane, and insanely unjust. We are much too civilized, much too rational to commit such wickedness. Instead, we simply vote for evildoers that we praise as political pragmatists and national defenders and progressive liberators. So we lock up Charles Manson (along with a lot of innocent people, by the way) while we unleash the hell of Bush and Barack and Trump upon the world.

We could never murder pregnant women. We could never rape children. We could never hack unborn babies to pieces in their mothers' wombs. We could never burn the flesh off innocent people's bones with atomic bombs and napalm and drones and scud missile fire.

We are much too enlightened to commit such horrific acts. That's why we elect politicians to do it for us. And that's why we call our murderers "soldiers." And that's why we call our baby killers "abortionists." And that's why we call our cultish depravity "God, Country, and Constitution." Abundant evil is cloaked in the abundance of euphemisms.

But Charles Manson is finally dead. And for some insane reason we now feel safer.

God help us.

1,487. ~ PROPHETIC DISRUPTION ~

These damn solitary fanatical souls on the street corner, waving their Bibles and shouting messages of repentance! Why can't these fundamentalist zealots keep their religion to themselves? How dare they disrupt my superficial peace with their convicting spiritual truth!

These religious radicals are interrupting the social anesthetization of salacious billboards and mesmerizing capitalist advertisements and intoxicating political propaganda. I'm trying to get comfortable here in Babylon, and these sidewalk prophets are seriously interfering with my hypnosis!

Thank God for them!

1,488. ~ REFLECTIONS on CONSERVATIVES and LIBERALS ~

Conservatives tell us we need fences: moral fences, spiritual fences, ethical fences, social fences, logical fences. They rightly remind us that 2+2 equals 4, and attempts to prove or live otherwise lead to chaos and confusion.

Liberals tell us we need to tear down fences. Barriers restrict, walls inhibit, rules and laws impede freedom and confine the human spirit. They rightly remind us that a caged tree cannot grow. True virtue cannot be conscripted, it must be allowed to blossom on its own. Liberals remind us that horrific evils in human history have emanated from those who in the name of "law and order" and "national security" and "moral values" committed unspeakable atrocities. And, yes, conservatives would be quick to respond that just as many evils have been committed by those who opposed religion and mocked moral values and rejected the concept of divine, objective, universal truth.

I am just a simple and uneducated man, but I see tremendous value in both the conservative and liberal philosophies. Some fences need to be left in place (or in fact built), and other fences need to be torn down completely. I suppose the debate will forever rage on about the construction and destruction of these philosophical, political, social, and metaphysical fences. And perhaps that's a good thing, because growth and progress never ensue from a lack of tension.

What I have noticed from both my liberal and conservative friends is that they all sincerely value human rights and social justice. They all want peace. They all want personal safety and collective security. They all extol the principle of freedom. They just have some profound disagreements about the definition and the achievement of these ideals.

One of the many reasons I love and admire Dr. Martin Luther King, Jr. is because he embodied the best and truest of both liberal and conservative values. He constantly envisioned, articulated, and advocated the goals of world peace, social justice, and authentic human equality. But he always did so by constantly appealing to immutable divine principles and objective universal truths. Dr. King preached and lived the true revolutionary liberation which is only to be found in the infinite caress and eternal compass of the Creator. His idealism was inseparable from his objectivity. For Dr. King, hate was the universal problem and love was the universal solution. And whether we lean left or lean right, we should all be able to see the truth in that.

So as I hear both sides out, being sympathetic to much of what each has to say, I urge them to begin by wedding themselves to love, life, and nonviolence. I urge them to let love, life, and peace construct the impenetrable walls of authentic security, true justice, and eternal security. And as we cultivate these divine walls we will see the barriers of hatred, violence, and death crumble into oblivion.

Before all, and above all, we must pray for love to fill our hearts and minds and souls. Because when love permeates our own lives then we will truly love peace, we will truly understand justice, and we will truly value all lives – born and unborn, enemy and ally alike. And I think that if we can at least agree on love and life, then we can all to come together to truly change things positively and permanently.

And that's exactly what politicians and the political system don't want us to do. There's too much power and money invested in keeping us divided and distracted. There's too much profit to be made from keeping us hating one another rather than loving one another.

But I believe that love and truth, and the truth of love, is much stronger than the lies and deception of politics.

It's up to us to choose what we will cultivate, what we will follow, and what we will live out. I pray and I truly believe that love will indeed win. In fact, I know for a fact that love has already won. So whether you're on the left or the right, why not join the winning side?

Love beckons.

"Above all, love one another deeply, because love covers a multitude of sins." [I Peter 4:8]

1,489. ~ POLITICS and GOODNESS ~

Political change can alter social circumstances, but it cannot fundamentally alter the human heart or the human condition. Wisdom and virtue are not evidenced by circumstantial manipulation, but rather by unwavering faith and positive character regardless of situations and circumstances. By all means, let us pray and labor for a society in which it is easier for human beings to be good; but let us also understand that true goodness is adhering to right even when everyone and everything around us is terribly wrong.

1,490. ~ EAST and WEST ~

The open spaces. The lack of judgment. The purple desert horizons. The mountains that rise in the distance but appear close enough to touch. The stillness, the emptiness, the quietude – so replete with the presence of God. My soul belongs to the East, but my spirit longs for the West. If I go far enough in both directions perhaps I will find heaven where they eventually meet.

1,491. ~ FIGHTING and FALLING ~

Anyone who fights long enough will eventually be wounded in battle. And when courageous social and spiritual warriors fall, those that never dared to enter the fray will be the quickest to condemn them. Cowards are the most judgmental of human creatures.

But the saints are never deterred by mortal opinions and human condemnations. They rise to fight again – over and over again. They are defined not by their sins and errors, but by their rising in faith from every failure.

Show me a person who has never truly fallen and I will show you a person who has never really fought.

1,492. ~ GALACTIC MYSTERIES and THE REVOLUTION of THE STREETS ~

Seek heaven. Contemplate the stars. Cultivate cosmic visions. Dream universal dreams. Let your mind venture to the peripheries of space; but keep your feet firmly planted on earth. Keep your hands ever ensconced in the soil of service. Let your heart be always attuned to the suffering of your neighbors. Never let galactic meditations distract you from the necessity of revolution in the streets.

1,493. ~ EMBRACE THE MYSTERY ~

Trust the Holy Mysteries. Trust the Holy Sacraments. Trust the consensus of the Saints and Church Fathers and Mothers. If you are looking for a perfectly consistent religion, the Orthodox Christian Faith ain't it. The fullness of God in a single man... infinite God Man without beginning or end, nevertheless born of a Virgin... three persons in One... life through crucifixion... salvation through suffering... bread and wine becoming Body and Blood... mystery abounds. And mystery is not irrational; mystery is simply that which is deeper and richer and fuller than human logic can express. So embrace the mystery, for there is salvation within.

1,494. ~ FIRE! WITHOUT APOLOGY! ~

We burn political idolatry with justice and truth. We burn militaristic devilry with life and love. With the nectar of angels we send demons to a brimstone flood. With JAH Bread and Wine we watch Babylon drown in Jesus' Blood.

You can run to the hills, you can flee to the sea, but you cannot escape the Creator's mercy. Divine love will either burn you or save you, but either way you shall not escape it.

So we offer God's love without apology. We offer God's love unconditionally. We offer God's love firmly and unceasingly. But what you do with such love is up to you.

The fool curses the fire because he is either too distant to receive its warmth, or else he gets burned trying to tame its flames.

God is a consuming fire, and His fire is love. You can confront God but you can't control God. You can run from His love, but you can't hide from His love. The Lord's fire is a terrifying and hopeful grace!

"Our God is a consuming fire." [Hebrews 12:29]

"God is love." [I John 4:8]

1,495. ~ WHO KNOWS FROM WHENCE THE DEMONS COME? ~

Who knows from whence the demons come? What stirs them up and makes them play? What gives them birth? What gives them life?

But there is no life in them. Only death. Yet they seem so alive, in some very real sense, dancing in the darkness of human minds and human hearts.

I don't know what awakened the demons on those awful childhood nights. Was it the liquor? Was it the psychosis? Was it the ghosts of generational heartaches and struggles and sins and pains? Was it a combination of all those things? I will never know. I was just a child, trying in my innocence to make my parents love each other.

And what confused me most was the fact that they actually did love each other. I could see it. I could feel it. So when the yelling would awaken me in the nocturnal hours, I did my best to make it stop. And since the yelling was often about *me*, I felt it was *my* responsibility to solve their problems.

One night I woke up to a violent argument, and I banged on the wall in angry protest (my room was right next to my parents' room.) I was only seven years old, but I was pissed off. I pounded on the wall in rage, hoping they would get the message. But the yelling continued. So I got up and I ran outside in my pajamas, barefoot, into the icy street. And as the gentle midnight snow fell, I screamed at Mama and Papa, and I screamed at the universe, and I screamed at God. I screamed into the cold callous night that I wouldn't come back inside until the fighting stopped. I was a quixotic little boy, tilting at cosmic confusion, seeking to conquer the wrongs that ultimately resided within my own sinful heart.

Such episodes too often occurred during my childhood. Perhaps that's why I have always felt responsible for the sins of the world; and perhaps that's why I've also felt responsible for the lack of peace in the world. I should have been a better child. I should have been able to make peace in my own home. I should have been a blessing rather than a burden. My own four children have all brought peace to our marriage and peace to our home. So why couldn't I bring the same peace to my own parents?

I was a selfish and rebellious child. I caused my parents much more pain than they ever caused me. So I am thankful for the love they always showed in spite of the tremendous grief I caused them.

And I have learned that, yes, I am indeed responsible for the sins of the world. I am indeed responsible for the lack of peace in the world. I am indeed responsible because I don't fight hard enough against my own sins and I don't sacrifice enough to bring peace and love to others. I remain a selfish, obstinate, slothful, judgmental, and self-righteous human being.

I have always known what is right. I have always felt the hand of God upon my life. Therefore I have no excuse for my sins. I must own them. I must repent. I have no justifications. I can't blame the innocence of youth, for even as a child I understood what was true, yet I too often followed lies. I cannot blame my parents – or anyone or anything else – for the sins and errors and failures that I chose of my own free will.

The world continues to disrupt me with its chaos and cacophony. I have been thoroughly conditioned not to sleep too well. My insomnia is God's gift to keep me vigilant and alert. How can I sleep deeply and peacefully when there is so much pain and suffering in this world around me? When I sleep, I dream of horrors; and when I am awake, I pray for sleep.

Such is the fate of spiritual warriors. We are tired and wounded and mournful and weak. But we rise up, with Christ; and we fight to the death. This world may kill us, but Our Lord will save the world.

May God forgive me, and may God strengthen me to be who He truly calls me to be. I pray for the courage to fight as vigilantly in my waking life as I fight in my dreams.

"Lord, Jesus Christ, Son of God: have mercy on me, a sinner."

1,496. ~ ON PACIFISM, RIGHTS, and THE KINGDOM of GOD ~

The Christian must not equivocate. Peace cannot be preached or lived with half measures. I am a pacifist because the Gospel demands and commands nothing less.

It is clear to me that the root of all violence and war is the human presumption of certain subjective, individual, political rights. The underlying cause of all domestic disputes, civil strife, international conflicts, and interpersonal enmities involve disputes about the definition and implementation and preservation of various incongruent rights. Human rights are trampled under civil rights; civil rights are trampled under states' rights; states' rights are trampled under individual rights; and individual rights are trampled under majority rights.

We live in a violent world and a violent society because people demand rights for themselves while denying rights to others. And how can any professed follower of Christ justify or defend violence of any kind, since the only right that Our Savior granted us is the right (and the responsibility) to lay down everything that we believe to be "ours" in order to follow Him and pursue His Kingdom?

Once we realize that nothing is ours and all is His – possessions, family, even our own bodies and minds and souls – then we understand that to sacrifice our own rights on the altar of Truth is what truly furthers peace on earth and justice in the world. As Aldous Huxley wrote: *"God's Kingdom will not come unless we begin by making our human kingdoms go."*

And with this realization it thus becomes impossible to violently rob any human being of their life for any reason at all. This realization also makes it possible for us to lay down what we once held to be "ours" in order to serve even our enemies and oppressors, who according to Christ are actually our *neighbors*. Love is the one and only force that will truly liberate both victim and victimizer. And in spite of what the "Just War" philosophers may say, it really is impossible to love those that you kill.

1,497. ~ HOPE ~

It seems that whenever I find hope, something happens to destroy it. But I've also learned that hope is the faithful antidote to misery and despair. Hope is actually a volitional choice, not a situational circumstance. We must choose to hope, repeatedly, and in spite of all the evidence that leads us to believe it is foolish to do so. And we must put our hope in the right place: not in people or in temporal security, but in the Christ who calls us to take up our cross and follow Him to eternal life.

"Still Life With Open Bible" is one of my favorite paintings by one of my favorite artists, Vincent Van Gogh. Here we see the little yellow book by Emile Zola – *La Joie de Vivre* *("The Joy of Life")* – resting before a large open Bible. Zola's book is weathered and worn, like the characters within, and like Van Gogh himself. The title is meant to be ironic. Zola's novel shows us that life is not joyful; it is instead fraught with misery and suffering.

To the right of the Bible is an extinguished candle, likely symbolic of Van Gogh's father who died shortly before Van Gogh painted this. Darkness looms in the background. The brightest light seems to emanate from Zola's little yellow novel, which contains not the hope of the Gospel but rather an account of human despair.

So why does Van Gogh give light to Zola's book rather than to the Holy Book? Is Van Gogh trying to tell us that the Bible is an ancient and irrelevant relic, an anachronistic icon that is ultimately unable to address the realities of the human condition? Is Van Gogh telling us that it is actually rather the harsh, pragmatic truth of Zola that is truly relevant and most real? Is Van Gogh declaring his rejection of an ancient and antiquated Christian Faith in favor of a naturalistic, humanist enlightenment philosophy?

Many have indeed interpreted it this way. But I don't see it like that at all. What I see is Van Gogh depicting himself through Zola's book, with all of its worn pages and suffering characters, in front of the open arms of Christ (the open Bible.) I see Van Gogh, who had a deeply troubled relationship with his earthly father, pointing to the unconditional and reconciling love of his heavenly Father.

Van Gogh thus portrays himself in Zola's *"The Joy of Life,"* because he understands the irony of the title all too well. Unrequited love, psychological torment, spiritual anguish, and tumultuous relationships with family and friends plagued Van Gogh throughout his earthly existence. In spite of what many have said about him, Van Gogh was very much the realist – a man who keenly observed and personally suffered from the pains, hardships, and betrayals of this very real world. And yet Zola's book is the most illuminated object in the painting. It's as if Van Gogh is telling us that yes, life is harsh and bitter and cruel, yet the light of Christ nevertheless shines upon us. We are fallen, broken, despondent, and wretched human creatures, but we nevertheless bear the indelible and glorious image of God.

Van Gogh portrays his father in the unlit candle. Between them both (between Zola's book and the unlit candle) the large – yea, eternal arms of God – are open wide to receive and reconcile progenitor and prodigal, sire and son. Van Gogh recognizes that the light of Christ is ever present in human suffering and human struggle. There is redemption in the pain. Between the obscure darkness of death and the clear miseries of life, the open arms of Jesus remind us that God's love is the ultimate, hopeful, illuminating reality of infinite existence.

I see Van Gogh prostrating himself before God and saying: "Lord, I very much relate these words of Emile Zola. They express my own grief, my own sorrow, my own doubt and despair. I have read them again and again. I would be imprisoned by them if I did not know that there are greater words, truer words, *your* words. So I prostrate my sorrows, my thoughts, my struggles, my fears, my pains, my philosophies, and myself before You and your unfailing grace. My earthly father is gone, my Christian faith is dimmed, and sometimes it feels like the candle of my soul has burned completely out. But your arms remain ever open to me. So I cast myself before You, in all of my brokenness."

This is what I see in this painting. But I'm not an art critic. This is just my own humble interpretation. And that's the wonderful thing about art: no one has a monopoly on what we may glean from it.

"I said, 'I am an artist,' which I won't take back, because it's self-evident that what that word implies is looking for something all the time without ever finding it in full. It is the very opposite of saying, 'I know all about it, I've already found it.' As far as I'm concerned, the word means, 'I am looking, I am hunting for it, I am deeply involved.'" ~ Vincent Van Gogh ~

"What is really wretched is loneliness, worries, problems, and the unfulfilled need for kindness and sympathy. Feelings of sadness or

disappointment undermine us more than dissipation – those of us, I say, who find ourselves the happy owners of irregular hearts."
~ Vincent Van Gogh ~

"Nearly everyone has a feeling for nature, some more, some less; but there are some who actually feel God. God is a Spirit, and they that worship Him must worship Him in spirit and in truth. It is written, 'The world passeth away, and the lust thereof,' and on the other hand we are also told about 'that good part which shall not be taken away,' and about 'a well of water springing up into everlasting life.' Let us therefore pray that we may grow rich in God. Let us ask that it may fall to us to become the poor in the Kingdom of God, God's servants. We are still a long way from that, however, since there are often beams in our eyes that we know not of."
~ Vincent Van Gogh ~

1,499. ~ GHOST SOULS ~

Ghost souls...
Trapped in two worlds
Too low for heaven
Too high for earth
Reaching for angels
And thirsting for dust

1,500. ~ POLITICS and "WE THE PEOPLE" ~

Politics is the art of convincing the people that one is for the people while one exploits the people for personal profit and power. So, as much as I despise politicians, it's we the people who are ultimately to blame.

1,501. ~ PEACE THROUGH LIFE and LIFE THROUGH PEACE ~

I believe in peace through life and life through peace. Where life is valued and affirmed, peace will naturally flourish. Where life is violated and denied, peace will never take root.

1,502. ~ CONVERSION ~

Jesus does not convert us; He rather calls us to conversion. The Cross is not a magic wand or a cosmic waiver. The Cross is the call to unite our own sufferings with Christ's sufferings so that through His holy Blood and holy tears our own mortal blood and mortal tears will be ultimately redemptive.

Make no mistake: there can be no conversion apart from the grace of God. But we must accept His grace, we must live in His grace, and we must in fact cooperate with His grace.

The paradox of the Gospel is that Christ alone saves, yet nobody is saved alone. The Cross alone redeems, yet there is no redemption apart from taking up our own crosses. God indeed does it all. There is no eternal hope apart from the Incarnation, the Crucifixion, and the Resurrection. Yet we must nevertheless work out our salvation with fear and trembling. We must pray and labor to be converted every day, every hour, and every moment of our lives. And by God's grace we have the certain hope that our salvation will be complete, because our salvation has in fact already been completed. We just have to keep on working it out until the angels escort us from this world to the next.

"Christ is the solution to all the problems of humanity, provided that humankind works with Him." ~ Archbishop Oscar Romero ~

1,503. ~ IF WE HATE MORE THAN WE LOVE ~

If we hate a single individual more than we love an entire righteous movement... if we hate a single person more than we love the countless people who suffered, sacrificed, and died for truth... if we despise one human being more than we cherish all of humanity... if we hate our ideological opponents more than we love *Love*... well, then we are on the opposite side of world peace, social justice, and human reconciliation. As Dr. Martin Luther King, Jr. said: *"Darkness cannot drive out darkness; only light can do that. Hate cannot drive out hate; only love can do that. Love is the only force capable of transforming an enemy into a friend."*

If we hate more than we love, we play right into the enemy's hands. Not only is hate feckless and ineffectual, but it invariably harms the one who hates more than the one who is hated.

1,504. ~ A RESPONSE to SOME QUESTIONS ABOUT ABORTION ~

In response to some questions posed to me, I would like to offer a few thoughts on abortion, leaving emotion and subjectivity out of it as much as possible (although I admit on the front-end, without apology, that I am biased towards peace, love, and life):

1. Regardless of whether the human fetus is a "baby," a "person," or a "child," it is undeniably a human life. The ethical question then becomes whether or not this nascent human life should be protected and accorded the legal right to life. I would argue that yes, all human life – regardless of race, gender, ethnicity, age, sex, religion, sexual orientation, social status, or stage of development – should be protected and accorded the legal right to live, from conception to natural death. History has demonstrably proven that great evils and injustices occur as a result of one segment of humanity determining that another segment of humanity is not fully human.

2. The circumstances and experiences of life are full of "grey areas," but the existence of life itself is biologically black and white. Life

either exists or does not exist. A human being (human *being*) is either alive or not alive. In fact, the word "being" implies life, existence, presence, and reality. So let's start with acknowledging that fact and then proceed from there. And I would argue that whenever and wherever we encounter "grey areas" on the path of existence, we should always err on the side of life. To err on the side of *not* killing is always the morally, ethically, and yes – spiritually – right thing to do. It is also the logically correct thing to do, because where life exists there is always the possibility of healing, improvement, correction, and empowerment. But the violent negation of life is the violent negation of all the possibilities, hopes, and joys that accompany life.

3. Abortion is not merely a women's issue. Every pregnancy involves at least three lives: the life of the mother, the life of the father, and the life of the unborn. Therefore, abortion is a *human* issue, not simply a women's issue. And like all issues of human rights, every conscientious human being has both a moral right and an ethical responsibility to affirm and defend the human rights of all other human lives. One does not need to be religious, or even a believer in God, to understand that protecting the objective rights of all human lives is ultimately the best protection of one's own subjective life as well.

4. Unborn lives are not parasites. Parasites derive their own sustenance at the expense of the host. But mother and unborn child are engaged in a symbiotic nurturing relationship that benefits both equally. The unborn human life is not an "invader." The unborn human life did not ask to be conceived. The unborn human life is innocent and helpless and completely at the mercy of another.

5. To answer the ultimate question that was asked: "Are we killing *babies* with abortion?" I personally think that yes, we are killing babies. But again, to leave such subjective terminology out of it, what is indisputable is that abortion violently destroys human life. There is no debate about that. So even if one is not willing to acknowledge the fetus as a "baby," they must at least acknowledge that the fetus is a

human life. And if we refuse to protect the most helpless, innocent, and vulnerable among us, then why should we presume to be safe ourselves? There is great truth in the cliché that a chain is only as strong as its weakest link.

6. As for the silliness I've heard about God supposedly aborting babies because women have miscarriages: well, I say let's leave life and death in the Lord's hands rather than taking it upon ourselves to kill. And that goes for war, capital punishment, and all other acts of killing, as well as abortion. We live in a fallen world, and therefore human existence will always be accompanied by deformities and sorrows and pains and death. But God forbid that we should be the ones to inflict deformity and sorrow and pain and death on others.

7. In summary, let me invoke the age old saying: *"Live and let live."* This is such a simple but profound concept. Let God do with life what He will; but let us always affirm, nurture, protect, and exalt life. Those who seek solutions in death ultimately seek their own sorrow and their own demise, along with the demise they bring to their victims. Those who seek to enrich their own lives by destroying the lives of others are the most pitiful, impotent, and impoverished of souls. There is no hope in killing. Never.

1,505. ~ LEARNING HOW to LOVE ~

I am thankful for my spiritual mentors who always remind me to err on the side of love, forgiveness, grace, and humility. I am full of fire and passion, and if I'm not careful I will burn my own soul in my efforts to burn Babylon.

I too often light righteous fires and then choke on my own smoke. But love is the fire that burns without killing, that purifies without harming, that divides without destroying, and that convicts and compels without condemnation or coercion.

I am still learning how to love. I have a long way to go. I am thankful for those who teach me and lead me in love through their divine words and constant forgiveness and holy example.

1,506. ~ "OTHER ISSUES" ~

I didn't oppose slavery, because I believed there were "other issues."

I didn't oppose segregation, because I believed there were "other issues."

I didn't oppose the bombing of innocent civilians, because I believed there were "other issues."

I didn't oppose the prison industrial complex, because I believed there were "other issues."

I didn't oppose executions, because I believed there were "other issues."

I didn't oppose the violence of militarism and war and police brutality because I believed there were "other issues."

I didn't oppose systemic racism because I believed there were "other issues."

I didn't oppose the legality of abortion, because I believed there were "other issues."

But when the violence and killing and injustice threatened *me*, then suddenly there were no "other issues."

1,507. ~ THEOLOGICAL KNOWLEDGE and DEMONIC INTERPRETATIONS ~

You can quote the Bible chapter and verse; you can be learned in Hebrew, Greek, and Aramaic; you can recite the Gospel in ten different languages; and you can have theological degrees coming out of your ears – but unless you side with life and unless you prioritize "the least of these," then you side with hell rather than heaven. Satan knows the sacred scriptures better than anyone, and many people follow his demonic biblical interpretations right into the abyss of Abaddon.

1,508. ~ ALWAYS... ~

Always have a book in your hand, a song in your soul, and a prayer on your lips. And always carry gratitude, forgiveness, and love in your heart. To be always learning, always creating, always praying, and always loving will carry us through life and usher us into heaven. I don't know much about much, but of this I am confident.

1,509. ~ LOVE UNTIL YOU BLEED ~

I've been labeled a "ne'er-do-well," an "underachiever," a "zealot," a "foolish idealist." I've been called "arrogant," "rebellious," "unteachable," and "touched," among other things. I've been dismissed, disparaged, ridiculed, and discounted by this fallen world.

Van Gogh wanted to preach and to paint, yet his family and friends told him to go into business, to find steady employment, to be practical so that he could "make something of himself." But he refused to compromise his passion for Christ and humanity and love and beauty. Thank God he didn't obey those who counseled him to temper his zeal and sell out to social acceptance.

I surmise that having read Dostoevsky, Van Gogh surely must have come across the great writer's words: "Beauty will save the world." And he gave his life to that saving beauty. And the world is richer because he spilled his paint and his blood and his heart and his soul.

So, love until you bleed, and then love some more. Love until you die, and then you will live on. Let your heart be crucified now so that your heart can be healed forever.

1,510. ~ KINGDOM POLITICS and WORLDLY POLITICS ~

Kingdom politics will never harmonize with worldly politics. While you vote for your rulers, we will follow our Lord. While you vote for your bondage, we will serve our Liberator. While you vote for your destruction, we will worship our Savior. While you vote for masters that cannot save, we will praise the God who can. While you vote for politicians and presidents and earthly princes, we will bow before the King of Kings. We invite you to join us.

1,511. ~ BLEEDING INTO HEAVEN ~

I give my heart,
I give my blood,
I give my life
I give my love
But it's not enough
No, not enough
So here I bleed
And here I cry
Killing myself
Trying not to die
Blood flows
From my mind
And from my soul
Bleeding into heaven

1,512. ~ CREATIVITY and THE CREATOR'S CONFLAGRATION ~

In order to create, one must first be free from the concerns of daily bread and the necessities of daily life. Yet the paradox is that beauty is often born from hunger and suffering, and creativity often blossoms from struggle and despair.

True art is rarely (and I dare say never) produced by those that have never doubted or hungered, that have never fought or been hurt, that have never loved or had their hearts shattered. Creativity withers in the confines of comfort and certitude.

The grape on the vine is sweet, and yes, we wish life would always remain sweet. But when the grape is crushed, trodden under foot, and set aside to ferment, it produces wine that pleases the palate and intoxicates the senses. Likewise, we too, as the images of God, are able to glorify Him more through hardship and pain than through comfort and ease.

The sun rises and sets with mystical intensity, painting the horizon with flame dawn and ember dusk; yet its cosmic fire brings peace to the human soul. We too must be burned with the love of God. And the soul that is chrismated with divine coals will inevitably produce cosmic creativity and ineffable works of imagination.

The true artist must dance in the Creator's conflagration until he himself becomes holy ash that is fuel for those that follow him.

But let us not think that fire is necessarily destructive. Divine fire is purifying and purgatorial, restorative and redemptive. The artist does not kill himself or even die for his art. Rather, the true artist, in truly creating, is crucified with Christ. And therefore his soul, and the art that his soul produces, endure eternally.

1,513. ~ OUR CONFESSION IS REBELLION ~

To confess Christ is to protest against all earthly and political powers that seek to usurp His authority and His Kingdom. Likewise, to profess allegiance to earthly and political powers is to fundamentally deny Christ and to betray His Kingdom. Our Christian confession is rebellion, revolution, spiritual and social resistance to all principalities and states that exist by violence, oppression, bloodshed and lies. When the gospel is our politics then we recognize all other politics as enemies of the gospel. Because of our eternal state, we are invariably threats to all temporal States.

1,514. ~ TO LOVE MORE and ARGUE LESS ~

So what if we win the argument or win the debate? Yes, we may come out looking smarter than our opponent. And yes, we may have prevailed in the "arena of ideas." We may have intellectually eviscerated the atheist, the homosexual, the Muslim, the liberal, the conservative, etc. But have we really advanced the Gospel? I doubt it. Usually all we have done is advanced ourselves at the expense of the Gospel. The Gospel is ultimately about love – not a weak, feckless, compromising love, but an active, vigilant, and sacrificial love. But it is nevertheless about love. And love needs no defense, because love cannot be destroyed. We would do better to love more and argue less. The gates of hell will not prevail against the Church, so God doesn't need us to fight His battles. What He wants us to do is love and love and love some more. After all, they will know we are Christians by our love.

1,515. ~ MORE REFLECTIONS on DIETRICH BONHOEFFER ~

There are lots of Christian preachers and Christian professors and Christian theologians and Christian churchmen that, like the young Dietrich Bonhoeffer, still do not truly know Christ. In fact, there are lots of Bonhoeffer scholars who have yet to truly understand the most important aspects of Bonhoeffer's life and teachings. I've met them and had lengthy conversations with them, and it's baffling how in spite of their vast academic knowledge of Bonhoeffer they nevertheless miss the most important aspects of his life and teachings.

Many learned theology professors and clergymen have secured for themselves comfort, prestige, security, and human praise by invoking the name of Jesus in the most unthreatening, stale, and anemic ways. They have risen to academic esteem with their dissertations on Christian prophets like Dietrich Bonhoeffer while dismissing or ignoring the very truths and convictions that defined their prophetic nature.

So please read Bonhoeffer's testimony below. And please read as much as you can of his other works, most especially *The Cost of Discipleship*. This was a man who could have easily used the Bible and the name of Christ to make a name for himself, to carve out a safe and profitable personal existence, to endear himself to the world rather than prophesying against the world. But when Bonhoeffer was confronted with the Gospel, he embraced it – along with its accompanying agony, suffering, and martyrdom.

Bonhoeffer took up the Cross and lived and died by it. And that was his greatness. And central to his understanding of the Gospel was his recognition of and intervention on behalf of the "least of these." Whether it was Jews being exterminated in Nazi Germany, African Americans being lynched and oppressed in the United States, or unborn children being unjustly and brutally aborted, Bonhoeffer's Jesus compelled him to speak out and sacrificially act on behalf of the suffering, the voiceless, and the innocent victims of violence and evil. And Bonhoeffer's Jesus compelled him to do so only by the methods and means sanctioned by the Lord he worshipped and served. Contrary to the popular narrative, Dietrich Bonhoeffer never rejected the pacifism of his true Christian conversion. Yes, he was certainly involved in proactive resistance to the Nazi regime, but he never embraced violence as a legitimate Christian solution to the evils he faced.

For all of Bonhoeffer's intellectual prowess, his ultimate genius is to be found in his keen love for the oppressed and his personal willingness to die – *but not kill* – for his victimized neighbors. In other words, Bonhoeffer truly followed Jesus Christ in the most profoundly personal and socially redemptive ways. As he wrote: *"We must 'speak out for those who cannot speak.' [Proverbs 31:8] Who in the Church today still remembers that this is the very least the Bible asks of us in times such as these?"*

May we all seek the grace to cultivate Bonhoeffer's true Christian courage and conviction.

*"I threw myself into my studies in a very unchristian and arrogant manner. A mind-boggling ambition that made my life difficult and separated me from the love and trust of my fellow human beings. That was a terrible time. I was terribly alone and left to my own devices. Then something happened that changed my life and turned it around permanently. I came to the Bible truly for the first time. And it is very difficult for me to say that, because I had already preached several times, been involved in the Church, given speeches about the Bible and written about the Bible. But I still had not become a Christian. I was an untamed child, my own foolish master. In a crazy vanity, I had turned this whole business about Jesus Christ into a personal advantage. I pray God, that it will never be so again. I had also never truly prayed. I was desperately lonely, and yet I was very self-satisfied and quite pleased with myself. It was from this bondage that the Bible – especially the Sermon on the Mount – freed me. That was a grand liberation. Since then everything is different. I now saw that everything depended on the renewal of the Church and of the ministry. **Christian pacifism,** which I had previously fought against with passion, all at once seemed perfectly obvious. And so it went further, step by step. I recognized and thought of nothing else. My calling is now quite clear to me. What God will make of it I do not know. But I must follow the path of Christ's peace. I believe the nobility of this calling will become plainly clear to us only in the events and times to come. If only we can hold out!"*

~ Dietrich Bonhoeffer ~

[For more in depth information on the subject of Bonhoeffer's pacifism, I highly recommend the book *Bonhoeffer The Assassin? Challenging the Myth, Recovering His Call to Peacemaking* by Mark Thiessen Nation, Anthony G. Siegrist, and Daniel P. Umbrel.]

1,516. ~ DARKNESS FELL AGAIN TODAY ~

Darkness fell again today
as it falls every day,
somewhere and in some way.

Another eclipse of peace and light,
so now I'm angry
and I say bring on the night!

I'm tired of forgiveness and love.
I want justice for the wicked!
Give them what they deserve!

I'm ready to take up arms,
to sow some bullets,
and spread some fear.
I'll give these blood shedders
a triple dose of our own tears!

I'll engage the darkness
with more darkness;
And I'll win, believe me!
I'll avenge all this innocent blood
by baptizing it in the blood of evildoers.

But NO, says my Lord.
No, it is not for you to do such a thing.
You must love anyway.
You must forgive anyway.
You must fight always,
but only with the wood of the Cross.

Can I do it?
I don't know.
Do I want to do it?
I don't know.

But I must pray
for the desire, grace, and strength

to meet darkness with light,
hatred with love,
violence with peace,
vengeance with mercy,
and retaliation with forgiveness.

After all, I am a Christian,
and this is what my Lord commands.

God help me.
God help us all.

1,517. ~ ABORTION, ECONOMICS, and BOURGEOIS PREJUDICES ~

Economically disadvantaged women are *not* more inclined than other women to abort their unborn babies, and to believe so is to harbor demeaning and prejudicial views about the poor. The real factors driving abortion are misogyny and materialism.

Many women are coerced and forced to have abortions against their wills by abusive, controlling, and cowardly men. But the abortion mills aren't interested in protecting these women's choices *not* to have abortions, because every abortion means more money for the abortionists and more revenue for abortion organizations like Planned Parenthood.

Consider the words of Margaret Sanger, the racist founder of Planned Parenthood, who promoted eugenics as a means of controlling the poor, "minorities," and the "unfit."

"We should apply a stern and rigid policy of sterilization and segregation to that grade of population whose progeny is tainted, or whose inheritance is such that objectionable traits may be transmitted to offspring." [Birth Control Review (April 1932, pp. 107-108)]

"Give dysgenic groups (people with "bad genes") in our population their choice of segregation or (compulsory) sterilization." [Birth Control Review, (April 1932 pg. 108)]

"Birth control must lead ultimately to a cleaner race." [*Birth Control Review, (April 1932 pg. 108)]*

"No woman shall have the legal right to bear a child without a permit, and no permit shall be valid for more than one birth." [*"America Needs a Code for Babies," March 27, 1934]*

"The most merciful thing that the large family does to one of its infant members is to kill it." [*Woman and The New Race]*

So every time you perpetuate the myth that the poor are more inclined to kill their offspring than the rich, you disclose your racism, bigotry, and bourgeois prejudices.

1,518. ~ JUSTICE, MORALITY, and "NUANCE" ~

It's interesting how issues of justice and morality are always full of "nuance," "complexity," and "grey areas" as long as they involve the lives of others, but when our own lives are violated or threatened, our sense of justice and morality suddenly becomes crystal clear, unambiguously black and white, and rigidly uncompromising.

1,519. ~ THE MYSTERY of THE CROSS ~

The more we try to explain the mystery, the less we will understand it. God's love cannot be systematized, rationalized, or reduced to a syllogistic equation. It can only be experienced, lived, and subsequently manifested. Century after century, scholars and theologians and philosophers have tried to make the folly of the Cross palatable to the worldly mind. We have painted it, polished it, gilded it, preached it, exalted it, tattooed it, and adored it. We love the Cross deeply, as long as we don't actually have to take it up and carry it. We love God's love as long as His love doesn't require our own crucifixion. The mystery of the Cross is that true love and true salvation are accompanied by sacrifice and suffering, and that in and through sacrifice and suffering we will find that mystical "peace which passes all understanding." (Philippians 4:7)

1,520. ~ "LAWFUL" and "UNLAWFUL" VIOLENCE ~

Violence begets violence. "Lawful" violence is just as unholy as "unlawful" violence. *"All those who live by the sword shall die by the sword." [St. Matthew 26:52]* Likewise, those who die by the Cross shall be saved by the Cross.

1,521. ~ IF NOT POLITICS, THEN WHAT'S THE SOLUTION? ~

Political ideologues on both the left and the right constantly ask me: "So if you don't vote and you don't support the political process, then what's your solution?" And here is my consistent answer:

Don't kill. Don't exploit. Don't oppress. And don't vote for politicians or support political systems that perpetuate violence and injustice and oppression. Love God and love your neighbors – in personal, sacrificial, tangible ways.

And this is not *my* solution, this is the Gospel solution. The issue at hand is whether or not we really want to understand and obey the Gospel. Most of us would rather vote for wolves than follow the Shepherd. And no, we cannot do both. So let's stop kidding ourselves.

1,522. ~ LOVE AND SALVATION ~

Love is the path and the purpose, the destination and the journey. Those that truly love life are those that truly live to love. Unless we bathe in God's love today, we will not bathe in His love in the eternal tomorrow. *"Whoever does not love does not know God, because God is love." [I John 4:8]*

But make no mistake, love is not easy; love is not always pleasant; and love is never passive. Love labors, sacrifices, agitates, and endures. As Dostoevsky wrote, *"Love in reality is a harsh and dreadful thing compared to love in dreams."*

Love may crucify us, but apart from love how else can we be saved?

1,523. ~ THE GREATEST ART ~

Sincerity is the greatest art. It doesn't matter how talented you are, it only matters that you are true.

1,524. ~ WESTERN TRIUMPH ~

The triumph of Western civilization has come at the expense of dehumanization, depersonalization, and human degradation. "Mankind" has set foot on the moon and touched the very tapestry of Mars, yet "Mankind" has never been further removed from humanity.

"Come then, comrades; we must find something different than the imitation of the West. We must abandon our desire to catch up with this so called 'civilization.' The West now lives at such a mad, reckless pace that it has forsaken all guidance and reason. The West is running headlong into the abyss, and we would do well to avoid it with all possible speed. When I search for humanity in the technique and style of the West, I see only a succession of human negation and an avalanche of murders." ~ Franz Fanon ~

1,525. ~ AVOIDING SIN and CONFRONTING EVIL ~

The Gospel is less about cautiously avoiding sin than about boldly confronting evil. In fact, when we are busy confronting evil we have little time to sin.

1,526. ~ CRUSHED into COMMUNISM ~

When those in power treat the powerless like dirt, it's just "business as usual," the "difficult but necessary process of getting the job done." But when the powerless dare to rise up, resist, and confront the powerful on a basic human and basic moral level, they are condemned as "communists," "socialists," and "violent subversives" that need to be crushed in order for the capitalist machine to keep on grinding.

After all, if our blood, sweat, and tears don't produce a substantial profit, then they are of no use to the corporate beast. And yet the laborers have always cried out: "But what about our souls? What about *our souls*?!"

And the capitalist machine has always responded: "If your souls can't make us money, then what use do we have for them?" And thus, in the irony of ironies, it has often been the "Christian" capitalists who have driven many workers to a godless communism.

1,527. ~ BABYLON ADVICE ~

They told Noah to listen to the weatherman. They told Martin Luther King to stick to the pulpit and stay out of the streets. They told Samson he needed a haircut. They told Bob Marley to sing but don't be baptized. They told King David to stop dancing before the Lord. They told Mother Teresa to tend to the poor but keep silent about abortion. They told John the Baptist to mind his own business. They told Vincent Van Gogh to get a job. They told Jesus to keep His teachings private, because if He made them public He would be crucified.

Babylon will always try to tell you what to do, what to think, and how to live. And the irony is that even when you obey Babylon, Babylon will still crucify you in the end. So you might as well die to Truth rather than killing yourself for a lie.

1,528. ~ THOSE WHO TRULY KNOW THEMSELVES ~

Those who truly know themselves will never be truly understood by this world. We are strangers, pilgrims, and disciples – passing through this terrestrial vale of tears on the road to Zion. We will never find true hospitality here. We have learned to find comfort in constantly being uncomfortable. We have made the Cross our home.

1,529. ~ LIFE OVER DEATH ~

Our philosophy doesn't need to be empirically, academically, or psychologically tested. It is tested in the streets, it is tried by reality, it is forged by existence, and it is sanctified by life. Our philosophy is peace and love and justice and truth. And this philosophy will always prevail; it will endure forever; it will eternally conquer. You can silence us, imprison us, kill us, and bury our flesh in the bowels of the earth; but our philosophy will emanate and echo throughout the corridors of infinity – because our philosophy is theology; and theology, at its essence, is Life over death.

1,530. ~ WRONG, EVIL, and HUMANITY ~

If the deliberate destruction of innocent life in the womb is not wrong, then nothing is wrong. If violently dividing a mother from her unborn child is not evil, then nothing is evil. If abortion is not a crime against humanity, then we have no humanity.

1,531. ~ FRIENDSHIP ~

A true friend is someone who calls you as much as you call them.

A true friend is someone who loves and supports you through good times and bad.

A true friend is someone who always tells you the truth but never judges or condemns you.

A true friend is someone who makes you laugh, makes you think, and makes you a better person.

A true friend is someone who endures and tolerates the major transformations in your life, even if they don't always understand them.

A true friend is someone with whom you can discuss anything and to whom you can divulge anything.

A true friend is someone who always sees the good in you, even when everyone else can only see the bad.

A true friend is someone with whom you never have to pretend, and who never has to pretend with you.

A true friend will rejoice with you, cry with you, pray with you, and struggle with you.

A friend may be a brother, and a brother may be a friend; but when friendship and brotherhood are inseparable, then a mystical fellowship has been born from the very hand of God.

I am blessed to have a few such friends in my life. I can count them on one hand, and yet that makes me richer than most. Such friendship, brotherhood, and love has not only blessed my life, but it has helped me realize that life is worth living.

"One who has unreliable friends soon comes to ruin, but there is a friend who sticks closer than a brother." [Proverbs 18:24]

"Friendship is born at the moment when one man says to another: "What! You too? I thought that I was the only one!"
~ C.S. Lewis ~

"Don't walk in front of me; I may not follow. Don't walk behind me; I may not lead. Just walk beside me; just be my friend."
~ Albert Camus ~

"I would rather walk with a friend in the dark, than alone in the light." ~ Helen Keller ~

"Friendship is the hardest thing in the world to explain. It's not something you learn in school. But if you haven't learned the meaning of friendship, you really haven't learned anything."
~ Muhammad Ali ~

"The glory of friendship is not the outstretched hand, not the kindly smile, nor the joy of companionship; it is the spiritual inspiration that comes to one when you discover that someone else believes in you and is willing to trust you with a friendship."
~ Ralph Waldo Emerson ~

"When I say it's you I like, I'm talking about that part of you that knows that life is far more than anything you can ever see or hear or touch. That deep part of you that allows you to stand for those things without which humankind cannot survive. Love that conquers hate, peace that rises triumphant over war, and justice that proves more powerful than greed." ~ Fred Rogers ~

1,532. ~ THE FIRST STEP TO FINDING PERSONAL PEACE ~

The first step to finding personal peace is weaning ourselves off of destructive ideologies and destructive habits and destructive people. Before we can step into the light we have to first step out of the darkness.

1,533. ~ WHEN THE RATS ARE FED ~

When the rats are fed
but we have no bread...
when the roaches have nests
but we have no beds...
well, that shit gets to our heads.

And when we can't eat
and when we can't sleep,
then we take to the streets.
And then the blood runs deep
and the blood runs red,
until we are fed,
until we too can sleep and eat and rest.

So rich man,
you best sleep with one eye open,
because our waking nightmare
will inevitably destroy
your peaceful dreams...

until you do right,
until you do right.

And that's all we want:
peace and life.
We just want what's right.

1,534. ~ WHEN THE SYSTEM TELLS YOU... ~

When the system tells you that their lies are the truth, you best believe that their truths are lies. When the system tells you that their wrongs are "rights," you best believe that their "rights" are wrongs. When the system tells you to side with the masses, you best have the courage to stand alone. When the system tells you to go to the polls and crucify Christ, you best cling to the Cross and say, "To hell with Babylon!"

1,535. ~ SOME COMMENTS on THE FLORIDA SCHOOL SHOOTING ~
[2/14/2018]

What can I say about today's tragedy that I haven't already said numerous times in numerous ways? But let me reiterate some of the basic points:

1. The spiritual law of the harvest applies equally to the social realm. A society that is established by violence, that is sustained by violence, and that thrives by violence will inevitably be a society that is internally plagued by violence. We cannot escape or evade prophetic truth: *"Be not deceived; God is not mocked: for whatsoever man soweth, that shall man also reap." [Galatians 6:7] "Put away thy sword, for all those who live by the sword shall die by the sword." [St. Matthew 26:52]*

2. The nature of violence is demonic (Cf. Enoch 69:6-7), and it cannot be tamed. Violence, regardless of how many people may believe it to sometimes be "just," always afflicts the innocent along with the guilty. Violence, like lust, knows no limits, boundaries, or restraints. Once it is unleashed it spreads like a virus, having no thought for the age or innocence of its victims.

3. A government that lectures the common populace about "gun control" while it steadily amasses nuclear weapons and spends billions of dollars on its military while its own citizens suffer from homelessness and hunger is not a government interested in peace. So dear Mr. President and Congress: when you put down your own guns then you can tell everyone else to put down theirs. And as disciples of Jesus Christ, we will proclaim the same message equally and unequivocally to both the civic rulers and to the common citizens of this land: "Thou shalt not kill. Mash your swords into plowshares.

Love your enemies and bless those that persecute you. That is the only real solution to the violence that plagues this society."

4. As long as we justify, defend, rationalize, and tolerate the legalized slaughter of the most helpless members of the human race – unborn children – then we have no reasonable right to be shocked and outraged by gang violence, school shootings, mass murders, and terrorism. Unless and until the weakest among us are safe, then none of us are safe. As Dr. Martin Luther King, Jr. said: "Injustice anywhere is a threat to justice everywhere. Whatever affects one directly affects all indirectly... Ultimately a great nation is a compassionate nation, and no nation can be truly great unless it has a concern for 'the least of these.'"

5. There is hope for our society and hope for this country. But the hope resides in individual, corporate, and national repentance from the sin of violence. As the people of Nineveh – "that exceedingly wicked city" (Jonah 1:2) – repented in sackcloth and ashes, so too can America repent and finally find the favor of God. But as long as we seek feckless solutions in half measures, restrictions, laws, and political measures designed to preserve power and to protect the "right" to violence while naively seeking to preserve social peace and national security, then we will continue to be plagued by the perpetuation of evils such as we witnessed today.

I pray for all the victims of this horrific act. I pray for their families and loved ones. I pray also for the murderer, that God would change his heart and redeem his tortured soul. And I pray for myself, that God would help me to live the words I preach, that He would create in me a heart of peace and a spirit of true Christian love for all people. *"Lord have mercy."* +++

1,536. ~ LEFT BOOT, RIGHT BOOT ~

Left boot, right boot: I refuse to be trod upon by either!

1,537. ~ THE TWIN PILLARS of BABYLON ~

Many well intentioned revolutionaries have embraced Marxist ideology and Machiavellian pragmatism as the means of achieving righteous and noble ends. But Marxist dialectics leads people to believe that revolution is not merely a means to an end, but the end in itself. And that's why Marxism invariably destroys its own adherents and ultimately negates its own philosophical assertions.

If revolution is not predicated upon God, directed towards God, and infused with the principles and power of God, then such "revolutionary" endeavors will inevitably end in ruin. Atheism and idolatry are the twin pillars of Babylon, the stale counterrevolutionary winds that seek in vain to quench the fires of authentic revolutionary change.

1,538. ~ UNBROKEN ~

Break my heart
But you can't break my soul
Make me weep
But I'll still be whole

Crush my pride
And I'll still walk tall
So put me down
But it's you who'll fall

Laugh at me
And enjoy your sins
The fool today
In eternity wins

1,539. ~ GOD SAYS / MAN SAYS ~

God Says:

"The earth is the Lord's and the fullness thereof, and all they that dwell therein." [Psalm 24:1] "Do not neglect to show hospitality to strangers, for thereby some have entertained angels unawares." [Hebrews 13:2] "The stranger who resides with you shall be to you as the native among you, and you shall love him as yourself." [Leviticus 19:34] "Now in case a countryman of yours becomes poor and his means with regard to you falter, then you are to sustain him, like a stranger or a sojourner, that he may live with you." [Leviticus 25:35] "This is pure and undefiled religion, to care for orphans and widows in their distress, and to keep oneself unstained by the world." [James 1:27] "Whoever oppresses a poor man insults his Maker, but he who is generous to the needy honors him." [Proverbs 14:31] "Whoever gives to the poor will not want, but he who hides his eyes from the poor will be cursed." [Proverbs 28:27] If you pour yourself out for the hungry and satisfy the desire of the afflicted, then your light shall rise in the darkness and your gloom will become bright like the noonday." [Isaiah 58:10]

Man Says:

"This is MY property! This is MY country! This is MY food! This is MY water! This is MY fruit! This is MY right! Go and earn your own land, your own food, your own water, and your own rights. And if you want your own country, then go and kill and rape and conquer and enslave just like my forefathers did. Otherwise, don't expect me to share with you!"

1,540. ~ PARENTS and CHILDREN ~

Being a good parent is not as much about teaching your children the truth as it is about letting the truth of your children shatter every lie in your life. All the truth I've ever needed to know has come to me through my children's eyes and my children's hearts.

Have you ever suffered from any of the things listed below? If you haven't, then fall on your knees and thank God for sparing you. But don't presume to tell the rest of us to simply "move on" and "get over it."

Racism
Child abuse
Poverty
Rape
Bullying
Parental neglect
Discrimination
Mental illness
Hereditary physical pathologies
Sexual abuse
Emotional abuse
Depression
Anxiety
Economic exploitation
Family rejection
Addiction
Loneliness
Heartbreak

I think 99.9% of us are really in the same boat. We have all suffered and continue to suffer from one thing or another. And instead of arguing about whose suffering is the worst, I think we ought to come together and help each other heal.

My pain is really not less or greater than your pain. So let me seek to comfort you as you seek to comfort me. Perhaps then we will find justice. Perhaps then we will find peace. Perhaps revolution begins with something as simple as this.

1,542. ~ TRANSCENDENCE ~

Let us transcend ignorance and fear and violence and hate. Let us transcend doubt and despair and depression and delusion. Let us, by grace, transcend the lies of hell and enter into the Truth of heaven. And in order to transcend, we must elevate one another. Christ alone rose alone. The rest of us must rise together.

1,543. ~ CHRISTIAN OUTLAWS ~

It is impossible to obey the holy commands of Christ while obeying the unjust laws of society. Christian discipleship inevitably brings us into conflict with worldly legalities, and society's laws invariably violate the imperatives of the divine will and order. As much as we wish to carve out a comfortable Christianity which safely conforms to a corrupt and evil culture, it is simply impossible to do so. We must honestly reckon with the fact that to remain within the Church is to remain outside of the law, and to remain within the law is to remain outside of the Church. The true followers of Christ will always be outlaws in this fallen world.

1,544. ~ FINDING THE PEACE THAT ELUDES US ~

Killing begets killing. Violence and death will never give birth to peace and life. Justice begins with peace, and peace begins with justice. There will never be one without the other. By killing those that kill, do you suppose that you will bring the dead back to life? Let us leave vengeance to God. Let us love our brethren, our neighbors, and yes, even our enemies. Then, and only then, can we hope to find the peace that continues to elude us.

1,545. ~ LIFE IN PIECES ~

Tear stained cheeks
And blood stained thighs
Empty wombs
And haunted minds

Broken hearts
And death scarred souls
Life in pieces
No longer whole

Crushed by Choice
Mother and child
Crucified both
By profit and lies

1,546. ~ THE ENEMY ~

Muslims are not the enemy. Socialism is not the enemy. Immigrants are not the enemy. Russia is not the enemy. The homeless are not the enemy. Science is not the enemy. Homosexuals are not the enemy. Religion is not the enemy. The enemy is a government, a system, and an ideology that supports the racist, oppressive, capitalistic abortion industry which profits from the exploitation of women and the legal slaughter of the most vulnerable members of the human race. Violence, bloodshed, death and destruction are the enemy; and all those who love life and value peace should unite to oppose the systemic injustice and evil of abortion. For until the weakest among us are safe and free, none of us will ever be truly safe or truly free.

1,547. ~ THE WICKED IN HEAVEN? ~

If I make it to heaven and see that slave owners, child molesters, and abortionists are also there, I won't be disappointed. I will rejoice that they too have found the perfect presence of God's perfect love – a love which burns away all evil desires, all wicked inclinations, and all insidious ideas. But if abortionists are in hell, I suspect I shall be there too, for I stood idly by while my unborn neighbors were mercilessly slaughtered. I ate and drank in apathetic torpor while the bloodshed of abortion was systematically executed day after day.

The guilt for all injustice and evil begins with me; for I have tolerated it, ignored it, and refused to sacrificially intervene to stop it. So I cannot demand judgment for others while asking mercy for myself. That is not what the Gospel commands. The mercy that I wish for myself I must also wish for others – *all* others, regardless of how wicked they may be. Because their evil does not exist in a vacuum. Their evil is somehow the product of my own sinful indifference to injustice, evil, and human suffering.

"Lord have mercy on us. Lord have mercy on us all."

1,548. ~ I AM A KILLER ~

I am a killer.
I come to slay.
I'm taking aim
at violence and hate.
So join me
or get out of my way.
Side with bloodshed
and die from the same.

1,549. ~ YES, JESUS LOVES YOU! ~

The Gospel means "good news;" and the glorious good news is that God does in fact love you – unconditionally and eternally. In fact, He loves you so much that He became a man in order to love sinners in the flesh. He loves sinners so much that He suffered and died on the Cross for them. And then He rose again to give sinners the hope of eternal life.

The Cross is not some magical, forensic transaction that appeased the wrath of an angry cosmic judge; it is rather the ultimate display of love conquering hate and sin and evil and death. The Cross is not some divine schizophrenic act whereby God somehow tortures and punishes Himself in order to enable Himself to love us. The Cross is rather the divine victory of life and love conquering everything that sets itself up against life and love.

Yes, how we respond to God's glorious love does indeed make all the difference. To reject and refuse it is to deprive ourselves of its eternally saving benefits. But to embrace and accept His love is to be positively transformed here and now and forever.

The Gospel is not a cosmic guilt trip. The Gospel is the Heavenly Father eagerly longing to embrace His prodigal children, missing them so much that He came to earth to bring them back home by way of the Cross.

That is the Good News. That is the Gospel. Jesus loves you! And anyone who tells you otherwise is speaking blasphemies from hell.

1,550. ~ WORDS ~

Give me true words, hard words, controversial words, and convicting words. Give me words that burn my soul and afflict my conscience. Give me words that rebuke and chastise and disrupt and confront. But in them all, and above them all, give me words of peace and love and life and hope. In all of your mortal words, give me the Incarnate and Eternal Word, who alone can save and redeem and heal.

1,551. ~ WASTING LIFE FIGHTING FOR DEATH ~

Whether one fights for militarism, euthanasia, war, capital punishment, or abortion, nothing is more tragic than wasting one's life fighting for death.

1,552. ~ ALL I KNOW TO DO ~

I close my eyes
and pray
to see another day.
But then I awake
to face more pain.
So I arise
from tear stained sheets,
to face cruelties
that make my soul bleed.
It's a cold world
but I'll keep the Faith.

Foxes have dens
and birds have nests,
but pen, paper, and prayer
are my only rest.
Disappointments
never seem to end,
and the pain is multiplied
when it's inflicted
by family and friends.

When times are good
do I not glorify your Name?
And when you bless me Lord
do I not give You praise?
So why then, Jesus,
do you let me suffer

again and again?
Why do you let me hurt so much
that I seek comfort in sin?

But I'll keep trying Lord.
And even though I fall,
I'll always rise anew.
This world is against me
but I'll cling to You...
always and forever.
Because that's all I know to do.
That's all I know to do.

1,553. ~ THE BURDEN of LOVE ~

Love is not fair, easy, or comprehensible. Love is not tidy, predictable, or comfortable. Love is painful, scary, confusing, and burdensome. Love is not safe. However, love is good. And God is Love.

"And now abide faith, hope, and love, these three; but the greatest of these is love." [I Corinthians 13:13]

1,554. ~ THE PAIN of FAITH ~

With faith things sometimes get worse. And sometimes I don't like faith very much. I want to take matters into my own hands. I'm tired of being hurt time and time and time again. So I'm tempted to divorce faith and live by what I know will work. I'm tempted to trade faith in for pragmatic certainties that are trustworthy even if destructive. At least then I won't be constantly disappointed.

So yes, at times I want to divorce faith and send it on its merry way to torment someone else. Faith wears me down. I get so tired.

And yet I can't bring myself to do it. I am a fool. I cling to this fickle mistress no matter how often she wounds me.

Faith, I have found, is a most unfaithful thing. It will crucify you if you let it. Sometimes I want to run away from it as fast and as far as I can. But here I remain, clinging to faith as if it were my salvation. Because in the end, in the very end...in eternity...I do believe that faith will be worth all the nails and thorns and splinters and scars. But the truth is that oftentimes faith just really hurts like hell.

1,555. ~ WORKING TO END HELL ON EARTH ~

When we begin working as hard to end hell on earth as we do trying to preach people into heaven, then we will become true Christians. As the apostle wrote, *"Let us not love with word and speech, but with action and truth."* [I John 3:18]

1,556. ~ WHERE WERE YOU? ~

Sunday is coming
But where were you
Friday afternoon?

Morning is rising
But where were you
In last night's tears?

Heaven is calling
But where were you
When I was in hell?

1,557. ~ PEACE, LIFE, and HERESY ~

If it doesn't affirm, value, and perpetuate unconditional peace and the unconditional sanctity of all human life, then regardless of the doctrine, label, or name by which it is called, it is heresy.

1,558. ~ "THE RIGHT SIDE of HISTORY" ~

What does it mean to be "on the right side of history" if you are on the wrong side of peace, the wrong side of life, the wrong side of justice, the wrong side of humanity, and the wrong side of eternity? I don't care where I stand in Babylon's history books, just as long as my name is written in the Lamb's Book of Life.

1,559. ~ POLITICAL ZIONISM and THE REJECTION of EVIL ~

Political Zionism is evil. So is saying: "To hell with the Jews! Let them be annihilated!" I refuse to side with evil. Period. I don't know where that puts me on the political spectrum, and I don't care. What I do know is that peace begins with rejecting evil and confronting evil – on all sides, wherever it may be found, regardless of the ideology or name by which it is manifested.

1,560. ~ POLITICIANS, PROPHETS, PERSUASION and GAINS ~

Rhetoric, charm, eloquence, and charisma may persuade the masses, but they cannot negate the indelible conscience that dwells within every human heart. That's why politicians gain votes but prophets gain souls.

1,561. ~ THE CLOUD of EUPHEMISMS ~

Calling abortion "medicine" is like calling rape "romantic intimacy." Violence is always committed under the cloud of euphemisms.

1,562. ~ TOXIC REACTIONARY MINDSET ~

If you think liberalism is the enemy, or if you think conservatism is the enemy, then you have succumbed to the toxic reactionary mindset that ultimately empowers politicians and disenfranchises the people. Nothing impedes authentic revolution like the myopia of political partisanship. It is a tragic irony of social history that the people themselves are often responsible for their own oppression and bondage. Believing that freedom is to be found in violence, death, division, and hate, the masses flock to the voting booth without realizing that they are actually entering the slaughterhouse.

1,563. ~ FALLING STARS ~

Stars fall
upon my soul,
burning but brightening,
purifying
to make me whole.
I taste their fire,
and it blisters my tongue.
But they scald
without mercy,
because I need to be purged.

I thank God
for the grace of falling stars.

1,564. ~ OUR COMMON CALLING ~

To humble the proud and exalt the humble... to convict the rich and comfort the poor... to burn politics and liberate the people... to abort death and give voice to life... to crucify violence and resurrect peace.

Who am I to do such things? I am no less or more important than you. And you are called to do no less or more than I am in this regard. This is our common calling. Let's get to work!

1,565. ~ GOODNESS and GREATNESS ~

To be truly great one must first be truly good. And those who are truly good are not concerned with greatness.

1,566. ~ TRANSCENDENCE ~

Let this be a transcendent day! Let us transcend ignorance and fear and violence and hate. Let us transcend doubt and despair and depression and delusion. Let us, by grace, transcend the lies of hell and enter into the truth of heaven. And in order to transcend, we must elevate one another. Christ alone rose alone. The rest of us must rise together. So rise up people of God! Rise up brothers and sisters of peace, life, love, and humanity! Rise up, and lift me up along the way!

1,567. ~ THE CHURCH and POLITICAL STABILITY ~

The Church is not called to be a stabilizing political influence; the Church is called to be an agitating, disruptive, unsettling, and revolutionary force that confronts systemic evil and convicts violent ideologies. The Church is called to peace, and true peace never appeases or cooperates with the status quo of injustice and oppression.

"There is no peace along the way of safety. Peace must be dared. It is the great venture. It can never be safe." ~ Dietrich Bonhoeffer ~

1,568. ~ RULERSHIP and BONDAGE ~

To be ruled by anything or anyone other than Christ is to be enslaved. Bondage has many names, and the Cross of salvation is the only true liberation. Satan is happy to oppress us with fascism, communism, democracy, or monarchy. It matters not to him what we call our oppression, just as long as we remain oppressed. The devil is willing to grant regime change, political change, "revolutionary" change, and governmental change – as long as he can keep us in chains by preventing the divine transformation of heart that alone leads to authentic freedom.

1,569. ~ PREACHING TO THE CHOIR ~

"You're preaching to the choir," say those on the right. "You're preaching to the choir," say those on the left. Well, I'll keep preaching to these choirs until they learn the harmony of peace, life, justice, and love. When ya'll learn to all sing in tune, then I'll stop preaching to you.

1,570. ~ BULLIES and BADGES ~

If you walk around with a gun, intimidating and bullying people, don't expect them to respect you just because you wear a badge. I will never respect anyone who demands answers or behavior from me by threatening me with violence. I might do what you say just to stay alive, but don't confuse that for admiration or respect.

1,571. ~ GIVING and TAKING ~

You want the land? Then take the land.
You want the gold? Then take the gold.
You want the power? Then take the power.
But know that you are only taking it because we are giving it to you. And in giving it to you we are gaining our souls and you are losing yours.

1,572. ~ UNSETTLING THE SETTLED ~

God has a way of unsettling the settled. Carrying our crosses and following Christ rarely lead to worldly security and temporal safety. If we are safe, settled, comfortable, and secure in our faith, then we should be prepared for God to shake us up and wake us up. His grace will disrupt and afflict, but it will eternally save.

1,573. ~ OPPOSING THE UNHOLY TRIUMVIRATE ~

We must oppose the unholy triumvirate of racism, poverty, and violence with the holy triad of peace, love, and respect for all human life. As long as we permit anyone to suffer from hunger, oppression, war, or abortion, then we permit the seeds of our own inevitable sorrow and demise. God has commanded peace, love, and life. And God is not mocked. He will not long tolerate our tolerance for injustice and evil. We will reap what we sow. We will suffer from the strangulating weeds of our own apathy. The blood of innocents stains our collective soul, and it shall not be cleansed until we demand an end to killing and oppression – until we demand an end to *all* killing and *all* oppression, in *all* of their insidious forms.

1,574. ~ TRANSCENDENT THEOLOGY ~

A theology that does not transcend the Church walls to penetrate the streets, saturate the labor fields, illumine the union halls, and permeate the workplace is no theology at all. It is nothing more than an empty superstition with the name of God attached to it.

1,575. ~ REVOLUTIONARY OFFENSES ~

Most people are more offended by the agitating voices of revolution than by the injustices that make revolution necessary. They curse the prophets for rebuking the sin of politics. They condemn the saints for condemning idolatry. They despise conscientious voices for afflicting their consciences. They do not want to be bothered with the horrors of bloodshed and injustice and oppression unless the injustice and oppression are happening to them, unless it is their own blood that is being shed. Then their consciousness is suddenly aroused. And then they beat their breasts, they curse the evil, and they cry out to heaven for the very justice they refused to others.

1,576. ~ EXTREMISM ~

Extremism is not the problem. The problem is extreme evil, and the only solution is extreme good. Jesus was an extremist. He gave Himself over to torture and death in order to conquer sin and evil. That was extreme. And He calls His disciples to follow the same extreme path. But most of us would rather settle into a comfortable and moderate "good" that sacrifices little and makes no demands. Yet what is truly good is always truly costly. Just as there is nothing moderate about wickedness, so there is nothing moderate about good. This is spiritual warfare, not a spiritual game. We must treat it as such. Moderation in Christian discipleship is no virtue; extremism in confronting evil is no vice.

1,577. ~ "PRO-CHOICE"? ~

Those who are truly, authentically, and consistently "pro-choice" would fight to ensure that women considering abortion had as much information as possible, both about the truth of abortion and about alternatives to abortion. Rather than shaming and shouting down Pro-Life activists, they would encourage women to receive the life-affirming information and assistance offered them. But they don't. Because they really don't care about "choice." They are merely servants of death and puppets of the capitalistic abortion industry, an industry that profits from pregnant women desperately in need of loving, life-affirming help. We know of what spirit they are, and it's certainly not the Spirit of peace, love, compassion, and truth. Their rhetoric of "choice" is nothing more than a euphemistic masquerading of bloodshed and murder. And like all lies and injustices and evils, theirs too will inevitably be burned up by the fires of truth, justice, peace, and love. Life will eternally conquer death, and wickedness will forever drown in the blood of the innocents.

1,578. ~ ORTHODOX CHRISTIAN THEOLOGY 101 ~

Orthodox Christian Theology 101:
Christ is greater than King David, greater than St. Paul, and greater than Emperor Constantine. Christ is greater than all the apostles and saints. The saints are saints because of their obedience

and faithfulness to the teachings and example of Our Lord. So if there is ever a discrepancy between something Jesus said and something anyone else said, always choose to obey the words of Jesus. And if there is ever a discrepancy between the actions of Jesus and the actions of anyone else, then always err on the side of emulating Jesus.

We will not be judged by whether or not we followed King David, St. Paul, or Emperor Constantine; we will be judged by whether or not we followed Christ.

1,579. ~ THE FIRST PRINCIPLE of PRIORITIZING THE CHILDREN ~

One of my first principles, which I am convinced is rooted in Our Lord's teachings and example, is that the love, care, protection, and interests of children are foundational to all aspects of authentic social justice. Any movement or ideology that is willing to harm innocent children in order to achieve the aims of adults is an unjust movement and an unchristian ideology. A society that does not prioritize the needs and welfare of children will never be a just and peaceful society.

1,580. ~ HUMANITY and FORGIVENESS ~

To be human is to need forgiveness. And to be human is to remain open to the possibility of forgiveness. No human is sinless, and no human is beyond the scope of God's mercy, grace, and redemption. We dehumanize ourselves if we think we don't need divine love, and we dehumanize ourselves if we think that God cannot possibly love us.

1,581. ~ THE VOICES GOD HEARS ~

If we don't lift our voices for the poor, the oppressed, and the voiceless unborn innocents during the week, then we have no right to sing our hollow hymns on Sunday. God is not impressed by the melody of the choir; He is rather attuned to the prophetic chords of conscious souls.

1,582. ~ HELL, UNIVERSALISM, and APOCATASTASIS ~

The Orthodox Church teaches that universal salvation is a legitimate Christian hope, but the Church condemns preaching it as a dogmatic certainty. I personally agree with those saints and Christian believers who expressed sound biblical reasons for the hope of the ultimate reconciliation of all created beings with their Creator. I personally believe that the victory of the Cross has atoned for all sins and conquered all evil. I believe with St. Paul that Christ has indeed reconciled all things to Himself (I Corinthians 1:19-20).

I also believe in hell. The scriptures speak of hell, and I believe hell is a serious reality. But I don't believe that hell is a physical place of conscious eternal torment. For one thing, such a notion contradicts the theological truth that God is omniscient and that His mercy endures forever (Psalm 136). There is no place where God is not. And where God is, His love is also present. Therefore I agree with St. Isaac the Syrian who said, *"The love of God is the fire of hell."* Those who reject God's love in this temporal life will experience His love as agony in the next. Yet there is nothing in Holy Scripture to indicate that human free will is negated at death. The departed soul may perhaps still cry out to receive the eternal love of Christ. That's one reason why we Orthodox offer prayers for the departed. God transcends time and space, and thus we offer our prayers for all souls with the conviction and hope that He hears and answers always.

As St. James the Apostle wrote: *"Is any among you afflicted? Let him pray. Is any merry? Let him sing psalms. Is any sick among you? Let him call for the elders of the Church; and let them pray over him, anointing him with oil in the name of the Lord: And the prayer of faith shall save the sick, and the Lord shall raise him up; and if he has committed sins, they shall be forgiven him. Confess your faults one to another, and pray one for another, that ye may be healed. The effectual fervent prayer of a righteous man availeth much. Elijah was a man subject to like passions as we are, and he prayed earnestly that it might not rain: and it rained not on the earth by the space of three years and six months. And he prayed again, and the heaven gave rain, and the earth brought forth her fruit." [James 5:13-18]*

So I believe both in the reality of hell and the reality of the Cross's victory over hell. I believe in the glorious paradoxical mystery that God created human beings with the freedom to reject Him forever, and yet His love is so powerful and pure that all volitional creatures will eventually and ultimately choose His love forever.

Our Lord said: *"Enter through the narrow gate. For wide is the gate and broad is the way that leads to destruction, and many enter through it. But small is the gate and narrow the way that leads to life, and only a few find it."* [St. Matthew 7:13-14] He also said, *"I am the door: by me if any man enter in, he shall be saved."* [St. John 10:9]

The path to heaven is indeed a narrow path, and Christ alone is the door to salvation. But nowhere in Scripture do we find any indication that the door will be permanently closed or that the narrow path will be forever blocked.

St. Paul writes: *"So when the corruptible shall has put on incorruption, and this mortal has put on immortality, then shall be brought to pass the saying that is written, Death is swallowed up in victory. O Death, where is your sting? O Hell, where is your victory?"* [1 Corinthians 15:54-55]

And Our Lord declared: *"I, if I be lifted up from the earth (Resurrected to heaven), I will draw all men unto me."* [St. John 12:32]

The Greek word "apocatastasis" (ἀποκατάστασις) means restoration or re-establishment. This word is found in the New Testament in the Book of Acts: *"Repent ye therefore, and be converted, that your sins may be blotted out, when the times of* refreshing shall come from the presence of the Lord; And he shall send Jesus Christ, which before was preached unto you: Whom the heaven must receive until the times of **restitution (ἀποκατάστᾰσις) of all things**, which God hath spoken by the mouth of all his holy prophets since the world began." [Acts 3:19-21]

Thus there is scriptural support for the belief that all of creation, and all created beings, will ultimately be divinely restored and eternally redeemed.

I maintain that if our theology leads us to renounce all violence, to hope in the universal redemption of all souls, all creatures, and all creation, and to emphasize the love of God to the exclusion of all hatred, fear, guilt, and shame, then we have truly understood the Gospel.

The King has prepared a banquet, and all are freely invited. Some receive the invitation with joy and immediately come running. But others say: "I don't need the King's food. In fact, I don't even believe the King exists. Enjoy your fictitious banquet; I will feed myself." But over time, these fools begin to starve. And the divine appetite with which they were originally imbued will inevitably override their recalcitrance and pride. The innate hunger for God shall prevail in their souls, and thus they too shall ultimately be found dining at Our Lord's eternal feast.

But it is important for me to clarify that this is simply my own humble opinion. I am not a priest, a deacon, or an Orthodox theologian. I am just one sinner working out my own salvation with fear and trembling. But I find comfort in the words of scripture and the words of the saints that point to this glorious universal hope.

"The greater part of Eastern teachers of the Church – from Clement of Alexandria to St. Maximos the Confessor – were supporters of Apokatastasis, of universal salvation and resurrection. Orthodox thought has never been suppressed by the idea of Divine wrath; and it never forgot the idea of Divine love. Most importantly, it did not define man from the point of view of Divine justice but from the idea of transfiguration and deification of humanity and cosmos."
~ Nikolai Berdyaev ~

Dear fellow American Christians: while you busy yourselves raising money to cross the oceans to save the "savage heathens," your own American neighbors are dying from hunger, suffering from homelessness, afflicted by untreated mental illnesses, brutalized by racism, intimidated and oppressed by a corrupt police system, and systematically murdered by legal abortion. I tell you that there is no more urgent mission field than this very land that you claim is a Christian country.

This does not mean that no American Christian is called to preach the Gospel overseas. Indeed, Christ commanded His disciples to *"Go into all the world and preach the Gospel." [St. Mark 16:15]* But we must be very careful not to view other nations and peoples as "savage heathens" while our own supposedly Christian nation is rife with inhumanity and injustices. We have a large beam in our own collective social eye, and it seems we should focus on removing that before busying ourselves with the splinters in other parts of the world.

1,584. ~ STILL "EMOTIONALLY DISTURBED" ~

"Anneewakee Treatment Center for Emotionally Disturbed Youth"...

I was sent there when I was 13 years old. I'm still not sure who or what objectively defined "emotionally disturbed," and no one bothered to explain it to me. And it didn't matter, because the $80 an hour was paid by my parents, not by me; so naturally Dr. Slaten (my atheistic psychiatrist) was sympathetic to their insights rather than mine. You know, don't bite the hand that feeds you.

Somewhere along the way I had wound up in "therapy" all by myself. My parents had begun going to marriage counseling when I was about 8 years old, and before long my sister and I were also brought in for "family counseling." But eventually I found myself going to "therapy" all by myself. No more marriage counseling. No more family counseling. Somehow it was determined that I alone had the problems and needed the help.

And that pretty much tells a child all he needs to know. All my parents' midnight screaming and cussing and alcoholism and violence and family dysfunction were somehow my fault. I must have caused it all. What other conclusion could be derived by a child?

So there I was, alone with Dr. Slaten, the godless psychiatric sage, week after week, as he tried to convince me that my faith in God was somehow responsible for all the trouble in my family and all the problems I had in school.

"Give up God and take this Ritalin," he essentially told me. "This will help you do better in school and it will bring peace to your family. And isn't that what you want? Haven't you caused them enough suffering? Your parents don't want to have to send you away again, and next time it won't be to a boarding school. Next time you'll be sent to Anneewakee. And I think you know what that means."

Talk about a threat. I knew exactly what it meant. I knew that Anneewakee was basically a juvenile detention center for drug addicts and criminals, of which I was neither. But I also knew that Dr. Slaten had a direct connection to Anneewakee, and if he could convince my parents to send me there then I knew that's exactly where I might end up. And while I can't prove it, I suspect he was well compensated for every child that was sent there by his recommendation.

But I wouldn't give into him. I refused to jump through his hoops or adhere to his atheistic philosophy. I never disrespected him, but I held my ground. And I can say without hesitation that I've never seen evil as clearly as I did in that callous, cold-hearted man. I'm sure he must have had a soul; but it was a dry, shriveled up soul that resulted in him being a shell of a human being with a shell of a human conscience.

I learned at a very young age that those who are truly psychologically disturbed often seek positions of power and authority behind which they can hide their own perversions and sicknesses. And I learned early on that the weakest and sickest among us often prey upon others in order to attain a semblance of order and control in their own lives. Those who are psychologically unstable often gravitate towards psychiatry, politics, or law enforcement. This is not to say that all psychiatrists, politicians, and policemen are power hungry and mentally disturbed people. But there is a significant correlation between psychological illness and the desire for authoritarian power. Those that cannot control anything else in their lives often seek ways to manipulate and control others.

So Dr. Slaten successfully persuaded my parents to send me away to this ostensible "treatment center" run by sadists and pedophiles. He won. He had the influence and the power, and he exercised it. I was just a child pleading in vain with my parents; but he had the shingle on his wall and the letters behind his name, so who were my parents to question his credentialed wisdom?

And so with tears in their eyes and broken hearts, my parents sent me away once again. It was not an easy decision for them. They knew better of course; but Dr. Slaten was a professional, an "expert." They had paid thousands of dollars over the years for his advice, and it's naturally difficult to act against such an investment. And Dr. Slaten understood that all too well. Thus all my pleading was in vain. All my thoughts and opinions and feelings and concerns made no difference. What does a child know compared to a learned PhD?

So off I went.

But God protected me from day one. Tears soaked my green robe as I sat in my solitary padded cell and prayed for strength. And God answered my prayers. And I survived. And I put the Ritalin pills under my tongue and pretended to swallow them. Then I hid them in my mattress and flushed them down the toilet when I was allowed to go to the bathroom. The godless man who tried to drive Jesus out of me with pills and lies and banishment to *"Anneewakee Treatment Center for Emotionally Disturbed Youth"* had only succeeded in driving me closer to the very God he denied.

I spent two and a half years at Anneewakee – three months locked away in a prison complex and the rest of the time in a rugged Florida panhandle wilderness. But my time there was easy compared to many people who suffered unspeakable torture and abuse from which they may never recover. God was with me every step of the way. And if I learned nothing else, I learned that no evil person and no evil circumstances can negate the faith I have in the love and goodness of my Creator.

But I confess, unapologetically, that I remain just as "emotionally disturbed" today as I was 35 years ago. I had emotions then, and I have emotions now. I was disturbed by the injustices I saw and experienced as a child, and I'm equally disturbed by the injustices I see and experience as an adult. And as unpleasant as it is, I pray that I will never become anesthetized to injustice or inured to evil. Let me suffer from anything except the soul crushing death of apathy and unbelief.

Dr. Slaten "counseled" me to stop talking about God. I told him he could prescribe any medication he wanted and send me to any school or "treatment facility" in the world, but I would never stop talking about God. So that atheist took me up on my challenge and did his best to drive God out of my spirit and my consciousness. But he only succeeded in making me love God more deeply; and all the suffering I endured only made me feel God's presence and love more strongly.

It was the Holy Spirit that gave me the wisdom to hide those Ritalin pills under my tongue and spit them out when they weren't looking. It was the Holy Spirit that empowered me to fend off the pedophiles and emerge from Anneewakee relatively unscathed. It was the Holy Spirit that enabled me to see through Dr. Slaten's deception and lies. Those godless "authorities" couldn't cure my faith in God back then, and they never will.

So yes, as I approach 50, I remain just as emotionally disturbed as I was when I was 15. And I dare to say that if you live in the same world I do and aren't emotionally disturbed by its inhumanity and injustices, then I think you are the one that's truly in need of psychological help.

Never let the fools fool you. Never presume that those with the power and authority possess inherent wisdom and grace. Cling to the truth with which you have been divinely imbued. Even if all the powers on earth criticize and condemn you, keep serving God, keep clinging to God, and keep loving others – *all* others, even those that would seek to drive God out of your life.

By grace I am still standing, still surviving, and still fighting this spiritual warfare. I realized long ago that it will never be easy. But the battle belongs to the Lord. And through the Cross and the Resurrection the victory has already been won. I simply need to keep living it out.

May God have mercy on Dr. Slaten, and may He have mercy on everyone else who sought to rob me of the spiritual truths that give life its meaning and purpose. I pity those people, and I pray for them. Perhaps they knew not what they were doing. I know my parents didn't know. There was no malicious intent on their part. I forgave them long ago. But I still pray to forgive Dr. Slaten and certain others who seemed to know exactly what they were doing. But I must find the grace to forgive them, because my own salvation depends upon it.

"Lord have mercy on us all." +++

1,585. ~ AESTHETIC TRANSCENDENCE ~

Great art weds heaven to earth. Aesthetic transcendence makes human flesh quiver and angels weep. There are rare occasions when eternity penetrates mortality through a sublime image, a sublime note, a sublime sentence, or a sublime taste. The genius of creativity is daring to grab God's attention and refusing to let go. The true artist – whether a painter, a musician, a poet, or a chef – always, on some level, infuses the temporal with the eternal.

1,586. ~ BETTER TO SUFFER from EVIL THAN TO BECOME EVIL ~

It is better to suffer from evil than to become evil. It is better to endure injustice than to be the cause of it. As Miguel de Cervantes wrote, *"God bears with the wicked, but not forever."*

1,587. ~ NONVIOLENCE and CHRISTIAN PROFESSION ~

If we say we will obey Christ's commands regarding nonviolence and love for enemies unless a sufficient threat arises to disregard His commands, then we are like vegetarians who say they only eat meat between meals. As meat eaters are not truly vegetarians, in spite of what they claim, so if we shed human blood we are not truly Christians, in spite of what we may profess.

1,588. ~ JUDAS, JESUS, and ME ~

If I was Judas I would betray Jesus. And if I was Jesus I would save Judas. But I'm not Judas and I'm not Jesus, yet they both live in me. But only Jesus will live in me forever. And that is the good news of the Gospel.

1,589. ~ TEMPORAL LOSSES and ETERNAL TRUTHS ~

I would rather lose today by defending eternal truths than be victorious with lies that damn my eternal soul.

1,590. ~ I'M ONLY BLEEDING ~

It's all right,
I'm not dying;
I'm only bleeding.
I'm surviving,
Yet I'm pleading...
Help me live!

1,591. ~ A GOSPEL ACCEPTABLE TO THE WORLD ~

The world will gladly accept a Christian gospel denuded of its imprecatory power. The world will gladly accept Christian love so long as it makes no demands of justice and truth. The world will gladly accept a crucified Christ who remains on the Cross – dead, powerless, and always unthreatening. The world will gladly accept a gospel that makes no judgments, has no standards, and invokes no imperatives. But the world cannot and will not accept the one and only authentic Gospel – the Gospel of truth, justice, power, and revolution – the Gospel of resurrection and redemption that incinerates all evil in its eternal wake.

1,592. ~ INSTABILITY ~

Some seek stability in socialism. Some seek stability in capitalism. But if you won't feed your neighbor and your neighbor won't feed you, then no political, religious, or social system can save you.

1,593. ~ THE MOST IMPORTANT THING TO ME ~

The most important thing to me is to hear my children's laughter, to see them smile, to know that they know that I love them. If everything else I strive to accomplish comes to naught, I will have succeeded if they feel and experience my love. My children are the truest, realest, and deepest proof of God's unfailing mercy. It is impossible for me to doubt my Lord's love, because I bathe everyday in the undeserved and unconditional love of my children. I don't have a bank account, and I literally have pennies to my name. But I am rich beyond measure when it comes to my children's love. I have failed in life in every possible way, but when I look at my children I realize that I have succeeded in all that truly matters.

1,594. ~ REBELLION, REVOLUTION, and RESURRECTION ~

Because Christ is Risen, we too can rise up. This is the greatest revolutionary truth there is. Any rebellion predicated on anything other than this will go no further than the grave.

1,595. ~ GRATITUDE for GOODNESS ~

I thank God for everyone who has fed my soul with good music, good art, good books, good food, good philosophy, good friends, and good times. I am thankful for all the good people who have turned me on to the many good things that make life worth living, that make life worth enduring. And most of all, I am thankful for the good people who have turned me on to the goodness of God, who is the beginning and end of all goodness and truth. So thank you good people! Keep sharing your goodness. I truly can't live without it; and I wouldn't want to.

1,596. ~ ART and AFFECTATION ~

If you are more concerned with impressing people with your talent rather than expressing an idea, then you will produce affectation rather than art. True creativity may not always be understood, but it is always felt – like the Creator's universe that defies rational comprehension yet nevertheless resonates in the soul.

Talent disconnected from truth is like a waterless well, like bread that can't be swallowed, like bullets that don't penetrate paper. Every artist has something to say, and that is what compels their creativity.

But there are many talented people who have never found their voice, who have no real conviction, and thus all they have to offer are lines and shapes and colors and notes that reflect nothing deeper than their own shallow egos.

1,597. ~ THE LABOR OF HOPE ~

How often we sow in hope
and reap in despair.
We toil, we dig, we plant
only to harvest sorrow.
We soak our pillows with tears
and offer prayers to the wind.
But our hope withers
and our hearts are fields of dust.

Why do we try?
What can we do?

Yet we put our hands back on the plow,
and we labor some more.
When hope abandons us,
we hope nevertheless.
Because there is a God who sees.
And in His eternal time,
our tears and sweat and blood and faith
will bear everlasting fruit –
sweet fruit that shall forever satisfy our souls.

But for now,
when we can no longer hope for ourselves,
others must hope for us.
And we too,
when others lose hope,
must somehow hope for them.
Because no one can labor for God's Kingdom alone.
No one can truly hope alone.
None of us can truly be saved alone.

Hope is a collective endeavor.
Hope is a cooperative work.

So please: help me to hope!
And I promise to hope also for you.

1,598. ~ GOD IS THE AUTHOR of REVOLUTION ~

Jesus lived, died, and rose again in rebellion against sin and death. The Prophet, Priest, and King rebelled against false prophecies, false religion, and godless kingdoms.

The Creator of the universe rebelled against the disorder and evil of a fallen world. God mounted an insurrection that began with His incarnation in the womb. He left the security of heaven to confront violence and hate with militant peace and sacrificial love. With a small band of followers, He revolutionized the cosmos and forever transformed human consciousness.

Satan pretends that he is the original rebel; but long before Lucifer was ever created, God was revolutionizing the darkness and bringing forth light, He was revolutionizing the void and bringing forth life. Eternally creating, eternally redeeming, eternally restoring, eternally loving – God is the Author of all true revolution, and Christ is the epitome of all true rebellion.

Our Lord's repetitive command was, "Follow me." And following Christ is not only the path of salvation, but it is also the path of revolution. Revolution and salvation are inseparable. We will not be saved apart from confronting evil, resisting oppression, denouncing violence, and loving "the least of these." We will not ascend to heaven above without laboring to lift our brothers and sisters out of their hell here on earth.

1,599. ~ IN AMERICA ~

In America the poor are blamed for poverty; war is the perpetual answer to the question of peace; political division is the only response to political division; the reality of racism is dismissed with rhetorical rationalizations; and the unborn are treated like weeds that need to be exterminated. So forgive me if I don't salute the flag or pledge my allegiance.

1,600. ~ **WHEN YOU TROD THROUGH BABYLON** ~

When you trod through Babylon
wear flowers in your hair.
Chant the Psalms
and don't bow to fear.
Make the sign of the Cross
and say your prayers.
For many revolutionaries
have become oppressors,
and there are many devils there.

1,601. ~ **WAR and REVOLUTION** ~

Wars are won by those who can inflict the most suffering, but revolution is won by those who can endure the most suffering. Those who kill for lies will eternally lose to those who are willing to die for truth.

1,602. ~ **THE TRUTH IS WITH THE "LEAST OF THESE"** ~

Whether the oppressor is Pharaoh, Herod, "Officer Friendly," Barack Obama, Donald Trump, or Planned Parenthood, I will always side with the victims rather than the victimizers. Regardless of deceptive political rhetoric or Machiavellian rationalizations, discipleship to Jesus Christ always means prioritizing the marginalized, the voiceless, the disinherited, and the oppressed. Whatever the issue or the cause may be, the truth is always with the "least of these." If confronted with moral ambiguities and social uncertainties, always err on the side of life affirmation. Always choose not to kill. Always stake your claim with those whose very lives are being threatened. Not only is this the path of basic Christian discipleship, but it is also the path of basic human survival.

1,603. ~ THE HEAVENLY CHILDREN'S TABLE ~

At the glorious heavenly banquet, we will all be seated at the children's table.

"Jesus called a little child to stand among them. 'Truly I tell you,' He said, 'unless you change and become like little children, you will never enter the kingdom of heaven.'" [St. Matthew 18:2-3]

1,604. ~ NO APOLOGY for A MILITANT PACIFISM ~

Sometimes I worry that my condemnations of war and the military may be a bit too strident. But then I meditate upon the innocent children who are tortured and killed in acts of war, and I realize that I have nothing for which to apologize. It is impossible to be too harsh in condemning acts that result in the severed limbs and burning flesh of innocent children and babies. It is impossible to be too harsh in condemning a military that commits such atrocities. It is just like abortion: how can we be too harsh in decrying the evil of murdering an innocent child in the womb? And I certainly will not apologize for unequivocally stating that acts of militarism, warfare, and abortion are diametrically opposed to the Gospel of Jesus Christ. No Christian should have anything to do with such atrocities. If anything, I fear that I have not been adamant enough in condemning the deliberate destruction of human life. So I pray for a militant pacifism that will conquer this apathetic passivity towards the injustices of warfare and killing. When you wage war against peace, you wage war against Christ Himself.

"I am not only a pacifist, but a militant pacifist. I am willing to fight for peace. Nothing will end war unless the people themselves refuse to go to war." ~ Albert Einstein ~

1,605. ~ LOVE IS A DANGEROUS THING ~

Love does not always come with smiles and kisses and flowers and happiness. Sometimes it comes with splinters and thorns and suffering and crucifixion. Love is a dangerous thing. As Dostoevsky wrote, *"Love in reality is a harsh and dreadful thing compared to love in dreams."* And yet, what is life without love? I'd rather suffer with love than die having never truly lived.

1,606. ~ RISE UP ~

Resist oppression, rebel against injustice, rise up to oppose violence and hate with peace and love. They can crucify us but they can never conquer us. Our blood and tears water the earth with truth and rights. Our righteous struggles will echo in eternity. Life over death! Good over evil! Christ over Satan! Rise up and live this truth today and every day!

1,607. ~ VIOLENCE and ANARCHISM ~

Violence is the fundamental and most effective tool of the state. If anarchists truly seek a peaceful, free, and just society, then they must first reject and renounce the fundamental tool of state oppression. Since anarchism is opposition to coercive power and control, authentic anarchism must necessarily be pacifistic. Seeking to subvert coercive power structures by violent means will only result in revolutionaries assuming the role of the oppressors they seek to depose. Thus violence is always counter-revolutionary and ultimately opposed to authentic anarchism.

1,608. ~ REBELLION is MY ANSWER ~

I have often had people say: "I agree with your political and social critiques, but what is the solution?" And I always answer the same way: *Rebel!*

Rebel against oppression.
Rebel against violence.
Rebel against racism.
Rebel against corruption.
Rebel against politics.
Rebel against death.
Rebel against propaganda.
Rebel against injustice.
Rebel against negativity.
Rebel against deception.
Rebel against lies.
Rebel against idolatry.
Rebel against hatred.
Rebel against inhumanity.
Rebel against despair.

Rebel against everything that sets itself up against the knowledge of God. (II Corinthians 10:5)

That's why this book is titled, *REBEL SONG*. Inherent in all of my social and political criticisms is the call to proactive, positive, and militantly nonviolent Christian resistance.

1,609. ~ ARGUING THAT "PACIFISM DOESN'T WORK" ~

Rejecting pacifism by arguing that it doesn't work is like refusing to cut your grass and blaming the lawnmower. Pacifism, like lawnmowers, only works when used. It's impossible to cut down the weeds of violence without taking up the mantle of peace.

1,610. ~ KEEPING AMERICA SAFE and FREE! ~

We kill people who kill people to prove that killing people is wrong. We incarcerate nonviolent law breakers to prove that we are a just and lawful society. We encourage usury, capitalism, and the exploitation of the poor to prove that the rich can always become richer in this country. We violently deny life, birth, and freedom to the weak and the voiceless to prove how liberated and empowered our women are. We honor our dead soldiers by recruiting more and more innocent young people to kill and die in our ever expansive wars. We spend more money on militarism and the prison industrial complex than we do on eradicating poverty and homelessness, because by God, we're keeping America safe and free!

1,611. ~ THE "YES" and "NO" of CHRISTIAN PACIFISM ~

Christian pacifism is as much of a "yes" to proactive, sacrificial love as it is a "no" to violence and hate.

1,612. ~ A PENTECOST MEDITATION ~

Ten years ago, on this blessed Pentecost Sunday, our family was baptized into the Ethiopian Orthodox Tewahedo Church. God gave me the baptismal name, Gebre Menfes Kidus, which means "Servant of the Holy Spirit."

My goodness, how I have struggled and failed to live according to my divine calling, according to my divine name! I am truly the weakest Orthodox Christian I know. I read and study and write a lot, but my actions lag woefully behind my words and convictions.

I have gone from being a super zealous Orthodox convert to someone who misses Divine Liturgy more often than not. But after ten years God has not abandoned me. By His grace I still cling to the

Cross and cling to the Orthodox Faith, even though sometimes I feel like I'm barely hanging on.

So say a prayer for me, and please pray for my family.

The Holy Spirit has descended upon His children, and He is not so fickle as to flee whenever we sin, struggle, and doubt. Rather, he pours His grace and love upon us all the more, pulling us nearer to His bosom the further we go astray. And perhaps that's why I feel so close to God at times, because I am so prone to wander, so inclined to give up the fight.

Lord, bathe me in your Holy Spirit. Cleanse me and renew my strength. I still have so much work to do.

1,613. ~ IF YOU WANT TO GET TO HEAVEN ~

If you want to get to heaven, you've got to dig into the earth. You have to toil, sweat, and bleed with your neighbors. You have to pray with dirt on your soul and tears in your eyes. You have to carry your cross; and more importantly, you have to help others carry theirs.

1,614. ~ VIOLENCE and IDOLATRY ~

Violence and idolatry are inextricably connected. To shed the blood of living human icons fashioned with the very breath of God, for any reason – even in defense of the Church – is idolatry.

To kill, even for a just cause, is to elevate an idea, an ideology, or an institution above the sanctity of human life. It is the ultimate idolatry and the most egregious form of iconoclasm. It is also a denial of the Resurrection, the fundamental theological hope of the Christian Faith; because it assumes that the physical body and the temporal life must be preserved at all cost.

When a professing Christian deliberately kills, they reject the Gospel of peace and salvation; they act diametrically opposed to Our

Lord who commands us to lead people to eternal life, not send them to physical deaths. As St. John Chrysostom said, *"Our duty is to make the dead to live, not to make the living die."*

One must simply choose the Cross or the sword. We cannot carry both. And what we choose will determine our salvation. Will we usurp the angelic role of divine avengers, or will we obey Our Lord's clear command to love our enemies and leave vengeance to God? Will we kill to preserve our earthly existence, or will we die to gain eternal life?

1,615. ~ REFLECTIONS on IRELAND'S VOTE TO LEGALIZE ABORTION ~
[5/25/2018]

We will gladly fight for our own rights. We will suffer and die for our own freedoms and our own liberation. We will organize, unite, and act in solidarity to pursue justice for ourselves. But if others are suffering, if others are oppressed, if others are being denied their lives, their freedom, and their rights, then we aren't really too concerned about it.

Bobby Sands and nine others starved themselves to death to protest British oppression in Northern Ireland. Their sacrificial protests helped change the course of history. But now that Ireland has legalized the violent slaughter of unborn babies, I wonder what the Pro-Life protests will be. What sort of opposition will be mounted? What sacrifices will be made in pursuit of justice? What subversive acts of rebellion and resistance will be undertaken? What extreme measures will be enacted to defend the innocent? What radical confrontation will there be against an unjust system that preys upon the weak and the voiceless?

I suspect the only response will be tears and prayers and laments like this one. After all, our own lives will remain largely unaffected; and it's not our children who are going to be mercilessly killed. So we will probably carry on as usual.

And that's what makes abortion so difficult to fight. It is human nature to rise up and raise hell when our own lives and rights are at stake, yet we flee from confronting evils done to someone else. We clearly see the injustices done to ourselves while remaining blind and indifferent to the injustices done to others. And I think we will surely be judged for such selfishness and apathy. For as Our Lord clearly said, *"Whatsoever you have done unto the least of these, you have done it unto Me."[St. Matthew 25:40]*

This is a dark day, and we have once again ushered in the darkness ourselves. Innocent blood will now be legally shed, and there is celebration in the streets. Yet as Tolstoy said, "God sees, but waits."

"There is a way that seems right to a man, but the end thereof is death." [Proverbs 14:12]

"There are two ways, one of life and one of death, and there is a great difference between the two ways." [The Didache 1:1]

"A voice is heard in Ramah, mourning and great weeping, Rachel weeping for her children and refusing to be comforted, because they are no more." [Jeremiah 31:15]

1,616. ~ THE GOSPEL IS BLOODY ~

You can't preach the Cross without preaching nails and thorns and splinters and scars. The Gospel is downright bloody. The road to heaven is an agonizing trod, but Jesus accompanies us every step of the way. There is grace in the pain.

1,617. ~ PRAY FOR THOSE WHO HAVE BEEN CRUEL TO YOU ~

Pray for people who have said and done cruel things to you. Try to understand that it might not even be their fault. Many people suffer from illnesses and circumstances beyond their control, and it may cause them to lash out at others who are not to blame. Yes, it hurts when people say mean and hateful things to us. I am a sensitive soul, and such things bother me more than they should. But I try to step back from it, examine my conscience, and then pray for those who have spewed venom and hate my way. I also try to use it as a lesson be more cautious with my own words.

I will never apologize for attacking injustice and evil in the harshest terms possible, but I must be careful not to attack individuals in the same way. Challenge them and confront them? Sure. Just as I too need to be challenged and confronted. But I don't ever want to personally disparage or demean someone else. That never accomplishes anything positive.

1,618. ~ REMNANT ~

There is a remnant, a divine remnant, a revolutionary remnant that follows truth when the masses follow lies, that pursues peace when the masses pursue war, that affirms life when the masses legislate death. God has His remnant – small, simple, prophetic souls who dare to proclaim right in a world gone wrong.

1,619. ~ THE SIMPLICITY of THE GOSPEL ~

The Gospel is pretty simple really. It's very difficult to truly live out, but it's not that hard to understand. The words of the saints and the witness of the martyrs throughout history are also pretty clear – deep, rich, and challenging, but eminently comprehendible. They affirm and accentuate the clarity of Our Lord's divine message.

Heresies are usually the result of human intellect trying to reduce sacred mysteries to mortal rationale. Rather than accepting and obeying the simplicity of sacred truth, the human instinct is to alter the truth and reduce it to something palatable to the sinful flesh and the temporal mind. We corrupt the simplicity of love with a thousand qualifications; we reduce the truth of peace to countless conditional demands; and we turn the mystery of faith into metastasizing sets (and sects) of systematic syllogisms.

Jesus tells us to love our enemies, and we find every reason to explain why He doesn't really mean it. Jesus tells us to put away the sword and take up our cross, but we find every reason to try and carry both. Jesus tells us the Kingdom of God is among us, yet we find every reason to continue clinging to the kingdoms of this world.

The Gospel is blessed good news, glorious news, the greatest news humanity will ever know. But we corrupt the Gospel and turn it into yet another human dogma of division and discord. The Incarnate God lived, died, and rose again to unify us with His peace, love, and grace. But we have taken the Name of Jesus and used it as a weapon of violence, hate, and condemnation.

In His holy Name we wage war, we exploit the poor, we foment political division, we promote nationalistic idolatry, we execute our neighbors, and we slaughter the unborn. And we dare to do so with the Bible in our hands and His very Body and Blood on our tongues.

We have forsaken the simplicity of the Gospel for earthly idolatries, seeking salvation in worldly politics and mortal philosophies. What fools we are: believing we can kill and vote our way to heaven.

1,620. ~ TO ALL PEACE WARRIORS, LIFE AFFIRMERS, & JUSTICE SEEKERS ~

To all my fellow peace warriors, life affirmers, and justice seekers: never lose hope! The battle belongs to the Lord, and those who fight against His truth will ultimately lose. So keep praying, keep struggling, and keep hoping. Keep loving your enemies, and keep loving even those who are committed to evil. Because love is eternally victorious. Christ is Risen! And every entity and force opposed to this truth is defeated at the outset. As the world gets darker, God's light shines even brighter! And in His mystical time, all temporal darkness will inevitably be swallowed up by His eternal love.

1,621. ~ EULOGY for MY FRIEND and BROTHER: CHRISTIAN SHEETZ ~
[Delivered at Indian Springs First Baptist Church, June 9, 2018]

I met Christian at Bible College in the early 90s. We formed an instant bond over our mutual love for Alabama Football and great music. But our friendship grew deeper and richer over the years, and he became one of my best friends in this world. It's hard to believe he's gone, but we know that he's with the Lord, and we will carry him with us always in our hearts.

In St. Paul's letter to the Philippians, he gave this exhortation: *"Work out your salvation with fear and trembling." [Philippians 2:12]*

I watched Christian work out his salvation over the years. His life was not easy. Like many of us, he struggled with his faith. At times he questioned God and questioned his value and purpose in life. Since I too struggle with similar doubts, it was a blessing to be able to share our hardships and pain with one other. But throughout his difficulties Christian never abandoned his faith. He continued to struggle valiantly, following Christ through good times and bad, and taking courageous steps to change the course of his life when necessary.

One of the many things I admired about Christian was the battle he waged against his addictions. A few years ago he had fallen prey to the darkness of chemical dependency. It deeply affected his view of God and his view of himself. But by the grace of God he refused to abandon his faith or give up on life. He took the brave step to enter rehab where he worked hard to conquer his demons and come out stronger, healthier, wiser, and happier. He cultivated a positive view of God, himself, and others that was quite infectious. That took tremendous courage, and it was a tribute to the strength of his character. I learned a lot by watching Christian struggle and overcome many things throughout his life. I pray that God would grant me the same grace to persevere and fight the spiritual warfare in my own life as well.

I also watched Christian's theology and convictions evolve over the years. Jesus became increasingly important and central to everything he lived and believed. He followed the admonition of the Beatitudes: *"Blessed are the peacemakers, for they shall be called the children of God." [St. Matthew 5:9]*

Christian became a true peacemaker. With his words, his actions, his philosophy, and his friendship, Christian honored the Prince of Peace and helped bring light to the darkness of this world. He admonished us to forsake the idolatry of violence and politics and killing and hate. He urged us to place our faith in the Kingdom of God rather than the kingdoms of this world. Not too long ago he wrote these challenging words on his Facebook page:

"Our enemy is Satan, and our shores were invaded in the Garden of Eden. Regretfully, we tried to handle that on our own, and the world has been hell ever since. In our modern day we Christians must ask ourselves: are we going to look to the United States for protection or to God?"

Following Jesus and living out the Gospel of Peace will bring us into conflict with this world. I watched Christian face ridicule and resistance because of his unconditional commitment to divine peace and true Christian love. I saw him face insult and opprobrium from political ideologues on both the left and the right. But Christian remained undeterred, growing closer and deeper in his relationship with Our Lord, the Lord who came not to kill but to bestow life abundant and eternal.

The essence of the Gospel is love for God and love for others. And there is no doubt that Christian truly loved God and truly loved other people. When the tornado devastated Tuscaloosa a few years ago, Christian went and spent a week there assisting with the recovery and restoration efforts. If there was an opportunity for Christian to help and serve someone else, he was eager to do so. Christian donated his body to science, proving that even in death he continues to serve humanity.

The help and encouragement he personally gave me over the years meant more to me than he probably ever realized. He supported my writing, promoted my books, and went out of his way to let me know that he had been deeply encouraged and influenced by my words and ideas. As I faced opposition and even lost friends because of my radical Christian philosophy, Christian let me know that my labors were not in vain. He gave me affirmation, and he encouraged me to continue writing and proclaiming the Gospel of peace and the Kingdom of heaven. Had it not been for his sincere encouragement and support, I may have given up writing years ago. I may have given up on many other things as well.

Christian's favorite movie was *We Are Marshall*, the true story of a football program and a community struggling to recover from a tragic plane crash that killed 75 people, including 35 members of the Marshall University football team in 1970. The movie is a portrayal of humanity's struggle to maintain hope, to find purpose, and to rise up from the ashes of despair. When I think about Christian's life – his own pains and struggles and ultimate perseverance – it is easy to see why this was his favorite movie.

A few other things about Christian:

~ His favorite TV show was *The Andy Griffith Show*.

~ His favorite musicians were Bob Marley and Carlos Santana.

~ He enjoyed smoking his pipe, and his favorite pipe tobacco was Captain Black.

~ Christian also loved cats, and one of his most beloved cats was named "Saban," named for Alabama football coach Nick Saban.

~ Christian also had a wonderful sense of humor, and he especially loved a good dose of scathing sarcasm.

~ And of course, anyone that knows Christian knows that next to his love for Jesus and his love for his family and friends, Alabama Football was truly his greatest passion.

Laughter is extremely important in life, and Christian always reminded me to laugh. You can't take yourself or life to seriously, or you'll go insane. Sometimes I'd call Christian or he'd call me, and we'd just start laughing. No words needed to be said. Laughter truly is healing medicine, and Christian's sense of humor was always a balm to my soul.

Christian drowned in a horrible kayaking accident, and that will always grieve those of us who loved him. But I must say that as unfortunate as his death was, I don't consider it a tragic death. Christian died having found peace in his life. He died doing something he loved with someone he loved. His marriage to Mary had given him tremendous joy, and I want to thank Mary for giving him the love and support he truly deserved. Mary, I want you to know what a true blessing you were to Christian. He spoke often of the happiness and peace he had found in his relationship with you.

I don't know why God chose to take him home at this particular time or in this particular fashion, but I can only think that it's because Christian had fulfilled his purpose and lived out his calling. And even if his only purpose in life was to befriend and love a struggling sinner like me, then he more than accomplished his calling.

I want to share a lyric from one of Christian's favorite Santana songs, a song called *"Somewhere in Heaven"*:

"Somewhere in heaven, there is a place waiting for you and for me. He made a promise, He shed every drop of blood, He died on the Cross so we'd be free."

Because of his faith in Christ and the struggle he lived out by clinging to the Cross, I know that our brother Christian Sheetz is truly free today. And that same freedom is calling out to all of us. May God grant us the grace to also one day say with our brother that we too have *"fought the good fight, that we have finished the race, that we have kept the faith." [II Timothy 4:7]*

Christian and I often spoke of "Babylon." The clearest definition of Babylon can be found in Revelation 18. I won't read it here, but it is essentially a biblical metaphor for confusion, evil, injustice, and oppression. Babylon represents anything and everything that sets itself up against the truth, peace, and salvation of Christ's Kingdom.

One of Bob Marley's most famous songs is called *Exodus,* and it urges the people of God to move out of Babylon and ever forward towards Zion. Christian's life was an exodus from pain, addiction, and despair, and towards peace, freedom, and salvation. Not too long ago he shared these reflections on his Facebook page:

"To be completely honest, I fear the process of death. However, once that is over, I will never have to live in fear again. It will be goodbye Babylon!"

I thank God for my brother Christian Sheetz. I will miss him more than words can express. But I believe in the fellowship of the Body of Christ, and I believe in the mystical communion of the Saints departed. So I know he is with us always. And by grace we too will one day make our own exodus from Babylon and into the Kingdom of Zion, where every tear shall be wiped away and suffering shall be no more.

Proverbs 18:21 reads: *"One who has unreliable friends soon comes to ruin, but there is a friend who sticks closer than a brother."*

The Book of Sirach states: *"A faithful friend is a sturdy shelter: he that has found one has found a treasure. There is nothing so precious as a faithful friend, and no scales can measure his excellence. A faithful friend is an elixir of life." [Sirach 6:14-16]*

And Psalm 132 says: *"Behold now, what is so good or so pleasant as for brothers to dwell together in unity? It is like fragrant oil running down upon the beard, the beard of Aaron, running down upon the border of his garment. It is like the dew of Hermon, running down upon the mountains of Zion."*

Thank you Jesus for loving me enough to give me a true friend and brother like Christian Sheetz.

I know that Christian would want me to end with these two phrases:

"ROLL TIDE!"

"CHRIST IS RISEN!"

~ Amen ~

1,622. ~ POLITICS of THE PALATE ~

The richest gourmet food was born from the proletariat palate. Food – like art and music – is inherently political. It emanates from the passions, the struggles, and the sensibilities of the people. As much as the aristocracy tries to separate it, monopolize it, and profit from it, they nevertheless taste the blood, sweat, and tears of desperation and survival. As the rich man dines on his sweetbreads, he inescapably ingests conviction into his soul.

1,623. ~ OUTLAWS IN BABYLON ~

The children of Zion are outlaws in Babylon. Those who belong to the Kingdom of God will always be viewed as subversives and insurrectionists by the kingdoms of men. We are spiritual revolutionaries – rejected, persecuted, outcast, and abandoned by the laws and gods and governments of this temporal realm. But rebellion against injustice is our divine passport, and confrontation with evil is proof of our heavenly citizenship. So we embrace our status as strangers, as pilgrims who are merely passing through this terrestrial vale, blazing the torch of Christ's love as we trod toward our salvation.

1,624. ~ BECAUSE CHRIST IS FIRST, HUMANITY COMES FIRST ~

For the record: I don't want children to be ripped away from their mothers at the border or at the abortion mill. I refuse to prioritize manmade nationalistic boundaries or the euphemism of "reproductive rights" over and above the sanctity of families and the inherent right to life. When the law supports social justice and affirms intrinsic human value, then I will support it. But when laws are unjust and undermine life, then I will condemn and oppose them – regardless of the constitutions, flags, or governments that undergird them.

I'm not sure where that places me on the political spectrum, but as long as I'm on the side of the Gospel then I don't care if I'm anathematized by the right or the left.

Because Christ is first, humanity comes first. And therefore I stand opposed to everything unjust and anything inhumane, regardless of its legality, constitutionality, or ideological purity. If it divides families, harms children, destroys life, and causes humanity to suffer, then it is wrong – despite what any law or government may say.

1,625. ~ TWO EQUAL MISTAKES IN INTERPRETING THE GOSPEL ~

There are two equal mistakes in interpreting the Gospel:

1) To believe that the Incarnate God who lived, suffered, died and rose again to conquer sin and death was somehow not the greatest revolutionary who ever lived.

2) To pervert the subversive, nonviolent, revolutionary love of Jesus into yet one more political ideology of worldly violence and humanistic hubris.

1,626. ~ HERETICAL THEOLOGY and POLITICAL CORRUPTION ~

The dehumanization of others is the surest indication of heretical theology and political corruption. To dehumanize anyone based upon race, religion, gender, age, sexual orientation, nationality, political affiliation, or birth status is to blaspheme God and commit crimes against humanity. Orthodox theology and social justice demand the preservation of human life and human rights from the womb to the tomb!

Babylon's godless democracies will never produce righteous rulers. As long as we continue to trust our own selfish collective will and vain desires more than the divine will and order, then our laments about the corruption and evil of our elected leaders will ring hollow to God. The fact is that our rulers are not righteous because we refuse to be ruled by righteousness. Period.

PSALM 101 – A Psalm of David:
I sing of love and justice;
to you, LORD, I sing praise.
I follow the way of integrity;
when will you come to me?
I act with integrity of heart
within my household.
I do not allow into my presence anyone who speaks perversely.
I hate wrongdoing;
I will have no friendship with those who act shamefully.
May the devious heart keep far from me;
the wicked I will not tolerate.
Whoever slanders a neighbor in secret
I will reduce to silence.
Haughty eyes and arrogant hearts
I cannot endure.
I look to the faithful of the land
to be my companions.
Whoever follows the way of integrity
they alone can enter into my service.
No one who practices deceit
can remain within my court.
No one who speaks falsely
can be among my advisors.
8 Morning after morning I clear all the wicked from the land,
to rid the LORD's city of all evildoers.

1,628. ~ RUN AWAY ~

We can run away.
We can run from it all.
But the faster we run,
the quicker we'll fall.
We can escape to space,
or flee to earth's edge.
But when we reach the end,
We'll still meet ourselves.

1,629. ~ THIS IS WHAT I SAW ~

I looked to the heavens
and this is what I saw:
A midnight tapestry
with a billion stars...
A blinding sun
that births blue skies...
Hawks soaring
on clouds so soft...
Strange night lights
and mysteries of dawn...
And manmade things
that litter it all.

Confront the unholy trinity of ignorance, fear, and hate with the power of peace, love, and truth. Don't be a pawn of the Babylon system that feeds upon folly and division. Make sure your anger is righteous, and then channel your anger into positive and redemptive actions. Revolution involves individual as well as social transformation. Too many of us expect justice to magically become a reality without intense self-examination, sacrificial love, and an unwavering commitment to the divine principles upon which justice is established. If we yell, chant, and march without love in our hearts, then we are nothing but clanging cymbals that only contribute to the discordant cacophony of Babylon.

1,631. ~ THE KINGDOM of GOD IS A POLITICAL KINGDOM ~

Make no mistake: the Kingdom of God is indeed a political Kingdom. The question is not whether or not to avoid politics, the question is which kingdom will guide our politics.

God descended from heaven and came to live here on earth. He calls His disciples to follow Him, and that call is most certainly a call to engage society with the divine imperatives of justice, peace, and human rights. But nowhere in the Gospels do we see Our Lord commanding His disciples to embrace worldly political ideologies, to pledge allegiance to earthly states, or to hate and do violence to those who are wed to different temporal political philosophies than our own. And nowhere do we see Our Lord commanding His disciples to force the will of God on unbelievers through the compulsion of democracy or the compulsion of the sword.

We cannot serve two masters. We must choose the Kingdom of God or the kingdoms of men. Through the Incarnation, the Kingdom of God came to earth. King Jesus Christ has conquered sin and death. He has liberated the captives. He has redeemed sinners and reconciled all things to Himself. But do we really believe it? Because if we did, then we wouldn't place our hope in perishing earthly kingdoms and feckless earthly politics that contradict the Kingdom of God.

And if you argue that Christians aren't living in the "real world" unless they vote and support godless governments, then you disparage the Incarnate God who lived, suffered, and died to transform the realities of earth with the realities of heaven.

1,632. ~ DEMANDS ~

We demand pothole free streets. We demand high speed internet. We demand our cable TV, our "safe spaces," and our functional democracy. We demand free sex without syphilis and sin without consequences. We demand countless self-indulgent "rights," but we don't demand justice. And the justice we deny, spurn, and ignore today is the justice that will haunt us in eternity. What we demand will either deliver us or damn us.

1,633. ~ LOVE IS STRENGTH ~

Hate begets hate, so let us not fall prey to this demonic cycle. We have to love our enemies and bless those that curse us. (St. Matthew 5:44) That's part of the cross we are called to carry as Orthodox Christians. (St. Luke 9:23) We must desire the repentance of the wicked, just as we ourselves must repent of our own sins and beseech God's mercy. (St. Mark 1:15; Psalm 136) We must remember the book of Jonah: Nineveh, that "exceedingly great and wicked city," repented in sackcloth and ashes; and God forgave their sins and blessed them abundantly. (St. Matthew 12:41) Christ came to redeem humanity and to reconcile all things to Himself. (Colossians 1:20) The evildoers are not beyond the hope of salvation. (II Peter 3:9) So we must pray for them. (St. Matthew 5:44) And yes, we must also confront and rebuke them; for righteous confrontation is also part of the Gospel. (Titus 1:13) But we must love the wicked nonetheless. (I Peter 4:8)

Love is not weakness; love is strength!

1,634. ~ NEVER GIVE UP! ~

Never give up on life and never give up hope. Never! Live until life kills you, and then live again forever in the Creator's eternal embrace. Hope until hope kills you, and then bathe forever in the faith of Christ's saving love.

1,635. ~ IF WE ARE SELF-ABSORBED ~

If the writer, musician, or artist seems self-absorbed, it's only because we are crying out to humanity to help us bear our pain.

1,636. ~ PRINCIPLES and IDOLATRY ~

If we love moral principles – even if they are divine, true, immutable moral principles – more than we love God and our human brothers and sisters, then we have turned moral principles into an idol and we have blasphemed Christ.

1,637. ~ CHRIST ALONE IS OUR COMMANDER IN CHIEF ~

Our Lord commands us to love our enemies. So how can we vote for any person or support any political system that promotes the acceptability or supposed necessity of killing one's enemies? Call us unpatriotic, but our allegiance is to Christ alone – without apology.

So you'll have to conduct your killing without us. And we anticipate that you may eventually kill us too in defense of your idolatrous states, your godless philosophies, and your demonic political parties. But we are prepared to die for peace. We are prepared to die for the Kingdom that endures forever. Christ alone is our Commander in Chief, and we refuse to serve any other.

1,638. ~ EVIDENCE of A LOST ARGUMENT ~

When they call you names and falsely accuse you, it's evidence that they've lost the argument. But continue to speak the truth, and love them anyway, because truth and love can never lose.

1,639. ~ POLITICS and THE PRINCE of PEACE ~

Too many Christians place way too much importance on political leaders and the political system. Those of us who profess the Prince of Peace have become despondent, we've come to despise one another, we've become consumed with hatred and rage because of our trust in godless political ideologies and corrupt politicians that cannot save. If the followers of Jesus would unite to truly live out the Gospel, then we would denude these oppressive political powers and we would affect authentic and lasting change. But instead, we trade our salvation and hope for a mess of political pottage. And then we dare to complain about the hell that we ourselves have manufactured.

1,640. ~ THE ONLY TRULY PRO-LIFE POSITION ~

The "consistent life ethic" is the only truly Pro-Life position. To be authentically Pro-Life and authentically Christian is to care about the sanctity, dignity, and rights of all human lives from the womb to the tomb. It is not a question of which particular human rights abuse is worse than another. The injustice done to families and children at the border is merely another manifestation of a wicked American government that has always oppressed certain groups of people throughout its history – from slavery, to Native American massacres, to segregation and Jim Crow laws, to abortion on demand and the oppression of so-called "illegal" immigrants. Apart from an unwavering commitment to the "consistent life ethic," our moral outrage will always be selective, myopic, and ultimately unproductive.

1,641. ~ THE DELUSION of DEMOCRACY ~

Democracy is the delusional belief that replacing old evils with new evils is "progress."

1,642. ~ RESIST BABYLON'S WARS ~

Cold wars, political wars, culture wars, bloody wars... the Babylon powers are depending upon our participation. Babylon can't wage war without us. So let us mount the resistance of peace, love, compassion, and humanity. Babylon is hell bent on self-destruction. Let us have nothing to do with such folly and evil, lest we too be destroyed by the brimstone that Babylon invites upon its own hubristic head.

1,643. ~ WHERE WILL WE GO WHEN WE DIE? ~

Where will we go when we die? Heaven or hell? The question is like asking where will we go right now, today, this very moment. Wherever we go we will nevertheless be. Heaven will not release us from ourselves, and hell will not destroy ourselves. It is not the location of our souls, but rather the condition of our souls that determines heaven and hell and everything in between.

As Bob Marley said, *"You're running and you're running and you're running away, but you can't run away from yourself!"*

And as Tolstoy wrote, *"It is not the place we occupy that is important, but the direction in which we are moving."*

1,644. ~ ON COMMUNITY and RELATIONSHIP ~

Nothing truly great was ever accomplished alone. Even the Savior of the world was born from a mother, raised by a father, accompanied by disciples, and inseparably united with the Holy Trinity. And when Adam lived in perfect sinless communion with his Creator, God nevertheless said, *"It is not good for man to be alone."* *[Genesis 2:18]*

It is a great temptation to think that we can accomplish more by ourselves than we can with community. But God has ordained relationship, and as difficult as it often is, we all desperately need it. That's why family, friendships, and the Church are so vitally important.

Community is never easy; but if we truly tried to live even a single day without relying on our fellow human beings, we would realize just how truly powerless we are alone.

In one of his most famous sermons, Dr. Martin Luther King, Jr. said:

"It really boils down to this: that all life is interrelated. We are all caught in an inescapable network of mutuality, tied into a single garment of destiny. Whatever affects one directly, affects all indirectly. We are made to live together because of the interrelated structure of reality. Did you ever stop to think that you can't leave for your job in the morning without being dependent upon most of the world? You get up in the morning and go to the bathroom and reach over for the sponge, and that's handed to you by a Pacific Islander.

You reach for a bar of soap, and that's given to you at the hands of a Frenchman. And then you go into the kitchen to drink your morning coffee and that's poured into your cup by a South American. And maybe you want tea: that's poured into your cup by a Chinese. Or maybe you desire to have cocoa for breakfast, and that's poured into your cup by a West African. And then you reach over for your toast, and that's given to you at the hands of an English-speaking farmer, not to mention the baker. And before you finish eating breakfast in the morning, you've depended on more than half the world. This is the way our universe is structured. It is interrelated in its quality. We aren't going to have peace on earth until we recognize this basic fact of the interrelated structure of all reality."

1,645. ~ WEALTH, POVERTY, and MIRACLES ~

It's interesting that many with an abundance of wealth often lecture the poor about the danger of running out of resources. "We can't just give you 'free stuff' – i.e. food and housing and healthcare – because eventually we'll run out of capital."

And I can understand how the godless would promote such a self-centered, callous, and exploitative concept; but it really disturbs me when I see professing Christians adopting the same cruel mindset. When Jesus commanded His disciples to feed the multitudes, He didn't lecture them about making sure everyone earned their right to eat. And when He multiplied the loaves and the fishes, He didn't lecture the disciples about making sure people didn't abuse the miracle.

But somehow, many professing Christians today feel that Jesus is no longer in the provision business, no longer in the miracle business. So rather than doing all they can to spread their wealth to others, they horde their wealth and justify it in the name of fiscal responsibility and economic pragmatism.

And maybe that's why we don't see many miracles today. Divine miracles are predicated upon divine obedience. And the first principle of divine obedience is to love our God by truly loving our neighbors.

The sky does not dry up by showering the earth with rain, and neither will we grow poor by giving to those in need. The more you help me, the more I'm able to help you; and the more we help each other, the more we are able to also help others. And that's the divine cycle we should be trusting and living out. That's how miracles are born.

1,646. ~ THE DEVIL'S DECEPTION ~

One of the devil's master strategies is not so much to deceive people with outright lies, but rather to deceive people with a plethora of information and facts that distract them from the most important truths. Satan is happy to let human beings know anything and everything, as long as they never truly know themselves and truly know their God.

1,647. ~ DOING WELL and DOING GOOD ~

When we pull ourselves up by our own bootstraps we have done well. But when we pull someone else up, we have done good. And when we become more concerned about doing good than doing well, we will then begin to cultivate a truly peaceful and just society.

1,648. ~ WHEN IN BABYLON... ~

When in Babylon, do as you would do in Zion.

1,649. ~ INDIVIDUALS, INSTITUTIONS, & THE COMMANDMENTS of CHRIST ~

In all of His divine teachings, Jesus never issued qualifications or distinctions between what He commanded for human individuals and what He commanded for collective human governments. The fact is that governments are not impersonal entities, magically immune and absolved from the moral imperatives of the Gospel simply because they form an institutional collective. Governments are comprised of individuals, and individuals that support or participate in government will be judged by the same holy standards as every other individual.

If it is wrong for a single individual to refuse to forgive, to take vengeance on their enemies, and to preserve his own life and welfare at the expense of the lives and welfare of others, then it is equally wrong for governments, nations, and all other collective human institutions to do so. On Judgment Day we won't be able to hide behind flags or constitutions or the consensus of the crowd. When Jesus asks, "What did you do for the least of these?" it won't suffice to answer, "Lord, I was only doing my job, fulfilling my governmental role, serving my country, and exercising my political responsibility."

1,650. ~ THE LOVE of TRUTH ~

Knowledge without love is dead. Understanding without personal engagement and sacrificial commitment is a shallow scholarship. The love of truth is only valuable if it is equaled by knowing how to truly love.

1,651. ~ LIVING IS AN ACT of REVOLUTIONARY SUICIDE ~

Choosing to live is an act of revolutionary suicide. To live even though one knows death is inevitable, to live even though one knows life is full of pain, to live even though one knows the worst possible death may await them – this is a most revolutionary act. By choosing to live – and by choosing not to kill – one revolts and rebels against the lie of death and embraces the truth of life eternal.

"The most important thing you do every day is deciding not to kill yourself." ~ Albert Camus ~

1,652. ~ HOW THE PRO-LIFE MOVEMENT SACRIFICED ITS MORAL FORCE ~

Ironically, the Pro-Life movement sacrificed much of its moral force when it shifted its focus from identifying abortion primarily as a human rights issue to identifying it primarily with an agenda of Puritanical morality. Pro-Life activism was largely denuded of its moral and persuasive power when it began to prioritize its alliance with rightwing political "values" above its solidarity with universal human rights. The tragic result is that the Pro-Life cause is now viewed as a politically conservative cause rather than a universal humanitarian cause.

Those of us who promote the "consistent life ethic," and attempt to link our opposition to abortion to our solidarity with all oppressed people everywhere, now have to overcome the connotation that being Pro-Life is synonymous with Republican politics and religious fundamentalism. Those that oppose abortion while flying the flags of "family values," political conservatism, and "American morality" only make it much more difficult for true Pro-Lifers to succeed in this epic battle for the restoration of basic human rights for the unborn.

1,653. ~ VISION ~

Ordinary people see mistakes. Artists see opportunities. The only thing separating "ordinary" from "art" is vision.

1,654. ~ THE WORDS and WITNESS of THE SAINTS REGARDING PEACE ~

The overwhelming biblical commentary of the saints and martyrs throughout history is not on Romans 13 and Old Testament justifications for violence, but rather on the words of Our Lord as recorded in the Gospels, words which compel us towards uncompromising nonviolence and unconditional enemy love. And as if their words were not enough, their exemplary lives of self-sacrifice prove beyond any doubt that they rejected both individual and state sanctioned violence in favor of peace, love, mercy, and martyrdom. Yet somehow, most Christians today dismiss their words and spurn their witness in favor of their own subjective justifications for violence and killing. We have inverted Tertullian's maxim that "The blood of the martyrs is the seeds of the Church" into "We will defend the Church by making martyrs of our enemies."

1,655. ~ ON GUNS and BADGES and UNIFORMS and MORAL AUTHORITY ~

I have no tolerance for the assumption that the guys with the uniforms, guns, and badges possess some sort of inherent moral authority. As far as I'm concerned, people that train and prepare and walk around ready to kill are oppressors and enemies of the Gospel – regardless of what sort of shiny objects they wear on their constabulary clothing.

People love to say: "If you just comply with the police then you won't get shot. And if you don't comply then it's your own fault if you wind up dead." Well, the same thing could be said about rapists, child molesters, and colonizers: just comply, and you'll have a better chance of living. But some of us (call us crazy) have been conditioned by life to be extremely distrustful of the privileged powerful who rely on violence to manipulate, control, and exploit the weak. And some of us (call us Christians) refuse to presumptively cede authority to those whose mercenary ethic and Machiavellian lifestyle blatantly contradict the Gospel of Jesus Christ.

1,656. ~ UPROOTING GOVERNMENTS ~

Governments are like weeds: it is foolish to think we can uproot them all; and we must remember that weeds actually serve a divine purpose. However, when we become more concerned with protecting weeds than with planting flowers and cultivating fruit, then we end up hungry people living in an ugly world. So keep your governments. It is no business of mine. My business is to cultivate the Kingdom of God.

1,657. ~ DISRUPTIVE and DISTURBING IMAGERY ~

Those who argue against showing the graphic reality of what evil does to the oppressed clearly reveal themselves to be allies of the oppressor. Their cowardly objection is, "That's in poor taste." But we respond, "Your injustice, inhumanity, and evil are in poor taste!"

Therefore, we will continue to show you the scarred skin of the victims of your "states' rights;" we will continue to show you the melted flesh of your "just wars;" and we will continue to show you the strange fruit of your "separate but equal;" and we will continue to show you the decimated unborn bodies of your "freedom of choice." May the sight of horrific truth penetrate and destroy your euphemistic lies!

If you insist on justifying evil, then have the guts to look at it squarely in the face. Then, perhaps, the terrible images of oppression will haunt your souls and drive you to repentance. That's why we will continue to disrupt, disturb, and confront you with our revolutionary imagery.

1,658. ~ LUST and LOVE ~

Lust can be gratified, but only love can be satisfied.

1,659. ~ INDIVIDUAL EVILS and SYSTEMIC INJUSTICES ~

Acts of individual evil will occur even under the most controlling of governments, but systemic injustices cannot be carried out apart from government. Rape, murder, and theft will perhaps always happen in our fallen world, and no government can prevent evil individuals from engaging in such evil acts. But the evils of war, slavery, fascism, genocide, communism, and the systematic slaughter of unborn babies can only be successfully executed by governments. Under governments that ostensibly exist to protect the good, the good constantly struggles to protect itself from governments.

1,660. ~ GIVE ME THE THINGS THAT BLEED ~

When you suffer, remember that the dead don't bleed. As Hemingway wrote, *"Because of his pain he knew he was alive."* So give me the things that bleed: saints and broken hearts and the Savior of them all. Life is in the blood (Leviticus 17:11), and unless we bleed we will never truly live.

1,661. ~ THE PATRIOT and THE REVOLUTIONARY ~

The patriot seeks to preserve the nation even at the expense of humanity. But the revolutionary seeks to preserve humanity even if it means the destruction of the nation.

1,662. ~ POWER and PURPOSE ~

Which is stronger: a razor or an axe? Well, try shaving with an axe or sawing a tree with a razor. Strength and power reside in purpose.

1,663. ~ BABYLON'S 3 POINT POLITICAL STRATEGY ~

Babylon's 3 point political strategy:

1. Promote evil.
2. Label the promotion of evil "freedom."
3. In the name of "protecting freedom," ridicule, condemn, persecute – and if necessary, kill – those that dare to criticize and condemn evil.

1,664. ~ EVIL PARTICIPATION ~

Seeking to change the evil system by participating in the evil system is like bathing in cyanide and expecting to cleanse the poison.

1,665. ~ NO PEACE, NO JUSTICE ~

It is often said that there can be no peace without justice. Well, the truth is that there can be no justice without peace. So the question is: are we going to continue trying to bomb, execute, and war our way to peace, or are we going to love, forgive, and reconcile our way to justice?

1,667. ~ DISCIPLESHIP IS DISSIDENCE ~

To be honest, true Pro-Lifers need to raise a lot more hell in this struggle for human rights. We remain apathetic because we're not the ones being violently ripped apart limb from limb in our mothers' wombs. We should always be uncompromisingly nonviolent in our righteous resistance, but let's not confuse resignation to evil and acceptance of the status quo for "peacefulness."

It is up to us to speak for the innocent, to give voice to the voiceless, and to cry out on behalf of the vulnerable and the oppressed. It is up to us to vocalize the silent screams of the countless unborn children who suffer violent and unjust deaths. So perhaps it's time to re-examine whether our gentle pleas for abortion to end are truly an appropriate response to the bloody and inhumane horror we oppose.

If we really believe abortion is murder then we should act like it. The time for politics and politeness is over. It's time to take to the streets and end this abomination! Revolution never comes quietly like a gentle rain; it comes rolling in with earthquake, thunder, whirlwind and lightning. Resist and revolt or get out of the way! This is literally a matter of life and death!

Dr. Martin Luther King, Jr. said: *"Our lives begin to end the day we become silent about things that matter. In the past, apathy was a moral failure. Today it is a form of moral suicide."*

Discipleship to Christ is dissidence to evil, confrontation with injustice, and rebellion against oppression. We cannot claim to follow Jesus if we neglect the cries of our suffering neighbors.

"Rescue those being led away to death; save those staggering toward the slaughter. If you say, 'But we knew nothing about this,' does not He who weighs the heart perceive it? Does not He who guards your life know it? Will He not repay everyone according to what they have done?" [Proverbs 24:11-12]

"Let justice run down as waters, and righteousness as a mighty stream." [Amos 5:24]

"I know your deeds, that you are neither cold nor hot. I wish you were either one or the other! So, because you are lukewarm—neither hot nor cold—I am about to spit you out of my mouth." [Revelation 3:15-16]

"Alone" is a very lonely word. The joys and truths and beauties of life are never fully experienced apart from others. To feel, to know, to enjoy, to understand... such blessings are best received in community, not in isolation. As Christopher McCandless realized and wrote – perhaps when it was too late – *"Happiness is only real when shared."*

1,669. ~ NUANCE and COMPROMISE ~

Social injustices and systemic evils have always been justified by appeals to "nuance" and "compromise." After all, Dred Scott wasn't completely inhuman. In fact, the Supreme Court was "enlightened" enough to deem that he was more human than not. They were "reasonable" enough to declare that he was actually 3/5ths of a person.

Nuance... Compromise...

And today, the same godless logic is invoked in the abortion debate. Most people who support the legality of abortion are not so heartless as to say that abortion is a great a noble thing. They acknowledge that the "fetus" has some semblance of life, even though not as much life as Dred Scott. So go ahead and kill ("terminate") the baby ("product of conception") as early as possible; and preferably only in extreme cases where the pregnancy involves rape or incest (or some other horrific tragedy, such as simply becoming pregnant when you didn't intend to become pregnant.)

Nuance... Compromise....

We are always willing to appear enlightened, reasonable, nuanced, and compromising as long as the lives at stake are not our own. But if we ourselves were to become subject to systemic injustice, legalized oppression, and violent extermination, then we would suddenly view the world in very stark, black and white terms. Our sense of justice and our understanding of human rights would suddenly become keenly unequivocal. God forbid that *we* should be nuanced to pieces like the innocent unborn babies we callously jettison and discard with our "enlightened" sophistry.

May God save us from nuanced lies! And may He give us the hard light of truth and understanding! Today the victims are the unborn innocents. Tomorrow we might become the victims. And unlike these precious unborn babies, we will in fact be guilty. For how can we cry out for personal justice when we personally denied justice to others? Compromise in the pursuit of justice is cowardice, an nuance in matters of life and liberty is evil.

1,670. ~ SACRIFICE ~

Sacrifice certainty for wonder.

Sacrifice judgment for grace.

Sacrifice yesterday for now and tomorrow for today.

Sacrifice killing for life, politics for peace, bloodshed for beauty, and deception for truth.

Sacrifice comfort for love.

Sacrifice security for salvation.

Let eternity fill the moment, and then suffer with joy as you are being redeemed.

1,671. ~ MELTING ~

Lava judgment...
burning flames...
scorching souls...
melting into...
Eternal mercy

1,672. ~ JESUS and EARTHLY POLITICAL AGENDAS ~

Jesus had nothing to do with the agenda of the Shah of Iran or the agenda of the Ayatollah Khomeini. He had nothing to do with the agenda of Salvador Allende or the agenda of Augusto Pinochet. He had nothing to do with the agenda of Fulgencio Bastista or the agenda of Fidel Castro. He had nothing to do with the agenda of Adolf Hitler or the agenda of Josef Stalin. He had nothing to do with the agenda of JFK or the agenda of Che Guevara. He had nothing to do with the agenda of Barack Obama and He has nothing to do with the agenda of Donald Trump.

Jesus has nothing to do with earthly kingdoms, with bloody revolutions and counter-revolutions, with political and legal force, or with temporal governments and human systems predicated upon the violent imposition of one mortal ideology over another.

Jesus' Kingdom has come to earth (St. Luke 17:21), and He calls His disciples to live, think, and act as citizens with no other allegiance or loyalty.

"A house divided against itself cannot stand." [St. Luke 11:17]

"No one can serve two masters. Either you will hate the one and love the other, or you will be devoted to the one and despise the other." [St. Matthew 6:24]

1,673. ~ KILLING, SALVATION, and SERVITUDE TO THE STATE ~

Whether we slay our neighbors with our own personal swords or with the States we serve... whether we slay our neighbors with bullets or with ballots... whether we slay our neighbors legally or illegally... whether we slay our neighbors with the guillotine or with the government – we have killed our neighbors and rejected Christ all the same.

If one man stabs his brother in the heart he is condemned as a murderer, but if a thousand men wear uniforms and follow orders then they can kill their brethren with impunity and even be hailed as heroes for doing so.

We won't be saved by whether we fought for our countries, fought for our political parties, fought for our constitutions, or fought for our governments. We will only be saved by the love of Jesus; and He will judge our love for Him by how we loved others – *all* others.

1,674. ~ CREATIVITY and CRITICISM ~

Don't disparage other people's art. Make your own. Criticism is the pastime of those who are too lazy to create anything themselves.

1,675. ~ FIRST PRINCIPLES of AUTHENTIC LIBERATION THEOLOGY ~

Peace and love are the first principles of authentic liberation theology. Without a Christian commitment to nonviolence and sacrificial love, all of our revolutionary endeavors will inevitably perpetuate the very evils and injustices we seek to redress.

1,676. ~ WHAT WILL I DO WHEN ALL IS LOST? ~

What will I do when hope takes flight? What will I do when faith betrays me? What will I do when love has waned? What will I do when life becomes too cruel to bear? What will I do when all is lost? I'll tell you what I'll do: I will hope and believe and love and live, even if it kills me. Because I know beyond all doubt that I dwell on the threshold of eternity.

1,677. ~ DEHUMANIZING IDEOLOGIES ~

Beware of any ideology predicated upon the insidious idea that "there are too many of 'them'." Babylon always justifies its evil in the name of some greater good: e.g. "They" are a drain on the economy... "They" are a drain on the nation... "They" are a drain on the planet... "They" are a drain on humanity...

Keep disparaging a certain segment of the human race until "they" are ultimately dehumanized, and then the bloodbath can begin in the name of "progress" and "enlightenment."

1,678. ~ REMEMBER TO SUPPORT GOD'S WORK ~

There are souls laboring for the Kingdom of Heaven that receive only suffering in return. So when you receive your salary, remember to help those that have no "job" but are doing God's work all the same.

We may say, *"If a man will not work, he shall not he eat." [II Thessalonians 3:10]* But we must be careful not to judge a person's labor by their occupation or income (or lack thereof.) For St. Paul also writes: *"The elders who direct the affairs of the church well are worthy of double honor, especially those whose work is preaching and teaching. For Scripture says, 'Do not muzzle an ox while it is treading out the grain,' and 'The worker deserves his wages.'" [I Timothy 5:17-18]*

St. Paul was a tentmaker, but John the Baptist had no vocation that we know of. And yet Jesus said that among those born of women there was none greater than John the Baptist (St. Luke 7:28). The blessed forerunner subsisted on a diet of locusts and wild honey, and he was beheaded for his righteous labors. I wonder how he would be received today, by those of us who profess the name of Jesus, with his prophetic tongue and homeless lifestyle. I suspect many "good Christians" would tell him to go clean himself up and get a job. And I suspect many "good Christians" today would tell Jesus: "God helps those who help themselves. We hate that you were crucified, but you only have yourself to blame."

If Jesus had simply found gainful employment and learned to submit to authority, He could have saved Himself. But instead He chose to save the world.

1,679. ~ BOOK of LOVE ~

I must now work on a book of love, because love covers a multitude of sins (I Peter 4:8). My polemics and judgments and condemnations and rebukes have done little to serve the Kingdom. It is thus time to focus on the discipline of love – and make no mistake, love is a discipline.

The pen I have previously wielded in self-righteous anger must now flow with the ink of love. Not a soft love, not a compromising love, not a love devoid of confrontational truth, but a love that prioritizes love above all else. As Dostoevsky wrote: *"Love in reality is a harsh and dreadful thing compared to love in dreams."*

I must trust love to do its divine work. I must trust love to convict and persuade and heal and redeem. I must let love permeate my words and thoughts and actions and life. I must let God crucify my ego so that love can save.

Because of the blessed encouragement of Father Deacon Michael Wilson (and many others) – who spoke through the Holy Spirit – I must now engage in the discipline of love. Pray for me to learn, to grow, and to mature in the love of Jesus Christ. Pray for me to know and experience and live and write words of love. My own salvation is at stake.

"To cheat oneself out of love is the most terrible deception; it is an eternal loss for which there is no reparation, either in time or in eternity." ~ Soren Kierkegaard ~

1,680. ~ WHO KNOWS JESUS? ~

Who knows Jesus? The blind one does.
Who knows Jesus? The harlot does.
Who knows Jesus? The sick one does.
Who knows Jesus? The addict does.
Who knows Jesus? The desperate one does.
Who knows Jesus? The sufferer does.
Who knows Jesus? The guilty one does.
Who knows Jesus? The sinner does.

Jesus came to save the weak and the sick, not the strong and the well. So ask yourself: do you really need Jesus, are you OK on your own?

"It is not the healthy who need a doctor, but the sick. I have not come to call the righteous, but sinners, to repentance." [St. Luke 5:31-32]

1,681. ~ I FOUGHT THE LAW ~

I fought the law, and JAH won. And I didn't even need a gun.

1,682. ~ A PRAYER ~

Dear Lord: Please lead me in righteousness and truth. Help me to remember that all agony, trials, and pains produce beauty and blessings when I offer them up to You. Calm the waves that crash against the walls of my soul. Temper the conflicts that disrupt and disturb my spirit. Give me a steadfast single-mindedness that seeks nothing more than to love you by loving others. Strengthen my heart to give, and to forgive, even when it hurts to do so. Sharpen my mind to correctly discern both myself and the world in which I live. Protect my heart and mind from the ubiquitous threat of self-deception. Grant me peace, and cleanse me, so that others will somehow see You in me. Guard me – and guard us all – from enemies both mortal and metaphysical. Bless me with the gift of hope at all times. Make my life a prayer to You. *In the Name of the Father, the Son, and the Holy Spirit, One God* ~ *Amen* ~

1,683. ~ THREE WORDS ~

These three words
I leave with you:
Peace, Love, and Life.
If all else is false
these things are true.

1,684. ~ DIG DEEP ~

Dig deep. And when life gets harder, dig deeper. Dig into your soul until you find Jesus there, and then cling to Him and don't let go. Because life is difficult. Damn difficult. And as Jim Morrison said, *"No one here gets out alive."* So we have to live until we die. No way around that. But if we die living for Christ and living for others, then we will not die in vain. We will live forever, on the other side, in the arms of our merciful God. And with all due respect to "The Lizard King," it is Jesus Christ, not Jim Morrison, who will ultimately have the final word.

1,685. ~ THE JUDGMENT of THE WRITER ~

I envy musicians and artists. I think there is great truth in the idiom, "A picture is worth a thousand words." And I think the same can be said for a song. We writers, speakers, and preachers will always be judged by our words. Our words will always be measured by our actions, and our actions will always fall short of the ideals we articulate and express with speech and pen.

Artists and musicians rarely face such judgment. People either like or dislike what they have created. But they don't say, "Picasso was a hypocrite!" or "Beethoven never truly lived according to the ideals of his symphonies!" Yes, they face judgment and critique and ridicule. But the judgment of their artistic creations rarely has anything to do with the sanctity of their lives.

I wish I could sing sad songs, paint beautiful strokes, play sublime chords. I wish I could give the world some beauty and poignancy that would not be appraised by the quality of my life. But alas, I am a writer. And I am a Christian. And I am a sinner. And my words will always be measured by how I live. And I will never truly be able to live according to all that I profess.

But I must write anyway. And I leave my words to God, so that He may do with them what He will. And as I said in the Introduction of this book, I pray that God will resurrect a divine melody out of any discordant notes I may have sounded with my words herein. St. Basil the Great said, *"Words are truly the image of the soul."* I suspect that those who read this book will realize that my soul still needs a lot of work. Pray for me.

I recently read these blessed thoughts from the journals of Thomas Merton, one of my spiritual heroes. And I really can't think of a more fitting summary with which to bring this book to a close. Forgive me for ending my own book with a quote from someone else, but Thomas Merton has summarized it all for me right here:

"What a fool I have been, in the literal and biblical sense of the word: thoughtless, impulsive, lazy, self-interested, yet alien to myself, untrue to myself, following the most stupid fantasies, guided by the most idiotic emotions and needs. Yes, I know, it is partly unavoidable. But I know too that in spite of all contradictions there is a center and a strength to which I always can have access if I really desire it. And the grace to desire it is surely there. It would do no good to anyone if I just went around talking – no matter how articulately – in this condition. There is still so much to learn, so much deepening to be done, so much to surrender. My real business is something far

different from simply giving out words and ideas and "doing things"
– even to help others. The best thing I can give to others is to liberate
myself from the common delusions and be, for myself and for them,
free. Then grace can work in and through me for everyone."

~ Thomas Merton ~

[The Other Side of The Mountain: The Journals of Thomas
Merton, Volume Seven]

The ***Christian Peace Army*** is enlisting all who are committed to nonviolently opposing injustice and evil.

MISSION STATEMENT

+ We believe that Christian love and Christian truth are the most effective weapons against inhumanity and oppression. (Cf. St. John 3:16; St. Matthew 5:43-48; Romans 8:37-39; Psalm 43:3)

+ We believe that apathy towards evil is a form of evil itself. (Cf. James 4:17; I John 3:18)

+ We believe that opposition to evil must be active and vigilant, but always nonviolent. (Cf. Psalm 82:4; Micah 6:8; Zechariah 4:6)

+ We believe that if worldly powers can manufacture weapons of destruction and amass violent armies, then the children of God can organize armies of nonviolent resistance and cultivate spiritual weapons that will bring down all wicked strongholds. (Cf. II Corinthians 10:3-4; Ephesians 6:10-18; I John 3:8)

+ We are a Christian army, and we obey Our Lord Jesus Christ who commands us to put away the sword and take up our cross. (Cf. St. Matthew 26:52; St. Luke 9:23)

+ As Christians we welcome, embrace, and stand in solidarity with all those who are equally committed to nonviolence and the sanctity of Life. Anyone, regardless of their religion or lack thereof, who is committed to the Christian imperatives of peace is welcome in our army. (Cf. St. Matthew 12:50; Acts 10:35)

+ The members of the ***Christian Peace Army*** are willing to offer our bodies, our service, and our lives in order to thwart violence, oppose injustice, and promote humanity. (Cf. Romans 12:1-2)

+ We oppose any and all ostensible solutions that are predicated on violence. We believe that a violent solution is no solution at all. (Cf. St. Matthew 5:9; St. Matthew 26:52)

✦ We oppose all war, and we believe that legalized abortion is nothing less than a declaration of war against the most innocent and helpless members of humanity: the unborn. We are therefore committed to a nonviolent revolution which will bring an end to this slaughter of innocents. There can be no peace in the world apart from peace in the womb. (Cf. Psalm 139: 13-16; Proverbs 24:11-12)

✦ We pray for the strength to sacrifice our own lives in pursuit of justice, but we refuse to sacrifice the lives of others, no matter how noble the cause. (Cf. St. John 15:13)

✦ The **Christian Peace Army** seeks to find creative, nonviolent, life-affirming solutions to the evils that plague our world. (Cf. Psalm 34:14; I Peter 3:11)

"Finally, my brethren, be strong in the Lord, and in the power of his might. Put on the whole armor of God, that ye may be able to stand against the wiles of the devil. For we wrestle not against flesh and blood, but against principalities, against powers, against the rulers of the darkness of this world, against spiritual wickedness in high places. Wherefore take unto you the whole armor of God, that ye may be able to withstand in the evil day, and having done all, to stand. Stand therefore, having your loins girt about with truth, and having on the breastplate of righteousness; And your feet shod with the preparation of the gospel of peace; Above all, taking the shield of faith, wherewith ye shall be able to quench all the fiery darts of the wicked. And take the helmet of salvation, and the sword of the Spirit, which is the word of God: Praying always with all prayer and supplication in the Spirit, and watching thereunto with all perseverance and supplication for all saints." [Ephesians 6:10-18]

"For though we walk in the flesh, we do not war after the flesh: For the weapons of our warfare are not carnal, but mighty through God to the pulling down of strongholds." [II Corinthians 10:3-4]

"Rescue those being led away to death; save those staggering toward slaughter. If you say, 'But we knew nothing about this,' does not he who weighs the heart perceive it? Does not he who guards

your life know it? Will he not repay everyone according to what they have done?" [Proverbs 24:11-12]

"In the nonviolent army, there is room for everyone who wants to join up. There are no racial or color distinctions. There are no examinations to pass, no pledges to take, except for this: whereas soldiers in the armies of violence are expected to inspect and keep their rifles clean, nonviolent soldiers are called upon to examine and polish their greatest weapons – their hearts, their consciences, their courage, and their sense of justice." ~ Dr. Martin Luther King, Jr.

"Our warfare is to make the dead to live,
not to make the living dead."
~ St. John Chrysostom ~

"I must first be disciplined myself by my own words.
This book itself is a judgment."
~ SOREN KIERKEGAARD~

"Today I am full of doubt about my book and
full of doubt about myself. But I have nothing
to say if people put me personally on trial.
Any defense becomes a self-justification."
~ ALBERT CAMUS ~

"I do not know you God because I am in the way.
Please help me to push myself aside."
~ FLANNERY O'CONNOR ~

"Blessed be the Almighty God,
ready to forgive all sins.
Blessed be Almighty JAH,
wherever you trod
keep the Almighty within."
~ GARNETT SILK ~

BIBLIOGRAPHY and RESOURCES on PEACE and NONVIOLENCE

(Please note: some of the web links listed below may have changed or been deleted subsequent to the printing of this book.)

THE ORTHODOX PEACE FELLOWSHIP
http://www.incommunion.org/

THE COST OF DISCIPLESHIP
By Dietrich Bonhoeffer

A DICTIONARY OF EARLY CHRISTIAN BELIEFS
By David Bercot

THE KINGDOM OF GOD IS WITHIN YOU
By Leo Tolstoy

AN ENCYCLOPEDIA of PACIFISM
By Aldous Huxley

THE DIVINE WITHIN: Selected Essays
By Aldous Huxley

DOROTHY DAY: Selected Writings
Edited by Robert Ellsberg

RESISTANCE, REBELLION, and DEATH
By Albert Camus

FAITH AND VIOLENCE
By Thomas Merton

GANDHI ON NON-VIOLENCE
By Mohandas K. Gandhi

DEFENDERS OF THE UNBORN: The Pro-Life Movement Before Roe v. Wade
By Daniel K. Williams

WHAT WOULD YOU DO? (If a Violent Person Threatened to Harm a Loved One.)
By John Howard Yoder

THE POLITICS OF JESUS
By John Howard Yoder

A CHANGE OF ALLEGIANCE: A journey into the historical and biblical teaching on war and peace By Dean Taylor

FIGHT: A Christian Case for Nonviolence
By Preston Sprinkle

PEACEFUL NEIGHBOR: Discovering the Countercultural Mister Rogers
By Michael G. Long

A FAREWELL TO MARS: An Evangelical Pastor's Journey Toward the Biblical Gospel of Peace By Brian Zahnd

THE CONQUEST OF VIOLENCE
By Bart De Ligt

ARGUING PEACE: COLLECTED PACIFIST WRITINGS, Volume Three: Biblical and Theological Essays. Peace Theology Books, 2014.
By Ted Grimsrud

IT IS NOT LAWFUL FOR ME TO FIGHT: Early Christian Attitudes toward War, Violence, and the State
By Jean-Michel Hornus

ELECTING NOT TO VOTE
By Ted Lewis

PEACE THEOLOGY [A website of nonviolent resources]
http://peacetheology.net/

WILLIAM STRINGFELLOW: Selected Writings
Edited by Bill Wylie-Kellermann

SAINT IN THE SLUMS: The Story of Kagawa of Japan
By Cyril James Davey

DISARMING SCRIPTURE: Cherry-Picking Liberals, Violence-Loving Conservatives, and Why We All Need to Learn to Read the Bible Like Jesus Did
By Derek Flood

BONHOEFFER THE ASSASSIN?: Challenging the Myth, Recovering His Call to Peacemaking By Mark Thiessen Nation, Anthony G. Siegrist, and Daniel P. Umbel

MYSTERY AND MEANING: Christian Philosophy & Orthodox Meditations
By Gebre Menfes Kidus

MINISTRIES and CAUSES to SUPPORT

Please consider supporting the following ministries with prayer and financial contributions. And most importantly, please help somebody you personally know that is in need of assistance. Give first to those in need within your own family, within your own Church, and among your own friends. Help them and love them unconditionally. And give to those you see begging in the streets. Our job is not to presumptively judge how they will use the tangible support we give them. Our job is to give freely and leave judgments to God. Christ has given abundantly and unconditionally to us, and we have all squandered His gifts in many ways; yet He continues to lavish us with His unconditional love. Therefore, let us give unreservedly to others. It is such a simple thing to give from what we have to those who lack. May God help us to help one another!

The Orthodox Peace Fellowship [https://incommunion.org/]

The Catholic Worker Movement [http://www.catholicworker.org/]

Debre Bisrate St. Gabriel Ethiopian Orthodox Church – Clarkston, Georgia [http://atlantagabriel.org/]

Holy Trinity St. John the Theologian Greek Orthodox Church – Jackson, Mississippi [http://www.holytrinitysaintjohnjackson.org/]

Pro-Life Mississippi [http://www.prolifemississippi.org/]

International Orthodox Christian Charities [https://www.iocc.org/]

Zoe For Life [http://www.zoeforlifeonline.org/]

Bethany Christian Services [https://www.bethany.org/]

Catholic Charities [https://catholiccharitiesusa.org/]

Christian Aid Ministries [https://christianaidministries.org/]

The Missions and Evangelism of Abba Gebre Tsadik of the Ethiopian Orthodox Tewahedo Church

The Milagro Foundation [http://milagrofoundation.org/]

New Wave Feminists [http://www.newwavefeminists.com/]

Nick's Kids [http://www.nickskidsfoundation.org/]

[I have listed these ministries because at the time of writing this book I know them to be life-affirming, peace loving organizations that comply with the values of the Gospel of Our Lord Jesus Christ. However, if any of these ministries ever deviate from these principles and begin supporting anything that is opposed to nonviolence and the sanctity of life, then I will no longer endorse them. But I trust that they will stay the course.]

> *"It is not the responsibility of knights errant to discover*
> *whether the afflicted, the enchained and the oppressed whom*
> *they encounter on the road are reduced to these circumstances and*
> *suffer this distress for their vices, or for their virtues: the knight's*
> *sole responsibility is to succor them as people in need,*
> *having eyes only for their sufferings, not for their misdeeds."*
> ~ Miguel de Cervantes ~

> *"Let us love our neighbors as ourselves. Let us cultivate charity and*
> *humility. Let us give alms, because such selfless acts cleanse our*
> *souls from the stains of sin. We lose all material things when we leave*
> *this world, but we carry with us into eternity the reward of our*
> *charity and our kindness to the poor. Those who truly give to others*
> *will receive from the Lord a due reward and a divine recompense."*
> ~ St. Francis of Assisi ~

> *"The bread you do not use is the bread of the hungry; the garments in*
> *your wardrobe are the garments of those who are naked; the shoes*
> *that you do not wear are the shoes of those who are barefoot; the*
> *money you keep locked away is the money of the poor; the acts of*
> *charity that you do not perform are so many injustices you commit."*
> ~ St. Basil the Great ~

ABOUT THE AUTHOR

GEBRE MENFES KIDUS is an author, activist, and public speaker who promotes the "consistent life ethic" and the Orthodox Christian Faith. The author and his family were baptized into the Ethiopian Orthodox Tewahedo Church in 2008, whereupon he received the baptismal name, *Gebre Menfes Kidus*, which means "Servant of the Holy Spirit."

For speaking engagements, panel discussions, or interviews, contact the author via the information below.

GEBRE MENFES KIDUS is also the author of ***"MYSTERY and MEANING: Christian Philosophy & Orthodox Meditations"***, which is available for sale at AuthorHouse Publishing:

http://www.authorhouse.com/bookstore/bookdetail.aspx?bookid=SKU-000365536

CONTACT INFORMATION:

Email: GebreMenfesKidus@yahoo.com

Facebook: https://www.facebook.com/gebre.menfeskidus

(Please note: this contact and order information may be subject to change upon the printing of this book.)